THE GREAT SHIPS

The Stackpole Military History Series

THE AMERICAN CIVIL WAR

Cavalry Raids of the Civil War
Ghost, Thunderbolt, and Wizard
Pickett's Charge
Witness to Gettysburg

WORLD WAR II

Armor Battles of the Waffen-SS, 1943–45
Army of the West
Australian Commandos
The B-24 in China
Backwater War
The Battle of Sicily
Beyond the Beachhead
The Brandenburger Commandos
The Brigade
Bringing the Thunder
Coast Watching in World War II
Colossal Cracks
A Dangerous Assignment
D-Day to Berlin
Dive Bomber!
A Drop Too Many
Eagles of the Third Reich
Eastern Front Combat
Exit Rommel
Fist from the Sky
Flying American Combat Aircraft of World War II
Forging the Thunderbolt
Fortress France
The German Defeat in the East, 1944–45
German Order of Battle, Vol. 1
German Order of Battle, Vol. 2
German Order of Battle, Vol. 3
The Germans in Normandy
Germany's Panzer Arm in World War II
GI Ingenuity
The Great Ships
Grenadiers
Infantry Aces
Iron Arm
Iron Knights
Kampfgruppe Peiper at the Battle of the Bulge
Kursk
Luftwaffe Aces
Massacre at Tobruk

Mechanized Juggernaut or Military Anachronism?
Messerschmitts over Sicily
Michael Wittmann, Vol. 1
Michael Wittmann, Vol. 2
Mountain Warriors
The Nazi Rocketeers
On the Canal
Operation Mercury
Packs On!
Panzer Aces
Panzer Aces II
Panzer Commanders of the Western Front
The Panzer Legions
Panzers in Winter
The Path to Blitzkrieg
Retreat to the Reich
Rommel's Desert Commanders
Rommel's Desert War
The Savage Sky
A Soldier in the Cockpit
Soviet Blitzkrieg
Stalin's Keys to Victory
Surviving Bataan and Beyond
T-34 in Action
Tigers in the Mud
The 12th SS, Vol. 1
The 12th SS, Vol. 2
The War against Rommel's Supply Lines
War in the Aegean

THE COLD WAR / VIETNAM

Cyclops in the Jungle
Flying American Combat Aircraft: The Cold War
Here There Are Tigers
Land with No Sun
Street without Joy
Through the Valley

WARS OF THE MIDDLE EAST

Never-Ending Conflict

GENERAL MILITARY HISTORY

Carriers in Combat
Desert Battles
Guerrilla Warfare

THE GREAT SHIPS

British Battleships in World War II

Peter C. Smith

STACKPOLE
BOOKS

Dedicated to two very special and wonderful people,
Pat and Jack

Published in paperback in 2008 by
STACKPOLE BOOKS
5067 Ritter Road
Mechanicsburg, PA 17055
www.stackpolebooks.com

For information on all of Peter C. Smith's books, please visit www.dive–bombers.co.uk

Cover design by Tracy Patterson

Printed in the United States of America

10 9 8 7 6 5 4 3 2 1

Library of Congress Cataloging-in-Publication Data

Smith, Peter Charles, 1940–
  [Great ships pass]
  The great ships : British battleships in World War II / Peter C. Smith.
    p. cm. — (Stackpole military history series)
  Originally published: The great ships pass : British battleships at war 1939–1945 / Peter C. Smith. 1977.
  Includes bibliographical references and index.
  ISBN 978-0-8117-3514-8
  1. World War, 1939–1945—Naval operations, British. 2. Battleships—Great Britain—History—20th century. 3. Great Britain. Royal Navy—History—World War, 1939–1945. I. Title.
  D771.S63 2008
  940.54'5941—dc22

                                                          2008003817

Contents

Introduction

In 1960, an almost-unnoticed event took place that to a few people seemed to symbolize the ultimate acknowledgment that Great Britain had long ceased to be a major naval power. That event was the consigning to the scrap yard of the HMS *Vanguard*, the last of the mighty battleships to fly the White Ensign.

Although by this date she represented merely an obsolete hulk of an era and age long passed—with her ironic name (*Rearguard* would have been more apt) and her forlorn isolation for many years sealed up in reserve in Portsmouth Harbor in full view of her most illustrious forebear, the HMS *Victory*—the physical act of severing the last link with Britain's former maritime greatness was a sad occasion.

The last British battleship went to the breakers about 100 years after the arrival of the first "ironclad" battleship, the HMS *Warrior*, had effected a revolution in warship design, but the lineage of the *Vanguard* and her kind went back much farther—back four centuries, in fact, before the armada of 1588.

In those four centuries, Britain rose to become the greatest power in the world, the richest nation on earth, and the most widespread and benevolent empire ever known. This unique position was achieved by command of the sea, and that command, for almost all of that long period, ultimately rested on Britain's great ships, its ships of the line, its battleships.

No weapon of war did more for Great Britain over such a length of time and so economically. Behind those forbidding but majestic bulwarks, Britain remained immune from the envy and hatred of the other lesser powers who sought to conquer and despoil it and subject its free peoples.

No tyranny succeeded in passing those defenses, though many tried. Spanish king, French emperor, Prussian emperor, German and Italian dictators—all failed. But in the end, decay came from inside, and the decline and passing of the battleship ultimately matched exactly in its timing and speed the passing of the British nation as a major power and factor in world events. This was undoubtedly a coincidence, but it was somehow apt. Over the centuries, neglect and shortsightedness had often threatened both. Finally, the will to maintain them was eroded, and battleship and national greatness passed into history.

The last brief years of the battleship saw them reach their zenith in size and power, but these same years were marked with acrimony and derision about the battleship's usefulness and purpose, and its ultimate passing went unmourned in Britain at large. All that remains of the battleship era are two 15-inch guns mounted incongruously on the lawn of a London museum. It is not enough.

A great many books have been written about the technical development of the battleship. The most worthwhile one is Dr. Oscar Parkes's magnificent volume, a worthy monument indeed. When one turns for a brief description of what these great ships achieved during the last two decades of their long development, the situation is less satisfactory. Whereas there are several books that purport to tell the full story of their achievements in the last years, few do so in any detail. Most books of this nature dismiss the years 1919-45 in a chapter or two at best. Battleships in World War II are generally presented as already obsolete. When they put to sea, they were sunk wholesale by bombers and submarines—or so the story goes. When not sunk, they achieved nothing at all constructive to the war effort. These are the usual generalizations.

Introduction to the 2008 Edition

I am very proud to have this revised edition of my book published for the American reader. The historical links between the Royal Navy and the U.S. Navy go back a very long time. After a brief period of mistrust in the 1920s, the ties grew very strong and were cemented during the period reviewed by this work, World War II. With four times the population and ten times the wealth, it was inevitable that the U.S. Navy would overtake the Royal Navy as the premier naval power. Aided by a series of mistaken decisions by Prime Minister Winston Churchill—bedazzled as he was by visions of German cities in ashes—the age-old priority given to Britain's sea defenses lapsed, and the United States' awesome and awe-inspiring construction program to build a two-ocean navy combined with British decline to make the U.S. the main maritime power from 1942 onward. This fact should not, however, distract from what the British battleship did during the final years of her 400-year-old history.

The nonsense written about British battleships in many history books is nothing compared to the deluge of inaccuracy, misinformation, and downright idiocy transmitted on television in both the United Kingdom and United States since the first edition of this book in 1977. The pure scale and regularity of this media babble masquerading as "factual history" makes a new edition of this book even more essential for some balance and objectivity.

Talking heads and voice overs reading puerile scripts, with sound bites by so-called "experts" to give the façade of accuracy, only add to the charade. I have seen the sinking of HMS *Barham* in the Mediterranean portrayed by the BBC as the sinking of a Japanese battleship off Leyte and by the History Channel as a sinking merchant ship in the North Atlantic. Such is the stuff served up as factual research on television today, while Hollywood, making up its own fabrications like *U-571*, *The Battle of Midway*, and *Pearl Harbor*, further perpetuates the rewriting of history. Nobody seems to care what is the truth anymore. This applies equally to the United Kingdom, with the television companies seemingly leading the stampede to dumb down history and steer it away from accuracy. Someone on the BBC's *The Word* program recently sneered, "History is dead." For them, that certainly would seem to be the case.

Unfortunately, for this legion of detractors, it is a stubborn and uncomfortable fact for them to face that, for all their hasty and superficial judgements, the British battleship took part in *more* actions, was engaged in *more* operations, and voyaged *more* miles in combat duties in World War II than at any period since 1805.

This new edition of my book attempts to redress the balance of knowledge and chronicle the final and neglected facet of the battleship's story.

Peter C. Smith
Riseley, Bedford, United Kingdom
June 2008

CHAPTER 1

Mistress of the Seas?

On November 21, 1918, there was enacted in the bleak wastes of the cold North Sea, some forty miles from lonely May Island in the Firth of Forth, a drama of awe-inspiring significance and magnitude. It was nothing less than the surrender of the German High Seas Fleet to Britain's Grand Fleet and this act of total submission of vanquished to the victor marked the supreme highwater mark of British sea power after three centuries of development and almost unbroken victory. But more than this, it marked the apex of supremacy of the battleship as the final arbiter of naval might after an equally long and successful period on the grim stage of sea warfare.

"You have given us their army," wrote Field Marshal Sir Henry Maitland Wilson to Adm. David Beatty that day, "and we have given you their fleet."[1]

There can be no doubt at all that the field marshal was speaking the plain truth. It had been the successful application of the blockade by the Royal Navy of Imperial Germany that in its slow, quiet but irresistible way had nullified the many great victories and feats of arms gained by that nation's soldiers in the four years of the bloodiest warfare yet known to man. Though her armies might strike deep into the heart of France and Russia and there consolidate, resisting all attempts to throw them back in countless massive assaults that bled the Allies white, behind the front lines starvation grew, and in its wretched misery, the German home front festered, grew rotten, and ultimately broke.

The German armies were finally defeated in the field by the British under Field Marshal Douglas Haig, but by that time, the whole imperial edifice built up by Kaiser Wilhelm II had become gutted spiritually from within until all that remained was the rotten core of a once-proud nation.[2]

British sea power had brought this about in four years. More particularly, the Grand Fleet which, though it did not come firmly to grips with its opponent once during that period of time, by its mere existence doomed the colossal efforts of Germany to dominate the continent. In the same manner, the great ships of the Royal Navy had cast their decisive influence over other tyrannical empires with similar ambitions, Napoleon's France and Philip's Spain in the centuries before.

1

The once imperial splendor of Germany followed these earlier examples to an equally decisive termination, laid low by the one force which they all tried to challenge but never were able to dominate: Britain's control of the sea. And this vital factor was guarded in 1918, as in 1805 and no less surely in 1588, by the battleship, the British battleship. At this supreme hour of its greatest and most complete victory, whereby an entire enemy fleet submitted without a shot being fired, how stood the battleship in the Royal Navy, in the fleets of the lesser sea powers and in the eyes of the world.

In Admiral Beatty's great fleet, that remarkable November day in 1918 was to be found the greatest assembly of British warships in her history. There were 150 lithe, sleek destroyers, flotilla upon flotilla, in that assembly—six squadrons of swift, pert light cruisers and one squadron of rugged armored cruisers swelled this total, but dominating all else were the great bulks of the battleships and battlecruisers; there were seven squadrons of these mighty vessels.

This massive armada of more than 200 fighting ships, with five American and three French representative vessels in attendance, steamed out to meet its German enemy in full fighting order. Each ship had its guns crews closed up for action with the guns trained outboard. At their battle stations, the men were issued with gas masks and asbestos clothing.

At 9:30 the "dirty and uncared-for ships"[3] of the High Seas Fleet were in sight, being led to the rendezvous by the light cruiser *Cardiff* and, on sighting her, Admiral Beatty formed his great command into two gigantic columns, each composed of two score or more battleships and cruisers.

The German fleet, which surrendered that day, consisted of their most modern vessels: nine battleships, five battlecruisers, seven light cruisers, and forty-nine destroyers. Large as this array was, it was totally dwarfed by the Grand Fleet, and this comparison illustrated perfectly the hopelessness of the German challenge to dispute control of the sea.

As the Grand Fleet came abreast of the German formation, Admiral Beatty turned the two long lines of British ships inward toward the German ships through 180 degrees, and in one brilliant maneuver, he placed his flagship, the battleship *Queen Elizabeth*, abeam Adm. Ludwig von Reuter's German fleet. Thus sandwiched between the two British columns, the German fleet was escorted back to the Forth, where both fleets anchored. The final seal on this memorable day was set by the signal sent by Beatty to Reuter at 11:00 A.M.: "The German flag will be hauled down at sunset today, Thursday, and will not be hoisted again without permission."

Seven months later, in a final act of self-degradation, the bulk of these surrendered German ships scuttled themselves in the still, quiet waters of Scapa Flow. This final drama was in fact an acknowledgement that their whole creation and purpose had failed utterly. As the last of the German ships slid below the water the work of the Grand Fleet was brought to its fulfillment, in a less spectacular, but far more complete and absolute, manner than the Battle of Trafalgar.

In 1918, then, there was no question in the minds of most senior officers of the Royal Navy that the battleship, as so often before, had been the main instrument with which this crushing victory had been secured. Nor was there much doubt then that as "Mistress of the Seas," her place was still secure for the foreseeable future.

Indeed, in 1918, in terms of battleship strength, the Royal Navy appeared to be in an unapproachable position. No less than seventy-one battleships and battlecruisers flew the white ensign in November 1918, a total that no other nation could even begin to approach.

It is true that many of these ships were elderly vessels, the so-called pre-Dreadnoughts, which had possessed little fighting value during the Great War and were destined for early visits to the breakers' yards in any event. But even without these ships, along with *Dreadnought* herself, which was destined for the same early termination, the number of modern fully battleworthy capital ships that the Royal Navy had in full commission was thirty-two battleships and nine battlecruisers, a total of forty-one heavy ships. This placed the Royal Navy way out ahead of any of her competitors in naval strength, especially as this ratio was maintained by cruiser and destroyer strength as well.

With the total elimination of the German and Austrian fleets from the world scene, only a few other nations retained even the semblance of a modern fighting fleet anyway. In order of precedence, these nations possessed the following the numbers of modern battleships and battlecruisers:

United States	15
Japan	9
France	7
Italy	5
Russia	5
Spain	3
Brazil	2
Argentina	2
Turkey	1

These nine nations totaled forty-nine modern capital ships against the Royal Navy's strength, on its own, of forty-one. Moreover, it was not only in numbers that the Royal Navy had a convincing preponderance of strength; equally, or perhaps more important, it was at a high pitch of training and readiness, and more than any of her rivals, the British fleet was fully attuned to modern battle conditions as they existed at that time. In numbers, in expertise, and in tradition, the Royal Navy in 1918 was undoubtedly the greatest maritime fighting organization in existence.

The figures thus presented appeared to confirm the continuing predominance of the British fleet in the postwar world and in the unshakeableness of the security of the empire, which had emerged even larger after the Great War, and whose ties were now strengthened as never before by the mutual sacrifice of the shedding of the blood of their sons in a common cause. British prestige was at its peak.

And yet within five years, this numerical superiority had been thrown away and was never regained. In ten years, the experience and expertise amassed from the Great War had been overtaken by new technical innovations with which the Royal Navy began to fall behind. Within twenty years, the utterly prostrate German enemy would once again be in a position to challenge Britain for control of the seas. How could this come about? There is no single answer but rather a series of interlocking factors that ensured the complete reversal of the 1918 position in so short a time. And the decline of the Royal Navy and the growth of her rivals are linked absolutely with the uncertainty of the future role of the battleship in sea warfare.

Presenting the numbers of capital ships completed and in service with the world's fleets as a yardstick (a now familiar phrase but one that was only just about to make its debut on the naval scene in 1918) gives a somewhat reassuring picture, but at the same time, it is a completely false one. Before proceeding, an explanation of the term "capital ship" as used in this book is desirable for the lay reader. This term was adopted to identify *both* the battleships and the battlecruisers of the fleets—a wholly misleading adoption because the two types had little in common, save for the main armaments. How the two types differed will be discussed later in this volume, but the United States had not actually built any of the latter at this time and wished to include those of other nations in the battleship totals. This led to frequent confusion in the minds of the public that they were in fact one and the same.

The true picture is only revealed when the actual numbers and types of capital ships then under construction are taken into account, and here the position was, for the British public—which regarded British dominance at sea as a fact of life, like breathing and taxes—far more alarming.

In 1918, in fact, work was in progress on only *one* British capital ship, the battlecruiser *Hood*. Originally one of a class of four, her sisters—*Anson, Howe,* and *Rodney*—had been cancelled earlier. Such was not the case with Britain's main rivals, the United States and Japan; both nations had already embarked on enormous building programs, which, once completed, would completely alter the rosy picture of British might at sea.

In 1916, the year of the battle of Jutland, the American Congress had voted through an enormous expenditure to allow for the rapid and unprecedented growth of the U.S. fleet, with the avowed aim of creating—to use their favorite phrase of the time—"a navy second to none." In fact, what the "big navy" men wanted was a navy superior to all, and in this, they were enthusiastically backed up by the steel and shipbuilding lobby, which foresaw an unprecedented boom in construction.

The aim, it was said, was to create a fleet that would be able to stand up to any British challenge in the Atlantic and any Japanese threat from across the Pacific—at the *same* time. Britain and Japan were linked by a strong treaty of alliance. Although this treaty was not directed at the United States when it was signed in 1902 but rather drafted as a brake on Russian imperialistic expansion into China and the Pacific, the very virulent and vocal Anglophobes in the American navy—and there were many at this time[4]—used this treaty as a threat to persuade the Congress to authorize this enormous program.

As a direct result, 1916 saw the beginning of construction in American yards of twelve of the largest and most powerful warships ever envisaged, vessels that, once built, would so completely outclass all existing capital ships as to somewhat nullify any temporary numerical advantage Great Britain might have. In addition, a further six equally enormous and awe-inspiring battlecruisers were laid down. The full program was as follows: twelve battleships— *Colorado, Maryland, Washington, West Virginia* at 32,600 tons; eight 16-inch guns, fourteen 5-inch guns, four 3-inch guns; and twenty-one knots; *South Dakota, Indiana, Montana, North Carolina, Iowa, Massachusetts* at 43,200 tons; twelve 16-inch guns, sixteen 6-inch guns; and twenty-three knots; and two other battleships; and six battlecruisers—*Lexington, Constellation, Saratoga, Ranger, Constitution, United States* at 43,200 tons; eight 16-inch guns, sixteen 6-inch guns, four 3-inch guns; thirty-three knots. The Colorado-class battleships were laid down on the stocks between 1917 and 1920; the Lexington-class battlecruisers were commenced in 1920 and 1921, as were the South Dakota-class battleships.

Nor was this program, ambitious as it was, the end of the story. In their eagerness to overtake Britain as the leading naval power, while that country was still fully focused on the German menace, the U.S. Navy actively considered even more far-reaching designs to produce the ultimate battleship. That summer, the American Senate directed the Committee on Naval Affairs to go ahead with research into the design of such a ship, which they aptly enough named the *Terror*. The ship was to have, in their own words "the maximum size, the maximum draft, and the maximum armament, and the maximum thickness of armor to make the very best battleship. or cruiser the world has ever seen or will see."[5] In their usual way, they stated that the creation of such a monster was not a threat to Britain or Japan but instead would be "the peacemaker of the world."[6]

Research work went ahead; the only limitations being put on the designers were the width of the locks on the Panama Canal. By October 1916, they had come up with a sketch design of the following characteristics: 70,000 tons; twelve 16-inch guns, twenty-one 6-inch guns; thirty-one knots.

It was not very surprising, therefore, to anyone but the Americans themselves that both Japan and Great Britain, when viewing this gigantic expansion of American seapower, tended to regard the *Terror* and even the more modest vessels already under construction, not as the world's peacemaker but as a determined threat against their very existence.

Whereas the American senators might consider themselves "better" than most nations and therefore ideally suited to wield such an instrument and be arbiter of events on the world's stage, both Japan and Great Britain took rather more worldly views on what they saw as a challenge. In this, the same reasons applied to the new American fleet as had been applied to the creation of the powerful German fleet before 1914. Great Britain had an enormous empire spread all over the globe. It had the world's largest mercantile fleet, which also had to be defended, and it was dependent on the importation of food and materials to an alarming degree, as the recent U-boat campaign had so convincingly brought home. Control of the sea was essential to the British, but to the Americans, completely self-sufficient at that time, it was not a necessity, merely an exercise in prestige.

It was a commonly expressed viewpoint in British naval circles, at all levels, that war with the United States was "unthinkable."[7] The reverse was quite often the case across the Atlantic, however, with many American admirals seeing Britain as the most logical future opponent in any new sea conflict, the clash of trading interests being the most likely cause of friction leading to such an event.[8]

Japan too was alarmed. It had been pursuing her own expansionist policies at the expense of her Chinese neighbor, and when told by the United States and Great Britain to curb these policies, Japan greatly resented it. It had reached the status of a first-rate power very quickly and largely by its own military prowess. Quite naturally, Japan saw what it considered its natural destiny being thwarted by the two western powers and acted accordingly. The only way the U.S. and Britain could reach Japan in the event of war was by sea, so Japan immediately initiated a great shipbuilding program of its own to counter that threat.

Although the earlier cordial relations between Japan and Great Britain were now wearing rather thin, the long-established ties between the two navies were still deep, and in particular, the influence of the world's greatest seapower in design was still strongly felt. British-built and British-designed warships predominated in the Japanese fleet, as did British methods. As in other areas, however, Japan was now becoming more and more self-reliant. This was reflected in its building programs.

As early as 1912, Japan had shown her newfound independence of thought with the magnificent Kongo-class battlecruisers. The lead ship was ordered from a British yard—Vickers, Barrow—while the three sisters were built in Japanese yards, but it was the design itself which most impressed. Indeed, Great Britain thought so highly of the *Kongo*, which so obviously outclassed the Lion-class of the current British program, that the *Tiger*, laid down soon after the launch of the *Kongo*, was redesigned to incorporate many of the design features of the Japanese vessel and, as a result, turned out to be one of the most successful vessels of this type ever built. Already, then, the pupil, Japan, was imparting lessons to the teacher, Britain. In the 1920s, this trend was accelerated still further.

Alarmed at the massive United States building program of 1916 onward, Japan was now ready to counter it. Although at war in 1914 alongside the Allies, Japan was never a very enthusiastic backer of their cause, the military caste in Japan having far more in common with the Prussians, who took over the German destiny during the Great War, than with the democratic nations she was linked to by treaty. Japan therefore made the maximum effort toward the war to qualify it for a major seat at the peace conference but undertook only such military expeditions that actually contributed to her own ambitions and strict self-interest. For example, to besiege and capture Tsingtao, Germany's main naval base in the Pacific, was a prize that she took quick action to secure. It was not so much the removal of German influence from China, however, as the establishment of Japan's own power there that had prompted this action, which was completed by November 1914.

Japan had solemnly promised the Chinese that she fully accepted the integrity of China, and that pledge influenced the Chinese, with whom Germany had been negotiating to return the port intact, knowing in any case that it could not be held against British sea power.

Once established, however, the Japanese did not yield this prize of war to its rightful ownership, and in 1920, it was still very much a Japanese base.

More than this, early in 1915, with a strong foothold thus established, with its allies fully committed in Europe, and with America apathetic and uninterested, Japan saw its chance to press on with the next stage of its program, and it had nothing to do with aiding the crusade against Germany.

Japan presented the Chinese government with a series of points aimed at giving itself a complete stranglehold over China's economy; if met in full, these points would give Japan absolute ascendancy and influence over that vast country, to the exclusion of all other foreign influences. The so-called Twenty-one Demands were made in secret, but when the British and American governments got wind of them, they combined to administer a stern warning to Japan to desist. But Japan ignored this and pressed on, and China, with little hope of material assistance at that time, was forced to accept the bulk of them. This gave the western governments a perfect indication of the probable course of Japan's future diplomacy, but there was little they could do to stop her between 1915 and 1918.

However, in overplaying her hand, Japan had made potential enemies out of what had hitherto been cordial friends, and as both these nations happened to be premier naval powers, Japan had no option but to speed her own naval defences. This she would have done anyway; the 1916 American program merely acted as both the spur and the necessary excuse for proceeding with her own rebuilding plans.

The Kongo-class battlecruisers had been followed by a steady stream of Super Dreadnoughts, through the *Fuso, Hyuga*, and *Nagato*, all designed and built to outclass the corresponding ships built by the United States over the period 1912-16. Once the American 1916 plans were known, however, the Japanese countered with their 8-8 Plan. This was the immediate construction of eight battleships and eight battlecruisers to be laid down between 1917 and 1927. Again, ship for ship, they were to be the match—or much better—than the American South Dakotas and Lexingtons.

The first two were completed in 1919 and 1920, and others were being built while more were still in the planning stage. The full program was as follows: eight battleships—*Nagato, Mutsu* at 33,800 tons; eight 16-inch guns, twenty 5.5-inch guns, four 3.1-inch guns; 26.5 knots; *Kaga, Tosa* at 39,900 tons; ten 16-inch guns, twenty 5.5-inch guns, four 3.1-inch guns; 29.5 knots; and *13, 14, 15, 16* (names unallocated). Yet a further class of four ships, the "Y Hiraga" design of 1921, were prepared with the following specifications: 47,500 tons; eight 18-inch guns, sixteen 5.5-inch guns, eight 4.7-inch guns; thirty knots. The eight battlecruiseres were the *Amagi, Akagi, Atago*, and *Takao* at 41,217 tons; ten 16-inch guns, sixteen 5.5-inch guns; and thirty knots; the *Kii, Owari, 11*, and *12* (names unallocated) at 42,600 tons; ten 16-inch guns, sixteen 5.5-inch guns; and thirty knots.

Thus it can be seen that with the introduction of these monsters—mounting 18-inch guns in the main against the 16-inch guns of the American ships—Japan was not only accepting the challenge but going considerably farther.

When compared with both these titanic building programs, the Royal Navy's completion of the battlecruiser *Hood* in 1920 was the pale termination of that service's expansion from the war programs. Compared with what had gone before, *Hood* was a fine addition to the fleet, but compared with the behemoths being built by Japan and the U.S., she had already been left far behind. *Hood*'s details were 41,200 tons; eight 15-inch guns, sixteen 5.5-inch guns; thirty-two knots.

Worse than the fact that her 15-inch guns were already being outclassed by existing 16-inch and projected 18-inch weapons was the fact that she was only one ship against the eighteen new American vessels and the sixteen new Japanese ships, without taking into account the ships of those two powers now being completed and joining the fleet from earlier programs.

Obviously, the Admiralty had to respond to this dual challenge, and respond it did. In 1921, Parliament sanctioned new naval estimates, which included this response. Four new battlecruisers mounting 16-inch guns were to be laid down at once, followed by a program of battleships with 18-inch guns. The details of the four battlecruisers were as follows: *1, 2, 3, 4* (names unconfirmed, although generally thought to have been *Inflexible, Indomitable, Indefatigable,* and *Invincible;* an alternative set of speculative names put forward at the time included *St. George, St. Andrew, St. David,* and *St. Patrick*) at 48,000 tons; nine 16-inch guns, sixteen 6-inch guns, six 4.7-inch and no fewer than forty 2-pounder pom-poms; and thirty-two knots. Known as the G-3 design, these four ships were approved in August 1921 and ordered on October 26 from the shipyards of Beardmore, John Brown, Fairfield, and Swan Hunter. The four battleships were designated *5, 6, 7,* and *8.* These four magnificent battleships, the N-3 design, were thought to have a designed tonnage of 48,500 tons and mount nine 18-inch guns, sixteen 6-inch guns, six 4.7-inch guns, and carry forty 2-pounder pom-poms, and have a speed of at least about twenty-three knots.

It is a thousand pities these eight ships were never built, for each one would have been worth two of older battleships that were eventually retained for World War II; the battlecruisers alone would have had the speed to accompany carrier task groups; but the Treasury was hostile and unsympathetic even without the machinations of Washington.

When details of these ships and the Japanese giants came to light, the American politicians, who had sanctioned their great program to ensure "the fulfillment of the United States' destiny as leader of democratic impulse,"[9] began to have second thoughts. It was one thing to undertake the construction of the world's mightiest battle fleet for use as the proverbial "big stick" with which to bring Great Britain to heel and browbeat the rest of the world into accepting a *Pax Americana* to replace the long-established *Pax Britannica*.

It was quite another when, after the spending of many millions of dollars on such vessels, that they would then be completely outclassed by both British and Japanese ships of the same type. They would have expended a great deal of taxpayers money and have been no farther forward.

If Great Britain and Japan could not be outbuilt in a new naval race, then might not an alternative way be found to ensure that America's "naval destiny" be fulfilled on the cheap? As Oscar Parkes related, "At an average cost of 7 million pounds apiece, these three powers were committed to an expenditure of 252 million pounds on capital ships alone."[10] The United States might be the world's richest nation, but there was a limit to what public opinion at home would stand, especially as many prominent American citizens were not as convinced as the big navy group that their nation really needed to replace Great Britain as the world's policeman, even for national prestige.[11]

In this new policy, they were aided by several important factors that now began to emerge. The first was the economic bankruptcy of Great Britain, which emerged from the Great War—which it had started as the richest country in the world—with vast debts, mainly to the United States. True, the amount owed Britain by other countries exceeded its debts, but when Britain's bills went unpaid, it was expected to pay up. Britain owed the United States a large amount of money, and the American authorities were making it clear that it must be repaid despite it having been spent, among other things, in keeping the United States safe from the German fleet, which in 1914 was second only to the British.[12]

This was not at first thought to have influenced the British politicians. In March 1920, for example, the new First Lord, Walter Long, addressed the house in terms that seemed to indicate that the traditional British policy of control of the sea would be maintained indefinitely. "I believe," he stated, "it is a fact that the naval policies of all past governments, whichever party they have represented, have at least included the common principle that our Navy should not be inferior in strength to the Navy of any other power, and to this principle the present Government firmly adheres."[13]

This was not, however, the same as saying that the government of David Lloyd George intended to maintain the old two-power standard, which was thought vital by most of its predecessors. When Sir David Beatty, now First Sea Lord, laid before Parliament the size of the postwar fleet he considered the absolute minimum, it was not well received.

Beatty's requirements were for an Atlantic fleet to be composed of a fleet flagship, two battleship squadrons, a battlecruiser squadron, two light cruiser squadrons, four destroyer flotillas, and three submarine flotillas, in addition to a powerful Mediterranean fleet which was once more to be reestablished after a lapse of several years. This did not seem excessive to the Royal Navy in view of the size of the old Grand Fleet, but to the economists, it seemed to be highly unrealistic. A total force of fourteen battleships in full commission in the balmy days of 1920, when not an enemy appeared in sight, was just not tolerated. The numbers were pruned to a total of six capital ships in the Atlantic Fleet and six in the Mediterranean; cruiser and destroyer strengths were cut even more, and the actual number of ships in the destroyer flotillas were reduced from one flotilla leader, one sub leader, and sixteen destroyers to one leader and eight destroyers only. This was as much a tactical consideration as an economic one, since war experience had shown that the larger numbers made handling flotillas in combat unwieldy.

The realities of economics soon made themselves felt in the navy in other ways. The summary reduction in the strength of the serving personnel from the wartime peak of 407,316 caused great resentment, especially in the clumsy and thoughtless way it was handled. This feature of the so-called Geddes Axe, named after the First Lord of the day, was to be repeated, in the high-handed way in which it was introduced, by a later government when cuts in pay were to become necessary and led to the Invergordon mutiny. Insensitivity when dealing with service matters and personnel had long been a hallmark of the British government, although it should have been expected, by the 1920s and 30s, to have acted with more thought and tact.

Allied to the economic factor was the strong feeling in the country that the Great War had indeed been the "war to end all wars." This feeling was common, and the widespread pacifism that swept the western world was in its way highly commendable. It was particularly strong in Great Britain, and the reasons are not hard to find. For centuries, this country had relied on seapower to protect her. A miniscule standing army had been built up, but this was, in the main, small in comparison with the continental armies, especially those that developed during the nineteenth century. Not only had the British not fought a major land campaign since Waterloo more than a century before, but it had always conducted its campaigns without conscription. Even the Crimea operations had not brought home to the bulk of the population how bloody and all-embracing land warfare had become. Seapower was not only effective, it was economical in the nation's most valuable asset, manpower.[14]

It was only when this policy was abandoned in the 1914–18 war and a huge conscript army sent to fight in the traditional continental manner that this aspect of modern warfare was brought grimly home to the nation.[15] The ghastly carnage of the Western Front naturally made a deep and long-lasting impression on all who took part, and an equally firm impression on those that had lost relations and friends—in 1920, this meant almost every household in the land. There was a fierce determination that such wholesale slaughter must never be allowed to take place again.

The logical answer would probably have been to revert once more to the old tried, tested, and reliable defense of the sea, but the natural reaction against the huge casualty lists of France and Flanders automatically embraced all forms of self-defense. The thought that all the suffering and hardship of World War I had been in vain, that naval rivalry with Germany, held by many to have been a contributing factor to the outbreak of the war, had been overcome only to be replaced by similar rivalry on an even vaster scale, was simply not acceptable. Politicians naturally reflected the will of the people and, even if they sincerely believed in the need to maintain Britain's defenses, found that the arguments for such a policy fell on deaf ears. It was not long therefore before excuses were being made in the House of Commons as to why Great Britain was falling behind in terms of battleship construction, and for the first time but unhappily not for the last, the reasons given were "the general, financial, and international situation prevailing."[16]

The United States, although hardly as affected in terms of casualties as Great Britain, shared the revulsion against warfare and further spending on arms, and the public climate changed sufficiently by 1921 that the American House of Representatives halved the naval estimates for that year, effectively putting an end to the immediate realizations of the big navy men. Despite Japanese aloofness from this general trend, it is not surprising that the two western powers began to make diplomatic approaches to each other to terminate the new race before it got fully underway.

Unfortunately for all these men of good faith and idealistic intents, the old lesson—that unilateral disarmament is futile and, more to the point, highly dangerous—was forgotten in the general euphoria of the time, which led them to believe that perhaps Japan might be persuaded to join them in a reduction in naval forces, providing that they led the way in making concessions. The argument ran that if it were demonstrated to the Japanese by example that they had nothing to fear from the British and American navies, then they would agree to cooperate in wholesale limitations. All well and good, then, but suppose such a power was to renege on any new pact and go all-out for world domination? Then it was argued that an international force based on existing armaments would provide the solution.[17]

Be that as it may, President Warren G. Harding's call for an arms limitations conference, made in 1921, was warmly welcomed in British circles, and only slightly less enthusiastically by the lesser naval powers, France and Italy. And why shouldn't it have been, for in any general agreement on naval disarmament, such powers could not help benefiting, in proportion of total strengths, at the expense of the premier naval power, Britain. It was Britain that had the most to lose at this time, and ultimately, it was Britain, or rather the men of her mercantile marine, who had to pay the price.

When this conference got underway at Washington in November 1921, the British delegation faced the knowledge that they would have to fight hard for a large enough fleet to protect the empire. Worse, they knew that at the same time as they were striving to prevent the whittling away of the navy to a dangerous level at the conference table in Washington, they faced equally fierce opposition from the Treasury at home. It was an unenviable position but one to which Sir David Beatty applied himself with the same devotion and patience as he had his seagoing commands during the war.

The nature of the Washington Conference was set by the opening speech of the American president. Instead of a carefully debated conference to discuss the best ways and means of limiting naval armaments, the Americans produced, out of the hat, a plan—a diktat, almost—aimed at ensuring that America achieved at least parity with Great Britain, thus leapfrogging herself to the top of the naval strength league. In one respect, Harding knew that his audacious outline was almost certain of ultimate acceptance, for the British government, in flat contradiction of their pious utterances in 1919, had already made it fairly obvious that they would not, after all, object to such a parity.[18]

What came as a complete surprise to the assembled delegates—and as alluring as it was unexpected—was the proposal that all the battleships and battlecruisers then in various stages of construction should be broken up on the slips forthwith and that no new construction of capital ships should take place for at least ten years. The lure was in the tonnage figures put forward.

Here it was seen that the United States was being virtuous and setting a wholesome lead for the other powers to follow, for she would scrap some 845,000 tons of new capital ships against 583,000 tons for Great Britain and 449,000 tons for Japan. These figures later included the tonnages for completed ships also to be dismantled at the same time. Of course, these tonnages did not reveal that, in making this concession, America was at this time well aware that the ships she was building were already far outclassed by those building in Japan and Britain, as we have seen.

Though these proposals went far, there was still more. On completion of the scrapping program, the Royal Navy would still be left with a slight tonnage margin of superiority:

Great Britain	22 ships	604,450 tons
United States	18 ships	500,650 tons
Japan	10 ships	299,700 tons

But any misplaced relief that the British representatives might have felt at even this small concession to her commitments was quickly eradicated as the American proposal went on to suggest that these figures were only temporary and that the final figures, to be achieved within the ten year period, were as follows:

Great Britain	500,000 tons
United States	500,000 tons
Japan	300,000 tons

It was clear from these figures on whom the final sacrifice was to be placed, for whereas the American and Japanese allocations remained much the same, still further reductions were to be made by Great Britain over this period. The final ratios for all the main powers would then come out as:

Great Britain	5
United States	5
Japan	3
France	1.75
Italy	1.75

If the nature of the fight before the British delegation was fairly obvious to them from the start, the position on the home front was equally precarious, as they well knew. Although in 1919 David Lloyd George had told the Americans that Britain would "spend her last guinea"[19] to ensure that the British fleet remained superior to the American, things were now very different. Leaving Admiral Chatfield and his staff to do their best in the face of the American proposals, Beatty hurried back to London, behavior which one historian has called odd, coming, as it did, in the face of such a threat across the conference table.

In the circumstances, there is little doubt that Beatty took the right course. Although big issues were at stake in Washington, ultimately it was the prime minister and the British government that would have to make the decisions, and knowing the strength of the forces at work in Whitehall to pare the armed forces to the bone, Beatty wanted to be at the center of affairs.[20] As Beatty recorded, "If it continues, we shall have no navy at all, Washington Conference or not!"[21]

Back at Washington, the caving in of the other nations to the American proposals was complete. None pretended to like it. Japan felt it a national insult to have her rapidly expanding navy frozen at 60 percent of its two potential enemies, and she gave way with bad grace. She was shrewd enough, however, to use her building program as a bargaining chip to give her mandates over the strategic islands of the Bonins, Kurile, Formosa, and the

Pescadores, which she undertook, no doubt with tongue in cheek, not to fortify. Moreover, the Americans were forbidden to fortify either Guam or
Manila, which meant that the closest fleet base available for their battle fleet
to work against Japan remained at distant Hawaii. This agreement virtually
gave the Japanese complete control of the Western Pacific, which was what
she desired in order to pursue her "forward" policy with regard to China.

If Japan was outwardly upset at, but ultimately accepted, the ratios proposed, then France was equally insulted. For more than two centuries, it had
been the main rival to Britain at sea, and up until the last decades of the nineteenth century, its fleet had maintained second place. It is true that this position was usurped first by Germany and then the United States during the
early years of the twentieth century, but France still had a strong tradition as a
major, albeit a seldom victorious, sea power. Her rank was now equal to that
of Italy, a nation with no large worldwide empire to defend. Moreover, France
had at this period the largest and best-equipped army in the world, and the
agreed ratios hurt her pride. She no doubt found solace in the fact that the
Washington Conference failed to agree on similar limitations for lesser warships, especially submarines, which Britain had wished to ban completely.[22]

But as another very perceptive historian has noted, none of these
nations really suffered at Washington, despite their protests:

> Britain lost on the deal. By accepting the main American ratios, she
> surrendered her long-standing sea supremacy among the nations of
> the world, she abandoned her ancient freedom to protect in the way
> she thought best her vital maritime communications, and she
> agreed to forgo her previous commanding lead over the Japanese.[23]

He added: "For the sake of a false semblance of naval equality with America, the British government gave away any chance of equality in the Far East,
where it mattered a great deal."[24] Whereas the judgment of history would
seem to uphold this opinion, another historian reaches quite different conclusions. The loss of this supremacy in terms of battleships was regarded as

> a considerable achievement. It failed to limit competition in sub-
> marines or military aircraft, both of which were potentially more
> important weapons than battleships, but this is more apparent with
> hindsight than it was in 1922; at that time battle fleets were generally
> regarded as the backbone of any navy, and it was reasonable to
> assume that the vicious, rising spiral of suspicion, response and
> counter-response had been cuts.[25]

It was this reasoning that provided the fuel to the third weapon in the pacifists' armory: "The battleship was on the way out!"[26] This third front against the Admiralty had been opened almost as soon as the war was over and reached the general public by way of a furious debate in the correspondence columns of the *Times* through the so-called battleship-versus-bomber controversy. Moreover, it was a feeling that, combined with the war-weariness of the nation, British governments were eager to back. That the battleship in 1945 was finally recognized as being finished by the development of air weapons should not cloud the issue of the decisions made in the 1920s. Informed naval opinion at this period was completely in agreement around the world that the battleship was still the main weapon of naval power. The Admiralty has been pilloried time and time again for the stand it took in the interwar years on this issue and is generally depicted as being run by ultra-conservative men with closed minds. Such a stance is wholly unacceptable but is made with distressing frequency. It cannot accord with the facts.

No responsible Board of Admiralty would press for the retention of the battleship in the face of tightening budgets had they not been convinced that it was a necessary weapon. Had it been demonstrably proven beyond doubt that the capital ship was outclassed and outmatched by aircraft in 1920 or by any other weapon, then surely such a weapon would have been adopted as quickly as possible by every nation aspiring to major status. In fact, the reverse was the case. It was not just Great Britain, with her long history of the battle fleet concept as defined by American admiral and naval theorist Alfred Thayer Mahan, who believed after comprehensive studies that the battleship remained supreme at this time, but the United States, Japan, and—when it again returned to the field—Germany also. Nor were the "lesser" powers—who were always outclassed and outnumbered in battleships and on whom restrictions would have placed a much lighter burden— in any less doubt that the battleship was still supreme at sea. The fact that all these powers came to the same conclusions at the same time would appear to negate the argument that the retention of the battleship was little more than "an Anglo-Mahan confidence trick, which eventually rebounded on its own innocent perpetrators."[27]

Right at the start of this long, drawn-out, and unhappy period of paper arguments, the Admiralty had made its position clear. After acknowledging the growing criticism of the keeping in commission a large number of capital ships, they stated: "The naval staff has examined this question with extreme care and as a result we profoundly dissent from these views. In our opinion the capital ship remains the unit on which sea-power is built up."[28]

The careful examination and the results that followed were not accepted by their critics however, and the press had a field day as the battleship was naturally denounced by the bomber enthusiasts, the pacifists, and—more alarmingly to the sincere men who were trying to give the empire the best defense they could—by many ex-naval men as well. Among the most vociferous of these were Adm. Percy Scott and Adm. John Fisher in England, both of whom were regarded as epitomizing the establishment of the big gun and the Dreadnought-class battleship, which both now regarded as finished. In the United States, this point of view was taken up by Adm. William Sims, an old friend of Scott's who had done as much for the efficiency of American naval gunfire as had Scott for his own service. That such men were combined in their disdain for the battleship in the 1920s provided powerful ammunition for the advocates of the heavy bomber who were stridently calling for the complete abolition of navies.

One concession wrung by Chatfield at Washington was that because other powers had 16-inch gun vessels completed, Britain was allowed to construct immediately two such ships to maintain the balance since her existing 15-inch-gunned ships were outclassed. These two vessels became the battleships *Nelson* and *Rodney*, laid down in 1922 and completed in 1927. Because the limit on displacement agreed to at Washington was 35,000 tons, these ships were far less powerful than the four battlecruisers of the original British postwar program. This was acknowledged in the fleet itself where the naturally perceptive sailors dubbed them the "Cherry Tree" class, because "they were cut down by Washington!" Their final details were 33,900 tons; nine 16-inch, twelve 6-inch, six 4.7-inch guns; and twenty-three knots.

As can be seen by comparison, these two vessels, in order to conform to the new limitations, sacrificed speed for armor in the old manner, and the unusual disposition of their main armament, with three triple turrets forward, was necessitated by the need to concentrate what armor protection they were allowed over the most vital sections of the hull. Although criticized for this, they did present the best compromise possible, and in foreign circles, especially America, their appearance was considered a disturbing factor because they appeared to outclass the most modern American ships.

In the then-current "fighting strength" table, drawn up by the U.S. Navy according to a complicated formula that involved both the life and hitting power of battleships, these two vessels rated as follows in comparison with the most recent ships in service at that time:

Nelson	British	20.4
Nagato	Japanese	18.8
Maryland	American	18.6
Hood	British	17.7
Arizona	American	17.6

Queen Elizabeth	British	16.6
Ise	Japanese	16.3
Texas	American	12.5
Repulse	British	12.5
Kongo	Japanese	12.0

It is interesting also to notice the high position of the *Hood*. Although designed as a battlecruiser rather than a battleship, her great displacement had allowed for extra armor to be worked in and had not affected her speed. She carried the same main armament as the Queen Elizabeth- and Royal Sovereign-class battleships as well. Between the wars, she was regarded as "Queen of the Fleet" and the "Mighty 'ood" in the Royal Navy and regarded with awe elsewhere. It was after her startling and sudden demise that opinion swung around squarely against her.

Although it was frequently stated that she was a post-Jutland ship and thus embodied in her great hull all the lessons learned from the tragic destruction of the three British battlecruisers at that battle, she was still suspect. Even in 1930, there were doubts about her, which obviously were still unknown to the compilers of the American table of strengths. Adm. Sir Frederick Dreyer, Director of the Admiralty Gunnery Division, stated: "It had become quite obvious to all of us that the improved type of 15-inch armour-piercing shell with which we had equipped the Grand Fleet in 1918 could easily penetrate and detonate in the *Hood*'s main magazines."[29] This was shown to be prophetic some ten years later, after nothing was done to rectify this weakness.

However much the appearance of the *Nelson* and *Rodney* in the Royal Navy's battle line might be welcomed by the Admiralty (five Iron Duke-class ships and the battlecruiser *Tiger* were soon afterwards scrapped in compensation), their arrival, or rather their very conception, aroused the battleship's critics to a crescendo of anger. R.Adm. Stephen Hall was one of those who expressed the opinion of the bomber-rather-than-battleship lobby in a letter to the *Times* in 1922, when the ships were announced: "By the time they [*Nelson* and *Rodney*] are completed, the inevitable development of air warfare will have left them entirely out of the picture."[30]

Others pointed to the dramatic demonstration of the bomber given in July 1921 by the American aviator Billy Mitchell, which seemed to prove their point beyond dispute. Both Mitchell in America and Maj. Gen. Sir Hugh Trenchard, at this time Chief of the Air Staff of newly independent Royal Air Force, represented the viewpoints of the air superiority faction. Both were convinced that not only was air power the most important factor in any future conflict between major powers, but that air power could do the jobs then and previously done by both armies *and navies*.[31] Both were extremely vocal in this extremist point of view, and the prevailing climate of the time, with air power being hailed as something new and exciting by the popular press against the old "sterile" (i.e., less newsworthy) forms of defense, ensured that their arguments, viewpoints, and wild statements received the maximum publicity.

Mitchell was particularly eager to force home his opinions, for America, unlike Britain, had not adopted a separate air force in 1918 but retained the three separate arms, the Marines, Army Air Force, and the Navy. Mitchell's crusade was for a unified, independent air force on the British pattern, and he knew the battleship would provide him with the most spectacular canvas of all on which to paint his vision of the future. The methods he used were doubtful in taste but successful, for in 1920, he was granted his first test, and the results proved so valuable to his cause that he successfully pressed for, and was granted, others in the following years.

His first success was against the ancient coastal defense battleship *Indiana*, a 10,200-ton vessel completed in 1895 that had been originally paid off in 1914 and used as a training ship on the east coast. In what were supposed to have been top-secret conditions carried out in November 1920, the bombers successfully dealt with the *Indiana*. Moreover, a mysterious source leaked to the British *Illustrated London News* two sensational photographs of bomb explosions and damage aboard the ship, which gained for the air faction a tremendous publicity boost. In vain did the Secretary of the Navy, Josephus Daniels, point out that the *Indiana* was merely "an ancient hulk."[32] She was a battleship to the press and to the public as a whole.

From this test, Mitchell made his usual claims. "We can tell you definitely now that we can either destroy or sink any ship in existence today."[33] The navy rose to the bait. A further series of tests was authorized, starting with smaller warships, a submarine, a destroyer, and then a light cruiser, all from America's share of the surrendered German Navy. Finally, the German battleship *Ostfriesland* was to be attacked in a series of strictly controlled test bombings, with pauses between each test so that damage and results could be carefully evaluated at each stage.

Mitchell agreed to the conditions, but as it turned out, he had no intention of keeping to them. The *Ostfriesland* was much more representative of the battleship type, for although obsolete by the standards of 1921, she was only ten years old, being one of Germany's first Dreadnoughts, with a tonnage of 22,800 and being completed in 1911.

The tests were held some seventy miles off Virginia Capes and commenced on June 20, 1921. In two days, three submarines were very quickly put down. A week later, a destroyer followed them with equal rapidity to the bottom, and finally, on July 18, the light cruiser *Frankfurt* sank after six hours of bombing by navy and army planes. But this was merely the buildup; the great attraction was the *Ostfriesland*, a very different proposition to the smaller targets so summarily dispatched to date.

The great battleship lay ready for her supreme trial in Hampton Roads on July 20, her 3-inch-thick armor decks bare and empty, her 11-inch armor sides equally clear.[34] The first waves came in just after 1:39 P.M., marine and navy aircraft again carrying 230-pound bombs. In all, three dozen of these small missiles were aimed at the *Ostfriesland*. A mere nine actually hit the stationary target, and of these nine hits, only two detonated. None penetrated the main deck. At 3:30, the tests resumed with heavier metal: six large army Martin bombers followed by navy seaplanes. The former carried two 600-pound bombs while the latter were equipped with 550-pound weapons. In fact, only nineteen of the twenty-four bombs were actually dropped, including eleven of the army bombs. Of these, the army scored two hits and one near-miss, and the navy fliers got three hits. At the end of it all, the *Ostfriesland* appeared unperturbed. None of the hits, although some penetrated the main deck, got through the protected deck and the battleship's stability and seaworthiness remained intact.

Her resistance was naturally not to Mitchell's liking. He still had his heaviest weapons in reserve, but under the strict test conditions, he feared the results might not be as dramatic as he had hoped. Under the conditions agreed to after each direct hit made by these larger bombs, a lull was to be made in the attacks while their results were analyzed by a boarding party. Mitchell had other ideas, hoping that a continued bombardment of hits and near-misses—which Mitchell believed caused a "water hammer" effect—would be almost certain of producing a more successful result. It was the publicity effect Mitchell wanted, not an analysis. He got his wish.

At 8:32 the next morning, the first army bomber came in and scored a direct hit with a 1,000-pound bomb. The observers prepared to go aboard to carry out their assigned tasks, but to their amazement and the fury of Adm. H. B. Wilson, the second army bomber immediately followed up with a near-miss. Meanwhile, Mitchell signaled Wilson, requesting him to prevent any navy aircraft from interfering with the operations of army planes.

Four more army bombers came in and between them scored another two direct hits and two more near-misses. Eventually, the observers got aboard the battleship, and there they found that not even three direct hits by 1,000-pound bombs had affected the watertight integrity of the ship. Mitchell concluded that a further bending of the rules would be necessary now. He was officially allowed three further drops using one-ton bombs, and then it was the navy's turn again. Mitchell had other ideas.

At 12:19 P.M., Mitchell signaled that his aircraft intended to attack and attack again with these big bombs until they scored two hits, but what he was really after was his "water hammer" effect with one-tonners. The first three bombs were misses, but the fourth shaved her hull on the port side forward and was followed by a second close by, both of which erupted beneath the *Ostfriesland* covering her heaving decks with great cascades of water.

It was this fifth bomb that did the vital damage; the sixth bomb was another miss. By 12:30, her aft gun deck was awash; by 12:37, she had listed over to port; and at 12:41, she rolled over, with her bows upside down out of the water, and sank. As she started her final lunge, another 2,000-pound bomb was dropped on her as a parting shot from Mitchell's jubilant airmen.

The reaction of the press was predictable enough; the New York *Evening Mail* can be held as typical. A battleship that had cost 40 million dollars and taken six years to build had been sunk "by six bombs carried by machines costing less than 25,000 dollars apiece."[35] Mitchell had got his scalp, but strangely enough, his methods resulted in the good points of his arguments being spoiled by his exaggerations. He did not get his Independent Air Force, but he did add considerable fuel to the already highly stoked bomber-versus-battleship fire.

The trials continued in the United States. In September 1921, the *Alabama* (11,600 tons, completed in 1900) was sunk; in September 1923, Mitchell also sank the battleships *New Jersey* and *Virginia* in similar tests. These two were also of the obsolete pre-Dreadnought type (15,000 tons, completed in 1906), and so the tests proved nothing new. In November 1924, the uncompleted hull of the new battleship *Washington* was also sunk, by bombs alone, in what was a more relevant test with regard to actual modern battleship strength of resistance. But even so, an end to the dispute was no nearer; instead, the battle lines merely hardened as the years went by.

As Capt. S. W. Roskill points out, the *Washington* was the only modern ship allocated to these trials, and "the fact that she proved very difficult to sink supported the views of those who argued that a properly defended modern battleship would survive the worst that air attack could do to her."[36] He conclude, however, that "the most important result of the whole series of tests was that every warship attacked with live bombs was sunk, and by bombs alone."[37]

This viewpoint is not shared by another postwar appraisal, this one by an airman. Wing Cmdr. W. H. Allen concluded that "the *Ostfriesland* was at anchor when the bombers struck, and naturally, she was without a crew and, therefore no guns were firing back. The exercise proved nothing."[38] There were no damage control parties to check the cumulative damage either. But more to the point, he added, "There is all the difference in the world between a capital ship at anchor and such a ship steaming fast, firing heavy barrages against the bombers, and maneuvering to put the bomb-aimers off the sighting."[39] Billy Mitchell would not have agreed with this; in fact, in one statement he is alleged to have asserted, quite seriously, that "the faster a water vessel goes, the easier it is to hit from the air."[40]

The question of costs raised by the *Evening Mail* also got its share of attention from the air enthusiasts. If the much cheaper airplane could sink the incredibly expensive warship, there was no answer in those days of economy and penny-pinching. For the price of just three modern battleships, asserted Mitchell, America could have no fewer than 3,000 military aircraft and be impregnable.

As usual, his was the extreme figure of cost-ratio to be thrown out in the argument and counterarguments. From Mitchell's 1,000 bombers for the price of a battleship, the estimates ranged down to a more modest ratio of 100 to 1. "Finally, in an attempt to get to the truth of this particular argument, the Admiralty and the Air Ministry got together and made a detailed study on which they both agreed. Between them they 'worked out an agreed figure of forty-three twin-engined medium bombers [*not* long-range heavy bombers] as the nearest approximation to the equivalent in cost to one battleship, taking into account all those overhead, maintenance, and replacement and similar charges which should be included to make an effective comparison during the life of one capital ship."[41]

Finally, the British also carried out a series of tests in more realistic conditions using the old pre-Dreadnought battleship *Agamemnon* (16,000 tons, completed in 1908), which had been stripped of her guns and fitted out as a radio-controlled target vessel. Her speed when brand new was only eighteen knots; nevertheless, she presented a moving target for the bombers. The results were not encouraging to the advocates of air supremacy. The tests were carried out during 1921-22 by RAF bombers using dummy bombs to test accuracy rather than penetration, for without the former the latter was useless. Tests were conducted from varying heights, and the percentage of hits scored varied from 0 to more than 50 percent, but the better figures were achieved only after the aircraft had pressed in at the point-blank height of 400 feet or less.

In 1924, another series of tests was made using the more modern battleship *Monarch* (22,500 tons, completed in 1912). Again, dummy bombs were used initially, then live bombs "at rest." She was then shelled by cruisers during the afternoon and by battleships, testing the new 15-inch armor-piercing shells, at night. Before dawn broke, the *Monarch* still floated, and the battleship *Revenge* had to put her down with deliberately aimed salvos.

From such experiments the Admiralty concluded that to put a modern battleship out of action by bombing would require at least twelve direct hits from bombs of over 500-pounds, and these bombs, to achieve the necessary penetrating power to pierce her armored decks, would have to be dropped from a height of 5,000 feet. The chances of this being achieved with the aircraft, crews, and bombing sights then in service they estimated at "seven in a hundred."[42]

To anticipate somewhat, the final verdict was given after the war by Wing Commander Allen:

> Yet through the whole of the Second World War, Bomber Command sank not one enemy capital ship at sea with free-falling bombs. It is an easy—and false—assumption to believe that a bomber is a cheap antidote to a battleship. But if a thousand bombers at 3,000 pounds each are lost in an unsuccessful attempt to sink a battleship the price is still 3,000,000 pounds. The bombers are a write-off but the battleship still remains an excellent weapons' system in various roles.[43]

But heavy bombers cost far more than 3,000 pounds each—more like ten times that amount.

Dive-bombing was far more accurate, of course, but apart from successful experiments being carried out by the U.S. Navy and later followed and improved upon by the Japanese Navy and the German Luftwaffe, these aircraft failed to figure in the estimations of the 1920s or indeed the 1930s, at least as far as the Royal Air Force was concerned.[44]

Torpedo-bombing was another matter. The threat from the torpedo had long remained the major one to the position of the battleship. Underwater damage was always recognized as being much more likely to cause the loss of any ship than either bombs or shellfire. The torpedo was not a new weapon by any means and had several times over the previous fifty years been hailed as the weapon to terminate the capital ship's long dominance.

As the torpedo had developed, however, and as the various craft designed to deliver it to its target had also grown more effective, so countermeasures had been adopted in the world's battle fleets. It was a weapon that had held out great promise but that promise had not been fulfilled, at least against modern battleships. Older warships and merchant vessels had proven only too vulnerable to it but the battleship had survived.

The hordes of torpedo-boats constructed by France in the 1870s and 1880s, as her final dying gasp as a major sea power, which were going to sweep the British battlefleet from the seas, had been countered by the quick-firing gun, the development of effective secondary batteries and by the adoption of the destroyer. As the destroyer took over the offensive from the torpedo boat so had the size of secondary armament grown to counter it. In neither the Japan-China conflict nor the Japan-Russia conflict had the torpedo come up to expectations, although the Japanese *had* used it to gain a temporary advantage against battleships moored and in an unprepared state of defence. At Jutland, the massed attacks by scores of flotilla craft on both sides had produced one hit on a British battleship and had sunk one old German pre-Dreadnought. However, the *fear* of the torpedo threat was widely held to have lost Jellicoe the *decisive*, rather than the ultimately acknowledged *strategic*, victory the nation expected of him.

Nonetheless, the threat of the surface-delivered torpedo remained a factor, but one that was considered under control. The arrival of the submarine on the scene, able to approach the most powerful battleship in secret and, in theory, destroy her with torpedoes, had been an even more startling threat. But here again the promise had not been born out by events. Although several older battleships had been sunk—this was not considered serious. No major battleship of the Grand Fleet had been sunk by a submarine and the combination of a powerful destroyer screen, high speed, and effective and constant course variations, zig-zagging, appeared to have gained as much control over the submersible threat as the surface one. With the further development of an effective (or so it was thought at the time) antisubmarine detection device (asdic in the Royal Navy, sonar to the Americans), the fear of the submarine was also beginning to fade.

The development of the ultimate torpedo-dropping vehicle, the torpedo-bomber, was a new factor. She had the speed and maneuverability that the destroyer and submarine lacked; moreover, the British battle fleet was ill prepared to deal with an aerial threat of this nature. Again, the expected answer was in the development of a quick-firing weapon of such range, and with such weight of shell, that no aircraft approaching its target at a low height and steady course (as a torpedo dropper must do), could survive within range. The result was the pom-pom, a multiple 2-pounder gun that fired an explosive shell. Great faith was pinned on this weapon, but very little equipment were developed until the 1930s. Until then, the torpedo-bomber was acknowledged as the major air weapon against which a battleship was vulnerable.[45]

Air Commodore A. V. Vyvyan warned the Post-War Questions Committee, set up under Adm. R. F. Phillimore in 1919, that the torpedo-bomber was by far the most dangerous form of attack to which the fleet would be subjected and particularly so when in harbor.

That the Admiralty and its foreign counterparts were not only aware of the danger, but that they took steps to provide defense against air attack, and particularly torpedo-bomber attack, in the late 1920s and early 1930s is clear. In the design of the *Nelson* and *Rodney*, great emphasis was placed on this factor. Not only was the horizontal protection increased to 6¼ inches over the magazines and ¾ inches over the machinery spaces, they were internally bulged against torpedo attack. (Bulges—blisters in U.S. Navy parlance—were originally fitted as external additions below the waterline. The theory was that any torpedo striking the vessel would expend the greater part of its destructive power against this double-skinned oil-cushion tank that extended over the ship's vitals below the main sloping armored deck. The Royal Navy later introduced them as an integral part of the hull, the first capital ships so equipped being the *Renown* and *Repulse* in late 1916. So far they had proved effective in practice and war service, but like armor protection against gunfire, as the power of the torpedo increased so the bulges had to be constantly improved and widened.) Furthermore, the ships' offensive power, in the form of gun armament, was also given an anti-aircraft slant never before attempted.

The elevation of the massive triple 16-inch gun turrets was raised to forty degrees. This far exceeded any existing heavy gun and was done especially to facilitate antiaircraft fire. It also gave her main armament a range of 35,000 yards, which again upset the Americans. Not only this, but the secondary armament of 6-inch guns was also given an elevation of sixty degrees for the same purpose, and this was in addition to the smaller exclusively antiaircraft guns. While some doubt was expressed in the use of such huge weapons as the 16-inch gun in an antiaircraft role, the *Nelson* and *Rodney* were to employ this method very successfully on at least two occasions during World War II.

This policy of ensuring that all new heavy ships, cruisers, and upward could use all their guns against aircraft gave the designers some headaches. For example, it was five years before the "teething troubles" in the Nelsons were overcome. In attempting to give the 8-inch twin turrets in the new County-class heavy cruisers the same advantages, the resulting mounting was so poor in service that further attempts were frowned upon as being "too complicated." That Japanese and American designers were able to produce effective dual-purpose weapons for their ships, right down to destroyers, seemed no spur to the British, and British flotilla craft went to war against the cream of the Luftwaffe twelve years later almost completely defenseless against bombing. Of course, just as the best ultimate protection against the torpedo-boat had proven to be the torpedo-boat destroyer, so—as Adm. Andrew Cunningham later pointed out—the correct way to "fight the air is in the air."[46] In other words, to protect its ships against bombers, the navy needed the fighter. This was recognized in all navies, but while Japan and the United States, after a long hard struggle, were able to go ahead with the development of an effective fleet fighter defense, the Royal Navy was crippled by the fact that control of aircraft was vested in a sister service, the RAF. Moreover, the obsession of the Royal Air Force with the strategic bomber ensured that the Fleet Air Arm received the minimum time and attention; as a result, the commanding lead held by the Royal Navy in naval air power in 1918 had vanished by 1930, and over the following decade, the gap, if anything, grew wider. This is not the place to chart the stormy history of the Fleet Air Arm, but the point should be made that in this the Admiralty had its hands tied. If they strove to perfect the battleship but did not produce a massive Fleet Air Arm, they could not be blamed. An aircraft carrier is, ultimately, only as good as the aircraft it carries.

The Royal Navy produced by 1940 a design of aircraft carrier that led the world. Fast, powerfully armed, and with an armored deck, the Illustrious-class ships were world beaters. But earlier RAF control ensured that these magnificent ships were forced to operate obsolete aircraft from their decks, which greatly reduced their efficiency in operations. Only the courage and dedication of the pilots and crews of these old aircraft raised them to such great heights. The Admiralty did the best it could. Nor could it have built more aircraft carriers than it did. When the charge is made that the Royal Navy fell behind in numbers of carriers, it is always forgotten that they were no more able to build more than 135,000 tons of such craft than they could build more battleships, for Washington had tied their hands in aircraft carrier tonnages in exactly the same way as it had in battleship tonnages. Nor was the Treasury any better disposed to grant additional funds for carrier construction than in any other field of naval rearmament.

Meanwhile, the Royal Navy concentrated on working its remaining battle fleet up to higher efficiency. The new 15-inch armor-piercing shell was tested and retested, and in the opinion of the board, it was a great success. Captain Dreyer, then director of gunnery, stated that there was no doubt that if such a weapon had been available at Jutland, "we should have sunk all, or at any rate four or five, of the German battlecruisers and some of their battleships."[47]

Night-fighting tactics were introduced and practiced until the Royal Navy became undoubtedly the most skilled exponent of night fighting in the world. The old fear of engaging capital ships in the darkness was replaced by a supreme confidence in their mastery of such techniques.

The search ahead of the battle fleet was entrusted to the deployment of the cruiser scouting force in the traditional manner (the A-K line), supplemented, but not replaced, by the still not completely reliable scouting float plane carried by many ships as the 1930s wore on. The massed flotilla attack by destroyers was also tested until the crews of these craft were welded into a highly trained team that had no equal anywhere. Based still on the power of the big naval gun, the swing established in the interwar years was toward more offensive use of every arm, a welcome change from the cautious and rigid attitudes of the Great War, and one which, when applied, was to reap rich dividends in the coming conflict. The very fact that the battle line itself was so much reduced probably helped in this factor, five ships being easier to control than the forty or so Jellicoe and Beatty had to deploy for action.

Again and again, this policy had been criticized as being unrealistic, but the enemy against which the battleships were being trained to fight was Japan, and her nine battleships constituted a battle line of considerable power and strength. Moreover, the very nature of this training resulted in a highly trained fleet, prepared to take risks to force a decision.[48]

As no new ships could be built until at least 1936 as a result of the later Washington conferences, work was put in hand in a modest way to modernize those that remained. In 1924, the American Congress authorized the modernization of its six oldest ships, and this included increasing the elevation of their main armaments from fifteen to thirty degrees and converting them from coal to oil. Similar plans were put in hand by the other nations, gun elevations went up, superstructure was modified and simplified to give better arcs of fire, bulges were fitted, and so on.

Criticism continued unabated. A familiar charge was leveled by other opponents of the capital ship: its size. Why, it was asked, did the Washington Conference not agree to further limit the tonnage of such vessels, 35,000 tons being the agreed figure? Why not, asked the critics, bring this down to 10,000 tons? Adm. Sir Herbert Richmond was the leading advocate of such a policy. In his book *Sea Power in the Modern World*, he stated that no warship need be larger than 7,000 tons, the size he considered necessary to combat an armed merchant cruiser.[49] On cost alone, his views earned him considerable attention. The Admiralty's answer to this, as it had been in previous years when the same question had been raised, was that the Royal Navy had to have ships of a size and power equal to those of their opponents' ships and that it was the opposition their ships had to face that dictated their size and not an arbitrary function. This ignored the fact that Richmond, supported by Admiral Scott and others, had proposed that *all* nations be tied to the same limit. These views were widely held to be responsible for the postponement of capital ship replacement at the London Naval Conference of 1930. The construction of new battleships was delayed until 1937, and further limitations on the total tonnages of cruisers and flotilla craft were agreed to.

This meant that existing over-age vessels would have to soldier on, and further extensive modifications were planned. In Britain, this involved the partial rebuilding of the *Warspite, Valiant, Queen Elizabeth*, and *Renown*, but neither the money nor the time were available for this program to be extended to the *Hood, Repulse, Barham, Malaya*, or the Royal Sovereign–class before the outbreak of the war. In all four modernized ships, gun elevation was further increased, new machinery was installed, heavier antiaircraft weaponry was mounted, and further modification of the superstructure was carried out on a vast scale. Opinions varied as to the results of this program. Capt. S. W. Roskill wrote of it, "Rarely can new wine have been more successfully poured into old bottles, or money have been spent by a navy to better purpose than in rejuvenating the *Warspite* and her sisters. It cost, in the case of *Warspite*, 2,362,000 pounds—less than one-third of the cost of the *Nelson* and far less than the later-built King George V–class, and it gave the navy what was virtually a new ship."[50]

On the other hand, Oscar Parkes was more critical: "The old adage 'Reconstruction never pays' would certainly have applied to the Queen Elizabeth–class had we been free to build new ships to replace them. But as the treaty precluded such, there was nothing for it but to press new wine into old bottles and make the best we could of them, and the results cannot be dismissed as bad bargains, because ships which had reached their allotted span could not be armored to withstand far heavier bombs than pre-war practice employed."[51]

Only 3,000 tons per ship were allowed to be added in this construction, but happily, improved machinery saved some weight, which could be more usefully employed. In the *Queen Elizabeth* and *Valiant*, but not in the *Warspite*, the old secondary armament of 6-inch casement guns was completely replaced by new 4.5-inch dual-purpose guns in countersunk turrets, and this was the weapon also adopted by the rebuilt *Renown*; each of these ships carried twenty of these most successful weapons, which were also the main antiaircraft defense of the new carriers then proposed. As for the other veterans, they went to war as they were.

Adm. B. B. Schofield wrote: "When the author joined one of this class, HMS *Malaya*, in November 1928, after undergoing a two-year refit she was, except for the anti-torpedo blisters with which she had been fitted externally and the unification of the two funnels, basically the same ship as had fought at Jutland twelve years previously."[52]

Yet another twelve years later, there was not much difference, for besides the addition of a hangar to house four seaplanes and the provision of a few additional antiaircraft weapons, she was *still* the same ship.

In contrast to this period of relative stagnation in the battle fleets of the major powers, a startlingly new and original development took place as the 1920s gave way to the 1930s. It was an ominous portent for the Royal Navy that this new impetus came from its old opponent—reduced to impotence in 1919, it was thought. Only a brief decade later, Germany produced its first pocket battleship.[53]

CHAPTER 2

The New Conflict

The reemergence of the German naval threat was remarkable in both its swiftness and its originality. It appeared almost as if British Admiralty policy had become so engrossed with its defense of the Royal Navy against attacks mounted by the U.S. Navy, the Royal Air Force, and the Treasury, that it had not noticed the reappearance of the German menace. This was not true; the blatant way in which the Versailles disarmament clauses were being evaded and ignored *were* known,[1] but if the Allied governments turned a blind and cynical eye to this, there was little the navy could do. In the main, however, Japan, who already *had* a large navy, was the immediate threat to world peace. It was realized that the rebirth of German seapower might complicate this already delicate balance, especially now that the Royal Navy had been so swiftly cut down from its position of strength to one of such weakness. But such had been the state of German forces after the war that it was felt that many years' respite lay ahead before this situation would arise, and by that time, the Japanese situation might have been resolved.

The results of the Versailles Treaty with regard to the German Navy would appear to have finished it forever as a major fighting force, and therefore, to discount its eventual reappearance for several decades was not too unrealistic at that time. What was not foreseen was the rapid manner in which the revival took place after 1933, with the rise to power of a nationalistic leader fired with the will and power to restore Germany to her former position in the world. Even so, the deceit, lies, and evasions of solemn treaties were as much a part of the "good" pre-Hitler Germany as they were part of the Third Reich. The Nazi Party did not *invent* these methods as a means of overcoming naval treaty restrictions; they merely improved upon them. Indeed, they were more open and honest about such tactics than their mentors of the Weimar Republic had been.[2]

The German Navy after 1919 stood as follows. Eight old pre-Dreadnought battleships were allowed to it for coastal defense. These had been obsolete, even in 1914, and required such large crews that only two or three were kept in commission anyway in the 1920s. To supplement these ancient vessels and give a semblance of a balanced fleet, eight light cruisers of equal vintage were retained, along with thirty-two old destroyers and torpedo boats. Total personnel was limited to a mere 15,000 men. Naval aviation and submarines were completely banned. It is to their credit that the commanders in chief[3] of this much reduced and decrepit force saw these limitations and restrictions not as a stranglehold and unalterable shackle upon the German Navy—as the victorious powers evidently thought they were—but as a challenge to be met by German skill and ingenuity.

The manpower problem was evaded by hand picking the 15,000 so that they, in effect, became a hard core, an elite of 15,000 potential officers for a revitalized fleet, and not simply a total head count of all stratas. Submarines were constructed abroad, and aircraft were tested in the Soviet Union, so that German design in both kept well to the forefront of modern developments. The treaty permitted the replacement of the light cruisers and destroyers, but in each case, the tonnage exceeded what was laid down—at first by just a hundred tons or so, but as the Germans grew bolder and the Great Powers less stringent, by thousands of tons. But it was in the field of capital ship construction that the Germans pulled off their masterstroke, turning a humiliating set of restrictions into their own advantage in a manner completely unforeseen by those who, in drafting the limitations, had thought to tie any future German Navy to the Baltic.

It will be recalled that the main points of the Washington Treaty, after the acceptance of the ratios for each nation, had been severe tonnage restrictions on individual ships in the major categories. For battleships, the upper limit was 35,000 tons and 16-inch guns; for cruisers, 10,000 tons and 8-inch guns; for aircraft carriers 27,000 tons and 8-inch guns. To prevent any double-dealing that could result in the arrival of a super-cruiser of the old armored cruiser or battle cruiser type, aircraft carriers were clearly defined as decked vessels primarily designed to operate aircraft.

Germany's navy was not even considered at the conference; it was in such a position of inferiority that it could be ignored, or so it was thought. Although the major powers had their battleship strengths limited by the ratio 5:5:3:1.75:1.75 for Great Britain, United States, Japan, France, and Italy, it was against the first two powers that battleship strength was effectively measured. Under the tonnage limitations, these had come down, by the 1930s, to fifteen battleships each for Great Britain and the United States and nine for Japan, giving the French and Italian navies an available total of five battleships each.

One historian has since stated that the accepted ratios were different from this: They "provided for a reduction in size of the battle fleets of Great Britain, the United States, France, Italy, and Japan, which on completion would have their relative strengths in capital ships in the ratio of 5:5:3:3:3,"[4] thus giving France and Italy equal tonnage with Japan. This bonus appears to have been unknown to those nations and five battleships was the figure accepted. It has already been stated how this gave offense to France, but Germany, by the fact that she was not involved in the conference, automatically leaped into an equal third place with these two nations, for Germany was allowed to replace its six old battleships. At a stroke, then, Germany could equal in numbers the battleship strengths of Italy and France, the two victorious continental powers. Moreover, at a time when every other nation had its shipbuilding potential at a standstill, Germany alone set off on a policy— and a legal policy at that—of building new battleships.

Here again the major powers were at first highly smug, just as they had been on manpower, because the tonnage allowed for German battleships was only 10,000, against the 35,000 of the major powers. Any six vessels that Germany produced must therefore be inferior in every way under such a limit. And to make it absolute the caliber of gun for the main armament was put at 11 inches against the 16-inch guns of the Washington powers. Little wonder, then, that they felt Germany was stymied at sea.

However, in the welter of self-congratulation on how clever they had been, two things were forgotten. First, Germany had showed a natural tendency to adopt the French *guerre de course* strategy—witness the *Goeben* and *Breslau* episode and the cruise of Adm. Maximilian von Spee's squadron across the Pacific, coupled with the work of her cruiser-raiders like the *Emden*. Therefore, in seeking to restrict Germany in terms of battle fleet encounters on the Jutland style, the Allies were forcing the country to adopt the mercantile raiding policy at which she had already proved more adept.[5] And second, despite their preoccupation with establishing a tonnage limit and an armament limit on British cruisers, they failed to impose a speed limitation on Germany's new ships. By combining the merits of the cruiser and the armament of a small battleship, adding unlimited range with the adoption of diesel power units, and cheating on the tonnage, the Germans produced a warship that could outfight with ease any of the world's heavy cruisers then under construction and could be brought to battle and destroyed by only eight of the world's capital ships then in existence. These were the four Japanese Kongo-class battle cruisers as well as the *Hood, Renown, Repulse,* and *Tiger* from the British fleet. Japan was hardly likely to ever be an enemy of Germany, and Britain, under the terms of the Second London Treaty, soon scrapped the *Tiger,* thus leaving itself three aging capital ships against Germany's three brand-new marauders. Moreover, whereas Great Britain could not even begin to replace its old, slow tonnage with new construction before 1937, Germany was at liberty to construct yet another three of the same type, again with complete legality, if it chose to do so. As David Woodward remarked, "the 10,000-ton limit was not really respected—the ships were actually about 14,000 tons, but the fact that on this displacement they mounted six 11-inch guns and that they had a speed of twenty-six knots was a *tour de force* for the German naval architects. That this was possible at all was due to the fact that the Germans deliberately sacrificed armor."[6]

As for their function in life, "when the design of the pocket battleship was first made public at the end of 1928, it was stated that the ship was designed to cover troop convoys between Germany proper and East Prussia, in the event of a war between Germany and Poland. Even the most naive could not help asking why for that purpose she was given a radius of action of 20,000 miles when the distance from Stettin to Elbing or Pillau was about 250 miles!"[7]

Why indeed! It is a common fallacy to blame the small size of the German battle fleet in 1939 on Hitler. Had he stayed his hand, the story goes, until 1948, the German Navy would have been ready with the completion of the Z-Plan. So it would, indeed, but it is hardly likely that Britain would have stood by and made no move to counter such a threat by simply outbuilding Germany as it had done before. It was quite within Britain's power to lay two or three keels to one against Germany over this period, and in fact, the position would have been worse, from the German point of view, had this happened. In 1939, it is true, Britain had few battleships built or being built, but those it had were old and slow. Germany's were, by contrast, modern and fast. By 1948, Germany would have trebled her strength, but Britain could have done the same, and then the bulk of its ships would have also been modern. Moreover, this criticism of the Hitler regime always omits the fact that he left almost all naval policy making to his admirals, understanding little about sea matters and caring even less.[8] What he did do was obtain for the German Navy an advantageous position first by means of the Anglo-German Naval Treaty, then by unlimited funding of fleet replacement to the absolute capacity of German shipyards, and finally by presenting his navy with the whole Atlantic coastline, from North Cape to Spain, so that they were free to roam the Atlantic at will. For all of these advantages, the German Navy was to thank him, after his death, with abuse, blaming their own lack of élan and flair in surface ship fighting on Hitler's restrictive orders, when in fact it was their own naval leaders and admirals who failed the many tests that came their way.

Meanwhile, the appearance of the first of the pocket battleships, the *Deutschland*, in the late 1920s, caused a furor in naval circles. She was quickly followed by two more, the *Admiral Graf Spee* and *Admiral Scheer*, and their names should have been enough to sound the warning bells in the Admiralty—the first being the admiral who ranged the Pacific in 1914, the victor of Coronel, and the second being the aggressive leader of the German battle cruiser force in the same conflict. They were the symbols of the best of the German fleet in the Great War; they were to be the cardinal points on which Germany's surface fleet policy was to be built for the second conflict with Britain.

For a totally defeated nation, the adoption of new techniques in ship-building was another revelation. "Novel features introduced in her construction, for a vessel of her size, were electric welding and main propulsion by diesel engines; both weight saving items, particularly the latter, which gave her a large radius of action on a modest bunkerage, and clearly marked her as a corsair intended to operate against trade."[9]

By 1935, the first three of these vessels had been completed, the pocket battleships *Deutschland, Admiral Graf Spee,* and *Admiral Scheer* at 12,400 tons; six 11-inch guns, eight 5.9-inch guns, eight 21-inch TTs; and twenty-six knots.

If Great Britain could not, by its own fetters, take up this challenge, then one of the lesser powers was determined to. Let Great Britain shackle itself and keep its eyes on the distant Pacific while Raeder and Hitler forged their own new navy unhindered, but France, under Darlan and others, was determined to ensure that her navy, albeit reduced in size, was to be the match of any continental rival. As a direct response to the three German pocket battleships, France laid down two new battle cruisers designed to outclass them in every way. Thus was started, almost imperceptibly at first, a new naval arms race. For when these two powerful ships were announced, the Italians, fearing their position in the Mediterranean was under challenge, laid down two large, fast battleships of their own in reply.

The French vessels were the 26,500-ton *Dunkerque* and *Strasbourg.* They were armed with eight 13.5-inch guns as their main armaments and were capable of better than thirty knots. This magnificent pair of fighting ships was complemented by the provision of a force of super-destroyers, of around 3,000 tons and armed with 5.4-inch guns or larger, capable of speeds of forty knots. These powerful ships were the first part of a replacement program planned to restore pride and efficiency in the French fleet after a long period of decline and staleness. In this, they were effective. They utilized the German trick of saving weight by carrying their heavy guns in fewer turrets. The accepted practice was for heavy caliber guns to be paired, but the Deutsch-lands had used triple turrets, and the *Dunkerque* now introduced quadruple mountings. They also followed the practice of the British Nelsons in carrying all guns forward to economize the armored belt. Their details of the battle cruisers *Dunkerque* and *Strasbourg* were 26,500 tons; eight 13.5-inch guns, sixteen 5.1-inch guns; and thirty knots.

In reply to these two ships, Germany immediately commenced work on two more heavy units, both ordered in 1934. They were originally to have been improved Deutschlands, but as they were now outclassed by the French pair, the Germans went one better and drew up plans for their own brace of battle cruisers.

Hitler had already torn up the Treaty of Versailles on the grounds that the powers had agreed to disarm further once Germany had been disarmed and they had not done so. No bones were made about the fact then that the two new ships were designed to outmatch the French battle cruisers. Later, as a sop to Germany, and in the absence of any other movement, Great Britain accepted a new naval agreement with the new Reich, giving the Germans the go-ahead to increase their total tonnage to 35 percent of the British total. This would place them *ahead of* France and Italy and meant that they could now go all-out on their naval rearmament. The two new ships were announced as 26,000-ton vessels and were to carry a main armament of nine 11-inch guns. In reality, they displaced some 31,800 tons and used the extra tonnage to incorporate extra protection, a main belt, and turrets of thirteen inches. This represented a new adaption of the battle cruiser concept, sacrificing weight of armament rather than protection for speed—a much sounder concept than Fisher's original ideas for the type. The Germans also showed a more ready appreciation of antiaircraft defense, and the heavy antiaircraft capability of these two ships, *Scharnhorst* and *Gneisenau*, with fourteen 4.1-inch guns controlled by four high-angled directors, was a greater advance in this direction over anything afloat up to that time. The vessels had a radius of action of 10,000 miles at nineteen knots and a top speed of thirty-two knots. Their basic details were 31,800 tons; nine 11-inch guns, twelve 5.9-inch guns, fourteen 4.1-inch guns; and thirty-two knots.

Meanwhile, Hitler's fellow dictator was nursing his ambition for the resurrection of the old Roman Empire, which meant dominance of the Mediterranean. Until 1935, Italy had been as alarmed as anyone else about Germany's new intentions in Central Europe. When Austria was first menaced by Hitler, it was Italy alone of the European nations that had taken any positive steps. On the assassination of Engelbert Dolfuss, the Austrian leader, it was Italy that noisily "mobilized four divisions on the Brenner Pass,"[10] thus causing Hitler to back down. But with the Abyssinian crisis a little later, Italy was turned from a common cause with France and Britain against the rising power of Germany by the introduction of sanctions in a weak attempt by Britain and the League of Nations to prevent aggression.

There is no need to go into the details of Mussolini's decision to invade Abyssinia on flimsy excuses or of the weak and vacillating policies adopted by the League, and Britain in particular, to stop it, except to comment on how it affected Britain's already weak position in terms of naval power.

If Italy were to be stopped from taking over that little country, then the main decision rested with Great Britain, especially the Royal Navy. As usual, France backed away when talk turned to fighting and action, so no help could be expected from her navy.[11] Could the British Mediterranean Fleet enforce the decision on its own against both the Italian Navy and the Italian Air Force? That was the first question. The second was that if it could, would the government of the day have the will to use it?

The British Mediterranean Fleet was at a high pitch under the inspired leadership of Adm. W. W. Fisher and was quite confident of its ability to decide the day very quickly. By September 1935, it had been reinforced to bring its strength up to five battleships against two Italian ships ready for sea, while two battle cruisers were stationed at Gibraltar.[12] In all other types of warship, the two nations were roughly equal; even in the air, the balance was far more favorable than that later appeared in 1940. However, it was airpower that made the British government cringe when considering whether to use the battle fleet. So heavily had the interwar claims by the air faction influenced political thinking that they feared for the safety of the British fleet in any such conflict. This was no doubt given weight by the parlous state of the warships' antiaircraft defenses. Sir Charles Forbes confided in the British ambassador in Cairo that his ships had only enough ammunition to shoot for fifteen minutes.[13] Another estimation was that the ships had enough ammunition "for one week" and that they were "properly caught with [their] trousers down."[14]

However much these figures weighed down those at home, the men on the spot were confident that they would be able to handle the situation, given the opportunity. As Admiral Cunningham later recalled:

> About a week before the fleet sailed, I was sent for by Sir William Fisher to his office in Admiralty House. I found him greatly incensed. He handed me a document, which I recognized as an appreciation of the situation by the Chiefs of Staffs Committee in London, and pointed out two or three paragraphs, which I was to read. I did so, and found they contained a very pessimistic, not to say defeatist, view of the Mediterranean Fleet's capacity to deal with the Italians. It was obviously this that had angered the commander in chief, and I must say I agreed with him. We had some discussion, which he closed by rising to his feet and saying in his most impressive manner: "Cunningham, I have sent a signal to Their Lordships telling them I disagree with every word of this pusillanimous docu-

ment. The Mediterranean Fleet is by no means so powerless as is here set out."[15]

But fear and pessimism held sway in Britain, even though the public reacted violently to the agreement made between Foreign Minister Samuel Hoare and French Prime Minister Pierre Laval that would have acquiesced to many of Mussolini's demands in Africa, and in the end, no move was made to oppose Mussolini, whose conquest went ahead without hindrance.

In fact, Britain's politicians had now got the worst of all worlds by their defense policies of the previous fifteen years. To satisfy the United States, they had reduced their own fleet to a dangerous level and had, at the same time and on the altar of the same indifferent god, turned a reliable ally, Japan, into a powerful potential enemy. In return, the United States turned its back on world affairs. In order to be ready to fight this former ally, the bulk of the truncated British battle fleet had to be preserved for use in the Far East. Because of this fact, any losses involved in opposing Italy's expansion in the Mediterranean would be prohibitive.[16] Thus, a second potential enemy was made of a previous ally, who was also an expanding sea power, with no gain on the balance to compensate for this fact. Finally, the old enemy, Germany, had been given full encouragement to build ships as fast as it could. The Royal Navy, however, was still hedged in by the various naval treaties, which only Britain was actually abiding by.

Italy now regarded Britain and France as enemies.[17] Like Britain, America, and Japan, both France and Italy were modernizing their old battleships to make them battleworthy, but unlike the major powers, the Italians now joined in the naval race initiated by Germany and seconded by France. To give herself some measure of local superiority over the British Mediterranean Fleet and to outmatch the Dunkerques, the Italians laid the keels of two new battleships of 35,000 tons, the *Littorio* and *Vittorio Veneto*. These were the most powerful warships built since the Nelsons a decade or more before, and their construction at one stroke heightened the new battleship race. For whereas the *Deutschland*, *Dunkerque*, and *Scharnhorst* were all smaller vessels, in tonnage and armament, than Britain's aging battle fleet, these two new Italian giants were designed to mount 15-inch guns and achieve speeds of thirty knots. Their final details were 35,000 tons; nine 15-inch guns, twelve 6-inch guns, twelve 3.5-inch guns; and thirty knots.

The laying down of these vessels coincided with the end of yet another round of naval limitation talks, the Second London Naval Conference. The results were predictable enough and were on par with those achieved five years before. The First London Naval Conference had reduced the Royal Navy, in the words of one historian, "to the lowest point reached between the two wars, in strength and efficiency."[18] Just how much had been shown up by the events of the summer in the Mediterranean. For the 1935 conference, the British again trotted out the two standard requests: one was the abolition of all submarine building, and second was Prime Minister Ramsay MacDonald's own pet adoption of Richmond's theory for the reduction in the permitted size of the larger types of warships and the guns they mounted (Britain's figures for this new top limit was 25,000 tons and 12-inch guns). As both the tonnage and the gun size had already been breached in plans by the French, Germans, and Italians, it is not surprising that this motion got nowhere at all.

The United States still hankered after its big navy and held out for limits of 35,000 tons and 14-inch guns. America was as wedded to the battleship concept as Great Britain; in fact, the U.S. showed itself to be more so. American Vice Adm. A. L. Willard stating after the 1932 fleet exercise that "the battleship is still the backbone of the fleet."[19]

In spite of such statements and foreign building, the critics still concentrated their darts on the British Admiralty for wishing to respond. "A battleship had long been to an Admiral as a Cathedral is to a Bishop," mocked one such distinguished observer.[20] Japan was at the conference, cynically observing the charade for the last time. It knew the value of the battleship, which was the only weapon in the armory of Japan's enemies that could threaten it in 1935. Without the battleship in play, Japan would be secure, and accordingly, she made the startling gesture of proposing that instead of seeking new limits on battleship building, why not abolish them altogether, along with aircraft carriers and heavy cruisers? Her proposal was received with the same coolness as MacDonald's equally unrealistic limitation proposal, especially by the United States. Japan withdrew in a huff and went its own way, which is what she had been doing up to that time anyway.

The feeling toward the future of the battleship in Japan was no weaker than elsewhere. The one major exception to this was Adm. Isoroku Yamamoto, who favored the naval air arm.[21] He had first come to prominence at the 1935 conference when he made it plain that Japan would no longer accept the old 5:5:3 ratio, and the failure of the conference to ultimately achieve anything positive was blamed on him. In fact, he was a realist, while British political attitudes toward defense must have seemed to him like something out of *Alice in Wonderland*. For instance, Ramsay MacDonald asked him, in all seriousness, "If the other powers agree to paper parity, will Japan promise not to build to, it?" to which the Japanese delegate could only answer politely and simply, as if talking to a child, "Very sorry, but no. If we have parity, we build."[22]

On the battleship question, Yamamoto was no less plain. "These ships are like elaborate religious scrolls which old people hang up iii their homes. They are of no proved worth. They are purely a matter of faith—not reality."[23] On another occasion, he declared that "these battleships will be as useful to Japan in modern warfare as a samurai sword."[24] However, in expressing this opinion, he was very much in a minority; the great weight of informed naval opinion in Japan, as in America, France, Italy, Germany, and Britain was for a renewal in the building of such vessels and incorporating the new defenses of armored decks and antiaircraft firepower, which the older ships lacked. As Yamamoto's biographer John Deane Potter wrote, "Yamamoto began to be criticized in Japan for his declared policy for the development of aircraft carriers at the expense of battleships. Many people thought the neglect of battleships was dangerous."[25] Certainly Yamamoto held his views until his death, and his handling of the battle fleet of Midway seemed to show that his feelings had gone too much that way, for he gave his battleship strength absolutely no chance to prove its worth one way or the other. However, his attitude did give Japan the most efficient fleet air arm at the outbreak of war, for which his nation should have been grateful. Nor did his opinions hold back Japanese battleship development; quite the contrary, on withdrawal from the conference, they felt free to go ahead to design and build the greatest and most powerful battleships of any nation. "The object behind these monsters was to give Japan a decisive tonnage lead because the naval planners banked on the fact that the United States was unlikely to build a ship which was too big to go through the Panama Canal. At this time, too, the Japanese began to disguise their naval plans. Twenty-foot fences shielded all this frenzied shipbuilding activity from view and the strictest security was enforced."[26]

The initial designs commenced in 1934, and the final plan was not approved until three years later after twenty-three different stages of development. Their object was simply to outrange and outgun any ship then afloat or being built, and it was hoped that such vessels would offset the numerical superiority that American battle fleets seemed they would always have. Over 860 feet long and with a beam of 128 feet, these gigantic vessels, when completed, displaced 69,500 tons—almost twice the permitted tonnage agreed to at Washington and London. They were thus able to incorporate a 16-inch-thick armored belt and 71-inch deck protection and carry the enormous triple 18.1-inch gun. They had a designed speed of twenty-five knots. Despite numerous public statements to the contrary, the keels were laid for the first two in 1937, and plans called for another pair three years later. Basic details of these Japanese battleships—*Musashi, Yamato, Shinano,* and *No. 111* (unnamed)—were 64,170 tons; nine 18.1-inch guns, twelve 6.1-inch guns, twelve 5-inch guns; and twenty-seven knots.

Back at the conference, the wrangling continued, and eventually, a confused sort of compromise was reached in which the United States, as usual, got its way. An upper battleship tonnage limit of 35,000 was agreed to. The caliber of the main armament was fixed at 14-inch guns, though with the proviso that if any of the contracting parties to the Washington Treaty failed to enter into an agreement to conform to this provision by April 1, 1937, then this maximum caliber could go up to sixteen inches, which is what the Americans wanted all along. Furthermore, no limit was placed on the numbers of ships each nation could build.

Again, this left Great Britain in an unenviable position when the Washington Treaty finally expired at the end of 1936. Neither Japan, which had walked out, nor Italy, which was to start on 15-inch-gun ships anyway, had been party to the 1935 agreement. America's patience ran out, and it started work on her 16-inch-gun ships. What should Britain do?

The first ships of the new American program for 1937 were the two ships of the North Carolina class, the *North Carolina* and *Washington* at 35,000 tons; nine 16-inch guns, twenty 5-inch guns; and twenty-eight knots. They were designed to meet the Pacific requirements of long range and heavy antiaircraft capability. Much heavier deck armor was fitted in common, and the superstructure was more concentrated to give clearer fields of fire for the host of skyward-pointing batteries. The North Carolinas' propulsion was by American-designed and -built turbines, and in practice, these proved far more economical than their British equivalents. Not only were these fine vessels more powerfully armed, faster, and longer ranging than the British ships of the same era, but their maneuverability was also far greater. Moreover, the Americans were able to build their ships much faster than the British. Thus, the Admiralty was obliged to think in terms of four or five years to design and build a battleship, which the Americans could construct in a little more than three years.[27]

The Admiralty, however, had to decide whether to go for the 14-inch gun as originally agreed or to adopt the 16-inch gun. On the face of it, there would seem to be no problem. It was true that, faced with the building programs of Germany, France, and Italy, a decision had to be made quickly, for it is the guns that decide the length of time a battleship takes to construct, but in view of the American decision, there should have been only one answer. In the triple 16-inch turrets of the Nelson class, Great Britain already had a tried and tested weapon, a decade in the proving, of equal power and merit to anything the Americans were producing. Moreover, it did not call for any new design or experimental work. It seemed the obvious solution to many, including Winston Churchill.

In a way, it was ironic that it should have concerned Churchill so much, for as much as any limitation by naval treaty, it was his policy, when he was at the Treasury, that had reduced the Royal Navy to its then-sorry straits. It was he who had introduced the "pernicious law,"[28] known as the "ten-year rule," that had given the Treasury a firm grip on the "economy axe"[29] with disastrous results. Consequently, for the next ten years, the very roots of Britain's naval existence—the dockyards, private shipbuilding, armament industries, and skilled labor in vital factories—were allowed to wither away.[30]

As one naval historian has emphasized, "the ten-year rule, a penny-pinching political formula which assumed that Britain could rely on ten years' notice of involvement in any major war, had had a crippling effect on the maintenance of the armed forces, let alone their modernization of development; and its suicidal fatuity was to be well demonstrated."[31] As Lord Lee of Fareham had already remarked with unhappy accuracy, "a great navy, once let down, cannot be' improvised in an emergency. It is not only the ships that take years to build; the training and instinct required to handle that amazing complex of machinery, a modern battleship, needs a generation to teach."[32]

The British were in a cleft-stick because the plans for 14-inch gunned ships were already prepared. To change over to 16-inch gunned vessels would mean another year's delay in completing the first British vessels, which meant they would not be finsished until 1941. But Britain already had both 16-inch and 15-inch designs, so why the delay and the decision? Lord Chatfield gave the answer that "on the 35,000-ton displacement, allowed by the agreement, a 14-inch ship was, we considered, a better balanced one than a 15-inch ship, taking into consideration air attack by the modern torpedo."[33] This still did not satisfy Churchill, but when told that Britain could not afford to wait one more year and that most of its skilled draughtsman had gone, he "grudgingly withdrew his objections."[34]

As originally designed, the five new British ships might not have been so inferior to foreign designs as their completed armament showed, for they were to mount three quadruple 14-inch turrets—a total broadside of twelve 14-inch guns. This would have given them a broadside weight of 8.6 tons against the American equivalent of 8.43. However, further testing with improved shells showed that extra magazine protection was required, and as a consequence, the B mounting was made a twin and the broadside reduced to ten guns and the weight of shell to 7.1 tons. Captain Grenfell explained the results:

> Where a fixed limit is placed on warship tonnage, there is a natural tendency to squeeze into the treaty maximum as much as possible in the way of fighting power, resulting usually in the attempt to squeeze too much. The endeavor to force ten guns into a ship that ought really to have eight actually led to her only having six, since the ten had such complicated mechanism that no more than two thirds of

them would normally go off at once; or at all events for the first five or six years of the new mounting's life, until numerous modifications had been made in the light of breakdown experience.[35]

Admiral Schofield, who commanded *King George V* later in the war, made no mention of these failures and rather stated that "had the alteration in the King George V class not been necessary, they would have compared very favorably with American South Dakota class"[36].

Nevertheless, in the 1937 and 1938 programs, Great Britain was finally allowed to replace—or slowly begin to replace—its aging tonnage of battleships. These five ships represented a total displacement of 175,000 tons but were only the first step in a complete replacement program. These ships' tonnage was designed to conform to the treaty limitations, but the war had actually broken out before they were completed. Like most contemporary battleships, they wasted a great deal of space to fit hangars and scouting aircraft with their launching gear. With the full development of aircraft carriers in the fleet, the provision for no less than six brand-new fleet types, and one mobile repair-and-maintenance carrier (*Unicorn*, in addition to the new *Ark Royal* then laid down), it would have been thought that ample scouting facilities were already available to the battle fleet and that such space could have been better utilized, by providing two more twin 5.25-inch gun mountings for example, but this was not done. The basic details of these five battleships—*Anson*, *Howe*, *Duke of York*, *King George V*, and *Prince of Wales*—were 35,000 tons; ten 14-inch guns, sixteen 5.25-inch guns; and twenty-seven knots. (It had at first been planned to name the *Anson* and *Howe* the *Jellicoe* and *Beatty*.)

Meanwhile, on the continent, further programs had been put in hand by the three powers that had started the ball rolling. In Germany, the first two battleships were laid down with the outward intention of matching those of the major powers—to a limit of 35,000 tons. These resulted from Germany's new-found liberty to build up to 35 percent of the British tonnage. Laid down in 1936, these two powerful vessels, *Bismarck* and *Tirpitz*, were actually of 42,343 tons displacement and, at that time, seemed to be the most well-protected battleships yet designed. In fact, their design allocated no less than 40 percent of her standard displacement to protection. They were 823 feet long, with a beam of 118 feet (compared with 103 feet for a King George V–class and 108 feet for a North Carolina–class ship). Their main armament was based on the well-proven 15-inch gun, with which the Germans had had some valuable experience during the Great War with the *Baden* and *Bayern*. Their total broadside weight of eight 15-inch guns was actually less, by 220 pounds, than the King George V–type ship, but they were far better protected against bomb attack, with a special 2-inch armored upper deck above the 4¾-inch-thick main deck, which was designed to detonate any bombs before they penetrated to the main armor itself. They had a side belt 16 feet deep and 12½ inches thick. Their speed was, at twenty-nine knots, slightly improved over the British design. However, their secondary armament was complicated by the fact that the Germans kept to the old principles of one caliber for surface protection and another for aerial defense. As usual, the antiaircraft system was vastly superior to British designs, but this mounting of two secondary calibers was a bad feature on an otherwise superb design. Britain and America, and to a lesser extent France showed a better appreciation of the advantages of dual-purpose weapons. Italy and Japan persisted with double batteries as Germany.

In response to these monsters, the French replied with two battleships of their own, the *Jean Bart* and *Richelieu* at 35,000 tons; eight 15-inch guns, nine 6-inch guns, twelve 3.9-inch guns; and thirty knots. They were also influenced by the need to counter the two Italian battleships now well advanced and so they designed their vessels to match, as far as the treaty allowed, both designs. Again, the concentration of the main armament in quadruple turrets forward to save weight of armored belt was adopted as in the smaller Dunkerque design. However, there was no question of repeating the same small-caliber weapon, and France decided to go for the 15-inch gun. This left Great Britain, alone of all the contracting powers to the Second London Conference, with ships building with 14-inch guns. The French, Germans, and Italians went for 15-inch, the Americans and (so it was thought at the time) Japanese for the 16-inch. So much for the usefulness of these conferences in restricting other powers.

The Italian answer was immediate and again highly predictable. Having outmaneuvered the League of Nations *and* the premier seapower in 1935, Mussolini was confident of his ultimate destiny as the new Caesar. The Mediterranean was, so he declared, an Italian lake, and to back up this claim and his well-ventilated claims for Corsica-Tunisia-Nice, he ordered the construction of two additional battleships based on the same general design of the Littorio class. These were the *Imperio* and *Roma* at 35,000 tons; nine 15-inch guns, twelve 6-inch guns, twelve 3.5-inch guns; and thirty knots.

Across the Atlantic, the United States followed up her initial battleships with a further class of four for the 1938 building program. These were the South Dakota-class battleships *Alabama, Indiana, Massachusetts,* and *South Dakota,* which featured the same main and secondary armaments as the North Carolina class, but their power was concentrated into a shorter hull—680 feet as against 729 feet—in a further effort to maximize protection over the vital areas. They were also given a single-funnel arrangement to further facilitate antiaircraft fire, but their complement remained the same at 2,500. They were built with great speed, and although laid down after the King George V-class ships, they were completed ahead of some of them. Their details were 35,000 tons; nine 16-inch guns, twenty 5-inch guns; and twenty-eight knots.

In reply to these developments abroad, the British came back in the 1938 and 1939 programs with battleships which, for the first time, began to really match their foreign opponents—and indeed, at least on paper, to outclass them. But before they could do this, they again had to fight off a new wave of criticism and hostility within their own country. Despite the fact that no fewer than twenty-three powerful capital ships were under construction in foreign yards, the Admiralty was bitterly vilified for embarking on its own battleship program. As usual, the howls of protest and rage were led by the indefatigable air lobby. Such criticism is usually reflected in postwar analysis of the situation, although, at least in these instances, the benefit of hindsight is extended to the other powers as well.

When the Washington Treaty finally lapsed in 1936, much of the effort and financial resources of the naval powers was extended on new, monster battleships, which would have been better diverted to the construction of aircraft carriers. France and Italy built no carrier.[37]

The Royal Navy's defense was simple. "Advocates of the extreme air view wished the country to build no more capital ships although other powers continued to build them. If their theories turned out well founded much money would have been wasted; if ill founded, we would, in putting them to the test, have lost the empire."[38]

Fortunately, the balanced view is sometimes heard through the storm of criticism and scorn, as with Charles Owen: "Chatfield has since been accused of infatuation with battleships but the battleship was the unit of naval power understood by the politicians; and the navies potentially hostile to Britain were still building battleships against which at that time the Royal Navy had no convincing alternative defence or weapon of destruction."[39]

The Royal Navy *was* building new aircraft carriers, eight of them: *Ark Royal, Unicorn, Illustrious, Formidable, Victorious, Indomitable, Indefatigable,* and *Implacable*—far more than any other naval power, including Japan and America. However, what critics overlooked is that a carrier is not now and was certainly not then a 100 percent reliable weapon with which to operate against battleships.

This "argument" ignores the fact that the aircraft could only operate in daylight in the first years of the war. Until radar and other navigational aids had been fitted they could not fly from carriers at night or in thick weather, so at night carriers become defenseless targets, requiring their protection to be provided by another source, and this could only be the battleship. Moreover, without radar, aircraft could not find their quarry by night or in poor visibility, nor could they hit it once it was found.[40]

Thus wrote Vice Admiral Gretton, and he went on: "Indeed in the first years of the war, the carriers could not face, at night, ships like the *Bismarck,* the *Scharnhorst,* or the *Gneisenau.* They had to be kept out of their way, and this situation would not have been altered if there had been more of them. Modern, fast battleships were needed."[41] But not only at night. Even during the day, the carrier could at times become frighteningly vulnerable to surface attack:

> Aircraft carriers are subject to awkward periods of operational paral-ysis, from which gun vessels are free. A battleship or cruiser which has been bombarding one target can switch its guns round to another in a matter of seconds, and can go on firing with hardly a break till its ammunition runs out. But the carrier, as at present con-stituted, suffers embarrassing lacunae when its aircraft are coming down, going up, or refueling and rearming, during which it is pecu-liarly vulnerable to attack. Even with skillfully planned and directed operations, these "dead" periods introduce an inevitably high degree of chance into carrier warfare.[42]

But these were far from the usual postwar viewpoints; most observers took the line that the battleship was as vulnerable and outdated in 1936 as it had become by 1946.

"What had happened, in effect, was that the aeroplane had displaced the gun as the main offensive weapon, thereby extending the range of battle from tens to hundreds of miles,"[43] stated Professor Lewis. He elaborated fur-ther: "This of course is why the battleship itself, traditional gun-carrier and long queen of the seas, has also lost her empire. Already fabulously expensive to build and increasingly difficult-to defend she was now being completely out-ranged in offence too. Her original *raison d'être* was gone, or at least, rap-idly going."[44]

However, the Admiralty Board was able to get permission to go ahead with the King George V–class ships, and it is as well that they did so. Wrote Gretton:

> In the light of full after-knowledge, however, I cannot agree that the decision to build the King George Vs was a mistake. Perhaps five was too many. But they filled a gap, short but important, when the car-

rier was unable to produce its own protection, and I tremble to think what would have happened if in 1940 the fleets had had to rely on the *Nelson* and *Rodney* and the Queen Elizabeths and Royal Sovereigns for their main source of strength. In 1945, the battleship was a useful adjunct to the carrier. In 1940, the battleship was an indispensable defence, and sometimes a substitute for the carrier on the many occasions when aircraft could hot effectively operate.[45]

The new British Lion-class battleships were the first to be designed free from the cramping restrictions of the treaties and, as such, were a much more well-balanced design than the King George V–class ships. Named the *Conqueror, Lion, Temeraire,* and *Thunderer,* they were of a designed tonnage of 40,000 tons, had an overall length of 780 feet and a beam of 105 feet, and could reach thirty knots. They featured a squared-off stern rather than the cruiser-stern as featured in the King George V–class vessels, such a feature saving weight and being conducive to better maneuverability. They carried three triple 16-inch gun turrets as designed and would have carried a 16-inch belt, of greater depth than their predecessors, with a 6-inch upper deck. They had a designed speed of thirty knots. These four ships would certainly have been a match for the Germans' Bismarcks. Some changes of name had been made, "the names originally chosen being *Lion, Temeraire, Conqueror,* and *Bellerophon*— a fine quartet. Later, objections were raised to *Bellerophon*—a loved and honored name to generations of British seamen from the glorious first of June to Jutland—on the grounds that it would be beyond the powers of the sailor of 1940 to pronounce, and another Trafalgar name, *Thunderer,* was substituted."[46] So there was no new Billy Ruff'n for the fleet![47]

By 1939, even these giants were overawed by the projected battleships of all the other major powers. By this time, the battleship building race had gone over the top and was now completely unchecked. After twenty years of frustration and pent-up wrath, the United States now saw its way wide open to naval dominance once and for all. All the old plans and theories were taken down and dusted off, and with the outbreak of war in Europe, no further excuses were accepted. Under the benign tolerance of President Roosevelt, America embarked on the most colossal warship building spree of all time, designed quite deliberately to give her the two-ocean navy for which it had been yearning for so long.

Pride of place in this great new fleet was, as always, the battleship. If the Americans had doubts about its role in any future war, then the size of their programs from 1939 onward hardly reflected them. Despite elaborate secrecy, the first reports of the new Japanese ships were beginning to filter into the west. Although this information was still very inaccurate (the British

Admiralty estimated that the *Yamato* and her sisters were of 42,500 tons displacement, with nine 16-inch and twelve 5-inch guns[48]), they were sufficient to spur the Americans on to designing even larger ships than those building. The first group to be laid down were the six ships of the Iowa class (BB 61-66) under the 1939 and 1940 programs: the *Iowa, New Jersey, Missouri, Wisconsin, Illinois,* and *Kentucky.*

They featured a 12.2 inch armor belt for their main protection, with 18-inch over the turrets. They were 887 feet long, this great extra length being provided to fit the new clipper bow and bulbous underwater hull form which gave them, together with the 212,000 SHP turbines, the incredible battleship speed of thirty-three knots. For a 45,000-ton vessel with such massive protection, this was a remarkable achievement by the American designers, engineers, and builders, and the resulting class of warships must rank as one of the finest, if not *the* best, battleships in the world. Despite their great size, they remained far handier ships than the British King George Vs, although a later British design was found to be much superior in seakeeping qualities—which was always the British warships' best feature anyway.

But large as the American ships were, they were only a beginning on the growing stage of the world's navies. The subsequent Montana class was even larger. Provided for under the 1940 expansion program, these ships were almost half as large again in tonnage as the Iowas, and although their speed came down to twenty-eight knots once again, they were designed to mount twelve 16-inch guns and have an overall length of 921 feet. The six ships of this class were *Montana, Ohio, Maine, New Hampshire,* and *Louisiana* at 60,500 tons.

Nor was this all, for word had reached the Americans that the Japanese were constructing a new class of battle cruisers on the lines of the *Dunkerque* and *Scharnhorst,* and in order to counter these projected vessels, the 1940 program also called for a class of no fewer than six more ships to swell the capital returns. Although listed as "large cruisers," they were battle cruisers, pure and simple. They had a 9-inch belt and a speed of thirty-three knots and featured a new triple 12-inch gun, which made them the masters of the German pair as well. These ships were *Alaska, Guam, Hawaii, Philippines, Puerto Rico,* and *Samoa* at 27,500 tons; nine 12-inch guns, twelve 5-inch guns.

The Japanese were no less ambitious. A fifth ship (Hull No. 797) of the already-building Yamato class was planned under the 1942 program. Furthermore, two even larger vessels were projected under the same year's construction plans, and these were to push the main armament size up to an impressive 20-inches. These two unnamed battleships (798 and 799) were to carry three triple mountings of such weapons and were to displace 64,000 tons and speed at twenty-eight knots.

The American naval chiefs were not misinformed about the projected Japanese battle cruisers. At least two were planned for the 1942 program, similar in appearance to the Yamato-class battleships with a long, flush-deck hull, two triple turrets forward, and one aft the central superstructure and single funnel. They were to feature a 7-inch main belt with 5-inch deck protection and have a length of almost 800 feet and speed of thirty-three knots.

By this time the naval race with regard to battleship tonnage appeared to simplify into three competing pairs who were building against each other in practice, if not publicly admitting the fact: America and Japan, Italy and France, and Great Britain and Germany. Although British war plans continued to be framed to take Japan into account as the main enemy at sea in any future conflict, it was realized that we were far more likely to be embroiled with Germany or Italy first, and taking into consideration their programs, there would be very little we could do about Japan if we had to tackle them at the same time.

Therefore, if war was with Germany only, Great Britain felt confident of her strength. If against Italy as well, then she could still be confident, especially with the French fleet by her side of equal size to the Italian one. But should Japan come in and America stay out—a not unlikely possibility in view of the American attitude over the previous two decades—then the Mediterranean would have to be left to the French, the old ships would have to somehow face the Germans, and the modern ships would go east. While the German navy was still heavily outnumbered, this was practical, if dangerous. However, the arrival of the *Bismarck* and *Tirpitz* on the scene would upset these fine calculations. They might be matched by the King George Vs but would leave only the older ships available for the Pacific (until the Lions were finished), and they were obviously not really suitable for this type of employment having neither the range nor the speed. Nor was the problem made any easier by the fact that the only naval base in eastern waters, Singapore, was not anywhere near completed. But the main complication was the lack of heavy ships themselves. Singapore had become an obsession with British defense planners as the means to halt Japan, but without sufficient heavy ships to form a balanced fleet to operate from it, it was, in the historic words of one observer, "a sentry box without a sentry."[49]

If the existence, therefore, of the two Bismarcks could cause such disruption to the long-standing illusion that Great Britain ruled the waves, then the intended full-strength building program, as developed by Germany under the guidance of Admiral Raeder, would have been its final unmasking.

There has been a great deal of controversy over this plan, the so-called famous Z (for *Ziel*, German for "target") Plan. Admiral Raeder stated that during the winter of 1938–39, he presented Hitler with two alternative plans on the future of the new navy. For a short-term war likely to take place within a year or so, he suggested a force "consisting mainly of submarines and pocket battleships—which could be produced relatively soon, and which, though admittedly unbalanced, could in the event of war present a considerable threat to Britain's lifelines."[50] Alternatively, for long-term policy, what could be prepared was "a force of great striking power, with capital ships of the highest class - which, though it would take longer to produce, could not only threaten Britain's lifelines but also engage the British High Seas Fleet with every prospect of success."[51]

Hitler promised Raeder that he would not need the fleet before 1946, and thus on January 29, 1939, the Z Plan was born. It was a massive program of new construction, one that was, like the Japanese and American plans, based firmly upon the battleship as its mainstay. The *Bismarck* and *Tirpitz*, although not due to be completed for another eighteen months or so, were giving the Admiralty headaches, but the new program called for six new battleships and three new battle cruisers to be completed by 1944–45. Further projections of the plan called for a total of twelve of the battle cruiser type and more battleships. Wrote David Woodward:

> From the *Bismarck* and *Tirpitz*, the Germans went on to ships of 56,000 tons with eight 16.25-inch guns; two ships of this type were actually laid down in 1939 and not definitely cancelled until two years later. . . . From these ships it was proposed to go on to 80,000 tons, and finally the height of the kolossal in naval architecture was reached with a design for a ship of 144,000 tons, full load, with a speed of thirty-four knots and eight 19.75-inch guns, but that design was so far off realization that it may be regarded simply as a piece of dreaming by a naval architect .on a grandiose scale.[52]

The battleships and battle cruisers that were firmly decided upon to go ahead with were colossal enough. The six battleships were of the so-called H type. Flush-decked and twin-funneled, they adopted diesel propulsion with a BHP of 165,000 giving them a speed of twenty-nine knots and a range of 16,000 miles at nineteen knots. Their main belt was 12½ inches thick with an upper 2-inch deck over a 4-inch main deck.

Their main armament was to be eight 16-inch guns, in four twin turrets, with the usual double secondary batteries for surface and air defense. These huge ships with their great range and endurance were designed "as support groups, able to keep the seas indefinitely, on which the raiding squadron could fall back when opposed by a heavier concentration."[53] Two of these battleships were named the *Friedrich der Grosse* and *Gross Deutschland*, with the other four left abandoned before names had been allocated.

The battle-cruisers reverted to the old policy of sacrificing protection for speed, while carrying heavy guns. Thus, they were designed to mount six 15-inch guns in three twin turrets in exactly the same manner as the twenty-year-old *Renown* and *Repulse* did; the Germans planned to re-arm the *Scharnhorst* and *Gneisenau* in this fashion. However, their deck protection against air attack was enhanced up to battleship standards, having an upper deck of 11 inches, a main deck of 3 inches, and a lower deck of 4 inches. They would have taken some stopping by bombing attacks. They had diesel propulsion units and had a designed top speed of thirty-three knots.

These nine capital ships, along with two aircraft carriers were all to be completed by 1944, and would have made life very difficult for the Admiralty. As David Woodward said,

> In 1939, Britain had fifteen capital ships, of which the five units of the Royal Sovereign class at least would have been obsolete by 1945. In addition, Britain would have completed five ships of the King George V class of 35,000 tons, and the four ships of the Lion class of about 45,000 tons. The last of these would probably have been ready in 1944, and there might have been other ships, laid down in 1941 and ready in 1944–45, once the size of the German naval construction effort had been seen. But whatever happened, we would not have had much to spare, for against thirteen modern German capital ships, we would have had ten obsolete ones, and somewhere between nine and thirteen new ones.[54]

When one realizes that the final program for the Z Plan called for, by 1948, six H-class battleships, twelve P-class battle cruisers, and eight aircraft carriers, the prospect seems highly alarming. However, postwar German naval historians are equally as critical of this German plan as British historians are of the King George Vs and Lions.

> The "verdict of history" that Raeder invoked has in fact gone against him. For one who held the supreme command of the Navy for over fourteen years, battleships remained a basic instrument of world-wide naval strategy. Though he accepted the aeroplane as a new and important factor, he regarded a naval air force mainly as an auxiliary to the fleet. That air power had brought to war a new dimension, rendering former naval concepts outmoded and virtually consigning battle-fleets to the scrapheap, was beyond him.[55]

So much for Raeder and Z Plan. The British would hardly have agreed with that "verdict of history" had his battle fleet of 1944 come to fruition; even the much smaller ships that the Germans did complete tied down the greater bulk of British naval strength in home waters, as will be seen.

Meanwhile, Italy and France continued to build against each other in a tit-for-tat situation, and the next pair of French ships to be projected—as answers to the Italian *Roma* and *Imperio*—were the battleships *Clemenceau* and *Gascogne* at 35,000 tons; eight 15-inch guns, nine 6-inch guns, twelve 3.9 inch guns; and thirty knots.

By the last years of the 1930s, battleship construction was at its peak, and in this period, the major powers were joined in this feverish activity by a surprise outsider, the Soviet Union. Since the revolution in 1917, Soviet Russia had not loomed large on the naval scene. The Soviet Union had retreated into herself, and when it had finally reemerged in the 1930s under the tyrannical rule of Stalin, it found itself an outsider whose hateful political creed and cruel dictatorship had left her beyond the pale to fascists and capitalists alike. The country was deliberately excluded from most of the naval conferences of the interwar period, although it is doubtful whether this can be termed a handicap in any way. The Soviets did, however, sign the Second London Treaty. It was irrelevant, anyway, for they built no major ships in this period. With the re-awakening of Germany, her Baltic position seemed perilously exposed and thus a new naval force was seen as essential.

In January 1938, the Russian Defense Council approved a program of new capital ship construction, which totaled four battleships and four battle cruisers. The battleships were laid down the same year for completion in 1941–42 and were the first capital ships to be built for the Russian navy since the revolution.

It is interesting to notice that the naval experts of this largely land-oriented nation came, quite independently, to exactly the same conclusions as all the other major naval powers had with regard to the continuing validity of battleship as a weapon of war in the 1940s. Like the Japanese designers, the Soviets gave their shipbuilders one main target to aim at in the construction of these four ships: to make them invulnerable. This they set out to do, and as a result, these ships, on paper anyway, ranked with the *Yamato* and *Iowa* in size and power.

Having an overall length of 890 feet (all dimensions are approximate since accurate and precise information on Soviet warship designs is still difficult to verify)[56] and a massive beam of 127 feet, 7 inches, they were engined to give 231,000 s.h.p. to attain a maximum speed of twenty-eight knots. An 18-inch side armored belt and three armored decks constituted her main protection. The estimated full load displacement for these ships was 65,000 tons and their main armament consisted of three triple 16-inch turrets. The first of these Soviet monsters was laid down at Leningrad in 1939 and the second followed a year later at Nikolajev. The second pair were due to be commenced in 1940. These four battleships were *Sovyetskayai Soyuz*, *Sovyetskakyai Ukraina*, *Sovyetskayai Belorussiya*, and *Sovyetskayai Rossiya*.

The four battle cruisers stemmed from the same program initially and were designed as 22,000 tonners, but with the appearance of the Scharnhorsts in the Baltic, they were redesigned in July 1938 and much enlarged, so that their final full load displacement was in the region of 35,240 tons. Some 816 feet, 9 inches, in length with a beam of 103 feet, they had a designed horsepower of over 231,000 to give them a planned top speed of thirty-three knots. Their main armament was to be three triple turrets, as in the battleship design; and the caliber of the guns was selected as 12-inch to match the German pair.

Final approval to go ahead with this quartet—the *Kronstadt*, *Moskva*, *Murmansk*, and *Sevastopol*—was given in the spring of 1940, just after the crushing of Finland had given the Communists greater security to their Baltic naval bases and shipyards.

Even the lesser naval powers had plans; the most important of these was the Netherlands, which, with a large Far Eastern empire to protect from Japan's rapacious ambitions, proposed a powerful squadron of three brand-new battle cruisers to bring her East Indies Fleet up to date. These ships displaced 28,000 tons and were to be based in the Dutch East Indies as a powerful deterrent to Japanese raiding squadrons sent to that oil-rich region.

In addition, and on a far more modest scale, Sweden proposed building two new coastal battleships in the late 1930s, but they were never completed.

And so as the world drifted into the Second World War in the autumn of 1939, all the major nations were busy constructing mighty new battle fleets.

However, if Hitler's invasion of Poland on September 1, 1939, set in train the British and French ultimatums and declarations of war some six years before he had promised Admiral Raeder, it also disrupted the building plans of almost every other nation as well. Thus not only Germany's cherished Z Plan evaporated that September day but ultimately the actual completion of no more than a handful of those seventy great ships then taking shape in the naval arsenals of the world.

And how was the Royal Navy to be found on this fateful day? Whatever the ghastly state of her other defenses, the claim by Winston Churchill, recalled to the Admiralty on the outbreak of the war, that at least all was well with the navy, did not withstand too close an examination. The bulk of its ships were old, its equipment was obsolete, its aerial defenses pathetic, and its numbers all too obviously inadequate. Wrote Charles Owen:

In 1939, when war broke out in Europe, the primary element of
British naval power was still the battle fleet; and the fifteen battleships and battle-cruisers forming it, all but two of them of First
World War vintage, although largely modernized, were in essence
what Fisher and Jellicoe had introduced, proved and refined during
the early years of the century. Thus the decisive naval weapon
remained the mighty turreted centre-line gun.[57]

This verdict has been endorsed by other highly distinguished historians
and naval experts. Thus, Capt. Stephen Roskill and Arthur J. Marder might
disagree on the way in which Churchill behaved as First Lord of the Admiralty, but they appear to be in harmony with regard to the position of the battleship in the service, despite all the foreign competition. Thus Marder writes,
"The excessive emphasis in pre-war training on a fleet action had considerable value for captains and other officers on the bridge in handling ships in
close company; but it bore little relation to what was to come in 1939. . . .
Naval strategy and tactics were largely conditioned by a determination to
make the next Jutland a Trafalgar—when a second Jutland was highly
improbable."[58]

Captain Roskill concludes that "it now seems clear that the balance
between the various traditional classes, the battle fleet, the cruisers and the
flotilla—had not been happily struck; and that too much faith continued to
be placed in the big gun as the principal arbiter of defeat or victory at sea,
and too little imagination had been shown towards the potentialities of ship-
borne aircraft."[59]

The judgment of our enemy, who it will be recalled planned to build thirteen new capital ships to our nine, was equally severe. As Rear Admiral Ruge
wrote, "England had always thought in terms of battleships, and saw no reason to change her ideas. It may be no mere coincidence that England lost her
status as the principal maritime power at the time when the aircraft carrier
replaced the battleship as the vital core of battle fleets."[60]

Nonetheless, the die was now cast, but even in battleships, Great Britain
was not fully ready. As we have seen some modernization had been undertaken, but it was far from universal. Much of it was still underway. So although
the Royal Navy went to war with a paper strength of fifteen capital ships, in
actual fact it was less.

The battleships *Queen Elizabeth* and *Valiant* were still in dockyard hands
completing their major refits as described, as was the battle cruiser *Renown*,
although she was almost ready for delivery. This left twelve active units, and
of these twelve, only two, the *Nelson* and *Rodney*, were of post–Great War
design, and they were now both past middle age. The *Hood* still held her aura

of invincibility, but in fact, she badly needed a modernization, and the British hoped to refit her on a comparable scale to *Renown*,[61] but it was not to be. Of the remaining units, only one, the *Warspite*, had been modernized enough to stand in a modern battle line. The other eight units—*Repulse, Malaya, Barham*, and the five Royal Sovereign–class ships—were unfit to stand up to modern enemy vessels and were handicapped still further by their slow speed. Of the nine new ships, only one, *King George V*, was expected to be completed within the coming year. The others were due two in 1941 and two in 1942, which might very well prove to be too late. As for the four Lions, the first ships of equal stature to the Bismarcks now completing across the North Sea, work had hardly got underway on any of these. And strangely enough, one of Churchill's first acts on becoming First Lord was to try to get work on these four ships stopped immediately.

On the plus side, Britain had the small but powerful fleet of France on its side. France had the old battleships *Lorraine, Bretagne, Provence, Paris*, and *Courbert* to back up Britain's own elderly battle line, and it had the two superb Dunkerque-class battle cruisers ready for action in the Force de Raid at Brest, with the aircraft carrier *Béarn* and three cruisers and ten large destroyers. Nearing completion were the *Jean Bart* and *Richelieu*, both due in 1940. While Italy hung back on the sidelines, much to Mussolini's humiliation and mortification,[62] Allied capital ship strength appeared overwhelming. Perhaps, then, Churchill was right to be so confident in 1939. That confidence, however, was not to last the first year of the war.

CHAPTER 3

Old Truths, New Lessons

On September 3, 1939, when Britain and France belatedly declared war on Germany, whose armies had been operating deep inside Poland for three days with their flanks almost wide open, the twelve great ships on which the main strength of Great Britain rested were mainly to be found in home waters. Only the three ships of the First Battle Squadron were overseas. These, the modernized *Warspite* and the unmodernized *Barham* and *Malaya*, lay at readiness in Alexandria harbor awaiting Italy's decision on whether it would join Germany in combat. In the event, economic considerations and the lamentable state of his armed forces made Mussolini postpone this decision for some nine months. The ships of the First Battle Squadron therefore began to return to home waters, their only Mediterranean activity being a warning sweep, conducted by Admiral Cunningham to the west of Crete between September 11 and 16, designed to enforce the *Duce*'s indecision. Italy, at this stage, was in an even worse position than Britain, for it had only two effective battleships on her strength[1] and could in no way dispute the Anglo-French control of the Mediterranean, despite the pessimistic viewpoint of Admiral Noble, which did much to boost Italian ego.[2]

The main strength lay at home and here was the Second Battle Squadron in readiness at the old Grand Fleet base of Scapa Flow in the lonely Orkney Islands. Under the command and control of Adm. Sir Charles Forbes, this unit comprised the *Nelson* (flag), *Rodney, Royal Sovereign, Royal Oak*, and *Ramillies*, the last only recently returned from the Mediterranean. Of these ships, only the *Nelson* and *Rodney* were fit to stand in line of battle against modern ships. All of the Royal Sovereign–class ships were unmodernized. Here it should be said that they were far from being "coffin ships," as Churchill once described them. They were still the equals of the many battleships of foreign nations of the same vintage but lacked deck armor, gun elevation, and speed—grave defects when pitted against the more modern ships and larger air forces of Britain's continental opponents. That they were far from valueless was soon proved in full.

Accompanying the Second Battle Squadron at Scapa, as part of the Home Fleet, was the Battlecruiser Squadron, consisting then of only the unmodernized *Hood* and *Repulse*. The modernized *Renown*, however, was soon to rejoin, and when the *Warspite* got home, Admiral Forbes would be able to utilize four modern, or at least modernized, battleships and as many unmodernized vessels for backups.

What Britain really needed to face the German ships—all of which were less than a decade old—was modern battleships of its own, but the prospects for this happy event were in September 1939 remote. The first of the King George V–class ships, the *King George V*, was not expected to join the fleet until the end of the following year at earliest. Against this, the Admiralty estimated that the more powerful *Bismarck*, then under construction by the Germans at Hamburg, might be ready for operations by the late summer of 1940, when the Royal Navy would have nothing in service that could either catch or destroy her.[3] As for the Lions, a much more worthwhile proposition, the position was even worse.

The first pair in this class, the *Lion* and *Temeraire*, had been laid down in June and July 1939, respectively, by Vickers Armstrong and Cammel Laird, while the second pair had only just been ordered, the *Conqueror* from Clydebank and the *Thunderer* from Fairfield, in August 1939. But already these vessels were under attack, not from any foreign enemy but by Britain's own First Lord of the Admiralty. One recent biographer, to whom Winston Churchill could commit few errors, has described the situation in connection with these ships in the following manner: "At the outset of the war the navy was involved in an enormous and elaborate construction program designed to remedy the neglect of the interwar years, and replace the often antiquated ships of the Fleet with new vessels of modern design and great power. Besides being expensive the construction program was likely to be slow. Churchill, seizing on the need of the moment, decided to scrap it."[4]

Although many authorities have claimed that Churchill, both as First Lord of the Admiralty and later as supreme British War Lord, was obsessed to the point of delusion with the power of the battleship as a weapon of war, his many actions in connection with the few great ships the Royal Navy had would seem to give the opposite picture. As another biographer put it, "Churchill had a fetish for the suicidal use of battleships."[5]

Numerous illustrations of this assertion will come our way, but certainly his initial action on the Lions was very much a test of the Board's loyalty and complaisance.[6]

It was on September 12, almost within a week of the brave and hopeful signal "Winston is back," that the Board was faced with the first of many fateful interventions, and made their professional reply.

Churchill had stated that, in his view, all battleship construction that could not result in a finished vessel by 1941 should be suspended for a year and work concentrated on more immediate problems. This scheme, would have meant the abandonment, albeit not forever, not only of the four Lions but also of the fifth King George (*Beatty*) and maybe even the fourth (*Jellicoe*). Thus, the Board was asked to go into the war with the prospect of only three of the proposed nine battleships joining the fleet. Not surprisingly the Board viewed Churchill's first foray into grand policy with some dismay. Their duty was to consider the long-range requirements of the Fleet and the nation rather than merely the short-term viewpoint. After waiting fifteen years before commencing a replacement program designed to bring the navy up to date, most of this delay having been brought about by the same politician when at the Treasury (a fact glossed over by his admirers), they were not prepared to jeopardize their careful preparations at the drop of a silken top hat.

The reply, from the First Sea Lord, Adm. Sir Dudley Pound, expressed this viewpoint quite clearly. While they agreed to the temporary delay of three months in the work in progress on the four Lions (because of the congestion caused by the conversion of unprotected liners into the grand-sounding "armed merchant cruisers" for patrol working), they would not agree to hold up any of the King Georges. Furthermore, they wished to recommence work on the four Lions as soon as possible. Japan, as always, dominated the thoughts of the Board. "It would be fatal to the Empire to emerge from this [German] war only with old battleships, when we might be faced with sending a fleet to the Far East."[7]

As usual, Churchill was not too happy with opinions that contradicted his own current viewpoint: "It is far more important to have some ships to fight with, and to have ships that Parliament has paid for delivered to date, than to squander effort upon remote construction, which has no relation to our danger!"[8] Unfortunately, both Japan and 1942 were not to be so remote as the First Lord envisaged in 1939, and when that time arrived, it was with obsolete Royal Sovereigns that he left his admiral to face the enemy rather than new Lions.

In the face of the most expert and specific advice, Churchill remained adamant. In vain would Pound reiterate that "before the war is over the scales may be more heavily weighed against us if we lose any capital ships."[9] Nor did Admiral Phillips's measured arguments have any effect. Although expense has been identified as one good reason for abandoning the program, Phillips argued quite reasonably that "war is a wasteful thing. At the end of the war there are sure to be millions upon millions of pounds' worth of army and air force material, which will be utterly and absolutely wasted. Not one penny put into our capital ship strength will ever be wasted."[10]

All work was halted—little had started, in any event—on the *Conqueror* and *Thunderer*, which would be reconsidered later that year. The King

Georges would be completed by 1942 at the latest. The *Lion* and *Temeraire* would also go ahead but at lower priority. In the event, these two vessels would be abandoned by 1945. All that remained was another Churchill innovation, the *Vanguard*.

In order that a battleship could be built to meet modern conditions and back up the inadequate 14-inch King Georges, Sir Stanley Goodall put forward the proposal that a ship be laid down in 1940 for completion by 1943. As the length of time taken to construct such a ship was dictated more by the availability of her main armament rather than her hull, he suggested they use the four spare 15-inch gun turrets that had been landed from the battlecruisers *Glorious* and *Courageous* in the 1920s. They had been retained to be utilized as 'spares' for existing battleships should they lose a turret in action damage. The verdict of this intervention by the First Lord was to be subsequently described by one fawning historian as "an insight not without shrewdness."[11]

Thus was born the *Vanguard* concept, the ship that was to be the final British battleship. The idea was sound enough when viewed as a backup for the King George Vs, but she could never be an adequate substitute for the Lions in terms of strength vis-à-vis foreign ships. As it turned out, her greatest attraction and asset, that of speed of construction, was thrown away through the slowness and enforced inefficiency of British shipbuilding techniques.[12] Thus, far from joining the fleet *before* the probable date of the four abandoned Lions, she did not finally reach service until two years *after* that time—not until 1946, by which time the war was over.

Ordered under the 1940 War Emergency Program in March 1941, the *Vanguard* was actually laid down at Clydebank in October of that year. It was not until November 1944—three years later—that she was even launched. In hull design and engine layout, she generally followed the King George Vs but had a longer armored belt, featured a cutaway bow and highly flared forecastle, which gave her more speed and a rakish appearance, enhanced by her funnel caps. The usual wasteful practice of providing hangars for scouting seaplanes was subsequently modified, in the light of wartime experience. Also, happily, the hodgepodge of (largely useless) short-range antiaircraft weapons that were such a shameful example of the unpreparedness of British men of war to face air attack was rectified, and she carried only 40-millimeter Bofors guns. Basic details of this vessel, the last British battleship to be built and completed, were 44,500 tons; eight 15-inch guns, sixteen 5.25-inch guns, thirty-three 40-millimeter guns; and thirty knots.

Two other ideas concerning Britain's limited numbers of battleships that fermented in the First Lord's fertile brain during his period of office should be mentioned at this stage. Both demonstrate the immense activity and interest in naval matters shown by Winston Churchill, an interest that went far beyond the normal hazy comprehension of most politicians appointed to that office. In this, the Royal Navy was fortunate, and this enthusiasm and driving force was to mark Churchill as the greatest Englishman of the century in the years ahead. Unfortunately, it was coupled with a single-mindedness and ruthlessness that resented opposition, however well-reasoned, and the tendency for Churchill to consider himself a greater naval planner and strategist than his service advisers on the Board was to lead to angry recriminations later, when his own power was absolute and once he had finally worn down his more thoughtful Sea Lord, Admiral Pound, was to involve him in one of the greatest disasters the Royal Navy was to suffer in World War II.

The first of the early schemes was, on the face of it, sound enough, although it placed a great deal of emphasis on the gullibility of the German enemy, a gullibility that was not born out in practice. This was for the creation of the fleet of dummy battleships in order to deceive the enemy about the strength and whereabouts of the main units of the Home Fleet.

Dummy battleships had of course been employed before, during the Great War, but one of Churchill's first acts on becoming First Lord was to bring the idea up once more. He felt that air reconnaissance had made the need for such deception even more essential. As regard to capital ships, he wanted dummies of six of them made at once—*Nelson, Hood, Renown,* a couple of Queen Elizabeth, and a Royal Sovereign. His proposal was that such mockups could be built atop barges and moored in appropriate harbors to deceive the airmen. Sir Dudley Pound had more confidence in the ability of the Luftwaffe to discern between such craft and the real thing. As usual he considered Churchill's idea in far greater depth and then gave his answer.

Admiral Pound felt certain that static dummy vessels would be quickly spotted for what they were, the mere fact that they were stationary for long periods would give the game away. Instead he proposed that typical warship superstructure should be built upon some merchant ships' hulls. This would give the photographic effect required from the aerial viewpoint, and would also give the ships the advantage of mobility.

This was agreed to, but as more pressing and urgent needs infringed upon the material and labor required, only three such dummies were actually constructed, much to Churchill's chagrin: two battleships and the aircraft carrier *Hermes.* There is no doubt that they fooled the enemy very little, although one historian suggests that at the time of the *Bismarck* sortie, the reporting of the two battleships at Scapa Flow may have deceived them for a while.[13] In the event, the fake *Hermes* was sunk off the east coast, where for many years her "distinctive" *Hermes* superstructure was an interesting, and no doubt puzzling, feature for the British convoys to negotiate.

The second great scheme involving battleships, one that was very dear to the heart of Winston Churchill throughout the first six months of the war, was the famed Operation Catherine. This plan has been much discussed and its merits analyzed elsewhere.[14] Suffice it to say, it resembled in many ways Admiral Sir John Fisher's equally audacious, but much more practical, scheme of the Great War in which a strong naval force, self-sustaining in the first part, was to force an entrance to the Baltic and then exercise a decisive influence over that sea, which Germany regarded, quite rightly as it subsequently turned out, as its own private domain.

Again this idea first saw light in the very first days of Churchill's appointment as First Lord. The backbone of this force was to be two or three of the Royal Sovereign-class battleships, whose replacements it will be recalled, Churchill had proposed to abandon. These ships were to be specially adapted for this mission, the first of many to qualify for Admiral Gretton's "suicidal uses." The battleships were to have two of their four 15-inch twin gun turrets removed and the weight thus saved was to be utilized to build into their old hulls the extra armored deck protection and the additional anti-torpedo bulges, along with extra anti-aircraft guns, to enable them to withstand anything the Germans could throw at them in their daring venture. To protect them from mines in the approaches to the Baltic specially fitted "mine-bumper" vessels were to go ahead of them and their accompanying fleet of one aircraft carrier, five cruisers, and two destroyer flotillas.

Such a fleet was to dominate the Baltic in the face of the Luftwaffe and the modern heavy ships of the German Navy and, by its presence and actions, to thus cut off Germany from the whole of Scandinavia, prevent her importing vital iron ore, influence Sweden to such an extent that she might join the Allies, and influence Soviet Russia as well. Such a scheme was vast in its implications and scale, especially so in the use of so many valuable vessels on what could only turn out to be a one-way suicide mission. The intervention of the German fleet was to be welcomed, for, even if it did result in the destruction of most of the British force, it would be worth it if they took the German Navy with them.

To lead this death-or-glory ride to almost certain destruction, Churchill found his man in the offensive-minded Admiral of the Fleet, the Earl of Cork and Orrey, but when *he* examined it in detail, he at once increased the numbers of ships required in all classes. Even if the Royal Navy had large numbers of ships to spare in this way, it would have been an immense gamble, but as it was, it did not. Although the idea was considered in depth, the First Sea Lord added certain basic conditions that could not be met in effect, and there were no spare carriers, no spare cruisers, certainly no spare destroyers, and the old battleships were finding vital, and certainly more enduring (if less spectacular), employment elsewhere. The plan was eventually shelved.

If Winston Churchill tended at first to underestimate the power of land-based bombers to influence operations in narrow waters by a battle fleet, and if this view was shared, in varying degrees, by the majority of the naval officers ashore and afloat at this time, then it was because their prewar doubts about the ability of the air forces of all nations to actually inflict damage on warships had been given almost complete and total backing by the actual performance of the mighty bomber itself.

Both Germany and Great Britain during this period had put severe restrictions on their bomber forces which prevented them carrying out any effective attacks on the strategic targets in either nation's homeland. Neither wished to be the first to start the long expected reign of terror from the air against civilians. Hitler because he expected to win the war without it anyway, and Great Britain because she had neither sufficient aircraft nor the ruthlessness to carry out such attacks (at this time at least). Therefore, the cream of the bomber crews were free to divert all their energy to carrying out the most cherished of their pre-war ambitions, to destroy at the outset of war the obsolete mammoths of the enemy fleets lying sluggishly at their anchorages.

The fact they could do this, and with contemptible ease, had been a corner stone of their policies for almost twenty years. Now they had the opportunity to prove themselves and both sides threw themselves into with eagerness. Just about the first major war operations by each side consisted of air strikes on the opposing fleets. The results hardly matched up to the heady predictions of Tedder, Mitchell, and Scott. In fact the first air attacks on warships resembled, more than anything else, the cruel and smashing massacres of the French Armies in August 1914 during the battles of the frontiers. Happily the casualties were slight in terms of men, but in actual results and in the exploding of a long-held myth, the effects were as shattering for the airmen.

In these first air attacks, it was the Royal Air Force that took the initiative, the Luftwaffe being tied up mostly in crushing the Poles. Although the RAF policy was to conserve its strength while a steady buildup took place, in order to throw it in at a decisive point, the restrictions placed upon them against attacking land targets prompted them to reconsider naval targets as alternatives. The RAF, although confident it could destroy all types of warships with ease, did not regard the destruction of the German Navy as anything other than a secondary target. However, the Air Ministry decided to see what they could achieve, with a limited force at this time, when little else was available to hit. Although Allied governmental restrictions forbade even attacks on dockyards, lest civilian casualties might result, bombing attacks were allowed against warships anchored in roadsteads or the open sea.

The bomber crews were eager to prove themselves and, on the first day of war, a reconnaissance report of German warships putting to sea in the Heligoland Bight led to the despatch of an air striking force against them. The result was to be depressingly familiar in the years ahead. Of the fifty-four bombers dispatched, not one so much as sighted the German ships, and all returned to base without accomplishing anything.

The next day, however, further patrols brought news that several large warships lay at anchor in Brunsbuttel, Wilhelmshaven, and the Schilling Roads. Radio faults delayed the receipt of this report for two hours and when it got through the weather conditions necessitated a low-level attack as the only one holding out promise of success. Accordingly, the 500-pound SAP (semi-armor piercing) bombs were taken off and replaced with 500-pound GP (general purpose) bombs. Then the strike took off. Altogether, fifteen Blenheim twin-engine bombers and fourteen Wellington twin-engine bombers, from Nos. 9 and 149 Squadrons, took part.

The Wellingtons' targets were the German battlecruisers *Scharnhorst* and *Gneisenau.* For the inauspicious results achieved, the British blamed the bad weather and fierce flak, whereas the Germans gave the credit to the flak and the work of the fighter unit 11/*Jagdgeschwader* (JG, or Fighter Wing) 77. The RAF claimed one possible hit for the loss of one aircraft. The Germans in fact suffered no damage to either battlecruiser and they in turn claimed to have destroyed two of the Wellingtons one by antiaircraft fire and one by fighters.

The Blenheims, from Nos. 107, 110, and 139 Squadrons, went in against the pocket battleship *Admiral Scheer,* which was anchored in the Schilling Roads. The five Blenheims of No. 139 Squadron failed to locate their target at all, but both the other units were more fortunate. Unfortunately, they attacked separately.

The five bombers of No. 110 Squadron, led by Flight Lieutenant Doran, made a very brave and concentrated low-level attack that achieved absolute surprise. They were initially mistaken for German aircraft by the ships, and approaching the *Admiral Scheer* from several angles at masthead height to split the defense, the first two aircraft scored one direct hit and two near-misses. None of their bombs detonated; all were duds. Doran's aircraft scored two of these, one bomb bouncing off the pocket battleship's armored deck into the water alongside, the other landing fair and square. The second bomber scored another near miss alongside. The bombs of the third and fourth Blenheims were also close to target. The last aircraft was caught in a hail of flak from the awakened defences that finally arose from the German ships and crashed into the sea. By the time No. 107 Squadron arrived, the antiaircraft defenses were in full spate, and they lost four of their five aircraft destroyed. One of these aircraft, having been hard hit by flak, spun into the bows of the old light cruiser *Emden* causing slight damage and about a dozen casualties.

Thus, at a cost of seven bombers from a total striking force of twenty-nine, the RAF had inflicted minimal damage on one pocket battleship and one light cruiser. The disappointment was immense. Wrote the official air historian:

> These operations of September 4 may be regarded as characteristic of our first attempts to damage the enemy from the air. The over-optimistic view of what might be achieved; the care taken to avoid harming the German civilian population; the large proportion of aircraft failing to locate the objective; the ineffective bombs and inconsiderable results; the expectation that crews would be skilful enough to find and bomb in atrocious weather a precise and hotly defended target on the other side of the North Sea; and the unflinching courage with which the attacks were pressed home—all these were typical, not merely of September 1939, but of many months to come.[15]

The Germans were not impressed, although had those three bombs not have been duds, the story would have been much different. But as it was, "hopes of striking a heavy blow at the German fleet at the very outset of the war had been frustrated. Virtually nothing had been achieved—at heavy cost."[16] "The Blenheims," wrote Captain Roskill, "had pressed home their attacks most gallantly, but the results achieved were not commensurate with the losses suffered. Fortunately, the enemy bombers did no better in their early attacks on our own warships."[17]

In the problem of hitting such elusive targets as battleships with bombs, the Germans had a more realistic approach than the British. They quickly realized that such attacks would call for a specialized bomber force trained to operate over the sea, and rather than merely detach such units from the main bombing force in the manner of the RAF, they allocated two special maritime bomber and strike units for naval cooperation duties.

Under the command of General Geisler, these two units, *Kampfgeschwader* (KG, or Bomber Wing) 26 and *Kampfgeschwader* 30, were equipped with the Heinkel He 111 and the new Junkers Ju 88 twin-engine bombers, respectively. These units were manned with picked crews and were trained to attack shipping. No previous background of experience in the bombing of warships existed, and the small band of enthusiastic officer pilots engaged in these operations "evolved and perfected their own methods."[18]

It can be seen that the Luftwaffe was, however, following the same false trail as the RAF in going for the bomb rather than the torpedo as the most effective means of attacking warships. However, as one of their aircraft, the Ju 88, was adaptable for dive-bombing and as their crews were of a high-standard elite and specially trained for the job, Geisler's force was potentially more dangerous to the battleship than the RAF squadrons, no matter how brave and gallant their crews. The German airmen were soon to be given their first opportunities to show whether they could, in fact, do better.

General Geisler's command, elevated to *Fliegerkorps* (Air Corps) X but still very much under strength due to the demands of the Polish campaign, actually consisted of some sixty He 111s of KG 26 and a few of the still largely experimental Ju 88s of I/KG 30, a total force of some seventy aircraft. Their chance to test their performance against British battleships at sea, rather than in well-defended anchorages, came towards the end of the month. The British submarine *Spearfish* had been so damaged off the Horns Reef that she was unable to dive and had to steer a slow, painful course back across the North Sea on the surface. To give her support a cruiser squadron and a destroyer flotilla was sent to her aid, and to cover these light units, the Battle-cruiser Squadron was also dispatched, the *Hood* and *Renown*, with light forces. Admiral Forbes took the *Nelson* and *Rodney* out as well, with *Ark Royal* and a destroyer screen. In the forenoon of September 26, the heavy ships were located by German flying boats but the only bombers available to the Germans were nine He 111s and four Ju 88s, the former armed with 1,000-pound bombs, the latter with 500-pound bombs. Both groups of aircraft attacked separately. As in the case of the British, no attempt was made to make a combined attack. "The attacks were quite uncoordinated and no attempt was made to concentrate on the most important target present."[19]

The Heinkels located the 2nd Cruiser Squadron that afternoon but failed to score any hits at all, but by far the most spectacular assault was carried out by the four Ju 88s. They took on the five big ships of the Home Fleet on their own. They arrived over the fleet in eight-tenths cloud cover at 9,000 feet, and each pilot made his dive-bombing attack separately. The first plane selected the *Ark Royal* as its target and was uncomfortably close with a near-miss off the carrier's bow. This led to the first of many German claims to have sunk her. Another pilot dived on the largest ship he could see, the largest in fact he could have found in any fleet, the *Hood*.

Reports from the German aircrew indicate that they took the British gunners by complete surprise, and in an attack from 6,000 feet this aircraft scored a direct hit on the battlecruiser. The bomb caught the *Hood* a glancing blow on her quarter and fell harmlessly into the sea. It was a chance in a million: a few yards farther ahead and the damage might have been serious. For a brief moment it had looked as though the bomb was coming clean for the quarterdeck.[20]

No damage was done and no aircraft was damaged in this first, historical sortie of bomber against battleship at sea, but, light though the attack was, it gave both sides much to ponder on. It was clear that the accuracy of the dive-bomber was under-rated by the Royal Navy, and even more important, the standard of antiaircraft fire was shown to be depressingly low. The antiaircraft gunfire of the fleet was, on this occasion, as ineffective as the bombing, and Admiral Forbes states in his despatch that "the control personnel were obviously unprepared for such high performance dive-bombing!"[21]

The RAF now tried again. Since the first daring attack Bomber Command had adopted the policy of carrying out armed reconnaissance patrols into the North Sea with groups of bombers, nine or more strong, Hampdens, Wellingtons, and the like. These groups were to rely on their own defensive gun armaments for mutual defence and were to attack any German submarines or heavy surface vessels encountered. On September 29, a force of eleven Hampdens from No. 144 Squadron located two German destroyers near Heligoland. Intercepted by German fighters, five of their number were destroyed without achieving anything.

"Thenceforward the reconnaissance in force was less popular," recorded the official historian, "but twenty-four Bomber Command aircraft stood by each day at the call of Coastal Command."[22] These heavier strike forces were not to get a chance to show their paces for several weeks. Meanwhile, it fell to the Germans to lay on a classic naval-aerial combined operation designed to lure the heavy ships of the Home Fleet back into the range of the reinforced arms of *Fliegerkorps* X. To do this, the battlecruiser *Gneisenau*, light cruiser *Köln*, and nine destroyers were ordered to sortie out towards the south coast of Norway between October 8 and 10. This was the first mission of the *Gneisenau*, but the orders given to her commander were explicit: he was to avoid contact with superior forces and merely act as a bait to give the bombers their chance.

The *Gneisenau* and her group duly sailed on the seventh under Admiral Btihm and were sighted the next day, as planned, off the Lister Light heading north. The bait was eagerly taken, and Admiral Forbes, who already had advance wind of the sailing of the German battlecruiser, assumed, naturally enough, that she might be breaking out into the North Atlantic. Accordingly he made his dispositions. The battlecruisers *Hood* and *Repulse*, with two cruisers and four destroyers, were sent from Scapa Flow to take up an intercepting position north-west of the Stadtlandet headland. A cruiser squadron from the Humber was sent into the Skagerrak from the Firth of Forth to prevent any doubling back, and finally, early on the eighth, Admiral Forbes sailed himself with the *Nelson* and *Rodney,* one aircraft carrier, one light cruiser, and eight destroyers to take up position north-east of the Shetlands. The battleship *Royal Oak,* with two destroyers, was sent to guard the Fair Isle Channel in case the Germans showed such audacity as to force this passage as a shortcut.

Nor was this all. It was hoped that the RAF striking force might also be able to inflict some damage on the German fleet, and during the afternoon of the eighth, twelve Wellingtons were accordingly sent out. Again, they failed to locate their target, and the shadowing Hudson also lost them that evening. After dark, the *Gneisenau* and her companions reversed course and by midday on the tenth were snugly back at Kiel. Meanwhile, the heavy ships of the Home Fleet continued to seek them far to the north. Throughout the ninth, the *Nelson, Rodney, Hood, Repulse,* and *Royal Oak* maintained their vigil, but it was unrewarded. Although the *Gneisenau* had proved the ideal bait to get the British heavy ships to sea, the conviction that the Germans were heading for the North Atlantic convoy routes meant that they confined themselves to waters far away from the Luftwaffe. Only the light forces of the Humber Force entered their domain, and against these vessels, the main weight of the planned decisive air attack was dissipated. No fewer than 148 bombers of KG 26, *Lehrgeschwader* (LG, or Training and Development Wing) 1, and I/KG 30, sortied out but failed to score a single hit.

As attempts to bring the heavy ships to the bombers had failed, the Germans now decided to do what the RAF had attempted earlier—strike at the navy in its own bases. The fast dive-bombing Ju 88s of I/KG 30 were given the task on October 16. Led by Captain Pohle, they attacked the naval forces in the Firth of Forth most gallantly, despite a late interception by British fighters. Two bombers were lost, but only light forces were found, no battleships. Two light cruisers and a destroyer were hit and put out of action for a while.

Obviously, the big ships were based at Scapa Flow, reasoned the Luftwaffe, and so a second attack was sent against that base. This took place on October 17, but once again, the German bombers, a mere four Ju 88s under Captain Doench, found that there were no big ships to attack when they got there. The fleet was at sea. Frustrated, they turned their attentions to the old demilitarized hulk of the *Iron Duke* and damaged her with a near miss. This was achieved for the loss of one bomber.

The discouraging results achieved by the Luftwaffe in this period almost exactly matched the achievements of the RAF. The disillusionment was just the same. As one German historian summed up: "The widely held belief that bombers and dive-bombers could drive the enemy's naval forces from the seas was not, at the war's outset, fulfilled. Bad weather, and lack of experience in nautical flying, spotting, recognition, and attack, were the contributory causes. Achievements were greatly overestimated."[23]

For the RAF to admit that such a cornerstone of their own invincibility was built on sand would be too much to expect. The lessons were not learned; it needed a greater shock before the truth would be admitted. These lessons were received before the year was out.

On December 3, another attack in force was launched against the German heavy ships off Heligoland. Twenty-four Wellington bombers, from Nos. 38, 115, and 149 Squadrons, took off that morning to strike at two light cruisers. Heavily engaged by flak and intercepted by fighters they bombed through cloud and escaped unscathed. Again, no major ship was so much as scratched. Nothing daunted, the RAF repeated the performance on the fourteenth of that. month. A strong force of Wellingtons and Hampdens was sent out against reported German warships in the same area. Again the Hampdens failed to find the ships at all. Twelve Wellingtons of No. 99 Squadron had better luck and carried out attacks on warships in the Schilling Roads. Again they were intercepted by defending fighters and this time half the bombers were destroyed, again without achieving anything, for the cloud base at 800 feet, was too low for attacks with SAP bombs to be effective.

This was bad enough, but four days later came the final eye-opener. Again, the Schilling Roadstead and Wilhelmshaven were the targets. The force consisted of some twenty-four Wellington bombers, from Nos. 9, 37, and 149 Squadrons. This time, as the Germans had been given ample trial runs on which to base their defences, it ended in complete disaster.

Two of the aircraft turned back early on. The remainder arrived over the target area and sighted several large warships, but no attacks were made, due, it is claimed, entirely to the need to avoid civilian casualties ashore. However this time the German fighters were already in the sky waiting for them and it is doubtful whether they would have been able to attack any ship at all, whether at sea or in dock. Attacked by wave after wave of single-engine Me 109s and twin-engine Me 110s, the Wellingtons were shot to pieces as they maintained their standard close formation, wingtip to wingtip. Of the twenty-two bombers that reached the target area, no fewer than fifteen were shot down, ditched, or crashed on landing. Incredibly, the RAF announced this as a great victory over determined fighter opposition; in truth, they had shot down but two fighters, and no German ship had been so much as scratched. December 18 marked the final lesson of the ability of the bombers then in service with the RAF to affect sea warfare. "The offensive (if such it can be called) against enemy warships during the long months of inactivity on land was singularly unimpressive in its immediate results," wrote the official historian. Bomber Command had made 861 sorties and dropped only 61 tons of bombs. The only damage had been that achieved in the first attack, and that was negligible, "not worth the loss of forty-one bombers."[24]

Even so stout an upholder of the power of the bomber over the warship as Vice Admiral Hazlet conceded that, during this period at least, "early bombing attacks by both sides on ships in harbour had proved remarkably ineffective."[25]

The chief reason for the equal early lack of success on attacks on ships at sea was simply that the wrong types of aircraft were using the wrong type of weapon. Torpedo bombers were what were required, especially against battleships. If prewar experience had proven anything, it was this. However the only such aircraft available to the RAF on the outbreak of the war were two squadrons of obsolete Vildebeest torpedo bombers with a top speed of 153 miles per hour and a radius of 185 miles. Nor was the Fleet Air Arm any better off with its equally antiquated Swordfish biplanes, and even their replacements, the Albacores, were of the same type. The Luftwaffe had no torpedo bombers at all, save for a few He 115 float-planes.

It should be noted that even these puny forces had shown that they could hit warships at sea or in harbor, even if at present they could not inflict much damage on them. It was only to be expected that as the potential of aircraft was developed at a far higher pace and speed than any corresponding defense could be adapted for the battleship, this initial impotence was merely a temporary factor. Any relief felt afloat after the attacks of 1939 was soon to be shown to be but a passing and untypical period of relative immunity.

The air factor having for the time being been shown to be a false alarm, what of the submarine? Great faith had been placed in the ASDIC (SONAR) detection device prewar as we have already noted. It was therefore regarded as a completely adequate defense against submarine attack on battleships, as much as the antiaircraft gun was against bombers. But the device was overrated and both submarines, and the techniques they used, had also moved on apace during the twenty years' peace. Similar lessons were therefore quickly learnt with regard to this weapon. The loss of the aircraft carrier *Courageous* so soon after the outbreak of the war showed just how potentially deadly a well-handled submarine could be against large vessels.

At this stage of the war, Germany had very few operational submarines. Moreover, those they had were bedeviled by unsatisfactory torpedoes. The ratio of torpedoes that hit their targets and failed to explode during the first three or four months of the war was nothing less than a major scandal.[26]

Nonetheless, even in the face of these twin difficulties, the German U-boats quickly made their mark. The fact that not a single modern battleship had ever been sunk by submarine attack gave a certain air of invincibility to even the oldest of the combatants' capital ships, and the addition of the bulges gave extra confidence. This confidence was rapidly deflated. One historian gave this scathing viewpoint: "The slow and clumsy battleship could no longer venture to sea without an escort of destroyers to screen her, the screen required became ever larger and more complex as the maneuvering and diving capabilities of the submarine improved."[27]

However, compared with the vast numbers of escorting destroyers which accompanied the Grand Fleet battleships on their sorties in World War I, some 120 ships to protect forty battleships, the Home Fleet did not have a marked increase in the numbers of flotilla craft allocated to it. The battleships of Admiral Forbes's command, for example, had at best the nine destroyers of the 8th Flotilla and the eight destroyers of the 6th Flotilla to protect them, seventeen destroyers in all. Other fleets we shall encounter had even fewer destroyers per battleship and so the ratio was not, in fact, increased at all over the Great War. Nor was the fastest submarine the German and Italians had in service anywhere near as fast as a modern battleship.[28]

In one respect, the conditions of the submarine vis-à-vis the battleship were the same in both conflicts and this -was in the vulnerability of the bases. In the Great War, Jellicoe had felt that his great ships were safer against submarine attack when at sea at speed, than when anchored in their "secure" base at Scapa Flow. Submarine alarms in the Flow were frequent, but no German commander ever actually penetrated the base in 1916-18 and gradually the defences were built up to a high pitch.

When the Home Fleet came back to Scapa Flow in 1939, all the great work done earlier had been allowed to wither in neglect. When, at the time of the Munich crisis in 1938, it was decided to again utilize the Flow as the main fleet base, this tragic state of affairs was revealed to Admiral Forbes. "It was a strange sight, which greeted him as he led his ships into the anchorage. A party of Royal Marines had just finished dismantling the last of the gun emplacements of the First World War while boom defence vessels were busy at work preparing to lay the anti-submarine nets ultimately required for the Second World War."[29]

Admiral Forbes made a tour of inspection of the base and found that it was virtually undefended. He was especially concerned about Holm Sound and personally bought a concrete barge, which he had sunk there to help close the gap. Despite repeated representations to the Admiralty in the intervening period, the outbreak of war found his base in virtually the same condition as the year before. "There is no doubt that the Admiralty did not make any strenuous effort to strengthen the defenses of Scapa Flow between the time of Munich and the outbreak of war."[30]

The price was extracted in full measure on October 14, 1939. The poor state of the Home Fleet's main base was not unknown to the Germans and the penetration of the fleet anchorage by a skilful and daring submarine commander was not considered beyond the bounds of possibility. Adm. Karl

Dönitz found his man in Lt. Günther Prien, captain of *U-47*. The plan was worked out with care and attention to detail.

Thus it was that, on a clear and moonless night, the *U-47* was painfully and patiently edged through northernmost passage of Holm Sound, to the north of Lamb Holm, past the sunken hulks and right into the sleeping anchorage. It was an act of extreme bravery, but once within Prien, far from being offered the choice of the whole Home Fleet, found the great open anchorage virtually empty.

It will be recalled how, after the sortie by the *Gneisenau* between the eighth and tenth of the month, all the capital ship strength of the Home Fleet had been taken to sea in a fruitless hunt. On conclusion of this operation the bulk of the British fleet had not returned to Scapa Flow but had instead taken itself to the alternative "secret" anchorage of Loch Ewe, on west coast of Scotland. The only major unit still remaining at Scapa that night was the battleship *Royal Oak* that had been patrolling close by in the Fair Isle channel earlier. The *Repulse* had left earlier for Rosyth.

In the strange glare of the northern lights, Prien took his submarine into the Flow on the surface and cast around for a target worthy of his attention. In this he was entirely unmolested. All that could be made out were two large vessels to the north of the anchorage and it was against these that Prien made his final approach at 12:58 A.M. The ships were the *Royal Oak* and the old seaplane tender *Pegasus*, but Prien thought that the latter was the *Repulse* or a similar capital ship. The myth has persisted to this day, that *two* battleships were hit that night, despite all the true facts long being made public.[31]

At a range of 4,000 yards, a four-torpedo salvo was fired. One torpedo stuck in its tube, but the other three sped towards their targets. With tension at a pitch of intensity the German crew waited for the crash of the explosions but all that came was one muffled detonation. Almost unbelievably, all had missed this sitting duck save for one, which had hit the battleship's anchor cable. The detonation was so slight and the damage so minimal that when the captain and a team of officers aboard the battleship made a check. They were convinced that it was caused by a small *internal* explosion forward.

No alarm was raised, and still surfaced and unmolested, Prien was able to turn *U-47* around 180 degrees and then fire his single stern tube at the great bulk of the battleship. Again, there was no result, the uncanny silence of the Flow remained undisturbed. It was with remarkable coolness that this fantastic situation left Prien still determined to finish his mission. He withdrew and carefully reloaded his torpedo tubes for yet a third attempt.

At 1:16, he was back in position and a further three torpedoes were launched. This time he was rewarded for two of them exploded under the *Royal Oak*, passing below her "bulges" as if they were not there, thus ripping out her bottom. Within thirteen minutes the huge vessel had rolled over and taken 833 of her officers and crew to their deaths.[32]

Despite difficulties with the current and falling tide the imperturbable Prien retraced his steps and by 2:15 that morning was in open sea and safe away. It was an incredible performance and there is no doubt that the captain of the *U-47* deserved all the accolades heaped upon him by his rapturous nation.

It was a disaster of the greatest magnitude for the Royal Navy. "Though all the battleships of the *Royal Oak* [*sic*], class were too slow, too old and too ill-protected to take their place in the line," wrote the official historian, "they did valuable work escorting convoys and covering landing operations later. But whether the ship herself be regarded as having great military value or not, the loss of so many valuable lives in such a manner was tragic."[33]

Typically the block ship that would have finally barred *U-47*'s entrance arrived at the Flow the day after the attack. But it was over a year since Admiral Forbes had first pointed out the danger. Nor were the German submarines any less determined in their efforts to torpedo battleships at sea, only their frequent torpedo failures prevented much more serious disasters in these opening months.

For example, when the Home Fleet moved its base to Loch Ewe, the Germans quickly became aware of the fact. Between the middle of October and November, a force of four submarines was stationed to the west of the Orkneys to intercept them. On October 30, one of these boats, *U-56*, under Lieutenant Commander Zahn, found himself by good fortune to be in a perfect attacking position when the *Nelson, Rodney,* and *Hood* crossed his path. He was actually inside the protecting destroyer screen and made his attack from point-blank range. He fired a spread of three torpedoes and after being timed to the end of their runs to the target, which Zahn claimed to be the *Nelson,* they were rewarded with the sounds of two of the torpedoes hitting. However it was not with enormous explosions that these successes announced themselves to the waiting submariners, but with the same metallic clangs as Prien had first heard. In his subsequent report, Zahn complained that they were all duds; in fact, so hard did he take the failure of this perfect opportunity that he was relieved of his duties immediately.[34]

There was little wrong with the torpedoes of the *U-30*, under Lieutenant Commander Lemp, however, when she encountered the *Barham* and *Renown* on December 28 in the North Minch. Easily penetrating the slender screen of five destroyers, she managed to hit the old battleship, and the resulting detonation caused heavy damage. On this occasion, the *Barham*'s protection was sufficiently strong to prevent this being a lethal blow but the resulting damage put her in dockyard hands in Liverpool for three months. She was considered an unlucky ship for, on her inward passage two weeks before she had rammed and sunk one of her escorting destroyers, the *Duchess*, with heavy loss of life.[35]

Despite the threat of bombers and submarines, the battleship continued to retain its position as the main unit of naval power during the opening months of the war. It is not generally credited with this fact but it is nonetheless true. On the German side indeed the battleship was playing quite an important role in the rapid defeat of Poland.

It will be recalled that after the Great War, Germany was allowed to retain eight ancient pre-Dreadnoughts in its fleet.[36] Of these eight, four were still serving in 1939, and although only two of them were operational, these old veterans had the unique distinction of firing some of the first shots of World War II.

These two were the *Schleswig-Holstein* and *Schlesien*, both of which had undergone some modernization, losing one funnel and four 5.9-inch guns and having four 3.9-inch antiaircraft guns added. They were retained for training purposes, but at the outbreak of war, they were immediately put to good use as coastal bombardment units. Their first action took place on September 1, when the *Schleswig-Holstein*, under Captain Kleikamp, shelled Westerplatte in conjunction with attacks by Stuka dive-bombers. The 11-inch shells from this old ship thus marked the opening of the war at sea.

The Polish defense positions here defended the estuary of the Vistula River and until they could be reduced the Germans could not use the port of Danzig, the alleged reason for the war, as a supply base for their armies' advance. Despite being weakly held these positions held out for a week. The *Schleswig-Holstein* repeated her bombardments on the fourth and seventh before the garrison finally gave in.

The peninsula of Hela was held by the Poles with equal gallantry in the face of overwhelming odds. In order to reduce it, the *Schlesien* was brought up to assist her sister. Between the seventh and thirteenth, the two old battleships carried out almost daily bombardments, but Hela held until October 2. On the nineteenth, the *Schleswig-Holstein* bombarded Polish troop concentrations at Oxhoft, Ostrowogrund, and Hexengrund, and again on October 25, 26, and 27, she and *Schlesien*, under Captain Utke, fired on artillery positions on Hela.

After their brief moment of glory, the two old battleships were once more relegated to harbor duties until the invasion of Denmark. But it was mainly in the training role that they served out their old lives through the war until almost the final days. The *Schlesien* was ultimately mined in May 1945 and scuttled off Swinemunde, while the *Schleswig-Holstein* was damaged by bombing at Gdynia in March 1945 and also scuttled. However, the true role laid down for the German heavy ships was war on British shipping in distant waters, and in readiness for this, two of them had already sailed before the outbreak of hostilities and were cruising in the "waiting" positions well before the Royal Navy could intercept them. Oilers and supply ships had already slipped though the net to sustain them but for a while they were held in check.

The first raider to sail was the pocket battleship *Admiral Graf Spee*, under Captain Langsdorff, which left Germany on August 21, passing through the Faeroes-Iceland channel undetected. She was followed by her sister, the *Deutschland*, under Captain Wennecker, on the twenty-fourth. Both had supply vessels in train. Although they evaded detection, neither went straight into the attack.

The pocket battleships were restrained because Hitler, underestimating the determination of England, hoped after his rapid Polish campaign to come to terms with the West. Consequently, until the end of September, the *Deutschland* remained off the east coast of Greenland, remote from all shipping, while the *Admiral Graf Spee* lay in the South Atlantic between St. Helena and Brazil.[37]

Not until the end of the month were the two pocket battleships given permission to commence raiding operations. They immediately set to work but their achievements were initially very poor to offset the enormous amount of work involved to get them into position. They were, in fact and of necessity, working in waters too remote from the main shipping routes; when they changed position results started to come.

However, in assessing the role of a surface raider it should never be the total tonnage of shipping actually destroyed that should be the prime consideration. The amount of disruption to normal shipping channels, the enormous concentration of all available resources that the Allies were forced to divert into hunting them down, the effect this had on already tight strategic dispositions, all weighed the balance in their favor.

The German raiders of the Great War had shown just what this involved and directly the first reports came into the Admiralty of sinkings involving surface warships they and the French immediately formed powerful hunting groups to bring the raiders to bay.

The *Deutschland* was the less successful of the two ships during this period. On receiving permission to begin operations on September 26, the *Deutschland* headed south from her waiting area to commence working on the Bermuda-Azores route. Her first victim was the *Stonegate* (5,044 tons) on October 5. Doubling back to the north, she operated to the east of Newfoundland, for a time between the ninth and sixteenth of that month, against the HX convoy route. During this period, her total achievement was the capturing of the American freighter *City of Flint* (4,963 tons), with the subsequent diplomatic uproar, and the sinking of the Norwegian steamer *Lorentz W. Hansen* (1,918 tons). The chief blame for this disappointing return was placed on the unreliability of her scouting aircraft and difficulties with her engines. Troublesome machinery, due often to the boilers with which these ships were fitted, was the reason why the third pocket battleship, *Admiral Scheer*, had not sortied to join her sisters. She was still not fully operational on outbreak of the war for this reason.

These difficulties led to the early recall of the *Deutschland* to Germany in mid-November, and she arrived safely back at Wilhelmshaven without further incident. Here, on November 15, she was officially renamed the *Lützow*, the reason being, it is said, that Hitler was fearful of the resulting propaganda opportunities for the Allies should a ship bearing the name *Deutschland* be destroyed in battle.[38]

The *Admiral Graf Spee* initially had better fortune, although even in her case the destruction of so many lone merchant ships by so powerful a vessel seemed pitiful rather than awe-inspiring.

But whether or not the dignity of the battleship was somehow mocked when put to such a use there can be no denial of the fact that the reporting of two pocket battleships at large on Britain's sea routes had an effect out of all proportion with the meager results in terms of tonnage destroyed that they were chalking up. This was considerable, and the Admiralty's problems in finding these proverbial needles in the vast watery haystacks of the North and South Atlantic Oceans were complicated, not only by their lack of sufficient cruisers, all of which were outclassed in everything but speed, but by the confusing reports of which ships were actually at sea. The *Admiral Graf Spee* frequently advertised herself as *Deutschland*, and the Admiralty did not know that that vessel was safely back in Germany until many weeks after she actually got there.[39]

The setting up of the various hunting forces to bring the German raiders to book was mainly an affair of cruisers, but several battleships and battlecruisers were, of necessity, involved, these being the only ships able to scare away the raiders by their mere presence with a convoy.

The *Admiral Graf Spee* sank her first victim on September 30, the *Clement* (5,051 tons), an elderly tramp steamer. To send this vessel to the bottom required the expenditure of no fewer than five 11-inch and twenty-five 5.9-inch shells, and this after demolition charges and a torpedo had failed to work. As a demonstration of German naval power, it turned into something of a farce. "With a mighty roar the 11-inch gun went into action. The first salvo crashed into the belly of the *Clement*. Two minutes later the ship's medium artillery followed suit. Three 8-inch guns [*sic*] spat their destructive metal towards the *Clement*. Through field glasses the *Spee* crew, crowding the rails, could see the jagged holes in the ship's side above the waterline. But the *Clement* continued to ride high. Not a shot had missed her, yet the *Clement* remained afloat."[40]

This incident took place off the Brazilian port of Pernambuco, but knowing that the *Clement* had radioed a report Langsdorff took his ship east towards the southern coast of Africa to avoid detection. In these waters, he fell in with his next three victims, the *Newton Beech* (4,651 tons) on October 5, *Ashlea* (4,222 tons) on the seventh, and *Huntsman* (8,196 tons) on the tenth.

Meanwhile, the formation of the Anglo-French Hunting Forces and the detachment of further ships for vital convoys was reaping a richer, if less direct reward, in the field of strategy. The battlecruisers *Renown*, *Dunkerque*, and *Strasbourg* were the capital ships directly involved with the aircraft carriers *Eagle*, *Ark Royal*, *Hermes*, and *Béarn*, and ten heavy and six light cruisers. Quite an achievement for one ship.

Still in the same water, the fifth victim of the German raider was the *Trevanion* (5,299 tons). Not wishing to press his remarkable good fortune in evading detection, Langsdorff switched areas again, doubling into the Indian Ocean. But here he found even less traffic than before, and the only result of a month's operating was the sinking of the tiny *Africa Shell* (706 tons) in the Mozambique Channel on November 15. The *Graf Spee* therefore returned to the South Atlantic. But now her time was running out.

As great an achievement as the disruption she caused was the remarkably smooth and efficient way her refueling and restoring operations were carried out. In the successful operating of such methods, in hostile waters and with limited resources, the German Navy showed itself far superior to the Allies, who had neglected their own fleet train and were soon regretting the fact.[41]

Back on the Cape route, the *Spee*, which had steamed some 30,000 miles on this voyage, began to experience engine defects similar to those of her sisters. Langsdorff therefore resolved to sink a few more ships here, cross the Atlantic to the potentially rich hunting grounds off the River Plate estuary for a final harvest and return home early in January 1940.

The first part of this scheme worked well enough, the *Spee* dispatching the liner *Doric Star* (10,086 tons) on December 2 and the steamer *Tairoa* (7,983 tons) on the third. The *Admiral Graf Spee* then headed west, encountering and sinking the *Streorrshalh* (3,895 tons) en route. This was her last victim, for on arrival off the Plate on December 13, the pocket battleship found not the easy pickings expected, but Force G, the heavy cruiser *Exeter* and light cruisers *Ajax* and *Achilles* under Commodore Henry Harwood, who had been waiting for him. Having outthought the German battleship, the three cruisers then proceeded to outfight her, despite her overwhelming superiority in weaponry (six 11-inch and eight 5.9-inch guns against six 8-inch and twelve 6-in guns).

Commodore Harwood had already decided on his policy and his cruisers, in two divisions (*Ajax* and *Achilles*; *Exeter*), went straight into the attack. Langsdorff had expected them to back off when confronted with his big guns and merely shadow him until something larger came up in support. It was a nasty surprise for him when they did no such thing.

The *Admiral Graf Spee* commenced firing at 6:18 A.M., concentrating her full main armament on the *Exeter*, her most powerful opponent; the *Exeter* replied with her own guns two minutes later. Meanwhile, the two smaller cruisers came in fast with their smaller batteries blazing.

As usual, German gunfire, in the initial stages, was very accurate and her third salvo was a straddle. Within a few minutes, the German battleship hit the *Exeter* twice, close to B turret, putting it out of action and killing almost the entire bridge complement. Another two 11-inch shells slammed into the *Exeter*, putting A turret out of action and starting a fire amidships. With only two 8-inch guns left in action, the *Exeter* seemed doomed, but she had scored in return.

The *Admiral Graf Spee* had taken three 8-inch shell hits, including one on her control tower. Her main battery remained intact however, and she was prevented from finishing the *Exeter* off only by the unwelcome attentions of the *Ajax* and *Achilles*, which were now close enough for concentrated fire by their twelve 6-inch guns to start taking effect on the lightly armored German vessel. Langsdorff was therefore forced to switch his whole main armament against these two vessels (at this time he did not divide his two triple turrets against both British divisions), and the *Exeter* was able to limp away. She fired two salvos of torpedoes, which further spoiled Langsdorff's maneuvering.

The German ship's main battery was again accurate, and both 6-inch cruisers were straddled but by skilful weaving avoided being hit by anything than splinters. Although then four 11-inch shells had put the *Exeter* out of the running, the *Admiral Graf Spee* was already, at 6:37 A.M., looking for a way out of the fight. Langsdorff turned away. The range, which had come down to 13,000 yards, now opened to 17,000, and the 6-inch shells of the two remaining British ships had no effect on the pocket battleship's hull, although her upperworks were being badly knocked about.

The damaged *Exeter* was therefore left relatively unmolested for a fifty-minute period, during which time her last turret kept up a steady fire, which further worried the German captain, even if no further hits resulted. The *Exeter* was finally forced to abandon her longstop role at 7:29 A.M. when the machinery of Y turret failed due to an electrical fault. By this time, however, the actual battle was just about over, and the action had developed into the incredible scene of a pursuit by the two little cruisers of their mighty adversary.

The *Graf Spee* made attempts to smash her opponents, turning at bay and engaging them at intervals with every gun. Thus the *Ajax* had both after-turrets blasted out of action by a single 11-inch hit at 7:25. But they continued to score hits in reply, no less than seventeen 6-inch shells striking the German ship causing thirty-six dead and fifty-nine injured.

Langsdorff now gave up trying to shake off his pursuers, and with some 60 percent of his ammunition gone, he headed for the temporary safety of the Uruguayan port of Montevideo to effect repairs. Harwood had already decided to break off the action and resume it after nightfall. He had a report that some 80 percent of his ammunition had been expended which influenced his decision, and, although he later found this to be incorrect, kept to this wise policy. The action of December 13 was followed by three days of political wrangling. Langsdorff, already humiliated by world reaction to his hasty retreat after ninety minutes of combat, eventually decided, after consulting Berlin, to scuttle his ship rather than make a final fight. Rumors were spread that the *Renown* was waiting for him, when she was actually thousands of miles away heading for Rio de Janeiro to refuel. Other major units were even further away.

The *Exeter* limped off to the Falklands and was replaced by another 8-inch cruiser, the *Cumberland*. But the German captain was convinced that he stood no chance. On the seventeenth, the *Admiral Graf Spee* sailed into the estuary of the Plate while the *Ajax* and *Achilles* stood ready. At sunset, the pocket battleship was blown up and settled in the mud, her upperworks a twisted mass of debris, her 11-inch gun turrets mute. Two days later, Langsdorff shot himself.

Besides being the first major surface ship action of the war, the River Plate battle is interesting because it established what was to be the accepted pattern of such warfare from the German (and later also the Italian) attitudes on one side and the British on the other. The Germans were reluctant to accept battle at all against a superior or equal force. Even when the odds were firmly on their side, they showed a remarkable degree of hesitance in forcing a decision. The British accepted battle at almost every opportunity, regardless of the odds. There were a few exceptions to this general pattern on both sides of course, some Axis commanders *did* show rare bursts of aggressiveness in the use of their heavy ships, while a few British admirals showed a marked caution in battle, placing secondary considerations above the primary function, destruction of the enemy, but such cases were rare.

Individual bravery did not really come into this divergence of attitudes, but the factor of morale did. At the battle of the Plate the Royal Navy reestablished its aura of initiative and superiority. This tradition of invincibility had been begun by Drake, Raleigh, and the like, through Hawke, Howe, and Nelson over three centuries of naval supremacy. It had been lost during the Great War by excessive caution, although a few—Beatty, Tyrwhitt, and Keyes—still showed the old flair was not dead. In the Second World War it flowered as never before. In a war of materialism and automation, it is remarkable just how much this factor of morale made the difference between defeat and victory at sea.

On the less satisfactory side, the marked tendency of Axis commanders to avoid battle can be explained by the fact that they were hedged in by strict orders not to hazard their ships unless victory was absolutely certain. Certainly most of the postwar vindication of their attitudes cites Hitler (or Mussolini) as the chief villain. It is remarkable, however, that such uniformity of reaction should have been maintained despite many outstanding opportunities for Axis admirals to score important victories at not too great a risk.

In the case of the German battleships at large on the world's oceans, there was justification in avoiding battle. They need not be sunk outright in such a duel; it needed only moderate damage, such as that suffered by the *Admiral Graf Spee*, to turn a powerful hunter into a crippled quarry. The establishment of control of the world's oceans by the Royal Navy meant that any damaged German battleship was terribly vulnerable and almost certain of final destruction. Damage had to be avoided, and this meant shirking any form of combat, no matter what the odds.

Finally, on the strictly material side, the need for British battleships was reinforced. Although the three smaller cruisers had cornered the larger hunter and brought on its destruction, we could not count, as absolutely certain, that all Axis commanders would run rather than fight, and a more resolute captain might have destroyed all three British ships and still got away. To illustrate this, let us finally examine the hits scored by both sides and the damage caused.

The *Admiral Graf Spee* had scored a total of ten hits, eight on the *Exeter* and two on the *Ajax*, with her 11-inch guns. The result of these was that the *Exeter* had all three turrets put out of action and was put out of the fight with severe damage, while the *Ajax* lost half her main armament. In reply the pocket battleship had been hit no less than twenty times, but of these, only one had pierced her armored deck (1-2 inches), and none her main belt (itself only 4 inches). Her guns were all intact, so was her battleworthiness. True, her extra-light upperworks had suffered and she had a hole in her bows, which would have made a North Atlantic voyage back to Germany a hazardous operation, but, where it really counted, the three British cruisers despite their bravery could not hurt her. She had not cracked, only her commanding officer.

Likewise, it was when he thought he would have to face the *Renown*, along with the *Ark Royal*, that he decided that it was hopeless and destroyed his still fully operational ship in a gesture of complete resignation. There was no way past the *Renown*; she was not within 1,000 miles of the *Graf Spee*, but the threat was enough. It is difficult to imagine Langsdorff coming to the same conclusion had he known all that faced him were likely to be cruisers of 7,000 tons and 6-inch guns.

Finally, it should be noted that of the ships that took part in the Plate battle, the only one that carried a radar set was the *Graf Spee*. None of the British cruisers were so fitted, and therefore one of the most common Axis excuses for defeat is also withheld from them. It did not contribute much to their gunnery, for its maximum range, 16,000 yards and its newness, the *Graf Spee* was the first major German warship to be fitted with the "mattress" aerial on her control tower, which meant that the Germans relied on their rangefinders. These were superb instruments, larger and far more accurate than their British counterparts, as indeed, they had been in the Great War.[42]

Thus, in the first attempts at *guerre de course*, the operations by the two pocket battleships had sunk a total of 57,041 tons of Allied shipping (eleven vessels) and at a cost of one of their number sunk. Such figures were hardly the success rate they were hoping for. Moreover, it is ironic that, although the purpose of these two ships was to draw off Allied warships into the further oceans, the pressure on the *Admiral Graf Spee* led to an operation by her two larger capital ships against British patrol lines between the Faeroes and Iceland, "to divert the enemy from concentrating his strength in the South Atlantic in pursuit of the *Admiral Graf Spee*,"[43] a complete reversal of the planned policy.

This operation, under the command of Vice Adm. Wilhelm Marschall, commenced on November 21, when, with the *Gneisenau* and *Scharnhorst*, cruisers *Köln* and *Leipzig*, and destroyers, he sortied out. The two cruisers and the destroyers were soon detached to carry out an antishipping sweep in the Skagerrak, but the two heavy ships pushed on northward throughout the night of the twenty-second. Both ships had been fitted with radar, and in increasingly bad weather conditions, which nullified aerial operations on both sides throughout the operation, they were able to penetrate the Shetlands-Norway passage without detection.

The Germans were well aware that the only ships they would be likely to encounter between the Faeroes and Iceland were the cruisers and armed merchant cruisers of the Northern Patrol. To make their plan effective, they only required to locate this patrol line and then, with their overwhelming advantage in gunpower, protection and speed, simply roll it up, sinking and destroying as they went. Such an operation entailed little risk for they intended to vanish into the northern mists and return home once they had caused enough devastation to influence Admiralty dispositions elsewhere.

We can agree with the official historian who described this as "not a very aggressive plan for two of the most powerful warships afloat to execute, since nothing more than a brush with patrols, followed perhaps by a chase, was likely to result."[44] Admiral Raeder, however, seemed to think the objective worth the effort, as did the crews of the two battlecruisers themselves.

By dawn of the twenty-third, the two ships were north of the Faeroes and sweeping steadily northwestward in clear visibility without sighting any activity whatsoever. It was late in the afternoon, at 4:07, that the first sighting report was received, from the foretop of the *Scharnhorst*, of a large steamer in the distance. In such waters, it could only be an armed merchant cruiser and elatedly the two great battlecruisers swung round to annihilate her.

It was in fact the AMC *Rawalpindi*, under Capt. E. C. Kennedy, a 16,697-ton ex–P & O liner armed with eight old 6-inch guns and with a top speed of seventeen knots. She had sighted the German vessel nearest to her earlier, and, on the look-out for the returning *Deutschland*, naturally took her for that ship, and so described her in a sighting report sent at 3:51. Captain Kennedy can have had no illusion as to his probable fate once sighted but he held to his duty, to evade destruction for as long as possible to enable further sightings to be sent to Admiral Forbes, to somehow hang on until help came from one of the regular warships of the patrol, who would be able to further shadow the enemy, and, when all else failed, to try and do his utmost to cause, somehow, damage to his mighty adversaries. On the German side, Marschall had found a sitting duck for a necessary trophy and it was in his best interests to finish her off quickly and move on. This is what he did.

Again, as with the first operations by the *Graf Spee*, this took longer than expected. The *Scharnhorst* commenced firing with her main armament at 8,000 yards range at 5:03, to which the *Rawalpindi* replied within seconds and then actually straddled the German ship. But the German gunners were soon into their stride, and massive 11-inch shells were slamming into and through the unarmored hull of the AMC. She was quickly ablaze from end to end, although her guns kept firing until hit, one scoring a direct hit on the *Scharnhorst*. This shell hit the battlecruiser's quarterdeck and caused some casualties from splinters.

This brave but one-sided duel could have only one ending, an ending made certain by the *Gneisenau* coming up into the battle and adding her firepower to that of the *Scharnhorst*. Some fourteen minutes after opening fire, the gallant *Rawalpindi* sank. A few boatloads of survivors managed to get clear into the raging seas and the oncoming darkness. Although certain that they had been reported, the Germans chivalrously decided to try to pick up these poor souls from the water. They were still so engaged, at 6:15, when they were sighted by the first warship to answer Kennedy's call, the light cruiser *Newcastle*, armed only with twelve 6-inch guns.

She was sighted by the *Gneisenau* a minute earlier and reported as a destroyer. Immediately, Admiral Marschall signaled to the *Scharnhorst* to get underway and break off the rescue operation. Despite the fact that this new arrival was little better equipped to stand up to him than the AMC he had just dispatched, the arrival of a real warship, any warship, at once terminated the thought of further operations by the battlecruisers. The one thought in Marschall's mind was to get away and hide in the northern mists in preparation for a break back to Wilhelmshaven at the earliest opportunity.

The *Newcastle* was not equipped with radar and so was unable to maintain contact with the German ships who vanished into a rain squall. Joined by the cruiser *Delhi*, the *Newcastle* searched to the north until dawn of the twenty-fourth but was unrewarded with a sighting.

Meanwhile, wide-ranging plans were put into effect by Admiral Forbes to stop the German ships from getting home. Although doubt about exactly what ships were out still remained, at least one of them was thought to be a pocket battleship.[45] Cruiser patrol lines were formed off Norway on both the twenty-fourth and twenty-fifth, and another was thrown across the Fair Isle Channel entrance. Submarines and other light forces were sailed from the Firth of Forth. Meanwhile, Admiral Forbes himself sailed from the Clyde with the only heavy ships he had available in the northern area, the *Nelson* and *Rodney*, a heavy cruiser and seven destroyers, to take up an intercepting position west of the Stadtlandet headland where they cruised between the twenty-fifth and twenty-ninth. Farther afield, other heavy units were moved into position in case a breakout into the Atlantic was in fact the real reason for the German sortie.

The battlecruiser *Hood* was sailed from Plymouth, together with the French battlecruiser *Dunkerque* on the twenty-fifth, to cover the northwest approaches. The *Warspite*, at sea escorting a Halifax convoy, was sent to the Denmark Strait, while even further afield the battlecruiser *Repulse*, with the carrier *Furious*, put to sea from Halifax and steered east. But it was all to no avail.

The German ships kept well to the north during the twenty-fourth and the daylight hours of the twenty-fifth while the British were beating to the south in vile weather conditions. At dawn on the same day, the German ships approached the Stadtlandet headland but, on finding the weather conditions too good for an attempt just yet, veered sharply back northward again and awaited an expected deterioration. This came on the following night and, hidden by the fury of a south-westerly gale, the two battlecruisers passed through the British cruiser lines on the forenoon of the twenty-sixth and by noon were far to the south of Admiral Forbes's storm-bound battleships. They arrived back at Wilhelmshaven early on the morning of the twenty-seventh unscathed save for some weather damage from the pounding they had received.

The *Nelson* and *Rodney* continued to patrol an empty ocean on the following two days. Ill luck dogged them further, with the *Rodney* developing serious rudder defects and having to be sent back to the Clyde and the *Nelson* continuing the fruitless hunt for another day and then returning home. Here while entering the new "top-secret" anchorage of the Home Fleet, Loch Ewe, the *Nelson* was mined and seriously damaged. German U-boats knew all about Loch Ewe and had sewn the whole approach with the new magnetic mines some time before. The *Nelson* was bottled up from the time of this incident, December 4, until January 4. For a whole month, then, the most powerful ship of the Royal Navy lay damaged and powerless until she could be sailed south to Portsmouth for repairs.

This marked one of the lowest ebbs of the Home Fleet, for during December 1939, it had been reduced to just one ship, the *Hood*. On the seventh, the *Warspite* arrived at Greenock and became flagship, but it proved how narrow was Admiral Forbes's margin of strength. Meanwhile, back in Germany, Marschall's brief foray was greeted with jubilation, with the sinking of the *Rawalpindi* being declared a major naval victory.

"The first operation had been successfully completed. The battleships had proved their worth," proclaimed one postwar historian. Although the clue to their rapture, which might escape Britain—used to control of the world's oceans—was contained in and earlier section of the same book: "It was to be a sweep against the patrol forces operating between Iceland and the Faeroes. Officers and men were taken by surprise; no vessel of the High Seas Fleet had ever ventured so far during the First World War."[46] Here is the key to the fervor this sortie provoked. With a naval history and tradition in which to cross the North Sea and get back at all was considered a marvelous achievement, actually to get as far as the Faeroes and back and sink an enemy warship (albeit a rather decrepit and phoney one) could indeed be considered an outstanding event. At all events, Admiral Raeder thought so, concluding that "the results of our first battleship operation may be rated very highly."[47]

This operation was in fact one of several mounted that winter, although none of the others got much further than the Skagerrak, where the only likely opposition was likely to be submarine patrols. On November 21–22, the newly renamed *Lützow* had ventured out, with the cruisers *Köln* and *Leipzig* and three destroyers, the same ships repeating the feint on the twenty-fourth and twenty-fifth of the same month. Not until February 18 did the Germans sail the *Scharnhorst* and *Gneisenau* again. This operation, Nordmark, saw both battlecruisers, in company with the *Admiral Hipper* and three destroyers, pushing up as far as the southern Norwegian coast in the hope of scoring a success against one of the Norwegian convoys, as had happened once in the Great War.

However, Admiral Forbes received news of this sortie, the convoys were withdrawn and the Home Fleet sailed. German air reconnaissance failed to locate such shipping as was in the area and the squadron of Admiral Marschall returned to Germany on the twentieth with nothing to show for its efforts. The ships became ice-bound due to the severe conditions prevailing but attempts to muster a heavy air attack on them failed as miserably as had earlier efforts.

So much for the few brief excursions undertaken by the German heavy units during the first six months of the war. Operating with limited objectives and for only brief periods, they had achieved little or nothing. Taking shape in Admiral Reader's brain at this time, however, was a role for his ships that was to prove to be as bold and daring as anything ever undertaken by German seapower.

In contrast to the limited operations of the Germans and the even scarcer sea experience of Britain's allies,[48] during this opening phase of the war at sea the capital ships of the Royal Navy had already steamed many thousands of miles in operations, much of it in the appalling weather conditions which marked it as one of the worst winters of the war.

Most of the British ships were in dire need of refitting, but during this winter, they remained constantly at sea. The fiction writer's image of the battleship, permanently "swinging round the buoy" in some snug anchorage, receives a rude shock when the true details are examined. The capital ships of the Royal Navy spent precious little time in harbour during the winter months of the so-called Phoney War. An Admiralty statement issued on February 2 gave the bald facts: "Battleships averaged twenty-five days at sea a month for the first four months of the war, steaming anything from 7,000 to 10,000 miles in most cases." It will be recalled how Admiral Forbes's fleet reached a low ebb during December 1939, when, for a brief period, only the *Hood* remained in the battle line. It is true that the *Warspite* and *Barham* had come home from the Mediterranean, although the *Barham* was soon damaged.

Most of the capital ships were employed in protecting the more important of the Atlantic or troop convoys during this period. The First Canadian Troop Convoy had as its escort the *Repulse* and *Resolution*, while Admiral Forbes had put to sea with the *Warspite, Hood,* and *Barham* in support on December 12. The *Revenge* provided the heavy escort for the Second Canadian Troop Convoy later the same month, while in February 1940, the Third Convoy also came unmolested across the North Atlantic under the guns of the *Valiant* and *Malaya*. The Home Fleet had sortied out on frequent operations to give the same support for the vital Scandinavian iron-ore convoys to Methyl on the Firth of Forth.

The *Ramillies* had covered the passing of the British Expeditionary Force to France and escorted other important troop convoys from the Clyde to Gibraltar in September, before sailing to Aden to cover Indian Ocean movements, while the *Royal Sovereign* also spent many weeks with the Halifax, Nova Scotia, Escort Force. The battlecruiser *Renown*, after long and distant voyaging into the South Atlantic with the *Ark Royal*, also took part in some successful interceptions of German blockade-runners from Spain during the period February 10 to March 3. Her unmodernized sister, the *Repulse*, had, by that month, spent a total of 130 days at sea since September. The *Warspite* acted as temporary flagship, after covering a North Atlantic convoy from December 6 to March 9, and during this period, on February 27, it had the honor of being inspected by King George VI in the Clyde.

Of the many ships refitting or repairing battle damage, the *Barham* did not rejoin the flag until late in the spring. The *Valiant* completed her working-up program, after her rebuilding, in the West Indies, then went to Halifax on convoy escort duties, and finally rejoined the Home Fleet in February. The *Rodney* also had her defects patched up and rejoined in March. However, the *Nelson* could not be expected to recommission until the August of 1940, while the *Queen Elizabeth*, whose major reconstruction was at an early stage, would not rejoin the fleet until at least January 1941.

By early March, when the defenses at Scapa Flow had been strengthened sufficiently to allow the Home Fleet to return there, Admiral Forbes had under his command the *Rodney* (flag), *Hood, Valiant, Warspite, Renown*, and *Repulse*. But almost at once even this force, which Churchill inspected soon after, was again reduced by the detachment of the *Hood* at the end of the month to Plymouth for refitting. Her speed had come down to only twenty-five knots and so this much-postponed refit could no longer be put off. She was not however to get the even more vital modernization that she so very much required. That had been delayed for many months, and now she was destined never to get it.[49]

Admiral Forbes's five heavy ships were almost immediately involved in the first moves of the Norwegian campaign as the war hotted up with the coming of spring. With the German invasions of Norway and Denmark the British battleships, far from being allowed a further period after the winter storms to refresh and refurbish ships and men, were to be thrown into battle at an even higher pitch and pace of activity than ever before.

The origins of the Norwegian campaign have been discussed in detail many times and this is not the book to rework the many arguments and counter-arguments. Suffice it to say that both Germany and the Allies had plans which required the involvement of that small nation in the conduct of the war and that, whereas the German plan was prepared first and envisaged total occupation, the Allies involved themselves in schemes of a less comprehensive nature but which were expected to result in at least partial occupation of certain strategic areas of that country. Both plans came to fruition at the same time but the Germans were better prepared and better equipped, had a decisive objective and, ultimately, the victory. What the campaign did bring out, as far as the battleship was concerned, was the first major challenge from an effective aerial opposition, which set the pattern for the rest of the war. At the same time the battleship again proved that it could have a decisive effect on events, if used correctly.[50]

The fighting off Norway during the campaign was confused, but certainly the initial clashes at sea demonstrated the superiority of the Royal Navy over its German opponent, for although the overall plan was bold in its form and bold, even reckless, in its execution, once the initial impetus was spent the German naval commanders displayed a remarkable lethargy in the conduct of individual actions.

Operation Weserübung, as finalized by the German Naval Staff, called for the participation of almost every active warship available to carry and support the troops. The aim was to take by surprise every major port in Norway (and incidentally Denmark as well, on whom the Allies had no designs whatsoever) and to proclaim they were there as "protectors" against Allied invasion. It was thought that a large portion of these "Nordic" nations would welcome them, but here the boasts of Quisling misled them, for hardly anyone welcomed the Germans as guardians.

In Norway, task groups were allocated to Narvik, Trondheim, Bergen, Kristiansund, Arendal, Oslo, and Egersund; in Denmark, to Korsor-Nyborg, Copenhagen, Middelfart, Esbjerg, and Tyboron. Because of complete lack of proper landing craft, the soldiers required that they be disembarked at proper harbors. It was essential therefore that complete surprise should be achieved.

The heavy units allocated to cover the occupation of Narvik, the most risky of the planned landings as it was so far north and vulnerable to counter-action by the Royal Navy, comprised the *Scharnhorst* and *Gneisenau*, under Admiral Lütjens. Their role was to act as heavy support for the ten destroyers of Commodore Bonte and also the invasion force for Trondheim, the *Hipper* and four destroyers, on their initial stages of the voyage north.

Allocated to the Oslo force was the *Lützow* but only after a whole series of conflicting plans for her future use. She was the only large vessel capable of resuming the raiding operations, cut short by the destruction of the *Graf Spee* and the repairs necessary to the *Scheer*, and it had been intended to send her out into the Antarctic to mop up the Allied whaling fleets, again creating the diversion of Home Fleet forces in classic manner. This was changed in March to a scheme whereby she would first take place in the Oslo occupation and then continue on into the Atlantic for raiding. It was then felt that to aid her in her breakout, Trondheim would be more suitable and she was allocated to that force, but shortly afterward, it was learned that she had cracks in her engine mountings. Her speed was at best twenty-four knots, and with this new development, her raiding plans were obviously not possible. Again she was switched back to the Oslo force, although when she sailed she had provisions for a nine month cruise.[51]

Finally, the old *Schleswig-Holstein* was again brought into active service under Captain Kleikamp for use as the flagship for the taking of the Danish port of Kdrsor-Nyborg. It was felt that her old 11-inch guns, which had broken Polish resistance, would serve equally well to overawe the Danes. Her sister ship, the *Schlesien,* under Captain Horstmann, was also to be readily available off the Danish coast if needed, operating from Kiel.

The German plans were completed by April 1, with the first groups sailing on the seventh; the combined landings were to begin on the ninth. But at the same time, the first British moves were underway. This was the mining of the Leads to bar the sanctuary of Norwegian coastal waters to the vital iron-ore trade of German ships. Codenamed, aptly enough, Operation Wilfred, it comprised two groups of minelaying destroyers to place live minefields, while off Bud/Kristiansund North two destroyers pretended to lay another. This was to take place on April 8. At sea, acting as heavy support for these groups of destroyers, was the battlecruiser *Renown,* flying the flag of Vice Admiral Whitworth, with four destroyers. As Norwegian reaction was expected to be hostile, troops were embarked ready for landing at Narvik, Bergen, and Trondheim, the R4 plan.

In fact the secrecy that Raeder considered so vital, had been lost on the seventh, for the returning aircraft of an RAF Bomber Command force actually sighted the main German force on the night of April 6–7, heading northward twenty miles north of Heligoland. A striking force of twelve Blenheims of 107 Squadron was sent off at 1:25 P.M. to hit this force but failed to inflict any damage whatsoever. The RAF historian notes that, even so, their sighting report was "of the highest value for it now gave the composition of the force as a battleship, a pocket battleship, two or three cruisers and a large destroyer escort."[52] Unfortunately, a radioed report failed to get through the ether and not until four hours later did word reach Admiral Forbes that such a large German fleet was at sea. Meanwhile, further strikes by two squadrons of Wellington bombers again failed completely because of bad visibility. The German formations were given ample shielding during the next twenty-four hours as the weather steadily deteriorated; by the eighth, a southwesterly gale had developed.

During the day, intelligence had been received which indicated the Germans were launching, an invasion of Norway but this was discounted. Admiral Forbes naturally assumed another break-out was under way and sailed with the bulk of his fleet from Scapa at 8:15 on the evening of the seventh to take up an intercepting position. Troops embarked aboard cruisers for Norway were hastily disembarked after they had just carefully completed their combat loading and the cruisers rushed out in support. By the morning of April 8, Admiral Forbes was plunging through heavy seas northeast of the Shetlands. He had with him the *Rodney* (flag), *Valiant*, and *Repulse*, as well as three cruisers and twelve destroyers. No carrier was available.

Meanwhile, the German groups had pressed on unmolested and the northern minelaying force on the British side completed its work. The southernmost force, however, had been recalled. The *Glowworm*, one of the *Renown*'s escorts, lost a man overboard in the heavy seas and fell behind to search. At nine on the morning of the eighth, she fell in with the Trondheim force of the *Hipper* and four destroyers, and after a gallant fight in which she rammed the German heavy cruiser, she was sunk. The German plans went ahead. Farther south, Allied submarines had managed to sink several of the German troopships but it did not affect the success of the plan.

The brief garbled signals of the *Glowworm* reached the Home Fleet and Admiral Forbes dispatched the *Repulse*, a cruiser, and four destroyers to her aid. At the same time, the *Renown*, north of the Lofoten Islands, swung around south to bar the approaches to Vestfiord. The British destroyers actually guarding the approaches were instructed to join Admiral Whitworth at sea, thus allowing Bonte's flotilla to slip in unnoticed and seize Narvik after sending the two ancient coastal defence warships of the Norwegian Navy to the bottom with torpedoes.

In the meantime, the *Scharnhorst* and *Gneisenau* had headed off north through heavy seas to take up their covering positions. At 3:37 on the morning of the ninth, they ran into the *Renown* and her nine destroyers. Weather conditions were appalling that night but began to moderate, although there were frequent snow squalls that shut down visibility again to nil. It was bitterly cold.

Admiral Whitworth was aware that the *Repulse* and her light forces had been told to concentrate on him, and in the terrible weather of that night had decided that his best policy was to rideout the storm ready for action on the morning of the ninth. He was unable to reach the entrance to Vestfiord for the mountainous seas made it impossible for his destroyers to keep in touch. Accordingly he had swung round northwest until midnight until conditions eased somewhat, and then resumed his southeasterly course. The

German ships were on the opposite course when first sighted and were at first taken for the *Hipper*.

In fact, it was the leading German ship, the *Gneisenau*, that was picked up, but the *Scharnhorst*, farther astern, was taken for the smaller heavy cruiser. The British had the advantage of the light and were not at first spotted in return.

> In the half-light of early dawn, the range was still too great for the layer in the *Renown*'s gun director to distinguish the target through his telescope. Captain Simeon swung his ship round to an easterly course to close the range and increased speed to twenty knots. The range-takers could soon see the *Gneisenau* in their lenses at 19,000 yards. The *Renown* turned again onto a course parallel to the enemy's; her six 15-inch guns in their turrets swiveled smoothly round and steadied on the target. A few last-moment adjustments of range and deflection, the clang of the fire-gongs, and the ship lurched and shuddered as the guns erupted in flame and blast at five minutes past four.[53]

The *Gneisenau* had spotted the *Renown* a little before but was uncertain of her identity. With the arrival of the first of the one-ton shells from the British battlecruiser there was no longer much doubt. At 4:11 A.M., the *Gneisenau* replied. Strangely enough, no word had been passed on to the *Scharnhorst* astern, and she was taken completely by surprise.

> In the early morning hours, the navigating officer on board the *Scharnhorst* was able to use the sextant. He had been unable to fix the ship's position by astronomical sights for some time and he intended now to make another attempt. He lifted the instrument and—instead of the expected star—got the red flashes of heavy guns in the mirror! "Alarm!" bells screamed the watches below rushed to action stations; orders from the bridge, signals from the flagship and first firing instructions came through in quick succession, and in a few minutes the barrels of the 11-inch guns were thundering at the vessel which hove into sight faintly silhouetted against the dark western sky. In dense swirling snow, the battleships withdrew north at top speed. The running encounter lasted from 0510 to 0659 hours (German time) with the *Scharnhorst* and *Gneisenau* firing from the stern. Heavy 15-inch shells exploded close to the *Scharnhorst* as her captain, by repeatedly changing course, managed to outmaneuver each new salvo. [54]

The German flagship was not so fortunate. A shell from the *Renown* scored the first hit of this duel, striking the foretop of the *Gneisenau* at 4:17 and putting the control system for the main armament out of action. Against the six heavy guns of the British vessel, the Germans could pit eighteen, but this hit reduced the odds. Lütjens had absolutely no intention of making a fight of it, however. At high speed, the two German battlecruisers turned away northeast. Two of their 11-inch shells scored hits on the *Renown*, which failed to cause any damage whatsoever, and in reply, the *Renown* put the forward turret of the *Gneisenau* out of action. A splinter from a shell burst entered the rangefinder hood, and the deluge of water coming in green at the high speed the German ship was moving flooded the turret. A third 15-inch shell smashed home on Lütjens's flagship before the two German vessels, flat out and firing directly astern at their pursuer, vanished into a snow squall.

The *Renown*'s speed was down to twenty knots, but the Germans were making twenty-eight, risking serious further damage to their two forward turrets. After a brief interval during which Whitworth altered course to the east in order to reduce the effect of the raging seas, the German ships were again briefly sighted. The *Renown* worked up to twenty-nine knots, her maximum speed at this time, and recommenced firing, but still the German squadron increased the range, and at 6:15, they had drawn far ahead and were finally lost to view again. Although the *Renown* kept up the pursuit for another two hours, Lütjens had won clear, and at nine, Whitworth turned back toward Vest-fiord to back up his destroyers. These latter had opened fire during the early stages, although far out of range, before the speed of the chase had forced them to drop out one by one. However, it is thought the flashes from their 4.7-inch guns may have been taken for larger weapons by the Germans and helped to reinforce their decision to run rather than fight the old *Renown*.

But as Captain Roskill summarized, in considering this brief action, "the honors must surely go to the single, slower, and more lightly protected British ship." We can only echo this and agree that "the enemy lost a great opportunity to destroy his slower and less well protected adversary. And it now appears that his loss of the tactical initiative was due to Admiral Whitworth's immediate engagement and vigorous pursuit under most difficult conditions of sea and weather."[55]

As if in mute agreement, most German historians either ignore the incident or take the line of Vice Admiral Ruge: "Early on the morning of the ninth, at the precise moment when the German groups were entering their allotted ports, the *Scharnhorst* and *Gneisenau* came upon the battlecruiser *Renown* and after an action lasting half an hour were able to disengage with only slight damage to themselves."[56] Put that way, it sounds like a major German achievement. In fact, the British did not realize that both the German battlecruisers were involved at first, only that one was a heavy cruiser. In the light of later knowledge, the handling of the twenty-four-year-old veteran is even more outstanding.[57]

Nor was the other German heavy ship more fortunate against the hapless Norwegians. While attempting to force the coastal defences of Oslo, the brand-new heavy cruiser *Blücher* was sunk with heavy loss of life, and the *Lützow*, coming to her aid, was also very roughly handled. The Norwegian coastal guns on Kaholm Island Fortress were 11-inch Krupps weapons and they scored three direct hits on the armored pocket battleship at close range; one destroyed the sick bay, another hit the port boat crane, but the main blow was a hit on the center gun of her forward triple 11-inch turret which completely immobilized it. As her after turret would not bear on the Norwegian fortress, the *Lützow* was therefore *hors de combat*, and her commanding officer, under Admiral Thiele's orders, quickly retreated back down the fiord out of harm's way. Not until noon on the tenth did she finally berth at Oslo.

This damage, coupled with her earlier defects, put an end to any thoughts that might still be had about an Atlantic sortie. The main concern was to try and get her home again in one piece. Again, the old lesson of warships versus shore-based guns had demonstrated the advantage lay with the latter in a straight duel. The *Lützow*, in much haste, therefore sailed from Oslo later that same afternoon at 2:20, and since no fast escorts were available, she sailed alone. It was hoped that her high speed would grant her the necessary immunity from attack to enable her to reach Kiel, even though many attacks by British submarines were being received hourly. It was a gamble that did not come off.

Like the *Graf Spee*, the *Lützow* was equipped with a gunnery ranging radar set, and at 1:20 A.M. on the eleventh, this set picked up a contact off her starboard bow which was rapidly drawing closer due to the *Lützow*'s high speed. An immediate alteration in course was made to avoid what was thought to be a British submarine, but ironically enough, it was this sudden alteration that drew the submarine's attention to her. She was the *Spearfish*, under Lt. Cmdr. J. H. Forbes, who at 1:29 launched a full salvo of six torpedoes at this high-speed target, which he had correctly identified as a heavy ship and not, as he first thought, a destroyer intent on attacking him.

After making a detour, the *Lützow* was just being brought back to her original course when one of these torpedoes struck her right aft almost completely blowing her stern away. Her momentum carried her over to port, and she started to settle in the water—in effect, a helpless hulk completely at the mercy of any subsequent attack. As a gesture of defense, a picket boat was launched and circled the *Lützow*, dropping small charges. She seemed doomed. It was fortunate for the Germans that the *Spearfish* was already herself badly damaged and, after scoring this hit, had limped homeward in the darkness. The helpless pocket battleship lay a sitting target for a further eight hours until a destroyer escort arrived with a Danish tug (Denmark had fallen without bloodshed), and she began the long trip back to Kiel.

Water kept coming in all through the voyage back and so perilous had become the situation at one stage that her captain considered beaching her. Further tugs came out, and she finally limped into Kiel on the evening of April 13. It would be a whole year before the *Lützow*, which many felt to be a jinx ship by this time, was ready again to put to sea.

Meanwhile, Admiral Forbes was off the southern coast of Norway with the *Rodney* and *Valiant,* after turning south to meet the reported German forces heading north, and the Admiralty had instructed the *Warspite* and the aircraft carrier *Furious* to join his strength. The *Repulse* rendezvoused with the *Renown* at 2:00 P.M. on the ninth off Vestfiord, and the five destroyers of the 2nd Flotilla under Warburton-Lee had gone into Narvik against the ten destroyers of Bonte's force, which had landed its troops.

Far to the north, the two German battlecruisers remained undetected. They had steamed northwest almost to Jan Mayen Island on the ninth and waited. It had been planned for them to pick up the ten Narvik destroyers for the return to Germany but this was overtaken by events. The Arado floatplane from the *Scharnhorst* was therefore sent to Trondheim for further instructions for by now the fuel situation was becoming precarious. They waited in the empty wastes throughout the tenth and then received instructions to return home, picking up the *Hipper* and the Trondheim destroyers en route.

On the night of April 10-11, they swung in a wide arc to within sixty miles of the Shetlands and turned south, once more shielded by bad weather and poor visibility. They met the *Hipper* at noon on the twelfth off Egersund while the Home Fleet was still scouring the seas far to the northeast. By late afternoon, they were deep in the North Sea on the way to Wilhelmshaven. Although located by a Hudson of Coastal Command off southwest Norway, they were not brought to bay. "The striking forces dispatched the same day, amounting in all to ninety-two aircraft, were once more frustrated by the weather."[58] An attempt by twelve Hampdens to attack a warship at Kristiansund was intercepted by German fighters with the resulting loss of half of the British bombers employed.

While the German warships were not unduly menaced by the RAF, the Home Fleet was experiencing its first taste of determined and prolonged bombing by units of the Luftwaffe. General Geisler's X Air Corps, comprising some forty-seven He 111s and forty-one Ju 88s, located Admiral Forbes's fleet around noon on the ninth in the latitude of Bergen in clear weather and with no fighter cover. For three hours that afternoon, the ships were forced to "sit and take it." As before, both sides showed a marked lack of expertise: only four bombers were shot down by the Home Fleet's massed antiaircraft fire after an enormous expenditure of antiaircraft ammunition. In return, the only warship sunk by all this air activity was the destroyer *Gurkha* and then only because her commanding officer, a noted gunnery expert, deliberately took his ship away from the protection of the cruiser squadron he was escorting in order to give his gunners a clear shot in better conditions of wind and sea. He paid the price for isolation very quickly, but this lesson does not seem to have been absorbed, and his mistake was repeated time and time again in the following years'[59]

The heavier antiaircraft batteries of the battleships proved of more deterrent value, and the only success achieved by the ninety German bombers was a single direct hit scored on the *Rodney*. A 1,100-pound bomb failed to penetrate her armored deck but caused fifteen casualties. This failed to cause any serious or lasting damage to her operational ability. All the same, the almost continuous and unopposed air attacks had a wearing-down effect on morale and proved that antiaircraft fire alone was not sufficient to provide a certain defence against determined bombing. This did not prevent the battleships from operating off the Norwegian coast, or even far inland up the landlocked fiords. Perhaps the most striking demonstration of the battleship's effect on operations took place on April 13 at Narvik, for here the *Warspite* was sent in, with nine destroyers, to finish off the eight surviving German destroyers holed up in the fiords around that port.

Air attack apart the hazards of risking a valuable capital ship in an assault of this kind against forewarned torpedo craft in restricted waters were many. For any but the Royal Navy the risks might appear unacceptable; indeed for many British Admirals lesser risks proved a deterrent to action, as we shall see in the next chapter. But Admiral Whitworth was one of the best afloat and he determined on attack. The decision and the risks were summarized thus:

> The previous evening, Admiral Whitworth had received a signal which released him from the storm-tossed monotony of his patrol off the Lofoten Islands and bade him go in and finish off the rest of the shipping in the Narvik fiords. Of the three capital ships now available to him—the battlecruisers *Repulse* and *Renown* and the battleship *Warspite*—the latter was chosen for the job, to the particular chagrin of *Repulse*'s company, who were itching for a chance at least as good as their sister ship's encounter with *Gneisenau* and *Scharnhorst*. But they had to admit *Warspite*'s claims; she was much more heavily armored against air attack and her guns were capable of greater elevation. To her, early on this morning, Whitworth trans-

ferred his flag—"with considerable difficulty," he reported, "owing to the heavy swell": a sidelight on the movements of admirals not without its humor even amid the grim business of war.

Even so, there were tremendous risks in taking this great and valuable ship into the land-locked fiords. Apart from the danger of air attack, she was vulnerable to submarines and ship-fired torpedoes, and it was by no means certain that there was no cruiser among the pent-up German forces. There were wrecks—the *Rauenfels, Hardy*, and the sunken German merchant ships and destroyers from the first battle. The mythical shore defenses still existed in rumor, and there were reports of a minefield on the way.[60]

All this made no difference to Whitworth's decision. The operation was planned with great care but there was no hesitation. An air attack from the *Furious* was a failure, but by noon of the thirteenth, the British squadron was well on its way into the fiords. Meanwhile, after several days of lethargy the German commander, having missed the opportunity of slipping away with at least his few undamaged survivors, now made his tardy dispositions to offer at least some resistance to the oncoming British units.[61]

The actual battle is described in detail in Captain Dickens's excellent book,[62] but let us examine briefly the German dispositions and the part played by the *Warspite*, which was predominant. The *Kollner* and *Kunne* were sent to patrol the narrows to give early warning of the actual approach of the British, and this they did at 1:00 P.M. The remaining six destroyers were to be divided between Ballangen and Herjangs fiords in the hope they would catch the British in the flanks if they concentrated on Narvik itself as Captain Warburton-Lee had done. However, their movements were sluggish and by the time Whitworth's ships were first reported none of these six had yet even raised steam. In addition to the destroyers, the submarines *U-25* and *U-65* were available, and it was hoped that they would be able to cripple the *Warspite* with submerged attacks, but again this did not happen.

The initial exchange of fire between the *Kollner* and *Kunne* and the leading British destroyers, some of which had their minesweeps out, was at long range and ineffective. The *Kunne* retired down the fiord while the damaged *Kollner* took up her ambush position in Djupvik Bay on the south side of the fiord. Her scheme was nullified by the *Warspite*'s spotting Swordfish, which had been launched earlier. She duly reported the *Kollner* lurking off Djupvik and then flew on up the fiord, reporting *Kunne*'s hasty retreat, and sighted the *U-64*, which was still lying full surfaced off Bjerkvik and, in a brilliant attack, hit and sank her with two 350-pound antisubmarine bombs. Damaged by flak, this indomitable machine returned from this assault and reported on the *Kollner*'s latest position just in time for decisive counteraction to be taken.

Admiral Whitworth was to write in his report that he doubted "if ever a ship-borne aircraft has been used to such good purpose" as had *Warspite*'s little Swordfish that day. We can only agree. The leading British destroyers trained their guns and tubes to starboard and both sides opened fire almost together, but the *Kollner* could only fire two salvos before she was shot, through and through by the *Bedouin* and *Eskimo*. A torpedo blew off her bows and then the great bulk of the *Warspite* nosed round the point.

> We can feel that we have increased speed as the ship has begun to vibrate. Heavy explosions shake the ship, and we hear that the destroyers are attacking a submarine. Suddenly comes the order "Salvos," and the right gun comes to the ready. Then, "Enemy in sight," and the sight-setters chant the ranges. It is just like a practice shoot. Our guns are nearly horizontal, so the range must be short. Then "ding ding" of the fire gong, the right gun moves a little, comes steady, and there is a "Woof," which rocks the turret. The left gun is now at the ready, and fires while the right gun is reloading. B Turret, firing over our heads, blows away our "blast bags," and the turret fills with smoke—like London on a November night. The turret officer calls out, "Tell the crew we have hit a destroyer and she is burning nicely."[63]

As Captain Roskill says, the unfortunate *Kollner* had the dubious honor of being the first target that the *Warspite* had engaged with her main armament since Jutland in 1916. They made no mistakes; the monstrous blast of her 15-inch guns split the air and went bellowing away, the thunder tossed back and forth from mountainside to mountainside. In a few minutes, the *Kollner* rolled over and sank.[64]

The first two German boats to get out from Narvik, the *Ludemann* and *Zenker*, joined the retiring *Kunne* and came into line and were joined by the *Arnim*. This quartet opened fire as the leading British ships pushed on toward them but kept the range at the maximum visibility. Consequently, accuracy was not great and a scrambling encounter followed, with the Germans retreating all the while ever deeper into the cul-de-sac of the fiord.

Whenever an enemy destroyer appeared briefly through the smoke and haze, the *Warspite* roared and her one-ton shells went smashing and tearing their way into the lightly built German vessels. Off Narvik, the Germans tried to stand their ground briefly, but all their torpedoes were combed, and the ammunition was running out. An attack by ten aircraft from the *Furious* at this point was as unsuccessful as the first and only served to confuse the issue, but after they had left, the *Warspite* and the destroyers went in for the kill.

The *Kunne* limped up Herjangsfiord and ran herself aground. She was finished off by a torpedo from the *Eskimo*. The *Giese* was the last of German boats to raise steam, and as she left the shelter of Narvik, she was saturated by the combined fire of six British destroyers. Abandoned and ablaze, she drifted into the main fiord and sank. One destroyer was berthed alongside Narvik pier and had not been engaged. At first it was thought her guns were a shore battery, but a salvo from the *Warspite* failed to silence them. She seriously damaged the *Cossack*, but when the *Foxhound* closed to deal with her, she was abandoned and blown up with two enormous explosions. And then there were four. These had retreated up the long narrow Rombaksfiord. Here the *Ludemann* and *Thiele* made their last stand, damaging the *Eskimo* before being heavily hit by the *Forester* and *Hero*. The *Thiele* was run aground, capsized and sank; the *Ludemann* joined the *Arnim* and *Zenker* right at the head of the fiord. But all the fight was gone from them; all were scuttled and abandoned. Every destroyer was wiped out. A torpedo attack by *U-25* failed, as did others by her and *U-48* the next day, because of the failures of the German torpedoes.

It was a decisive battle. As Admiral Whitworth later wrote, "The cumulative effect of the roar of *Warspite*'s 15-inch guns reverberating down and around the high mountains of the fiord, the bursts and splashes of these great shells, the sight of their ships sinking and burning around them must have been terrifying." Unfortunately, the demoralized German defenders, who took to the hills in the time-honored manner, were given ample time to regain their courage and resolution by the dilatory manner in which the subsequent land campaign was conducted. Moreover, the *Warspite* had only been able to operate thus without opposition because the Luftwaffe was more busy in the south. As the dive-bombers drew closer as the weeks passed, that immunity vanished and operations by all warships became a very hazardous operation, not only in the land-locked fiord with no room to take avoiding action, but also far out at sea.

Nonetheless, the *Warspite* remained in Vestfiord for several more days, ready to support the assault on Narvik when it could eventually be mounted. On April 24, she took part in the bombardment of the German defense works around Narvik and in the port itself. It was hoped that merely this shelling by monster guns would induce the enemy to surrender, but more than a week had passed, the Germans had new strength, and no troops were landed to follow up the effects of the bombardment itself.

For three hours, the thunder echoed and re-echoed among the tumbled mountains and the houses of the little town shook at the blast and concussion. But little else resulted. Under their mantle of snow, few military targets could be distinguished nor could the results of the shell bursts be seen. Recurrent snowstorms frequently reduced visibility to a few hundred yards. Conditions made any reconnaissance impossible, and there was no way of judging what moral effect had been produced on the defenders. A wireless station was destroyed as well as a few sheds and railway rolling stock, and a ferry steamer was sunk. The machine-gun nests could not be located, while the strongpoints guarding the harbour waterfront were in any case forbidden targets.[65]

An attack on Trondheim occupied the First Lord's mind at this time, urged on by Keyes. Typical Churchillian memos winged their way across the ether to Admiral Forbes urging him to take his precious battleships right in under the wings of the Luftwaffe to achieve Operation Hammer.

Like that of April 15: "High-explosive shell for 15-inch guns has been ordered to Rosyth. *Furious* and First Cruiser Squadron will be required for this operation. Pray, therefore, consider this important project further."[66] Admiral Forbes, who was daily learning of the capabilities of the German air force and the limitations of his defenses (the *Suffolk*'s bombardment of Stavanger was a typical incident),[67] did his best to bring a note of reality into the situation. "The naval force required would be *Valiant* and *Renown* to give air defense to *Glorious* [by which he meant provide the necessary antiaircraft protection]; *Warspite* to carry out bombardments as she is the only 15-inch ship in the fleet with 6-inch guns; at least four antiaircraft cruisers; about twenty destroyers and numerous landing craft."

Thankfully, the *Hammer* was abandoned, but nonetheless, operations against Narvik continued at a slow pace. With the threatening attitude of Italy, the *Warspite* left Norwegian waters for home and then the Mediterranean on April 28, but she was replaced by the *Resolution*. On May 12, she took part in the operations that resulted in the fall of Bjervik to the Allies, but the contributions of her big guns were lost soon afterwards. On the eighteenth, Ju 88s of II/KG 30 made determined attacks on her and were rewarded by a single direct hit with a 1,000-pound bomb. She was off Tjeldsundet, and about fifty heavy bombs were aimed at her. The one that hit penetrated three decks, killing two of her crew and wounding a further twenty-seven. She was sent home for repairs. It was clear that even this far north, the long arm of the Luftwaffe could reach out, and while the battleships could take such punishment without serious loss of fighting capacity, the little cruisers and destroyers, unarmored and undefended, began to suffer severe losses.

Meanwhile, out at sea, Admiral Forbes's fleet was beginning to adapt itself to this new form of air-sea warfare. This should be recorded, for the

Royal Navy was not often given credit for foreseeing that these new circumstances required new formations.

> Shortly after the bombardment at Narvik, we joined a force comprising the aircraft carriers *Ark Royal* and *Glorious,* the battleship *Valiant,* and the cruiser *Berwick,* screened by twelve destroyers. This squadron was the forerunner of the well-known Carrier Task Force of today; and it must, I think, have been the first such squadron ever to operate in war. It was a beautifully balanced squadron, with its two big carriers, the heavy guns of the battleship, and the speed and eight-inch guns of the cruiser, fully screened against submarines.[68]

However, operations on land went sadly amiss. Ill-equipped troops flung ashore without proper plans were gradually pushed back by the German troops and armor, constantly supported by dive-bombers and covered by fighters. Finally, only Narvik remained in Allied hands and by the beginning of June, events in the south, the collapse of Holland, Belgium, and France, and the evacuation of the British Expeditionary Force from Dunkirk forced the abandonment of that port as well. In all this, the navy had provided the army with the only support it had and had taken heavy casualties in so doing.

> Mr. Churchill, the First Lord, had dreams of a battleship with its main armament exchanged for antiaircraft guns, making it a sort of floating hedgehog to accompany the Fleet. This might indeed, have worked, because battleships alone had the heavy horizontal armor which made them more or less immune to the bomber—although how they would be able to replenish the prodigious expenditure of ammunition that would be called for, or how they would cope with the rapid deterioration of gun barrels, firing an unheard-of quantity of rounds in a very short space of time, is more arguable.[69]

However, one final incident that took place during the evacuation of Norway served to illustrate that the power of the battleship was far from finished and it also showed just how vulnerable the new capital ship of the future, the aircraft carrier, was without heavy ship support.

The dire straits that the isolated German force around Narvik had been reduced before the Allies finally withdrew aroused considerable concern in Germany. Although the German Navy had achieved all that had been asked of it during the occupation, and in so doing had suffered casualties from which it was never fully to recover, there was felt that one last effort must be made to help take the pressure off General Dietl's troops. On May 23, Hitler, in an effort to arouse some enthusiasm among his reluctant naval staff, wrote, "In the great struggle for Germany's destiny, the navy can only fulfill its task by showing an uncompromising offensive spirit and a resolve to inflict damage on the enemy whatever the risk to itself."[70]

Unfortunately for Germany's destiny, the German surface forces were never very successful in doing this. Admiral Raeder was against risking what precious few operational warships he had left to him on a nebulous enterprise of this sort, but finally agreed to mount an offensive sortie against Allied shipping off Vestfiord. The Germans had as yet no idea that the Allies were already pulling out every man, plane and ship from Norway anyway. Unfortunately, the orders given to the fleet commander, Adm. Wilhelm Marschall, were rather ambiguous. On the one hand, Raeder told him that it was designed to "relieve Force Diete by effective engagement of British naval forces and transport in the Narvik-Harstad area." But on the other hand, Navy Group West instructed him that his mission was "a surprise penetration of the And and Vaags Fiords (Harstad)" and that the object was "the destruction of enemy warships and transport there encountered, as well as of beachhead installations."[71]

It is not surprising then that Marschall complained he had been given two objectives which were "far apart operationally and geographically," but which had to be carried out at the same time.[72] Nor is it surprising that when further attempts at getting Raeder to clarify the position resulted in nothing positive that Marschall should ultimately have chosen the former. With the fate of the 4th Destroyer Flotilla and the *Blücher, Königsberg,* and the like, we can understand that to venture some 400 miles up into British held territory into waters dominated by the Royal Navy, (or so it was thought at the time), seemed unattractive. Nonetheless Admiral Marschall was to achieve for his nation perhaps the greatest triumph to date at sea, for in disarray, as were his instructions, the British system was full of even more loopholes. By the afternoon of June 7, the German force was in position, and undetected, in the latitude of Harstad, having left Kiel on the fourth. Here Marschall prepared himself for the strike on Harstad itself, but the following day, having received reports of two groups of Allied ships at sea in the area, he instead decided to operate against these rather than venture inshore into what might be a trap. Initially, he was only modestly rewarded. His force consisted of the *Scharnhorst, Gneisenau,* and *Admiral Hipper* escorted by four big destroyers—the *Galster, Lody, Schoemann,* and *Steinbrinck*—and the naval tanker *Dithmarschen.*

What of the British Home Fleet? At this time, it had been reduced, by damage and departures, to the battleships *Rodney* (flag) and *Valiant,* the battlecruisers *Renown* and *Repulse,* and the carriers *Glorious* and *Ark Royal.* However, both the battlecruisers had been dispatched under Admiral Whitworth to cover the Faeroes-Iceland route following a mistaken report by a Q ship of German ships, possibly raiders, steering northeast. This left only the *Rodney* at Scapa Flow and *Valiant* at sea covering the evacuation convoys with the *Ark Royal*. Such protection was hardly adequate, for there were no fewer than three convoys in that area steaming home with troopships laden with exhausted soldiers. The first convoy, consisting of six great liners, had only the old training cruiser *Vindictive* as escort; 15,000 troops were aboard. Fortunately, they reached Scapa without incident on June 8. The second convoy, consisting of seven liners with a further 10,000 troops aboard, left Harstad on the seventh with two light cruisers and five destroyers. At the same time, a convoy of store ships also left, eight transports and tankers escorted by two destroyers and some smaller escorts. Nor was this all. Sailing on her own was the heavy cruiser *Devonshire*, with the king of Norway aboard, and several independently routed transports and hospital ships. To protect this mass of highly vulnerable shipping, only the *Valiant* and *Ark Royal* were operating. Toward this wide-open target steamed Marschall with his three big ships and four destroyers. It was not surprising that Juno turned out to be a victory for the Germans; what *was* surprising was that the massacre was not far greater than it was.

One other Allied squadron was in the area: the aircraft carrier *Glorious*, which had just landed the brave pilots of RAF Squadrons 263 and 46—Hurricanes and Gladiators—without hooks or experience of deck landings at sea. The skill and bravery of the young pilots in achieving this only makes the resulting tragedy even more poignant. On completion of the landing-on operation, *Glorious*, with her two escorting destroyers, was due to rendezvous with the convoy escorted by the *Southampton* and *Cairo*, but she never did.[73]

Marschall's ships were now steering a course which took them across the tracks of all these groups. The second large troop convoy, with the *Valiant* providing close escort, passed ahead of the German squadron and reached safety. The slow store ships passed astern of the German ships and they too got home. Perhaps the luckiest escape was that of King Haakon aboard the cruiser *Devonshire*, for at one time, the German battlecruisers were within a mere eighty miles of him and his government. Moreover, through their excellent intelligence and wireless-intercepting units ashore, the Germans knew perfectly that the *Renown* and *Repulse* were far away on a wild-goose chase.

On the morning of the eighth, the incredible British good luck, somewhat undeserved because of their lack of precautions it would appear, finally ran out. The *Hipper* sighted an oil tanker, the *Pioneer*, and her escorting trawler, the *Juniper*, at 5:55 A.M. These were summarily shelled and sunk, the tanker being finished off by a torpedo from the *Schoemann* at 8:00. While this one-sided engagement was taking place, Marschall received further instructions reminding him that his main objective remained Harstad (by this time abandoned and containing nothing worth shooting at) and that any ships encountered at sea were to be left to the *Hipper* and the destroyers. Despite this, Marschall continued to concentrate his big ships on targets afloat, which was with the light of hindsight a remarkably wise decision.

The *Gneisenau's* secondary armament had contributed to the demise of the British tanker, but otherwise, the battlecruisers had little to do. The next victim to come into their view was the troopship *Orama* (20,000 tons), together with the hospital ship *Atlantis*. While the *Hipper* and *Lody* dispatched the former, the latter, under international law, was allowed to proceed unmolested, and she made no warning signals in return.

The rest of the day was spent in following up a false lead to the southeast, and on the ninth, the *Hipper* and the destroyers were sent into Trondheim to refuel. The *Scharnhorst* and *Gneisenau*, however, continued to hunt. At 4:45 that afternoon, they were rewarded, smoke being sighted on the horizon. "Asked for a more detailed description by the Captain [of *Scharnhorst*], the lookout, Midshipman Goss, explained: 'It was a short blast of smoke, like blubber when there's a bit of trouble with the boilers. Bearings are precisely laid.'"[74]

It was the *Glorious* that had in turn sighted the battlecruisers and was working up to full speed in a vain attempt to escape. How she came to be so caught out with no anti-submarine flying patrol in the air has been recorded elsewhere.[75] As it was, she was doomed.

At a range of 28,000 yards, the 11-inch guns of the German battlecruisers boomed out. As usual, their accuracy was spot on, and soon the heavy shells began tearing into the carrier's unprotected vitals, punching through the thin flight deck and turning hangars and aircraft into a blazing shambles. It was clear that no air strike could ever be mounted amidst that early devastation. In the target area, the first covering salvo straddled the flight deck, which was packed tight with aircraft. Angry flashes flared into dazzling sheets of red flame, and an enormous pall of smoke enveloped the luckless carrier.[76]

Squadron Leader Cross of the RAF was among the few survivors. The last moments of the *Glorious* are described by Bernard Ash from his viewpoint:

> He had barely reached the quarterdeck when another shell ripped into the bridge, killing the captain and putting the carrier out of control. It was only half an hour since the first shots had been fired, and now she was a sitting target. Before very long more accurate gunfire had holed her aft and she clearly had not long to live: at 5:20 the order to abandon ship was given. Cross went over the side with others, and was able to get on to a Carley float.[77]

The Germans described the first moments of the battle thus:

At the start of the battle, Admiral Marschall, through the rangefinder on his bridge, personally saw three or four of the carrier's aircraft hoisted to the deck, followed by feverish attempts to get them airborne. It seemed that the British commander had changed his plan. Before, however, he could turn the *Glorious* into wind, the planes had already been destroyed by shell-fire. Evidently, the accuracy and rapidity of this, even at extreme range, prevented any British counteraction.[78]

Desperate attempts at making radio signals were also blocked by the Germans; only the *Devonshire*, some hundred miles away, picked up garbled references to two pocket battleships, but because of his guests aboard, Vice Admiral Cunningham aboard the British cruiser decided not to break wireless silence. Meanwhile, the *Glorious* was dying. At 5:40 P.M., she sank with almost her entire crew, only forty-three surviving from the ship and the RAF personnel aboard.

While the two German battlecruisers had been making "undisturbed target practice" on the luckless carrier, her two tiny destroyer escorts, in the best traditions of the destroyer service, had been making heroic efforts to shield her, even at the cost of their own lives. Both the *Ardent* and *Acasta* tried to shield the crippled *Glorious* with smokescreens, all the time under heavy fire from the secondary armaments of the battlecruisers, which far outranged their puny 4.7s. The *Ardent* then tore through the smoke to carry out a torpedo attack. It was suicide. All the torpedoes were avoided and this only caused a short pause in the battle. Meanwhile, the *Ardent* was smothered with shells at very short range and capsized, a blazing wreck, and went down with all but two of her gallant crew.

By now, the *Glorious* had gone also, and only the tiny *Acasta* remained. Leading Seaman Carter, her sole survivor, has described the last moments of his very brave ship and her crew:

On board our ship, what a deathly calm, hardly a word spoken, the ship was now steaming full speed away from the enemy. Then came a host of orders, prepare all smoke floats, hose-pipes connected up, various other jobs were prepared. We were still steaming away from the enemy, and making smoke, and all our smoke floats had been set going. The Captain then had this message passed to all positions: "You may think we are running away from the enemy, we are not, our chummy ship has been sunk, the *Glorious* is sinking, the least we can do is make a show, good luck to you all." We then altered course into our own smokescreen. I had the order stand by to fire tubes 6 and 7. We then came out of the smokescreen altered course to starboard firing our torpedoes from the port side. It was then I had my first glimpse of the enemy; to be honest it appeared to me to be a large one and a small one, and we were very close. I fired my two torpedoes from my tubes, the foremost tubes fired theirs, we were all watching results. I'll never forget that cheer that went up; on the port bow of one of the ships a yellow flash and a great column of smoke and water shot up from her.[79]

It was a hit, at 6:39 P.M., according to German records, but it was actually scored on the *Scharnhorst*'s starboard quarter, not her port bow as Leading Seaman Garter's graphic account stated at first. The *Acasta*'s torpedo had hit the battlecruiser just below the rear triple 11-inch turret, which had so far not fired a shot. "The explosion hurled the men on the turret's lower platform to the deck, while within seconds sea water and oil from a pierced fuel tank flooded the compartments below, at a cost of forty-eight lives."[80]

The center and starboard engine rooms of the *Scharnhorst* were flooded and the after turret put out of action by this hit. Her speed was reduced to twenty knots, some 2,500 tons of water was shipped. Although the gallant *Acasta* sank soon afterward, torn apart by shells with only one survivor, she had done her job. The German admiral had no choice but to abandon his sortie and make for Trondheim at his best speed to effect repairs. This almost certainly saved the slow convoy from annihilation. The Germans entered Trondheim on the ninth, and although the *Gneisenau* and *Hipper* were almost at once ordered back to sea to complete the operation by making another sortie toward Iceland, they returned next day without accomplishing anything, for, by this time, the Royal Navy had large concentrations of heavy units at sea.

Once again, the appearance of British battleships proved to be sufficient deterrent to further German operations, although yet again they were too late to bring the raiders to book. What had happened was that the *Atlantis* met the *Valiant* early on the ninth and reported the sinking of the troopship. The *Renown* was recalled from the north and concentrated with Admiral Forbes in the *Rodney* from Scapa Flow. The *Repulse* was also brought back from the waters off Iceland to join the convoy's protection. The *Ark Royal* joined Admiral Forbes on the tenth, and the Home Fleet cast first east then northwest on the eleventh. The next day, they returned south and at midday steered directly towards the Norwegian coast. In the early hours of the thirteenth, a strike of fifteen dive-bombers was launched from the *Ark Royal* against the damaged *Scharnhorst* at Trondheim. They were intercepted by fully alert German fighter defences and were badly cut up, with eight Skuas being destroyed. They managed to obtain one direct hit on the *Scharnhorst*, with a 500-pound bomb on her upper deck, but the bomb failed to explode, and damage was minimal.

However, the German squadron was not to get away without damage. In order to divert British air reconnaissance, while the damaged *Scharnhorst* slipped home, the *Gneisenau* and *Hipper* again sortied out from Trondheim on June 20, heading for the Iceland-Faeroes passage. While still only some forty miles from the Norwegian coast that same night, they were intercepted by the submarine *Clyde*, under Lieutenant Commander Ingram, which made a brilliant attack. One of the *Clyde*'s torpedoes found its mark on the *Gneisenau*'s bows, tearing a huge hole "as high as a house." The German squadron therefore broke off the sortie and returned to Trondheim. Although the *Gneisenau* eventually got safely back to Germany, she was out of the war for six months at a crucial period. So was her sister. The *Scharnhorst* made her dash for safety on June 21, with four destroyers and four torpedo boats as escorts. While off Utsire on that date, she was subjected to the usual air attacks.

> For nearly two hours on end wave after wave appeared as the RAF attacked the Force with bombs and torpedoes off the Isle of Utsire. But the dense hail of AA [antiaircraft] shells repelled all attacks. Many of the bombers, hit by AA fire or shot down by fighters, crashed into the sea leaving long trails of smoke behind them. In the *Scharnhorst* alone, the expenditure of ammunition during this defence action ran to 900 rounds of 4.1-inch, 1,200 rounds of 37mm and 2,500 rounds of 20mm shells![81]

Although undamaged by these attacks, the *Scharnhorst* put into Stavanger for a time to avoid a reported interception by the Home Fleet. She resumed her voyage next day and reached Kiel without further incident. The next day came the surrender of France, and Great Britain was alone.

The Norwegian campaign was over, as was the first shock of war on land on the continent. Everywhere Germany had struck she had been victorious. Even in Norway, it had appeared that the tiny German fleet had successfully challenged the might of the Royal Navy and got away with it. More, they and the Luftwaffe had inflicted heavy casualties in the process. The truth was that never more than a fraction of the Royal Navy's entire strength was utilized in Norway. (By this time, the *Hood* and *Ark Royal* had left for the Mediterranean, as had the *Warspite* earlier.) Although the Royal Navy's losses were serious, they were not crippling by any means. On the other hand, the German Navy had almost been wiped out during the Norwegian campaign; those ships not sunk had been crippled.

The final balance sheet showed that for the vital operations of invading the British Isles and guarding the supplies of the invading armies Germany had, at the zenith of her power in June 1940, no navy at all worth the name. Of her heavy ships, the *Scharnhorst, Gneisenau,* and *Admiral Scheer* were out of action for repairing serious battle damage or refitting. None could be ready before September or October. The *Lützow* likewise was refitting and could not be ready for action until April 1941. Lesser units had suffered a similar attrition rate.

The sacrifices had not been in vain. Heavy ships could be spared for the Mediterranean to face the new Italian Navy with confidence. The crippling of the German Navy gave the fully stretched Royal Navy time to adjust to the loss of the French Navy as an ally and its transformation into a hostile neutral as well as the addition of Italy's fleet.

Admiral Marschall, despite his brilliant coup in destroying the *Glorious,* was not received as a hero by Raeder; instead, he was berated for failing to carry out his orders. In the meantime, the RAF, tired of failures at sea, again repeated their attempts to hit the heavy ships in dock. Heavy raids were mounted in July and August and continued into September and October. 1,042 bomber sorties were mounted and 683 tons of bombs dropped on German naval targets during this offensive. The total result was two bomb hits on the new cruiser *Prinz Eugen* on July 1-2 and a hit by a single dud bomb, and the *Lützow* a week later. Again, the heavy bomber had shown itself impotent against heavy warships.

As we have seen, the sortie by the *Scharnhorst* for home on July 27 had led to the dispatch of the *Renown* and *Repulse* to intercept her, but this had failed. Although Admiral Forbes's strength had been drained by the dispatch of heavy ships to the Mediterranean and other duties, he still had enough to cope with the true state of the German Fleet, although the completion of the *Bismarck* and *Tirpitz* was causing concern. There also arose some friction between Admiral Forbes and Churchill over the correct dispositions of the Home Fleet to meet the impending invasion. This we will return to in depth in chapter 5. For now, we must leave the grim waters of the North Sea and Arctic and the now-hostile waters of the Channel and examine events farther south. Here in the landlocked waters of the Mediterranean, the lessons learned off Norway were to be underscored, and the war at sea, as far as the battleship was concerned, was to reach a new peak of activity and combat.

CHAPTER 4

Mediterranean Battleground

On June 10, 1940, when the Italian nation finally lurched into the war after nine months vacillation, the naval threat mounted by her modern fleet seemed potentially dangerous. On paper, the numerical balance between the Italian Navy and the Allied squadrons available was tipped in Italy's favor by virtue of three other factors: Italy's central commanding position in the Mediterranean; its overwhelming superiority in air strength, which many felt would be *the* decisive element in naval operations in such waters; and the scandalous lack of defenses, especially aerial defenses, available to the British Navy and the small army in the Middle East.

Nonetheless, the strictly naval balance was not too one-sided, and in capital ship strength, with which we are mainly concerned in this volume, the balance appeared overwhelmingly in favor of Britain and France. Of the six Italian battleships (four old and modernized vessels and two brand-new 15-inch-gun ships just completing), only two of the oldest were actually ready for operations at the beginning of June. By contrast, the Allies enjoyed a striking margin in this category. At Alexandria lay the ships of the Mediterranean Fleet under Admiral Cunningham. By this date, he had his old flagship, the *Warspite*, back on station together with the elderly *Malaya*, *Royal Sovereign*, *Ramillies*, and the French *Lorraine* of similar vintage. Only the *Warspite* of this battle line was modernized, but it still represented a solid backbone for command of the western Mediterranean—one that the Italians were unlikely to challenge in direct combat,[1] even when they had brought their strength up to full.

Over in the Western Basin, the situation was equally reassuring, for here the French had deployed the bulk of their fleet. Here were the *Dunkerque* and *Strasbourg*, their best vessels, modern and fast, filled with élan. They were backed up by two more veterans, the battleships *Bretagne* and *Provence*.

As Captain Roskill relates, Mussolini had, in March 1940, already issued a directive instructing the navy to adopt a stirring, if somewhat vague, policy of maintaining from the outset of hostilities "the offensive at all points in the Mediterranean and outside." Count Ciano, the Italian foreign minister, confided a somewhat less cheerful opinion in his diary on the day Italy joined in the war: "The adventure begins. May God help Italy!"[2] His forebodings were more realistic than Mussolini's vain ambitions, and it was the battleships of the Royal Navy that were to inflict the first lessons.

Certainly, if the situation appeared rosy at the outset as "Bartimeus" recorded,[3] the situation soon changed abruptly with the collapse of France a few days later and the signing of the armistice. But at the start, it was the Allies who seized the initiative in the Mediterranean, as well as outside.

"We had the news of the Italian declaration of war at 7 P.M. and the fleet at once went to two hours' notice for steam, and the *Ramillies* abandoned her refit."[4] By midday on June 11, Admiral Cunningham was already leading his fleet out to sea to seek the Italians in the central Mediterranean. The *Warspite* and *Malaya*, with the *Eagle*, two cruisers, and nine destroyers, swept northwest to Crete and then westward, hoping to catch Italian shipping in the central basin. They returned on the fourteenth, having sighted nothing whatsoever of the enemy on the sea or in the air, but they lost the elderly light cruiser *Calypso* to a skilful and daring submarine attack on the way back. The *Royal Sovereign*, *Ramillies*, and *Eagle* sortied out at the end of June covering convoys also.

The pace was maintained during the following days. Two British cruisers bombarded Tobruk on the twelfth, and four French cruisers from Toulon shelled Genoa on the fourteenth. On June 20, the French battleships made their first warlike sortie, with Admiral Tovey taking the *Lorraine* from Alexandria with two British and two French cruisers and a mixed screen to carry out a bombardment of Bardia. This duly took place on the night of June 20–21 with little or no opposition. Unhappily, this firing of the French battleship guns at the Axis enemy was the first and the last time, for, on the twenty-second, the armistice was signed at Compaigne, and a valuable naval ally vanished from the Mediterranean, leaving Great Britain in such a perilous position that for a short period, the abandonment of the whole area was seriously considered.[5]

Resolution prevailed, and to replace the gap caused by the French defection—which left the Western Basin naked—Admiral Somerville had already been appointed to command a powerful force to be based upon Gibraltar, Force H. The *Hood* arrived at Gibraltar on June 23, with the *Ark Royal*, and they were joined by the battleships *Valiant* and *Resolution*, the cruisers *Arethusa* and *Enterprise*, and four destroyers (the screen being supplemented by the older ships of the 13th Flotilla already based there for the earlier operations). The setting up of a virtually independent command at Gibraltar was a typical example of British vagueness because the relationships of command between Somerville's force and the flag officer in the North Atlantic, Admiral North, whose base at Gibraltar was never firmly established and was to lead to a particularly nasty complication within a very short time.

Force H was a brave investment in the faith and future of Britain and certainly more than adequately filled the hole left by the French surrender. Unfortunately for Admiral Somerville, he soon found that the first mission this magnificent command of his was to carry out was against his former ally. There is no need, in this volume, to go again into great depth as to the decisions that led up to the fateful bombardment of the French fleet at Mers-el-Kebir save perhaps to give a brief outline and give sources for further study.[6] Suffice it to say that it *was* deemed necessary, ultimately, to carry out this operation, and that the British commander instructed to do so was firmly opposed to it. Such a combination was therefore fated to produce a highly unsatisfactory result and such indeed was the case.

Vice Adm. Sir James Somerville was a popular and sensitive officer who did his utmost to see that the original bleak alternatives offered to the French Admiral Gensoul were made more palatable. In this, he was successful, and on July 2, he received a signal containing the new alternatives. These were, briefly, that the French could continue the fight under their own colors alongside the British from British ports; they could take their ships to the safety of British harbors and lay them up, the crews being repatriated if they so wished; the fleet could sail to a French West Indian possession and be demilitarized under neutral supervision; or they could themselves scuttle their ships at their moorings. Alternatively, the French could render their ships unserviceable for war operations at Mers-el-Kebir under Somerville's direction. Failing agreement on all these points, Somerville was left in no doubt as to his duty, however repugnant that might be: "If none of the above alternatives are accepted by the French, you are to endeavor to destroy ships in Mers-el-Kebir but particularly *Dunkerque* and *Strasbourg*, using all means at your disposal."[7]

Both Admiral North ashore at Gibraltar, Admiral Cunningham at Alexandria, and the majority of Somerville's staff afloat were in agreement that if actual physical action against the French Fleet could be avoided, it should be. Adm. Sir Dudley North made his feelings on the matter as plain as any other, and for this, he almost lost his command and certainly earned Churchill's animosity.[8] Nonetheless, the worst eventuality had to be allowed for, and prior to sailing from Gibraltar, Somerville and his officers considered how best such an attack could be carried out in such a way as to minimize loss of life.

Somerville's hopes that torpedo attack might be used rather than gunfire were dashed by Admiral Wells's objection that this could only be successful from the air if the antiaircraft defences of the port were first silenced. Destroyer attack was ruled out by the presence of net defenses. Seeking for some way to avoid the massacre he foresaw, Somerville decided that in the case of Mers-el-Kebir, where the main French ships lay, a few rounds should first be fired, aimed not to hit but "to show that we were really in earnest." If this failed to bring the acceptance of the terms, there would be a limited bombardment to induce the French to abandon their ships, final sinking being accomplished by torpedo aircraft or demolition.[9]

Although showing an understandable concern for French life, this really seems to show a lack of understanding of the French themselves, particularly their commander. If they rejected the four quite reasonable alternatives that Somerville was to convey, they would hardly be likely to back down, in any form whatsoever, once British shells, however carefully aimed to miss, started falling in their harbor among their ships. *L'honneur*, which had calmly accepted unilateral surrender to Nazi Germany, was bound to bristle up yet another notch in their minds at being dictated to by the British. And so it turned out.

Thus, on the afternoon of July 2, Somerville, "with a heavy heart," led the ships of Force H out from Gibraltar and set course for Mers-el-Kebir just across the horizon. [10] Under his command, he had an imposing force with which to make Britain's will known. He flew his flag in the *Hood*, with the *Valiant* and *Resolution* as battle line. The *Valiant* was modernized; the *Hood* was the fastest vessel; the *Resolution* was neither—but their combined broadsides of twenty-four 15-inch guns would seem quite sufficient to do the job if necessary. The *Ark Royal* was there to provide spotter aircraft and lay a minefield across the entrance of the harbour. It was thought that in the unlikely event of the French making a run for it her torpedo bombers would be able to hit and slow them down in time for the British heavy ships to engage them, for both the main French ships, the battlecruisers, could show clean pair of heels to the *Hood*. In addition, Somerville had two light cruisers and a composite destroyer screen totaling eleven destroyers, one of which, the *Foxhound*, was sent ahead to carry Captain Holland to open negotiations with Gensoul. [11]

All attempts at reaching a peaceful solution proved impossible, mainly because of the intransigent attitude of Gensoul. By 10 A.M. on the third, Gensoul had sent a written reply stating that "French warships will meet force with force." Holland persevered, but Gensoul still refused to meet him face-to-face. Moreover, it was obvious to the watching British aircraft that the French ships were raising steam and clearing for action. Once they got to sea, the French squadron would no longer be a stationary target to be dealt with by a firm police action, but a full-fledged fighting fleet. The outcome would probably result in the almost equal destruction and damage to *both* fleets, a risk Britain just could not afford at this stage of the war.

Somerville was still reluctant to take the final step, however. Although the *Ark Royal*'s aircraft were given the go-ahead to lay their mines across the entrance (ineffectually as it turned out), he put back his deadline to 1:30 P.M.

Holland was still laying off the port at 1:15 aboard the *Foxhound* when Somerville again signaled him to see if there was no alternative. Holland proposed to try once more, and the final deadline for carrying out Catapult was again put back, this time to 3:00. But it was not until 4:15 that Gensoul finally allowed Holland aboard his flagship, the *Dunkerque*. As he went aboard, Holland "noted with dismay that decks were cleared for action and that gun directors and range finders were trained on our ships. Tugs were standing by to unberth the capital ships."[12]

Once aboard, Holland listened as Gensoul again repeated his assurances that his ships would never fall into Axis hands. In turn, Holland tried to explain the British government's fears. Although the word of the French admiral was taken as sincere, the British could not—as recent events had made only too clear—trust anything that the Germans or Italians said. French reliance on a treaty point was just not good enough. Hitler had violated every treaty he had ever signed, and Britain's life was at stake here. There was just no way that the two viewpoints could be bridged it seemed. By 5:00 P.M., they were no closer a solution, and Somerville knew he must act quickly before dusk gave the French an excellent opportunity to slip from his grasp. He fixed the new deadline as 5:30 and signaled Holland accordingly. Meanwhile, back in London, the cabinet was getting even more anxious. A signal arrived at 4:46 urging Somerville to "settle matters quickly or you will have reinforcements to deal with." There was fear that a powerful French cruiser squadron at Algiers was preparing to sail to Gensoul's aid forthwith.

Churchill later acknowledged the cruel dilemma that faced the commander of Force H. "The distress of the British admiral and his principal officers was evident to us from the signals, which had passed. Nothing but the most direct orders compelled them to open fire on those who had been so lately their comrades. At the Admiralty there was also manifest emotion."[13] Nonetheless, as he also recorded, "there was no weakening in the resolve of the War Cabinet." There may have been some fears that Somerville had already left it too late, a signal sent from London at 6:26 urged, "French ships must comply with our terms or sink themselves or be sunk by you before dark." But by the time Somerville received this prod, the action was almost over.

The order to open fire was finally given at 5:54, and the first broadsides crashed out from the British heavy ships at some 15,000 yards range, the maximum visibility in the conditions then prevailing. The French ships were anchored abreast inside the northern mole, below the forts of Mers-el-Kebir and du Santon, in the following order: *Dunkerque, Provence, Strasbourg, Bretagne,* and the airplane tender *Commandant Teste,* with their bows facing away from the sea. At right angles to them, across their bows, were the large destroyers *Kersaint* and *Tigre*. The other big destroyers *Mogador*, *Volta*, *Lynx*, and *Terrible* were anchored behind the antisubmarine nets below Roseville, on the western side of the harbor. Both sides had had ample time to range in on the other before fire was commenced, but the French ships' positions, masked as they were by the forts themselves and hampered by the need to try and slip their cables once the battle commenced, made poor practice.

No British ship was hit by French shells, although, at the start, one or two salvos did achieve a straddle on the British line: "During the action, the *Hood* was straddled several times, one officer and rating being wounded by shell splinters. There were no other casualties. Even the excitement of being under fire for the first time, and of hearing the screeching wind of heavy shells falling about them, could not efface the fact that it had been little more than slaughter."[14]

The British squadron in line ahead the *Hood*, *Resolution*, and *Valiant*, with the *Arethusa* and *Enterprise* astern, by contrast made good shooting, steering from the northwest on a steady easterly course from which they were on the starboard quarter of the French capital ships and fired in over the Mers-el-Kebir point. The salvos of 15-inch shells soon fell right in among the French vessels, and within a few minutes, the *Dunkerque* had been struck by three shells out of a four-shell salvo. This put one of her gun turrets out of action at once, damaged a boiler room, and destroyed one of the main generators, cutting off her power immediately and effectively silencing her armament. She was steamed slowly out of line and anchored off the village of St Andres at 6:13 P.M. She was reported as being firmly aground but on an even keel. However, the French Admiral Esteva made a broadcast in which he claimed she was virtually undamaged.

The old *Provence* was likewise hit by several 15-inch shells, which caused considerable damage. She was forced to cease firing as well, and, like the French flagship, struggled across the harbour in a deluge of shells and ran aground in shallow water below Roseville. This beaching saved her from sinking in the harbor.

More positive in results, as far as British gunnery was concerned, was the destruction of the *Bretagne*. She was underway from the mole when the third salvo from the British squadron plunged into her vitals detonating one of her main magazines. Ablaze along her whole length astern the bridgework, with steam and smoke forced out of her boilers by the concussion, she suddenly turned turtle at 6:09 and went down with most of her crew.

Caught in the battleship line, the unprotected airplane carrier *Commandant Teste* also took splinter hits which set her ablaze, while among the smaller vessels that caught the "overs" from the British battleships, the destroyer *Mogador* had her whole stern blown off by a direct hit from a 15-

inch shell but managed to keep afloat long enough to be beached in the Bains de la Reine.

In fifteen minutes, the British ships had fired thirty-six 15-inch salvos, and three out of four of the French heavy ships were put out of action. The *Hood* then switched her gunfire to the French forts, but signals from shore by wireless and searchlight requested the British to cease fire, and Admiral Somerville to do just that at 6:12.[15] By so doing, he hoped that the surviving crews from the damaged French ships might be able to make their way to safety without further needless loss of life. At the same time, Somerville turned his battle line sixteen points to port together to open the range from the fire of the forts, which had begun to straddle his ships, and avoid counteraction by submarine attack. At the same time, he signaled back, "Unless I see your ships sinking I shall open fire again."

The harbor entrance was left clear, but Somerville was confident that the French would make no attempt to escape. This was self-delusion, for the appeal to cease fire made by the French was a ploy enabling the *Strasbourg*, which had not been hit in the brief action and had by this time raised steam and gained the deep water channel, to make a dash for the open sea.

The magnetic mines in which the British placed their faith to act as a deterrent in just such an eventuality played no part because while the long period of negotiation was underway throughout the third, Gensoul had craftily ordered the antisubmarine nets south of the gate to be demolished, thus giving an uncluttered escape route to the *Strasbourg*, alone now but with her fighting power intact, and the five undamaged super destroyers that accompanied her.

The watchful aircraft from the *Ark Royal* reported, "One Dunkerque left harbor and steering east" at 6:20. Somerville ignored this, and not until ten vital minutes later, when a second aircraft confirmed this fact, did he realize his mistake. By that time, the *Strasbourg*, mistaken for the *Dunkerque* at first, was steaming hard at twenty-eight knots for Cap de L'Aiguille far to the east.

Taking the *Hood* and his fight ships off for a long, and somewhat tardy, stern chase, Somerville took a huge gamble in leaving the *Valiant* and *Resolution* unscreened for a while, which in view of his earlier fears of submarine attack seem to show he fully realized his tactical error in not keeping farther east with his big ships earlier. Indeed, he readily admitted this in his report.

Meanwhile, the *Ark Royal* flew off two striking forces of aircraft, six Swordfish armed with bombs and a further six with torpedoes, escorted by Skuas, in an attempt to hit and reduce the speed of the French battlecruiser. Both attacks failed, although the airmen reported that one from first attack and one from the second had struck home. Actually, the *Strasbourg* evaded both groups and reached Toulon harbor on the evening of July 4 unharmed and was given a triumphant reception. Her escape was indeed a magnificent achievement for the Vichy. Admiral Somerville confided to his wife that he expected to hear more about his tactical error before long: "Afraid I shall get a colossal raspberry from the Admiralty for letting the battlecruiser escape. In fact, I shouldn't be surprised if I was relieved forthwith."[16]

The reported hits led Somerville to chase on with the *Hood* for a considerable time, and not until late in the evening, at 8:20, did word reach him that the *Strasbourg* was now some twenty-five miles ahead of him and drawing steadily away. He therefore abandoned the pursuit and returned with his whole force to Gibraltar on July 4.

Force H then prepared for the next stage of the elimination of the Vichy fleet—the destruction or crippling of the brand-new battleship *Richelieu*, which was then at Dakar. However, when the Admiralty received reports that the *Dunkerque* was not disabled for certain, they instructed Somerville to return and finish the job. The bombardment was to take place on the sixth with only the *Hood* and *Valiant*. Somerville was once more "horrified," and when it was learned that the *Dunkerque* was aground close to the small hamlet of St. André and that French civilians might be killed, he managed to substitute a torpedo-bomber attack in place of the bombardment.

The aircraft flew off the *Ark Royal* some ninety miles from their target, in three waves at 5:15 on the morning of the sixth; they braved heavy flak and fighter defenses to make their strikes. The total of twelve aircraft reported a total of five certain hits and three possible hits. Even a percentage of such a high success rate would have ensured the French ship's elimination as required, and Somerville duly wrote that, in his opinion, the *Dunkerque* "must be completely knocked out"; in fact, she "could be written off for the rest of the war." A great champion of the Fleet Air Arm, Somerville was over-optimistic about the results they achieved. If five or six of these torpedoes were hits, many did not explode, for the main damage received was when one torpedo crippled the patrol boat *Terre Neuve*, which sank some thirty yards from the *Dunkerque*'s starboard side. "A torpedo in the second wave hit the wreck of the *Terre Neuve*, setting off her forty-four depth charges. The seven tons of TNT triggered by the explosion opened a great breach in the *Dunkerque*'s hull and killed and wounded four officers and 150 men."[17]

The only Vichy battleship left unaccounted for in the Mediterranean was the *Lorraine* of Admiral Godfroy's squadron at Alexandria. She at least had fired her guns at the Axis enemy, but Godfroy was as adamant as Gensoul that she would not continue to do so. Happily, Cunningham was patiently able to negotiate a satisfactory agreement (to the chagrin of Darlan and Laval), whereby the French battleship would be demilitarized by the unloading of their oil fuel, removal of their breechblocks, and other measures. That this was achieved was due to the personal intervention of Capt. H. T. Baillie-Grohman of the *Ramillies*, who boarded the *Lorraine* while covered by the battleship's guns. Here she remained until May 17, 1943, when Godfroy finally decided to rejoin the Allied cause.

With "this mournful episode" (as Churchill put it) completed, the British at both ends of the Mediterranean could now concentrate on tackling the Italians, and this they set about with a will. During July 6 and 7, a series of convoy operations were set in train by both the Italians and the British which resulted in the first tests of power for both. Malta was the keystone to Britain's Mediterranean position, for this island was in the center of Italy's main supply routes to her North African possessions. In common with so much of Britain's defense, the island had been neglected woefully, so much so in fact that the RAF and army felt it was indefensible. Churchill and the navy thought otherwise and were ultimately justified, but the need to build up the island for both defense and offense *after* the outbreak of war, instead of before, was to result in much costly effort in the years 1940–42.

The British operation, commenced on July 6, was for the sailing of two convoys from the island to evacuate noncombatants and give them protection during their voyage. Admiral Cunningham sailed with his main forces late on the evening of the seventh. They sailed in three groups. Force A consisted of five light cruisers and a destroyer; Force B, the battleship *Warspite* (flag) and five destroyers; and Force C, the battleships *Malaya* and *Royal Sovereign*, with the carrier *Eagle* and ten destroyers.

On the morning of the eighth, Admiral Somerville sailed from Gibraltar with Force H in order to create a diversion and attract a proportion of the Italian strength westward away from the convoy. This squadron consisted of the *Hood* (flag), *Valiant*, and *Resolution*, with *Ark Royal*, three light cruisers, and ten destroyers. It was suggested that Force H strike either at Taranto or Augusta with *Ark Royal*'s carrier planes or alternately make a strike on Naples. This Somerville declined to do, having a healthy respect for the potential of the Italian Air Force. Instead, he contented himself with a foray towards Sardinia and an air attack on Cagliari.

While these initial movements were underway, the Italians were running through a similar convoy operation of their own. Five merchant ships were sailed from Naples bound for Benghazi. They were covered by a cruiser squadron and destroyers and sailed on the sixth. False reports of a British cruiser squadron at Malta led to the dispatch, on the seventh, of six heavy cruisers, three light cruisers, and sixteen destroyers as additional protection, while Admiral Campioni put to sea with the battleships *Conte di Cavour* (flag) and *Giulio Cesare*, eight light cruisers, and twelve destroyers. Thus, with two battleships, six heavy and thirteen light cruisers, and forty-eight destroyers, almost the entire active strength of the Italian Navy was involved. The Italian Air Force was also held in readiness at maximum strength to strike at the British fleet should it put in an appearance. Long-range reconnaissance flights were flown and these soon picked up both British squadrons. The stage was thus set for the first encounters between British battleships and Italian battleships and between British battleships and Italian heavy bomber squadrons. Both proved to be classic duels of their type and set the pattern for future operations.

Both the British convoys and the Italian one passed off relatively quietly and without loss. Throughout the daylight hours of July 8, the various forces of Admiral Cunningham's fleet were subjected to prolonged and accurate high-level bombing attacks mounted by the Italian three-engine Savoia-Marchetti SM 79-II "Sparviere" aircraft of the air force's crack units.[18]

Here then was the supreme test of the theory that the heavy altitude bomber could sink, with ease, the battleship operating in restricted waters, with virtually no air cover. Although the *Ark Royal* and *Eagle* were operating with their respective fleets, carriers themselves are not an answer to aerial attack. It is always forgotten that an aircraft carrier is merely a platform and floating base, that a carrier's defense is only as good as the fighters she can put up and maintain. The *Ark Royal's* Skuas—few though they were—were dive-bombers as much as fighters and had hardly any speed margin over the Italian bombers. They claimed to have destroyed four bombers. The *Eagle* had just two obsolete biplane fighters, Sea Gladiators, with which to combat more than 400 modern bombers, which were faster than they. Both fleets, then, really had little or no aerial defense at all, and the air attacks were mainly a straight contest between the aircraft, making undisturbed practice at a great height, and the massed fire of the fleet. Both proved ineffective. Of the hundreds of bombs aimed at the ships, there was one single hit—on the bridge of the cruiser *Gloucester*, which was able to continue to operate. Of the thousands of rounds of antiaircraft shells fired off by both fleets over the five-day period, few, if any, caused damage to the Italian bombers.

On the British side, it was thought that "if they did not bring down many aircraft they certainly forced them to keep at a good height, and probably succeeded also in disturbing the bomb-aimers."[19] On the Italian side the inexperienced airmen made fantastic claims of success. In common with the German and RAF crews before them and the U.S. Army Air Force later, they proved unable to distinguish between hits and near misses from such heights and always erred on the side of optimism in their reports.

High bombing had the advantage that large aircraft could be used and so heavy attacks on warships could be made far out to sea. The terminal velocity of the bombs was sufficient to penetrate armored decks and the aircraft were practically immune from anti-aircraft fire. Nevertheless fast-moving ships were difficult targets and with a time of flight of half-a-minute or so they had time to take avoiding action. With a similar time of flight and size of target, naval gunfire had never expected to hit with the first salvo and this is what the bombers were trying to do; it is not surprising therefore that they seldom succeeded.[20]

This is Vice Admiral Hezlet's summing up of the problem that faced the Italian Air Force at this time. He concludes that "the British can correctly be said to have thereby surrendered the command of the sea in the central Mediterranean. They neither could use the central Mediterranean for their own traffic nor deny it to the Italians. The Italian Air Force, therefore, without a fight, exerted what was probably the greatest influence of aircraft over sea power to date."[21]

Here I must, with respect, part company with the admiral. The effect of prolonged bombing, it is true, was nerve-racking. Admiral Cunningham has fully admitted the concern he felt during this period of the vulnerability of his old ships.[22] Nevertheless, I feel that this conclusion should be qualified considerably. The effect that the Italian bombing had varied according to the attitude adopted by the naval commander on the spot. In these first test cases is a classic example of that. The heavy bombing did not prevent Cunningham, fully aware of the danger as he was, from thrusting boldly on into the central Mediterranean and giving battle to the Italian fleet. Nor did it prevent him sending heavy ships and convoys in Malta, nor at any time did he shrink from putting to sea with his battle-fleet in search of the enemy. The British continued to use the central Mediterranean—with enthusiasm—in the months that followed. It was the Italians who were constantly concerned about the appearance of British warships on their short sea routes to Libya rather than the British cowering from the Italian Air Force.

On the other hand, in justification of the admiral's argument, bombing on about a half the scale received each day by Cunningham had a profound effect on Somerville. Far from penetrating toward Sardinia and striking at Cagliari, his experience of July 9 caused him to abandon his operation after dusk that same day and retire to Gibraltar. In making this decision, he had the full support of his seagoing staff, who also deemed it prudent. Cunningham, on the other hand, never considered any retirement, despite the weight of attack. This is not to praise one commander and criticize the other for their respective decisions, but merely to show that accurate altitude bombing was *only* a deterrent if the reaction to it was caution not contempt."[23]

Certainly, it was an exhausting ordeal for the ships' crews to have to undergo for hours on end.

"Here they come again!"

"Alarm to arms! Hostile aircraft bearing Red Three Oh. Opened fire at 1825."

How a ship shakes and thunders when all her anti-aircraft guns are firing! The noise was tremendous: the pom-pom-pom of the "Chicago pianos"; the sharp rattle of the multiple machine-guns; the bark of the 4-inch. Under the hot sun the sweat trickled down the sailors' bodies. They wore clean overalls with the trouser ends tucked into their socks, and anti-flash gear covering their faces and hands. Before action of any kind every man was supposed to change into clean underwear so that if he were hit there would be no dirty material driven into the wound. This precaution could not be taken against aircraft attacks, which might develop at any hour of the day, and in this respect were unlike a surface action, where the whole ship could strip preparatory to the fight.[24]

Force H was fortunate in several respects. In addition to having slightly better fighters embarked, they also had the radar warning set of the modernized *Valiant* and her superb new antiaircraft battery to help beat off the attacks. The *Valiant* now boasted twenty Mark III type 4.5-inch guns in twin turrets, which could elevate up to 80 degrees; four multiple pom-poms; and four Mark III quadruple .5-inch machine guns—all controlled by the pom-pom directors for close-range fire. By the standards of the day, this was quite an imposing defense. However, the decision having been taken, Force H returned to Gibraltar on the tenth, losing the destroyer *Escort* to submarine attack on the way back.

Meanwhile, Cunningham's fleet had pushed on into the central Mediterranean, with the cruisers deployed ahead in the classic manner, supplemented by Swordfish searches from the *Eagle*. At the same time, the Italian fleet had concentrated in the Ionian Sea in the hope that the British would be lured over submarine traps and decimated by bombing to such an extent that a limited action could be fought against any survivors that got through. Cunningham was aware from flying boat patrols from Malta that enemy big ships were out and he set course to cut them off from their base at Taranto.

At dawn on the ninth, another flying boat brought the news that two battleships, twelve cruisers, and numerous destroyers were some 145 miles to the west of the British fleet. Undeterred by the odds—or the bombs—Cunningham held on toward them at his best speed.[25]

Admiral Cunningham later recalled how the battle actually developed "almost exactly" like the battle studies fought out on the table at the Tactical School at Portsmouth before the war—"a tribute to the nature of the studies and instructions received there."[26] It was a refutation of the many critics of prewar battle training. There was the long-range air contact, the follow up pin-pointing by the Fleet Air Arm planes, the torpedo-bomber strike from the carrier (on this occasion, as in so many others at this period of the war, without result), followed by surface contact by the cruiser scouting line and the beginning of the actual surface action proper. Vice- Admiral Tovey's four 6-inch cruisers, despite being faced with overwhelming odds, pressed home their initial sighting of the various Italian forces, made at 2:52 P.M., and were soon hotly engaged. In order to give them support against the 8-inch salvos of the Italian heavy cruisers, Admiral Cunningham took the *Warspite* on ahead with five destroyers, leaving the slower *Malaya* and *Royal Sovereign* some ten miles astern with nine other destroyers. The *Eagle* acted according to her flying needs, screened by the *Gloucester* and the oldest destroyers.

The Italian concentration had taken place around 1:30 P.M., giving Campioni a force consisting of two old (modernized) battleships against Cunningham's three (one of which was modernized), the Italian vessels having a speed superiority of several knots over the *Warspite*, the fastest British ship. In other categories, the Italians were vastly superior in numbers, having six 8-inch cruisers and ten 6-inch cruisers against the British five 6-inch vessels, and thirty-two destroyers against the fourteen British flotilla craft in the attack groups. After concentrating, the Italians turned northward towards the coastline of Calabria, on the instep of the boot of Italy, leading Cunningham right up to the noses of the Italian airfields that abounded there. Utilizing the *Warspite* as a battlecruiser, Cunningham brought her into action against the Italian heavy cruisers at 3:26, with the *Malaya* and *Royal Sovereign* still some ten miles astern. Her first target was an 8-inch cruiser bearing 265 degrees at a range of 26,400 yards. The *Warspite* loosed off ten salvos at this target and others as they presented themselves. A possible hit was claimed from the last salvo, and although this is not substantiated by the Italians, the *Warspite*'s 15-inch shells were dropped accurately enough to force the Italian cruisers to hastily turn away behind a smoke screen and retire. The *Warspite* was unable to continue to engage them over this because of the fact that her spotting aircraft had been damaged by the blast from X turret and had thereafter proved unusable and was jettisoned as a fire hazard.

Meanwhile, the *Malaya* had been making the utmost effort to hold her position, and in order that she might close on the flagship, the *Warspite* was put through a complete 360-degree turn to starboard, at 24½ knots. The last time she had performed such a maneuver was in front of the High Seas Fleet at Jutland in 1916, although then her famous "windy corner" episode had been involuntary rather than designed.

A squadron of 6-inch cruisers was then observed attempting to work its way around to get at the tempting prize of the old *Eagle*, and the *Warspite* took these ships under fire between 3:33 and 3:36, firing four salvos each at two of them, which was sufficient to cause the abrupt termination of that bit of bravado. Twelve minutes later, the *Warspite* catapulted off her reserve scout plane, and shortly thereafter, six Italian cruisers were sighted ahead of the Italian battle fleet. The Italian ships were still heading at high speed to the northeast, but the *Warspite*, cutting the corner, had caught them at extreme range.

At 3:53, the *Warspite* commenced firing on the right-hand ship of the two Cavour-class battleships sighted. This was the flagship of Admiral Campioni; she was bearing 287 degrees from the *Warspite*, and the range was an enormous 26,000 yards. This was the great moment Cunningham had been waiting for. Even as the *Warspite*'s mighty guns erupted at full elevation, the ripple of flame and smoke from both her adversaries showed they were fighting back.

Both Italian battleships chose the *Warspite* as their target—not surprisingly, since she was the only British heavy ship in action—and initially, they made good shooting, straddling within a very few salvos, but soon falling off. The majority of the Italian 12-inch shells fell within 1,000 yards of the *Warspite* but were reported as nearly all having a large spread. The British flagship, however, was ranging well in reply. The closest that Campioni's battleships came to the *Warspite* was one salvo that landed about two cables length off her port bow.

The gallant old *Malaya* was doing her utmost to get into the action in support of her flagship sister and fired some four salvos at the enemy battleships from a position astern and to port of the *Warspite*, but despite firing at her maximum elevation, her salvos fell some 3,000 yards short of the enemy. The *Royal Sovereign* was falling farther behind during this period and could not get into the fight at all. So the *Warspite* was on her own against the two Cavours. The decisive blow came at 4:00 P.M.: "The *Warspite*'s shooting was consistently good. I had been watching the great splashes of our 15-inch salvos straddling the target when at 4 P.M., I saw the great orange-colored flash of a heavy explosion at the base of the enemy flagship's funnels. It was followed by an upheaval of smoke, and I knew that she had been heavily hit at the prodigious range of thirteen miles."[27] To continue:

The damage that this hit caused to the *Giulio Cesare* was, in fact, considerable. Apart from wreckage among the light armament on her upper deck, she had four boilers put out of action and suffered 115 casualties. Her speed was temporarily reduced to 18 knots. The tactical consequences were quickly observed from *Warspite*, for the enemy at once made a large turn away. As we had previously captured the Italian naval codes we were now able to read their admiral's signal to his destroyers to cover his retirement with smoke. Our aircraft watched, with some amusement, the confusion which this maneuvered caused in the enemy's ranks.[28]

By 4:04, this smoke had forced the *Warspite* to again cease fire after seventeen salvos. The plucky *Malaya* got off another four of her own—again well short—before also ceasing four minutes later. But almost at once, one of the fleeing Italian cruisers ran clear of the smoke in her haste to get away northward, and the *Warspite* sped the Italian on her way at 24,600 yards with six further salvos, before she hastily ducked back into a smokescreen once more.[29]

At 4:05, the counterattack by the Italian flotillas manifested itself, and they were observed from the *Warspite* moving across to starboard from the van of the enemy fleet. Five minutes later three torpedo tracks were observed by the British destroyers, who were moving in to counterattack them; they had evidently been fired at very long range. "Half-hearted and never pressed home" was how Cunningham described the Italian destroyer attacks, and soon the British flotillas, which had been released from screening duties by their respective battleships, "moved joyously ahead at full speed, dodging the overs from the Italian battleships."[30]

As the Italian flotilla craft appeared fleetingly in and out of their smoke screen, they were engaged by the 6-inch guns of the *Warspite* and *Malaya*, between 4:30 and 4:41, before they vanished in the wake of the bigger ships. Meanwhile, Cunningham had intercepted frantic plain-language signals from the Italian flagship announcing that they were "constrained to retire" and warning of a submarine line ahead. The *Warspite* therefore worked her way to the windward of the great pall of smoke, but by the time they broke clear of it to the north, there was no sign of the Italian fleet, although the coast of Italy was clearly in view twenty-five miles away.

There was clearly no chance of catching the Italians, who were last reported at 7:05 P.M. steaming toward Messina in considerable disarray. This was partly because of the reappearance of the Italian bomber squadrons. Between 4:40 and 7:25, they delivered a series of heavy bombing attacks, again concentrating mainly on the *Warspite* and *Eagle*, although later, at 5:05

and 6:57, they switched their assaults "with a pleasant impartiality" against their own fleet, against which they were equally unsuccessful.

Master of the field of battle, Cunningham casually cruised with his whole fleet to the south of Malta during the next twenty-four hours and sent in his destroyers in relays to refuel there. Even the battleship *Royal Sovereign* put into Grand Harbour on the night of the tenth for fuelling. On the eleventh, the fleet again reconcentrated, but at 9:00 A.M., the *Warspite* pushed on ahead to Alexandria with four destroyers, leaving the *Royal Sovereign*, *Malaya*, and *Eagle* to follow on. Despite almost continual bombing attacks on the eleventh and twelfth, all ships returned safely without suffering a single hit, and the *Malaya* was able to make up her failure to hit a Cavour by scoring hits on two Italian bombers with antiaircraft fire, although no planes came down. Meanwhile, on the thirteenth, the *Ramillies*, with four destroyers, was sailed to cover the convoy, returning to Alexandria on the fifteenth.

The results of this brief engagement, known as the Battle of Calabria, were noted by Admiral Cunningham in his report:

> *Warspite*'s hit on one of the enemy battleships at 26,000 yards range might perhaps be described as a lucky one. Its tactical effect was to induce the enemy to turn away and break off the action, which was unfortunate, but strategically it probably has had an important effect on the Italian mentality.
>
> The meager results derived from this brief meeting with the Italian Fleet were naturally very disappointing to me and all under my command, but the action was not without value. It must have shown the Italians that their Air Force and submarines cannot stop our Fleet penetrating into the Central Mediterranean and that only their main fleet can seriously interfere with our operating there.
>
> It showed that high level bombing, even on a heavy and accurate scale experienced during these operations, yields few hits and that it is more alarming' than dangerous. Finally, these operations and- the action off Calabria produced throughout the Fleet a determination to overcome the air menace and not to let it interfere with our freedom of manoeuvre and hence our control of the Mediterranean.[31]

The battle certainly did have "a moral effect quite out of proportion to the damage." As Cunningham said later, "Never again did they willingly face up to the fire of British battleships, though on several subsequent occasions they were in a position to give battle; with a great preponderance in force."[32]

The Italian admirals and air marshals, however, were completely unabashed and announced a stunning victory over the combined fleets of

Cunningham and Somerville. Mussolini swallowed it whole, saying "that within three days the Italian Navy has annihilated 50 percent of the British naval potential in the Mediterranean."[33] Perhaps it was exaggerated, but even Count Ciano, to whom Mussolini made that boast, was not really fooled. Nor was he impressed at the equally glowing accounts given by the bomber pilots: "Admiral Cavagnari maintains that our air action was completely lacking during the first phase of the encounter, but that when it finally came it was directed against our own ships, which for six hours withstood the bombardments of our aeroplanes."[34] Evidently, the admiral was making the most of this indignity to help explain away the navy's rapid withdrawal; after all, most of the bombers attacked the British ships, although perhaps enough did not to justify Ciano's conclusion that "the real controversy in the matter of the naval engagement is not between us and the British, but between our air force and navy."[35]

The photographic evidence produced with a flourish in the Italian press was also rather counterproductive when it was revealed that a picture claiming to be a direct hit on a British battleship was really an upside-down print of the old *Royal Sovereign* steaming flat-out under a pall of smoke to get her crack at the Italian fleet. In Force H, the reaction was similar: "In the course of the action in the area of the Balearic Islands, Italian aircraft caused heavy damage and set HMS *Hood* on fire," recorded one broadcast; the *Hood*'s subsequent departure for England and replacement by the *Renown* some week later caused Italians to believe this, quite without foundation.

Calabria did indeed set the pattern, and the Italian fleet showed the same healthy respect for British battleships as did the German, and before them the German High Seas Fleet and the French Fleets of Napoleon. Their very success thus presented the British battleships in World War II with the same problems that had beset their forebears in 1914, 1800, and earlier—how to catch, lure, or ensnare a reluctant enemy into battle. In truth, it was not necessary, for the result would be the same whether the enemy remained skulking in port or was destroyed on the seabed. Britain's naval supremacy was equally vindicated by both results, although in the latter case there was always the unsatisfactory uncertainty exercised by the "fleet in being," that one day it might venture out. This meant constant vigilance and maintenance of a strong enough battle line to deal with it should it do so. The weather-beaten ships of Anson, Hawke, Jervis, Nelson, Jellicoe, and Beatty had spent long weeks and months of fruitless patrolling to maintain such a vigil, but this exercise in maritime dominance was not understood, or tolerated, in the 1940s; only actual battles were taken as the datum points on which the ultimate power of the battle fleet was based, and criticism of the lack of "results"—i.e., sinkings of actual enemy battleships—was the only yardstick used by the mass of critics from Churchill down to the press and many postwar historians.[36]

It was clear that with the ships he had, Cunningham was not going to be able to bring such a coy opponent into his sights except by chance of a lucky torpedo hit from his air striking forces (which, up to that time, had been attempted often and failed every time) or by long-range fire. Range and speed were the urgent requirements of his battle line as he himself made clear to Sir Dudley Pound soon after.

As neither the *Malaya* nor the *Royal Sovereign* had crossed the target, he informed Pound that his requirements were, at the minimum, "one more ship that can shoot at a good range."[37] At the end of July, Pound gave him the good news that this wish was to be granted, for the *Valiant* was to come east to him from Gibraltar, along with a new carrier and two antiaircraft cruisers. That such a modernized battleship was needed to support the *Warspite* was emphasized by the fact that Pound's two older ships badly needed refitting. The *Royal Sovereign*'s boilers had given out after her prolonged bout of all-out steaming, and she took part in only one more operation before being sent for a refit. The *Ramillies*, which had actually started and abandoned her refit in June, was having similar troubles, while the *Malaya* was not to be relied on in an emergency, because of condenser troubles. Fortunately, both the *Warspite* and *Malaya* could be docked in August.

On July 19, the Australian cruiser *Sydney*, with some destroyers, caught two Italian cruisers off Cape Spada and sank one of them as they fled at high speed. On hearing of the action, the Mediterranean Fleet put to sea in the hope of intercepting the survivor and also covering convoy operations in the Aegean. Cunningham sailed with the *Warspite*, *Malaya*, and *Royal Sovereign* once more, but apart from more heavy air attacks, which caused no damage save one unexploded bomb on a cruiser, and a successful torpedo-bomber strike from the *Eagle* against Tobruk, nothing untoward took place. Following this, the *Royal Sovereign* was sent through the Suez Canal and thence via the Red Sea for a proper refitting before joining the North Atlantic escort force. En route she was attacked by the Italian submarine *Ferraris*, on August 13–14, with no results whatsoever. There was a brief lull in the eastern basin while the big ships were docked.

Meanwhile, Somerville's Force H made another foray south of Sardinia to provide escort and diversion for the passage of the old carrier *Argus* that flew off much-needed Hurricane fighters to Malta in Operation Hurry. This took place between July 31 and August 4 and incorporated the previously planned air strike from the *Ark Royal* on Cagliari, which took place on the second. The *Hood*, *Valiant*, and *Resolution* once more provided heavy cover to

the carriers. This was the last time the original heavy ships of Force H operated together; the *Hood* was sent home with the *Valiant* and *Ark Royal* on the
fourth, and the *Resolution* went off to take part on the Dakar operation. At
home, Somerville transferred his flag to his new flagship, the *Renown*, and
she returned to Gibraltar with the *Ark Royal*.

Between August 20 and 29, the cruiser *Sheffield* and destroyers of the 8th
Flotilla arrived to complete the new smaller Force H, and the famous combination was born of one battlecruiser, one aircraft carrier, one light cruiser,
one flotilla leader (the *Faulknor*), and eight destroyers of the world's most
famous task force. Also arriving at Gibraltar at this time were the *Valiant*,
Illustrious, the antiaircraft cruisers *Calcutta* and *Coventry*, and four destroyers
destined for Admiral Cunningham's command.

Meanwhile, that fleet had ended its brief period of inaction in spectacular style. As the war on land had not actually resulted in any movement, Cunningham offered to wake things up by bombarding Italian positions on the
Libyan coast with the battle fleet. The targets selected were the supply port of
Bardia and the guns of the Fort Capuzzo, which guarded Sollum. The fleet
sailed on August 16: the *Warspite*, *Malaya*, and *Ramillies*, together with the *Kent*
(an 8-inch cruiser sent out to stiffen the 6-inch cruiser squadron, with
another, the *York*, to follow). On the morning of the seventeenth, the three
battleships and the heavy cruiser duly appeared, undetected, off the enemy
shore and opened fire. As Cunningham recorded: "Everything went according to plan. Bardia and Fort Capuzzo were subjected to twenty minutes deliberate bombardment from a rain of 15-inch, 8-inch, and 6-inch shells, which
was a satisfactory spectacle to watch."[38]

Another attempt by the Italian air force to intervene resulted in an even
greater humiliation than previously; besides failing to score any hits, the Italians lost twelve bombers to antiaircraft fire and the *Eagle*'s fighters working
from desert airstrips.

The next operation was a combined one, called Hats, in which the
Valiant, *Illustrious*, and light forces sailed from Gibraltar in company with the
Renown, *Ark Royal*, and the rest of the regular Force H. They were met by the
Warspite, *Malaya*, and light forces from Alexandria that penetrated the Sicilian
Narrows and took over. A mercantile convoy was passed through to Malta
from the east at the same time, and although both British commanders would
have welcomed a test of strength, this time nothing resulted, and both con-
tented themselves with tiny carrier attacks on Italian bases as consolation.[39]

On the return of Force H, the *Ark Royal*, *Resolution*, and light forces were
detached to take part in Operation Menace against Vichy forces at Dakar,
along with the *Barham* and Home Fleet units. This left Admiral Somerville

with only the *Renown* and six destroyers at Gibraltar (three old destroyers and three modern ones, but of these one new and one old boat were refitting). It thus happened that when a Vichy squadron, consisting of three 6-inch cruisers and three large destroyers, sailed through the straits, all they met was a *bon voyage*. Both Admiral North and Admiral Somerville had interpreted the rather confusing orders they had previously received as a need to maintain what is today termed a "low profile." Unfortunately for Admiral North, this was *not* the feeling of the Board and proved to be the final incident in a chain, beginning with his written objections to Catapult, that led to a loss of confidence in his ability to command at the Rock. When he was subsequently relieved, there was considerable indignation, and Admiral Somerville unhesitatingly claimed that any fault was his, rather than North's. He considered that in any event, the *Renown* and six destroyers "would not have been up to the job" of stopping the six French warships.[40]

If this seems a little pessimistic compared with Admiral Whitworth's handling of the same ship against the two German battlecruisers six months before, then it must be remembered, as Somerville himself added, the loss of the *Renown* "at a time when we were very short with the large and modern Italian Navy having just entered the lists against us, would have been a disaster of the first magnitude."[41]

It is an academic point anyway, for the order to intercept was not given and the Admiralty decision was subsequently upheld, although the manner in which it was carried out was seen, much later, to have been less than fair to North's honor, and he was duly exonerated from any charge of negligence.[42] Somerville's unselfish defense of his old friend was, however, to lead to further complications with London before very much longer.

Admiral Cunningham's new arrivals were given their first taste of action in mid-September when the *Valiant, Kent, Calcutta,* and *Coventry* provided the escort for the *Illustrious* for aerial torpedo and minelaying operations against Benghazi and Bardia, which resulted in the sinking of two destroyers and two freighters, the only British casualty being a torpedo hit on the *Kent* by Italian torpedo bombers of their new Aerosilurante arm. As yet small, and only just formed with adapted SM 79s, in a few operations these units were to cause more damage (although very little actual loss) than all the long-range, altitude bombers combined. At the end of the month, Admiral Cunningham received another letter from London telling him that other reinforcements were being sent to him, the main unit being the *Barham,* on the conclusion of the Menace operation.

Meanwhile, Cunningham continued to utilize the central Mediterranean at will. Between September 28 and October 3, a reinforcement of Malta took

place with 2,000 troops being carried into Grand Harbour aboard the cruisers *Gloucester* and *Liverpool* while the Mediterranean Fleet's "First Eleven"—
the *Warspite*, *Valiant*, and *Illustrious*, with light forces—provided the heavy
cover. During the afternoon of the twenty-ninth, these ships were, as usual,
subjected to prolonged altitude bombing by the Italian Air Force, despite
the busy work of the new Fulmars, but once again this routine irritation had
no effect whatsoever on the Mediterranean Fleet's planned movements,
although it was later claimed that in spite of their apparent impotence, the
Italians still denied the British the full use of the sea.[43]

If they did, it was not apparent in these operations, nor did the
much-strengthened Italian fleet influence matters either. During is operation,
it again put to sea to dispute the passage of Cunningham's small force. The
Littorio and *Vittorio Veneto* of the new 9th Division and the *Cavour*, *Cesare*, and
newly rebuilt *Caio Duilio* of the 5th Division formed the Italian battle line on
this occasion, supported by seven heavy cruisers, four light cruisers, and two
dozen destroyers—about double Cunningham's strength. This great array was
spotted by the *Illustrious* aircraft some 120 miles to the north. What happened
then is described in one recent "objective" account thus: "When reconnaissance aircraft from the *Illustrious* report the Italian Fleet only nine Swordfish
aircraft are available. But they cannot be employed because of Italian air
superiority. In consequence the Italian Fleet returns on September 30 unmolested."[44] Which must be the most novel way yet of saying that a fleet twice as
large *and* with admitted air superiority beat it back to port before it could be
attacked. It even sounds like a major triumph. As Admiral Cunningham put
it: "They had four [actually five] battleships out this time, including the *Littorio* and *Vittorio Veneto*, fine new ships of 35,000-tons armed with nine 15-inch
and a speed of 31 knots. After some thought, we decided to press on with the
main object of landing the troops in Malta, and no more was seen or heard of
the Italians."[45]

A similar operation was carried later in the month, between October 8
and 14, the object being the safeguarding of a four-ship supply convoy to
Malta from Alexandria. Because the Italians were now at maximum strength,
there was some hope of a major fleet action ensuing, and in readiness for this
Admiral Cunningham put to sea with his total force. Never before, and never
again, did the Mediterranean Fleet field such numbers. The battle fleet comprised the *Warspite* (flag), *Valiant*, *Malaya*, and *Ramillies*, the carriers *Illustrious*
and *Eagle*, the 8-inch cruiser *York*, five light cruisers, and sixteen destroyers.
However, the passage was made in rough weather conditions and the convoy
reached Malta undetected.

When a return convoy was identified by Italian reconnaissance, it was too
late for them to intercede with their heavy units apparently, but a flotilla of

destroyers ran into the light cruiser *Ajax*, which dealt with them in a summary manner sinking three out of seven and damaging a fourth, which was dispatched the next day by the *York*. The carriers again made strikes against the Dodecanese airfields in return for which a torpedo bomber damaged the light cruiser *Liverpool*, but Admiral Cunningham recalled how a similar attack in strength on the battleships was beaten off by their heavy barrage and that the subsequent entry into Alexandria harbor at 1:00 A.M. on the fifteenth "at high speed firing a blind barrage on both sides with our guns flashing and the sparkle of bursting shell" was spectacular. [46]

Further excursions followed with a similar lack of surface action, but once more, the battleships of the Mediterranean Fleet continued to use the central Mediterranean with impunity. On October 25, a convoy to Greece was covered by the Second Eleven—the *Malaya*, *Ramillies*, and *Eagle*—and following Italy's attack on Greece, all four battleships and both carriers were again at sea between October 29 and November 1 seeking action which was not forthcoming. It was, however, yet another example of how "Cunningham's great concourse of ships had held complete control of the eastern and central basins."[47]

An even more striking demonstration was to follow of how the British Fleet dominated the whole length of the inland sea of the Mediterranean from west to east. This was a combined operation involving convoys from Alexandria to the Aegean and Malta covered by the Mediterranean Fleet; the passage of further reinforcements to Cunningham; and the *Barham*, the 8-inch cruiser *Berwick* (to replace the *Kent*), and three destroyers (plus one to refit at Malta). This was Operation Coat, and the escort by Force H provided three minesweeping destroyers to help them through the Narrows and laid on an additional air strike at Cagliari in Sardinia, which the *Ark Royal*'s aircraft had visited before. Once the *Barham* had joined the flag, further moves were planned. First, the *Illustrious* was to strike at the Italian battleships lying snug at their moorings at Taranto; during the same night, a cruiser squadron was sent in against Italian supply routes to Albania; and finally, the *Ramillies* was to refuel at Malta and provide the heavy escort for an eastbound convoy from that island to Alexandria. Such a complicated plan, or series of operations— all to be carried out in the heart of the Mediterranean—surely belied any postwar claims that the Royal Navy did not hold command of these waters.

All these movements took place between November 4 and 14 and were achieved entirely without loss save for two Swordfish torpedo aircraft. The *Barham* and her consorts sailed from Gibraltar on November 7 with part of Force H, but the *Renown* had been detached for duty in the Atlantic at this time. The only Italian reaction to this and the bombing of Cagliari on the ninth by the *Ark Royal*'s aircraft was a single bombing attack, during which the *Barham* and others received the usual near-misses which did not affect them materially at all.

Meanwhile, in the east, Admiral Cunningham had put to sea fielding the *Warspite, Valiant, Malaya, and Ramillies* as his main strength, with the *Illustrious* and light forces in company. Under this shield, the convoy operations to and from Malta proceeded to plan and without event, other than ineffective bombing, and the fleet arrived off Malta as arranged. The *Ramillies* entered Grand Harbour for refueling equally unruffled, as in peacetime, despite a claimed attack by an Italian submarine.

The fleet cruised west of Malta on the tenth, and the *Barham* and her consorts rendezvoused in the middle of the morning, whereupon the whole force steered northeastward, again brushing aside bombing attacks on this day and the next. On the eleventh, the cruisers penetrated the Straits of Otranto and wiped out a convoy of four freighters after their two escorts "departed at high speed." But the stroke that really distinguished this series of operations was the attack by the *Illustrious*'s aircraft against the Italian battleships at Taranto. Here, for the loss of only two obsolete Swordfish, these gallant young men put three torpedoes into the brand-new *Littorio* and one apiece into the old *Caio Duilio* and *Conte di Cavour.*

Photographic reconnaissance confirmed this brilliant attack; the *Littorio* was heavily damaged and was reported as down by the bows with her forecastle underwater and a heavy list to starboard. The *Caio Duilio* was also down by the bows. Both these ships were eventually salvaged, repaired, and put back into service, but the *Cavour*, although refloated much later, was in a bad way and became effectively a total loss. Still, for six months, the battle fleet of the Italians was halved, and this attack showed, as had the loss of the *Royal Oak*, that against torpedo attack, the protection of the old battleships was inadequate. The *Littorio* had stood up to three hits well enough for her to be put back in service but only a single hit had disabled each of the older units so badly that they settled on the seabed. It also showed, as at Scapa, that the great ships were far safer out at sea and steaming at speed than they were immobilized in harbors, stationary targets. Torpedo-bombers were the only aerial attackers that could hurt the big ships (although not yet destroy a modern vessel), but they had to date only been able to hit ships at rest; the many attacks on heavy ships at sea had all ended in failure. As Captain Roskill stated:

> Although from the nature of this attack it was not to be expected that the ships would be permanently disabled, the results achieved by so few Swordfish were not only remarkable in themselves but were accomplished at a singularly fortunate period when, with grave uncertainty still surrounding the future of the French fleet, the bal-

ance of maritime power by no means rested firmly in our hands. In spite of the failure of the Italians ever to use their battleship strength effectively, account always had to be taken of its existence, and by this 'well conceived and brilliantly executed' attack one threat to our maritime control in that theatre was greatly reduced.[48]

An Italian war communiqué stated the next day that "only one unit was in any way extensively damaged. There are no victims. Six enemy aircraft were shot down." Ciano was shaken. Strangely enough, Mussolini was not: "A black day. The British, without warning, have attacked the Italian fleet at anchor in Taranto, and have sunk the battleship *Cavour* and seriously damaged the battleships *Littorio* and *Duilio*. These ships will remain out of the fight for many months. I thought I would find the *Duce* downhearted. Instead, he took the blow quite well and does not, at the moment, seem to have fully realized its gravity."[49] It was soon to become apparent to him.

The immediate Italian reaction was to remove the surviving battleships to the port of Naples, leaving the central Mediterranean to be covered by only a heavy cruiser squadron based on Messina for a time. This eased Cunningham's situation considerably: he could retain control with the *Warspite*, *Valiant*, and *Barham*, thus enabling the *Malaya* and *Ramillies* to be dispatched to other vital areas denuded of battleship cover.

Encouraged by the ease of its previous passages, Force H was also becoming more active in the western basin. Between November 15 and 20, the *Renown* again led them as escort for the carrier *Argus*, which flew off fighters for Malta, but although unopposed, this failed because the planes were flown off at extreme range and meeting strong headwinds ran out of fuel and fell into the sea. A planned air strike from the *Ark Royal* was also aborted.

Meanwhile, Churchill had been pressing for the direct transportation of vital war supplies, especially tanks, from Britain straight through to the Army of the Nile, and the dominance of the British Fleet now led him to insist that this be done instead of sailing round the Cape of Good Hope. Before this was done, time was taken to dock the *Warspite* at Alexandria. It must be emphasized that even while in harbor and supposedly at rest, the work of the battleships continued. In fact, so poor was the Egyptian manned antiaircraft defense of Alexandria that the main burden of the port's defense rested almost entirely on the battleships' antiaircraft batteries. Thus, gunners who had spent days beating off prolonged air attacks at sea got no respite when the battleships got back to harbor—a highly unsatisfactory state of affairs.[50]

The convoy operation, Operation Collar, finally got underway toward the end of the month. Although both Cunningham and London thought it unlikely that the Italians would attempt to dispute the convoy's passage with their fleet, Admiral Somerville thought that, on the contrary, they might chance their arm to avenge Taranto. He was right. In view of his expectations, Somerville pressed that the *Royal Sovereign*, which had made her way around the Cape of Good Hope and was undergoing a much-needed refit in Gibraltar dockyard at this time, should be added to his Force H for this next operation. The Admiralty agreed to this, but as it turned out, the battleship could not be got ready in time. She thus missed her final chance of landing a 15-inch shell on her old enemies before she left for the Atlantic convoy routes.

Thus it was that when the convoy of three fast motor vessels sailed, the *Renown* once more represented Somerville's sole heavy metal, whereas the Italians could in theory attack with three battleships. In addition to the *Ark Royal*, Force H had two light cruisers, the *Despatch* and *Sheffield*, with two others, the *Southampton* and *Manchester*, passing through with them to Malta, as well as eleven destroyers, three of which were bound for the east.

Meanwhile, several convoys and subsidiary operations were to take place in the eastern basin designed to ultimately mesh in with the convoy's movements. The *Ramillies*, on the first leg of her journey home, was to be escorted through the Narrows to link up with, and return with, Force H on November 27. The convoy would be taken over by Cunningham's fleet in return for the last lap to Alexandria.

Escorting the *Ramillies* and the cruisers *Berwick* and *Newcastle*, which were returning with her, and the antiaircraft cruiser and five destroyers to meet the convoy was the *Barham* and *Malaya* group, whose carrier, the *Eagle*, was to strike at Tripoli on the twenty-sixth en route. They sailed on the twenty-fourth. Two days later, the *Warspite* and *Valiant* put to sea, with the *Illustrious* and the cruisers, to cover a convoy to Crete and to attack air bases in the Dodecanese. Another supply convoy was to pass through to Malta with cruiser escort. Other local convoys were at sea also in the eastern basin, but they found little opposition, and Cunningham stated that the Mediterranean Fleet's part in these complicated movements was unique in being the only occasion that the *Warspite*, or any other ship of his command, had cruised around the central Mediterranean for several days and not fired a single gun.

However, over in the western basin on the twenty-seventh, things fell out very differently, and it was Admiral Somerville's turn to put the Italian battle fleet to the test of surface action. On receipt of the news of the British operations, the Italian Naval Command (*Supermarina*), ordered Admiral Campioni to sea once more from Naples with a powerful force. Flying his flag aboard the *Vittorio Veneto*, he was supported by the *Guilio Cesare*, now repaired after her knock from the *Warspite* in July. In addition, Campioni had six heavy cruisers, fourteen destroyers, and the support of submarines and bombers on station in readiness. These ships were sighted by aircraft from the *Ark Royal*, and what resulted was a hard, stern chase later dignified by the title of the battle of Spartivento.[51]

At dawn, the convoy was some 120 miles southwest of Cape Spartivento (the tip of Sardinia), with the bulk of Force H ahead and to the north of it interposed between the merchantmen and the enemy coast and line of advance. Not until 10:05 that morning did the first sighting reports reach Somerville on the *Renown*'s bridge that the Italian fleet was, in fact, at sea. When it did come, it merely reported the ships, and there was some confusion that they might be reporting the *Ramillies* and her group, which had penetrated the Narrows, brushed off a destroyer attack, and were steering to the rendezvous. Amplifying reports soon made it clear that this was not the case, and Force H realized it was up against at least two Italian battleships in one group and several large cruisers in another.

By 10:15, Somerville was concentrating his limited firepower around the *Renown*, leaving the convoy with light protection and the *Ark Royal* to organize a torpedo strike independently. He then set course to cut the corner and meet the *Ramillies* to the eastward. Once he had concentrated his forces, he would have two heavy ships—one fast, one slow—to match the Italians, but would only have one 8-inch cruiser, the *Berwick*, and four 6-inch cruisers to oppose the Italian heavy ships. On learning soon afterward that the *Ramillies* was some thirty miles away and closing, Somerville reduced speed to twenty-four knots to await events. He placed the protection of the convoy above the desire to bring the Italians to battle, but as he later reported, the two objects at this time were not opposed.

According to Somerville, "whatever the composition of the enemy force, it was clear to me that in order to achieve my object . . . it was essential to show a bold front and attack the enemy as soon as possible." This he now proceeded to do with a will. The Italians had also concentrated at this time, knew the composition of both British forces from reports from their scout planes and were some thirty miles east-southeast of Sardinia. However, this boldness evaporated once they realized that the two British forces were about to join. This caused a change of heart, as did the knowledge that the *Ark Royal* was about to launch torpedo bombers. In his own words, Campioni now, around noon, considered that, far from taking on Somerville "in conditions favorable to us" (as he thought two hours earlier), with Somerville's two capital ships closing fast, the situation was changed. "I decided not to become involved in a battle."[52]

Somerville, on the contrary, was holding on toward the enemy, feeling that "the prospects of bringing the enemy to action appeared favorable." As the torpedo-bomber striking force went to the attack on the Italian battle fleet just over the horizon, spirits in the British ships were high. From one of the British destroyers, in the van as they thrust on at best speed towards the now fleeing enemy, a war correspondent recorded the scene as the *Ramillies* got into the chase for a brief time:

> She was magnificent, her great-beamed hull thrusting along, throwing on either side of her enormous bows a fair half of the middle sea—*Ramillies* driving her twenty-five-year-old engines to unheard-of pressures. Even twenty-five years ago she had a speed of twenty-two knots only. We went past her as a swallow past an eagle. Her guns were trained already, elevated as if they were trying to reach over the barren sea towards the enemy. All the way down her sides the spray leapt high in a succession of angry flourishes. Her wake was as broad and as tumbled as the well-trodden pathway of the Fs. From her mainmast she flew already her battle flag, a vast white ensign, stiff as a metal banneret upon the wind.[53]

At 12:07 P.M. came the signal "Smoke and mast bearing 000." Far in the distance, the speeding enemy could be made out going at high speed. These were the Italian heavy cruisers and thirteen minutes later they opened fire, narrowly missing the *Manchester*. The British replied in kind, but first honors went to the Italians, who scored a hit with an 8-inch shell on the *Berwick*, which put her after turrets out of action. This was followed shortly afterward by another direct hit, but she held her place in line and her after turrets were not required in this action anyway. Only her forward turrets would bear as the Italian cruisers made smoke and turned away toward the shelter of their battle squadron, as both the *Renown* and *Ramillies* added their heavy guns to the duel.

> *Ramillies* opened fire, but she opened fire beyond effective range. In spite of the magnificent efforts of her engine-room she could not make the grade. She cannot be considered as having taken part in the action proper at all. *Renown* opened and her first salvos were well amongst the Italian ships, but she dropped slowly out of range. She would have dropped in any case, for the Italians had all the advantage of speed, but actually *Renown* ran a bearing in the last stages of the chase, and could not make her normal speed.[54]

The *Renown*'s first salvo was actually fired at 12:24 at the right-hand ship of the heavy cruiser division; the range was 26,500 yards. Some six salvos were got away at this target before they vanished behind smoke.[55]

The *Ramillies* opened at 12:26 with two salvos at her maximum elevation to test the range. She attained a maximum speed of 20.7 knots at this time, and she held this throughout the action, dropping steadily astern in the *Renown*'s wake but there, ready in support, should the Italians show a little spirit and close for a gun duel.

Once the Italian cruisers had been lost sight of, Somerville brought the *Renown* around to starboard in order to bring the enemy battleships into view and in so doing sighted briefly the heavy cruisers once more. Two further salvos were loosed against these before they again took cover. A further turn to starboard was made to open up the *Renown*'s A arcs on a heavy cruiser bearing 356 degrees, and eight salvos were pumped out at this ship before she too was lost in smoke at 12:45.

While the Swordfish were attacking, the *Renown* was worrying around the edge of the smoke seeking further suitable targets and was rewarded with the glimpse of two large ships steering west. The three twin 15-inch turrets were already swiveling round to lock onto these when, just in time for them, they were identified as three-funnelled Vichy liners, which had blundered across the battlefield. Fire was checked in time to prevent another rift in Anglo-French relations from taking place.

With the enemy out of view for the time being, the *Renown* fell back to concentrate with the *Ramillies*, but as she did so, they took a fleeting view of the two scurrying Italian battleships, and these were taken under fire with two ranging salvos at 1:11. Both of these fell well short, and the range was opening fast. (The Italian vessels were in fact cruisers, *not* battleships, which were well out of action by this time). In view of this and after carefully considering all the alternatives open to him, Somerville called off the chase and returned to the convoy.

And thus it came about that the Italians again ran clear, the Swordfish once again failing to score any damaging hits on the enemy ships to slow them down enough for any British vessel to come up to them. One hit on a heavy cruiser and damage to a solitary destroyer, which had to be later towed home in a sinking state, were the only reward and, fast approaching the Italian coastline with its abundant airfields, and with his convoy left far astern and poorly defended, Admiral Somerville broke off the pursuit at 1:20, after one hour and twenty minutes of action.

As usual, the fleet was attacked by bombers later in the day. On this occasion, it was by a total of only twenty aircraft, half of which concentrated on the *Ark Royal* and straddled her with bomb bursts, but she emerged unscathed, as did the rest of the force. The Italian Air Force claimed to have hit an aircraft carrier, a battleship, and a cruiser, while a British battleship was reported as being stopped with a fire aboard. This was the old *Royal Sovereign* trick again, and, although the *Ramillies* was equally as slow, she was not hit and certainly did not slow to a complete standstill at any time during this operation.

The results were disappointing, but the convoy got through safely, the Italian fleet was run off once more, and British morale was high—in fact, at a peak. The subsequent intervention by London tended to take some of the edge off this euphoria, but when Admiral Somerville was cleared, as expected, the feeling in the ships was one of defiance against the enemy *and* Whitehall.[56]

Thus, 1940 ended on a high note for the British battleships in the Mediterranean. As one German commentator put it, "Up to this date, the British Mediterranean Fleet could do practically anything it wanted."[57] This view from the other side contrasts starkly with the postwar view postulated by Admiral Hezlet. While the Italian Navy reorganized its command structure and remaining forces—including the battleships *Vittorio Veneto*, *Giulio Cesare*, and *Andrea Doria*—the navy supported the Army of the Nile in its victorious advance into Libya. The *Barham* provided the heavy support for the inshore squadrons operations between December 9 and 17, and at the end of that time, yet another large operation involving both Force H and Cunningham's fleet was planned. This was perhaps the most audacious stroke to date, for after covering convoys to and from Malta between December 16 and 18, the *Warspite* and *Valiant* were detached to carry out the bombardment of the Albanian supply port of Valona through which passed the bulk of the troops and supplies for the Italian armies, which were in full retreat from the tiny Greek army. By 1:15 A.M., the two great ships were in position, undetected, off the port, only 100 miles from Taranto itself, and opened fire with their main armaments.

The two battleships were firing, without spotting, by indirect fire over the intervening hills some 2,000 feet high, for the *Illustrious* was not present. This probably reduced the effectiveness of their salvos, but the *Warspite* fired fourteen, and the *Valiant* fired a similar number into the port installations and airfield, totaling 100 15-inch shells and destroying a score of aircraft. There was no answering fire from the startled defenders, and as the two battleships steamed away through the "beautiful, clear moonlit night and flat calm, though bitterly cold" to the south, the only reactions seen were searchlights probing the seas far astern of them.

Meanwhile, the *Malaya*, transferring west, had given protection to the convoy bound for Malta, and on the twentieth, she headed into the Narrows with three destroyers, evading an attack by an Italian submarine force on the way. The *Renown* and Force H had sailed from Gibraltar on the same day, having been busy in the Atlantic, and they rendezvoused with the *Malaya* and were back in Gibraltar by the twenty-fourth, together with two empty steamers from Malta; they had convoyed back with no opposition whatsoever.

In the meantime, Admiral Cunningham had taken his flagship into Valletta harbor to refuel, raise morale, and confer with Vice Admiral Ford and the governor. "It was a stirring encouragement to the Maltese to see the flagship in Grand Harbour once again, even if the former cynosure of the fleet was now dazzle-painted, scarred with rust and her guns blistered from recent use."[58] By Christmas Eve, both British forces were safely back in harbor.

The new year opened in much the same manner. The British had been held up in front of Bardia and planned to mount an assault to take this vital port on the Libyan coast on January 3. To provide heavy support, Cunningham put to sea on the second with the *Warspite, Valiant, Barham*, and light forces, and this time, the *Illustrious* was on hand to provide fighter cover and spotters. The fleet's target area was in the northern part of the battle zone, and the object was to prevent troops here catching the attacking Australians in the rear during their push. At times, the zone into which the one-ton shells were dropped was surrounded on three sides by friendly troops, which made accuracy essential.

From 8:10 until 8:55 A.M., the three battleships "drenched" the target area with their twenty-four 15-inch shells; the Italian shore batteries replied bravely but without scoring any hits. While at Malta, Cunningham had unearthed some of the 15-inch shrapnel shells, which had caused great execution amongst the Turkish infantry at the Dardanelles in 1915 and which it was hoped would prove equally unpalatable to Mussolini's warriors. Unfortunately, they proved ineffective and failed to burst in the required manner as the balls inside had rusted together into a solid mass during their twenty-five years interment at Malta.

Despite this, the fire from the battle-fleet proved invaluable: "It was not particularly spectacular from the sea, merely the thick clouds of smoke and dust flung up by the bursting shell. What it must have been like to the Italians I cannot imagine; but as all enemy movement ceased I imagine our task was successfully accomplished."[59] On the fifth, the remnants of the garrison of Bardia surrendered with 25,000 prisoners.

Another through operation was planned almost at once, Operation Excess. This involved the passing of a convoy from Alexandria via the central Mediterranean to Malta and Greece, as well as light forces for the eastern basin. As usual, the *Renown*, reinforced by the *Malaya*, which had now joined Force H, provided the heavy metal from the west, with the *Ark Royal* and light forces. They sailed on January 6 and met little opposition except for Italian bombers. The convoy and reinforcements were joined by two light cruisers and destroyers from Cunningham's fleet on the afternoon of the ninth, and Force H returned to Gibraltar.

The Mediterranean Fleet was, as usual, engaged in several subsidiary operations during the passage of the convoy, with Cunningham sailing on the seventh with the *Warspite* and *Valiant*, *Illustrious*, and destroyers. Various cruiser forces were deployed: *Gloucester* and *Southampton* in taking troops to Malta and then picking up the Greek part of the convoy; four light cruisers joined Cunningham on the ninth; and an empty convoy was brought out of Malta at the same time. All went well until the tenth, when the main fleet was attacked by a group of Ju 87 Stuka dive-bombers commanded by Captain Hozzel and Major Enneccerus, which, unknown to the British, had earlier been sent to Italy with the specific task of attacking the Mediterranean Fleet and saving the tottering Italian armed forces from final collapse. For weeks, they had been training to ensure that their pinpoint accuracy was at its peak for its first assault.

They were meticulous in their planning and perfect in the execution of their first task. First, a feint by Italian torpedo-bombers drew away the defending fighters down to sea level. Next, a portion of the Stukas concentrated their attacks on the two battleships, thus pulling away the most powerful anti-aircraft defenses. Their bombs were too light to sink the battleships, of course, but their assault did have the desired effect. The *Warspite* was struck by only one bomb, which hit the starboard anchor with a glancing blow, but the resulting detonation did practically no damage, other than damaging the starboard paravane chains and the bower anchor. The *Valiant* was near-missed and took three casualties from bomb splinters. The *Illustrious*, on whom the brunt of the attack fell, was severely damaged by no less than six direct hits. Only her armored deck saved her. Despite further attacks that day and later while she was repairing at Malta, she finally managed to reach Alexandria and from there to the repair yards of America. She was replaced by the *Formidable* as soon as that vessel could get round the Cape of Good Hope and through the Canal. The next day, Stukas of the same unit bombed and sank the *Southampton* and damaged the *Gloucester*. It was clear that with the arrival of these deadly aircraft, the old halcyon days had departed.[60] Wrote one historian:

> The bombs that smothered *Illustrious* were like a handful of pebbles flung into still waters. Long after the splashes had died away, the waves of repercussion continued to ripple outward. For *Fliegerkorps* [Air Corps] X, that fateful January afternoon, did far more than

deprive Admiral Cunningham of his most valuable ship; they achieved an important strategic victory, they sealed off the Central Mediterranean to anything heavier than a cruiser. Not for close on two years did an Allied battleship or aircraft-carrier penetrate the Sicilian Narrows; and if anyone suggested a convoy to Malta might be escorted by capital ships right the way through to the island the fate of *Illustrious* was a counter argument that brooked no contradiction.[61]

This was absolutely correct, but in a more detailed examination, it showed that the dive-bomber, although far more accurate than the horizontal bomber against a fleet with no fighter defenses, lacked the payload to sink a capital ship. The *Illustrious* took six hits when the Germans had estimated that three would be enough to put her down. She survived, albeit badly damaged, and so did the battleships on countless occasions. Not disputing the gallantry of this attack, nor its long-term strategic effect, what it proved once more was that bombs were still not the correct weapons to use against capital ships. The altitude bomber had the bombs heavy enough to cripple a battleship but not the accuracy to hit them at sea; the dive-bomber had more than enough accuracy, but not the bombs heavy enough to cause fatal damage. It was, in fact, the ships of cruiser size and below that were the most vulnerable to such attacks, especially the latter, and heavy losses were to follow. But the battleship, it must be remembered, was especially built to take hits, to absorb the severest punishment and still be able to continue functioning.

This was the purpose of the battleship after all, the reason for her existence. Battleships did not just happen; they evolved, as did every other type. The case for scrapping the battleship because they could be hit from the air by dive-bombing could not be maintained because they did not sink when hit. Cruisers and destroyers *did* sink—in large numbers—from dive-bombing, but there was no call to scrap these types; only the battleship was singled out. Nor did the damage to the *Illustrious* bring a cry to scrap the carrier fleet: nor should it have done. As David Howarth put it, "The big ships survived the particular threat that had been argued so hotly between the wars. No capital ship was sunk by bombs from aircraft [at sea]. They came through thousands of bombing attacks in the course of two years."[62]

Captain Roskill sums up the effect this new form of attack had on Admiral Cunningham: "The check received in January made no difference to Cunningham's determination, and early next month he was again in the central basin."[63] While the fleet returned to Alexandria, Rear Admiral Rawlings had put to sea on the twelfth with the *Barham* and *Eagle* to strike at airfields in the Dodecanese once more, but bad weather caused this to be abandoned, and the *Barham* was back in port the next day.

A more serious incident happened inside Alexandria harbor when the destroyer *Greyhound* came into collision with the *Warspite* on the night of January 31. The battleship's bulges were slightly damaged by this knock and were patched up by emergency repairs.

Meanwhile, Force H—its commander reprieved from an abrupt recall in the same manner as North[64]—was making preparations for more aggressive action in the western basin after the failure of a Fleet Air Arm attack on the Tiso dam in Sardinia, during which sortie, between January 31 and February 4, the *Renown* and *Malaya* had provided heavy cover. As the air attacks had not worked, it was decided that the battleships should be given the opportunity to show what they could do; the target selected was the Italian naval base at Leghorn, deep in hostile waters surrounded by the bases of Italy and Vichy France. It was thought that the damaged *Littorio* might be repairing at the Genoa dockyard and thus present a worthy spin-off target for the British ships, while there were oil storage depots at Leghorn and Spezia for the *Ark Royal* to launch an attack on.

Bad weather thwarted the first attempts at carrying out this audacious plan, but on February 6, the three big ships, with the cruiser *Sheffield* and a screen of ten destroyers, sailed from Gibraltar and, on the morning of the ninth, arrived completely by surprise off Genoa. An Italian force, consisting of the battleships *Vittorio Veneto*, *Giulio Cesare*, and *Andrea Doria*, with three 8-inch cruisers and ten destroyers had in fact sailed to the south of Sardinia in the expectation of another convoy operation and were completely deceived, although at one point the two fleets passed within fifty miles of each other.

Dawn broke on the ninth to reveal the Gulf of Genoa completely undefended and wide open as the two British heavy ships took up their bombardment positions in calm seas under a clear blue sky. Admiral Somerville described the opening scene thus: "Not a sign from shore, not a ship except our own on the sea. We steamed up to the beginning of the run-about ten miles off Genoa—and then crash went the broadsides."[65]

It was indeed a "cleverly disguised foray," one that achieved complete success. The great ships belched flame and smoke as they made deliberate practice upon the dockyard and harbour installations. In fact, it was the *Caio Duilio* that was repairing there, but she escaped without receiving a hit. However, the deluge of 273 15-inch shells that struck the area sank five ships in the harbor and damaged others, while other targets hard hit were the Ansaldo electric works, the main power station and railway marshalling yards as well as dockyard installations. Severe damage was caused in the city itself from the overs from the mighty salvos, some 144 casualties being reported. Return fire from the Italian coastal batteries, when they finally awoke, was completely ineffective and once again the old argument, that battleships were ineffective in a duel with coastal guns, received a hard knock to the contrary, despite the Dardanelles.

The old *Malaya* was ranging accurately on the target area with great gusto and from her port yardarm proudly flew the Malayan Jack in the traditional manner (the *Malaya* had been a gift to Britain from the Malay States, and so she flew their flag in battle). As was noted, there was a marked resemblance between this flag and the Peninsular and Orient Steamship Company house flag, a point which was not lost on Somerville. He signaled to the *Malaya*, through the thunder and roar of the bombardment: "You look like an enraged P and O!"

The targets had been pinpointed earlier by using a large-scale model of the area prepared by Mr. Scillitoe, commissioned gunner of the *Renown*, but after a while, the enthusiasm of the gunners and total lack of opposition led to an extension of their interest along the shore line. Somerville made a general signal during the action: "Who knocked that lighthouse down and why?"

The *Ark Royal*'s aircraft laid mines off La Spezia, and on this object lesson in the daring use of sea power and heavy ships in the face of a superior enemy, Somerville led his force home again, breaking radio silence two days later to inform the delighted Admiralty at home, "Bombardment completed. From all accounts Genoa is in a bloody fine mess." It was, and so was the Italian Fleet, which turned north to search for the British squadron but missed them completely, although whether it was their misfortune or good luck that they failed to find Force H is debatable. By February 11, Force H was back in harbor unscathed.

Coupled with Valona, Genoa was a great morale booster back home. And not only at home. In occupied Europe, too, it was news that the Royal Navy was still on the offensive even if most of the continent was under the heel of Germany and Italy. As Churchill later broadcast, "If the cannonades of Genoa, rolling along the coast, reverberating in the mountains, has reached the ears of our French comrades in their grief and misery, it may cheer them with a feeling that friends are active, friends are near, and that Britannia rules the waves."

The Mediterranean Fleet continued to operate; it sortied out in February to create a diversion for Force H and acted as distant cover to the convoys of troops being sent into Greece and Crete the following month. On the nineteenth, it sailed to cover a convoy to Malta, returning to Alexandria on the twenty-fourth. These operations encountered no resistance whatsoever.

Meanwhile, great events were looming. The Luftwaffe had claimed to have hit two battleships in a torpedo bomber attack on the fleet on March

16, and this report, although totally false, led the Axis into a false sense of security. Under pressure from the Germans, the Italians finally agreed to use their heavy ships in an offensive operation against the troop convoys to Greece. It was an operation planned with great caution by the Italians and only undertaken on the understanding that the Luftwaffe would be out in strength in their support. It did not materialize.

On March 26, Admiral Iachino, after much heart searching, put to sea to carry out the plan. He flew his flag in the battleship *Vittorio Veneto* and had under him a powerful force consisting of six 8-inch and two 6-inch cruisers with thirteen destroyers. These concentrated the next day south of the Messina Straits and set course towards the south of Crete. He held on toward the Aegean until midday on the twenty-eighth, and then, uneasy at the absence of the promised air support and searches, he turned back for home still far short of his target area. It was a prudent move, for Cunningham had received intelligence of this sortie and had sailed with the bulk of the Mediterranean Fleet on the evening of the twenty-seventh. With him were the battleships *Warspite* (flag), *Valiant*, and *Barham*, and in support were the carrier *Formidable* (taking *Illustrious*'s place) and nine destroyers. Already out at sea and scouting for the enemy was a cruiser squadron of four 6-inch ships with a further four destroyers. The stage was thus set for the clash that finally decided the merits of the respective fleets once and for all: the battle of Cape Matapan.[66]

The initial stages of the battle are briefly disposed of since they did not directly affect the battleships. Pridham-Wippell's four light cruisers ran into the heavy cruisers of the Italian force and fought a running duel with them, leading them back on Cunningham's fleet before the Italians broke off the action and fell back on the *Vittorio Veneto*. In closing, the British cruisers came under heavy and accurate fire from all the Italian heavy ships and were in great peril but a torpedo bomber attack threw the Italians into confusion and got them off the hook. Later air attacks scored hits on both the *Vittorio Veneto* and the heavy cruiser *Pola*, but whereas the Italian battleship managed to absorb this punishment as she was designed to do and continued her flight to safety without further molestation, the *Pola* was badly damaged and stopped. Iachino, not realizing because of poor reporting from air reconnaissance that the British Battle Fleet was so close behind him, sent back the *Zara* and *Fiume* of *Pola*'s division to assist her to safety, with an escort of four modern destroyers. This powerful force turned back confident of meeting only destroyers. In fact, Cunningham's big ships were rapidly closing in the night and were only some fifty miles away. Radar reports from the advanced British cruisers had left Cunningham with the hope that a stopped ship reported was the *Vittorio Veneto*, and by the time he took in this report, at 9:00

P.M., the estimated position was some twenty miles ahead of him. The battle fleet's speed was restricted to the twenty knots of the *Barham*, his slowest vessel, and for a night action with a modern capital ship, whose armament was probably intact, Cunningham was determined not to split his fleet. With a pair of destroyers on either flank as a token screen, the British battle line approached the stationary *Pola* through the blackness, their radar set giving constant readings and checks.

The British ships were deployed in line ahead: the *Warspite, Valiant, Formidable,* and *Barham.* At 10:03, the *Valiant* picked up a firm echo on her modern radar set showing the stationary vessel nine miles on the port bow of the battle squadron. Six minutes later, this was confirmed as being a large ship six miles off the port bow. In a brilliant deployment, Cunningham altered course 40 degrees to port *toward* the enemy. This turn into the target at night in order to quickly identify and dispatch the plotted vessel—rather than the automatic turnaway of the battle line from a possible torpedo attack danger, as was standard instruction since Jutland and before, and the accepted interwar reaction in a night battle—was a masterstroke. Indeed, it was the first time in either peace or war that it had been done. It sealed the fate of the Italian squadron. Guns were already trained round on the correct bearing, all ready to open fire. The twenty years of diligent training and retraining for a night action that the British battle fleets had undertaken were now to receive their just fulfillment.[67]

In pathetic contrast, the main armaments of the Italian heavy cruisers, also closing the stopped *Pola* on a converging course with the British fleet, were trained fore and aft, much to the later astonishment of the British observers. The Italian Navy had early on rejected the principle of night fighting with heavy ships; their only training had been in the repulsing of night destroyer torpedo attacks. Thus, only their secondary armament was ready for action. In serene confidence at their immunity, the *Zara* and *Fiume* steamed into the muzzles of the three British veterans.

These two heavy cruisers, led by the destroyer *Affieri*, in order *Zara* and *Fiume*, then the destroyers *Gioberti, Carducci,* and *Oriani*, were picked up at 10:20 by the *Valiant*, then three minutes later by the destroyer *Stuart.* At 10:25, Commander Edelsten, the chief of staff on the *Warspite*'s bridge, searching the horizon off the starboard bow, impassively reported that there were two large cruisers, with a smaller one ahead, crossing ahead of the battle line. Everyone turned away from the *Pola*, "and there they were." Instantly, Admiral Cunningham brought his great ships back into line-ahead by short-range wireless signal. The huge guns tracked silently round towards the enemy ships now less than 4,000 yards distant and from the director-tower came the unruffled message that they had the target in view, an unspoken hint, as Admiral Cunningham acknowledged later, that his finger was "itching on the trigger."

The destroyers *Greyhound* and *Griffin*, exposed on the engaged side of the battle line, were told to make themselves scarce quickly, and the carrier was likewise ordered out of the way to safety as there was nothing she could contribute to a proper surface action other than present a large, ungainly target for enemy torpedoes. As the *Greyhound* pulled clear, her searchlight beam shone out and shone unblinkingly on the *Fiume*, third ship of the Italian line. As it did so, the first massive salvos crashed out from the three British battleships.

The time was 10:27 when the *Warspite* and *Valiant* loosed off almost simultaneous broadsides, illuminating with their own searchlights as they did so. Three of the flagships turrets were bearing and this first salvo was an outstanding one. From a range of about 2,900 yards, five, or even six, of the 15-inch shells smashed straight into the *Fiume*, and the *Warspite*'s 4.5s added their weight to the devastation. Within seconds, the 6-inch battery was also firing at point-blank range. The effect was memorable. Admiral Cunningham wrote: "Our searchlight shone out with the first salvo, and provided full illumination for what was a ghastly sight. Full in the beam I saw our six great projectiles flying through the air. Five out of the six hit a few feet below the level of the cruiser's upper deck and burst with splashes of brilliant flame."[68]

Observers saw the whole of the Italian ship's Y turret aft blown overboard. A second 15-inch broadside from the *Warspite* followed at once in the light of a starshell, and three rapid-fire 6-inch salvos went to the same target. Astern of the flagship, the *Valiant* had also selected *Fiume* as her initial target, and she rapidly pumped a four-gun 15-inch salvo into this unfortunate vessel, before finding that her two after-turrets, like the *Warspite*'s X turret, would not bear. The range of her opening salvo was 4,000 yards.

The *Fiume*, a mass of flames and with a heavy list, drove out of line and into the darkness, a blazing charnel house. Both leading British battleships immediately switched targets to Admiral Cattaneo's flagship, the *Zara*. The *Valiant*'s second broadside at this ship equaled the *Warspite*'s first, and several hits were at once scored. Nicely locked into the *Zara*, the *Valiant*'s main armament then proceeded to give an awesome demonstration of their skill and accuracy. In the space of just a few minutes, her gunners poured five 15-inch broadsides into the *Zara*.

Again, Admiral Cunningham describes the scene:

When the *Warspite* shifted to the other cruiser, I watched the *Valiant* pounding her ship to bits. Her rapidity of fire astonished me. Never would I have believed it possible with these heavy guns. . . . The

plight of the Italian cruisers was indescribable. One saw whole turrets and masses of other heavy debris whirling through the air and
splashing into the sea, and in a short time the ships themselves were
nothing but glowing torches on fire from stem to stern.[69]

Once the *Formidable* had cleared her bows, the *Barham* also was able to
add her quota of 15-inch shells to the Italians' discomfiture. She had been
aligning up on the stationary *Pola*, which would have rapidly shared the two
sisters' fate but for their sudden advent on the scene. This saved her for the
time being, for the *Barham* shifted her attention to these vessels. Although
both of the *Barham*'s searchlights shattered and went out on the initial salvo,
there was enough illumination for her to make accurate practice on her own
account without them. It was, recalled her gunner, the best night shoot that
she had ever carried out.

Her first broadside had been against the leading Italian vessel, the
destroyer *Alfieri*, and from 3,100 yards, these shells were also almost all direct
hits, turning the destroyer into a blazing shambles within seconds before she
hauled out of line. The *Barham* then added six 15-inch broadsides and seven 6-
inch salvos to the concentration of fire, hitting the *Zara*. In all, about two score
one-ton shells pulverized this once-proud heavy cruiser. Again, her forward
gun turrets were seen spinning over the side as she took on a heavy list, and
with her bridge and hull a mass of flames and smoke, she heeled over to port.

Just after 8:30, the rear of the Italian line, the three destroyers, was
observed, and the *Warspite* again shifted target to pay her attention to the
leading one, the *Gioberti*. At 2,500 yards range, a combined 15-inch and 6-
inch broadside was sent against her and was seen to straddle. The British
destroyer *Havock* was also straddled when the battleships turned 90 degrees
to starboard to avoid a possible torpedo attack, but she escaped unscathed.
Likewise, the ungainly *Formidable*, scuttling off to the north, was taken into
sight by the battle fleet's searchlights, and only hasty action prevented her
also being on the receiving end of a 6-inch salvo.

At 10:38, on completion of their emergency turn, the battleships
resumed their course 280 degrees in line ahead, being rejoined by the carrier later. All the flotillas had been sent off on their own to finish off the Italian fleet, which it was hoped, still included the Italian battleship. The big
ships steamed on through the night completely unescorted, at eighteen
knots, to await the dawn.

But although the *Pola* joined the *Zara*, *Fiume*, *Affieri*, and *Carducci* on the
seabed that night, the commander in chief did not have the satisfaction of
sending the Italian flagship to the bottom alongside them. She gained clear
to safety. It was nonetheless a magnificent victory achieved without a single

casualty to the British fleet. It set the seal on the firm establishment of the dominance of the British battleship in the Mediterranean. What Calabria had initiated and Spartivento had reinforced, Matapan finalized. Never again did the Italian battle fleet venture out against British force when it was known that a battleship was included in the force. Once it was established in all future operations that a heavy ship was present, the Italians turned back. It was a supreme vindication of the battleship in waters that before the war, experts had claimed would be untenable.

CHAPTER 5

The Broad Atlantic

During the whole course of the Great War, the German High Seas Fleet had never gained the high seas. Despite its grand name and the towering ambition of its founders and admirals, the farthest it ever got from its German base ports was south of the latitude of Bergen in Norway. But already, by the summer of 1940, German pocket battleships had ranged as far afield as the Indian Ocean, and their two main units had penetrated the northern patrols to the south of Iceland. What would happen if these long range vessels, the *Scharnhorst* and *Gneisenau*, ever broke clean and got in among Britain's Atlantic convoy routes hardly bore consideration; the implications were too fraught. Should they evade the British Home Fleet, which in poor weather conditions was a practical proposition, then all they had to stand between them and mass slaughter of every convoy they happened upon were the few isolated and obsolete British battleships that were allocated to the defence of the most important of these great assemblies that daily crossed the great, broad ocean.

Certainly, none of the normal escort forces could oppose them for they were made up of old destroyers, corvettes and similar escorts, whose major function was anti-submarine defence. The torpedo armaments of most of the destroyers had either been cut down or taken out altogether in order to mount more and more weaponry for use against the U-boats. They offered no serious threat at all. The smaller escorts of course were even more impotent in the face of serious surface attack; most of them barely had speeds, at best, of seventeen knots, while the two German battlecruisers had a comfortable speed of over thirty. Should these two be joined by their even larger sisters now fast approaching completion, the *Bismarck* and *Tirpitz*, then they would present the Admiralty with a headache of enormous proportions against which, with their severely stretched and mainly obsolete forces, and the enormous area to be protected, they had no real answer. The decision taken by the German Navy before the war to go ahead with the construction of new battleships was therefore very quickly and obviously vindicated. Against the *Tirpitz* or *Bismarck* at large in the wide Atlantic, there was no answer from land-based bombers, from 8-inch or 6-inch cruisers, from short-ranged fleet aircraft, or from local escorts. The only deterrent, which was both available and effective, was the British battleship. No other factor prevented the German big ships from doing as they pleased among the convoy routes. Although the ships they encountered were usually the older vessels, with far less speed and armor, it was still sufficient to save the convoy by threat alone.

Of course, their easy conquests on land gave the new German Navy unrivalled opportunities to conduct such operations, with bases in Norway and the French Atlantic coast outflanking completely the traditional British blockade points across the North Sea outlets. Their magnificent support organization, cooperation by the submarine arm, and long-range aerial reconnaissance all added greatly to their advantages. Their only defect was that it all came their way too soon. All the benefits were offset by the galling fact that far from building too many of the derided and "obsolete" battleships for Atlantic raiding, they actually had completed too few of them to cash in on all their unexpected assets. Nevertheless, with two battlecruisers, two pocket battleships, and two heavy cruisers on hand, they were able to consider an offensive that would leave the pitifully small British Home Fleet stretched as never before. And when the *Bismarck* and *Tirpitz* were ready . . .

However, there had been a long lull since the early days of the raids by the pocket battleships while the conquest of the continent took place. The damage suffered by the main units here prevented them from mounting their first serious sorties for many months which gave the Admiralty some time to absorb the entry of Italian battle fleet and to concentrate the units in home waters on the more imminent problem of how to meet a very real and vital threat of invasion. This brought another sharp clash of opinion between Churchill and his naval commander, Admiral Forbes, over priorities and dispositions. The issues were also complicated over the possible fate of the French battleships, nearing completion in their Atlantic ports as the Panzers raced to the sea, and, later, with the prime minister's obsession to strike at the Vichy in French North Africa and elsewhere, which further diluted Britain's limited battleship strength for a period. It is perhaps as well that the Italians were overawed so quickly by Cunningham and that the German battle fleet was not yet ready to sortie forth in earnest. Let us consider each of the problems in rough order of timing.

It will be recalled how much importance the Admiralty placed on the early completion of the new French battleships *Jean Bart* and *Richelieu* to compensate for the expected delays in getting the *King George V* and *Prince of Wales* to sea. The French had responded with a will, and although not yet fully complete in June 1940, these two giants were seaworthy and were being completed at the Atlantic ports of Brest and St. Nazaire, respectively. Ironic as it now seemed, their very state of near-completion now weighed very much as a minus factor in the distribution of naval power now that France's defeat and subjugation were certain. Should these two vessels be taken over by the Germans and added to the *Bismarck* and *Tirpitz*, then the balance of seapower would shift overwhelmingly to the Axis. They would then be able to show two brand-new German battleships, two brand-new Vichy battleships, and four equally brand-new Italian battleships against the first two King Georges, both of which were, ship-for-ship, inferior to each of the Axis vessels. No wonder Churchill and the cabinet considered the most desperate measure necessary to ensure that they either sailed to safer waters or were destroyed where they lay.

Fortunately, Darlan's attitude at this moment in time was politely hostile. No one was going to tell France what its could or should do with its navy, but at the time, it was still allied with Britain. The French were down but not quite out, and the dockyards made supreme efforts to get the ships away in time. By magnificent efforts, it was done.

Certainly, when Alexander and Pound met Darlan at Bordeaux on the afternoon of June 18, the Frenchman seemed willing to cooperate to the limit. He promised that should an armistice take place between France and Germany, his fleet would fight to the end and, further, that "anything that escaped would go to a friendly country or would be destroyed." He added that in the case of the *Jean Bart*, this latter possibility must be quite likely, for if she failed to sail from St. Nazaire before the twentieth, the tide conditions would immobilize her there for another month. She would be destroyed then, rather than let the Germans capture her; plans were ready for this eventuality. The *Richelieu* at Bordeaux was more happily placed and should have that day have sailed for the safety of Dakar in French West Africa. Not only did Darlan promise this, but he also went so far as to recommend that ultimately the *Richelieu* should continue her completion in a North American dockyard, secure from German bombing before taking her place in the Allied line. And so it fell out, or at least the first part of the pledge.

The *Richelieu*, which had just finished running her trials, was hustled away on June 18 and reached Dakar in safety five days later. With the *Jean Bart*, it was touch and go. The Admiralty knew enough of Darlan's mental processes to make sure that they had on hand some insurance should his change of heart take place too soon, and accordingly, they sent over Vice Adm. T. J. Hallett aboard the destroyer *Vanquisher* to make absolutely certain that one of the two options taken by the French was carried out. Tugs were sent ahead to aid the French to undock the great vessel, and they finally got her clear. Anthony Heckstall-Smith described the dramatic scenes that accompanied this escape:

One boiler had been ready since June 11, but only two of *Jean Bart*'s four propellers were in place, and while their turbine drives had been installed, their engines had never been turned over under their own power.

But at 3:30 A.M., with all hands manning the capstan bars, for there was still no power to work the winches, surrounded by tugs, the great ship began to move slowly.

Inch by inch, foot by foot, the tugs nudged and hauled her clear of the dock.

Then, in the pitch darkness, she missed a fairway buoy in the narrow winding channel, and ran aground.

It took six tugs, including those sent in by Vice Admiral Hallett, more than half an hour to shift the huge vessel, and by the time she was afloat again the eastern sky was already lightening.

At 4:40, as *Jean Bart* reached the entrance of the Loire, Ronarch anxiously scanned the sky for the squadron of Moraines due to give him fighter cover. Instead, he saw Stukas winging their way towards him out of the rising sun.[1]

The *Jean Bart* beat off this dive-bomber attack and, thanks to the help of the tugs the British had thoughtfully provided, got away, refueling as she went and watched by the *Vanquisher* until she steered south. She arrived at the French Moroccan port of Casablanca on June 22.

Elsewhere, too, the French Navy still fought the enemy with resolution and bravery. Although flight was the main concern for the bulk of the heavy units at Cherbourg, at least one French battleship used her guns against the Germans at last, when Admiral Abrial utilized the *Courbet* as part of the port's defenses, and the old veteran fired on Rommel's approaching tank columns to some effect. Alas, it was the only time.

On July 3, when Operation Catapult, the taking of the Vichy ships or their destruction, was put into effect, only two French battleships were still in British waters. These were the *Courbet* at Portsmouth and the *Paris* lying at Plymouth; both were taken without loss of life. Both had as uneventful a war as their sisters, being utilized solely in the role of depot ships or antiaircraft batteries for most of the conflict. The only time one put to sea was on her final voyage back to France, for the ancient *Courbet* was one of the many obsolete vessels used as part of the artificial harbors constructed off Ouistreham to supplied the Allied armies freeing her homeland.

On July 7, the *Richelieu* was tackled for the first time. A small task force, consisting of the small carrier *Hermes* and light forces, arrived off Dakar and presented similar terms to those offered at Mers-el-Kebir. They were treated with equal contempt and a gallant attack was made by a motor boat from the *Hermes*, which dropped four depth charges under the *Richelieu*'s stern, designed to immobilize her by destroying her rudders. This failed because of the shallow water of the harbor, but a torpedo-bomber strike later detonated these charges with the desired effect. The repairs took a year to complete, but unfortunately, her armament was not affected, and she was to have ample revenge for this humiliation in due course.

The *Jean Bart* at Casablanca was also scheduled for similar treatment at the hands of Force H, but this was subsequently cancelled when it was realized that with no main armament shipped, and little likelihood of it being put aboard in the foreseeable future this vessel posed no great threat. The vigil maintained by the destroyer *Watchman* was called off. She was to receive the treatment planned for her at a later date, although it was from an American battleship and not a British one when the time came. This episode behind them, the Royal Navy could concentrate on the more pressing problems of defense against the expected German invasion.[2]

While France was still showing some semblance of resistance, the Admiralty had been considering their options in case of the worst. On May 17, they made the startling suggestion that the Home Fleet's main strength should be transferred to Plymouth. Admiral Forbes regarded this suggestion as quite wrong and said so. A long discussion followed on the best employment of the British capital ships while the invasion threat loomed over the islands. As Captain Roskill has stated at some length, this was a problem that had been discussed before, but now the factor and apparent supreme danger of air power clouded earlier clarity. [3]

Vice Admiral Hezlet points out that off Norway, the Home Fleet had been worsted when only lacing one German *Luftflotte* and that any invasion attempt would be covered by no less four such aerial armadas.[4] This seemed to show that the Royal Navy's task was an impossible one. However, it somewhat ignores the fact that once the British ships were in among the enemy's slow-moving invasion convoys, they could wreak havoc and, at the same time, be almost immune from air attack through fear of the German airmen sinking their own ships. Also, Britain had 1,500 small craft, from destroyers downward, on hand to take this drastic action, and even had the entire Royal Air Force have been wiped out during the battle of Britain, enough of these warships would have got through to the convoys, even in daylight, over the short distance required, to ensure their annihilation, Luftwaffe or not. Of course, British ship casualties would have been heavy, provided that the German troop-carrying ships were on the bottom and the Luftwaffe could bomb at will once more, but the point is that the invasion would have been defeated, about 150,000 of Germany's finest troops would have been drowned and all their landing craft, which had taken much effort and scraping of barrels to assemble, would have been gone for good. It is hardly likely that the Germans would have wished to repeat the experiment, even if another fleet could have been built. The Luftwaffe might have had the satisfaction of sinking twenty or thirty destroyers and a host of irrelevant small craft, but the invasion would have never taken place.

Let us go further and assume first that the RAF had been annihilated completely, a remote possibility, and also that after heavy fighting in the English Channel, about half of the German landing barges had gotten through in sufficient numbers for the German Army to effect a landing and establish a beachhead. How would they then have been supplied, let alone reinforced? For even had all the invasion protection craft have been destroyed in the process, the Home Fleet was still intact, and there were still more destroyers, at least another forty, plus many more small craft to be employed. It could have possibly succeeded had the German Navy been strong enough to provide some sort of fighting strength on the surface to guard them, but after Norway, the German fleet had, for several months to come, ceased to exist as a fighting force at all, save for the U-boats.[5]

While trusting in the Royal Air Force to hold firm and making all available preparations to repel the German landing should it come against all the odds, Churchill was quite confident that as before, the Royal Navy would provide the sure shield that it always had. "Seapower, when properly understood, is a wonderful thing. The passage of an army across salt water in the face of superior fleets and flotillas is an almost impossible feat."[6]

A very perceptive naval historian, writing at the very time when the Germans were—or seemed—poised to deliver their final knock-out blow, had enough confidence in his service to accurately predict:

It can therefore be said with confidence that, in these modern days, the combination of sea and air power affords as great a safeguard against seaborne military invasion as has ever existed before. The point is important in view of the opinion the writer has heard not infrequently expressed by civilians in the last few years that if the Germans could manage successfully to invade France, they would then be in a position, somehow or other, to invade England. So long as we remain superior at sea and reasonably well equipped in the air, such a contingency can be discounted.[7]

Churchill was of the same opinion. In a reply to an MP enquiring how the defence of London was to be conducted he replied with characteristic undauntedness: "You may rest assured that we should fight in every street of

London and its suburbs. It would *devour* an invading army, assuming one ever got so far. *We hope however to drown the bulk of them in the salt sea*" [emphasis added].[8] It is also typical that, even then, when Great Britain still had the world's largest navy and the bulk of the population, even members of Parliament should have overlooked this obvious point. The natural instinct for defense by sea, before the enemy ever stepped ashore at all, had been largely eroded by 1940 in most of the nation. Luckily, the prime minister still had it, and Britain still had a navy capable of carrying it out.

However, the fact that all the German heavy ships were either under repair or refitting, at this crucial moment in our history was not known for certain by the Cabinet or the Admiralty. It was thought probable that the *Scharnhorst* and *Gneisenau*, with the other bigger cruisers, would be utilized in the invasion as a feint in the North Sea to draw the bulk of our heavy ships away from the Channel. It was to deal with this prospect that Admiral Forbes determined upon retaining his battleships in the north. He agreed to the dispatch of considerable numbers of valuable light forces south, light cruisers, and fleet destroyers, to back up the anti-invasion flotillas, although their ultimate dispositions and the duration of their stay caused further commotion. However, in the positioning of the heavy ships, final accord was reached at an early stage.

The Admiralty had followed the Plymouth suggestion with one that at least two of the Home Fleet battleships should be sent to Liverpool, even though Admiral Forbes had agreed to sail his main strength down to Rosyth should the Germans seem ready to sail an invasion fleet across the North Sea. This second Admiralty suggestion went the same way as the first and Admiral Forbes kept ready at Scapa his heavy ships. Because of his failure to catch the German battlecruisers during the first winter of the war, Admiral Forbes had received the cruel and unjustified epithet of "Wrong-Way Charlie" from those who did not understand the problems involved. From his spirited defense of what he believed to be correct policy for his fleet during this difficult period, he certainly deserved a more fitting title, for he was proved absolutely correct in his interpretation of the situation.

The need to reinforce the Mediterranean had led to a further serious inroad into his limited strength at this time although by mid-July it was hoped to add both the *Nelson* and *Barham* to his strength once they had worked up following their refits from battle damage received earlier on,[9] but the earliest the first of the new battleships could now hope to join his flag was mid-October, when the *King George V* would be ready. Further complications would ensure that the *Barham* did not join Admiral Forbes's flag that summer.

Closer to the English Channel, the battleships contributed some indirect support, for two of the 13.5-inch guns from the demilitarized *Iron Duke* were to be adapted as part of the coastal defence system and mounted on railway mountings, while four of the *Hood*'s obsolete 5.5-inch secondary armament were also commandeered for a similar purpose on the south coast. The battleship *Revenge* was brought south to Plymouth and then Portsmouth to provide heavy gun support for Churchill's anti-invasion counterstrike, as was the old "dummy" battleship *Centurion*. The *Revenge* soon made her mark.

On September 13, the battleship put to sea, escorted by the destroyers of the 5th Flotilla. Her destination was enemy-held France; her target, the massed ranks of the invasion barges moored at Cherbourg. Silently, the *Revenge* slipped across the black waters of the channel with her ring of destroyers around her. The squadron achieved complete surprise. Aboard the destroyer *Javelin*, leading the screen, her commander, later Rear Admiral Pugsley, recorded the scene as it unfolded:

> To seaward, on the bridges of the British ships, which have remained apparently undetected, bearings of navigational marks seen in the light of gun flashes and bomb bursts, are read off on the compass cards and positions carefully plotted on the charts.
>
> In single line ahead with the battleship in the middle of the line, we lead round on to the firing course and prepare to open fire. As the order to do so reaches us, from the dim, black mass astern which is the *Revenge* suddenly erupts a blinding sheet of flame from the great fifteen-inch guns. A few seconds and then the sound and shock reach us, followed by the diminishing rumble of the huge shells, each a ton in weight, as they hurtle shoreward.
>
> It is an awe-inspiring sight. In this era of nuclear bombs, it would be as puny and out-moded a use of explosive as one of Nelson's broadsides seemed then. But these things are relative and, in the darkness of that still September night, it is an impressive exposition of controlled explosive power.[10]

That same day the invasion scare reached its peak as the air fighting mounted. From Scapa, Admiral Forbes sailed the *Hood*, *Nelson*, and *Rodney*, with two cruisers and eight destroyers, to Rosyth to meet the threat. But all remained quiet. In fact, the following day, Raeder was explaining that the invasion was best put off as things were not developing as hoped. They never did.

Well before this date, Hitler had turned his attentions to a greater priority. He had never wanted to fight Britain anyway: his bitterest enemy was Stalin, at that moment his loyal and helpful ally. It was against this tyrant that Hitler's thoughts had already turned long since. A land campaign he could conduct with confidence. A descent on Britain—defiant and growing in strength across waters he could never control and under skies he was failing to control—was not to his taste at all. And so the crisis passed.[11]

However, even before September, a new facet had been added to the Royal Navy's widespread commitments with the reemergence once more of the "Vichy problem" onto the scene. The ramifications and arguments that led to the mounting of the hastily prepared and ill-fated Dakar expedition, at the insistence of Churchill despite the more pressing needs of the moment, have been fully examined in a recent volume by Marder.[12] There is no need for me to delve into this subject; suffice it to say that an expedition was so mounted, codenamed Operation Menace, in which it was aimed to peacefully disembark Free French forces, under the imperious General de Gaulle, at the Vichy port of Dakar, Senegal, in French West Africa. It had great strategic importance and it was hoped that the occupation would the first step in a bloodless reestablishment of the French African Empire back on the side of the Allies. It was still not realized at home just how much the defeatist and pro-German Vichy factor had become the dominant voice in the French colonies. To provide a force of arms that would be both overawing and—should it come to a limited use of force—decisive, the Royal Navy was ordered to supply the escort and bombardment force for this first demonstration of Gaullic charisma. Accordingly, a force was to be assembled off Dakar, Force M, drawn from available units of both the Home Fleet and Force H at Gibraltar. This mixed group, under the command of Vice Adm. J. H. D. Cunningham, was given the go-ahead on August 29, and two days later, the warships and transports sailed from Scapa, Liverpool, and the Clyde to rendezvous with the Gibraltar section on September 13.

The most important of the warships of this force were the battleships *Barham* and *Resolution*, the aircraft carrier *Ark Royal*, the heavy cruisers *Devonshire* and *Cumberland*, and the brand-new light cruiser *Fiji*, together with four modern destroyers from the Home Fleet (the *Inglefield, Echo, Eclipse,* and *Escapade*) and six from Force H (the *Faulknor, Foresight, Forester, Fortune, Fury,* and *Greyhound*), all under five years old. Considering the shortage of modern flotilla craft at this time and the scarcity of battleships and carriers, this force represented quite a slice of modern British naval strength for such a distant diversion. Nor was that all for the greater part of the troops embarked ultimately turned out to be British.

There was never any chance of a peaceful occupation of Dakar; Vichy policy was firmly in control there, reinforced by the events at Mers-el-Kebir and the British blockade of France. The hopes that the appearance of such a majestic fleet over the horizon would persuade the Vichy that resistance was futile were equally sanguine, despite the impressive pen-portrait that Churchill sketched out. In the event when the fleet did arrive it was in the thick off-shore mist and fog that characterized this part of the West African coast and a chance for Hollywood-type dramatics was lost in the haze, both actual and, as it turned out, mental, that beset this operation.

Other more dramatic events also helped frustrate the hopes of the British and Free French. In addition to the coastal defense guns installed at Dakar (nine 9.4-inch, four 6-inch, four 5.4-inch, and six smaller guns manned mainly by native troops under French officers), the battleship *Richelieu* still lay in the harbor, protected by the breakwater. She was immobile because of the damage received in the earlier attacks, but her nominal armament of eight 15-inch and sixteen 6-inch guns was potentially an alarming factor. In fact, although mounted, most were not in a fit state for firing and her effective armament at the time of the attack was one twin 15-inch turret (B turret) and one triple 6-inch turret. There were also three submarines, the *Ajax, Bévéziers,* and *Persée,* which were a menace because Force M's slender destroyer screen. Churchill had not forgotten the *Richelieu,* but he viewed her as much a bonus prize, should the operation go as hoped, rather than as a deterrent.[13]

Then there was the escape of three Vichy light cruisers and three large destroyers past Gibraltar. As it turned out, they were bound for Dakar, after a short stop at Casablanca, in order to reinforce Vichy prestige there after the fall of had to the Free French earlier. Nothing was known of the descent of Force M upon Dakar at that time, and the dispatch of his squadron, known as Force Y, was merely coincidence. In London, of course, it was assumed that the worst had happened, that the Vichy had full details of the Menace operation, and that they were dispatching the warships, laden with experts and gunners, to stiffen the defenses. The accurate and spirited resistance put up by the colonial native gunners added to this suspicion afterwards.

After the *Renown* and her flotilla had sailed too late to stop the French ships from reaching Casablanca safely, various cruiser forces were sent posthaste to stop them from going any farther. The heavy cruisers *Australia, Cumberland,* and *Cornwall* and the light cruiser *Delhi* were all added to Cunningham's fleet (the *Fiji* had been torpedoed and badly damaged by the *U-32* on the first and had to return home for a refit lasting five months). Despite much huffing and puffing (but not shooting, the only *effective* method of persuading the Vichy), most of the French squadron eventually reached Dakar intact. This gave the defense the additional protection from the 6-inch cruisers *Georges Leygues* and *Montcalm* and the heavy destroyers *L'Audacieux, Fantasque,* and *Le Malin;* the last was much larger, faster, and more heavily armed than the British destroyers present.[14]

In truth, Operation Menace was beset with disaster and ill fortune from the beginning, and as the operation continued, the muddle and indecision got worse, and the casualties mounted with nothing to show for them except increased Vichy confidence.

After de Gaulle's peaceful approaches had been rebuffed on the morning of September 23, it was decided to see whether the battle squadron could persuade the French that the fight was hopeless. Accordingly, the heavy ships led in through the fog just before 9:00 A.M. All the advantage of the British battleships longer-range 15-inch guns was rendered null and void by the mist and haze, and it was at the close range of only 9,000 yards that Cunningham finally turned his battle line into position, under sporadic fire from both the forts and then the *Richelieu*.

At 11:04, the British ships finally commenced returning the fire; the *Barham* and *Resolution* between them fired more than 100 15-inch shells at the forts and the French battleship through the murk, in an engagement lasting about half an hour. The damage caused to their targets was virtually nonexistent. Rather than persist in this type of aimless bombardment, and ever mindful of his orders to use no more force than necessary, Cunningham broke off the action and withdrew. However, the French had made better practice in reply and had scored a hit with a 9.2-inch shell on the heavy cruiser *Cumberland* that seriously damaged her engine room and wrecked her main switchboard. Her speed reduced to ten knots, the *Cumberland* limped away to Bathurst for repair. The shell had penetrated her thin side plating above her armored belt, and she was thus effectively out of the battle within thirty minutes. Nor was this all. The submarines *Ajax* and *Persée* sought to attack and, in pursuing them, the destroyers *Inglefield* and *Foresight* got in too close, and both were damaged by shore fire.

The *Persée* was taken under fire by the *Barham*'s secondary battery and sunk by the destroyers after being damaged by a 6-inch shell. The only other hit scored by the battleships was a single 15-inch shell, which damaged the freighter *Porthos*. Despite the lack of success scored by the heavy guns, the accuracy of *Barham*'s shooting against the Vichy submarine shows what could have been done had the conditions for spotting been more favorable. It also reflects credit on her gunners, especially when it is remembered that she was taking part in this operation after having only just recommissioned from her refit and that this was instead of the normal shake-down cruise customary to enable the crew to work together as a team once more.

Nonetheless, it had been a disappointing start and this poor showing was compounded that same afternoon when an attempt by the Free French to get their troops ashore under cover of the mist failed when communications, both visual and electronic, broke down. The force withdrew for the night somewhat dispirited.

On the twenty-fourth, the ships of Force M again closed Dakar following the rejection of an ultimatum by the Vichy commander. The mist was still present, although visibility was slightly better than on the twenty-third. The fog was still sufficient however to rule out, yet again, any attempt at long-range fire to nullify the defenses. It was hoped that aircraft from the *Ark Royal* would be able to bomb targets in conjunction with the renewed cannonade from the sea, and Skua dive-bombers were dispatched with 500-pound semiarmor-piercing (SAP) bombs in an attempt to put the *Richelieu*'s one active turret out of action. These attacks were also thwarted by the poor weather conditions, and the Skuas could do no more than report two near-misses on the battleship. Nor did further attacks, using Swordfish with puny 250-pound bombs, have any better luck. As Marder rightly records: "One cannot imagine that the 250-pound SAP bombs of the British aircraft would have much effect on a battleship so heavily armored (belt, 9 to 16 inches, deck, 8 inches). "We might as well have dropped bricks!" the commanding officer of the squadron, Lieutenant Commander Johnstone, ruefully remarked. I imagine the aim was to do very temporary damage only to the ship by breaking up control facilities—bridges, aerials, boats, etc."[15]

If that was indeed the aim, it was to no avail, nor did air attacks on the forts have the slightest effect whatsoever. Meanwhile, the Vichy submarines had sortied to attack the battle line. In this first attempt, they were frustrated, for the destroyer *Fortune* picked up an asdic contact, warned the battle fleet, and dropped a single charge to keep the submarine down. So accurate was this solitary charge placed that within seconds the Vichy submarine *Ajax* bobbed up with a white flag flying. She was boarded, her crew taken captive, and she was scuttled by the British. The *Fortune* then dropped a depth charge pattern on her hulk to make quite certain.

While steaming to rejoin the formation, the *Fortune* was taken under heavy and accurate fire by a 6-inch cruiser, to which she could make a limited, although spirited, reply with her 4.7s. The destroyer's position was an unenviable one, because the British squadron could not see what was going on through the murk, and the *Fortune* was being straddled. However, all the time, she was closing the gap between herself and the battle line, and eventually the heavy ships were able to repay her earlier good work in kind. Her captain later described the incident thus: "The cruiser steadily closed on us, and thus it was that she was presently sighted by the *Resolution*. The battleship's 15-inch turrets trained on her swiftly, and fired a broadside in a great cloud of tawny cordite smoke and a thunder of sound. The cruiser thought little of this treatment, and promptly and wisely retired at high speed. For ourselves, the *Resolution* became one of our dearest friends from that moment."[16]

The second bombardment lasted not much longer than had the first the previous day and the results were equally unrewarding. The French batteries opened fire at 9:35 A.M., to which the two British battleships and two heavy cruisers immediately replied. Both British ships fired salvos at the *Richelieu* initially, and she received one hit from a 15-inch splinter, which penetrated her hull above the waterline but caused no serious damage. The *Resolution*'s director training gear failed after ten minutes, which did much to nullify the effectiveness of her shooting. The *Resolution* later shifted target to engage the guns of the Cape Manuel battery but failed to silence them completely. The air-spotter work was ineffective and all fire was hampered by the mist, made worse by a thick smoke screen laid by a French destroyer, which eventually hid the target completely.

Despite firing almost another 100 heavy shells, not a single hit had been scored on the fifty-odd merchant ships packed in the harbor or on any battery. On this occasion, the return fire was equally as ineffective, and in fact, the most serious damage sustained by the Vichy in this engagement occurred when one of the guns of the *Richelieu*'s solitary active turret burst. She was able to resume firing with the remaining pair, however, but no hits were scored on the British ships, which were working from between 13,600 and 15,000 yards out from the harbor.

Cunningham again broke off the action at 10:24 and withdrew to again consider the position. It was not promising. All that the two bombardments had achieved seemed to be a stiffening of Vichy resistance and a boost to their already considerable ego. At 1:00 P.M., the British line again moved in to resume the duel. Fire recommenced from 17,000 yards at 1:05, and the *Resolution* took on the battery while the *Barham* re-engaged the *Richelieu*. The heavy cruisers were not involved. Again the action was brief, the smoke-screens again hid the targets within minutes and not a single hit was made on either battleship's target.

By contrast, the *Richelieu* made excellent practice, as did the forts. Although the two 15-inch guns of the former failed to hit, the smaller guns of the forts caused considerable inconvenience. The *Barham* was hit by four medium-caliber shells, 9.4- or 6-inch, during this action. Although too puny to hurt a battleship, the hits were a blow to British pride. The *Resolution* was also straddled at this time, but there were no casualties. By 1:26, Cunningham had had enough of this humiliation and yet again pulled out. Vichy morale reached a new peak as they departed and justly so. There seemed to be no will to make a determined and full-blooded assault and end it all decisively, probably due to the fact that the spilling of French blood on the scale of Mers-el-Kebir was to be avoided. However, Churchill had signaled the commanders to "stop at nothing," but that didn't stop the bombardment fizzling out under heavy, if erratic, French air attack, after another two hundred rounds of heavy shell had been shot away into Africa in vain.

That evening, de Gaulle went aboard the *Barham* for a conference with Cunningham and General Irwin. After agreeing that the operation should be called off, as he was clearly not to be welcomed ashore as a liberator after all and the British could not force the issue on the present showing, de Gaulle returned to his headquarters ship and broke the news to his staff. However, completely inaccurate reports from the Fleet Air Arm made the two British commanders change their minds and decide on one last effort the next day, much to the general's surprise and Churchill's delight.

Dawn on the twenty-fifth seemed to bear out their wisdom in deciding to try again. The haze and mist had gone, the weather was fine and the visibility was perfect. Now at last the two British battleships would be able to use their superior range and finally knock out the courageous and effective French guns and thus decide the day. Alas, it was not to be, this unlucky. and muddled operation was to end on the same low-key as it had begun.

The targets allocated to the *Barham* and *Resolution* were the same as those of the previous day, and at 6:00 A.M., the big ships were steaming steadily towards the shore once more ready to go into action at 9:00, but this time, the 8-inch cruisers *Devonshire* and *Australia* were also allocated targets. Fire commenced at 8:58, with the *Richelieu* again taking the lead with her two-gun turret with the range down to 23,000 yards, and the batteries joined in soon after, although it was beyond their effective limits.

Meanwhile, the standing air patrols sent out from the *Ark Royal* had been driven off by French fighters and thus failed to spot the sole surviving Vichy submarine, the *Bévéziers*, from Dakar, which had taken up a patrol position on the probable line of approach of the British force. Nor did the destroyer screen detect her in time. The Vichy captain was able to use his intimate knowledge of British signals, from the time when both had fought Germans instead of each other, to good advantage against his former ally.

As the flag hoist "Blue 7," signifying the turn onto the bombarding course, was hauled down from the *Barham*'s yard at 9:01, the *Bévézier* fired a full salvo of torpedoes at the turning point from only 2,500 yards range. The four oncoming tracks were instantly spotted by the British ships, and the *Barham* combed them and got away with it. The *Resolution* was not so fortunate, however. As her great bulk slid around under full helm, two torpedoes passed under her hull, and a third struck her fair and square on her port side amidships. The resulting explosion tore a huge hole in her side and she listed over to port alarmingly. Her port boiler room was flooded which reduced her speed to only twelve knots. Several local fires broke out but were soon under control. Listing and forlorn the gallant old veteran limped away out of the fight for good, shielded by a smokescreen from the destroyers, who had failed to sink the Vichy boat in reply.

Meanwhile, the *Barham* continued the duel on her own, commencing to return the *Richelieu*'s fire at 9:05 from a range of 21,000 yards. It should be remembered, however, that this was well within the Vichy battleship's modern guns' range (31,500 yards at 35 degrees elevation as against the 23,400 at 20 degrees elevation in the two unmodernized British ships). Nonetheless, ten minutes after opening fire, the *Barham* was rewarded with a 15-inch shell hit on her larger opponent. The damage was small, and within a short time, the *Richelieu* had returned the compliment, again without serious injury, to the British ship. At 9:12, the *Barham* again ceased firing and broke off the action for the last time. Cunningham was concerned with the condition of the *Resolution* and took his flagship south to protect her. The last salvo left the *Barham*'s guns for Dakar at 9:21. After covering her withdrawal, Cunningham finally decided that enough was enough, and the operation was finally—and humiliatingly—terminated. The chances of resuming the action and putting the *Richelieu* out of action for good were rejected. Churchill was duly notified but he took it well. "There is an age-long argument about ships versus forts," he later wrote in connection with this sorry episode.[17] Nelson had said that a six-gun battery could fight a 100-gun ship of the line. Balfour, in the Dardanelles inquiry, said in 1916: "If the ship has guns which can hit the fort at ranges where the fort cannot reply, the duel is not necessarily so unequal."

This is so and proven to be correct many times during the latter course of the war. However, nothing went right at Dakar, and, in any case, for such an operation the wrong battleships had been sent. Hitting small targets like batteries mounted high up ashore, or the *Richelieu* snug behind her breakwater inside the harbour, takes a skilled and fully competent gun-crew with ideal weather conditions (or did before radar). As we have seen, the *Barham* was expected to do all this on her working-up trip straight from the repair yard and with a completely inefficient system of aerial spotters. This and the dismal weather conditions (besides the haze, it was stifling hot and muggy— very exhausting conditions in which to fight a 15-inch turret), there was about this operation, as about anything to do with the French at this stage of their history, an almost tangible feeling of resigned failure. As with Somerville off Mers-el-Kebir, North at Gibraltar later, and elsewhere, the British commanders on the spot seemed to lack the killer instinct to finish the job. Or as Churchill later phrased it, they appeared not to have "the root of the matter" in them when it came to dealing with the Vichy.

The homeward voyage of the two battleships was a melancholy affair. Although the *Resolution* appeared to be getting the situation under control, Cunningham was forced to take her in tow of the *Barham* early on the morning of September 26, and thus, at a dismal seven knots, they plodded on, reaching Freetown without further incident on the twenty-ninth. Here the *Resolution* lay for six months while sufficient repairs were effected to enable her to sail for home.

She finally arrived at Portsmouth in March 1941 and underwent air attack without being further damaged. The following month, she left Portsmouth for the Philadelphia Navy Yard where, under Lend-Lease, she underwent a proper refit and some modernization; this included, among other things, the elevation of her two forward gun turrets being increased to 30 degrees. Perhaps *the* lesson of Dakar had been applied in her case.[18] But her damage had kept her out of the war for a full twelve months, for she did not rejoin the fleet until September 1941. The *Barham* soon patched up her slight damage and rejoined Force H for a short period before going through the central Mediterranean to join Admiral Andrew Cunningham's main fleet at Alexandria. Her early exploits with that fleet we have already described. She was to have more action yet.

One unfortunate side effect of the failure at Dakar was that it resulted in "reprisals" by the Vichy against Britain. These took the form of two days heavy bombing attacks on Gibraltar on September 24 and 25. In the first, with some sixty bombers operating from Morocco, their target was the *Renown*, the only large ship left on station to poor Admiral Somerville. He felt the failure deeply, for he had courageously made it quite plain that he regarded any operations against the French as both unnecessary and deeply repugnant. Now it was upon him that the blows of vengeance were falling. The *Renown* was nearmissed by two bombs but not damaged. The antiaircraft defense was not effective, and Somerville decided that the safest place for his ships was at sea where they could dodge and rely on their own defenses. "The *Renown* had gone through the north entrance with every antiaircraft gun of her heavy armament blazing. The men of Gibraltar still speak of that tremendous sight."[19]

Somerville's force had spent the next few days "on fruitless patrol" and were thus well out of it when the bombers of Vichy returned in even greater strength the following day. In all, eighty-one twin-engine bombers attacked in waves for over three hours. Some 300 bombs were dropped and many buildings wrecked causing civilian casualties, but no lasting damage was done to the vital dockyard installations and three bombers were shot down in return. The trawler *Stella Sirius* was sunk alongside the outer wall; the only other warship present, the destroyer *Firedrake*, added her quota to the defence barrage and claimed one of the bombers brought down. Four French destroyers also made a sortie to attack British destroyers on patrol in the Straits on the night of September 24–25 without success.

Force H had been based on Gibraltar because of the flexibility that sea power had. Although known mainly for its sterling work in the Mediterranean, Somerville's command was as much at home in the eastern Atlantic at this period of the war. At home, there was still considerable anxiety that the *Richelieu* and *Jean Bart* might both be sailed back to Toulon for their completion, and there combine with the *Strasbourg* to make an impressive Vichy force. The cabinet was determined to prevent this by every means at its disposal. As a result, Force H was again sent out on patrol on September 26 and 27 to intercept the *Richelieu*, but she did not sail. The *Renown* and *Barham* repeated this operation at the end of September.

Ultimately, this problem was solved by diplomacy: Churchill wrote to Roosevelt pointing out to him that "we have been much disturbed by reports of intention of French Government to bring *Jean Bart* and *Richelieu* to the Mediterranean for completion. It is difficult to exaggerate potential danger if this were to happen, and so open the way for these ships to fall under German control."[20] Roosevelt shared that view, and the United States applied pressure on the Vichy, which resulted in both battleships staying put for the next two years. It was an enormous relief, and the solution was found only just in time, for by now, back in Germany, the big ships of the real enemy were beginning to stir from their long hibernation. The potential threat was about to become a very real problem.

During July, the German Navy issued a memorandum dealing with what form the fleet should take now that the war was approaching its termination. They were a trifle premature on that point, but this document, entitled *The Construction of a Post-War Fleet*, positively reaffirmed the German position with regard to the battleship. Despite the poor showing of their big ships to date, the Germans remained confident that "the main protagonist in the war against the enemy's ocean communications is the battleship itself."[21] But in the meantime, they had to fight with what they had. By October 1940, the position for the Germans had vastly improved over July, but there were still few ships that were actually ready to sail; the refits of most of them however were rapidly approaching completion.

To test the water, therefore, the heavy cruiser *Admiral Hipper* was sent out on a raiding mission by herself. This start was far from auspicious for future operations. She left Kiel on September 24 on the first leg of the breakout route up the coast of occupied Norway undetected, but on the twenty-seventh, while at sea to the west of Stavanger, the old trouble with her engines recommenced, and she was forced to break off her sortie. By the end of the month, she was back in port, not St. Nazaire, which had been her destination, but Kiel once more.

The Admiralty information on the *Admiral Hipper* was late, and not until the twenty-eighth did Admiral Forbes sail with his main strength to intercept her. Not surprisingly she was not found. A month later, the pocket battleship *Admiral Scheer* was again ready for deep-water raiding and this time her initial sailing went perfectly. Complete secrecy was achieved when she put out from Brunsbuttel on October 27, having passed through the Kiel Canal from the Baltic earlier. She reached Stavanger on the twenty-eighth without sighting or mishap and then continued northward, evading the heavy air patrols over the North Sea and being equally fortunate in escaping detection when she passed through the Denmark Strait on the last day of the month. Some of her success was thanks to her radar, but most of it was attributable to the atrocious weather conditions that shielded her. She lost two of her crew in the storm, but by November 1, she had escaped safely into the North Atlantic. For four days, she cruised in search of her prey, secure in her complete cloak of anonymity. On November 5, she struck.

In the early afternoon of that day, the *Admiral Scheer* fell in with the independently routed steamship *Mopan* (5,389 tons) while en route to a convoy her reconnaissance plane had sighted earlier in the day. Deciding on boldness, the German captain, Krancke, steered straight for this vessel and ordered her to halt. This order was complied with, and much to the relief of the Germans, no raider warning signal was sent. Dispatching this vessel with shellfire after her crew had taken to the boats Krancke pressed impatiently on toward the convoy. The *Mopan*'s silence had doomed many proud ships that afternoon, for shortly afterward, the *Admiral Scheer* came across the great concourse of thirty-seven fully laden freighters and tankers that was Convoy HX 84 like a bolt from the blue.

The solitary escort for this mass of valuable shipping was the auxiliary cruiser *Jervis Bay*, a 14,000-ton liner armed with 6-inch guns. It was a floating death trap, like the *Rawalpindi*, with no speed, no armor, no defense against submarines, and just a few old pop-guns. As the *Jervis Bay* made repeated challenges, the *Admiral Scheer* continued to approach head-on at high speed as before. Krancke needed to make a quick clean job of the escort, and to do this, he wished to employ both main and secondary armament together in stunning combination. At 4:40 P.M., the pocket battleship swung round and opened fire. The captain of the *Jervis Bay*, the gallant Captain Fegen, at once ordered the convoy to scatter, which they did with commendable expertise, laying smoke to cover their withdrawal, while the *Jervis Bay* closed her mighty opponent and engaged with her guns. The unequal contest did not last long, and by 5:00, she rolled over and sank, shot through, a mass of flames. Her brave captain earned the posthumous Victoria Cross, and his sacrifice saved the bulk of his convoy, for it delayed the *Admiral Scheer* long enough in the failing light to prevent her following up the many diverging tracks of the fast-vanishing vessels.

And here the invalidity of those prewar arguments were shown up in all their short-sightedness and hollowness. One cry urged that navy's build only warships up to a size large enough to engage an armed merchant raider and scrap all large warships, especially battleships. The *Jervis Bay* could probably have stood up to such a vessel all right, but what use was that against even a small battleship like the *Scheer*. Bravery was not enough, and Fegen went to his death in a totally unsuitable substitute for the battleships Britain had failed to build—or had scrapped prematurely—to ingratiate herself with senators from Wisconsin.

The *Admiral Scheer* now attempted to damage as many merchantmen as she could before the light failed, hoping to finish them off later once disabled. In all, some five ships totaling 33,331 tons went to the bottom under her gunfire while another three were damaged before darkness called a halt to the slaughter. One of these wounded vessels was the large tanker *San Demetrio*, whose crew abandoned her, but later reboarded and got her safely home with most of her cargo. It was an unsatisfactory start in some ways for the *Admiral Scheer*, but certainly six good ships plus a quasi-warship had been dispatched without any damage to herself in a single afternoon. Her sudden appearance in the midst of the North Atlantic was dramatic proof of the soundness of the German planning and the weakness of the British defense. What else might she achieve and where would she turn up next?

The reaction of the Admiralty was immediate once the news came through. Convoys were either delayed or diverted from the danger area, and Admiral Forbes dispatched his big ships to cover the probable escape routes should the *Scheer* be heading either back to Germany or to France. The battlecruisers *Hood* and *Repulse* were sent at high speed from Scapa Flow to interpose themselves between the pocket battleship and French bases of Brest and L'Orient. Admiral Forbes sailed with the *Nelson*, *Rodney*, and light forces to patrol the Iceland to Faeroes bolt-hole. These were logical dispositions to make after such an event. The *Scheer* was hardly likely to linger in the area after such a coup. However, the Admiralty thought otherwise and changed Admiral Forbes's plans, sending part of the battlecruiser force straight to the last known position of the raider and detached the *Rodney* to give direct support to some homeward bound convoys at sea. This was not the first, nor by any means the last, time that the commander in chief's dispositions were overruled in this manner, but in this event, it had no grave consequence because the *Admiral Scheer* was a long-legged ship and not bound to one ocean; she sped south toward new hunting grounds in the South Atlantic.

Again, it was the *effect* this solitary ship had rather than the actual tonnage she sank that made the greatest impact on Britain's economy. As Captain Roskill concisely summed up: "Many ships were thus delayed, and the assembly ports became seriously congested. The normal convoy cycle was not resumed in the North Atlantic until HX 89 sailed on November 17. The loss of imports caused to this country by the pocket battleship's sudden appearance on our principal convoy route was, therefore, far greater than the cargoes actually sunk by her."[22]

The only sure solution was the battleship escort for the more important convoys. Several hunting groups were formed, and the carriers *Formidable* and *Hermes* were utilized to this effect, but they were too few and the oceans too large for them to have any effect. It was the same problem in that respect as the old theory about the hunting-groups, as opposed to the convoy escorts, in antisubmarine warfare. Groups of cruisers and the odd carrier could search for weeks in the vastness of the North Atlantic, the South Atlantic and Indian Ocean without ever catching a glimpse of one raider or even several of them. The one sure place of eventually finding them would be in among the vital convoys, just like the U-boats, and, just like the U-boats, here they could be brought to battle or made impotent and scared away; the effect on the convoys would be the same. But to do this, battleships were required and there were just not enough of them. However, the danger presented was so great, and was to become greater still, that even the main units of the Home Fleet were allocated to this task in the months that followed, seriously restricting the narrow margin of strength Admiral Forbes enjoyed.

For the crews of the battleships on North Atlantic escort duty, it was a dreary and wearisome time. Although they knew that their presence ensured the safety of innumerable merchant seamen and thousands of tons of essential supplies, the week-in-week-out plod back and forth across the Atlantic with convoys that were usually much slower than even the Royal Sovereigns, made it a chore of monotony for them. Only for a lucky few of these old veterans was this dull slog enlivened by sight of the enemy, and all the while the U-boat packs were snapping at their heels in the hope of a shot at a battleship for a change instead of an insignificant (in terms of prestige) merchantman. It did have the desired effect however. Paymaster Lieutenant Allen recalled the work of the *Rodney* while thus employed:

> The routine was almost invariably the same. We would leave home with a destroyer screen, which returned to base after some days in our company.[23] They had seen us through the most densely packed U-boat hunting-grounds and we proceeded on our way to rendezvous with the convoy. Then came day after day of steaming with

the convoy. Everything seemed the same, and as Shipwright Burns, who had recently joined the ship, remarked, the only time there was any variety was the day when the fog came down, throwing a dense blanket over everything, and we lost the convoy.

The ship's company bore this long strain admirably. They were in two watches and, during the danger periods, which lasted from five to six days, the 16-inch turrets were required to keep two out of three closed up all the time. This meant that many men were closed up for roughly twenty out of twenty-four hours a day. So a routine was worked whereby one turret at a time was stood off from eight o'clock in the evening until dawn when, of course, the whole ship went to dawn action stations. Those who were attached to the 16-inch turrets were, therefore, almost in a world of their own for long periods of time together, and they managed to work up a tremendous *esprit de corps* to break the monotony.[24]

The great ships, then, played their part and proved themselves as essential to the battle of the North Atlantic as elsewhere, despite the somewhat disparaging generalisations that have been made since about their role in this theatre of operations, which was, in reality, Britain's major lifeline.[25]

So the *Admiral Scheer* sped south into the waters of the mid-Atlantic where, because Force H was occupied in the Mediterranean, she was left undisturbed until it suited her purpose. By now, she was not alone. On the night of December 6–7, the *Admiral Hipper* again sailed forth to try her luck. Taking advantage of the furor caused by the *Scheer*, the *Hipper* had sailed from Brunsbüttel up the Inner Leads without disturbance and that night she also got through the Denmark Strait undetected. Her orders were specific. She was to deliberately attack the Halifax convoy route, whereas the *Scheer* was mainly to concentrate against independently routed vessels in distant waters from now on.

Initially, despite her success at getting out without British interception, she was no luckier than before. She operated too far south to come up against her expected prey and, thus thwarted she moved against the Sierra Leone convoys, with equal lack of results. Her short endurance continued to be a curse, and the number of supply ships necessary to keep her operational was a heavy burden on the splendid German organization.

Meanwhile, the *Admiral Scheer* continued to roam at will, and her score steadily mounted up. On December 18, she came upon the British refrigerator ship *Duquesa* (8,651 tons). She had already dispatched the *Port Hobart* on November 24 southeast of Bermuda and the *Tribesman* on December 1 west of Bathurst, but in this case, as deliberate policy, the *Admiral Scheer* gave the victim time to radio a full and complete radio report before boarding her.

This was to divert the British hunting groups from the *Hipper*'s activities to the north and was successful in diverting at least two carriers, two heavy cruisers, two light cruisers, and an AMC into her area. From all this concentration, she slipped away as easily as before into the South Atlantic wastes, taking the *Duquesa* along as a prize.

The *Admiral Hipper* finally found the scent on Christmas Eve 1940, but yet again her luck was right out. She picked up a very large convoy that evening and shadowed it all night in eager anticipation of some easy killing to celebrate the Festive Day. At dawn, the *Hipper* closed to empty her Christmas stocking, but alas, she found that she had bitten off far more than she could chew. What she had attacked was Convoy WS5A, a "Winston Special" en route to the Middle East with troops for the desert. As might be expected, this was one convoy that was heavily guarded and no place for an 8-inch cruiser with unreliable engines to linger.

The escort included the carrier *Furious*, 8-inch cruiser *Berwick*, and light cruisers *Bonaventure* and *Dunedin*. Of these, only the *Berwick* was a match for the *Hipper* in a straight fight, and in the first exchange of shells, the *Berwick* was hit badly and two of the convoy's fifty ships slightly damaged. The carriers were laden with aircraft for Takoradi and could not help much so things might have gone very badly had the *Hipper* been handled more resolutely. As it was, the convoy was hastily, and somewhat prematurely, scattered, but the German ship, with its main adversary the *Berwick* already damaged at Spartivento and now hard hit again, allowed herself to be driven off by the 6-inch cruiser (which was twenty-two years old) and the antiaircraft cruiser, with her 5.25-inch popguns; the *Hipper* took refuge in Brest, sinking a lone merchantman she ran into on the way. This single ship, of 6,078 tons, was the *Admiral Hipper*'s sole trophy for all the voyaging and refueling her sortie had entailed. As usual, British reaction was too late, although the *Renown* and Force H sailed from the Rock into a severe gale to try to bring her to book, and the *Repulse* was sent out from Scapa in case the *Hipper* was heading back into the Atlantic. Admiral Tovey took the Home Fleet out on his first operation since relieving Admiral Forbes.

The Home Fleet that Admiral Tovey took over was now in a better state than before as regards heavy ships strength. At Scapa and Rosyth, he had under his control the *Nelson*, *Rodney*, *Hood*, and *Repulse*, which were joined in December by the newly commissioned *King George V* as his flagship. He also had the prospect of the *Prince of Wales* joining him early in the New Year. The frequent convoy escort operations already described had the effect of reducing almost permanently the total strength actually available to him at any specific time.

These reinforcements were most opportune, for the German surface fleet was now about to reach the zenith of its power. On December 28, the German Admiral Lütjens prepared his two battlecruisers, the *Scharnhorst* and *Gneisenau* for their own sortie in the wake of the *Scheer* and *Hipper*, and this time, there was to be no turning back south of Iceland—or so it was planned. The month of January 1941 marked the opening of an even more dangerous phase in the battle for the North Atlantic convoy routes. The *Admiral Scheer* continued to score steady victories in unexpected places. After a hunt for WS 5A, continuing what the *Hipper* had started, had proven abortive, she captured another prize in the form of a Norwegian tanker, fully laden, which she sent back to Bordeaux with its rich cargo. Captain Krancke then changed his tactics and abandoned the night approach for one of daylight boldness once more, utilizing the signals of British warships. This policy soon reaped dividends. Operating on the Capetown to Freetown route, the *Scheer* next captured the Dutch *Barenfels* on January 20, followed by a British merchantman. These three victims added another 18,738 tons to his credit, and no signal was sent by any of the merchantmen. The Admiralty thus had no idea that the *Admiral Scheer* was the cause of their disappearance.

Krancke then refueled from the *Nordmark* before heading for fresh pastures. [26] On February 1, he was west of Cape Town, and by the end of the month, the *Scheer* had completed a long swing around the Cape of Good Hope and up the east coast of Madagascar before steering for the northern entrance to the Mozambique Channel, where the raider *Atlantis* had advised of rich pickings. This new hunting ground soon bore fruit, and on February 20, the pocket battleship sank the Greek vessel *Grigorios* (7,187 tons) and captured the British tanker *British Advocate* (6,994 tons). The next day, she sank the *Canadian Cruiser* (7,178 tons), but this ship was more aware than her earlier victims and managed to get off a sighting report. On the twenty-second, a Dutch freighter was taken but she too made a raider report and this convinced Krancke that he must again make a move to safer waters. She had also received orders to return to Germany in any case by the end of March, and so the *Scheer* doubled back on her tracks. In doing so, she narrowly evaded being brought to book when the spotter plane from the cruiser *Glasgow* sighted her on the twenty-second.

Various cruiser forces were in the area and these—the 8-inch *Australia* and 7.5-inch *Hawkins*, along with the 6-inch *Emerald* and *Enterprise*—at once started to close on the *Glasgow*. Also allocated to the hunt by the Admiralty were the carrier *Hermes*, the 8-inch cruisers *Canberra* and *Shropshire*, and the *Capetown*, an antiaircraft cruiser. It seemed that if only the *Glasgow* could hold the *Scheer*, she would be overwhelmed as had the *Graf Spee*, but alas, the spotter plane lost contact soon after and never regained it.

After evading her hunters, the *Admiral Scheer* again refueled and stored and also refitted her engines. All this she completed by March 11 and then started on her long voyage back to Germany. It was a lonely and uneventful passage, and she was not sighted during the whole journey although she crossed most of the major convoy routes as she steamed steadily north. By March 25, she was off the Denmark Strait, and after waiting for the weather to worsen, she made the passage without incident and finally anchored off Bergen, Norway, on the thirtieth. By April 1, she had reached Kiel to a great ovation. In her classic sortie, the *Admiral Scheer* had shown just what *could* be done with a skillful commander and a reliable ship. In a voyage of 46,419 miles and five months, she had sunk the *Jervis Bay* and sixteen merchant vessels totaling 99,095 tons.

Her less useful companion, the *Admiral Hipper*, had by now finally found her feet. On February 1, after being reported at anchor by air searches, she left Brest under Captain Meisel for her second sortie. She headed straight out 1,000 miles west of Finisterre to her refueling rendezvous and there idled awaiting a suitable opportunity. After a U-boat pack had severely mauled Convoy HG 53, it was thought that the *Hipper* would find employment among the survivors, and she was thither dispatched. All she could find was one lone straggler on February 11. That evening, however, her luck finally changed for the better, and she came across Convoy SLS 64, a slow, completely unescorted convoy of seventeen ships.

When dawn broke on the twelfth, the *Admiral Hipper* was able to move in among these sheep with complete abandon and in a few hours of deliberate slaughter sent down seven ships totaling 32,806 tons and damaged two more. Only lack of fuel prevented further kills being made, and by February 15, the *Hipper* was back in Brest with eight scalps and no damage. Here she was bombed and bombed again by the RAF to no effect save a few near misses. Her short endurance and unreliable engines had made the German Navy determined to bring her home however, despite her last sortie's good results, and accordingly, she again left Brest on March 15, refueled south of Greenland, and passed through the Denmark Straits on the twenty-third, even though detected by cruiser patrols, reaching Kiel on March 28, just two days ahead of the *Scheer*.[27]

Meanwhile, the Admiralty had larger problems on their minds. In what seems in retrospect like a procession or unruffled parade, two more German big ships had penetrated the Denmark Straits, both heading west this time. The *Scharnhorst* and *Gneisenau* had sailed from Kiel on January 23, and after steering well to the northwest up beyond the Iceland-Norway area, they turned their sharp stems westward to break though to the Atlantic. But the Admiralty had been forewarned as early as the twentieth that such a breakout was contemplated, and Admiral Tovey had made his dispositions accordingly. This first warning was repeated on the twenty-third from what Captain Roskill calls "definite intelligence"—probably resulting from the breaking of the Enigma codes[28]—that a sortie by the two German battlecruisers was underway and that they had passed through the Great Belt. Accordingly, Tovey put to sea with the *Nelson, Rodney*, and *Repulse* at midnight on January 25-26 to an intercepting position south of Iceland. It seemed the trap was firmly set and must be sprung. Two light cruisers were patrolling the strait both equipped with the last word in radar sets of that time.

At first, it seemed that this must be so, for in the early hours of the twenty-eighth, one of these ships, the *Naiad*, did pick up the *Scharnhorst* and *Gneisenau* on her set and reported them to Tovey. The trap was sprung, but the jaws closed on thin air. The Germans had sighted the *Naiad* before she sighted them and at once turned away from this little vessel as they had been instructed to do. After this let-off, the two German ships again refueled, from the tanker *Adria*, east of lonely Jan Mayen Island. This completed and with brimming tanks, they again entered the Denmark Strait on February 3–4, and this time, their probing coincided with the return of the Home Fleet to Scapa on the first, and thus they got through without hindrance or detection. Proudly, Admiral Lütjens was able to signal to his force: "For the first time in history, German battleships have succeeded in breaking through to the Atlantic. Now go to it!"

Lütjens's orders seemed specific enough; he was to concentrate his efforts not just on lone stragglers but mainly to attempt no less than "the destruction of merchant shipping bound for Britain," by which Bekker infers that it was actual sinkings of large tonnages that were the priorities rather than mere disruption of convoy systems in general.[29]

Refueling off Greenland on February 5–6, the two German battlecruisers were now ready for extended operations. But in one respect, Lütjens remained the holder of one special card, which the Germans and Italians were to play to the full, time and time again: combat with equal naval forces was to be avoided at all costs. The captain of the *Scharnhorst* interpreted this to mean if the odds were evenly matched but his fleet commander took a wider view, he would avoid the slightest hint of battle, even if the opposing warships were either fewer in number or inferior in fighting power. (In most cases, they were both.)

Such was the case when the two battlecruisers came up against their first potential victims in the form of the ships of Convoy HX 106, at dawn on February 8, heading east along the Halifax convoy route at slow speed. First sighting was made by the *Gneisenau* at 8:35, and Lütjens split his force to make a pincer attack, the *Gneisenau* from the south and the *Scharnhorst* waiting to the north to ambush the fleeing victims. However, it did not turn out quite that way, for at 9:47, the *Scharnhorst* sighted the distinctive triangular fighting tops of a British battleship accompanying the convoy—disaster.

The *Scharnhorst*'s captain, Kurt Hoffmann, did not consider this to be so. His plan was to deliberately close the British ship and then lure her away from her charges, using her ten knots' extra speed to keep out of harm's reach. He accordingly continued to close the convoy. Such a tactic did not appeal to Lütjens at all, and he sharply signaled the *Scharnhorst* to break away at once and withdrew at high speed to the south.

The *Scharnhorst* had correctly identified her adversary as the battleship *Ramillies*. After her earlier adventures in the Mediterranean, she had been employed on escorting troop convoys and had, that previous month, guarded WS 5B bound for North Africa. Now, as she raised steam to attain her maximum twenty-one knots and her 15-inch guns elevated and swiveled round toward the single enemy ship, she seemed set for even greater glory. But this one fleeting glimpse was all that was allowed her of the new German Navy in action. As Bekker put it: "The ancient *Ramillies* had only to let off a few angry puffs of smoke and both German battleships—despite their modern fire-control and the proven effectiveness of their guns—even at long range—sought safety in escape."[30]

The *Ramillies*, unfortunately, reported the enemy ship as possibly a Hipper-class cruiser, and so, fortunately for them, the *Scharnhorst* and *Gneisenau* gained an extra respite of anonymity. The Home Fleet was deployed to prevent a break home by the *Hipper* or *Scheer*, which involved another spate of futile steaming. Lütjens refueled his ships and then cast further to the west. On the twenty-second, he was rewarded with the sighting of several ships from a convoy, which had recently dispersed, as was the custom then, some 500 miles east of Newfoundland to head for their various destinations in North America. This so-called "safe" zone proved to be anything but in this case and these unfortunates were deliberately sunk with very little effort, five ships of 25,784 tons total were dispatched. Lütjens then turned south once more after several of these vessels had made raider reports. These were picked up ashore, thus finally alerting the Admiralty. Refueling in the central Atlantic en route, the German squadron moved on down toward the Sierra Leone convoy routes.

Here they soon came upon a convoy, some 350 miles north of the Cape Verde islands, at dawn on March 8. The convoy was SL 67. Their escort consisted of two Force H destroyers, the *Faulknor* and *Forester*; a corvette, the *Cecilia*; and on detached convoy escort duty from Force H, the battleship *Malaya*, fresh from her exploits off Genoa. It was her scout plane that actually first sighted the two German heavy ships approaching and duly gave warning. For Lütjens, it was a repeat of the *Ramillies* episode:

At 4:45 P.M., the enemy was in sight from the *Malaya*'s fighting top and her 15-inch guns rose to full elevation, waiting for the range to come down, her twenty-five year old hull straining as she churned onwards at her best speed of twenty knots. The *Forester* took station ahead with the *Faulknor*, their lean hulls thrusting forward, torpedo tubes trained outwards in anticipation; while, down in the engine room, they prepared to make a smoke screen which would shelter them if, the *Malaya* being unable to cope, they were called on to make a suicidal dash into the enemy's guns.

But, directly after being sighted, the enemy was discovered to be altering course away, rapidly increasing speed, their gun turrets apparently still trained fore and aft. Once again the incredible had occurred—with the odds high in his favour, the enemy again refused combat. The poor old *Malaya* had no hope of matching the Germans' top speed, so after a brief pursuit all three British vessels turned back towards the convoy in case the enemy should decide to work round behind them and annihilate it. In fact, Admiral Lütjens had no such intention; well aware that he had been sighted and his position reported, his chief aim was to get as far away from the area as he could. Signaling the latest position of the convoy to two U-boats in the vicinity, he sped northwards.[31]

The German squadron now retraced their tracks to again attack the vital Halifax route, sinking a solitary Greek merchantman on their journey north-west. Admiral Tovey's heavy ships were sent to cover vital convoys during this period, both the *Rodney* and *King George V* being thus employed and leaving only the *Nelson* to patrol south of Iceland.

Further fueling and replenishment in mid-Atlantic ensured that the German ships were in top condition to resume their sortie, and on March 15, they came across another large group of dispersed ships from a convoy and quickly dispatched six of them. "With surprising speed the gun crews developed a technique for sinking the ships with shots accurately placed on the waterline. The ground swell and rough sea often impeded the picking up of survivors from their lifeboats."[32]

These easy pickings continued the next day when another unescorted group was located and another ten merchant ships went to the bottom. In just two days, the *Scharnhorst* had sunk six vessels of 35,080 tons; the *Gneisenau*, seven of 26,693 tons. Three tankers had been taken as prizes amounting to an additional 20,139 tons. It must have come as a gratifying surprise to the Germans to find that this suicidal policy of dispersement was still being operated by the British despite the losses inflicted the previous month in these waters.

Again many raider reports were sent out, and on the next day, March 16, the German ships had another narrow escape when another brief brush with a British battleship took place. The *Rodney* was escorting HX 114, and Paymaster-Lieutenant Allen recalled the incident as follows:

> A distress signal from SS *Demeterton* was received at the same time as the upperworks of a large unidentified warship was sighted closing from the north-east. Half the hands were at tea, and were closed up at the double with the rest. The stranger was recognized just in time as the *Royal Sovereign*, short of fuel and proceeding to Halifax. She was able to remain with the westerly convoy. An hour later, *Laconia* was sighted, having reversed the course of her convoy, and after twenty minutes she reported continuous gunfire to the south-eastward. At the same time, SS *Chilean Reefer*, thirty-three miles away to the south-east, made W/T Raider Distress signals, and then was not heard again. *Laconia* left to rejoin her convoy and we steamed for the last reported position of the *Chilean Reefer*.
>
> At 6:00 P.M., a merchant ship was sighted, later recognized as a German auxiliary, and shortly afterwards we saw another on fire, with a third ship alongside, momentarily discernible as a warship against the darkening eastern sky. We were probably silhouetted like a mountain against the light in the west, and after chasing first the warship and then the auxiliary, both of which disappeared in the gloom, we turned to the burning wreck. Twenty-seven men were picked up from an open boat. Half-an-hour before they had been bobbing up and down alongside the battlecruiser *Gneisenau* which had left in too much of a hurry even to haul them inboard.[33]

It was a close thing indeed, although the German version reads somewhat differently: "In rescuing the survivors of her last victim, *Gneisenau* is surprised by the British battleship *Rodney* employed in escorting Convoy HX 114; *but by skillful feinting, she is able to avoid an engagement with the slower but superior-armed opponent*" (emphasis added)[34]

The *King George V* at once sailed from Halifax, and the *Renown* sailed from Gibraltar with Force H to cut off their retreat to the French coast. On the seventeenth, this squadron came within an ace of heading the two German ships off for one of the Swordfish actually glimpsed them, only some 110 miles northwest of the *Renown*, which was steering north. Unfortunately, no word of this reached Somerville because of the failure of this aircraft's wireless, and when it eventually returned and flashed the sighting report by signal lamp, it was too late in the day for an air strike to be mounted against them by the carrier. The next morning brought thick fog in the area in which Force H was operating, and by this time, as Lütjens had jigged his course to throw off the scent after being sighted, the lead they had established was too great. The *Renown* returned to Gibraltar on March 24, having been at sea continuously for fifty days out of the preceding fifty-six; she refueled and sailed back into the Atlantic the same day for the two German ships were still not located.

In actual fact, Lütjens had already been given instructions to leave the North Atlantic, so that the *Scheer* and *Hipper* could break for home waters, and the German Naval Staff wished for both the battlecruisers to refit and refurbish in a French port in readiness for a combined assault, in conjunction with the planned sortie by the *Bismarck* and *Tirpitz*, which was now under active preparation. So the two ships steamed to Brest and arrived there safely on the morning of the twenty-second.

Far behind them in the waters of the eastern Atlantic, they left Admiral Tovey's forces scouring an empty sea. By this time, both the *Hood*, which had just refitted and was officially still on trials, and the *Queen Elizabeth*, which had finally finished her rebuilding on February 21 and was equally not worked up, had joined the *Nelson* south of Iceland. The rushing into service in the face of this emergency of these two valuable ships before they were fully battleworthy was a considerable risk by the Admiralty, but shortage of big ships forced them to do this again and again. The next time it was to have tragic results.

Admiral Lütjens skillful handling of his squadron in evading interception and fooling the British about his destination (his actual presence at Brest was not confirmed until almost a week later) was, for the Germans, the crowning achievement of what was the most potent demonstration of battleship raiding influence so far exhibited. As Captain Roskill wrote: "Admiral Reader's congratulatory message to Lütjens was certainly well merited and the jubilation of the German Naval Staff over the results accomplished appeared to be well founded."[35]

In cold, hard figures, this achievement included the sinking, or capture, of twenty-two merchantmen totaling 115,622 tons. The dislocation they caused and the potential threat their presence at Brest made to future convoys were all plusses on this balance sheet, to which their detractors wisely turned a Nelson-like blind eye when analyzing it as a wasted effort. On the very slender plus side of the British, the failure of air reconnaissance—first to locate the Germans during their breakout, then to hold them when later found—and the large extent to which air operations were limited by weather conditions were offset only by the fact that "the Admiralty's policy of giving as many convoys as possible close escort by battleships had certainly saved two of them from disaster."[36]

This latter policy had its dangers, however. For the big ships to be tied to slow-moving convoys, with poor escort screens and unable to zig-zag at speed, meant that considerable risks were run with these valuable ships at the hands of the wolf packs. It is as well that the undersea threat proved to be much less than predicted earlier, even so the torpedoing of the *Malaya* by the *U-106*, even if the result of an unintentional attack on such a target (she was aiming at the convoy and did not even see the *Malaya*) emphasized the risks being taken. The old veteran was some 250 miles west-northwest of the Cape Verde islands on March 20 when the torpedo slammed into her port side and caused great damage. Her convoy was subsequently scattered, as she could no longer offer it her protection, while the *Malaya* proceeded to Trinidad to carry out immediate repairs. It was fortunate for the overcrowded and much-bombed shipyards of Britain that in April 1941, Lease-Lend came into effect, and the *Malaya* was one of the first major units to go to the United States for major refitting under this scheme, being joined later by the *Resolution* and then by the *Warspite* as the tempo of war increased. The *Malaya* rejoined the fleet in June 1941.

Meanwhile, events of great importance had taken place in the Atlantic. The sortie of the *Scharnhorst* and *Gneisenau* was both the most successful, and also the last, sortie that German battleships would make across the face of that broad highway.

The mounting of Operation *Rheinübung* (Rhine Exercise)[37] was from the first the brainchild of Grand Admiral Erich Raeder, who is specific about it in his memoirs: "responsibility for sending out the *Bismarck* was mine." [38] It is clear that his continued faith in the potential of the battleship was the main driving force all along. Like all plans made in time of war, however, *Rheinübung*, when finally set in motion, was a much-reduced compromise of the original germ of the idea.

It was the intention of the German naval staff that the operation should take the form of a combined sortie by the newly completed battleship *Bismarck* and the brand-new heavy cruiser *Prinz Eugen* from home waters through the Denmark Strait in the now-traditional manner, coupled with a new sortie by the *Scharnhorst* and *Gneisenau*, once refitted, from Brest. Both these powerful squadrons would rendezvous deep out in the Atlantic, take on oil and supplies, and then descend in overwhelming strength on any convoy it wished. It was felt that such a combination would be more than enough to cope with the single battleship escort that had hitherto nullified their earlier efforts.

The sortie was to take place toward the end of April, and in preparation, the usual efficient back-up system, now perfected by the German Navy, was set in motion. Five tankers were sent out to their allocated waiting stations along with two supply ships, while selected U-boats and spy ships were briefed to provide extra intelligence on convoy movements and escorts. Once more in command was to be Lütjens, this time flying his flag in the *Bismarck*. Should any convoy approached be protected by an old battleship, the *Bismarck* was quite capable of dealing with her alone—or if need be, with one of the battlecruisers—while the *Scharnhorst* or *Gneisenau* and the *Prinz Eugen* would be able to concentrate on wiping out the small escorts and the in merchantmen as a team.

The ability of the *Bismarck* to summarily disable or sink one of the older British battleships was not held to be in much doubt. Her fully laden displacement came out at over 50,000 tons. She was built for strength and had a 12½-inch armored belt of Krupp steel and had a double system of armored decks of 2-inch and 4-inch thickness and a speed of more than thirty knots. Her main armament of eight 15-inch guns was similar to most of the British veterans, except for the *Nelson* and *Rodney,* and was adequate, although the duplication of secondary armament in both surface and antiaircraft batteries was a German flaw that resulted in wasted tonnage as compared with the dual-purpose methods adopted by Britain and the United States. However, her antiaircraft battery was controlled by a superb system, far in advance of that aboard British vessels, thus increasing their actual effectiveness in combat.

Raeder held that once this squadron got to work in earnest, the disruption caused by the little *Scheer* or by Lütjens's earlier exploits would be nothing compared with the chaos such a battle fleet would cause. It was expected that in order to track down such a mighty fleet, even the battleships of the Mediterranean Fleet might have to be pulled out, with the subsequent enormous boost to Italian morale, which was now at rock bottom after Matapan. With the invasion of Crete looming and the vital part expected to be played by Cunningham's ships in its defense, this might have been overly optimistic of the Germans, but in the event, even half the force planned pulled in warships from everywhere, including Gibraltar.

The *Scharnhorst* and *Gneisenau,* however, were not finally able to participate in the operation at all. In fact, they never sortied into the North Atlantic area again. In the case of the *Scharnhorst,* it was found that the defects to her machinery were greater than at first thought; a constant problem of all German surface ships from pocket battleships and battlecruisers down to their large destroyers, it was their Achilles heel in design during World War II. Although the French Naval dockyard at Brest had been taken over by the efficient Wilhelmshaven dockyard, they were unable to get the *Scharnhorst* ready for sea again until July 1941.

The *Gneisenau* was put out of action by the valiant and persistent bombing operations of the RAF, which after an enormous amount of effort and heavy losses were finally successful in hitting and damaging a stationary battleship in harbour, even if they still lacked the weapons to sink her. Thanks to the gallantry of these bomber crews, the *Gneisenau* was made inoperational for a very long period. It was up to the *Bismarck* and *Prinz Eugen* to carry out Raeder's project. Despite reservations about whether the operation ought to be postponed for some time until either the battlecruiser's repairs were completed or the *Tirpitz* joined her sister,[39] and despite some last-minute tinkering by Hitler when he was finally told of the operation, it was with these two ships that *Rheinübung* finally commenced on May 18, 1941, when the two giants glided out of the port of Gdynia.

Fortunately for the British, they had friends in neutral countries and an efficient spy ring to make use. Thus, when the Swedish cruiser *Gotland* chanced to sight the German ships in the Skagerrak on May 20, it was not long before this vital information—that "two large warships, escorted by three destroyers" were heading on a northwesterly course—was passed on to London and thence to Admiral Tovey at Scapa Flow. For many weeks, he had been expecting this news. Now that it had come so early in the Germans' planned sortie, it was to be expected that the Home Fleet would take rapid steps to forestall the German moves. What was available to Admiral Tovey on that fateful day?

We have seen how on numerous occasions the main strength of the battle fleet had been dispersed on other operations, and that, as a consequence of this policy, added to the normal calls of refitting and repair of ships, this actual strength on hand at Scapa was often far less than that theoretically available on paper. In this, the employment of the older ships as convoy escorts remained the chief factor but there was also the employment of even the largest and latest of our battleships in lesser roles, which seemed an unnecessary risk to take. For example, the brand-new *King George V* had taken Lord Halifax to the Chesapeake Bay in the United States between January 15 and 24, hardly a vital mission or one that could not have been done by a less important vessel. It is true that on her return trip, she acted as ocean escort for a valuable tanker convoy, but she did not return to Scapa until February 6. A three-week absence of his best ship in order to impress the Americans was a risk Admiral Tovey could have done without.

Ocean escort was essential, however. In addition to the *Rodney* and *Malaya*, the *Ramillies*, *Revenge*, and *Royal Sovereign* were all thus employed during the opening months of 1941, despite repeated attempts by Winston

Churchill to nag the Admiralty into withdrawing at least a pair of them and refitting them on the lines of his earlier totally impracticable and misconceived "Catherine" plans.[40]

In May, too, the battlecruiser *Hood* was sent to Hvalfiord to provide similar heavy cover for convoys passing south of Iceland, but she had returned to Scapa Flow by May 20.

The *Repulse*, with the new carrier *Victorious*, was earmarked to escort Convoy WS 8B to the Middle East, and the *Repulse* was actually in the Clyde awaiting the start of this operation. The *Rodney* was en route to the United States for her long-overdue refit and was providing protection for the liner *Britannic* along the way. The *Ramillies* was escorting an eastbound convoy while the *Revenge* was at Halifax waiting to sail with another. The *Renown* was at Gibraltar with Force H, and apart from Admiral Cunningham's ships and those older units refitting or repairing, all that was left to Tovey were the following ships: the *King George V, Hood,* and *Prince of Wales.* Of these, the *Hood* was in bad need of a refit, was twenty years behind the times, and was a battlecruiser, *not* a battleship.[41] Conversely, the *Prince of Wales* was at the other end of the scale, having joined the fleet only two months before; many of the civilian contractors were still aboard, while two of her gun turrets had only been handed over three weeks earlier. The new-design 14-inch guns were not proving a success and constant "teething troubles" made her an asset of questionable value. The main armament of the two British battleships was the 14-inch gun, which was inferior to the 15-inch gun of the German, French, and Italian ships and the 16-inch of the American vessels built at the same time. However, they were designed for strength, and their armor protection was, on paper at any rate, as good as any of their opposite numbers.[42]

Once the first sighting report was received, the Admiralty made a series of well-conceived preparations to deal with the worst. The *Repulse* and *Victorious* were added to Tovey's forces, thus enabling him to utilize his four capital ships in two squadrons and maintain an old battlecruiser-new battleship balance between them: the *Hood* and *Prince of Wales,* the *Repulse* and *King George V.* Taking into account the strengths and weakness of the four ships he had, these were the most sensible of the possible combinations available. Both of these squadrons were the rough equivalents of the *Bismarck* and *Prinz Eugen* pairing, taking into account the brand-new designs and strengths of the German vessels against the lighter main armament of the German heavy cruiser.

Cruiser patrols were established in the likely breakout areas: the 8-inch cruisers *Norfolk* and *Suffolk* in the Denmark Strait and the 6-inch cruisers *Birmingham* and *Manchester* in the Iceland-Faeroes gap. Four more smaller cruisers lay in readiness at Scapa. Tovey now awaited more detailed reports of the German movements, composition and intentions.

The German squadron had meanwhile had an uneventful passage through the Great Belt and Skagerrak and put into Korsfiord, near Bergen, on the twenty-first to top off with fuel. It was here that they were finally sighted and reported by a Coastal Command reconnaissance plane, who reported them as two Hipper-class cruisers. When the photographs were developed, however, it could be seen that although one was indeed a Hipper, the other colossus was more than twice as big. It had to be the *Bismarck*.

Tovey at once sent Vice Admiral Holland to sea with the *Hood, Prince of Wales*, and six destroyers to Hvalfiord.[43] The RAF laid on air strikes against the German ships, but of the twelve bombers dispatched, six Whitley's and six Wellingtons, only two actually found the fiord and these bombed through poor visibility and failed to come even close to their targets. Another attempt was mounted with eighteen bombers also failed to penetrate the murk and again only two of the aircraft reached the target area at all, and these could not see whether the ships were there or not. It was the old familiar story. They dropped their bombs at random, and far out to sea, Lütjens looked back at the flashes of the explosions with the satisfaction that he had again thrown the British off the scent.

At 5:00 A.M., off Trondheim, the German squadron sent back the three escorting destroyers and headed for the Denmark Strait at high speed; Lütjens decided on this route, instead of the alternative recommended by German naval command, at the last minute. Back in Germany the fate of the two ships hung in the balance. An uneasy Hitler, well-known for his "premonitions," had last-minute doubts about the sortie, including its effect on the timing of his assault on the Soviet Union and American opinion. Raeder had a hard time persuading the führer to allow the operation to go ahead but in the end won him over. It was about the only time he did, and the results of the sortie must have convinced Hitler that his opinions of his admirals were in complete harmony with his opinions of his orthodox and, at least to Hitler, timid generals.

The two German heavy ships were still at sea and their position and intentions unknown to the British. The sortie seemed set fair for a good beginning if only their luck would hold in the penetration of the Denmark Strait, the southern end of which, thanks to British minefields and the icepacks, was only some thirty miles wide. Still in the usual poor weather conditions of that lonely stretch of water it was to be expected that where others had gone they too would pass unseen. The advances in British radar were to completely nullify this false sense of security however. Once the raid was over indeed, the *Bismarck* was to return to Germany again to the north—so confident were the

Germans of the penetration of these routes. Only if she was damaged would the German leviathan make for a French port; otherwise, she was to go home to join the *Tirpitz* for a repeat performance at a later date.

Because of bad weather, all reconnaissance patrols had to be cancelled by Coastal Command, and no intelligence from them was therefore available. Admiral Tovey did not finally get the confirmation that the German squadron had put to sea until 10:00 P.M. on the twenty-second, and then the report came from a target-towing Maryland of the Royal Navy rather than from Ultra or from Coastal Command. Once the news was digested that the anchorages around Bergen were empty, Admiral Tovey lost little time in setting in motion the next stages of his plan to prevent a breakout into the Atlantic. By 11:00 that night, the *King George V*, four light cruisers, and seven destroyers had left the Flow and were steering west through the Pentland Firth to take up their covering position. The *Repulse* was ordered up from the Clyde to rendezvous with this force at 7:00 the next morning off the Butt of Lewis. The carrier *Victorious* also sailed with the fleet. No word of this concentration of power reached Lütjens, nor could he suspect that the *Hood* and *Prince of Wales* were already steering toward his breakout point. The German squadron held at twenty-five knots.

At 7:10 A.M., the *Repulse* joined the flag with three destroyers (one of Tovey's escorts, the brand-new *Lance* had already turned back with boiler defects), and Tovey steered northwest in order to cover both possible escape routes. Air searches were carried out across the Iceland-Faeroes channel despite poor conditions, but the weather was so bad over the Denmark Strait that no aircraft could operate. The commander in chief therefore remained without any fresh information on which to base his further movements. Although the Germans had tankers waiting to fuel them, the Royal Navy, the world's premier naval power, had none at sea to support her fleet, her main fleet at that. The conservation of his oil fuel had already become a major factor in everything Tovey did. It was to become dominant as the operation moved to its climax.

Meanwhile, Churchill was immediately cabling Roosevelt with the news and asking for help in locating the German squadron—neutrality aside, of course. "We have reason to believe that a formidable Atlantic raid is intended," he signaled. "Should we fail to catch them going out, your navy should surely be able to mark them down for us. Give us the news and we will finish the job.'[44] This assistance was not necessary as it turned out. One German authority states that Admiral Lütjens was not caught by surprise but was well informed of the situation as a result of his own intelligence operators, under Commander Reichart, who were monitoring and deciphering the signals of the British cruisers *Norfolk* and *Suffolk*.[45] The Germans were thus ready for them and the guns prepared to open fire.

However, most British sources state that it was not the superior Type 284 radar carried by the *Suffolk* that first made contact with the *Bismarck* at a range of seven miles at 7:22 P.M. on May 23. The German ships were hugging the edge of the ice pack and were actually first seen by Able Seaman Newell, the *Suffolk*'s starboard after lookout.

> The captain and most of those on the compass platform rushed over to that side of the bridge and saw through their binoculars what was undoubtedly the *Bismarck* and a cruiser with her. They were no more than about 14,000 yards away, a dangerously close range to enemy guns that could shoot up to 40,000 yards. Captain Ellis put his wheel over on the instant to make for the fog. But it had taken him two or three minutes to reach it and he thought it extraordinary that the *Bismarck* had apparently failed to notice him during that time. As he turned, Captain Ellis ordered an enemy report signal to be sent out.[46]

Once in the cover of the mist, the radar took over and enabled the tracking to begin. If the Germans were aware of the *Suffolk* at this stage, they took no avoiding action but sped on south through the Strait at almost 30 knots despite the risks. A little while later, the *Norfolk* arrived on the scene and, having inferior radar, almost walked straight into the enemy ships. The *Norfolk* made a sharp turn at six miles range under cover of smoke, narrowly escaping annihilation from accurate 15-gun salvos from the German flagship that were close enough to bring splinters aboard.

The two cruisers then began a skillful shadowing of the German squadron, and the *Norfolk*'s sighting reports were the first to get through to Tovey in the *King George V.* As they clung to the *Bismarck* throughout the hours, their constant stream of reports acted like a homing beacon to the big ships of Tovey's command. Perhaps Lütjens was not too worried at this; the two cruisers were an irritant but not a threat to his force and could be annihilated in the event of good visibility for his gunners. What the German admiral still did not know was that Tovey was already at sea.

Moreover, Vice Admiral Holland's two great ships were even closer, still with the destroyer screen intact. The *Hood* had picked up the earlier signals of the *Suffolk*, which put the enemy squadron 300 miles north of him. At 8:45 P.M., he increased the speed of his own squadron to twenty-seven knots to make contact at first light on May 24. The feeling in the battlecruiser squadron was one of quiet confidence in the outcome of the morrow's battle. The grave misgivings about the the *Hood*'s protection were not generally known in the service any more than by the general public. An eyewitness aboard one of the escorting destroyers summed up the feeling as the great ships raced to close the gap between them and their mighty adversary:

> *Electra* had worked with *Hood* in every type of weather and in every condition of war. But never had the battlecruiser looked more impressive than she did today—as she drove towards Iceland and her destiny, as she narrowed by half a mile a minute the distance between her and the fateful German guns. *Hood*, when we steamed out of Scapa, was no longer the world's largest warship, for unbeknown to us, the new German battleships had exceeded their published displacement by 10,000 tons. But, as the cold dawn broadened over the slate-grey sea, and as *Electra* bucketed through the creamy fringes of the squadron's wake, we waited with confidence and pride the outcome of the voyage. With *Hood* beside us, we felt we could tackle anything.[47]

One person to whom the *Hood*'s faults were not hidden was Vice Admiral Holland, who was well aware of the danger to his gallant old flagship from long-range plunging fire. It should not be surprising, then, that he wished to close with his powerful adversary quickly and then engage at a range that would minimize this effect. Although the *Prince of Wales* was equipped to absorb such punishment—to soak it up and still be able to retain her place in line and continue handing it out herself—Vice Admiral Holland was acutely aware of her shortcomings in the readiness of her armament. By getting in relatively close early on, he would be giving both his ships the best chance to minimize their defects. Although severely taken to task for this decision later, it was surely the only sensible course for him to have adopted with the ships he was given. True, an end-on approach would reduce his theoretical gun advantage from eighteen-to-eight to ten-to-eight but it was hoped this would be for a brief period only. Also his head-on approach would give the German gunners a smaller, and more difficult visually, target to lock on to. With the common knowledge of how accurate the German first salvos always were, this was another point worth considering. Such an approach gave the whole length of the ship as a target for shots going over, but this was the lesser of two evils.

Once the range had come down and both British heavy ships could swing broadside-on to their enemy, their 12-inch plus armored sides could take the punishment and three times the number of big guns could give back any such injury with extra interest. Alas, for Holland, there now came two events that upset this carefully constructed compromise. Both concerned the shadowing British cruisers. First, their presence irritated Lütjens enough for him to order the *Prinz Eugen* to exchange places so that she and not the *Bismarck* became the leading vessel. This gave the Germans the chance to warn off the two shadowers with some very accurate salvos from their heaviest guns whenever they inadvertently got too close or were revealed by the mist. But it also gave the German force a much more priceless bonus later when the *Hood* opened fire on the *Prinz Eugen*, thinking her to be the flagship at the head of the German line. This reduced the number of guns employed against the *Bismarck* still further in those vital opening minutes, to a theoretical six-to-eight advantage to the Germans, and with the *Prince of Wales*'s defective guns, the odds were even higher in the "weaker" squadron's favor. Thus, their policy of building ships with the same beautiful overall profile paid off yet again—in this case, in the biggest way possible.

The other unforeseen circumstance—although in those early days of radar it was always a grim possibility—was that the British cruisers actually lost contact with the German squadron for a crucial period of time. It was just on midnight when the regular sighting reports coming into Holland's bridge suddenly stopped. Up until then, the British ships were holding steady a course, which, at daybreak, would find them closing fast on the *Bismarck*'s bow. Suddenly, the safe assumptions of her future movements during the remaining hours of darkness were swept away.

Now Holland had to abandon his carefully worked out approach and adopt a policy of regaining contact in the minimum of time. He therefore altered course, at 12:17 A.M. on the twenty-fourth, and headed north at twenty-five knots to cut the corner in case the German ships had swung around behind their shadowers and were cutting back astern of them. In fact, the German ships continued on southwest without deviation. At 2:00 A.M., Holland again turned his big ships south to mark time until daylight, but to cover all eventualities he detached his destroyer screen with instructions to continue to sweep north to hedge his bets. This was the second grave mistake and they played no further part in the battle, where their torpedoes might have proved invaluable. Holland's intentions on sighting the enemy were to concentrate the fire of both his ships on the *Bismarck* while the *Prinz Eugen* was similarly assailed at odds of two-to-one by the *Norfolk* and *Suffolk*. Again, this failed to materialize for neither of the British ships were so informed and, once they had regained contact, they still kept their distance, wisely in the circumstances, of some fifteen miles. They were thus powerless to add their sixteen 8-inch guns to the coming duel and left the *Prinz Eugen* free to add her own eight such weapons to the pounding of the *Hood*.

Two other criticisms have been made of the final dispositions of Holland's battle squadron at this time. First, contact was resumed with the German ships by the cruisers at 2:47 A.M., and for several hours, he knew again exactly their course and speed, his angle of approach however still was neither one thing nor the other. It was too steep to enable his after turrets, totaling four 15-inch and four 14-inch guns, to bear on the German squadron, and it was too shallow to offer the minimum target to the enemy's full broadsides of eight 15-inch and eight 8-inch guns, presenting as it did a three-quarter bow view to their rangefinders. It was therefore not the best of both worlds but the worst. Nor did his going into action in close quarter formation allow the *Prince of Wales* any freedom of action at all in the ensuing engagement.

On the final approach, the *Prince of Wales* was ordered to use her gunnery radar set to sweep the horizon ahead but when this malfunctioned; like so much else on the new British battleship, the use of the search set was forbidden in case it gave away Holland's position prematurely. It had also been thought desirable by Captain Leach of the *Prince of Wales* that his more heavily armored ship should lead during the dangerous run-in period of the approach, but he did not pass his thoughts on to the admiral at the time. As the Germans throughout the action mistook the *Prince of Wales* (which they had not thought ready yet—in many ways they were right) for the *King George V*, this ruse would have almost certainly have worked and the Germans would have concentrated their fire on the apparent flagship which could have taken the punishment better. But all these arguments and suggestions came *after* the battle. As the German squadron came into view that misty May morning at 5:35, few would have given Lütjens and his men much chance of surviving that fateful day.

The German vessels had sighted the fateful smoke on the horizon at 5:30. Lütjens's orders were to engage convoys with battleship protection but to avoid getting entangled with superior force. There was little doubt that Holland's ships represented a superior force, although at first it was hoped they were merely cruisers (Lütjens had still not been informed that Scapa Flow was empty). His surprise as two capital ships loomed up on an intercepting course must have been most unpleasant. Had he have been able to avoid the action, he undoubtedly would have done so, as so often before, but their position made it clear that there was no avoiding a fight. That being so the German planned to give a good account of themselves. All the other surprises that morning were to come to the British.

At 5:37, the *Prince of Wales* reported "enemy in sight distant seventeen miles," and Holland ordered both his ships to turn forty degrees to close the enemy as planned. The *Prince of Wales* was then placed on a bearing of eighty degrees, and at 5:49, both British ships turned twenty degrees to starboard and were told to concentrate their fire on the leading enemy ship. It was fortunate indeed that the gunnery control officer of the *Prince of Wales* realized that an error in identity had been made and rapidly switched his broadsides to the *Bismarck* astern. Not until her last salvo did the *Hood* appear to reach the same conclusion. At 5:52, the *Hood* led the action with her first salvo at an estimated 25,000 yards, followed within half a minute by the *Prince of Wales*. The two German ships were slightly slower in their replies. The *Bismarck*'s first salvo crashed out at 5:53, and the *Prinz Eugen*, her lighter weapons firing more rapidly but well within her range, began at 5:59. The die was cast. Both flagships fired accurately right from the start.

"As seen from the distant *Norfolk* and *Suffolk*, the *Hood*'s firing seemed excellent. Her first two salvos were very close to the enemy, and the third looked like a straddle. The *Prince of Wales* was taking longer to get on. Her first salvo was over. Corrections were made, but it was not until the sixth salvo that a straddle was obtained."[48] All well and good, but the *Hood* was firing at the wrong ship, and the *Prinz Eugen* does not seem to have been overawed by the *Hood*'s shooting. Her own fast reply salvos were equally on target and it is thought that she in fact scored the first damaging hit on Holland's flagship. It was at once apparent from the ships in company that she had been struck. A large fire broke out by the *Hood*'s mainmast, which spread rapidly forward and blazed up high above the upper deck. To the watchers in the cruisers, it appeared as a big semicircle of flame, very like a top half of the setting sun, and they held their breath wondering whether it would be humanly possible to get it under control. Then it died down somewhat and afterwards seem to "pulsate up and down."[49]

This was a remarkable hit by the cruiser, and the British cruisers were unable to make a similar contribution to the fighting. When the *Suffolk* tried a few salvos they all fell well short. Meanwhile, the *Prince of Wales* was fighting valiantly for a brand-new ship. We had seen how she had switched target to the *Bismarck* early in the action and on her sixth salvo she got a straddle on her enemy. The *Bismarck* was even quicker and after only two initial salvos, straddled the *Hood* with her third, the first being ahead and the second astern.

At 6:00, it seemed as if the British squadron had victory in its grasp, for the worst moment—the approach with half the guns masked—was to be terminated by the execution of Holland's signal to turn another twenty degrees to port and thus come broadside-on to the enemy. Before the flag could be run down, however, and the vital turn made, disaster struck. The fifth salvo had just left the *Bismarck*'s guns and the *Hood* was just firing her own reply when a huge sheet of flame shot up from Holland's flagship, followed by an enormous explosion. Aboard the *Prinz Eugen*, an eyewitness tried to describe the scene:

As a whole salvo of 15-inch shells from the German flagship reached its target, there was an explosion of quite incredible violence, between the second funnel and the mainmast. The salvo seemed to crush everything under it with irresistible force. Through huge holes opened up in the grey hull, enormous flames leaped up from the depths of the ship, far above the funnels, and blazed for several seconds through an ash-colored pall of smoke, which spread terrifyingly towards the ship's bows. And this grey mass fringed with red, composed of smoke, fire and steam, was seen to form two billowing columns spreading upwards and outwards, while just below them formed a kind of incandescent dome, whose initial low flat curve rose higher and higher, finally culminating in an explosion of burning debris. The aft magazine blew up, shooting into the air a molten mass the colour of red lead, which then fell back lazily into the sea—it was one of the rear gun turrets that we thus saw rising into the air for several yards. All the inflammable objects in the area at the time—rafts, boats, and deck planking—broke loose, and even as they drifted continued to burn, drawing a thick cloud of smoke over the sea's surface.

And in the midst of this raging inferno, a yellow tongue of flame shot out just once more: the forward turrets of the *Hood* had fired one last salvo.[50]

.

The absoluteness and suddenness of this tragedy stunned friend and foe alike: "If ever a ship died in action, the *Hood* did. Her last salvo was in the air at the moment when she received the final blow. Every man was at his post; the breeches had just slammed behind shells and charges for a further salvo; she was steaming still at twenty-eight knots; and then the sea and the darkness covered her. One minute she was alive, the next minute dead."[51]

Captain Leach and the crew of the *Prince of Wales* did not long take in this stupendous turn of events. Turning hard to starboard in an effort to clear the great cloud of death and the forward section of the shattered flagship as it reared up out of the water in a final death plunge, they suddenly found themselves the new solitary target for all those lethal German guns that had just brought about this smashing blow to all their hopes.

In the ensuing twelve minutes of hell, the *Prince of Wales* was heavily hit. The range was down to 18,000 yards, and so the secondary armaments of the German ships were able to add their quota of shells to the total. Two minutes after the *Hood* had been torn asunder, the *Bismarck*'s deadly accurate gunners showed that it had not been a "lucky hit," as the British press later called it, but that the Germans were the best. A one-ton 15-inch, armor-piercing shell slammed straight into the British battleship's bridge, tore through it with contemptible ease, and exploded as it left the other side. In its wake, it left utter carnage, leaving every man there, except for Captain Leach and his Chief Yeoman, dead or wounded.

Three more 15-inch shells came roaring out of the sky and struck the *Prince of Wales*, as did three 8-inch projectiles from the *Prinz Eugen*. But here her stout construction showed up well. The 5.25inch secondary armament directors forward were put out of action by one 15-inch shell, but the guns were taken over by the after director.

Another hit the aircraft launching crane where the fragile old Walrus was about to be catapulted off for spotting. Splinters made mincemeat of it and the remains were quickly dumped over the side before they caught fire. A third heavy shell penetrated the ship's side below the waterline and passed through several bulkheads and the British ship took on 400 tons of water.[52] Her toughness prevented a repetition of the *Hood* disaster, but it was clear that if she stayed in line under such punishment she would be knocked about and perhaps in time disabled.

With the *Prinz Eugen* carrying torpedoes and with the U-boats on the look for such a juicy target as a crippled battleship, and with his main armament reduced by repeated failures and breakdowns to three guns only at times, Captain Leach made the only possible decision—to break off the action. It was 6:13, the range was down to 14,500 yards, and the enemy appeared unharmed. Leach altered course to 160 degrees, and as she came about, the *Prince of Wales*'s after 14-inch turret jammed solid. Her speed was still a good twenty-seven knots, however, and she was thus able to offer the two shadowing cruisers some protection as they resumed their former role to patiently await Admiral Tovey and his squadron to pick up the action again. Meanwhile, Admiral Wake-Walker, as senior man on the spot, took over the battered squadron. To the relief of the British, the German admiral did not press his advantage to its logical conclusion and destroy two British capital ships in one action. At the time, it seemed inexplicable but later the reason why was learned.

The *Prince of Wales* may have been a new ship and may have taken a beating, but she herself had inflicted telling damage on her German opponent during the course of her first, brief action. Unknown to her weary gun crews, struggling again to get their 14-inch maverick guns back into working order, their contribution was to be a decisive one in the final outcome of the battle. They had, in fact, made two hits on the *Bismarck* in reply. One entered the hull, piercing two compartments, putting a dynamo out of action, and damaging number 2 boiler room. The other was the more fateful one. This also pierced two compartments and opened up a fuel tank. This caused severe leakage and contamination; doubly serious due to her failure to refuel earlier while at Bergen. Her speed was reduced to twenty-eight knots, but the only casualties were five wounded.

An eyewitness aboard the *Prince of Wales* made light of her injuries: "By about twenty-five past six we were out of effective range of each other, and the action was broken off—a temporary lull only, we all hoped, for the role of watching and waiting was galling in the extreme."[53] Captain Leach was more realistic, but within a short time, he was able to report to the *Norfolk* that his ship was ready for action again, although still with her full armament not functioning.

Admiral Wake-Walker's prudence in not immediately reengaging did not go down well with the impatient Churchill, however.[54] The *Bismarck* and her consort continued their well-plotted course southwest during the forenoon of the twenty-fourth, with the *Suffolk* pacing her by radar from the starboard quarter with the *Norfolk* and *Prince of Wales* long-stopping to port. Poor visibility was no bar to the *Suffolk*'s radar watch, and constant alterations of course to throw the British off her trail availed the *Bismarck* nothing, especially as the oil slick from the *Prince of Wales*'s 14-inch shell hit left an easy track to follow. At 1:20 P.M., the *Bismarck* turned south, still with the *Prinz Eugen* in company; at 3:35, a British reconnaissance aircraft was also in company.

The Admiralty had in the meantime set in train wide-ranging movements of ships the length and breadth of the Atlantic in order to avenge the *Hood*'s loss. The *Rodney* was told to leave the *Britannic* with one destroyer as escort, take the remaining three with her, and close the *Bismarck* on a westerly course. As one of her crew recalled: "It was three years since the *Rodney* had been refitted, and the long hours spent at sea in heavy Atlantic gales had placed a great strain on her structure and on her engines." When the news was received that they were to refit in Boston in the United States, the crew were elated. When she finally sailed, she had many guests aboard for the same destination. There were many drafts for the Falklands, and for Halifax, and naval cadets for Bermuda. They even included an American naval officer and two CPOs. Altogether, there were about 500, and one can understand the torpedoman who remarked, "They seem to think we're the *Queen Mary!*"[55]

Her long-overdue refit now abandoned, the *Rodney* turned her great, long forecastle toward the enemy. But she was but one of the Royal Navy's big ships to receive the urgent summons from London. In Gibraltar, Admiral Somerville had been waiting aboard the *Renown* with the carrier, light cruiser, and six available destroyers of his famous command ready with steam up for just such an eventuality. When the word came, they cleared the Rock and headed northwest. In far-distant Freetown, the *Rodney*'s sister ship, the *Nelson*, was told to make her best speed to take the *Renown*'s place at Gibraltar in the remote possibility of the *Bismarck* attempting to break into the Mediterranean in order to give the Italian Fleet some backbone in time for Crete.

The *Ramillies* was told that the *Bismarck* was some 900 miles north of her and that she was to leave her convoy and place herself to the west of the enemy. Her sister, the *Revenge*, sailed from Halifax, Nova Scotia, as additional backup. A great circle of guns was being drawn around the German leviathan; it remained but to pull it tight. But once again, Lütjens proved himself adept at the art of outfoxing his opponents. His first task was to provide a diversion to allow the *Prinz Eugen* to break away and continue her sortie. In this, however, he was already admitting that the *Bismarck* had been thwarted. Despite the stunning blow he had inflicted on Holland's squadron, the hits he received in return were such to abandon his own mission, and his overriding concern was to get his damaged vessel safely into the haven of Brest.

It is interesting to notice that the leaders of both Germany and Britain were dissatisfied with their admirals for their conduct this day. Hitler, when it was all over, asked why Lütjens had not finished off the *Prince of Wales* when he had the chance, thus sinking two British heavy ships. Churchill remained optimistic despite the news of the *Hood*'s loss. "The *Hood* has blown up, but we have got the *Bismarck* for certain," was his first response to the news. But later he grew more restless at the way things were going and it seems likely that it was at his urging that a series of 'prodding and niggling' signals started to pour out of the Admiralty, growing ever more bizarre as the operation proceeded. The first of these was to Wake-Walker enquiring his intentions about the *Prince of Wales*'s reengaging the enemy. This was far from Wake-Walker's intentions at the time but it seemed to have caused him to reconsider. As a result, he commenced the concentration of his squadron in fighting formation, pulling *Suffolk* over to join his other two ships. Before this had been effected, the *Bismarck* gave him an unlooked-for opportunity to comply with Pound's apparent wishes.

At 6:38 P.M., the *Bismarck* suddenly rounded on her pursuers and almost took the *Norfolk* by surprise. Her salvos fortunately missed the thinly armored cruiser, although two near-misses caused some leaks. The *Prince of Wales* came up in support, and the two battleships exchanged a few brief salvos before the *Bismarck* again hauled round. But the *Prinz Eugen* had vanished into the Atlantic wastes. Lütjens was now on his own. His next task was to elude his shadowers and then get under the protection of the Luftwaffe and U-boats off France before he could be brought to battle.

Now the alterations of the British squadron's dispositions proved fatal. At 8:56 P.M., Lütjens informed his superiors ashore he was making direct for Brest because of his fuel situation. But he was to have another scare first. The *Victorious* had been sent on ahead of the *King George V* and *Repulse* to launch an air strike in order to slow her down even more, and this she set in motion at 10:08. The old aircraft—all torpedo-bombers—found the German giant at 11:30 and made their attack ten minutes before midnight with eight planes. They scored one hit, which did not damage, but the high-speed turns made by the *Bismarck* to evade this attack opened up her old wound, causing number 2 boiler room to be abandoned, and her speed reduced to sixteen knots for a time. The German ship looked doomed.

But the *Suffolk* lost contact again at 3:06 on the morning of the twenty-fifth, and all was in the melting pot again. At first, it was thought that she would be picked up again, but Lütjens had carefully studied the *Suffolk*'s zig-zag legs, and on one such outward turn, she had put her helm hard over to starboard and turned a complete circle almost to come about on an easterly course far astern of Wake-Walker's three ships. Lütjens was once more at liberty. The tragedy for him and his crew was that, at this triumphant moment, he did not realize it.

There then came a long and testing period of nerves and temper while the various British forces grouped their way around the Atlantic in order to relocate the *Bismarck*. Several false hares were started through confusing intelligence over the next hours. Not until 6:05 P.M. did the Admiralty order the *Rodney* to steer an intercepting course for Brest, and Admiral Tovey complied five minutes later—although by now he was some 150 miles astern because of a faulty interpretation of Admiralty bearings given him in the form of the D/F bearings and not as the worked-out position.[56] Meanwhile, the ever-vital factor of fuel was affecting the British warships as much as the *Bismarck*. Thus, the *Repulse, Prince of Wales*, and most of the smaller ships dropped out of the chase through lack of fuel, and only the *Rodney* and far astern the faster *King George V* remained to keep up the almost hopeless stern-chase. The *Bismarck* was sighted at last by a Coastal Command Catalina at 10:30 A.M. on the twenty-sixth, 700 miles west of Brest.

Fortunately, Admiral Somerville had all along stood out for Brest and Force H still remained between Lütjens and sanctuary. The *Renown* was no match for the *Bismarck* in a straight fight, despite the unrivalled confidence of her crew, but the *Ark Royal*'s aircraft, a more experienced team despite their previous failures against big ships, might have better fortune than the *Victorious* in slowing her down. Thus, thanks again to the gallantry of these young pilots, it fell out. Night attacks by the 4th Destroyer Flotilla, though equally as bravely carried out, were not decisive. But the *Bismarck* was brought to bay, crippled and unable to maneuver, but with her guns still very much intact, on the morning of May 27, 1941. The final act of the drama was now played out with the *King George V* and *Rodney* given the stage to bring about the ultimate execution.

Other ships were in the vicinity. The heavy cruiser *Norfolk*, which had managed to stay in the hunt to the end, sighted the *Bismarck* again at 7:53 A.M. at a distance of nine miles, and a little later, she was acting as a visual link to Admiral Tovey when the *King George V* was sighted twelve miles off to the south. Another 8-inch cruiser, *Dorsetshire*, had also hastened to be in at the kill, leaving her convoy some 600 miles astern. She was to achieve her ambition in no uncertain way, but for the moment kept clear. Admiral Somerville and the three ships left to Force H—the *Renown*, *Ark Royal*, and *Sheffield*—also kept clear, Tovey telling Somerville to stay at least twenty miles south of the enemy to enable his ships to have unrestricted room to manouevre.[57] The *Ark Royal* flew off a Swordfish to spot for the commander in chief, but weather conditions forced her to return, and a torpedo striking force was not sent off for the same reason. Several of the Tribal-class destroyers were still in contact after their night shadowing, forming a box around the crippled giant, while two more, the *Mashona* and *Tartar*, had joined up. In all the British ships, the problem of oil fuel was acute. This problem was occupying Admiral Tovey's mind as it had done since the operation began, but it can hardly have improved his concentration to have the prime minister again chipping-in with his viewpoint on matters: "*Bismarck* must be sunk at all costs and if to do this it is necessary for *King George V* to remain on the scene, she must do so even if it means subsequently towing her home," ran Churchill's signal from the Admiralty.

Admiral Pound later apologized to Tovey for allowing it to be sent, and Captain Roskill has already explained why he omitted this from the official history, despite Captain Grenfell's criticism for so doing.[58] We can leave the matter there as self-explanatory of the way Churchill felt about such matters as the fate of the most modern and efficient battleship in the Royal Navy in the U-boat infested seas of the western Atlantic. Luckily, the action was over, and Tovey was on his way home before this "singular" signal was taken in.

The *King George V* and *Rodney* approached the *Bismarck* from the west-northwest, and though a northwest gale was blowing, the visibility was fair to good from the flagship's bridge. Tovey gave the *Rodney* a free hand during this approach by telling her to assume open order about six cables from the *King George V*, in contrast to Captain Leach in the earlier battle. It was planned to approach the *Bismarck*, which was making an estimated ten knots away from France, on an opposing course and engage at 15,000 yards.

At 8:43 A.M., their quarry was sighted almost dead ahead some 25,000 yards off, and some four minutes later, the *Rodney* led off the firing.

There was a sort of crackling roar to port; the *Rodney* has opened fire with her 16-inch guns, and an instant later, the *King George V* lets fly with her 14-inch. I have my glasses on the *Bismarck*. She fires all four guns from her two forward turrets, four thin orange flames. The Germans have a reputation for hitting with their early salvos. Now I know what suspended animation means. It seems to take about two hours for those shots to fall! The splashes shoot up opposite but beyond the *Rodney*'s forecastle.[59]

Despite their reputation, the Germans did not straddle until the third and fourth salvos, but the *Rodney* was carefully handled by Capt. Dalrymple Hamilton and avoided being hit. "Nothing worse than a near-miss was experienced, which was so close that a fragment of shell passed through the starboard side of the director, smashed the cease-fire bell, passed through a tin hat which was hanging up, carved the Trainer's telescope in half, hit the fire gong which is attached to the director itself and shot to the rear, grazing the Trainer's wrist on its way."[60] This is the sum total of the damage done to the *Rodney* by the *Bismarck*, although the damage caused by the blast of her own triple 16-inch guns was considerable.[61]

But the *Bismarck*'s gunnery soon began to fall off and never seriously worried the British battleships again—which was perhaps just as well, for now the *King George V* began to experience the same difficulties with her main armament as had the *Prince of Wales*. One gun was out of action for thirty minutes and two others for briefer periods. As Admiral Beatty said on another famous occasion, there truly was "something the matter with our bloody ships," something that the twenty years' peace had done nothing to rectify.[62]

Nonetheless, the two British battleships now began scoring hits. The first was recorded by the *Rodney* at 9:02 and was confirmed by a German survivor: "At 9:02, both forward heavy gun turrets were put out of action. A further hit wrecked the forward control post, the rear control post was wrecked soon after—and that was the end of the fighting instruments."[63] Aboard the *Rodney*, the chief boatswain's mate was observing the battle from the armored director:

A turret on the *Bismarck* went first, and then he saw B turret split open and a large sheet of flame come out of it. He saw the spotting top disintegrate. The range was now so close that he could clearly see the remaining turret, X, elevate her guns as he prepared to fire once more. As she did so, a salvo from the *Rodney* landed on the turret, and when the smoke had cleared he saw that the guns were at full depression. He could see the fires glowing inside, and bodies and debris were hurled in the air, while men fortunate to be alive leaped over the side.[64]

By this time, the *Norfolk* had joined in with her 8-inch at 22,000 yards from the *Bismarck*'s starboard bow. After her long wait, it was appropriate that she should add her quota to the vengeance of the *Hood*. The *King George V* had altered course just after 9:00 at 16,000 yards range to open up her A arcs. 14-inch salvos now rained down on the German vessel, and the *Rodney* complied with the flagship's movements soon after, opening the gap between them to twenty-one miles. The *Bismarck* was forced to switch her main armament to counter Tovey's flagship, thus leaving the *Rodney* free to make relatively undisturbed practice. Tovey's method of fighting was shown thus to be ideal, although the considerable clouds of cordite drifting over the battlefield made spotting difficult although the radar helped somewhat.

Despite the carnage being wrought in the *Bismarck*, Tovey was not satisfied that they were hurting her enough to bring the engagement to the speedy close his fuel situation called for. "Close the range; get closer, get close—I can't see enough hits," Tovey said, according to one eyewitness,[65] while Bennett states that he was "sufficiently exasperated to tell his fleet gunnery officer that he would have a better chance of hitting if he threw his binoculars at her."[66]

The *Dorsetshire* was now firing into the *Bismarck*'s starboard quarter from 20,000 yards range. The *King George V* opened up briefly with her 5.25s, and the *Rodney* even took advantage of this opportunity to fire in anger—for perhaps the first and last time by a battleship—her two 24.5-inch torpedoes, but without scoring a hit.[67] The *Norfolk* also fired four torpedoes but again without result.

Soon after 9:15, both British ships turned 180 degrees to commence a rerun at their target by then drawing aft. The *Rodney* restarted her main armament firing at the point-blank range of 8,600 yards, while the *King George V* opened again from 12,000 and then, at 10:55, went in to within 3,000 yards to blast the *Bismarck* with several deadly salvos. Not surprisingly, the German ship was now slowing down; her gunfire, again directed against the *Rodney*, was ineffectual.

By 10:10, all the *Bismarck*'s guns had fallen silent, and she lay wallowing in the Atlantic swell, little more than a floating scrap yard, her guns askew, her superstructure carved into distorted shapes, huge holes in her upperworks from which spewed flames and smoke. Aboard, it was a scene from hell, with mounds of dead and dying and all machinery spaces filling with fumes and smoke. But despite all this, her engines remained intact, and she would not sink.

Tovey just did not have the time to spend in putting her down by gunfire alone. If he did not leave the area soon, his ships were almost sure to be left stranded long before they reached port. At 10:15, therefore, he ordered the two battleships to break off the action, just 100 minutes or so after it had started, and steer for home, leaving the assembled cruisers and destroyers to administer the *coup de grace* with torpedoes. And this was finally carried out by the *Dorsetshire*, which put three deliberately aimed torpedoes into the drifting, burning hulk of the once-proud *Bismarck* at 10:36. The great vessel then fell over to port and started to settle by the stern. Some four minutes later she rolled over and went to the bottom of the ocean she had sought to terrorize.[68]

In his report of the action, Admiral Tovey paid tribute to the manner in which the *Bismarck* had fought her last action: "The *Bismarck* had put up a most gallant fight against impossible odds, worthy of the old days of the Imperial German Navy, and she went down with her colors flying."[69] To which, in return, the Admiralty—again probably influenced by Churchill— sent him a dignified raspberry.[70]

But despite Churchill's bad grace in victory, it *had* been a gallant fight. It was also more than that, it was the end of an era. For the last time had the German heavy ships challenged British naval power in the Atlantic. Never again did they sail against the weakly protected convoys of that great ocean artery. The disruption of Britain's trade was left to the skulking U-boats, against which different defenses were required. As at Matapan in the Mediterranean, as at Jutland in the North Sea, the British battleships had done their job, had done it well, and had done it for keeps. The challenger was knocked down, and he stayed down. And although the cruisers, the destroyers, and the aircraft had tracked him and hurt him, had dogged him and hamstrung him, it was the battleship that had administered the knock-out blow.

For this, it received scant thanks from posterity.

The *Royal Oak* firing a broadside.

The *Queen Elizabeth* completed a major rebuilding early in the war and joined the Mediterranean Fleet in 1941.

The *Barham* at Scapa Flow. She was considered an unlucky ship, being damaged by a U-boat, in a collision, and by shore fire off Dakar and finally sunk with enormous casualties in the Mediterranean.

The *Repulse* "taking it green" in the North Atlantic. An unmodernized battlecruiser, she was the weakest of Britain's big ships—but also one of the fastest.

The *Nelson* was the flagship of the Home Fleet for much of the earlier period of the war but was damaged by a magnetic mine. She and her sister mounted nine 16-inch guns, the most powerful broadsides of the whole British Fleet, but they were painfully slow.

The huge armored bridge structure of the *Rodney* early in the war. Note the heavy and light anti-aircraft weapons, directors, and early radar mat mounted.

Looking forward along *Rodney*'s forecastle. Notice the earlier primitive additions to her light antiaircraft weapons mounted atop B turret.

The *Malaya* and *Ramillies*, resplendent in early dazzle paint scheme, sail forth in the eastern Mediterranean to carry out the bombardment of Bardia. In the distance is the 8-inch cruiser *Kent*.

The battlecruiser *Hood* returning to Scapa Flow in the autumn of 1940 after operations with Force H at Gibraltar that included Mers-el-Kebir.

The flagship of Admiral Cunningham's Mediterranean Fleet was the famous *Warspite*. Victor of the battles of Calabria (July 1940) and Matapan (March 1941), she was damaged off Crete in May 1941.

Another famous ship in action: the battlecruiser *Renown* firing a 15-inch salvo at full speed in pursuit of the Italian fleet at the Battle of Spartivento, November 1940.

The unmodernized *Malaya* bombarded Genoa and served well in the North Atlantic and Force H.

The *Revenge*, seen here in the Indian Ocean.

The brand-new *Prince of Wales* at Scapa Flow. Still not fully completed, she was sent against the *Bismarck* and, although damaged herself, scored the vital hit with her 14-inch shells that doomed the German giant.

The *Nelson* covered Malta convoys Substance and Halberd and, during the latter, was hit forward by an aerial torpedo. She is seen here badly down by the bows as a result.

The mighty but ill-fated *Hood* seen here at Scapa before her last sortie. She blew up with only three survivors in her duel with the *Bismarck*.

The *Valiant* was one of the two battleships badly damaged by Italian "human torpedoes" at Alexandria in December 1941.

The *Barham* seen here at sea with the 1st Battle Squadron in the Mediterranean. While patrolling in the Gulf of Sirte, she was hit by three torpedoes fired by a U-boat and sank quickly.

After the attack, the *Barham*, still moving through the water, rolled over on her beam ends. Seconds later, a main magazine detonated, blowing her asunder and ssending her to the bottom with heavy casualties.

The *Prince of Wales* arriving at Singapore Dockyard, December 1941. Part of a small, unbalanced force with no air cover, she was meant to awe the Japanese, who had ten battleships and ten carriers.

The *Repulse* sails from Singapore on her last sortie. On December 10, she and *Prince of Wales* were sent to the bottom of the South China Sea by Japanese naval torpedo-carrying aircraft.

The hastily assembled East Indies Fleet fortunately avoided a battle it could not win in April 1942. Seen here are the *Warspite, Royal Sovereign,* and *Revenge* with the carrier *Illustrious.*

Survivors abandoning the doomed *Prince of Wales* and boarding the destroyer *Express* alongside.

The old *Resolution* puts on a brave front in the Indian Ocean in 1942. Note Walrus aircraft on the after turret, funnel cap, and dazzle scheme.

In Arctic water, the *King George V* rammed and sank the destroyer *Punjabi*. As the destroyer sank, her depth charges exploded below the battleship's bows, causing considerable damage.

The landings in the Mediterranean at Sicily and Salerno were covered by powerful British fleets, but the Italians failed to appear. Here the *Valiant* fires a few frustrated salvos astern of the *Illustrious* while on patrol.

The *Anson* on trials.

The *Royal Sovereign* with the Eastern Fleet. One by one, the older battle-ships returned home, and some went into reserve. A strange fate befell the *Royal Sovereign*: she was handed over to the Soviet Union for four years.

The *Royal Sovereign* flying the Soviet naval ensign as the *Arkhangelsk*.

The *Howe*, on patrol in the Arctic, tests her pom-poms. The 8-inch cruiser *Berwick* is in the background.

The *Rodney* brings her main armament into action against enemy shore batteries and troop concentrations with good effect.

The *Duke of York*, in the darkness of the Arctic night, took on *Scharnhorst* in the last classic duel by British and German heavy ships and pounded her to defeat.

The *Ramillies* in action in 1944 bombarding German coastal batteries during the landings in southern France.

The *Warspite* continued in action despite grievous damage. Here she is pounding the German batteries on D-Day, June 6, 1944, off the Normandy beaches.

After refitting, the *Queen Elizabeth* went out to the East Indies station once more.

The *Renown* also served out her days in the Indian Ocean as the fastest capital ship in the fleet before returning to home waters in 1945.

The British Pacific Fleet took the war back to Japan and carried out bombardments of the Tokyo suburbs toward the end of the war. Here the *King George V* arrives at Guam in 1945.

The surrender of Japan was followed by the liberation of the former empire. Here *Anson* is anchored in Victoria Harbor, Hong Kong, in September 1945.

The last of the line: the *Vanguard* fires a 15-inch salvo. She was delayed so much the war had finished by the time she was completed.

CHAPTER 6

The Fleet in Being

The destruction of the *Bismarck* in May 1941 not only marked a turning point in the role of the battleship in World War II from the Axis point of view, but it also was a watershed in the history of the British battleship's long story. It was, in fact, the end of the old era. By establishing their complete dominance over the heavy ships of the two enemy powers, the British battleship had confounded its interwar critics and seemingly emerged as decisive an influence on naval warfare as it had always been. Far from being an impotent white elephant, unable to leave the sanctuary of its own bases, the British battleship had been used in a whole variety of roles around the world, with minimum casualties and with complete success. But with this very success, it had forced the Axis to adopt the very policies predicted for all battleships before the war: the "fleet in being," a distant mailed fist to be husbanded and used only with care and caution but nonetheless exercised as a menace to British commerce and trade so great that it could not be ignored. By the same token, Britain was forced to seek out these reluctant combatants by the same methods that the Axis now adopted as their alternative policy of attrition against the seapower they could not destroy in direct ship-to-ship surface combat.

In the transition period that followed—roughly from the mid-months of 1941 through to the end of 1942—the battleship continued to be a major factor in maritime warfare but in a different way. Still the backbone of the fleets, and holding great political importance as major pawns in the game, the big ships became the targets of both the underwater and aerial arms of the opposing nations. How successful these alternative means of controlling events at sea were—both in achieving the immediate objective of sinking battleships and in the longer-term objective of gaining control of the seaways (or removing that threat from the seaways)—varied from nation to nation, depending on what weapons they adopted to achieve it.

This policy was adopted by both Germany and Italy, whose main strengths anyway lay in their underwater and air arms. In both cases, British battleships ensured that the vital convoys of foodstuffs, oil, and war materiel that passed into Britain, Malta, Egypt, or later north Russia remained relatively immune from surface attack. The hope that the enemy would, sometime, accept combat, always sustained them in this long vigil, as did the alternative hope that the Axis fleets would ultimately surrender as a result of their impotence. But like the Grand Fleet battleships before them, the waiting for either of these events to materialize seemed interminable, although ultimately the Royal Navy was to be granted *both* those objectives.

The wearing-down of the British battle fleet, already at full stretch anyway, was made easier for the Axis by the fact that the Royal Navy never flinched from utilizing these vessels to the full, even in the face of growing odds. This was also in contrast to prewar predictions.[1]

But by keeping their own big ships tucked away in safety, and thus forcing the British to adopt the same alternative measures to remove the threat they presented, the Axis powers were more successful since they were rarely out at sea for British submarines to strike at, whereas British battleships were constantly employed and thus offered far greater opportunity to the U-boats. In the same way, British battleships acted as the linchpins of the fleets, the solid rock on which the lesser ships, including aircraft-carriers, fell back when hard pressed. Even so, British battleships were more open to air attrition than the heavily camouflaged German and Italian battleships snug behind their rings of nets and antiaircraft batteries. It is little wonder then that, in this critical period, British losses mounted and the fleet reached its nadir whereas Axis casualties were minimal.

It is also relevant to remember that, in the main, all the combatants continued to persist during this period with roughly the same policies of air attack on ships as they began with. The bombers got larger, as did the weight and size of bombs they could carry, but the method of attack only slowly changed. This second round of bomber versus battleship was long drawn out and this time the honors were more evenly shared. But only in very special circumstances, and by the adoption of specialized forces using the correct weapon, the air-carried torpedo, did the air arms finally put a modern battleship on the seabed. Against the older, less well-protected, vessels, the rapid development of the bomber and the bomb slowly but surely began to tip the scales in the direction of the air, but even here, the effort required just minimal successes, and the heavy losses made it far from the foregone conclusion of the prewar experts or the postwar historians. The battleship's resilience continued to make a mockery of these judgments in the period covered by this chapter, although the punishment taken was exceptional.

Thus, the Luftwaffe continued with the dive-bomber and showed again that this method was the most certain way of hitting ships at sea, even if it could not sink big ships. Development of special heavy bombs eventually resulted in the combination of the two methods and, finally, three obsolete and static battleships succumbed to the Stuka. But this was not the way. The Royal Air Force continued, almost as an act of religious faith, to pin their hopes on the heavy altitude bombers as they had all along. The bombing aids got more sophisticated, the bombs grew larger, a few minor successes were achieved, but never a sinking. This was not the way either, but still they persisted. The Italians had already learnt that altitude bombing was futile and had switched a far greater proportion of their effort from this method towards the real answer, known and feared as long ago as 1919, the torpedo-bomber. Fortunately the wretched economy and organization of the Italian war effort meant that their torpedo-bomber forces were used in "penny packets" and by an elite group of pilots. Their success rate grew against the smaller vessels, but against the battleship, numbers were the key, not simply skill and bravery.

This was not new and had been much discussed before the war. The torpedo-bomber was known to present the greatest threat to the battleship; indeed, they had ensured the introduction of the dual-purpose secondary armaments of all the new vessels and the adoption of the multitude of close-range automatic weapons that began to sprout and bristle on big ships at that time. The Royal Navy had demonstrated its effectiveness enough by 1941, at Taranto and elsewhere, but it was only during this period that the air forces of Britain, Germany, and Italy began to really develop this arm, and consequently, it did not achieve much.[2]

One air force, however, had not only developed the torpedo-bomber to a far greater extent than was ever realized in Europe but had spread its development over the widest field possible. Not surprisingly, this was a naval air force, that of Imperial Japan. By the period covered in this chapter, Japan was the only country to have combined both land-based and carrier-based torpedo-bomber squadrons of great skill and accuracy designed for the job from the very beginning, rather than the hasty adaptions of existing land-bomber types in the RAF, Luftwaffe, and Italian Air Force.[3] This was the opponent, and its methods were described by prewar critics as decisive.[4] It was in 1941–42 the only force of its kind.

If the British air marshals were slow to change their policies or accept that the more heady of their expectations were still not within their reach, then the admirals, too, were shown to be still out of step with modern war conditions, despite the bitter shocks they had received at the hands of the Luftwaffe in Norway and off France the year before.

It was to take a great deal more slaughter and heavy sinkings of priceless warships before the lessons finally sank in. Among these was that antiaircraft firepower on warships, even on battleships, was by no means sufficient in deterring determined air attack by large numbers of planes in resolute hands. Antiaircraft firepower was required to be tripled in British ships before they reached some degree of immunity, but even then, it was never the nearly 100 percent immunity many had hoped for before the war. Another was that fighter protection was the most certain way of ensuring the protection of a fleet beset by continual air assault. Unfortunately, the development of a suitable fighter in sufficient numbers to be effective lagged far behind the actual building of carriers to transport them into battle. This deficiency was never resolved by Britain; only the introduction into the fleet of American types, built for the job under Lend-Lease, produced the results, but not for another two years.

These lessons were, then, all worked over on a grander scale once more, and to supplement them, new weapons were thrown into the battle, both in the air and beneath the seas; all of them aimed mainly at the battleships of the warring nations. The first of these traumatic confrontations took place in the eastern Mediterranean at the same time that the *Bismarck* was fighting her battles far away in the North Atlantic.

Mussolini's unfortunate gamble in invading Greece against Hitler's wishes in order to gain some prestige for his tattered empire had resulted in a series of even greater disasters for Italy. Not only had the humiliation of her navy continued unabated, culminating in the Matapan disaster, but the tiny Greek army had bundled the Italians out of their country in short order and even threatened to drive them into the Adriatic by taking Albania. Stalin had had his greedy eyes on the Balkans, and Hitler, preparing for his long-sought showdown with communism, was determined to ensure the safety of his Romanian oil supplies. Germany was therefore not willing to see British air bases set up in Greece just over the border. That being so, he had little alternative but to bail his Axis partner out of trouble yet again, even though it meant delaying his own schemes. While British diplomacy worked with the dignity and speed of the elephant and while the Italians bribed and schemed with the various Balkan nations leaders to exert their influence there, Germany acted with her usual speed and efficiency. By the spring, all these nations and their own petty squabbles, had been subordinated to the German Reich, either through alliance (Hungary, Bulgaria, and Romania) or through force (Yugoslavia). Only Greece remained, with a small British army hastily thrown in from the Libyan desert at the height of their victory there. In April, these were crushed by the usual blitzkrieg tactics[5] and driven out to the island of Crete, a vital base to keep if the British wished to hold onto the eastern Mediterranean. General Student of the German Luftwaffe's airborne forces asked to be allowed to try the novel idea of taking a well-defended island, ringed by superior seapower, by the air alone. As it would not unduly interfere with Operation Barbarossa, Hitler's planned invasion of the Soviet

Union, and would round off his conquests in southeast Europe conquests, Hitler agreed. In the event, some seaborne follow-ups of heavy equipment were deemed necessary even for such a limited operation but these were on a small scale. The British were certain that no island could be taken by air power alone and expected large invasion convoys to back up the initial attack. Admiral Cunningham was therefore instructed to take his fleet to sea and ensure that this did not take place. The stage was set for one of the bloodiest air/sea battles in history.[6]

On the island of Crete, the British forces consisted of some 28,500 troops who had a month to prepare themselves for the attack. The German invasion forces consisted of 15,000 airborne troops, who would land there, and 7,000 seaborne troops, who would never make it. In the air, the balance tipped the other way: "As against the puny force of a dozen or so Hurricanes, Gladiators, and Fulmars, the Luftwaffe had available, under *Fliegerkorps* VIII for the supporting operations and *Fliegerkorps* XI for the actual invasion, no fewer than 650 operational aircraft, 700 transports, and 80 gliders. Of the 650 operational machines, 430 were bombers, 180 fighters."[7]

Pitted against these 650 aircraft, Admiral Cunningham matched the Mediterranean Fleet, which at this time consisted of the battleships *Warspite* (flag), *Queen Elizabeth, Valiant,* and *Barham;* the carrier *Formidable;* eight 6-inch cruisers; three antiaircraft cruisers; a minelayer; and, ultimately, thirty destroyers. The Italian fleet, although still superior in every arm, made no attempt to intervene in the battle. As one historian commented, "It is true to say that what little success was achieved by the British during the naval operations off Greece and Crete was made possible by the devastating broadsides of the battleships during the night action of the battle of Matapan."[8] The duel would be the long-anticipated and straightforward one of warships versus aircraft. That contest opened at dawn on May 14, 1941.

Admiral Cunningham disposed his forces in four groups. Three striking forces of cruisers and destroyers (Forces B, C, and D) were sent to patrol off Crete to prevent the passage of any invasion convoys heading for the beaches and ports of that island which all lay to the north. In support of these light forces, Vice Admiral Pridham-Wippell sailed with the *Queen Elizabeth*[9] and *Barham* with five destroyers for a screen and cruised to west of Crete to interpose itself between the Italian fleet and the protecting cruiser squadrons. Apart from a few minor incidents, these forces were not molested, nor did they encounter the enemy in any strength. On May 18, Force A1, under Rear Adm. H. B. Rawlings, sailed from Alexandria to relieve Force A. Force A1 consisted of the *Warspite* and *Valiant,* one cruiser, and a screen of eight destroyers. Admiral Cunningham was directing his fleet from ashore at Alexandria during this battle.

The *Warspite* and *Valiant* took over the supporting watch on the nine-teenth, and the following day, the actual German invasion commenced at first light. The German invasion convoy bound for Maleme put to sea from the Piraeus that night. Meanwhile the cruiser patrols continued to prowl north of Crete by dark and withdraw southward during the hours of daylight. During the twentieth, the Luftwaffe was almost exclusively employed in soft-ening up the land defences and by nightfall a substantial number of German paratroops were established ashore and much confused fighting was contin-uing. Sweeps by the light forces had driven off an Italian E-boat flotilla but discovered no convoys in the area.

On the twenty-first, Admiral Rawlings and his two battleships and escorts were some sixty miles west of the Antikithera Strait steering southeast to ren-dezvous with one of the returning cruiser squadrons. All forces, including those in transit to and from the battle zone and the base at Alexandria, had orders to concentrate for safety during daylight, but in the event this was not completely effected. The destroyer *Juno* was lost during the day as the scale of air attack increased but this was the enemy's sole victim. Rawlings contin-ued to cruise southwest of Crete and received further reports of enemy inva-sion convoys on their way. "With the concentration of such a large force, it was possible to put up an antiaircraft barrage over the fleet which effectively reduced the severity of the dive bombing attacks and inflicted casualties," wrote one historian. But at the same time he added, "The wear and tear and fatigue had been enormous, and the expenditure of ammunition was on a scale that could not be maintained indefinitely."[10]

That night, the cruiser striking forces returned to the north of the dis-puted island and there set upon, and turned back with losses, both the intended sea-borne reinforcements. The Royal Navy had certainly done its job, but the price it was now asked to pay was exorbitant. At first light on the twenty-second, these cruisers and destroyers, running short of anti-aircraft ammunition and fuel, were still deep in hostile waters and engaged to the hilt in finishing off the convoys. It was on this day that the Germans decided to switch the bulk of their bomber forces against the fleet and the fight began in earnest.

The cruiser forces received the first attentions of the eager Luftwaffe pilots. Several ships were damaged by hits and near-misses, and the expendi-ture of antiaircraft ammunition soon left the ships with little else to fire but practice ammunition. The German bombers ran an almost continuous shut-tle service between their bases and the fleet and thus the ships were almost constantly in action. On receiving the news of the heavy attacks being mounted, Rawlings decided to abandon his waiting position and move further into the danger area to give the hard-pressed light forces some relief. In doing so he brought down the wrath of the Luftwaffe on his own squadron.

Throughout the morning, the two battleships had stationed themselves some thirty miles west of the Kithera Channel, where, as he later reported, he served "some useful purpose by attracting enemy aircraft." At 12:25, he swung his great ships round and set off at twenty-three knots into the Aegean. It was a calculated risk of great daring, although the antiaircraft position of the two battleships was somewhat better than the cruisers, being 66 percent in the *Warspite* and 80 percent in the *Valiant*. Withdrawing damaged and under heavy attack, the cruisers were sighted at 1:12, and the two forces joined together twenty minutes later and commenced their withdrawal. Almost at once, the battleships became the center of the Luftwaffe assault as their distinctive bulks made inevitable.

As well as the Ju 87 Stukas, the true dive-bombers, the Germans were using conventional twin-engine bombers and fighters, some of the latter carrying bombs in a new role as fighter-bombers. It was three of the latter—Me 109s of III/KG 77, led by Lieutenant Huy—that inflicted the first damage. At 1:32, they hurtled out of the low cloud base, through the burst of flak some 2,000 yards ahead of the *Warspite* at an altitude of 800 feet, and attacked along the fore and aft line of the ship, avoiding the worst of the flak which was mounted in the broadside batteries further aft.

> The captain put on full port wheel, two bombs fell 50–100 yards clear and did not damage; but the third one hit the ship on the starboard side of the forecastle deck, and burst right on the starboard after 4-inch gun. It was probably a 500-pound semi-armor-piercing bomb, and the damage it caused was severe. A dangerous fire was started in the starboard battery, and all four 6-inch guns were put out of action; the starboard forward 4-inch antiaircraft twin mounting was blown completely overboard, and one boiler-room had temporarily to be abandoned. One officer and thirty-seven men were killed, or died of wounds, and thirty-one wounded.[11]

With her boiler room intakes damaged, the flagship's speed was reduced to eighteen knots but her large fires were brought under control and she was able to keep her place in-line for the rest of the day. Unhappily her sacrifice did not save her less well-protected companions for the concentration of ships was broken up with the sighting of a lone caique. The destroyer *Greyhound* was detached from the main body to sink her, which she did, but she was then alone and unsupported when set upon by eight Stukas at 1:51. Hit by three bombs she quickly sank by the stern. Admiral King then compounded this error[12] by sending out the cruisers *Fiji* and *Gloucester* with two destroyers to act as support. These too were caught beyond the protective barrage of the battleships and quickly overwhelmed and sent to the bottom.

Meanwhile, the battle fleet had undergone further assault between 1:20 until 2:10, during which time the *Valiant* was also hit. A high-level attack at 4:45 scored two hits with medium-size bombs aft, but they failed to penetrate her armored deck and caused little damage. At 6:00, the battleships steered south and then east, so they gradually drew out of range of the questing bombers. Nonetheless, at the day's end, the Royal Navy had lost two modern light cruisers and a destroyer, and had two of their only four battleships damaged, one badly, along with two more cruisers. The enemy's losses were not more than a dozen aircraft, which was no compensation, and ashore the fighting was going badly with the Germans now firmly entrenched and flying in reinforcements nonstop with no opposition from the air.

Despite this, further destroyers patrols were again sent to the waters north of Crete that night, to bombard enemy-held airfields, search for survivors from the sunken ships and maintain the surface blockade. Again, they ensured that no Axis shipping got through, but once more, the price paid was to be a heavy one. When word got through to Admiral Cunningham, ashore at Alexandria, of the perilous state of the remaining stocks of the fleet's antiaircraft ammunition, it caused the withdrawal of all the British forces back to Alexandria to replenish. In fact, the antiaircraft position of the *Warspite* and *Valiant* was adequate, and the signal was shown to Cunningham and his staff as stating these ships were "empty" when the signal should have read "plenty." The *Warspite* and *Valiant* therefore followed the cruisers back to Alexandria, and thus, Lord Mountbatten's three destroyers were left unsupported while withdrawing early on the twenty-third. Two out of three were bombed by Stukas and sunk, while the third was damaged but managed to crawl home.

The destroyers *Decoy* and *Hero* had that same night embarked the king of the Hellenes, the British minister, and other VIPs, and to prevent a similar calamity overtaking them, Admiral Rawlings had ordered them to join his screen. This wise instruction received no thanks from the important personage himself, but it ensured his safe arrival at Alexandria.

In order to try to reduce the scale of Stuka attacks on the fleet, it was determined to try to eliminate some of the aircraft based on Scarpanto, whether in response to the unrealistic signals pouring in from Whitehall or not is not clear. The carrier *Formidable* was therefore sailed to launch an attack with her striking force of four Albacores and four Fulmars. Escorted by the *Queen Elizabeth* and *Barham*, with eight destroyers, she therefore left Alexandria at noon on the twenty-fifth and launched her aircraft early the following morning from a position 100 miles south-southwest of Scarpanto. Although surprise was achieved, damage was limited, and the force withdrew after recovering its aircraft. Counter air strikes were beaten off by the few remaining Fulmars, but soon after being joined by a cruiser force, the whole fleet was instructed to provide cover for a convoy of reinforcements running into Crete. Because of this change of course, the fleet was located by a Stuka formation some ninety miles east of Bardia.

The twenty dive-bombers attacked before the *Formidable* could deploy her fighters and hit the carrier twice. A destroyer also had her stern blown off. Although the *Formidable* was able to continue to operate her aircraft for the rest of the day, on her return she joined the forlorn group of crippled ships awaiting the opportunity to sail south through the Suez Canal for repairs. Despite the departure of the *Formidable*, Admiral Pridham-Wippell continued to cruise with his two battleships off the southeast of Crete during the night and, at dawn on the twenty-seventh, set course for the Kaso Strait to the east of the island to cover a group of light ships who had landed further reinforcements at Suda Bay that night.

When within 190 miles of Scarpanto—supposedly out of action—the fleet was attacked in strength by fifteen medium bombers from the Greek mainland. Despite a heavy barrage, they broke through and scored a direct hit on the old *Barham*. The after 15-inch turret took the brunt of this blow and was put out of action. Two near-misses pierced her bulges and flooded them. The ensuing fire raged aboard for two hours before it was brought under control thus forcing the fleet to steer a southerly course downwind to assist the fire-fighters. Soon after 12:30, Cunningham recalled Pridham-Wippell's ships, and the *Barham* limped into Alexandria harbor.

These sacrifices were in vain, for ashore the decision had been to evacuate. Thus, the worn-out crews and damaged warships of the Mediterranean Fleet, already at the end of their tether, had to be sternly ordered back by Cunningham to save their comrades of the Army and Air Force. To the memorable exhortation that "it takes the Navy three years to build a ship but three centuries to build a tradition," the ships and the men went back to further casualties and further losses.

When the last man had been landed safely at Alexandria on June 1, Cunningham surveyed the broken ships that had been his proud fleet of a month before. He had left ready for service and to hold the whole of the eastern Mediterranean just two battleships, the *Queen Elizabeth* and *Valiant*, and five destroyers. Every other ship afloat was damaged to a greater or lesser degree.[13] Thus ended the battle of Crete.

There has never been much dispute about the results of this battle. On the German side, Gen. Albert Kesselring was exultant: "The result was abundantly clear. I was convinced that we had scored a great and decisive victory."[14] Admiral Ruge went even further: "Had the German Stuka crews been more experienced in attacking ships, or had torpedo-bombers been used, the cost to the British would have been even heavier."[15]

All of which accorded with most British postwar verdicts. Crete showed, wrote Vice Admiral Hezlet, that "shore-based air power when in sufficient strength could defeat a fleet of warships. General 'Billy' Mitchell may have overstated his case in the early twenties, but by the early forties, his assertion had certainly come true."[16] Another writer stated flatly that "the outcome of the Cretan battles, predicted in the interwar years, gave overwhelming victory to the Luftwaffe. The Royal Navy withdrew from Crete bombed to defeat."[17]

The only voiced opinion to the contrary came from the man on the spot at the time: "The hasty conclusion that ships are impotent in the face of air attack should not be drawn from the Battle of Crete. The struggle in no way proved that the air is the master of the sea."[18] Perhaps, but the judgment of history has gone against Admiral Cunningham, for good or ill, and his other conclusion has been equally ignored: "If shore-based, long-range fighters cannot reach the area in which the ships must operate, then the navy must carry its own air with it."[19]

Crete certainly proved that dive-bombers could sink warships, but still, the battleship had shown that it could take this sort of punishment, albeit with heavy damage, and still remain afloat. The battleship still remained the firm rock for the lesser vessels to fall back upon when hard-pressed. It can be fairly stated that had the battleships not been there to give this support, the casualties among the flotilla craft would have been much higher. Had the Italian battleships intervened, their presence would have been vital.

In all events, as Churchill has stated, the casualties suffered by the Mediterranean Fleet presented the Italian Navy with its best chance of challenging Britain's dubious control of the eastern Mediterranean. Not until the return of the *Barham* in July could Cunningham again mount a battle line to equal theirs—and then only of older ships. In view of the vital importance attached to the *Barham* during this difficult period, it is perhaps just as well that the Admiralty's earlier plans to sacrifice this valuable vessel were thwarted by the commander in chief.[20] For even three old battleships were sufficient to prevent the Italians from venturing forth in earnest again. Not until all three had been eliminated did they consider it prudent to sortie with their own heavy ships. Thus, for another six months, the eastern Mediterranean held out. The dive-bombers of the Luftwaffe at Crete—as in the Sicilian Channel five months before and off Dunkirk and Norway over a year before—had dealt the Royal Navy some heavy blows. Because the British ships disdained to stay in harbor and fought it out with the bombers within a biscuit toss of their home airfields, the Stukas had been given an ideal opportunity to show their strength and accuracy.

How were the German heavy ships coping in their very different circumstances? True, they lay in port and partially concealed, but they were unable to maneuver in the face of attack, had to sit and take it week after week, and were not up against the Ju 87 with its single bomb but were faced with annihilation by the whole weight of RAF Bomber Command, a command which, more than any other, believed itself capable of destroying warships from the air with the heavy bomber. With the *Scharnhorst* and *Gneisenau* bottled up in Brest, under close blockade by sea and undersea arms, with their machinery defects requiring months of skilled attention before they could consider breaking for the open sea anyway, the two German battlecruisers—joined later by the *Prinz Eugen*, which had accomplished nothing since leaving the *Bismarck* to her fate earlier—were the ideal targets for the heavy bomber.

Already, in an attack on the night of January 8–9, 1941, Wellington bombers, operating from Malta, had made their mark. They bombed Naples where lay the three Italian battleships that had escaped Taranto, and, although once more they did not hit any of them one bomber scored three near-misses on the old *Guilio Cesare*, which was enough to start some serious leaks in her ancient hull. Alarmed, the Italians quickly moved these vessels, including the *Cesare*, out of range to La Spezia. It seemed a fitting precedent, but alas, the Germans proved somewhat tougher opponents than the unhappy Italian Navy.

It will be recalled that the *Scharnhorst* and *Gneisenau* actually entered Brest on March 22, but they were not discovered there immediately, and as a result, the RAF heavily attacked Kiel and Wilhelmshaven on the night of March 18–19 without result. The fitting out of the *Tirpitz* was also causing grave anxiety at this time, and it was hoped she might also be damaged in these attacks.

But it was the two battlecruisers that caused the greatest anxiety at this period, for the extent of their machinery defects was obviously unknown here.[21] At any time, they might again sortie out and create havoc. The very day they entered Brest, Churchill was stressing to Alexander and Pound just this danger and the measures to be taken against it: "If the presence of the enemy battlecruisers in a Biscayan port is confirmed, every effort by the navy and the air force should be made to destroy them there, and for this purpose, serious risks and sacrifices must be faced. If however unhappily they escape and resume their depredations, then action on the following lines would seem to be necessary, and should be considered even now."[22]

The prime minister then outlined schemes for the formation of three hunting groups combining a battlecruiser and a carrier: the *Renown* and *Ark Royal*, the *Hood* and *Furious*, and the *Repulse* and *Argus*. Each of these groups was to be accompanied by one or two tankers fitted out to refuel them at sea in the German manner. Churchill was not impressed with the arguments that the Royal Navy could not do this when the German Navy had shown it could do it with ease. But until the German battlecruisers ventured out, the responsibility for their damage—or even better, their destruction—lay with the RAF Bomber and Coastal Commands. They had often boasted of how they would carry out a task like this and how simple it would be. The talk and letters of the 1920s and 1930s now had to be made good.

Photo reconnaissance finally located the two German battlecruisers on March 28. Following Churchill's directive of March 6, the RAF was already forced to concentrate more on the battle of the Atlantic than they wanted to, and now they had a target that appealed even to them. The first attack took place on the night of March 30–31. More than 100 bombers took part in this raid against the two ships; no hits were scored. This massive attack was repeated on the night of April 3–4, with the same result. There was one side effect of great moment, however, and that was the discovery, after these raids, of an unexploded 250-pound bomb by the Germans in the area. They immediately moved the *Gneisenau* out of the dry dock into the outer harbor. This move took place on April 5 and was at once reported by air reconnaissance. In her new position, the German giant, although no more vulnerable to altitude bombing than before, might be open to torpedo-bomber attack. The *Gneisenau* was moored against the northern end of the harbor protected by the curving arm of the mole and with light flak in position to cover all approaches. It meant a suicidal mission, but Churchill had stated that all risks were to be run, so it had to be tried.

The Beauforts of 22 Squadron were the aircraft chosen for this daring attack; it was one of the very few units of the RAF actually equipped as torpedo-carriers. The squadron took off to carry out their mission but only four aircraft actually located the German battlecruiser at all. There were 270 flak guns on the hills around the anchorage, three flak ships moored in the outer harbor, as well as the *Gneisenau*'s own light guns. Despite these impossible odds, one brave aircrew endured it all. The Beaufort of Flying Off. Kenneth Campbell went in alone. Flying in under masthead height over the mole itself, he steered between the flak ships and dropped his torpedo at a range of 500 yards. Caught in a hurricane of fire, this lone aircraft was torn apart, but the missile ran straight and true, smashing into the stern of the battlecruiser and crippling her starboard propeller shaft. This damage incapacitated her for many months. One brave torpedo-bomber crew had rescued the tattered reputation of Bomber Command, and no man more deserved his posthumous Victoria Cross than did Campbell.

The *Gneisenau* was redocked on the seventh, and repairs were begun again. On the night of April 10-11, the RAF returned once more with the big bombers. This time they were successful. They hit the *Gneisenau* three times, with as many near-misses. Fifty casualties were inflicted on the exposed flak gunners, many of them young midshipmen just posted to her crew for training, and the damage to dockyard installations was also great. It was a day of jubilation for the RAF, but the *Gneisenau* did not sink; even though her upperworks were badly knocked about and one turret was damaged, she remained afloat and capable of repair.

The *Scharnhorst* escaped this attack unhurt, but at least the RAF had shown that, given an all-out effort with every plane they had and provided the ship kept absolute motionless, they could hit her. All that was required now were the bombing-sights accurate enough to hit them more often and bombs (and bombers) large enough to actually sink them. All these things would come, but meanwhile, the prime minister was growling about their lack of results, perhaps somewhat inaccurately and unfairly considering the circumstances. He wrote to the chiefs of the air staff on April 17:

> It must be recognized that the inability of Bomber Command to hit the enemy cruisers in Brest constitutes a very definite failure of this arm. No serious low-level daylight attack had been attempted. The policy of the Air Ministry in neglecting the dive-bomber type of aircraft is shown by all experience to have been a grievous error, and one for which we are paying dearly both in lack of offensive power and by the fear of injury which is so prevalent afloat.[23]

With all of this, the unbiased historian must agree absolutely. Nonetheless, the air marshals remained unrepentant, and until the American-built Vultee was finally developed for the RAF, even the few remaining with the Fleet Air Arm were shortly relegated to the side-lines, the navy using torpedo-bombers, like the Barracuda and the Avenger, as dive-bombers instead of the proper aircraft.[24]

Despite this success, there was evidence that the RAF was finding the whole task both more difficult and more costly than they had hoped. Air Marshal Sir Richard Peirse in April was demanding whether there was any end to it or must he continue "to cast hundreds of tons more on to the quays and into the water of Brest harbour."[25] Somewhat revealingly, the official historian has stated that the air marshals in general much preferred the much more massive, and passive, targets presented by the German cities and their civilian populations. "Operations against the north German ports proved a much more profitable affair than repeated assaults against the *Scharnhorst* and

Gneisenau."[26] Nonetheless, both the Admiralty and the prime minister continued to see these vessels as worthy targets, and the attacks continued for a while yet. On the night of June 13–14, for example, 110 heavies raided Brest without result. The following month saw another large effort—the heaviest so far mounted. The reason for this is that the *Scharnhorst* had now completed her refit to the extent that she was again ready for her sea trials.

Just before midnight on July 21, the battlecruiser had moved out of dock at Brest and sailed south to La Pallice for these to be carried out of sight of prying eyes. But on the twenty-second, the photo-reconnaissance Spitfires noted her absence, and by the twenty-third, they had relocated her in her new home. Evening and night attacks were mounted at once by the RAF but went unrewarded. So great did the danger seem that it was decided to risk the heavy bombers in a daylight attack on the German ship, for the first time in almost two years.

The risk was amply justified by events. More than forty aircraft had not hit her during the hours of darkness, but the striking force dispatched on July 24—fifteen of the new four-engine Halifax bombers with a massive fighter escort—caught the *Scharnhorst* just after she had returned from her trials, during which she had again reached her thirty knots with ease. She was clearly fully mobile again but this brief state of affairs did not survive the daylight attack. At a cost of five of the big bombers, one third of the attacking force, the Halifax squadron put five large bombs into the *Scharnhorst.*

Two of the bombs with armor-piercing capabilities failed to explode, but the damage caused by the other three was serious, at least according to the British official historians. A German historian, however, was more sanguine about this impressive attack: "Flooding caused by the three heavy bombs was however quite considerable. The ship took in 3,000 tons of water, but the list could be compensated and the cable defects were promptly repaired. But even now good luck had not deserted the *Scharnhorst,* for there were, miraculously, no casualties. She returned to Brest at twenty-seven knots and in spite of recurrent air-raids and frequent shifts of berth the dock repairs to the two battleships were almost completed by the turn of the year 1941–42."[27]

Captain Roskill states that "a survey revealed that at least eight months would be required to effect permanent repairs,"[28] which was far more pessimistic than the German evaluation. An attack by a torpedo-bomber on the *Scharnhorst* as she sailed back to Brest was fended off and the Beaufort destroyed. There followed a lull in the RAF attacks on the two German battlecruisers. Up to this point in time, these attacks had been made by 1,875 bombers, in addition to 364 minelaying sorties. Total losses were thirty-four bombers, and for this, the *Gneisenau* had been hit by one torpedo and four bombs, and the *Scharnhorst* by five bombs. However, for the rest of the summer, the immediate threat they posed was nullified.

By September, however, the ships were again considered to be approaching operational status. By now, the air marshals had won their strategic victory, and it was against towns that they were concentrating their main efforts rather than battleships. In this, they were having no more success; the photographic evidence brought back after these great attacks showed that no more than one bomber in every three even got within five miles of its target city. This fact was hushed up, and it was only with great reluctance that the RAF again briefly diverted their main force from this task and again applied them to the crippling of the "Salmon" and "Gluckstein," as the two ships were nicknamed.

A particularly heavy attack was mounted on the night of September 13–14 without result. But by December 1941, all the signs were that the infamous pair were yet again almost ready for sea. Bomber Command was therefore ordered to make them once more their primary concern. The final rounds then began. Minelaying was stepped up from the air after December 11 and plans laid for further daylight missions.

On December 15–16, the most ambitious attack yet was launched. It called for a precision daylight attack to follow up within a short time a massed night bombardment. When aerial photos showed the *Prinz Eugen* undocking, this "right and left" was put into effect. On the night of December 17–18, 101 heavy four-engine bombers attacked, and the afternoon of the eighteenth saw the Manchesters, Halifaxes, and Stirlings—forty-one in all—again sweep in broad daylight under fighter protection. Six of the big bombers were lost in this daylight attack. The achievements were merely splinter damage to the *Gneisenau*'s hull and a hit on the lock gate that held the *Scharnhorst*.

A further daylight attack took place on December 30, the risks involved being accepted because of the dangerous position the Royal Navy had suddenly found itself in with regard to heavy ships. No hits were made.

As Captain Roskill summarizes, from the start of August to the end of the year a further 851 heavy bombers had attacked the two German ships, had lost eleven of their number in so doing, and, although they had razed the dockyard of Brest almost to the ground, had not hit the ships once.[29] This total lack of achievement is in no way detrimental to the aircrew who carried out these attacks. Quite the reverse. "To press home an attack on a well-camouflaged warship protected by fighters, balloons and one of the heaviest concentrations of anti-aircraft guns in Europe, and to know that as it was in dry-dock not even the best-aimed bombs could sink it, demanded the very highest qualities of morale."[30] Nobody would argue with this. It is, however, a slightly different story to that rosy picture hitherto presented.[31]

The Luftwaffe were finding also that battleships, even ancient and obsolete battleships, were not quite that push-overs as they had expected. Even though their dive-bombers were smaller, less costly, and far more accurate than the giant heavies employed by the RAF, the ratios of effort required to results and losses sustained were having a depressingly similar ring to them. After a similar concentration of effort, they did manage to put another battleship on the seabed in a more final and complete manner than their RAF counterparts. This particular confrontation took place in the September 1941 at the besieged Soviet naval port and base of Kronstadt, near Leningrad, and was equally as bloody as the encounter off Crete.

When Hitler's armies had crashed across the frontier of his former ally to once and for all rid the world of communism and also eliminate Britain's one potential ally left on the continent, it was expected by most "experts" that the huge armies of Soviet Russia—although outnumbering their Axis opponents by three to two in men, tanks, and aircraft all along the line—would crumble as swiftly and as completely before the German blitzkrieg as had the armies of France, Holland, Belgium, Britain, Yugoslavia, and Greece.[32] Indeed, at first, it did look like that and Soviet losses in men and all forms of material were stunning to the mind of the British, used to thinking in terms of six division armies for centuries. However, Stalin had a premium in both men and land and could afford to squander both while playing for time. Thus, it was not a six-week battle that Barbarossa launched but a four-year campaign in which the German armies bled to death. By September, the campaign had already lasted longer than most had expected, and still all the main prizes lay beyond the Germans grasp. Moscow and Leningrad almost fell but remained tantalizingly out of reach.

Near Leningrad—which was besieged on almost all sides and which the enraged Hitler had sworn to destroy utterly brick-by-brick as the birthplace of communism—was the great Soviet naval base of Kronstadt and the great shipbuilding yards of the Baltic. Here was concentrated the largest fleet Soviet Russia had, and here was it building the bulk of the new fleet. As the German armies closed in for the kill, it was from this fleet that the fiercest resistance was encountered, not at sea, but by the accurate long-range gunfire of the ships at anchor.

On paper at least, the Soviet Baltic Fleet looked impressive: two battleships,[33] three cruisers, forty-seven destroyers, ninety-six submarines, and a host of small craft. But the German Navy had little trouble in containing them to the far end of the Baltic. They retreated behind their minefields and barrages and refused to come out in the time-honored manner. The Germans, however, were made aware of their existence as their troops began to fight their way into the suburbs of the city. "The view from Bald Hill extended as far as Kronstadt. One could see the port and the powerful Soviet battleship *Marat*, which was shelling land targets with its heavy guns. The hits of the 30.5cm shells sent up fountains of earth as high as houses, especially in the sector of the 58th Infantry Division, which was making a hell-for-leather drive for the coast, in order to close the Leningrad trap in the direction of Oramenbaum."[34]

The power of a battery of heavy naval guns was a lesson that was to be many times reemphasized later in the war to the German infantry, but this was their first taste of it and they did not appreciate it. When the huge guns of battleships were correctly directed, they could saturate any section of coastline with their enormous shells to a depth of up to twenty miles, and the Wehrmacht had no answer. However, they could, as always, call on the Luftwaffe to redress the balance by utilizing the unique capabilities of their "flying artillery" units, the deadly Stuka dive-bombers. And this is what they did at Kronstadt.

Stukageschwader (Stuka Wing, or StG) 2, the so-called Immelmann Wing, so prominent at Crete barely four months earlier, was now called upon to eliminate these two smoking giants. Their attacks took place over a two-week period starting on September 16. For their part, the Russians had assembled 600 heavy flak guns to protect their fleet—a concentration of fire that equaled, if not exceeded, that at Brest harbor.

The German aviators were well aware of the problems in tackling battleships, even old ones, with aerial bombing. One young pilot described his briefing before the attack:

> There is no question of using normal bomber aircraft, any more than normal bombs, for this operation, especially as intense flak must be reckoned with. He tells us that we are awaiting the arrival of 2,000-pounder bombs fitted with a special detonating device for our purpose. With normal detonators the bomb would burst ineffectively on the armored main deck and though the explosion would be sure to rip off some parts of the upper structure it would not result in the sinking of the ship. We cannot expect to succeed and finish off these two leviathans except by the use of a delayed-action bomb which must first pierce the upper decks before exploding deep down in the hull of the vessel.[35]

The needs of the army, however, resulted in the Stukas being pressed into action before the arrival of the special bombs in an attempt to damage the ships if not sink them. These attacks took place on the sixteenth, and in them, the *Marat* was struck by a 1,000-pound bomb, which caused large fires but failed to put her under.

On September 21, the bombs arrived at the airstrips of the Stuka units, and the same day, aerial reconnaissance reported the *Marat* in Kronstadt harbor undergoing repairs. The Ju 87s at once took off in large numbers and this time made no mistakes. Hans Ulrich Rudel gives a graphic description of the dive-bombing attack that finished off the *Marat*:

> My Ju 87 keeps perfectly steady as I dive; does not swerve an inch. I have the feeling that to miss now is impossible. Then I see the *Marat* large as life in front of me. Sailors are running across the deck, carrying ammunition. Now I press the bomb release switch on my stick and pull with all my strength. Can I still manage to pull out? I doubt it, for I am diving without brakes and the height at which I have released my bomb is not more than 900 feet. The skipper has said when briefing us that the two thousand pounder must not be dropped from lower than 3,000 feet as the fragmentation effect of the bomb reaches 3,000 feet and to drop it at a lower altitude is to endanger one's aircraft. But now I have forgotten that! I am intent on hitting the *Marat*. I tug at my stick, without feeling, merely exerting all my strength. My acceleration is too great. I see nothing, my sight is blurred in a momentary blackout, a new experience for me. But if it can be managed at all I must pull out. My head has not cleared when I hear Scharnovski's voice: "She is blowing up, sir!"
>
> Now I look out. We are skimming the water at a level of ten or twelve feet and I bank round a little. Yonder lies the *Marat* below a cloud of smoke rising to 1,200 feet; apparently the magazine has exploded.[36]

Indeed, this hit had detonated the *Marat*'s forward magazine, and the whole bow section broke off, causing the old ship to settle on the bottom of Kronstadt harbor. Later on, the Soviets managed to get three of her main turrets operational as stationary batteries but without mobility they were of little value.[37] Striking in its contrast is the success achieved by the two-seater Junkers Ju 87 dive-bomber attacking accurately in daylight, with the almost total failure of the RAF's prolonged high-level heavy bombers campaign against Brest. But the propaganda from the Air Ministry continued to be that dive-bombers were "ineffective" and the Stuka in particular was "obsolete fighter bait." The difference between the words coming from Whitehall with the combat results continually being achieved by the dive-bombers just could not have been starker. This trend was to continue.

The mass Stuka attacks continued in this manner for several more days. During the course of them, the second battleship, *Oktyabrskaya Revolutsiya*, was hit by six medium (500-pound) bombs, which damaged her upperworks but failed to sink her. A solitary 2,000-pound bomb, which also hit her, failed to explode and thus she was reprieved, but two cruisers were badly damaged, as were five destroyers and two submarines by these attacks before the Stukas were switched south to the Moscow front at the end of the month.

Earlier, in view of the influence these two old battleships were exerting and the desperate position they ultimately found themselves in, hemmed in by mines and bombed daily, Hitler expected the Soviet Baltic Fleet to make a desperate attempt to break out and seek sanctuary in the neutral harbors of Sweden. To forestall this he ordered Vice Admiral Ciliax to form the German Baltic Fleet in the Aaland Sea.

The main strength of this formation rested on the newly operational *Tirpitz* and the recommissioned *Admiral Scheer*. They were supported by the light cruisers *Köln*, *Nürnberg*, *Emden*, and *Leipzig*, as well as eight destroyers. Almost immediately after their formation, however, the severe damage inflicted by the Stukas eased the position; none of the big Soviet ships was in any fit state to sail anywhere, and the German heavy ships, after leaving Swinemünde on September 24, were duly recalled. Both sides were then satisfied to accept the stalemate position in the Baltic for the next two or three years, and thus, the *Tirpitz* and *Scheer* again became an exclusively British problem again.

Before leaving the Russian front, the position of the third and final Soviet battleship in the Black Sea is of considerable interest. With the progress of the land campaign in the south, German and Rumanian forces quickly cleared the northern shoreline of the Black Sea in late summer, cutting off the base of Odessa and capturing the important shipyards of Nikvlaev on August 16. Here they found rich booty. On the stocks lay the gaunt skeleton of the 45,000-ton battleship *Sovetskaya Ukraina*, and the first plates assembled for the battlecruiser that was to follow her, as well as a heavy cruiser, four destroyers, and three submarines incomplete.

Thus, the only remaining heavy ship in the whole area was the *Parizhskaya Kommuna*,[38] a sister ship of the two Baltic veterans. With the steady advance of the panzers, she was hustled away from Sevastopol at the end of October to the safety of the Caucasian ports , leaving the shore bombardments to the five modern cruisers and some twenty surviving destroyers of the Russian Black Sea fleet.

The *Parizhskaya Kommuna* may have been old and obsolete, but in the Black Sea, she became a legend. The Axis forces had nothing afloat larger than a destroyer with which to tackle her afloat and despite repeated attempts to eliminate her she took part in a whole series of pin-prick operations and became a running sore on the flanks of the German forces besieging the Crimea. A heavy air attack was mounted on the *Parizhskaya Kommuna* during her flight to safety, but no hits were taken, and she began to fight back. During the second half of November, she was employed in bringing her guns to the support of the Soviet forces defending Sevastopol with good effect. On November 28, under the command of Captain Kravchenko, she fired 146 of her 12-inch shells into the Axis positions around Sevastopol. A month later, on December 29-30, the *Parizhskaya Kommuna* was employed in bombarding duties, her gunnery breaking up all-out German attacks in the Belbek, Kamyshly, and Verkhne areas when Hitler ordered the fortress to be taken by Christmas. It held out. The battleship also evacuated more than 1,000 wounded soldiers when she pulled out.

At the beginning of 1942, another series of bombardments was carried out by the *Parizhskaya Kommuna* at Isyumovki and Stary Krym on January 12, 1942, and flying the flag of Rear Admiral Vladimirski, she covered the Russian counterattacks when they landed troops behind the Axis lines. She was used in supporting the subsequent offensives on the Kerch Peninsula on the nights of February 26 and 28 and repeated this performance on the nights of March 20 and 22 at Feodosia. At the end of this splendid series of army-support operations, the gallant old vessel had worn out the barrels of most of her guns and had to retire from the fight for a while. She was docked at Poti to effect repairs and ship new mountings.

And so, even in a limited role, in a small, air-dominated sea, one ancient battleship played quite a prominent role in the defense of her nation and showed what ships could achieve if correctly used. But while the *Parizhskaya Kommuna* kept the Axis on the run in the Black Sea, the great ships of the Royal Navy were no less employed in the larger oceans of the world.

For the Home Fleet under Admiral Tovey, the destruction of the *Bismarck* in May and the continued immobilization of the two battlecruisers for most of the year eased their problems considerably. Not only by the bombing of the *Scharnhorst* and *Gneisenau* did the RAF contribute to this state of affairs. Although the growth of the torpedo bomber had been left late and still fell behind the development of other arms, the RAF was gradually expanding this arm and many of the pilots were a natural elite among bomber crews now swelled with enormous numbers of fresh recruits. One of the greatest successes these gallant young men achieved was a strike on the pocket battleship *Lützow* on the night of June 12–13, 1941.[39]

The fate of the *Bismarck* did not at first deter Raeder from his conviction that surface raiding by heavy ships still remained a viable proposition. All he lacked at this time was the ships in good enough condition to do so. Only the *Lützow*, her engines now repaired, fit the bill, and so, at the beginning of June, she proceeded on the first leg of a voyage that was planned to take her into the Indian Ocean. On her first leg toward the southern coast of Norway, she had a powerful escort, the light cruisers *Emden* and *Leipzig*, with five destroyers. But even as she slid out of the docks and into the North Sea, the

Admiralty in London was preparing to intercept her, for British intelligence sources were now working at a high pitch of efficiency. At first, these sources indicated that it was the *Tirpitz* on the way out, but by the evening of June 11, the *Lützow* had been positively identified.

At the same time, Admiral Tovey's strength was at an all-time low. The *Prince of Wales* was repairing her battle damage. The *Rodney* was again on her way to her American refit, and the *Repulse* was off Newfoundland on convoy protection work. At Scapa Flow, therefore, lay only the *King George V*, shortly to be joined by the *Nelson* from Gibraltar. It was only with these that Tovey could prevent the breakout.

Air searches were flown to locate and pinpoint the German force, but yet again, she proved elusive and evaded them throughout the daylight hours of the twelfth, when the two light cruisers were detached to Oslo. The *Lützow* herself with her destroyer screen turned west, away from the coast and out of the Skagerrak.

Meanwhile, the full strength of Coastal Command was being vigorously deployed in a combined search and strike role. Fourteen Beaufort torpedo-bombers from Nos. 22 and 42 Squadrons took off from the bases in Scotland in the hour before midnight and headed east. These aircraft, twin-engine monoplanes, represented just about the main front-line strength of the torpedo-bomber arm of the RAF in England and were now about to prove their worth.

Just before midnight, a Blenheim reconnaissance aircraft sighted the *Lützow* and made her report, and two hours later, a Beaufort of No. 42 Squadron homed to it. This lone aircraft, piloted by Flight Sgt. R. H. Lovett, made a very brave and determined attack taking the German squadron completely by surprise at 2:18 A.M.[40] His torpedo ran straight and true and hit the *Lützow* fair and square amidships. The pocket battleship at once assumed a heavy list and came to a halt.

Two more Beauforts from the same unit found her in this condition and attacked, but they were unrewarded. After hard work by the crew, the *Lützow* managed to effect temporary repairs and set off for safety at her best speed. After an interval of another two hours, an aircraft from 42 Squadron found her. By this time, the sky was light and a standing patrol of fighters was overhead. Notwithstanding these odds the brave pilot carried out his attack, but his missile ran wide, and the Beaufort was quickly destroyed.

One final attack from the air followed at 5:00 A.M., this time by Blenheims armed only with bombs. No hits were made, and by June 14, the damaged *Lützow* had limped into Kiel. She was in dockyard hands for six months, not reentering service until January 1942.

With the bulk of Raeder's cherished surface fleet thus out of action from air attack of one form or another, only the *Tirpitz* and *Admiral Scheer* remained as an immediate threat, and both these were retained in the Baltic for the time being to counter the Soviet Navy. Thus, the balance was maintained and the period of the Home Fleet's greatest weakness was fortunately matched by a corresponding lull on the German side.

Further help for the British in their watch on the North Atlantic sea lanes came from the United States at this time. The establishment of their neutrality zone, patrolled by their warships with sink on sight orders, effectively sealed off the western half of the Atlantic to German surface forays. Not surprisingly, this was viewed with great bitterness by the Germans since it went far beyond the accepted bounds of neutrality. It was made all the more difficult for them by Hitler's orders that every effort was to be made to avoid provocative acts against American warships while the Russian campaign was still underway. The Americans also took over the occupation of Iceland from the British, who nonetheless still could avail themselves of the full use of its naval anchorages and airfields. To show that considerable strength lay available to back these acts, the American Atlantic Fleet was deployed in full strength on patrol and escort duties, and the backbone of the fleet was the presence of the old battleships *Arkansas, New Mexico, New York*, and *Texas*.[41] On June 1, the First Marine Brigade was transported to Iceland and Rear Admiral Le Breton's covering Task Force 19 centered on the *Arkansas* and *New York*.

All these factors—increased intelligence efficiency by the British, the active contribution of a large American battle fleet, the realization of the greater efficiency of British radar at sea, and the withdrawal of the bulk of the Luftwaffe to the eastern front—helped to influence German thinking on future practicability of surface raiding operations by their heavy ships. Although this was still the cornerstone of Raeder's thinking, Hitler became more and more opposed to this type of warfare, the benefits being too nebulous and long-range to suit his temperament and the risks—in terms of German prestige every time a big ship went down—too great.

Not only these considerations weighed the German leader down; there was also a more thoughtful argument that was increasingly dominating his thinking, the safety of his Norwegian flank to counterattack. To his mind, it seemed quite a logical step—and one still within their capability with his armies tied up elsewhere—for the British to invade Norway and regain the enormous strategic benefits her coastline provided, while at the same time establishing a common front with their new-found allies. "Every ship that is not in Norway is in the wrong place," Hitler was said to have told Raeder, for with his soldiers and airmen fully committed in the wastes of the Soviet Union the main defence of Norway would have to fall upon the German Navy.

The divergence of their views on the use of heavy ships led to repeated rows between the grand admiral and the führer, which, not unusually, Hitler finally won.[42] But the final decision did not come right away, and Admiral Tovey was not privy to these discussions. He still therefore had to plan and guard against a breakout into the Atlantic even though the emphasis of his work now began to shift more and more to the protection of the convoys of war material that were being shipped by Britain to Russia's northern ports of Murmansk and Archangel.

One such scare occurred in September. The *Admiral Scheer* was reported missing from her anchorage at Swinemünde on the fourth of that month, and further aircraft and reports tracked her progress across the Great Belt and into Oslo fiord. All the signs of the same pattern that she, the *Bismarck*, and *Lützow* had followed before seemed to fall into place. Bombing attacks were launched on two days; the RAF pressed into service some of the new American Fortress four-engined bombers they had recently taken delivery of which boasted improved sighting equipment, but to no avail. Then, on September 10, the *Admiral Scheer* vanished, and the tension increased. Air searches were flown over the usual breakout routes with never a sign of her. Not until over a week later was she again spotted, back at her old berth at Swinemünde again. It would seem that this short excursion was to test her seaworthiness and efficiency after a long refit period, but the anxiety caused was proof enough of the danger she still presented. In fact, Raeder was anxious to send her out to the South Atlantic and Indian Ocean to take the place of the unhappy *Lützow*. This type of operation had to be cleared with Hitler and led to yet another clash of wills, from which the grand admiral retired a beaten man.[43]

It was at this time that Admiral Tovey began to flex his new-found air strength by a series of carrier strikes by the *Victorious*, protected by the Home Fleet. Results were sparse, but this activity all helped harden Hitler's mind about Norway being a "zone of destiny."

It was just as well that the German threat lay dormant at this time, for the even greater menace of Japanese expansion in southeastern Asia—her scarcely hidden ambitions and veiled threats being matched by sanctions and equally severe warnings from both Britain and America—indicated quite plainly that it was only a matter of time before the war spread to the Pacific. The American Pacific Fleet was reinforced, and Britain was also determined to build up a powerful fleet in that theater to counterbalance the great potential of the Imperial Japanese Navy.

The long sequence of discussions on what form this fleet should take and where it was to be based we will examine shortly. The way in which they affected the Home Fleet's strength in the late summer of 1941, well before the actual outbreak of hostilities, indicates the delicate balance of maritime defense at a time when the Royal Navy was fighting on a shoe-string.

In October, Tovey was informed that the *Prince of Wales* was to be taken from his fleet, which she had not long rejoined,[44] and sent east. Not only that, but the *Repulse* was to join her there. This left the Home Fleet with only the *King George V* capable of standing up to the *Tirpitz* should she come out. The *Prince of Wales* had actually sailed from the Clyde on October 24, when just such an operation appeared to be on the cards. The possibility of the *Tirpitz*, perhaps accompanied by the *Admiral Scheer* as well, breaking out loomed large at the beginning of November, and Admiral Tovey sailed with his main strength, the *King George V, Victorious*, three heavy and two light cruisers, to take up covering positions off Iceland.

Luckily, the Americans proved willing to cooperate to the full. Admiral Giffen sailed with the battleships *Idaho* and *Mississippi* and two heavy cruisers to patrol an adjacent area, thus giving a welcome margin of strength. In the event, the *Tirpitz* did not move, and Tovey returned to Scapa Flow toward the end of the month. Resources were never stretched quite as tight as that again, and Tovey could look forward to the welcome addition of the brand-new battleship *Duke of York* when she had worked up in December.[45]

The *Duke of York* did not join the flag until later. Churchill was eager to meet with Roosevelt after America had been finally pushed into the war on December 7. It was felt that an air passage across the North Atlantic was too perilous, and the prime minister decided to cross in Britain's latest battleship. Churchill and his party embarked in the Clyde on December 12, and the *Duke of York* carried him through the U-boat-infested seas in eight days, through a succession of heavy storms. She then proceeded to the West Indies to work up further and remained at Bermuda for the rest of the month and into January, waiting to carry Churchill home. Ultimately, this wait was in vain as he decided to fly. Thus, the *Duke of York* did not join Tovey's command until later that month. At the beginning of the year, therefore, the Home Fleet had only the *King George V, Rodney*, and *Renown* for their heavy metal.

Nor was the continuing watch on the Atlantic and Arctic the only task in which the battleships of the Royal Navy were applied. As well as Admiral Cunningham's depleted fleet in the eastern basin of the Mediterranean, Force H at Gibraltar assumed more and more of the responsibility for the safe and timely arrival of the great store and munitions convoys to Malta, the bulk of which took place from the west. To enable this to be carried out in the face of an Italian fleet, which, although supine, was still hugely superior in numbers, Admiral Somerville's strength was frequently supplemented during this period by the heavy ships of the Home Fleet, as and when they were available.

The fact that the Tiger convoy had met with so little opposition naturally led to demands that it be repeated, and on a larger scale, both to relieve Malta and reinforce her defences. In addition there were continuous air-ferry operations to be carried out. For these latter, it was usually just the stalwarts of Force H—the *Renown, Ark Royal, Sheffield*, and the 8th Destroyer Flotilla—that provided the escort for the various carriers employed; often, the *Ark Royal* carried out the task alone. Thus were Operations Splice (May 19–22), Rocket (June 5–7), Tracer (July 13–14), and Railway (June 26–July 1) carried out under the cover of the *Renown*'s heavy guns and *Ark Royal*'s aircraft.

For the passage of the next big convoy, Operation Substance, the battleship *Nelson* was added to Somerville's strength along with additional cruisers and destroyers and a minelayer, all from the Home Fleet. As a diversion, Admiral Cunningham cruised in the eastern Mediterranean with his big ships. The convoy of six freighters passed through the Straits of Gibraltar on July 20–21, but a troop-carrying vessel ran aground at Gibraltar when the Home Fleet contingent joined up with Force H the next day. The various ruses adopted to fool the Italians about the nature of the operation were so successful that the convoy was unopposed until the twenty-third. Not until then did the Italian Navy tumble to the fact it was a convoy right through to Malta and not just another ferry trip. By that time, it was considered too late for the Italian battleships to sortie out to stop them, nor was the possibility of bringing Force H to action on the return journey taken up. Thus, on this occasion, the *Renown* and *Nelson* had to content themselves with the role of providing the main antiaircraft firepower of the escort to ward off several torpedo-bomber and conventional altitude attacks.

Together with the *Ark Royal*'s faithful fighters, this duty was accomplished although a light cruiser was damaged and sent back and a destroyer was damaged and sunk. At 4:45 that afternoon, the convoy reached the mouth of the Skerki Channel. "Here, as always, the heavy ships of Force H had to turn back to remain with the *Ark Royal*, for whom there was inadequate sea room to operate her aircraft between the minefields thickly sown on either side."[46]

The convoy reached Malta, the escorting cruisers returned, and an empty convoy was brought out. The only casualty was a single destroyer damaged by bombing attack. No attempt was made by the Italians to send their indolent battleships against these scattered groups for whom the two capital ships of Force H could give only partial cover until they concentrated. The *Renown* and *Nelson* marked time on the twenty-fourth, and the returning cruisers concentrated on them the next day after ineffectual air attack without loss.

As always Somerville displayed the human touch that so delighted the men of his command. The destroyer *Firedrake* had been taken in tow by the destroyer *Eridge*, and the two little ships were making slow progress to the west all alone and hundreds of miles from the nearest friendly landfall. They seemed forgotten. "Then, as they watched, Force H came up to them in a superb sweep, a long perspective of magnificence and power. And as each ship passed, the *Firedrake*, limping along, the great hole in her side open to the sea, listing a little, battered, worn out and exhausted, the great ships cleared lower deck, brought every man to the open, and cheered her as they went past."[47]

No sooner had they returned to Gibraltar than they were off again. The *Renown*, *Nelson*, and *Ark Royal* gave their cover to Operation Style between July 31 and August 4, when the troops, left behind in an earlier mishap with the *Leinster*, were taken into Malta aboard the cruisers. At the end of this operation, which was again virtually unopposed, there were some changes in Force H. The *Sheffield* had already left, being replaced by the modern antiaircraft cruiser *Hermione* with her more suitable dual-purpose armament for Substance and later operations. Many of the 8th Flotilla's destroyers were damaged or in need of refits. They, too, were gradually replaced by the brand-new destroyers of the Laforey class, which also had heavy dual-purpose guns. Now it was the turn of the *Renown* to leave Gibraltar. During her many patrols in the Bay of Biscay in terrible weather, and during her chase of the *Bismarck* earlier, her hull had taken a battering. Now her bulges began tearing away for a considerable length along her hull and it was deemed necessary to dock her as Gibraltar could not undertake such a major refit. Accordingly, in September she arrived back to repair and then join the Home Fleet. Meanwhile, on August 8, Somerville had hoisted his flag in the *Nelson*, which, although slower was more powerfully armed and already fitted as fleet flagship for more than thirteen years, was more comfortable.[48]

The first operation with the new lineup of the *Nelson*, *Ark Royal*, and *Hermione* was on August 22–26, Operation Mincemeat. The minelayer *Manxman* was sent out to lay a minefield off Leghorn, which she did undetected. To cover her, Force H cruised to the north of Sardinia, and Swordfish attacked Tempio airfield as a diversion. This time, the Italians determined to intervene with their battle fleet. Admiral Iachino put to sea on August 23 with the modern battleships *Littorio* and *Vittorio Veneto*, four 8-inch cruisers, and nineteen destroyers to offer battle. Against such a force, Mincemeat had an ominous ring to it as Somerville only had one old battleship, one carrier, one small cruiser, and five destroyers with him.

The Italians did not guess the target, however, and assumed that another Malta convoy was in train, and Iachino took his two battleships south of Sardinia while Somerville was to the north. A light cruiser squadron was also sent out to make contact from Palermo, submarine patrols were reinforced and MTB flotillas put to sea. All in vain. When the Italian fleet was sighted by a British submarine, Somerville dallied awhile hoping to lure it westward from under the cover of the the Italian Air Force to even up the odds a little. But Iachino returned to harbor on the twenty-fifth, having one of his heavy cruisers damaged by a submarine torpedo on the way back.

Force H had gotten away with it, although the outcome of the battle, despite the odds, makes interesting speculation. It did seem to show that the Italians were beginning to act more aggressively, and thus even greater account had to be taken in subsequent operations that their battleships would, eventually, be brought to battle. Somerville duly warned Whitehall that the odds were mounting, but the only reaction was to order yet another large convoy into Malta, Operation Halberd which was to take place at the end of the month. But if the Italian battleships were going to take a more active role then this was to be welcomed; a fleet action this time would find Force H on more even terms, for reinforcements were again sent to Gibraltar with the merchantmen.

The battleships *Prince of Wales* and *Rodney* were the backbone of these welcome additions, along with four light cruisers and ten destroyers. The two battleships, together with the *Nelson* would, "make up a battle squadron capable of engaging Iachino's capital ships on equal terms should the Italian with his much faster ships accept action."[49]

The Italians meanwhile had plans of their own to cripple the big ships of Force H. At the end of the Great War, they had made quite startling developments with a new underwater arm, known as the charioteers or "human torpedoes." These penetrated enemy harbors on small two-man submersibles and attached powerful explosive charges to the undersides of the ship targets. Their most spectacular victory had been achieved on the last day of the previous war. Their main rival at sea had been the Austro-Hungarian Navy, which had completed a class of four power Dreadnought battleships for their fleet in the Adriatic. When the Austro-Hungarian Empire fell apart in the latter months of 1918, the flagship of this squadron, the *Viribus Unitis*[50] had been handed over to the newly formed government of Yugoslavia and lay berthed at Pola as no crew could operate her in the chaos of those days. It was this vessel that the Italians attacked, entering Pola undetected and placing a large explosive charge to her hull. The resulting explosion tore out her bottom and she sank with the loss of over 400 men.

Since that time, the Italians had worked on this weapon and were far in advance of other nations in its design and training. They had already made attacks on Gibraltar, and one attack, on the *Barham* in the autumn of 1940, had almost succeeded; the chariot got within seventy yards of her before detonating her charge. Fortunately, no damage was done to the battleship at that time.

Now the Italians decided to try again, and on September 19, the submarine *Scire* launched three chariots against the *Nelson*, *Ark Royal*, and the cruisers lying at the south mole. Two of the chariots selected the *Nelson* as their target and penetrated the mole's southern entrance. However, since the previous attempts a standing protection of dropping small explosive charges by patrol boats around the harbour had been adopted by the British and these were sufficiently daunting to make the Italian charioteers switch targets. They sank the tanker *Fiona Shell* and severely damaged the *Denbydale* and *Durham*. Their bravery and persistence was to pay off in a big way within a few months at the other end of the Mediterranean, but the *Nelson* was reprieved for the time being.

Again, elaborate deceptions were carried out to hoodwink the Italians into thinking that only the usual small force was to be employed. The *Rodney* arrived to refuel at Gibraltar in daylight on September 23, and to make it appear as if she was relieving the *Nelson* and not reinforcing her, Admiral Somerville and his staff made a special show of visiting her and hoisting his flag aboard her. He returned to the *Nelson* more quietly, and then she put to see without his flag at the masthead and with her band playing "Rolling Home" on her quarterdeck, to all accounts and purposes heading home. Even a signal from Somerville was sent from the *Rodney*, bidding his old flagship adieu. With darkness, Somerville's flag was rehoisted on the *Nelson*, and she joined the escort.

All this secrecy was not without its humorous side on deceiving the British matelots either. Security demanded that even the ships' companies should not be informed of what was going on. They knew that the *Rodney* was expected, however. This resulted in another little incident, which tickled the admiral's sense of humor. He shared the joke again in his official report: "As the dim form of the *Prince of Wales* was first sighted, hands on watch on the admiral's bridge of the *Nelson* exclaimed enthusiastically, 'Good old *Rodney*, here she is at last!' This was quickly changed to 'Gawd, she's one of them new bastards,' and the Nelsons had to guess again."[51]

The tale of Halberd was the usual one. The convoy of six freighters and liners sailed under direct protection of the Home Fleet units while Force H kept some miles away to further confuse the enemy. Thus, they did not realize that three British battleships were with the convoy. Accordingly, Iachino took his main fleet to sea on the evening of the twenty-sixth to attack, once the convoy and escort had reached the area of the Italian Air Force. He again had the *Littorio* and *Vittorio Veneto*, along with three heavy and two light cruisers and fourteen destroyers.

The battle with the Italian Air Force was joined on the twenty-seventh, and heavy and skillful torpedo-bomber sorties were made throughout this day as well as numerous submarine attacks. Iachino was off Cagliari in Sardinia under the umbrella of fighter cover waiting a favorable moment to intervene. The air attacks were pressed home with some determination by the Italian airmen some twenty-seven torpedo-bomber assaults being made over a four-hour period but the majority were broken up by the barrage of the screening destroyers. One group of the four was made of sterner stuff however and got through the outer flak wall concentrating on the *Nelson* from her starboard beam. Two of the SM 79s were caught by the antiaircraft guns of the big ships and turned away, but two pressed on with great bravery and dropped. The *Nelson* turned hard to starboard in order to comb their tracks, and one passed harmlessly to starboard. Both these aircraft were shot down, one by the *Nelson's* pom-poms, which broke her in three, and the other smashed into the water dead ahead of the flagship. Her missile continued to run the torpedo having gone deep. This torpedo suddenly appeared again as a line of bubbles only 120 yards dead ahead of the battleship and there was no question of any further avoiding action being taken at all, and it exploded on the battleship's bows throwing up a huge column of dirty water.

An eyewitness described the attack in this manner later:

> We had been getting used to the pattern of the attacks when one came in that, from the start, looked different from the others. Someone on the home aerodrome must have been giving the boys a pep talk. This one was carried out with far more determination; the planes came in so low they seemed to be skating over the water like giant dragonflies. They went through the barrage, and one bomber held on, when, by some miracle, it came through. There were the usual wisps of spray as the torpedoes were released, and we thought for a moment that all had missed when a sudden column of water sprouted up from the *Nelson* right forward. It was the single bomber, which had scored the hit, and it escaped over the fleet. Its crew deserved their medals. The *Nelson* never so much as faltered, but lumbered on as if nothing had happened.[52]

Somerville says the great ship "whipped like a fishing rod" when hit but managed to keep up eighteen knots. Gradually, the inrush of water brought her bows down and her speed gradually dropped to fourteen knots, at which she was able to keep up with the convoy but was not fit for a fleet action. This was the stroke of good fortune that Iachino had been long awaiting for Somerville still had no firm news that the Italian battle fleet was actually at sea. Some 120 miles separated the two forces, but Iachino was still unsure of the correct composition of the British escort.

As one historian has written: "The hit on the *Nelson* was a phenomenal piece of luck for the enemy. To explode its warhead the torpedo had to strike the sharp stem of the battleship with geometrical accuracy or it would have glanced off without actuating the warhead firing pistol. It was the only success achieved by the thirty or more attacks delivered. Six aircraft were shot down by the gunfire of the Fleet, four more by *Ark Royal*'s fighters."[53]

This torpedo hit was more fortuitous to the Axis cause than was first apparent, as we shall discuss shortly, but in the immediate term it put the two battlefleets on terms favorable to the Italians. Thinking that only one battleship remained to Somerville, Iachino now acted with a rare boldness and set course to close, expecting a general action against the solitary *Rodney* to commence around 3:30 P.M.

This brief flash of resolution did not last the hour. As he sped toward the convoy, he began to have second thoughts. A haze reduced visibility to about five miles, the fighter escort failed to show up as usual, and he worried about the *Ark Royal* intervening. At 3:00, he came to his decision, the helms of his two battleships and their companions were put hard over, and once more the Italian fleet refused battle. He retired at high speed throughout the rest of the afternoon concluding that he was up against at least three British battleships.

In actual fact, it was two. Somerville had received reports of the Italian fleet at 2:02 in the midst of the aircraft attacks, some seventy miles northeast of him steering an intercepting course at twenty knots. At once, he formed his three battleships in battle line at eighteen knots sent his cruisers and six destroyers out ahead, and steered to interpose himself between the convoy and the enemy. The *Ark Royal* meanwhile prepared her striking force of Swordfish. This brave front soon had to be adjusted as the *Nelson*'s speed came down, and Somerville took her back to the convoy as long-stop should the Italians break through. Vice Admiral Curteis sped on toward the Italians at increased speed with the *Prince of Wales* and *Rodney*.

As we moved away, the *Prince of Wales* hoisted a signal which meant that we were to proceed at twenty-eight knots, and caused a great deal of amusement on board, because it was several knots faster than we had ever done in our prime. She did not wait for us, however, but rushed ahead after the Italian Fleet, leaving us to plod along behind, while Swordfish from the *Ark Royal* prepared to deliver a torpedo attack. Reports at first were encouraging. We really thought we were going to bring the Italian Fleet to action at last, but once again they disappointed us when they found we were coming towards them, and retired to the safety and comfort of Naples, and we were denied even the sight of them until they surrendered some two years later.[54]

And so it indeed fell out. The *Ark Royal*'s aircraft went the wrong way and returned without sighting the enemy, and at 5:00, Somerville called off the pursuit. Almost at the same time, Iachino got reports that the Italian bombers had "sunk a cruiser and possibly a battleship and had damaged two other cruisers," and with this good news, he reversed course and returned to give battle. Thus, the two fleets had formed a procession first to the north and then the south again without seeing each other, and at sunset this charade was terminated when Iachino himself, was recalled by the Italian naval command to a waiting position off Sardinia. Force H marked time off the Skerki Bank, and the convoy went through with local escort for the loss of one ship damaged. All three battleships were back in Gibraltar by the thirtieth, the damaged *Nelson* having been sent on ahead.

Admiral Cunningham signaled Somerville: "Please accept a slap on the back from me to compensate for a slap on the belly with a wet fish," to which he answered: "Thank you, Andrew. At my age a kick below the belt is not of much significance." Somerville transferred his flag to the *Rodney*, and in her, he gave cover to another air-reinforcement sortie and the passing of Force K to act as a surface striking force from that island between October 14 and 19. On conclusion of this operation, the *Rodney* sailed, not for home but for Iceland.[55]

Somerville was forced to shift his flag yet again, this time to the *Malaya*, a move that did not please him. On November 10, the *Malaya* put to sea with the carriers *Ark Royal* and *Argus*, the cruiser *Hermione*, and destroyers for yet another ferry run, Operation Perpetual. Again, the three dozen Hurricanes were flown off successfully, but on their return to Gibraltar, the luck of Force H finally ran out, and the *Ark Royal* was hit by solitary torpedo on the thirteenth, sinking in tow the following day. This was but the first of a whole series of disasters that now overtook the British heavy ships in the Mediterranean basin.

We will return to the fate of Admiral Cunningham's battle line later, but first, we must examine how the Admiralty was planning to use its slender resources in view of the obvious threat looming up in the Far East with the onward march of Japan. With the application of sanctions, especially the oil embargo, applied by Britain, Holland, and the United States against Japan in a futile effort to persuade it to withdraw from China and French Indochina, it was clear that if the Japanese did not decide to surrender all their vast gains of the previous decade, then they would be at war within a short period. Surrender by a first-class power with a high military potential and record of victory was clearly not a serious possibility.

The American Pacific Fleet could, it was thought, be relied upon to shoulder the burden of the defense of the central Pacific, but the defense of Australia and Malaya—to say nothing of Burma and India—was Britain's responsibility. Fully committed as she was, the only way this could be done against a major seapower like Japan was by the commitment of a major British fleet. Indeed, this had long been British policy,[56] and we have seen how this weighed in the balance in prewar strategy with Italy.[57] But what form this fleet should now take, and where it was to be based, caused a considerable amount of heart-searching during the latter part of 1941. The active intervention of Churchill did nothing to ease the Admiralty's burden; indeed, it made it that much harder, for in the event, it reduced itself to a straightforward argument between Churchill on one hand and Pound and the naval staff on the other. Their ideas of the best type of fleet were in total opposition.

On August 25, Churchill wrote to the First Lord and the First Sea Lord about the menacing situation and set forth his feelings on how the Royal Navy should react to it once circumstances allowed. Right from the start, there was agreement about the need for a deterrent against Japan but not on how it should be composed or where it should be based. The prime minister's ideas called for "the smallest number of the best ships." He envisaged such an elite force having the same effect on Japan as the *Tirpitz* had on Britain, but the situations were totally different.

Churchill was aware of the need to retain at least three powerful ships at Scapa to combat the *Tirpitz*, and he suggested two King George Vs and a Nelson for this task. If the name ship and the *Prince of Wales* were thus allocated, the newly completed *Duke of York*, which was not not yet worked up, could be sent to the Indian Ocean and there be joined by either the *Renown* or *Repulse*, as well as an armored carrier. "This powerful force might show itself in the triangle Aden-Singapore-Simonstown," wrote Churchill, who added, "It would exert a paralyzing effect upon Japanese naval action."[58] This was to be done by the end of October. He was against sending the four Royal Sovereigns out east at all. Of course, as a politician, the prime minister had forgotten how his own orders canceling of the four Lion-class battleships and delaying completion of two of the King Georges had led to this sorry situation. His political short-term thinking did not seem quite so shrewd in the harsh light of the reality of the situation two years down the road.

The Admiralty had already been toying with their own plan, and when they presented this to Churchill in reply on August 28, the battle lines were clearly drawn. Far from a small, modern force to overawe the Japanese, the Admiralty were thinking in terms of overall strength. After all, the Japanese had a battle fleet of ten ships and were hardly likely to be deterred by a mere two. Pound was against sending a King George V overseas without a correct work-up on the firm grounds that if they did so, she would never get the opportunity to work-up correctly. The Admiralty argued that to contain the *Tirpitz*, all three King Georges were essential at Scapa. The Nelsons were seven or eight knots slower, and such a combination—although used out of necessity on the *Bismarck* sortie and the Halberd convoy—was not really satisfactory. Two King Georges were needed to cope with the *Tirpitz* and a third to allow for refits, damage, and other issues. If necessary, one of these could replace the *Malaya* as Force H's flagship since she would be available for Atlantic operations. The *Malaya* was allocated to the Home Fleet as a reserve ship for Atlantic escort duties on completion of her refit at the end of September, but as we have seen, the damage to the *Nelson* meant she went to Force H instead.

As the new American dispositions freed the Royal Sovereigns from Atlantic duties, it was proposed they go to the Indian Ocean to fulfill a similar function there and be on hand for a full fleet concentration. The main units of the new Eastern Fleet would be the *Nelson*, *Rodney*, and *Renown*, which would be based on either Trincomalee in Ceylon or Singapore, according to the situation at the time. In any event, an armored carrier was to accompany them as soon as the *Illustrious* and *Formidable* had repaired and the *Indomitable* had been completed. The unarmored *Ark Royal* would have been better for that area, but she was to be withdrawn for a refit in November—an ironic touch.

The *Warspite*, on completing her refit, would rejoin Cunningham, and the *Repulse* would be a spare ship for emergencies. She was to be retained in Home Waters until September and then sent east, escorting Convoy WS 11 en route. The *Repulse*'s lack of protection and modern antiaircraft firepower made her use in the Mediterranean out of the question. She had been offered to Somerville earlier in the year but he refused to use her on the Malta route because of these inadequate defenses.

But Churchill would have none of this. "It is surely a faulty disposition to create in the Indian Ocean a fleet considerable in numbers, costly in maintenance and manpower, but consisting entirely of slow, obsolescent, or unmodernised ships which can neither fight a fleet action with the main Japanese force nor act as a deterrent upon his modern fast, heavy ships, if used singly or in pairs as raiders," he rejoined. As for the Royal Sovereign-class ships, they would be useful as convoy escorts against heavy cruisers, but if the Japanese sent instead "a fast, modern battleship for raiding purposes, all these old ships and the convoys they guard are easy prey. The Rs, in their present state, would be floating coffins."[59] He then returned to his previous argument regarding these ships stating that 'even at this late date', they could be re-armored against bombing and used in the Mediterranean to defend Malta indefinitely. He considered the provision of three King Georges as lavish. To send one to the Indian Ocean, however, "might indeed be a decisive deterrent."[60]

In a letter to the leaders of Australia, New Zealand, and South Africa at the end of October, Churchill stated that the Admiralty's plan to base the *Nelson, Rodney,* and four Rs on Singapore had been spoiled by the damage to the *Nelson,* whose repairs would take three to four months. In the interim, however, Britain was "dispatching our newest battleship, *Prince of Wales,* to join *Repulse* in Indian Ocean. This is being done in spite of protests from the Commander-in-Chief Home Fleet and is a serious risk for us to run." Although adding that the movements of the *Prince of Wales* were to be reviewed when she arrived at Capetown, Captain Roskill states that nowhere on file is there any indication that this was done. As usual, Churchill, like Hitler with Raeder, had gotten his way.[61]

The *Repulse* therefore sailed off; its modernization that was so long delayed was now abandoned forever.[62] By October, she was in the Indian Ocean. At a meeting on October 20, Pound tried once more to retain the *Prince of Wales* at home, but Churchill, backed by Anthony Eden, stressed that a modern ship must go out East as well, and Pound gave way, the Admiralty informing the appropriate authorities the next day that the *Prince of Wales* was sailing for Singapore. The die was cast.

The battleship actually sailed from the Clyde on October 25 with two destroyers, and later, the *Repulse* was sent to Ceylon with two more—all that could be spared from the eastern Mediterranean. The two ships were to join up there and proceed in company to Singapore. In command of these two heavy ships of widely different capabilities, known as Force Z, was Adm. Sir Tom Phillips, glad to again feel a deck under his feet after several hard years as assistant chief of naval staff.[63]

The two British heavy ships duly arrived at Singapore in the late afternoon of Tuesday, December 2, Admiral Phillips having flown ahead to confer with his opposite numbers and the Americans. But between the time of their departure from Cape Town and their arrival at Singapore, much had happened. All the delicate juggling of capital ships on paper and the hopeful plans made regarding their future use had been negated by a series of disasters at sea unparalleled in recent history. Already, in fact, Admiral Cunningham's battle fleet had suffered a cruel blow.

Force K, which had been established at Malta earlier, had been operating with great success against the Axis supply lines to Libya, but ashore, Operation Crusader, the British offensive on which so many hopes were pinned miscarried after a promising start, and the Germans went over to the offensive.

Not surprisingly, Admiral Cunningham started to be inundated with signals from London demanding more offensive action on his part to interrupt the vital supplies of oil reaching Rommel. In vain, he tried to point out that with his forces at a low ebb he was doing what he could to rectify the situation. The exchange of signals is fully recorded in both Cunningham's autobiography and Churchill's memoirs and need not be repeated here. Suffice to say, they reached a crescendo toward the end of November. The upshot of it was that from Alexandria on November 24 sailed a striking force of five light cruisers and four destroyers to cooperate in intercepting two Italian convoys reported bound for Benghazi. Force K, at sea in the central Mediterranean, returned to Malta to refuel and then sortied out in conjunction. Because of the importance of these two convoys at this critical juncture in the desert, it was strongly suspected that the Italians would sail their main strength in support; to offer the British light forces protection against this type of intervention Admiral Cunningham sailed with his main force at 4:00 on the afternoon of the same day.

In fact, no Italian battleships did sail, and Force K made its interception and kill without assistance, but the eastern Mediterranean was thick with Axis submarines stationed there for just such a move by Cunningham's fleet. Three Italian and three German submarines were waiting as the *Queen Elizabeth* (flag), *Valiant*, and *Barham* steered west into the waters between Crete and Cyrenaica. And at 4:30 P.M. on November 25, one of these boats, the *U-331*, commanded by Lieutenant Tiesenhausen, made a skillful attack on the *Barham* with devastating effect. Penetrating the slender destroyer screen of only eight boats from the port side she fired a full salvo of torpedoes at the second ship in the battle line, the *Barham*, which as luck would have it was the least protected of her three possible choices. Three torpedoes from this salvo struck the battleship and tore through her bulges and into her innards. One observer described it: "The poor ship rolled nearly over on to her beam ends, and we saw the men massing on her upturned side. A minute or two later there came the dull rumble of a terrific explosion as one of her main magazines blew up. The ship became completely hidden in a great cloud of yellowish-black smoke, which went wreathing and eddying high into the sky. When it had cleared away the *Barham* had disappeared."[64]

Another eyewitness account of the old veteran during her last minutes of life gave a vivid description:

> A great tower of water had leaped up amidships on the *Barham*, so that only her bows and stern were in sight. I yelled to the captain, who was just below in his sea-cabin, and we swung round and increased speed to try to find the attacker by tell-tale torpedo tracks.

We were "outside left" on the screen, and at the time I imagined that a torpedo had been fired from long range. I had only seen one plume of water, so I thought she would be fairly safe, as battleships can stand more than one torpedo, and reach port with ease. I could not watch her much myself, for I was searching for tracks to starboard as we raced towards her. Then to my amazement I heard someone say, "God, she's going!" I took a quick look at her, and she was listing heavily. Actually, the submarine had dived clear under the screen, and surfaced to periscope depth to find himself within a few hundred yards of the *Barham*. He immediately fired at least three torpedoes, and they had struck almost simultaneously and so close together that only a single splash had gone up from the three of them.

The submarine was blown to the surface by the explosion and passed close to the *Valiant*. The destroyers closed the *Barham* and then "suddenly she started heeling over quickly, but before she had gone far she was rent by a colossal explosion, and completely disappeared in a vast puff of smoke, which reared its head a thousand feet into the air like a cobra about to strike."[65] The whole sequence of the loss of this ship was filmed. Her forecastle was crowded with survivors just before the magazines wiped them out in an instant.

Thus passed the *Barham*. She was the first British battleship to be sunk at sea after more than two years of warfare. Her loss was shielded from the public for several months by an anxious Parliament. Her captain and the enormous total of 861 men perished with her, the destroyers rescuing a further 451, including Admiral Pridham-Wippell, commander of the First Battle Squadron. Her attacker escaped without harm. Admiral Cunningham later commented to Admiral Pound that "it was a most daring and brilliant performance on the part of the U-boat, which fired from a position about two hundred yards ahead of the *Valiant*. If there is anything to be learned from it, it is that our antisubmarine vessels are sadly out of practice."[66]

After "a very unhappy night," during which time large numbers of aircraft passed close by the fleet without recognition signals and Cunningham had to restrain the *Queen Elizabeth*'s captain from opening fire on them in case the gun flashes gave the ship's positions away, the Mediterranean Fleet—now reduced to two capital ships—returned to Alexandria harbor.

The *Ark Royal* sunk, the *Indomitable* damaged, the *Barham* sunk—thus passed November 1941. These casualties, though extremely hard blows, were not yet fatal to the British cause, however; things were to become much more serious very quickly. The *Prince of Wales* and *Repulse* reached Singapore in a great blaze of (one-sided) publicity.[67] The American fleet at Pearl Harbor was put on an alert, and the Japanese had not yet, apparently, gone over the edge. Negotiations were still continuing in Washington. The buildup in the Indian Ocean could continue according to the Admiralty plan in the meantime.[68] Then came December, and the Japanese finally moved—with stunning speed and ruthlessness. Within a week, the whole scene had changed dramatically for the worse.

The day after the arrival of the British squadron at Singapore, Admiral Phillips announced his intention to fly to Manila and confer with the American navy and army commanders on the spot on how to coordinate their future strategy. He left for the Philippines on December 4. In order to further bolster Australian morale with a show of strength, the *Repulse* was ordered to sail for a short visit to Port Darwin on the fifth, with two of the fit destroyers. The *Prince of Wales* stayed to have some extra light antiaircraft guns mounted by the dockyard, while the other two destroyers went into dock as they were hardly battleworthy.[69]

The *Repulse* sailed as ordered; within a few hours, this movement was countermanded, and she returned to Singapore on the sixth. At home, Churchill and the Admiralty were both having second thoughts. Far from exerting the required deterrent value, the two ships were now dangerously exposed, and as General Smuts had written, "If the Japanese are really nippy there is here an opening for a first-class disaster."

The great ships, said Churchill, must go to sea and vanish among the innumerable islands. But it was too late for that now. The Japanese had already made their own plans. They decided that the main American fleet at Pearl Harbor in the Hawaii constituted the main threat to their strategy and had planned a knock-out blow to eliminate it at the very onset of hostilities. Admiral Nagumo had already sailed, on November 26, with a striking force of six carriers escorted by the *Hiei* and *Kirishima* and light forces. At dawn on December 7, his aircraft hit the Americans in two waves combining dive-, torpedo-, and altitude bombing in perfect combination against the moored battleships of the U.S. Navy.

Complete surprise was achieved, and by the end of the day, they had made sure that the two British capital ships were really on their own. The *Arizona* had blown up with appalling loss of life; the *Oklahoma* had sunk; the *West Virginia* and *California* were resting on the harbor bottom; and the *Tennessee* and *Nevada* received severe damage. Only two battleships came through—damaged but still in battleworthy condition—the *Pennsylvania* and *Maryland*. The old demilitarized battleship *Utah*, used as a target ship, was also sunk. 2,400 men were dead and 1,178 wounded. The Japanese had lost just 29 aircraft, the Americans 188.[70]

The *Repulse* had been recalled because a large Japanese invasion convoy had been sighted steaming across the South China Sea towards the Gulf of Siam. Any doubts that the Japanese meant business were shattered by the stunning news from Hawaii. Admiral Phillips therefore now had to determine what steps his squadron could take to retrieve the rapidly deteriorating situation. After consultations, he determined on action. What he was up against can be seen by examining the Japanese naval forces at sea in his area.

The Japanese invasion convoy for Malaya consisted of eighteen transports with 26,400 troops embarked and they had a close escort of one heavy and one light cruiser and twelve destroyers. In support was a heavy cruiser squadron of four 8-inch cruisers and three destroyers. But also at sea from the Pescadores was Vice Admiral Kondo with the *Haruna* and *Kongo*, two more heavy cruisers, and ten destroyers.

The convoy was at sea on the morning of December 4 and was later joined by an additional five transports escorted by a light cruiser, a minelayer, and seven small escorts. Equally formidable were the large numbers of specially trained bomber units of the land-based 22nd Naval Air Flotilla, deployed on Vichy French bases south of Saigon; they totaled some 123 bombers, 36 fighters, and 6 reconnaissance aircraft. In addition, the Japanese had ten submarines covering the most likely routes to the invasion beaches from Singapore.

Against this great mass of material, Admiral Phillips could deploy only his two capital ships and a scratch force of four (soon reduced to three) destroyers. Nonetheless, he determined to do something to help the army, and at 5:35 P.M. on December 8, the *Prince of Wales*, *Repulse*, and the screen sailed from Singapore and set a course northeast. Admiral Phillips thought that if the RAF could provide fighter protection over the beachhead and aerial reconnaissance ahead of his force, he would stand a reasonable chance of inflicting decisive damage to the transport fleet before the heavy ships could intervene in force.

Whether he realized the nature of the aircraft opposition he might have to face is doubtful; their numbers and quality were to be an equal surprise to the Allied defenders over the whole vast Pacific theater of operations in the humiliating months to come. Admiral Phillips and his squadron had the misfortune to bear the first shock of that revelation.

Phillips's small squadron required one other thing: luck. If he could evade detection until he got in among the transports, he might get away with it. This was not granted. As the big ships steamed down channel, a signal was taken in by the *Prince of Wales* informing Phillips that no fighter protection could now be given by the RAF at all in the area he expected to operate; the fighters had all been pulled back in the face of overwhelming bombing of their forward bases. Phillips decided to press on anyhow, even though he was also warned of strong Japanese bomber forces established in Indo-China. He still had the element of surprise on his side. At 2:00 P.M. on the ninth, even this was, unknown to him, taken from him, for the British squadron was sighted and reported by the submarine *I-65*.

Force Z intended to make a fast foray into the Gulf of Siam at dawn on the tenth and there destroy all the reported shipping providing he had not been sighted by enemy aircraft. But alerted by the *I-65*, the Japanese airmen had been straining every nerve to locate the British force. Just how worried they were by Admiral Phillips's bold attack has since been revealed. "The Japanese plans for the Malayan invasion were seriously threatened by the unexpected appearance of the two powerful British warships in the area,"[71] concluded one Japanese historian—an opinion that *totally* ignored the fanfare of publicity that had accompanied the arrival of these two ships at Singapore.

One of the bomber pilots, worn out and tired after constant searches for the British ships when the submarine lost contact, had described his own personal anxiety at the time thus: "It was possible that the British warships had broken through our air-sea screen and might even now be hurling their shells against our transports lying off Kota-Bharu. That was our greatest fear."[72]

These fears were unfounded, for on being detected by Japanese aircraft, Admiral Phillips duly broke off his sortie as he had stipulated he would do and set a retirement course for Singapore. The Japanese airman had already discussed plans for a massed torpedo attack on the battleships in Singapore harbour, but this would have been at the extreme limits of their range in the face of fighter opposition. Nonetheless it would have been attempted. Fate was to decide otherwise. Just before midnight on the ninth, while the British squadron (less the destroyer *Tenedos*, which had been detached earlier) was steaming south toward the Anamba Islands, a message was received from Admiral Palliser stating that another Japanese landing was taking place at Kuantan on the central part of Malaya's east coast.

It seemed a logical move on the part of the Japanese to outflank the British defenders farther north in Thailand. It was not too far out of the way of the British ships' present course, and it was more than 400 miles from the nearest Japanese air base in French Indochina. Moreover, with the RAF fighters withdrawn to the south, there was the possibility of air cover. It seemed too good a chance to pass up, and accordingly, Force Z altered course to the southwest. Expecting the staff ashore to anticipate his movements, he made no signal, fearing to give his ships' positions away prematurely. Unfortunately, the landing report turned out to be false, and no steps were taken to provide fighter cover over the area at dawn on the tenth.

A second Japanese submarine sighted and unsuccessfully made a torpedo attack on Force Z in the early hours of the tenth. Her sighting report, stating the British squadron was steering south, was picked up ashore. Kondo's battleships cleared for action, and back at Saigon, the aerial striking force was again dispatched to locate and damage the British ships before they made contact. Soon some thirty altitude and fifty torpedo bombers were in the air speeding south. These formations overshot and turned back north again. Ashore, a second striking force was prepared to take up the search. The tension increased as the morning wore on with no sign of the British squadron.

Around 8:00 A.M., Admiral Phillips arrived off Kuantan and sent the destroyer *Express* in to investigate. After a short delay, she reported the area as quiet as a wet Sunday afternoon. Phillips moved on down the coast for a while and then swung back north-east to investigate some small craft sighted earlier. Soon afterwards came a report from the *Tenedos*, far to the south, that she was being bombed heavily. The fleet was ordered to first-degree antiaircraft readiness, and course was again altered to the south and speed increased to twenty-five knots. Just before 11:00, a Japanese scout plane was picked up on the radar of the *Repulse*, and at 11:13, the first units of the 22nd Air Flotilla came into sight on their homeward course—nine twin-engine high-level bombers in line-abreast. The final hours had come.[73] Recorded one eyewitness:

> Nine aircraft were seen approaching, flying very high. They gave the *Prince of Wales* a miss and carried out a high-level bombing attack on the *Repulse*. I was in my turret, port side 5.25-inch, and the *Repulse* and ourselves opened fire practically simultaneously. One bomb hit the *Repulse*; it did some damage, caused considerable casualties, and started a fire on the catapult deck. This was quickly got under. But that was only the opening chorus.[74]

It was an impressive start from an enemy from whom not much was expected in the way of accuracy compared with the Luftwaffe. The attack was carried out from a height of 10,000 feet, and the *Repulse* was moving at almost thirty knots, Captain Tennant handling his 32,000-ton ship like a destroyer. This hit, although no more fatal than scores of others of the same type, was shattering to morale because of its very unexpectedness. One eyewitness described it:

> It was the most impressive pattern we had ever seen. It horrified us, destroying all misconceptions in its thunder, for in that brief instant *Repulse* had disappeared, had disappeared completely, in a "forest" of cascading bomb-bursts which, merging together, were replaced in

seconds by a giant wall of water. It was a fantastic, near-incredible spectacle, and then, after a shocked silence, a spontaneous cheer went up. For out of the chaos charged the "lost" *Repulse*, with black smoke pouring from a hole in her deck; but otherwise seemingly intact, and with the bright orange flashes flaring angrily from her side as she hurled yet another defiant salvo at the enemy.[75]

Commander Dendy could report that the bomb had hit the armored deck beneath the hangar but there had been no penetration and no serious damage. There was a lull for twenty minutes or so and then another formation came into view. They were quickly identified as torpedo-bombers. Again, the guns cracked and flashed along the long gray ships' hulls and the sky became pockmarked with ugly black explosions. One, two of the twin-engined aircraft were hit, flamed and smoked briefly and smashed down into the sea. There were cheers and yells of encouragement.

Both the big ships were given attention in this attack and as it developed came the second shock of the day for the British. The Japanese torpedo-bombers dropped their missiles from a height of between 300 and 400 feet instead of skimming down to wave-top level as was British and Italian practice. Thus they could evade the worst effects of the thunderous wall of flak from the myriad of light weapons. Nobody had expected that and it could be quickly observed that such tactics had no adverse effect on the accurate running of the torpedoes. In clusters they sped toward the weaving giants at more than forty knots.

From the attacking aircraft, the scene was equally as spectacular:

We began the attack at an altitude of 1,000 feet and about a mile and a half from the enemy. No sooner had we emerged from the protection of the clouds than the enemy gunners sighted our planes. The fleet opened up with a tremendous barrage of shells, trying to disrupt our attack before we could release our torpedoes. The sky was filled with bursting shells, which made my plane reel and shake.

The *Repulse* had already started evasive action and was making a hard turn to the right. The target angle was becoming smaller and smaller as the bow of the vessel swung gradually in my direction, making it difficult for me to release a torpedo against the ship. It was expected that the lead torpedo-bomber would be compelled to attack from the most unfavorable position. This was anticipated, and it enabled the other planes following me to torpedo the target under the best of conditions.[76]

Because of the clear waters of the South China Sea, the tracks of the torpedoes were clearly visible from the ships, and by a smart piece of ship-handling, the *Repulse* was able to avoid all those aimed at her in this assault. Not so the flagship. She commenced a turn to port to comb the tracks heading her way but was too late to avoid one of them. This torpedo struck the *Prince of Wales* on her port side aft, abreast P3 and P4 5.25-inch turrets.

> Even inside the turret and well above the water-line it shook us up terribly, and the damage was appalling; so much so that a consensus of subsequent opinion was that we had been hit twice simultaneously, here and further aft. We flooded my guns' magazines. Quickly the ship took a big list to port; our speed was reduced by half, and— this I heard afterwards—the steering gear was so injured that from then onwards we were never properly under control. Also the 5.25-in. guns were nearly all out of action from either electric current failure or the list.[77]

So far, almost three-quarters of an hour had passed since the attacks started and no signal requesting assistance or reporting that the fleet was under assault had been transmitted by the fleet flagship. Captain Tennant assumed that some technical fault aboard the *Prince of Wales* was responsible for this, and so, at 11:50, the *Repulse* sent her own report, which reached Singapore ten minutes later. Ashore, the RAF sent a squadron of fighters into the sky and out towards the position of the fleet off Kuantan. But it was too late now.

Another high-level attack took place, and once more, the old *Repulse* was thrown about the ocean like a greyhound under full helm. Even so, this attack was as accurate as the first, and two 550-pound bombs fell very close alongside and shook the battlecruiser up but caused no damage. Tennant then observed the plight of the flagship, which had hoisted her "not under control" signal. She had a list of eleven degrees, and repeated signaling from the *Repulse* produced no reply from her bridge; she was clearly in a very bad way.

Almost at once another torpedo-bomber attack developed, the aircraft making a divided approach with great determination and splitting their assaults between the two big ships. One group made a feint toward the *Prince of Wales* while the other pressed in on the *Repulse* from her port bow. The battlecruiser and the battleship were now close together which gave the Japanese airmen their chance. As the *Repulse* veered to starboard to comb her new assailants' torpedo tracks, the other aircraft swung back toward her and dropped from her port beam. Caught between these two attacks, the *Repulse* could obviously not escape punishment. As it was, only a single torpedo struck her, punching into her port side abreast her after funnel and detonating. The ancient battlecruiser shook and whipped but came back strongly. The damage was rapidly controlled and she could still maintain twenty-five knots. All her guns were still operational.

Not so the *Prince of Wales*. Already a cripple with hardly any anti-aircraft defence left she had to sit and take it all. An easy target, three more torpedoes slammed into her starboard side in quick succession but she stayed afloat, a defiant heavy-weight absorbing punishment and unable to retaliate, but refusing to submit. The *Repulse* had already dodged nineteen torpedoes before her first hit but she would be unable to stand up to the type of devastation being slammed into her big sister. So far she had side-stepped with the skill and agility expected of a professional but then the next wave of bombers arrived and this time she was simply overwhelmed.

> Up to now, Captain Tennant had found the game of trying to outwit the Japanese torpedo droppers and afterwards of spotting and combing their torpedoes an absorbing and rather fascinating one. This time, however, there were too many flights attacking at once for much dodging to be possible. Torpedoes came streaking in from several bearings, together and there was no hope of avoiding them all. One torpedo hit well aft just by the gun-room. It evidently jammed the rudders, because the ship could no longer steer. Three more hits came quickly, two on one side and one on the other.[78]

The battlecruiser was not built to take this type of punishment. She quickly took on a heavy list, and Captain Tennant ordered "Abandon ship." "The ship's steering went, and she veered round blindly staggering, tormented and powerless to evade her punishment. A third, a fourth and a fifth explosion registered on the battlecruiser's side, and her decks became alive with men. Slowly she began to roll, and then to sink . . . her smaller guns firing until the moment when she plunged"[79] An eyewitness described the scene: "When the ship had a list of 30 degrees to port I looked over the side of the bridge and saw the Commander and two or three hundred men collecting on the starboard side. I never saw the slightest sign of panic or ill-discipline. I told them from the bridge how well they had fought the ship, and wished them good luck. The ship hung with a list of about 60 or 70 degrees to port and then rolled over at 12:33."[80]

Thus passed the gallant old *Repulse* and with her 427 officers and men of her crew of 1,309.

From the air, as the *Repulse* went down the flagship still appeared intact. She was therefore selected to the next assault, once more from a squadron of altitude bombers. Despite the fact that she was almost stationary, only a single 1,100-pound bomb hit from a salvo of fourteen aimed at her, and it failed to penetrate her armored deck. Right to the very last, the high-level bomber had proved itself impotent. But that hardly mattered now for the well-trained torpedo-bomber had proved itself beyond all comparison.

Admiral Phillips had sent a signal requesting tugs as the later hits had brought her back on an even keel, but her stern was under water, all four propellers were out of action and all electrical power and hydraulic systems were finished. The destroyer *Express* was ordered alongside her starboard quarter and the steady transfer of survivors began. This was done with considerable skill by the *Express* and at some considerable danger to herself when the battleship took her final plunge over and her great bilge keel came up under the frail destroyer threatening to capsize her also. It was at 1:20 P.M. that the *Prince of Wales*, whose hit on the *Bismarck* earlier had sealed that ship's doom and who was the home of the Atlantic Charter, heeled sharply over to port, capsized, and sank. Of her crew of 1,612, the majority (1,285) were rescued by the three destroyers, but neither her captain nor the gallant Tom Phillips was among those picked up. "The time and date, 1:20 P.M. on December 10, 1941, are worth particular note, since they form a landmark in the history of the British people; indeed of the world.,"[81] Winston Churchill later recorded. "In all the war I never received a more direct shock."[82]

There were more shocks still to come. Denuded of a fleet to deny the seas to the enemy, Malaya, Singapore, and the Dutch East Indies quickly went the way of Hong Kong, as did the Philippines. Soon Burma fell, and the Japanese Army was threatening the sprawling land mass of India. To the east, the tentacles of the same monster devoured the islands north and east of New Guinea, and Port Darwin in northern Australia was bombed as a foretaste of things to come. Never has the loss of two ships heralded so enormous a disaster. Now indeed the economies of the Treasury and the myopic policies of successive governments earlier were presented with a bill of reality in terms of humiliation and the lives of countless British subject and dependants.

Nor was this the end of the sorry tale. Back in the Mediterranean, the very nadir of Britain's fortunes at sea was reached with yet another disaster. The failure of the brave and persistent Italian "human torpedo" attacks on Gibraltar had not stopped them from pressing ahead with this idea, and on December 18, three of these tiny craft were launched from the submarine *Scire* from Leros off Alexandria at 8:00 P.M. They all reached the harbor, and luck was with them, for although charges were being dropped as standard practice, a flotilla of destroyers from Malta entered the main gate, and they followed them in. Despite the fact that something unusual was spotted in the wake of the *Gurkha,* nothing was reported and were able to go about their business with deadly efficiency.

One fixed their charges to the propellers of the tanker *Sagona,* but the other two selected the prime targets of the *Queen Elizabeth* and *Valiant.* Below the *Valiant,* the two Italians were unable to affix their charges to the battleship's bilge keels; instead, it fell to the harbor bed some fifteen feet directly below her. These two were later found perched on the *Valiant's* buoy, arrested, taken ashore, and then later brought back and locked in cells deep below the waterline aboard the *Valiant.* As their time fuses ran out, they made representations to the battleship's captain and warned him to evacuate his ship as a large explosion was imminent. The pair who attacked Admiral Cunningham's flagship got ashore and away by train, although they were subsequently arrested.

All this had taken place despite the fact that a warning of some sort of underwater attack on the two remaining big ships was being planned for the 18th by the Italians. The charges under the tanker went up at 6:00 P.M., close alongside the *Queen Elizabeth,* badly damaging the tanker and the flotilla leader *Jervis* alongside. Nothing could be done in time, and twenty minutes later the charges lying below the *Valiant* went up below her forward turrets. The battleship immediately went down heavily by the bows, the explosion damaging her for a length of some eighty feet including her keel.

Four minutes later, while Admiral Cunningham stood right aft watching the *Valiant* settle, the *Queen Elizabeth* was shaken by a similar explosion. A great cloud of soot was forced up from her funnel and she listed abruptly to starboard. Three of her boiler rooms were flooded by this detonation, which tore a hole forty feet square in her bottom. Counter-flooding rectified the list but she was immobilized and without power until two submarines were brought alongside.

It was a heavy blow. The *Valiant* needed immediate docking as it was estimated that at least two months were required even for the temporary repairs required to send her south for more permanent docking. The *Queen Elizabeth* ultimately went into the floating dock for her repairs but for a time Admiral Cunningham continued to use her as his flagship with all due ceremony in the hope that her damage might be concealed from the enemy.

Elaborate attempts were made to continue this policy, but it is doubtful that the Italians were fooled, and there was no hiding the *Valiant's* injury. While it was in dry dock, several bombing attacks were made on the *Queen Elizabeth* without success. Not until April 1942 was the *Valiant* patched up sufficiently to take her place in line again, and then she was needed elsewhere. The *Queen Elizabeth* was finally sent to the United States in September 1942 and was not fully operational again until June 1943.

In a secret session of the House of Commons some time later, Churchill broke the news of this and the loss of the *Barham* earlier. "In a few weeks we lost, or had put out of action for a long time, seven great ships, or more than a third of our battleships and battlecruisers."[83] Admiral Cunningham wrote to Admiral Pound: "We are having shock after shock out here. The damage to the battleships at this time is a disaster."[84]

One postwar historian disagreed with the commander in chief on the spot. He expressed the view that the loss of these last two battleships was "of small moment compared with the lack of an armored carrier."[85] Things looked very different at the time, for it was plain—both to Cunningham and the Italians—that with no British battleship to stay their hand, their own heavy units could once more put to sea with confidence. Just how their new-found freedom would influence the future of Malta and their destinies in the Middle East we shall examine in the following chapter, but the dawning of 1942 found the two great oceans of the Mediterranean and the Indian almost denuded of the much-derided capital ship. How that affected naval strategy and what consequences resulted will also be examined.

CHAPTER 7

Broader Horizons

When discussing the Washington Treaty, a distinguished postwar historian considered that it was "a recognition of the strategic facts of the situation at that date: British naval power remained strong enough to dominate, as she actually did, the eastern Atlantic, the Mediterranean, and the Indian Ocean."[1] But at the beginning of 1942, the picture presented was far bleaker than this. The Washington Treaty might have in theory left the Royal Navy in such a position, but the actual wartime reality when the rosy statistics were translated into hard facts was that the Royal Navy dominated the eastern Atlantic but only barely clung to the Mediterranean at all, and if she dominated the Indian Ocean at this period—which is questionable—that dominance was soon to be put to a practical test proving quite the reverse.

As well as being at full-stretch with regard to numbers of capital ships available to plug the many gaps now appearing in Britain's maritime defenses, there was now the uneasy feeling that what few modern ships it did have were, after all, inadequate. When it is remembered that the King George V class sacrificed part of its main armament in order to carry extra protection, the loss of the *Prince of Wales* came as a double shock.[2]

But even questionable battleships were better than no battleships at all, and the situation in the eastern Mediterranean at the end of 1941 now bore ample proof of this. The Italian battleships put to sea in strength for the first time since the summer and this time their very presence on the field of battle brought them some successes against the hard-pressed convoys to Malta, which the previous factor of even old British battleships had hitherto denied them absolutely.

This new attitude of boldness first manifested itself during the passage of a vital convoy operation to take eight transports into Benghazi at all costs between December 13 and 19. The ships sailed in three groups with local escorts, but lost two of their number almost at once to the submarine *Upright*. The remainder sailed on December 13, and in support, virtually the whole of the main Italian fleet put to sea. The close-support group consisted of the *Duilio* and *Doria*, with five light cruisers and nine destroyers. The two heavy ships sailed from Taranto. From Naples sailed the *Littorio* and *Vittorio Veneto* with a screen, ultimately, of eight destroyers under Admiral Iachino. This great assembly was opposed by the light cruisers and destroyers of the Mediterranean Fleet, which hoped to snap up the merchantmen under their noses as before.

Even with odds like these, there was a certain lack of confidence in Rome as the operation got underway. Count Ciano recorded in his diary that day that his warships and admiral were once again on the wrong end of a naval disaster in the Mediterranean. What he was recording was the brief night battle off Sfax and other encounters during which destroyer and cruiser forces operating from Malta played havoc with Mussolini's supply lines. Two light cruisers, fully laden with gasoline and oil for the desert armies, were sunk with heavy loss of life by four Allied destroyers, while Force K and Malta-based submarines dispatched two vital tankers and the supply ships *Greco* and *Filzi* with their cargo of tanks. An even larger convoy to be given battleship protection was in the offing but Ciano was gloomy as to its chances even then. "The fact is that our naval losses become more serious everyday," Ciano bewailed, wondering if the war wouldn't outlast his navy. What was happening to the navy he found "baffling" unless it was paralyzed by an inferiority complex. [3]

In any event, this operation did not survive the day, for the submarine *Urge* caught the Naples group on the evening of December 14 and, after a skillful attack, put a torpedo into the *Vittorio Veneto*, causing damage that put her out of action for several months after she had struggled back to Taranto. At once, the operation was cancelled and all the forces put back to port. This did not save further losses for two of the remaining merchantmen collided during the turn round and were damaged.

The British light forces used the opportunity to run the fast transport *Breconshire* into Malta, and on the sixteenth, the Italians tried again. Two convoys sailed from Taranto, and Admiral Bergamini once more took the *Duilio* out with the three light cruisers of the 7th Division and four destroyers. Ditching the crippled *Vittorio Veneto* and taking on the *Doria* in her place, Iachino came out with the *Littorio*, which was escorted by two heavy cruisers and ten destroyers.

Both British and Italian covering forces clashed after heavy air attacks had been made on the British group, which consisted of six light cruisers and sixteen destroyers. Iachino's battleships made fleeting contact with these at dusk on the seventeenth at 5:45 P.M. The Italians briefly opened fire, but when the British cruisers and destroyers moved out to close with them, they drew off to the north again and both sides lost contact. This skirmish was known as the first battle of Sirte, and both the British freighter at Malta and the remains of the Italian convoy at Tripoli reached their destinations, although in a subsequent search for the latter Force K came to grief on a minefield.

Three further small convoys got to Malta during the first months of 1942 under cover of Admiral Vian's small cruisers; these reached their destinations by the skillful use of "something of a bluff, forced on us by the simple fact that these were the most powerful ships on the station; and the enemy could, had he accepted the many challenges offered, have called the bluff by forcing close action."[4] In January, the return of the Luftwaffe added to the hazards that these small forces had to contend with and during a further attempt to get three fast merchant ships through in the middle of that month lost two ships sunk and one, damaged and sent back as a result of bombing.

Conversely, the Italians were sending more and more supplies into Libya to fuel the fire of Rommel's new offensive; the *Duilio* was out between January 22 and 25 escorting one such convoy. Admiral Bergamini was also at sea in an abortive hunt during the passage of Convoy MF 5 from Alexandria to Malta. He had with him the *Duilio,* two heavy cruisers, two light cruisers, and twelve destroyers, but he failed to make contact, and later the same month, the *Duilio* also gave cover to two convoys that got into Tripoli.

Force H at Gibraltar could not at this period offer any alternative. The only heavy ship on that station was still the *Malaya,* and much of her time was spent watching over Brest. Still, in early March, she protected a flying-off operation by the *Eagle* and *Argus,* which saw the delivery to the hard-pressed defenders of Malta of their first large batch of Spitfires. This was repeated on two occasions at the end of the month.

The continued efforts by Vian to get supplies into Malta, now undergoing its worst blitz of the entire war and nearing the end of its tether, were bound to lead to another direct confrontation between his 5.25-inch cruisers and the Italians, and this took place at the second battle of Sirte on March 22. The British convoy consisted of four supply ships escorted by four light cruisers and sixteen destroyers, to be joined by a further light cruiser and a destroyer from Malta. This convoy had to ensure constant dive-bombing and submarine attack as it made its way westward but had only lost one destroyer to a U-boat by the twenty-second.

Early on the twenty-second, Iachino had sailed from Messina with the *Littorio,* two heavy and one light cruiser, and ten destroyers to intercept. A storm was brewing as both forces bucketed towards their rendezvous and two of the Italian destroyers were sent back damaged. At 2:24 P.M., the heavy cruiser squadron located the convoy and the battle commenced in and out of the large smoke screens laid by the British ships. Leaving the convoy to fight off the continued heavy air attacks with one antiaircraft cruiser and the Hunt-class destroyers, Admiral Vian formed his remaining light forces into six divisions and conducted a skillful fight against the Italians, which kept them at arm's length for several hours. Frustrated, the cruisers drew off, and Vian returned to his convoy, but at 4:18, the *Littorio* appeared on the scene and interposed herself between the merchantmen and Malta, thus forcing them farther south, still under constant air attack.

Between 4:40 and 7:00, a series of engagements took place in a rising gale and between enormous clouds of smoke. At one time, the *Littorio* got within a mere eight miles of the convoy—a stone's throw for her nine 15-inch guns— but a division of four destroyers pluckily engaged her and drew her fire on themselves; one, the *Hero*, was hit by one of her shells and sent back severely damaged. For half an hour, the remaining three destroyers dueled with the *Littorio* and the heavy cruisers, and then Vian's cruisers came back and commenced fire in their turn at some 13,000 yards range. "The tactics pursued by the several divisions were to emerge from the smoke-screen, engage the enemy until the fire of his heavy guns became dangerous, and then re-enter the pall. In this way only light cruiser *Euryalus*, astern of her sister *Cleopatra*, and the destroyer *Kingston* were struck by 15-inch shells, the former by splinters."[5] This was Admiral Vian's low-key account of the battle; an eyewitness aboard the destroyer *Legion*, armed with eight 4-inch guns and torpedo tubes, had a more graphic account of what it was like to engage a modern battleship at the point-blank range of under 5,000 yards:

> The *Littorio* was a magnificent sight. She must have been going at thirty knots but in spite of the heavy sea was putting hardly any spray. She was dividing her fire. I only saw one full broadside. Her 15-inch shells made a great mushroom of flame but her 6-inch secondary armament one could not see because of their flashless propellant. The splashes from the 15-inch seemed immense, their ranging appeared good, but the spread was bad. [The destroyers continued to close.] The enemy then appeared to shift his fire from the *Kingston* to us. The first salvo was well over, the next nearer and the third impressively close, most unpleasantly so. We altered towards this one in the approved style. I wondered when on earth we were going to fire torpedoes. We seemed, at 4,400 yards, to be almost within pistol shot. Eventually we turned and fired, Chief putting up a nice drop of smoke. We were fired at three more times and one 15-inch brick fell alongside—most unpleasant, and it smashed up a Carley float.[6]

These resolute torpedo-attacks were not to the Italians' liking at all, and at 6:58 P.M., Iachino broke off the engagement and retired to the northwest, returning home and losing two destroyers to weather conditions on the way. It was a decisive defeat for the *Littorio*, for in the condition prevailing, she not only had overwhelming firepower and range but also could maintain a higher speed than the smaller British adversaries. When she put about on the evening of the twenty-second, the Italian battleship had lost its best opportunity ever to inflict a lasting and crushing blow on the Mediterranean Fleet.

Nonetheless, by the fact that the *Littorio* had not been opposed by a ship of equal size, she had successfully delayed, if not destroyed, the convoy, and this gave the Luftwaffe ample time to do her work for her. Two of the four merchant ships were sunk off Malta the next morning and the following two in Valletta harbor later before they could discharge. The *Littorio* therefore had, by delaying the ships' arrival until the daylight hours, exercised a decisive influence over the operation.

If March had been a bad month for Malta, then April 1942 was far worse. The air attacks reached a new peak and damaged ships were sunk in the docks or hurried away to safety. The fighters were destroyed wholesale on their ruined airfields and the courageous submarine flotilla was eventually driven away from Malta for a period. The Italian convoys now reached Libya in comparative immunity. In April, the *Renown* returned to her old beat briefly when she guarded the American carrier *Wasp*, which made two air reinforcing runs from Gibraltar in April and May, but such was the pressure of events elsewhere that a plan to run a convoy from that end of the Mediterranean had to be postponed.

Admiral Cunningham had left the Mediterranean Fleet on April 1, and Adm. Sir Henry Pridham-Wippell hoisted his flag in the damaged *Valiant* until Adm. Sir Henry Harwood arrived. But there was still no battle fleet for him to take to sea nor the prospect of one for a considerable time. The *Warspite* was now needed in the Indian Ocean, and there were no other ships to spare. Admiral Harwood hoisted his flag aboard the crippled *Queen Elizabeth* on May 20 and prepared to try another major attempt at convoy relief for Malta in June. The Mediterranean Fleet at last received some reinforcement, but only of light cruisers and destroyers.

The June convoy operation was to be a double one, a convoy sailing from each end of the Mediterranean in the hope that by forcing the enemy to divide his forces one or the other might get through. From Gibraltar, Force H would guard the passage of four store ships and a tanker; this was Operation Harpoon. From Alexandria, the Mediterranean Fleet would escort some eleven supply ships in Operation Vigorous. The only British heavy unit available for these two convoys was the *Malaya*, the flagship of Force H.

Harwood was given something else with which to deter the Italian Fleet, the old *Centurion*. She had been converted into a passing likeness of the *Anson* after being under active consideration as an alternate block ship for Tripoli a year earlier. Armed with Bofors and pom-poms, she had voyaged forth to the Indian Ocean and had been based at Bombay. She had made the 20,000-mile journey under her own steam, and although she had not fooled the Japanese, it was considered that she might fool the Germans and Italians. She therefore sailed back to Alexandria, had a few extra antiaircraft guns mounted, and was ready for Vigorous by June 11.

Both convoys were on the move on the eleventh of that month, Harpoon passing the Gibraltar Straits on that night and the diversionary convoy from Port Said leaving with a small escort, to be followed later by the main force from Alexandria. The Harpoon convoy's fortunes will be followed first under the cover of the *Malaya*. The escort included the two old carriers *Eagle* and *Argus*, three modern light cruisers, an old antiaircraft cruiser, and seventeen destroyers. Also sailing with the convoy were four fleet minesweepers and six minesweeping launches bound for Malta. This convoy was the smaller of the two and was sighted first by the Axis on the twelfth. To oppose its passage, they deployed twenty-two Italian and six German U-boats, numerous aircraft from both nations (predominantly Italian torpedo-bombers), and a cruiser squadron of two 6-inch ships and five destroyers; this sailed from Cagliari, put into Cape Bon after being sighted by British submarines, and later sailed once more from that port on the fourteenth, to fall on the survivors off Cape Bon.

Adm. A. T. B. Curteis flew his flag in the cruiser *Kenya* for this operation and disposed the *Malaya* at the rear of the convoy inside a novel screen of the four fleet minesweepers. His theory was that here her volume of antiaircraft firepower would be best deployed to enable her to maintain a flak umbrella over the convoy ahead of her. This she was certainly called upon to do, for the two old carriers were so slow that when they turned into the wind to fly off their fighters they had great difficulty- rejoining the fleet once more. The Axis submarines were impotent and achieved nothing despite their numbers, but during the heavy and prolonged air attacks on the fourteenth, several ships came to grief, including the cruiser *Liverpool*, which was hit by an aerial torpedo and sent back and one of the six merchant ships sunk.

Nonetheless, the bulk of the convoy reached the Narrows intact, and the *Malaya*, the carriers, and the two surviving cruisers turned back as normal. But only one antiaircraft cruiser and a few destroyers carried on with the merchantmen, which proved insufficient against the two 6-inch cruisers that the Italians attacked them with the next day. Thus, the destroyers drove them off in constant attacks and made them retire, but while they were thus employed, the Axis dive-bombers returned in force, broke through the weakened antiaircraft screen, and soon had sunk another merchantman and damaged the tanker, which was subsequently sent to the bottom by British forces. Further air attacks and minefields decimated the rest, and only two store ships reached the island. The *Malaya* and the carriers had meanwhile returned to Gibraltar. Harpoon was a flop, but Vigorous turned out to be a disaster.

Again, the main reason for this was the new-found aggressiveness of the Italian fleet with no battleship opposition. On the twelfth, they were located, and dive-bombers of I/KG 54, under Major Linke, damaged one large ship, which had to be sent into Tobruk. The next day, two more merchant ships and two corvettes developed engine failures and were also sent back, again the Stukas from Libya sank one of them before she could make it. Throughout the night of June 13–14, the convoy was constantly shadowed by enemy aircraft. Early morning air attacks were kept at bay for a while by long-range fighters from the desert but soon the convoy passed beyond their limit of endurance, and the Luftwaffe was free to do as it pleased.

The air attacks increased during the afternoon and another supply ship was sunk and others damaged. By evening, the escorts had expended some fifty percent of their antiaircraft ammunition. E-boats also sailed to harry the convoy during the following night, at first these were held at bay, but then, just before 2:00 A.M. on the fifteenth, Admiral Vian received the worst news yet: the Italian fleet was reported as being at sea on an intercepting course. Harwood therefore ordered the convoy to reverse course, and while this complicated operation was being complied with, the E-boats slipped in and torpedoed the cruiser *Newcastle* and sank the destroyer *Hasty*.

Bombing had not stopped the convoy's onward progress, but the news that the Italian battleships were out did. They were thus committed to spend the daylight hours of the fifteenth plodding up and down in "bomb alley," affording the Luftwaffe all the time in the world to make as many attacks as they wished. All the while, the antiaircraft ammunition drained away. Never has a more convincing example of the power of the battleship to influence events been shown. As the day wore on, the cruiser *Birmingham* was hit and damaged, the destroyer *Airedale* hit and sunk, and another merchant ship sent back with engine trouble. Further attacks from dive-bombers so damaged the destroyer *Nestor* that she had to be sunk, and the U-boats, which had already sunk the destroyer *Grove* on the twelfth, sent the cruiser *Hermione* to the bottom.

The ships that caused this havoc were the *Littorio* and *Vittorio Veneto*, now repaired, under Admiral Iachino, who had sortied out on the fourteenth with two 8-inch and two 6-inch cruisers escorted by twelve destroyers. By dawn on the fifteenth, this fleet was within 200 miles of the Vigorous convoy and closing at high speed.

If there were no British battleships to stop this force, what was the alternative? This was heavy and prolonged attacks by the full weight of the RAF in the Middle East, the very type of forces, which had, it is supposed, made battleships obsolete. Air Marshal Tedder had been cooperating to the fullest extent with Admiral Harwood in fighting the convoy through, and what was available to him he threw in without reservation. The results were disappointing.

For a start the total strength available was small, only forty aircraft: four-engine Liberator bombers from the Suez Canal, eight in all, to make high-level bombing attacks; four Wellington bombers with two torpedoes each from Malta; and Beaufort torpedo-bombers from that island and from Egypt. Early on the fifteenth, they made their assaults in succession.

The four Wellingtons of No. 38 Squadron were the first to locate the Italian fleet at 3:40 A.M. On their approach, the Italian ships presented their sterns to the aircraft, and only one Wellington was able to get into a position to launch her torpedoes. Both missed by 200 yards. A Beaufort strike force left Malta at 4:00 and attacked about an hour later. Nine selected the battleships as their targets, pressing in with great bravery and dropping as close as 200 yards from the great targets, flying over the ships at low level afterwards. They claimed to have scored two torpedo hits on each battleship; their actual score was nothing. Three others hit the cruiser *Trento*. Then came the eight giant Liberators at the enormous height of 14,000 feet; immune from flak and with the latest bomb sights, they made unhurried and undisturbed practice on both battleships and the undamaged 8-inch cruiser.

> Their bombing was very accurate, and the warships at which they aimed disappeared in a flurry of bursting bombs. The Liberator crews—unbelievable as it sounds—claimed to have made twenty-three hits. In fact, they made one: a single bomb which burst on the *Littorio*'s A turret, killed one man, and did no damage whatsoever except for shaking the *Littorio*'s seaplane off its launching platform. The rest of the "hits" were near-misses, which merely deluged the battleships in harmless columns of spray. The Italian fleet held course.[7]

Another twelve Beauforts scrambled off from a desert airfield, but of these, only five got through after being intercepted by German fighters en route. These five aircraft also made extremely brave attacks head on at the Italian big ships. The watching Liberators claimed that the Beauforts hit a cruiser and destroyer. Actually, they had scored no hits. As Admiral Harwood later ruefully admitted: "Events proved with painful clarity that our air striking force had nothing like the weight to stop the Italian Fleet."[8]

At the time, however, the commanders back at Alexandria believed the reports of the RAF aircrews and considered that the air attacks had not only caused enormous damage to the Italian ships but that they had turned back.

At 7:00 A.M., therefore, they told Admiral Vian to again reverse course. The two groups were thus on a collision course, and not until 9:40, with barely 150 miles between them, did Admiral Harwood find out that, far from retiring in defeat, the Italian battleships were pressing on south at high speed. At once, Vian was told to come about again.

Meanwhile, the Malta Beauforts had landed and they converted their single damaging hit on the *Trento* into a claim to have hits on both battleships, and Harwood told Vian to reverse course to the west once more. Hardly had they done so than another signal, timed at 12:45, again turned the convoy back to the east. By the late afternoon, the two forces were within 100 miles of each other, and no reports were reaching the British commanders at all. Harwood left it to Vian's discretion whether to hold on or retire.

Fortunately, at this juncture, Iachino again was ordered to retire with success almost within his grasp, and on the way back to Taranto, he lost the damaged *Trento* to torpedo attack from the submarine *Umbra*, and a final torpedo-bomber attack by the Wellingtons from Malta scored a hit on the *Littorio* at night. This hit, although bravely achieved by Pilot Off. O. L. Hawes of No. 38 Squadron, unfortunately came too late to save *Vigorous*, and by the evening of the sixteenth, the battered and defeated convoy was limping back into Alexandria. Not a single ship had made it through.

As Captain Roskill summed up: "In the March convoy, for all the brilliance of Admiral Vian's action, it was the lack of heavy cover, which delayed the arrival of the merchantmen and gave the Luftwaffe the chance to destroy the *Breconshire* and *Clan Campbell* close off Malta. In the June operation, *the lack of the same element of maritime power was decisive*" (emphasis added).[9]

While this series of misfortunes had befallen the Mediterranean commands, events nearer home had brought home much more forcefully the same conclusions on the differences between Axis airpower and Britain's in relation to heavy ships at this period of the war, for in a daring operation, the *Scharnhorst* and *Gneisenau* had navigated the English Channel in broad daylight and returned in triumph to Germany.[10] Before we briefly describe that traumatic experience, we must return to the lonely waters of Scapa Flow and examine the difficulties besetting Admiral Tovey and the Home Fleet, for in view of the criticism directed against this force, their situation at this point of the war is relevant.

The Home Fleet was at very low ebb as 1941 gave way to 1942. Tovey had at his disposal only the combat-ready *King George V*, *Rodney*, and *Renown*, along with one carrier and ten cruisers. The *Duke of York* was still not fully worked up enough for her to take her place in line, and the *Nelson* was undergoing a refit. This was not all, for of the three great ships actually on hand, one of these, the *Rodney*, was shortly to be detached to help escort a WS convoy of twenty-six ships carrying 40,000 troops from the Clyde in February.

The *Scharnhorst, Gneisenau*, and *Prinz Eugen* at Brest were now thought to have repaired their earlier bomb damage and could sortie out into the Atlantic at any time. The *Admiral Scheer* and *Admiral Hipper* were thought to be operational in German ports, as was the *Tirpitz*. Between them, these four capital ships and two big cruisers could mount a pincer movement against Britain's Atlantic convoys, against which previous raids would be as nothing. Therefore, while the RAF was brought back into action against the Brest squadron to try to immobilize it, Admiral Tovey and Coastal Command increased their vigilance in watching and preparing for the next movements of the other three. With only three heavy ships, Tovey could clearly not guard against both at the same time, although this is what was subsequently suggested.

It was Hitler who sent in motion the next sequence of events; his insistence that every big ship should be in Norway led, on January 12, to ordering the *Tirpitz* to sail to Trondheim. Admiral Raeder set out for his leader exactly what she would do once she got there. The *Tirpitz* would "protect our position in the Norwegian and Arctic areas by threatening the flank of enemy operations against the northern Norwegian areas, and by attacking White Sea convoys." Her mere existence there would "tie down heavy enemy forces in the Atlantic so that they cannot operate in the Mediterranean, the Indian Ocean and the Pacific." All of this was very true and almost immediately proven correct.

Despite the increased watch over the Baltic and North Sea, the *Tirpitz* reached Trondheim later the same month. She had been quietly brought through the Kiel Canal to Wilhelmshaven earlier, and on the night of January 14–15, she sailed north with a fast escort of four destroyers, arriving completely undetected on the sixteenth. Here she was unable to proceed farther because to fulfill the second part of the plan, the bringing of the battlecruisers home and then up to join her, the destroyers were needed in the Channel. Nonetheless, she was now based in Norway. Not until the seventeenth did the Admiralty warn that the *Tirpitz* was at sea, and Admiral Tovey moved his main strength up to Iceland in anticipation of a breakout. Not until January 23, almost a week after she had arrived there, was the *Tirpitz* located by air reconnaissance in Aasfiord, fifteen miles east of Trondheim, behind strong net defenses.

Churchill, who had earlier expressed the opinion that it was safe to detach the *Prince of Wales* to the Far East because the *Tirpitz* was unlikely to leave the Baltic, now growled to the chiefs of staff: "The presence of the *Tir-*

pitz at Trondheim has now been known for three days. The destruction or even the crippling of this ship is the greatest event at sea at the present time. No other target is comparable to it." He added that "a plan should be made to attack both with carrier-borne torpedo aircraft and with heavy bombers by daylight or at dawn."[11] This took no account of the fact that the position she was anchored in made torpedo-bomber attack impossible. Altitude bombing was possible, although at extreme range.

The precedents were hardly encouraging, but the attempt was made. It was hardly a "maximum effort." Nine Halifaxes and seven Stirling four-engine heavies made their bombing runs on the night of January 29–30. No hits were made; no damage was done. It was not immediately repeated, for the bombers' attentions were drawn south for a chance against moving targets, but well within range.

At the same conference at which the *Tirpitz* had been sent north, Hitler had presented the still reluctant Raeder with a final ultimatum on the big ships at Brest: move them north through the Channel or break them up *in situ* was more or less the choice the grand admiral faced. Not surprisingly, he chose the former alternative. At once, highly detailed planning commenced. Channels were swept and kept open up the long route; extra destroyers and escorts were slipped south in readiness; special Luftwaffe fighter groups cooperated to an extent never before witnessed by the German Navy in the coordination of fighter and flak protection for the ships; extra flak gunners and guns were placed aboard the ships and the tide and moon tables were studied with intense care. By early February, the preparations for Operation Cerberus were almost finalized.

When the risks involved were pointed out, the German leader replied that if the ships stayed at Brest, they would sooner or later be hit from the air again. He compared the squadron to a patient with cancer, "doomed unless he submits to an operation." He also showed a greater appreciation of his enemy than his admirals, for he was convinced that the British would not react fast enough to stop the ships once underway.[12] In this, he was to be absolutely correct, and the muddle and indecision that marked British actions during the escape showed that not much had changed at home since the days of May 1940 or May 1941; it was still a case of "muddle through somehow."

That Hitler was also probably right about the need for the big ships to get out of Brest was brought home to the German Navy by the renewal, on a large scale, of the Royal Air Force's bombing attacks on the ships. For this, once more, it was the dynamic prodding of Winston Churchill himself with his "prayers" and "action this day" memos rather than any sudden understanding of maritime affairs by the air marshals with their gaze fixed steadily on the German cities.

The bombers came back and on the evening of January 6. The *Gneisenau* was near-missed by a bomb, which exploded alongside her in dock, flooding two compartments and peeling off part of her armour.

For the British, their naval preparations for an operational sortie by the Brest squadron more immediately concerned the safety of WS 16. Churchill had told Pound that this convoy was of vital importance to the land war in the Middle East and that it had to get through with as little loss as possible. "What is happening about the Brest ships?" he asked, showing his fears that they might intercept the convoy on its way across the Bay of Biscay.

Pound signaled Tovey to send the *Rodney* to the Clyde by the fifteenth in order to provide the necessary deterrent, but the *Rodney* had spent long lonely months at Iceland, and her overdue refit had not taken place. She was now in very poor condition, and eventually, the *Renown* had to take her place as WS 16's escort. The carrier *Formidable*, en route to Far East with Admiral Somerville, was also tacked on to their escort, and Force H was warned to stand by as German battlecruisers might be tempted to operate in Atlantic.

Meanwhile, the extra German naval activity had not escaped the watchful gaze of Coastal Command. Sir Philip Joubert warned in an appreciation dated February 8 that the conditions of weather, tide, and moonlight, taken in conjunction with the increased numbers of destroyers reported and the fact that the big ships had been spotted carrying out exercises in open water "would seem to indicate an attempt to force a way up Channel . . . any time after Tuesday, 10th February."[13]

The German squadron with the *Scharnhorst*, *Prinz Eugen*, and *Gneisenau* actually sailed to carry out Cerberus at 8:45 on the night of February 11, after another air attack had caused a three-hour postponement. Steaming at twenty-seven knots through the dark night, the squadron passed Ushant just after midnight and set course up the English Channel, passing Alderney at 5:30, and as the sky grew lighter the first wave of Luftwaffe fighters started circling overhead in anticipation of the opening bombing raids. They didn't come.

The RAF had available in the south of England about 240 day bombers and 550 fighter aircraft. Coastal Command had three squadrons of torpedo bombers totaling some 33 Beauforts plus a few Hudson medium bombers. In addition, No. 825 Squadron of the Fleet Air Arm was standing by at Manston with six Swordfish. The Luftwaffe maintained a standing patrol of sixteen fighters over the squadron at all times, reinforced during the passage of the Dover Straits, from a total force of 250 machines. The German air defenses were therefore outnumbered by two or three to one, but impressive as the

RAF totals seemed, they were badly equipped to emulate the Japanese off Malaya or the Germans off Crete.

> The weakness lay in the small proportion of torpedo-bombers, and in the lack of training of the heavy bomber for the work, which might be needed. It was perhaps now that the consequences of the long delay in providing Coastal Command with a properly trained and well-equipped torpedo striking force were most seriously felt; and that the prewar preference of the Air Staff for the bomb, as opposed to the torpedo, as the main weapon for use against ships was shown to have been mistaken.[14]

If it was realized, it did not show, and one RAF senior officer made the confident statement that if the Germans tried such an operation it would present the airmen with "a unique opportunity." Indeed it did.[15]

The Admiralty "appreciation" issued on February 2 correctly forecast that if the German ships did move, then the Channel was the most likely way for them to go. An Atlantic foray was considered unlikely as the ships' crews were not fully worked up for such a hazardous voyage, nor were the ships themselves. "We might well find the two battlecruisers and the eight-inch cruiser with five large and five small destroyers and . . . twenty fighters constantly overhead, proceeding up-Channel," they had warned. Dawn on the twelfth found just that.

To provide early warning against such a sortie and an adequate striking force to deal with it if it happened, the elaborate Operation Fuller had been drawn up with submarine patrols, air searches, and radar watch. All failed. The first sightings were by routine fighter sweeps over the channel and by this time the German ships were past the mouth of the Somme and going flat out for the most dangerous section of the voyage. The two Spitfires, which flew over the ships, landed back at their base at 11:09 A.M. and broke the news; at 11:30, the wheels of Fuller began to grind creakingly into motion. The result was a succession of small attacks by torpedo-bombers, heavy bombers, coastal batteries, motor torpedo boats (MTBs), and a destroyer flotilla from Harwich. All were gallantly carried out, all suffered heavy losses, all failed utterly to hit, let alone stop, the German ships.

At 12:18 came the first challenge. The guns of the Dover batteries came into action and fired a total of thirty-three 9.2-inch shells at the German squadron, the nearest of which landed about a mile off their port sides. At 12:25, five MTBs from Dover attacked from long range since without stronger MGB support, they could not break through the outer E-boat screen or the inner destroyer screen. One boat broke down the other four fired from about

5,000 yards, no hits were scored, and three more MTBs from Ramsgate achieved nothing more.

A little after 12:45, the six Fleet Air Swordfish attacked with the utmost gallantry, pressing in right over the screen and through the German fighter defenses. Only one of the five fighter squadrons assigned to their defenses was with them, and all six obsolete biplanes were destroyed by the flak and the fighters within minutes. No hits were made by any of the torpedoes they managed to launch. The self-sacrifice of No. 825 Squadron earned Lieutenant Commander Esmonde immortality and a posthumous Victoria Cross. For the Germans watching, the slaughter it was pathetic. In the cold, unemotional words of Vice Adm. Otto Ciliax's battle report on the efforts to stop his ships is a fatalistic disbelief that this was the best the British could do:

> According to reports from the leader of the Luftwaffe formations overhead, the first air wave is arriving and consists of eight torpedo-carrying planes with eighteen to twenty Spitfires. Under pressure of the German fighters, the torpedoes are released from a great distance, seemingly without target. The Luftwaffe is responsible for shooting down three aircraft, the *Scharnhorst* for one and *Prinz Eugen* for three of the four bombers which directly attacked the ships.[16]

Next came the torpedo-bombers of No. 42 Squadron. Fourteen Beauforts were sent south from Leuchars, but only nine had torpedoes. Of those nine that left for Manston, all took off at 3:30 P.M. accompanied by Hudson bombers, and seven managed to carry out their attacks fifteen minutes later when the German ships were off the coast of Holland. By this time, much had happened.

At 2:31, off the mouth of the Scheldt, the *Scharnhorst* had struck a mine. It had been laid earlier in eighteen fathoms of water and the explosion blew a large hole in the battlecruiser's starboard side flooding two double bottom compartments. The impact was enormous. "Right up to the commander's bridge, everything was flung about. Many of the crew were literally lifted off their feet and then smacked violently down. A few seconds later reports came in from all sections: Electric installation failed. No light on the ship. Rudder does not function. Gyro-compass out of action. Turret Anton making water. Fires in all boilers extinguished."[17]

Admiral Ciliax and his staff transferred to the destroyer *Z 29* and hurried on after the rest of his squadron, leaving the *Scharnhorst* wallowing helplessly in the gathering dusk; a group of four escort destroyers stood by her. Just twenty-five miles away, a British destroyer flotilla was steaming in their direction. It seemed only a matter of time before the sky would be teeming with bombers. Nothing happened. At 2:49, the boilers were working again, and soon after, she was on her way again at twenty-five knots, her echo sounders out of action but being guided through the sandbanks and shallows by her escorts.

Five of the six destroyers under Captain Pizey from Harwich made their attack at 3:43, one having already turned back with engine failure, which was not surprising because all dated back to the 1914-18 war and were more than twenty years old. It is not surprising that Ciliax was reported as saying, "The English are throwing their mothball navy at us now, apparently." They were, and with great courage, the *Campbell* and *Vivacious* fired torpedoes from 3,000 yards, followed by the *Mackay* and *Whitshed*, while the *Worcester* pressed in even closer and was deluged with a storm of. shells which reduced her to a floating wreck. Like the Swordfish, this heroism went unrewarded; none of their missiles struck their target.

Meanwhile, the big planes of Bomber Command attacked in three waves. Although low cloud and poor visibility ruled out any chance of high-level attack with armor-piercing bombs, it was confidently expected that ordinary low-level bombing attacks would devastate the big ships upperworks. 242 bombers thundered off the runways and out across the Channel to exploit the unique opportunity to the full. Thirty-nine bombers of this assembly actually made contact with the German ships and carried out attacks. Fifteen were shot down, and no hits at all were scored.

Finally, additional Beaufort torpedo-bombers were dispatched, being ordered up from St. Eval in Cornwall to Coltishall to collect fighter escorts. None materialized. They then flew down to Thorney and were sent out against the German fleet on their own at 5:40. It was almost dark when they left and it is hardly to their discredit that they failed to find the big ships at all. Two were lost, and the others returned with their torpedoes.

Fighter Command operated continually throughout the day, dispatching 398 aircraft and losing 17. All the MTBs and destroyers returned, many with appalling casualties and damage, and some having survived attacks by friendly aircraft en route. But with the coming of darkness, the British effort was spent.

Only the minefields could now halt Ciliax's racing squadron. At 7:55, the *Gneisenau* hit one, which brought her to a halt. Again, however, the delay was only of brief duration. She was six miles off Terschelling, in her own backyard, when she struck. Within half an hour, the damage had been patched up, the hole in her stern blocked with a steel collision mat, and soon she had worked up to twenty-three knots again. Both she and the *Prinz Eugen* reached the mouth of the Elbe by 7:00 A.M. on the thirteenth.

Meanwhile, Ciliax himself had been having adventures of his own. The *Z 29* had to stop when a flak burst broke a steam pipe, and he transferred over to another destroyer, the *Hermann Schoemann*. As he did so, he saw his flagship come storming up astern. "Boys," he later told her crew, "when I saw you looming out of the mist with your white moustache in front, I could have shouted with joy."[18]

The *Scharnhorst* was still not out of the woods. She passed the marker boats off the Friesians at 9:14, and at 9:34, she hit another mine in almost the same place that the *Gneisenau* had. Again, all the lights went out, the starboard main engine was damaged, and many compartments on the starboard side were flooding fast. The *Scharnhorst* took on a seven-degree list and began to be carried by the currents in towards the shoals of the coastline close by.

Despite these excessive injuries, her indefatigable engine room staff and damage-control parties had her operational again soon, although her main armament was out of action and she reported ready to steam at twelve knots. She had her port engine inoperational and had taken on 1,000 tons of water, but at 7:00 A.M., she limped triumphantly into Wilhelmshaven.

The mine-damage to both battlecruisers had to be kept from the public, Patrick Beesley reveals in *Very Special Intelligence*, since it was only "known to OIC from Special Intelligence and could not for that very reason be revealed." In his report to Raeder and Hitler, Ciliax stated, "Now that the three ships have put into German estuaries the Operation Cerberus is ended. With it closes one day of the war at sea, a day which will probably go down as one of the most daring in the naval history of the war. In spite of the damage sustained by *Scharnhorst* and *Gneisenau*, it can be said that the success achieved was above all expectations."[19]

For once, the Germans were not exaggerating. At 1:00 A.M. on the thirteenth, Adm. Sir Dudley Pound lifted the private telephone that gave him a direct line to Churchill. "I'm afraid, sir," the admiral said into the mouthpiece, "that I must report that the enemy battlecruisers should by now have reached the safety of their home waters." At the other end of the line, he heard a solitary word: "Why?" A board of inquiry was immediately set up to answer that question, which was being asked with some vehemence up and down the nation, from *The Times* to an anxious Parliament. It was a greater shock to national pride than the fall of Singapore two days later. The board sat and, as such boards usually do, blamed nobody. Churchill told Roosevelt that far from a disaster, the general naval situation "in home waters and in the Atlantic had been definitely eased by the retreat of the naval forces from Brest."[20]

This was true enough but hardly enough to satisfy the public, to whom matters of grand strategy mattered less than yet another humiliation and defeat. Since then, there have been many other post mortems on this unhappy episode. One historian analyzed the Bucknill Report and bluntly headed his chapter, "The Whitehall Whitewash."[21] Maybe it was, but what mattered to Admiral Tovey and his hard-pressed fleet was that he could now concentrate his attentions on the Arctic with the Atlantic, the main lifeline of the nation, secure from surface attack. Even the Germans realized this quite quickly: "Within a few days we received news that the British battleships had been withdrawn from the North Atlantic convoy service and were assembled in the north of Scotland," read their naval war diary.

The placing of the blame will be left to others; here we are only concerned with the position of the battleship's part in all this. One historian has placed the blame fairly on the Admiralty in not moving the big ships south. "The root cause, however, was that the Royal Navy having predicted the enemy's intention accurately, virtually left the whole operation to the RAF and the warships they provided were quite incapable of stopping the German ships."[22]

We have already examined the state of the Home Fleet at this time and the equally pressing commitments it was being asked to undertake. The other point to remember is that it was because the Germans feared an encounter with the heavy ships of the Home Fleet that Cerberus was undertaken. The battleships of the Home Fleet had, by their very existence, blocked one main route to the fatherland; there were not enough of them to block both and that had to be left mainly to the RAF, who themselves were eager to prove they could do it alone. If anything then, the Channel Dash might be claimed to have proved the case for the battleship rather than serve, as it has, as one more case of their impotence. Certainly without them, the *Scharnhorst* and *Gneisenau* would have taken the Atlantic route back home and probably annihilated a convoy or two, including the vital WS 16. Lord Chatfield's hypothesis can therefore be held to still have some relevance at the beginning of 1942: "The British battle fleet is like the queen on the chess board; it may remain at the base but still it dominates the naval game. Properly supported by other weapons, it is the final arbiter at sea; to lose it is to lose the game."[23] Just how great an influence even a single battleship could exert, even when remaining at its base, the *Tirpitz* was to prove in the months and years to come.

Hitler had got his "queen" into position; now he had "castled" his Brest squadron with considerable enthusiasm. It remained for the Germans to move up the rest of their heavy "pieces" in support, and this they now set about doing.

Intelligence reached the Admiralty on February 20 that the first of these moves was underway and the torpedo bombers of Coastal Command were alerted. The German ships involved were the *Admiral Scheer* and *Prinz Eugen*, escorted by three destroyers, which sailed from Brunsbuttel and were sighted at 11:10 A.M. on the twenty-first, steering north at high speed. German fighters shot down the shadowing aircraft, and the Beauforts sent to intercept the squadron off Utsire failed to find them; a solitary aircraft, which made a bombing attack, was shot down by flak. At 3:00 A.M., the Germans were again found at anchor in Grimstad Fiord near Bergen but sailed again the same evening.

Meanwhile, the carrier *Victorious* had been dispatched posthaste to launch a torpedo-bomber strike the following morning, and Admiral Tovey sailed in support with the *King George V.* The carrier planes failed to locate the enemy in thick weather, but four British submarines had been deployed and one of these, the *Trident,* found them entering the Inner Leads off Trondheim and put a torpedo into the heavy cruiser. Although badly damaged, the *Prinz Eugen* finally managed to reach the safety of Aasfiord where the *Admiral Scheer* and *Tirpitz* were already anchored.

Admiral Tovey's earlier predictions that the Germans would soon be able to confront him with "a considerable battle fleet" were thus being realized. The Germans were discovering that the building up of a balanced fleet was more difficult than they expected. With the mining of the two battle-cruisers and the torpedoing of the heavy cruiser, all the success of bringing the Brest squadron north had been nullified almost at once.

Worse was to come, for in a heavy bombing raid by RAF Bomber Command on Kiel on the night of February 26–27, the heavy bombers redeemed earlier disappointments by catching the *Gneisenau* in dry dock. A heavy bomb struck the battlecruiser forward, causing enormous damage by igniting a magazine. Almost the whole of the ship's bows was destroyed, and the fire spread to a liner, the *Monte Sarmiento* (13,625 tons), and burnt her out.

It had been the intention of the German naval command to rearm both these vessels with three twin 15-inch turrets when time permitted; these guns were made before the war, but time had never been found to fit them. Thus armed, the two battlecruisers would have been more than the equals of ships like the *Repulse.* Now with the prospect of many months of repair work in front of them, this project was revived for the *Gneisenau.* She was therefore towed away to the Baltic port of Gotenhafen (formerly the Polish Gdynia) for the work, which included lengthening the hull, to commence. However, the chronic shortage of skilled labor meant that this work proceeded with a very low priority during the rest of the year.[24]

Although it was now considered less likely that the *Tirpitz* would be sent out into the Atlantic like her sister ship the year before, the possibility could not be ignored. If she did so sortie and reach France, then the only dry dock large enough to take her was at St. Nazaire. This had been especially built to accommodate the liner *Normandie* before the war and was in the form of a lock, which led from the estuary of the Loire to the Penhoet Basin. A daring raid was mounted to destroy the lock gates and thus render the dock itself useless. An old ex-American destroyer, the *Campbeltown*, was filled with explosives, and on March 27, after a gallant approach in the face of determined opposition, this old ship rammed the lock gates. The next day, she blew up as planned, taking more than 300 German soldiers with her and putting the dock out of action until the end of the war.[25]

Despite the *Tirpitz*, the damage to the Brest squadron ships gave Admiral Tovey a short respite and the opportunity was taken to refit the *Rodney* at Liverpool during March; her place in line was taken by the *Duke of York*, although Churchill had the Indian Ocean in mind for her later. The prime minister was keeping a close watch on the capital ship situation, and on April 14, he was in touch with Admiral Pound on the matter: "Give me the latest dates for completion of repairs to *Nelson* and refit of *Rodney*. Has work been proceeding night and day on these two ships and the two Ansons, as ordered by the War Cabinet four months ago?"[26] He also wanted to defer the refitting of the *King George V* and was concerned about Admiral Somerville's unfavorable reactions to the *Malaya* joining his fleet in the East Indies. "What is her speed?" asked Churchill, "and in what respect is her radius of action less than *Valiant*? Are her guns cocked up?"[27] Admiral Somerville had turned down the offer of the *Malaya* "because of her short endurance."

The Germans, frustrated in building up the fleet to the size they wished, nonetheless were still determined, in Raeder's words, to use the heavy ships there unconditionally for the disruption of the shipment of supplies to Russia. Shortage of oil fuel was becoming a major problem for the two Axis navies, but enough was on hand in Norway to enable the *Tirpitz* to be blooded. Her first targets were the merchantmen of Russia convoys PQ12 and QP8.

Admiral Tovey had again evaluated the situation with some skill, and in his opinion, an attack of this nature was well on the cards on the Russia route, the most likely areas being between Jan Mayen and Bear Island. Each convoy therefore now involved a major fleet operation and the Home Fleet would have to cover both outgoing (PQ) and homecoming (QP) convoys for the last half of the route, leaving the final leg to the close escorts. It was in fact the Malta convoy situation once again with the German big ships and the Luftwaffe substituting for the Italian Navy and the Regia Aeronautica with Luftwaffe assistance.

What made the Russian route potentially more dangerous to the capital ships of the Royal Navy was not so much the proximity of the German bomber bases as the fact that during 1942, it was here that the first full-fledged torpedo-bomber units of the Luftwaffe were concentrated. The Admiralty might have been reluctant to send the Home Fleet close in to the Norwegian coast against bombers and dive-bombers, but, with the recent example off Malaya fresh in their minds they were resolutely opposed to taking on torpedo-bombers en masse. This was balanced by an almost identical and over exaggerated fear of the same type of attack held by the Germans of our old carrier-borne torpedo planes. Thus a delicate balance was maintained and only the side, which took the risks, or exploited the situation more wisely, could bring about a decision.

To help him provide worthwhile cover, Admiral Tovey asked that both the PQ and QP convoys should sail at the same time so he could protect both, and thus, on March 1, both put to sea, due to pass each other on the seventh; Admiral Tovey had his full strength in position between them and Trondheim on the sixth, with the *King George V* (flag), *Duke of York* (now fully operational), and the *Renown*, along with the carrier *Victorious*, an 8-inch cruiser, and twelve destroyers. It was a well-balanced fleet and quite capable of facing the entire German strength in those waters with confidence. Unbeknown to the British at that time, the Germans were about to oblige them with a highly worthwhile target.

Flying the flag of Admiral Ciliax, the *Tirpitz*, with an escort of three destroyers, put to sea on the evening of the sixth from Trondheim and steered northward; as she did so, she was sighted by the submarine *Seawolf* at long range; the report reached Tovey at sea just after midnight. At 8:00 A.M., the fleet came to full steam and swung east in anticipation of a classic battle, which would send the *Tirpitz* to the bottom alongside her sister. For once, Tovey could be confident that he had the strength to do it; all that remained was to get a firm fix on her and bring her to battle.

Alas, this was what could not be done. The advantages of the carrier were enormous, but they also suffered from grave disadvantages as well as we have already seen. Once their strike aircraft were airborne they were merely huge defenseless targets of little value and considerable worry; this the *Glorious* had proved.

The other thing that rendered them impotent was bad weather. Whereas the battleships could shoulder through the huge waves with comparative ease and still bring their guns to bear, the carrier just could not operate in such conditions. Not a single aircraft could leave the pitching reeling deck of *Victorious* throughout March 7. The *Tirpitz* was similarly handicapped; she could not launch her scout plane, and the Luftwaffe air patrols were completely negated by these appalling conditions. Ciliax therefore only had the vaguest idea of where his target convoy, PQ 12, was, and he was blissfully unaware that he was steaming into the welcoming muzzles of three British capital ships.

At noon on the seventh, the convoys, the Home Fleet, and the German squadron were within eighty miles of one another, but they might have been the world apart. Ciliax missed the convoy by a hair's breadth, and the Home Fleet was therefore denied the location that such a resultant attack would have revealed. The three German destroyers had been detached to search for the convoy, and while the *Tirpitz* passed ahead of the target, they passed astern, close enough to catch and sink a Russian straggler, the *Izhora* (2,815), which one destroyer promptly sank, though not before it had dispatched a distress signal. This was picked up by Tovey but could not be made out clearly. The three destroyers, having come so close and failed, were then sent back to fuel, and the *Tirpitz* continued the hunt in solitary splendor. Luck remained with her, although wireless bearings were received by the Home Fleet, and six destroyers spread on line of search. But at this time, their quarry was some 150 miles north of them. Still, Tovey was ideally placed between the *Tirpitz* and her home base, if only the weather would ease or a firm contact be established. Neither condition was fulfilled.

At midnight, Tovey took the fleet south and then east to get his carrier within air strike range of the Lofotens by dawn in case the *Tirpitz* should come down that way. In fact, the *Tirpitz* continued to hunt north and west on the eighth, only just astern of the QP 8, and did not finally give up until 8:00 that evening, when he turned south, toward the Lofotens. By this time, Tovey was convinced that she had in fact already slipped past his guard, he had therefore taken the fleet west away from this area towards Iceland to pick up some more destroyers. The Admiralty had evaluated the position more accurately than the commander in chief and at 5:30 ordered him to steer back northeast, which Tovey did. A further report from London at 2:40 A.M. was also right in predicting that the *Tirpitz* was now coming south, and Tovey once more headed for the Lofoten Islands. At this point, the two forces were 200 miles apart, and through this gap, the *Tirpitz* slipped undetected.

At first light on the ninth, the *Victorious* launched her striking force of twelve Albacores, which finally sighted their giant quarry at 8:00 A.M. All now rested on them. The *Tirpitz* was alone and unscreened, protected only by her own considerable firepower. The torpedo-bombers went in at 8:40, but the *Tirpitz* had sighted them first and was ready.

By rapid and skillful maneuver, the great battleship managed to avoid all the torpedoes aimed at her, and her gunners destroyed two of the aircraft who had thrown away some of their advantage by attacking from astern and into the wind instead of normally ahead and with the wind with them. All the same, the margin by which the *Tirpitz* avoided a damaging hit—which, with the three heavy ships pounding up from the west, would have spelt her doom—was narrow. "On the bridge of the *Tirpitz* were Admiral Ciliax, still commanding. the battleships of the German fleet, and the Commander of the ship, Captain Topp. In the midst of the British attack the German admiral suddenly ordered the ship's helm to be put hard a starboard; Topp interrupted him, countermanded his order and put the helm hard a port. Then he announced firmly that he commanded the ship and that the admiral did not."[28]

Thus the fleeting opportunity passed for Tovey to preside over the death of both German giants. Never again would the British battleships in such strength come so close to a decisive finale with the *Tirpitz*. She on her part abandoned plans to head straight for Trondheim but instead put into the nearest port, Narvik, where she arrived that evening. Tovey and his disappointed heavy ships arrived back at Scapa next day and although a destroyer flotilla was sent out to sweep the Norwegian coast up to Vestifiord on the thirteenth; the *Tirpitz* had already left Narvik and reached her old haven of Trondheim the night before. Here she was finally sighted by aircraft on the eighteenth.

Both sides were given food for thought in this encounter. The British now had a perfect example of how vulnerable the Russian convoys were to surface ship attack, and how they could not rely on their carriers to bring the enemy to book without fail. So much attention had been given to the hits scored by the torpedo bombers during the *Bismarck* action and before Matapan that it tended to be overlooked how often they had failed to score any hits at all, such as Calabria, Spartivento and the like. Nor could the anticipated reinforcing of Somerville's Indian Ocean fleet by the *Duke of York* take place she was still quite clearly needed at Scapa Flow.

On the German side the narrowness of their escape led to some rethinking, with Admiral Raeder stating on March 12 that "this operation reveals the weakness of our own naval forces in the northern area. The enemy responds to every German sortie by sending out strong task forces, particularly aircraft-carriers, which are the greatest menace to our heavy ships." He also criticized the poor showing of the Luftwaffe in shadowing the British convoys and in not locating the British Fleet until it was almost too late, nor in pulverizing it when it was close in once they had found it.[29]

With all this, Hitler surprisingly agreed. Work was restarted on the much-delayed aircraft carrier *Graf Zeppelin*, which was lying forlornly on the slipway at of Gotenhafen, and eventually, the Norwegian fleet would be built up to include the *Tirpitz, Scharnhorst, Graf Zeppelin*, and the two pocket battleships, as well as lighter craft like cruisers, destroyers, and others. Actually, the completing of the first German carrier was subjected to the same delays as the rebuilding of the *Gneisenau*, and although her hull was well forward, Göring saw to it that so many obstacles were placed in the way of the air group assigned to her that she would not be ready until the end of 1943.[30]

Meanwhile, the fleet would have to operate with what was available and the first reinforcements of cruisers and destroyers would be sent north as soon as possible. The Luftwaffe force was being expanded with torpedo-bombers[31] and recce aircraft, and their commander, Stumpf, was ordered to extend his co-operation to the fullest. However, one vital factor prevented the big ships from further exploiting their position for some time: the lack of oil fuel. The March sortie by the *Tirpitz* and three destroyers had used up 8,100 tons of precious fuel oil. Operations by larger groups would be more costly and come at time when Germany's oil imports were falling. Like the Italian battleships at this period of 1942, the shortage of fuel kept them chained in their pens at the very time when they had the most in their favour and the least opposition to their aggressive use. For a period operations were to be conducted with destroyers only; meanwhile the buildup was to continue and the heavy ships were to await a good opportunity. The cruiser *Admiral Hipper* reached Trondheim on March 21 without being attacked. But against the next pair of convoys, only three destroyers were sent to back up air and submarine attacks.

The buildup of the German fleet was very worrying to the Admiralty and more so to Admiral Tovey, who was now told to consider that the safety of the convoys was of greater importance than the destruction of the enemy ships. This he objected to in no uncertain terms, but it must be remembered always when discussing the Russian convoys that their passage was not essential to this nation at all but mainly an exercise in political expediency. The Russians—to whom these convoys were dispatched, full of tanks, aircraft, and supplies that might have saved Malaya and Burma had Britain used them itself—provided only the barest protection for them within sight of their own coastline.

At the end of March, Bomber Command returned, yet again, to the fray. Thirty-three four-engine Halifax bombers from No. 4 Group were sent against the *Tirpitz* on March 30. Bad weather resulted in most of them not finding their target at all. Those that bombed at all missed completely and five of the bombers were shot down.

They came back on April 28. The plan was for twelve of the new Lancaster bombers to make a high-altitude attack against the *Tirpitz* and the flak batteries, to be followed up at once with a low-level assault by thirty-one Halifaxes dropping mines and depth charges, which, it was hoped, would roll down the sides of the fiord and explode around the battleship. The weather this time was perfect, a bright moonlit night and clear skies. Complete surprise was achieved by the first wave and then the Halifaxes went in to be met by fierce flak. Five more heavy bombers were lost; no hits were made. The next night, the raid was repeated with the survivors—eleven Lancasters and twenty-three Halifaxes. Two bombers were destroyed, and no hits were recorded.

Between the end of April and May 12, another pair of convoys was run, PQ 15 and QP 11. Again torpedo-bombers and submarines took the brunt of the attack duties and once more it was only a small surface force of three destroyers that took part, with some small success. The big ships again stayed in port.

But the Home Fleet did not, although its strength had waned since the March episode. In order to rectify this, the Americans brought Task Force 99 to Scapa, which was a very welcome addition of strength. Under the command of R.Adm. Robert C. Giffen, this force was built around the new battleship *Washington*, with the carrier *Wasp*, two 8-inch cruisers, and six destroyers. The *Wasp* was later sent off to carry out fighter reinforcement runs to Malta, but the *Washington*, fast and armed with nine 16-inch guns, gave Tovey's battle line a powerful punch.[32] It was with this ship and his own flagship, the *King George V*, one carrier, the two American heavy cruisers, and a British 6-inch ship that the Home Fleet sailed to cover these latest convoys. The *Duke of York*, flying the flag of Vice Admiral Curteis, was still lined up for the East Indies and stayed at Scapa.

Unfortunately, the only result of this foray was a tragic accident. In thick weather, the fleet flagship collided with the destroyer *Punjabi*, and as the destroyer sank, her depth charges exploded. The damage to the *King George V*'s bow was severe, and she was out of service for three months for repairs. Her place was taken by the *Duke of York*.[33]

It was fortunate that at this period there was still no German activity other than the continual buildup, which went on despite major efforts to prevent it. On May 9, the *Admiral Scheer* sailed from Trondheim with the fleet tanker *Dithmarschen* and two escorts to take up position at the forward base at Narvik. On the sixteenth, the damaged *Prinz Eugen* also sailed with an escort of four destroyers, south to Kiel for more lasting repairs. Heavy attacks were mounted by the torpedo-bomber forces of Coastal Command, with twelve Beauforts, six Blenheims, and four of the fast new Beaufighters attacking on the seventeenth and losing three aircraft without result. A second wave of some thirty planes was intercepted by fighters and lost four aircraft. The *Prinz Eugen* survived it all and reached port on the eighteenth.[34] On the same day, the pocket battleship *Lützow* sailed north to take her place with a solitary escort.

Moving carefully in stages via Kristianund and Trondheim, she was brought without hindrance to Narvik and joined her sister there on May 25. They did not stir from here, however, when the next convoys, PQ 16 and QP 12, the largest to date, passed by, but Tovey was forced to divide his covering ships, using a cruiser squadron east of Bear Island to guard against the two pocket battleships while cruising with the Home Fleet further south in case the *Tirpitz* came out. Tovey's resources were now stretched to breaking point for he also had to provide from his own flotilla craft most of the increasing numbers of destroyers needed to cope with the heavier air and underwater attacks.[35]

On June 16, Raeder had consulted with Hitler and obtained his blessing to finally unleash his heavy ships against the next Russian convoy, expected in June or July. The operational plan was code-named the Knight's Move and was exhaustive in its detail, its main objective was the annihilation of the PQ convoy, and although the surface ships were to act in conjunction with the Luftwaffe and submarine forces they had the prime task. Raeder had requested special efforts from these other two arms in the matter of reconnaissance and this was promised him. The command of the operation rested with Adm. Otto Schniewind aboard the *Tirpitz* for tactical operations, but the operational control was under General-Admiral Carls back at Kiel, who would also assume command of all naval forces during the sortie. It was a complex setup but the British were even more liable to direct intervention from home headquarters as had been shown before. During the prior episode against the *Tirpitz*, the Admiralty's directions had been shown to have been far more accurate than the assessment of the man on the spot because of the intelligence supplied; it therefore created a dangerous precedent.

The German attack was to be two-pronged, utilizing just about every operational warship they had in Norway. The Second Battle Group—comprising the two pocket battleships *Lützow*, flying the flag of Vice Adm. Oskar Kummetz, and the *Admiral Scheer*, screened by the five destroyers of the 8th Flotilla—was to sortie out from Narvik up to the far-northern base of Altenfiord once the preparative order had been issued.

Likewise, the First Battle Group, the *Tirpitz*, the 8-inch cruiser *Hipper*, and the five destroyers of the 5th and 6th Flotillas would move north from Trondheim to Vestfiord. Once these advanced bases had been reached, the destroyers would refuel and once the convoy had been firmly located both groups would sail and rendezvous about 100 miles north-west of the North Cape in order to fall upon their victim east of Bear Island, secure in the knowledge from previous operations that the main British battle fleet never ventured that far.

The *Tirpitz* group was assigned the task of wiping out the Allied cruiser squadron known to accompany the convoys while the two pocket battleships mopped up the close escort. Only when the escorts had been finished off with the help of the destroyers would the squadron set about the task of sinking the defenseless merchantmen en masse. It was a plan which showed every prospect of success, although Hitler firmly laid down that should an enemy carrier be located close enough to inflict crippling damage to any of the big ships then the operation would have to be broken off at once. As for the actual attack on the merchant ships, it was to be a quick operation: the big ships would content themselves with hitting as many as possible and bringing them to a halt; they could then be finished off later by submarines and aircraft. The big ships were to hurry back to Norway before any retribution could descend in the shape of the Home Fleet.

The representations of Admiral Tovey against sailing the convoy with the balance all in favour of the enemy, or of at least sailing it in two smaller groups were both rejected due to political pressure at the highest levels. As one historian was to note: "The Cabinet had given the British Admiralty a task which it could not possibly perform."[36]

Nonetheless, it had to try, and though the convoy's protection would have to, rely even more on early detection of the enemy's movements, it was still hoped that either the submarine screen off their ports would manage to get a hit on the big ships if they came out or, alternatively, that the Germans might be drawn further west and into the arms of the Home Fleet. This latter proposition was a doubtful one, for the Germans had up to now avoided that situation on every occasion it had presented itself.

Tovey put to sea with the *Duke of York* (flag) and *Washington*, with the carrier *Victorious*, one heavy and one light cruiser, and fourteen destroyers. The cruiser covering force under Rear Admiral Hamilton consisted of four 8-inch ships with three destroyers, and although ordered not to proceed east of Bear Island, it did in fact hold on for a little longer close to the convoy to offer as much protection as it could. Tovey cruised between the north of Jan Mayen island and Spitzbergen through the early passage of the convoy, which was attacked by both submarines and aircraft between July 1 and 3, though with little effect, and a torpedo-bomber attack by the Luftwaffe on the fourth, although well pushed home, caused only light casualties. Meanwhile, the German heavy ships were on the move.

The First Battle Squadron arrived intact in the Lofoten Islands on July 3,[37] but less fortunate was the voyage north of the two pocket battleships. While entering Tjeld Sound in thick fog, the *Lützow* touched bottom and severely damaged her hull resulting in the flooding of several watertight compartments. Kummetz was forced to transfer his flag to the *Admiral Scheer*, and the crippled ship was sent back to Bogen Bay.[38]

It had not been an auspicious start to such a vital operation but when the news was reported to Raeder in Berlin he felt that the operation could still go ahead as planned. The German U-boats had been maintaining constant touch with the convoy, save for a few brief gaps, and the Germans knew exactly the speed, composition and course of PQ 17 on July 4. Unhappily, back in London, the whereabouts of the German units—in particular the *Tirpitz*—were less clear. (See Patrick Beasley, *Very Special Intelligence*, for the full details of Admiralty intelligence and PQ 17.)

By the afternoon of that date, it was estimated that the pocket battleships were up at Altenfiord, but there had been no firm news of the First Battle

Squadron since they had slipped out of Trondheim on the second. The move to the new forward base was not known; what was considered was that this group was out at sea heading steadily towards the convoy, and this at a time when British air patrols had lapsed due to an accident. But by 8:30 P.M., intelligence placed the *Tirpitz* at Altenfiord with the others, and it was estimated that if they sailed then, they would reach the convoy at 2:00 A.M. on the fifth. The decision was then made to order the convoy to scatter and signals were sent to that effect but in such a sequence that their arrival and wording caused the local naval escorts on the spot, the cruiser squadron and the close escort, to assume that the *Tirpitz* was in fact, almost upon them at that time and that at any moment her masts would be sighted coming over the horizon. The convoy was duly scattered much to their dismay and the two naval forces combined to offer forlorn battle in the hope that while they were sacrificing themselves the merchant ships might have time to win clear of the immediate danger. But as they sped westward and cleared for action, nothing happened at all.

The Home Fleet was still northwest of Bear Island on the fifth, but early that day, it turned back for Scapa. Firm reports were then received that the *Tirpitz* was out some 300 miles from the point where PQ 17 had scattered the day before.

What had happened was that the *Tirpitz*, *Admiral Scheer*, and *Admiral Hipper* had concentrated at Altenfiord, and when Hitler's approval had come through, they had finally sailed just after 11:00 A.M., escorted by seven destroyers and two small escorts. At 5:00 P.M., she was reported and attacked by the Soviet submarine *K-21*, without effect off the approaches to Altenfiord. At 6:15, she was sighted by an air patrol steering east beyond the North Cape, and just over two hours later, she was again spotted by the submarine *Unshaken*. By that time, however, the whole object of her mission was finished; there was no longer a convoy as such to attack. What remained of it—isolated groups and single unescorted ships—were being hunted down and sent to the bottom in short order by the unopposed submarines and U-boats. Of the thirty-seven ships that had formed the convoy, only thirteen finally got through, much later, to Russia. It was the greatest victory the Germans had achieved, and it resulted solely from the threat of the *Tirpitz* and her big sisters. Prior to their sortie, the convoy and escort had more than held their own against both underwater and air attacks.[39]

Churchill recalled that "although the naval force at Trondheim was only half as strong as Hitler had hoped, it riveted our attention."[40] He had written to an uninterested Stalin on May 9 that "on account of the *Tirpitz* and other enemy surface ships at Trondheim, the passage of every convoy has become a serious fleet operation."[41] After the disaster, he again attempted to spell out the facts of seapower to the Russian leader, who knew nothing about it and cared even less. "If one or two of our very few most powerful battleships were to be lost or even seriously damaged while the *Tirpitz* and her consorts, soon to be joined by the *Scharnhorst*, remained in action, the whole command of the Atlantic would be temporarily lost."[42]

It was because the British refused to risk their battleships east of Bear Island where the Luftwaffe could attack them that the Germans were thus granted immunity; and here I would agree with Admiral Hezlet absolutely that the Luftwaffe exercised a telling effect. But without the heavy ships to back this up with the real power this would not have mattered a great deal to the convoys. Churchill proposed that for the next Russia convoy the two 16-inch battleships (presumably the *Nelson* and *Rodney*) should in fact go right through with the convoy and fight it out with the enemy. They were to be protected from air intervention by the fleet carriers *Indomitable*, *Victorious*, *Eagle*, and *Argus*, plus five escort carriers, all available antiaircraft cruisers of the Dido type, and a screen of twenty-five destroyers. All well and good, except that a fleet of such proportions to carry out an operation of far from vital importance to the British themselves was beyond Britain's capabilities after its losses in Pedestal.

If fear of what the *Tirpitz* would do to a convoy and its close escort caused the disaster of PQ 17, was it an overrated fear? The official historian is inclined to think it was: "As we look back on this unhappy episode today, it is plain that the enemy was never likely to risk the *Tirpitz* in close attack on a convoy protected by an escort, which was heavily armed with torpedoes."[43] The study of the Knight's Move shows, however, that he had every intention of doing just that. When Captain Roskill goes on to cite the instances of German big ships' reluctance to attack a guarded convoy, it must be remembered that in these cases the convoys were guarded by British battleships and that they were the deterrent, not the light escorts. Finally David Woodward makes the points on both sides of this argument:

> It has several times been stressed in this narrative that the presence of the *Tirpitz* pinned down Allied heavy ships which were needed elsewhere.
>
> In view of the fact that when she did make her one big sortie the Allied heavy ships did not try to intercept her, because of the risks involved, it may be asked whether it was worthwhile keeping Allied heavy ships in north Atlantic or Arctic waters.

The answer to this must be that the loss of most of PQ 17 represented only a minor disaster to the Allies compared to what might have happened had the German battleship made for the open waters of the Atlantic.

The essence of the war at sea was that on one hand there were things that capital ships could not do and, on the other, there were things that submarines and aircraft could not do - witness their failure to stop the Atlantic convoys.[44]

The strong torpedo force theory of Admiral Tovey was tried out when the next Russian convoy sailed in September, but was not put to the test on that occasion. But before we examine that episode and the *Tirpitz*'s subsequent exploits, we must again switch to another ocean and backtrack in time three months to see how the battleship was affecting the issue as the Japanese swept westward into the Indian Ocean.[45]

What remained of Allied seapower after the loss of the *Prince of Wales* and *Repulse* had been insufficient to hinder the systematic Japanese seaborne invasion and conquest of the Malayan peninsula, and in February, Singapore island, the mythical fortress of white supremacy in the east, surrendered to a smaller Japanese army after resistance of less than a week. The American fortresses at Corregidor held out longer, but they too ultimately fell, and meanwhile, the whole of the Dutch East Indies was overwhelmed in a series of brilliant operations. At the battle of the Java Sea, the last organized naval resistance was snuffed out by a Japanese cruiser force with no loss to themselves.[46] What surviving warships there were—a few old cruisers, destroyers, and submarines—fled to the safety of Indian and Australian waters. The long years of Japanese occupation settled down over this whole vast region. Now the frantic Australians prepared themselves to defend New Guinea, last barrier before their own continent was laid waste.

Vice Adm. Geoffrey Layton had left Singapore before the fall to organize the defense of the Indian Ocean with what ships there were, leaving behind him a rather unfortunate signal but little else.[47] The original Admiralty plan of building up a balanced fleet of older battleships with carriers, cruisers and destroyers to take on the Japanese in equal numbers, so scornfully rejected earlier, was now taken out of store hastily and put into effect with the best speed possible. To command the new fleet, Adm. Sir James Somerville was selected and told by Churchill that he enjoyed his complete confidence. On the Indian border, Gen. Archibald Wavell prepared to defend the subcontinent as Burma was evacuated confident in the belief that the Royal Navy would soon demonstrate complete command of the sea once more. He therefore threw most of what he had on to the border leaving the east coast almost denuded of troops. When Somerville arrived and viewed the motley assembly that passed as his fleet, he had quickly to disillusion the military commander.

As we have already seen, Admiral Somerville sailed aboard the carrier *Formidable* from the Clyde on February 17, reaching Freetown, Sierra Leone, on the twenty-ninth. Already in the Indian Ocean were the battleships *Ramillies* and *Royal Sovereign* and a few equally ancient D-class cruisers and S-class destroyers that had escaped the debacle of Java Sea earlier. Churchill noted how the current plan against any Japanese move against Ceylon, as a natural preliminary to the invasion of India, would be countered by these two old battleships based at Colombo under a massive fighter umbrella. In actual fact, there were only five fighter squadrons in the whole of Ceylon, and all these comprised aircraft far inferior to the Japanese Navy Zero.

Reinforcements were on the way, both long-term and short-term. The *Formidable*, with Admiral Somerville aboard, sailed on to Capetown, and here rendezvoused with the *Resolution*, which was flying the flag of Algernon Willis. The *Revenge* was also to join up. The carriers *Indomitable* and *Hermes* were already on station. The former had been running in fighters to Malaya and Java, but thanks to Admiral Layton's foresight, she had landed her last consignment in Ceylon rather than squander them on a lost cause; otherwise, there would have been hardly any modern fighters at all. The latter was old, slow, and unsuited for fleet operations. She had been employed in the Indian Ocean on raider hunting and badly needed a refit. She was added to Somerville's immediate strength for the time being. The *Warspite* was allocated as Somerville's flagship.

The *Warspite* had complete her long refit following her damage off Crete on December 28, 1941, and had sailed on January 7 from the United States to work up at Vancouver, leaving there on the twenty-second and arriving, via the Pacific, at Sydney a month later. Here the Japanese got wind of her arrival and made a midget submarine attack on the harbor on the night of May 31-June 1, during which they claimed, in great detail, to have sunk her. In fact, she had only stopped over at Sydney a short while, sailing on February 26 and voyaging via Adelaide to Ceylon, arriving at Trincomalee on March 22. Somerville hoisted his flag aboard her five days later.

The Eastern Fleet, when thus assembled, presented a powerful and workmanlike force to the casual glance with a battle line of five ships, three aircraft carriers, two heavy and five light cruisers, and sixteen destroyers. A closer inspection revealed its glaring deficiencies, however. The four Royal Sovereign-class battleships had not been modernized, and therefore their main armaments of eight 15-inch guns, although presenting a powerful concentration of firepower, could, in fact, be outranged by the 14-inch Kongos. Worse, their speeds were, at best, only eighteen or nineteen knots, and their water distillation plants were inadequate to replace the high loss rate that a prolonged bout of high-speed steaming would ensure. This was their gravest defect, because their fresh water supplies would be exhausted even before their oil fuel stocks. They were tied to their bases by this fact as the navy still had no afloat-support vessels to accompany them to sea.

Churchill had labeled them "coffin ships" earlier and lost no opportunity to attach this label to them at every opportunity subsequently.[48] The prime minister's highly selective memory could never bring him to admit that by being part of a government that cancelled the four proposed Invincible-class battlecruisers in 1922 and, almost two decades later, cancelled the four Lion-class battleships in 1940, he had *twice* thwarted attempts by the Royal Navy to replace these old ships, which had been built in 1916–17 to fight in the North Sea. By doing so, he—and his equally blind compatriots in the House of Commons—had left his sailors with nothing but "coffin ships." Both quartets of cancelled ships would have carried 16-inch guns and been capable of more than thirty knots, but they had both been dustbinned by the same Churchill who was now sending such churlish signals. Admiral Somerville was also depressed that the Royal Sovereign-class represented his backbone. "So this is the Eastern Fleet," he had signaled. "Never mind, many a good tune is played on an old fiddle. . . . My old battle-boats are in various states of disrepair and there's not a ship at present that approaches what I should call a proper standard of fighting efficiency."[49] Nonetheless, should it come to a slugging match, he would be glad for them to back up the *Warspite.*

His carriers, which everyone expected to predominate after the Japanese example, were in not much better state. Carriers are only as good as their aircraft, and the aircraft of the *Indomitable* and *Formidable* were still the obsolete Fleet Air Arm types. His main striking force, which was to replace the battle fleet, was still based on the Albacore torpedo-bomber for example. It is always assumed that if the Royal Navy had built more carriers like *Indomitable*, they would have been able to exercise command of the Mediterranean and the Indian Ocean, but those who thought this way always assumed that British carriers could deploy highly skilled groups of fighters, dive-bombers, and torpedo-bombers like the Japanese and American navies, able to take on all-comers with some guarantee of success. British carriers, no matter how numerous, simply could not do that. Their fighters, like the Sea Hurricane and Fulmar, were totally outclassed, laughably so; they had not one single, solitary dive-bomber, and the torpedo-bombers were the Fairey Albacore and Swordfish, plank-winged biplanes from another era. Twenty, thirty, or even fifty 150-mile-per-hour Albacores would not have made much difference in either the Mediterranean or the Indian Ocean in 1942, even if their aircrews had been skilled, and events in 1942–43 were to prove that the rapidly expanded Fleet

Air Arm was just not up to the standard of those of the world's other carrier-based aviators in all but a few rare cases, as Somerville's diary duly recorded.

Nonetheless, it represented quite an achievement, in view of the enormous losses suffered earlier, for the Admiralty to mount a force of such size. They were certainly a fleet that the Japanese could not ignore, because of its very size. If the Japanese wanted Ceylon and India, they would have to match the British fleet in ships and destroy it. If Somerville could hold on and perhaps inflict some damage on the enemy in his much cherished moonlight torpedo-bomber attack, he might have a chance. Further reinforcements were promised, including the *Duke of York*, *Nelson*, and *Rodney*—ships with a much better chance of coming through a fleet action and giving as good as they got—but none of these could arrive for some time.[50]

A more constructive reinforcement would be the *Valiant* once her repairs were completed, and Churchill kept prodding to get her to Somerville before it was too late. But the Japanese did not wait for the British to get their ships into shape and order before carrying out the next stages of their expansion. Even as the ships of Somerville's fleet exercised and got to know each other across the other side of the ocean from Addu Atoll, the navy's secret base in the Maldives, they were busy consolidating their positions without hazard.

Between March 19 and 25, the Japanese 56th Infantry Division was transported from Singapore to Rangoon in a huge convoy while another force occupied Port Blair in the Andaman Islands; they were covered by a light carrier and a heavy cruiser squadron. The plans for the attack on Ceylon and the elimination of the British Fleet to keep them quiet on their flanks while they turned east to Midway and the Solomons was underway on March 26 when the 1st Carrier Fleet, under Nagumo, set sail from Staring Bay in the Celebes. He had under his command the elite force that had smashed Pearl Harbor—the five big carriers crammed with modern fighters, torpedo-bombers, and dive-bombers, and four fast battleships of the 3rd Battle Squadron, as well as the *Kongo*, *Haruna*, *Hiei*, and *Kirishima*, two heavy and one light cruiser, and nine destroyers. On April 1, this powerful force refueled south of Java and headed west.

Admiral Somerville had actually got wind of this attack on March 29, but it was expected to actually take place on April 1. The Eastern Fleet was therefore hastily assembled ready to concentrate south of Ceylon and carry out Somerville's plan. He had information of the Japanese force and in view of the lack of training of his own ships abandoned any concept of a daylight fleet action between the opposing capital ships, even though he had a numerical superiority of five to four here. Instead, his policy would be to keep within striking range of the enemy, without himself being spotted, keeping his distance during the day while the Japanese dashed themselves at Ceylon's

defenses. Then when the enemy had expended himself he would close to torpedo-bomber range at night and launch his antiquated planes by moonlight
in the hope of evading the defending fighters and delivering a telling blow.

At any rate, both Somerville and the authorities at home were agreed on
the vital need not to squander his fleet in an action against superior forces
needlessly. His was the second Eastern Fleet assembled; there were not
enough ships to form a third if that went the way of the first.

Somerville had already decided to split his force into fast and slow divisions to carry out such a plan. Force A consisted of the *Warspite* as fleet flagship, along with the *Indomitable* and *Formidable* for air, two heavy and two fast
light cruisers (the *Cornwall, Dorsetshire, Emerald,* and *Enterprise*), and six destroyers. Force B consisted of the four Royal Sovereigns under Willis, *Hermes* for
air, three light cruisers, and eight destroyers. The latter would operate in support of Force A, keeping to the west of it in case the Japanese battleships
broke through. The whole fleet was in position some eight miles south of Ceylon on March 31, ready for the battle. The men had complete confidence in
Somerville, and knowing full well the odds he faced and the danger he was
in, he kept his fears to himself. As one historian put it, all of a sudden "there
were no more hesitations about the R-class "coffin ships."[51]

On April 1 and 2, the Eastern Fleet cruised in this position awaiting events
and hoped for early air reconnaissance reports of his adversary. Nothing happened. As we now know, Nagumo was refueling in readiness, and the same
day, Admiral Ozawa put to sea with his light carrier and cruiser squadron to
penetrate the Bay of Bengal and create diversionary havoc among the unprotected merchantmen there.

Somerville spent these two tense days exercising his fleet, and they certainly needed it. "A fleet can be made up of individually efficient ships and
still be a mediocre instrument if it has not been exercised as a whole," wrote
one observer.[52] This was indeed the position of the Eastern Fleet whereas
Nagumo's ships had been operating continually for five months of unbroken
victories as an integral unit. On the second, the destroyers refueled from the
two heavy cruisers and the oiler *Appleleaf.* "This should have set the fleet up
for several more days at sea, but for another shortage which now proclaimed
itself; that of fresh water."[53]

The R-class battleships, Somerville recalled, "confessed with salt tears
running down their sides, that they must return to harbor quickly as they
were running out of water."[54] As they were "useless encumbrances" in any
event, this should not have presented too much of a problem, but perhaps
they were not as nonessential after all. The fleet would have felt rather
exposed without their comforting thirty-two 15-inch guns to back them up,
no matter what their shortcomings. If the battleships had to go back, then

Somerville decided that the whole fleet must go to and all refuel together at the same time.

Lack of any aerial reports seemed to indicate to everyone that either the earlier intelligence reports were wrong, or, more likely, that Nagumo knew they were waiting for him and had pulled back to rethink. The next choice for Somerville was where to take his fleet. He had the choice of Colombo, Trincomalee, or Addu. He was under no illusions as to the state of the defenses at the two nearer bases. Addu might be 600 miles to his rear, but at least it was secure; there would be no chance of being "Pearl Harbored" there.[55]

And so the fleet steamed back to Addu. But not all of it: a few ships were detached to Ceylon after all; the heavy cruiser *Cornwall* was sent to resume her refit at Colombo, while her sister was to act as escort for a troop convoy to Australia due to arrive there on the eighth. The *Hermes* and the destroyer *Vampire* as its solitary escort were sent to Trincomalee to fit out for the Madagascar operation for which she had been assigned. Churchill later considered this dispersal in the face of possible enemy action was imprudent, but Alexander and Pound defended these movements furiously.[56] They were to have tragic results nonetheless.

Somerville actually had little choice if these ships were to be got ready as required, for apart from Ceylon, the only other base he could have sent them to was Bombay, a thousand miles away, and he wanted them were he could concentrate them again quickly if need be.

On the morning of April 4, the main fleet reached Addu and commenced replenishing. Although defined as a naval base, what met their gaze was described in one account as "Scapa Flow—with palm trees."[57] The atoll was merely a small ring of near-barren islands of coral with a deep-water anchorage inside. There were still gaps in the anti-submarine defenses, recalling Scapa indeed, protected only by "an extempore guard of anti-submarine obstructions of some kind, but there was nothing to stop enemy submarines sitting outside and firing torpedoes through the holes. Also, the fleet was fully exposed to gun attack from ships out at sea."[58] The anchor cables of Admiral Willis's battle-squadron had barely roared through the hawse-pipes, and motor boats bringing flag officers and captains to conference in the *Warspite* were still converging on the flagship, when a signal came in that a large enemy force had been sighted by one of the scouting Catalinas, 360 miles southeast of Dondra Head, heading northwest.[59]

The aircraft had no time to report the composition of this force before it was shot down, but it was clearly Nagumo's expected fleet. The Eastern Fleet had been caught well and truly flat-footed 600 miles from the enemy and with its fuel and water-tanks empty.[60] Nothing could be done until this had been rectified and under the blistering heat the fleet worked flat-out to get ready. As the ships of the 'fast' squadron could be got ready quickly (less the two 6-inch cruisers) Somerville decided not to wait for his heavy metal but to sortie out immediately they were able and attempt the night torpedo-bomber attack on the retiring enemy as previously planned. The 'slow' division would follow the next day in support.

At Colombo, all preparations that could be made were made; the two 8-inch cruisers were sailed to join the flag once more, and the *Hermes* hustled out to sea from Trincomalee in case the enemy struck there first. Force A finally cleared Addu and headed east at 2:15 A.M. on April 5, the slow squadron not following until seven hours later. Somerville sailed east at nineteen knots through the night with the intention of carrying out his original plan, but at 8:00 that morning came word of the attack on Colombo.

From Nagumo's carriers, a powerful force of ninety-one bombers and thirty-six fighters hit the port. They were met by forty-two RAF and naval fighters. In the fierce air battles that followed, great slaughter was thought to have been inflicted on the Japanese, twenty-one being claimed shot down. In actual fact, the Japanese only lost seven aircraft and shot down nineteen of the defending fighters. In addition, a squadron of six Swordfish arrived in the middle of the battle and were summarily dispatched. Nonetheless, they prevented the bombers from doing worse damage, and only the AMC *Hector* and the old destroyer *Tenedos* were actually sunk there.

This was only the beginning, for the *Dorsetshire* and *Cornwall* were sighted by the Japanese, who sent a striking force of dive-bombers against them, and in under ten minutes, both 8-inch cruisers were sent to the bottom without loss to the Japanese Vals. About two-thirds of their crews survived this ordeal—and later the sharks—and were rescued.

The scale and accuracy of these blows gave Somerville and the Admiralty pause for thought. Air searches by his two carriers did not locate Nagumo's five, nor was he himself sighted. Outnumbered by five to two in carriers and four to one in battleships, it is not surprising that Somerville now decided that, perhaps after all, the protection of the R-class battleships might be more welcomed than at first thought.[61] Accordingly, the two forces rendezvoused early on the sixth.

Nagumo had withdrawn to the east to take stock of the situation having failed to flush out his main quarry. Somerville was equally frustrated at not being able to firmly pinpoint his opponent and thought he might be working round behind him against Addu. Not until 11:00 A.M. did the Eastern Fleet return to the atoll to once more replenish, and again, the Japanese returned to the fray off Ceylon. This time they hit Trincomalee early on the ninth. Only twenty-two fighters went up to meet them this time. They claimed fifteen Japanese destroyed but in fact again only ten failed to return.

Great damage was done to shore installations. A counterstrike by nine Blenheims of No. 2 Squadron was decimated, losing five aircraft and scoring no hits on any Japanese vessel. They ran into the returning Japanese strike and lost yet more aircraft and most of the survivors were so badly damaged that they were writeoffs on arrival back at base.

Worse still, the *Hermes* was again sent to sea for safety without air cover. She was sighted and crushed by a dive-bomber assault, along with the *Vampire*, the corvette *Hollyhock*, and two tankers. Meanwhile, Ozawa's carrier and cruisers had dispatched no less than twenty-three merchant ships (112,312 tons) in their sweep into the Bay of Bengal, while Japanese submarines sank ten more.

Somerville had meanwhile made the hard decision that he could not offer a direct challenge to such a powerful enemy fleet. The R-class battleships were sent to Mombasa on the East African coast while he took the fast squadron up to Bombay to exercise the role of the "fleet in being." It seemed as if the whole of the Indian Ocean was now a Japanese lake and the fall of Ceylon must follow. But the crisis was now over, and although it was hidden from the British for some time yet, Nagumo was steaming for home to refit in readiness for the Coral Sea and Midway operations in the Southern and Central Pacific. He had given the British a numbing lesson in the correct use of air and seapower, and the limitations of the battleship—if it was kept at arm's length through fear of air attack—was strikingly demonstrated.[62]

Somerville still felt the need for more modern battleships with which to regain control of the area, but he rejected out of hand the offer of the *Malaya* because of her short endurance. The *Valiant* was more welcomed, and it was hoped that the *Nelson* and *Rodney* would also join his flag. Nonetheless, there was still the worrying thought that the Japanese could always outnumber the British in capital ships if they so chose to do so—and not only with the old Kongos either; a very large building program was known to be in hand, although the prime minister, suspiciously, questioned the Admiralty intelligence reports that placed most of these with the active fleet at this time.[63]

And so the two fleets drew apart by many thousands of miles, and the battle of the Indian Ocean was never fought. Nonetheless, it has been accepted as the final turning point in the role of British battleship in attempting to influence events at sea. The same lesson appeared to have been inflicted in the Pacific, for the U.S. Navy had initially withdrawn what battleships it had to the west coast of the United States. Here they were based in San Francisco. The seven old veterans viewed this move with much disgust and were badly treated ashore because of it. It was deliberate policy, however; they were too slow to accompany the thirty-knot carriers in the hit-and-run raids being conducted at this stage of the war, and were therefore left behind. Even when the Americans received news of the Japanese assault on Midway, they were not brought into the plan of battle, for time would not allow it; during the vital battle itself, they had to content themselves with a lonely foray under R.Adm. William S. Pye into the eastern Pacific.

Thus, the battle of Midway was fought purely as a carrier duel and when the Japanese lost four big carriers to the Americans' one. The Japanese commander in chief, Adm. Isoroku Yamamoto, allowed himself to become so overawed by the potential of the remaining U.S. Navy dive-bombers that he abandoned plans to close by night with his nine battleships and reverse the tide of fortune by surface action, against which the Americans had nothing but almost-empty flight decks and 8-inch cruisers.[64] The verdict of history was therefore completed by the three actions of the Pacific War: Malaya, Indian Ocean, and Midway—all had been won by naval aircraft while the battleships had either been sunk or rendered ineffectual. As late as the second half of 1941, an authorative writer like Bernard Brodie could state that "the carrier is not likely to replace the battleship." Within a few months, Midway had altered all that, in a manner plain for everyone to see. From a couple of carriers and a few cruisers, a battle fleet the likes of which had not been seen since Jutland, mounting more than 100 guns of 14- 16- and 18-inch caliber, turned about and ran away.[65]

Unbeknownst to Yamamoto, American Adm. Raymond Spruance was down to his very last three torpedo-bombers, the only aircraft able to hurt any of the ten Japanese battleships. They had nothing to fear but fear itself, and Yamamoto blinked first. But was it so clear-cut and final as all that. Let us examine things a little more closely. First, although the Americans did not use their battleships at Midway, it was the last time they left them behind. They withdrew the fast battleships from the Atlantic and used them in support of their carriers, and on their own when needs be. The older ships were renovated and again used in shore bombardment roles. But why did they need the fast battleships if they were so obviously obsolete? The truth was they could still be decisive. Both the American admirals at the battle of Midway were acutely aware of what would happen to their task forces should the nine Japanese heavy ships get within gun range.

For that reason they made very certain that they kept well clear during the hours of darkness and only continued their attacks after careful searches had failed to locate the Japanese big ships anywhere nearby. Nor did they allow themselves to be drawn to far to the west in the subsequent actions, for exactly the same reason. If the Japanese battle fleet was impotent at Midway, it was because Yamamoto was primarily focused on the air, doubted the battleship, and did not use it correctly in any event. Instead of keeping it hundreds of miles astern of his carriers, he should have placed it several miles in front. Then the Americans would have been faced with an agonizing choice.

If they struck at the enemy carriers first, it left their own carriers wide open to destruction by the surface fleet. If they aimed their attacks at the battleships, there was no certainty that the heavily armored ships would all be sunk by bombs as simply as the big carriers with their wooden flight-decks, and the Japanese bombers would have been able to operate unmolested.

Theory perhaps, but the lack of heavy gun support worried the Americans enough to ensure that they were never again to be left without it, and the Japanese too, having muffed the main chance, used their heavy ships with much more vigor for the rest of the war. Indeed, it was the old lesson learned by the British—that the battleship still provided the basic rock on which all other units rested and retired on, the light forces when hard-pressed by superior numbers or by overwhelming air attack, the carrier when her aircraft were away or on the many occasions when bad weather rendered them helpless to operate their squadrons anyway.

This is not to deny that the main long-range striking power of a fleet was now firmly established with the carrier-borne dive- and torpedo-bomber, but only to emphasize that the current vogue to dismiss completely the many premier uses of the battleship completely is a shallow and false conclusion. The battleships were to play a great part yet in the war at sea, and to fight many of the fiercest battles in their entire history, ship-to-ship and ship-to-air. The events of December 1941 to June 1942 were certainly a watershed in the long history of the heavy ship, but they were by no means the final chapters. Indeed, one of the first of the British battleships to prove that they had a useful service to still perform was one of the much-despised "coffin ships" of the R class.

With the *Warspite* and the two armored carriers at Bombay—to be joined by the *Valiant* when fully worked-up—the four old Royal Sovereign-class ships were based for a time on Kilindini, near Mombasa in Kenya. Here they could protect the many important convoy routes round the Cape, to the Middle East and across to Australia later. But outflanking all these positions lay the Vichy French bastion of Madagascar, in particular the fine naval anchorage and base of Diego Suarez in the north of the island. The Vichy were as hostile as ever to the Allied cause and there was no guarantee that, should the Japanese venture there at the moment of their choosing, they would not be made equally as welcome as they had been the year before in French Indochina.[66]

Churchill and the chiefs of staff determined to forestall any such move; the prime minister aimed to secure the western half of the Indian Ocean no matter what. Gen. Jan Smuts of South Africa heard the news with relief, although warning that they didn't want another Dakar. Churchill was also ensuring that this was a success and not a fiasco. Ample forces were to be provided under determined commanders. The bulk of the operation was to be carried out by Force H under Vice Adm. E. N. Syfret, but ships were allocated from all over the world. The *Malaya* went to Force H, which was en route to the East Indies, but was rejected by Somerville.

In addition to the carrier *Illustrious*, one heavy and one light cruiser, and nine destroyers of Force H, the Eastern Fleet contributed the *Indomitable* and two more destroyers, and Admiral Syfret hoisted his flag aboard the *Ramillies* at Durban on April 22. Somerville was to refuel at the Seychelles and interpose his fleet between the islands to the east in case the Japanese intervened, but this did not happen.

The actual landing and capture of Diego Suarez took place smoothly on May 5–7. Two convoys from Durban met west of Cape Amber the night before the landing and were led into their anchorages for the landing by minesweepers following channel routes navigated and buoyed out by the destroyer *Laforey* with great skill.

The *Ramillies* proved to be the star of the show despite her age. The troops got ashore with complete surprise and no casualties. They were covered by the fighters from the two carriers at daybreak, and despite the usual French heroics to defend their base to the very end, they made good progress until they came up against the fortified positions protecting the naval base of Antsirane on a peninsula across the channel from Diego Suarez town itself.

At the request of the army commander, Admiral Syfret ordered the destroyer *Anthony* alongside the *Ramillies*, and a detachment of her Royal Marines—fifty strong, under Captain Price—were embarked with full fighting kit. At 3:45 P.M., the destroyer left the main fleet and steamed around the top of the island. At 8:00, she entered the narrow Oronjia Pass leading to Diego Suarez bay itself and guarded by a host of gun batteries located around the Oronjia Peninsula. Taken unawares, the Vichy guns did not start firing until the *Anthony* was through. With great skill and under fire, the destroyer berthed on her own in the darkness, and the *Ramillies*'s Marines got ashore safely and made their way into the pitch-black town.

They took the Vichy artillery general's house and entered the main naval depot, whereupon its commandant surrendered and released some British prisoners. Far from fighting to the last man, the little band of Royal Marines soon found themselves hopelessly outnumbered by the hosts of Frenchmen waiting to lay down their arms. The diversion was therefore a great success, and when the army assault reopened from the west, resistance soon collapsed. By 3:00 A.M., Diego Suarez was Britain's; the commanders of the Vichy naval and land forces surrendered.

The batteries on the Oronjia Peninsula, however, still dominated the harbor mouth, and no transports could enter without the risk of being blown out of the water. To terminate this state of affairs, Syfret took the *Ramillies*, then the *Devonshire* and *Hermione* and four destroyers, and formed a line of battle off the peninsula. The *Ramillies* opened fire at 10:40 A.M., but only a few 15-inch salvos proved sufficient to knock the heart out of these artillerymen, and ten minutes after the first broadside, fire was ceased and the transports were able to file into the harbor that afternoon—a lone attack by a Vichy submarine resulting in her sinking by Swordfish from the *Illustrious*.

The capture of this important base after only sixty hours of fighting was a remarkable achievement. It was only after Ironclad was over and the bulk of the ships dispersed once more that the enemy struck a blow in return for thwarting his hopes. The *Ramillies* had been retained at Diego Suarez, and, at 8:30 on the night of May 29, an enemy seaplane appeared over the anchorage making a reconnaissance of it. It was intercepted or brought down by gunfire. It was assumed to have come from a Japanese cruiser or raider that had slipped past the Eastern Fleet and clearly preluded some sort of attack. Despite this, the worst happened. Although in Churchill's words "extreme vigilance was ordered," this does not seem to have been extreme enough. The *Ramillies* weighed anchor and steamed slowly round the bay for a while. Nothing happened.

The aircraft had been launched from the submarine *I-10*, part of a daring attack force. In company were two sister ships, the *I-16* and *I-20*, each carrying a midget two-man submarine of the type used unsuccessfully at Pearl Harbor and, later, at Sydney against the mythical *Warspite*. But in this instance, they were a success for the enemy, for the following evening, both the *Ramillies* and a large tanker were hit by torpedoes. The tanker sank, but the tough old battleship survived, although severely damaged by the blow.

At first, the Vichy were suspected of helping the enemy, but this fear on this occasion proved unfounded, and Churchill paid generous tribute to the two brave Japanese officers, both of whom were killed ashore soon after the attack. The *Ramillies* was patched up at Diego Suarez, sailing on June 3 and reaching Durban on the ninth. Her repairs kept her out of action for several months, but the old veteran was far from finished yet.

Her three sisters were also gainfully employed during this period, mainly escorting important convoys. In February 1943, their final major duty with the Eastern Fleet found the *Resolution* and *Revenge* guarding the big troop convoys that transferred the Australian Division from Suez home to Australia. The *Ramillies* herself was sufficiently repaired at Durban to make the long voyage back to Plymouth, leaving South Africa in September and spending a year in dockyard hands before returning to the Indian Ocean.

It is convenient here to cover the work performed by the remaining capital ships of Somerville's command during this period, for as the Japanese became ever more embroiled in the Pacific and the threat to Ceylon vanished, its number diminished almost daily as its ships were recalled to more active theatres. In May, Churchill was still telling Roosevelt that it was Britain's intention to build up a powerful battle line comprising the *Warspite, Valiant, Nelson,* and *Rodney,* but in fact, only the first two were active there.

In August 1942, the Americans asked for a diversionary raid by the Eastern Fleet carriers against the Andamans to coincide with their move into the Solomons, but Somerville replied that the *Illustrious* and *Formidable* were still equipped with aircraft that could not stand up to Japanese shore-based planes, and he contented himself with merely making a feint involving dummy invasion convoys toward the east, Operation Stab, with his flag in the *Warspite.*

In September, the *Warspite* also covered the final landings that completed the occupation of the remainder of Madagascar (Operation Stream) but was not called upon to fire her guns in anger. Opportunity was taken to dock the *Warspite* at Diego Suarez in October, and meanwhile, the *Valiant* had joined the flag after a long working-up period, which aroused Churchill's ire.[67]

More pressing commitments, mainly in the Mediterranean, led to the departure of the *Indomitable* and three destroyers, and when she was damaged that August, the *Formidable* was taken away as her replacement, so that by August, only the *Warspite, Valiant,* and *Illustrious* remained of Somerville's fast squadron.[68]

Meanwhile, Churchill, who had strained every nerve to build up that fleet earlier when the Japanese threat loomed large, now chafed at the idleness of these three powerful ships in so quiet a theater of war; they were needed in the Mediterranean, where the fighting was, he told Pound. It was the need to sustain Malta at first which took the *Indomitable* away and terminated the *Nelson*'s and *Rodney*'s move east, but when the tide later turned there, Churchill wanted to employ the big ships in the Eastern Basin as before to overawe the Italians. Pound argued, but in the end, the Eastern Fleet was further run down; the *Illustrious* sailed for home in January 1943, followed by the *Valiant* a month later and finally the *Warspite* in April. [69]

By this time as well, the R-class ships were recalled; Churchill agreed that "it would be a very sensible thing to bring the old Rs back and lay them up in some safe harbor, using the crews to man new vessels." He could not resist a final dig at these ships: "They are only coffin ships, and a cause of grievous anxiety the moment any modern enemy vessel appears. If these ships are brought home one by one, the crews who have been shipwrecked or have been out a particularly long time could be given passages in them."[70] He conveniently forgot the number of times that their mere presence had saved

Atlantic convoys from destruction. He had never forgiven the Admiralty for not converting them as he had requested so often earlier in the war. And so one by one, the Rs came home from the Indian Ocean and were used in more humble duties; only the newly refitted *Ramillies* reversed the trend.

The *Resolution* and *Revenge* returned in September 1943 and together were laid up as the *Imperieuse* stokers' training establishment, initially at Gairloch, then in May 1944 at Southampton, and finally at Devonport.

The *Ramillies* and *Royal Sovereign* both came home in January 1944, but their days as fighting vessels were not yet over. They may not have been able to stand up to modern opposition by the standards of 1943, but the *Ramillies* had shown that in the role of a highly mobile, armored gun carrier, their long-range firepower was of high value in supporting army operations ashore, a role that was confirmed by American experience in the Pacific also. Diego Suarez had been a striking success, but when a heavy ship was not present to lend such weight to an assault the story was very different: This was one of the most valuable lessons that combined operations learned from the disastrous Dieppe raid in August 1942. "The presence of a capital ship at Dieppe might have made all the difference,"[71] wrote the historian of combined operations in his analysis, while Captain Roskill was more specific: "Off Dieppe heavy guns of long-range bombarding ships . . . were shown to be as essential as adequate air cover."[72] And again: "Hence, after the Dieppe failure the formation and training of heavy bombarding squadrons became a matter of first importance in Allied plans; and by far the best ships available to meet the need were the battleships."[73]

In the Arctic and in the Mediterranean, however, in the autumn of 1942 and the spring of 1943, the battleship was still needed to counter enemy fleets. It is for this reason that the *Nelson* and *Rodney* were both recalled in July 1942, to help fight through the greatest Malta convoy of them all the following month, Operation Pedestal.[74]

The *Nelson* and *Rodney* sailed from the Clyde at the end of July, escorted by six destroyers and carried out antiaircraft practice in the Pentland Firth on the way out. Although included as the main deterrent against the Italian fleet, past experience had shown that the chances of their engaging this shy opponent were few, but their powerful antiaircraft batteries would provide a massive addition to the convoy's flak defenses. On August 3, the battleships rendezvoused with the convoy and began the long Atlantic leg of their voyage with the intention of fooling the enemy into thinking this was just another important WS convoy for the Cape. During this part of the journey, the battleships helped to fuel the short-range destroyer escorts.

In fact, the Italian naval command had already made the decision not to commit their six battleships against the next Malta convoy. This decision was in the main forced upon them by the acute lack of oil fuel available to the fleet at this time. There was only sufficient to enable one battleship to sail, and they came to the conclusion that to use one heavy ship on her own against a heavily escorted convoy was to invite her destruction.

All six therefore remained in harbor, and the task of destroying Pedestal was left to the Axis air forces, strong submarine patrols and numerous E-boats stationed in the Narrows. Once all these forces had whittled down the convoy and escort, and once the heavy covering force had turned back as it had always done, then they planned to finish off the survivors with a cruiser striking force of three 8-inch and three 6-inch ships escorted by a destroyer flotilla.

On August 11, the convoy and escort had reformed inside the Mediterranean at full strength. As well as the *Nelson* and *Rodney*, there were the fleet carriers *Victorious*, *Indomitable*, and *Eagle* to provide fighter cover and a torpedo-bomber strike force, the old carrier *Furious* to fly off further fighters to Malta, seven light cruisers, and thirty-one destroyers—as well as corvettes, oilers, and a fleet tug to escort the convoy of fourteen merchant ships. Against them were ranged 320 Italian and 227 German aircraft, 18 Italian and three German submarines, 19 Italian and 4 German E-boats, and the cruiser squadron. It was an epic battle.

The convoy was first sighted by an Italian submarine early on the eleventh, but the first air attacks did not take place until later that day. Meanwhile, the German submarine *U-73* drew first blood by sinking the *Eagle* with four direct hits. The main battle commenced early on the twelfth, and for the rest of that day, the convoy forged steadily east beating off a deluge of bomber and submarine attacks. Two U-boats were sunk by the destroyers, and many aircraft were shot down. By dusk, when the heavy ships turned back, the convoy had lost no ships sunk. The carrier *Indomitable*, however, had been badly bombed and the *Victorious* slightly damaged by air attack, while one destroyer had been damaged. Considering the massive scale of attack, this was a gratifying achievement in which the battleships had played a good part; although much of the long-range interception work had been done with great gallantry by the outnumbered Fleet Air Arm fighter squadrons so enormous were the numbers of enemy bombers involved that many got through to the fleet and had to be tackled by the warships' barrage, which was the most impressive yet mounted by a British force in the war to date.

One of the most spectacular forms of defense against the low-lying Italian torpedo-bombers was the splash barrage laid down by the battleships' 16-inch guns at their extreme range. This alone deterred many from pressing in to a dangerous range and many dropped outside the effective range of their missiles. Others were made of sterner stuff, however. One eyewitness aboard a freighter described how one such aircraft, an SM 79, kept boring in with great bravery through the splash barrage, the destroyers' barrage and then the close-range flak. She had selected the *Nelson* as her target and never flinched. The gunners homed in on this aircraft, and it had been hit and had all its engines on fire before the torpedoes were released. A minute later, this aircraft smashed into the sea in a hail of debris.

Equal bravery was shown by the Italian pilot of a Ju 87 that selected the *Rodney* as its target. This aircraft was seen approaching in a shallow dive rather than the normal near-vertical approach favored by these aircraft. Captain Rivett-Carnac ordered immediate starboard full rudder, and the bomb, which failed to detonate, fell about twenty yards off the port side. Almost at once, the *Rodney* was switching target as further torpedo bombers slammed in from the port side of the screen.

An extract from the *Rodney*'s log on the twelfth gives some idea of the scale of events this day:

0745: Two torpedoes passed ahead. We combed their tracks.

0915: Large cloud of smoke on horizon. Red 10. (Shot down bomber)

0916: Bombs dropped on Starboard bow. Smoke coming from Destroyer Red 10. Bombs on Starboard bow (these were not close just direction)

0920: *Indomitable* firing at aircraft. Aircraft to port. Aircraft on star board quarter. Some firing. They go away.

0953: Track of torpedo crosses our bow from Port to Starboard. (questionable). We stopped Starboard engine and swung altering course before hitting convoy.

1015: Torpedo passed ahead from Starboard.

1045: Torpedo passed astern from Port bow.

1213 Four aircraft approach on Starboard bow. Everything opens up. Crosses over and leaves on Port quarter.

1216: Bombs ahead, astern and to Port of screen destroyer on Port beam.

1217: One aircraft shot down on Port side.

1242: Nine torpedo bombers coming in outside screen. Red 40.

1243: 16-inch open fire to port. It looks as if they exploded short. One torpedo bomber in water on Port bow/beam.

1245: Torpedo dropped on Port bow.

1246: Six torpedo bombers on Port beam. Looked as if quite a few
      torpedoes dropped.
1248: One torpedo bomber shot down by Fighter. Red 10. Starboard
      side of convoy undergoing heavy attack.
1303: Activity on Starboard side of convoy against torpedo bombers.
1305: Depth Charges on Port bow (screen). Port 4.7" guns open up
      at aircraft Port quarter.
1307: Cruiser firing astern. More depth charges on Port bow.
1315: Enemy aircraft approaching Green 75.
1317: Bomb astern *Nelson*. We are firing with everything we've got.
      Bombs fall across our bows close. Two to Starboard and one to
      Port ahead. They fall diagonally.
1320: More bombs to Starboard.[75]

And on throughout that blazing hot summer's day, with the clear blue
Mediterranean sky pock-marked with flak bursts, and scarred by trailing
flames of aircraft, the bright sunlit sea burst asunder by bomb, torpedo and
depth charge.

All this violent alteration resulted in the *Rodney* accentuating a long-
established boiler defect which reduced her speed to eighteen knots before
they finally turned for Gibraltar and left the still intact convoy plodding on
eastward as the dusk deepened. Once out of their protection, the Axis
bombers renewed their assaults and damaged several of the merchant ships
while Italian submarines picked off many of the close escorts. During the
night, the E-boats homed in and sank several more, and the next day, the
bombers took over again, but the Italian cruisers never turned up. Finally,
five of the merchant ships got through to Malta and their cargoes kept the
island going until the end of the year, by which time the whole picture had
changed in the Mediterranean.

If the Italians did not send their battle fleet out to dispute Operation
Pedestal, it was not expected that they would keep them in harbor the next
time Force H put to sea, for this was when they acted as the heavy covering
force for Operation Torch, the landings in French North Africa. The two
western Allies had agreed that they could not yet storm ashore into France
but that they had the power to take the initiative in the Mediterranean and
so this great series of amphibious operations was planned and executed on
November 8.

Not only had the Italian fleet been husbanded during the preceding
months and was therefore presumably ready for action in good order. It was
known that the third and fourth of their new battleships were almost ready
to take position in line. In fact, the *Roma* was ready.

But there was another complication—in fact, an old one—which assumed a new significance: the capital ships of Vichy France. As it was French territory that was to be invaded, it was fairly certain that their reaction would be as hostile, if not even more so from past experience, as the Axis's. There was even the possibility of concerted effort by the two navies, and even if not, the fact that both would be offering resistance would make attacks from three different directions under air feasible; from the Vichy North African ports, whose hatred of the Royal Navy had festered over the past two years; from the Italian Fleet, at a peak strength in capital ships; and from the Vichy Fleet at Toulon, which was under command of the French Admiral de Laborde, was well-known for being "fanatically anti-British." Not last, there were Gensoul's ships at Alexandria, whose loyalty to Vichy had grown stronger rather than the reverse during the long years of sullen isolation.

It was necessary therefore for the two western Allies to devote the strongest possible covering forces for their landings. The Americans had as their objective the west coast of Africa, with Casablanca as the prize. They planned to land at three spots north and south of that port and close in by land. At Casablanca lay the *Jean Bart*, still unfinished but with four guns operational. It was she, supported by a heavy cruiser and a large number of destroyers, that posed the greatest threat to direct assault. But farther south, at Dakar of ill memory, lay the powerful *Richelieu*, her sister ship, fully operational, with a light cruiser squadron and some big flotilla leaders. There were several submarines on hand at ports close to the landing zones the Vichy were sure to utilize also.

The Americans took no chances, allocating one of their brand-new battleships, the *Massachusetts*, to the covering force off Casablanca along with two heavy cruisers and four destroyers. Two of their old battleships, the *New York* and *Texas*, were also to take part as covering ships for the landings at Safi to the south and Mehdia to the north. In addition to this heavy metal, U.S. Task Force 34, under Adm. H. Kent Hewitt, contained one fleet carrier and four escort carriers for air cover, four more heavy cruisers, one light cruiser, and thirty-four destroyers.

The British landings were to take place inside the Mediterranean, with the objectives of Oran and Algiers, to be followed by Bougie farther east and hopefully Bone as well; these landings would have to face not only light local opposition but the possible intervention of the Italian and Toulon fleets. The initial landings were to be protected by Force H and were to be split into two task forces, center and eastern, under Commodore Troubridge and Rear Admiral Burrough, respectively; each would have their own local bombarding and escort vessels. It was obvious that Force H must be at a high strength, a fact of which Churchill was acutely aware. On September 25, he sent Alexander and Pound a memo: "I trust that not only *Renown* but also one of the KGVs will be assigned to Torch. It is most necessary to overawe the enemy by superior strength, and especially to deter the Vichy French. With three KGVs at Scapa Flow, you have ample margin."[76]

The commander in chief of the Home Fleet might not have agreed on this point, but nonetheless, the composition of Force H shows how exactly the Admiralty followed Churchill's wishes. The ships of Force H all left from home waters during October, with the *Rodney* and three destroyers sailing from Scapa on the twenty-third; she was reported as an American battleship by a U-boat on the twenty-sixth.

Force X, consisting of the *Duke of York*, *Nelson* and *Renown*, left Scapa Flow three days later and rendezvoused with the carriers *Victorious* and *Formidable* on the thirty-first. Finally, the *Furious* joined up to give Force H a powerful base of four capital ships, three fleet carriers, three light cruisers, and seventeen destroyers, under Admiral Syfret.

When the landings went in, the local opposition was tough at first. With the usual chest-clasping and affirmations about their honor being violated, the Vichy fleet at all three target ports resisted to the utmost. Fortunately, neither the British nor the Americans were prepared to put up with this sort of nonsense at this stage of the war and dealt with the Vichy attacks with the utmost efficiency.

In Morocco, the Americans were perhaps even firmer than the British in putting a stop to it. The cruiser *Primauguet*, flotilla leaders *Albatross* and *Milan*, and destroyers *Boulonnais*, *Brestois*, *Fougueux*, and *Frondeur* sortied with much enthusiasm, but they were annihilated by the American covering force, during two no-holds-barred actions during the forenoon of the eighth. The cruiser itself was shot through and through and "reduced to a wreck," while six of the seven flotilla vessels were sunk, disabled or driven ashore.

Nor did the eight Vichy submarines fare any better; they narrowly missed the *Massachusetts* and the cruiser *Brooklyn* but in return were decimated by the destroyer escorts, only three surviving to limp into Dakar and Cadiz. The *Richelieu* and the cruisers at Dakar stayed put. They refused absolutely however to later come over on the Allies' side against the Axis, and de Gaulle was reported as offering them cash inducements to do so which they scorned.[77]

The *Jean Bart* was a different proposition however. On the ninth, she dueled with the *Massachusetts* and was bombed by the carrier's Dauntless dive-bombers to good effect. The first bombing attack scored no hits on the ninth, but at 8:18 A.M., one bomb hit her quarter-deck, starting a fire, and carried on through the ship vertically and holed her below the waterline, locking her steering gear. A near-miss on the quay alongside flooded her bilges. Then the *Massachusetts* joined in with her 16-inch salvos. At 8:25, one of these straddled the *Jean Bart*. One shell pierced the bridge structure and penetrated both upper and lower armored decks, detonating in an empty compartment. From the next salvo, one shell hit the funnel and holed the superstructure and hull above the waterline.

The third salvo landed close but there were no hits; the fourth scored two direct hits on both the French vessels' turrets. One hit the operational turret locking its training gear; the second hit the armored casemate for the other mounting, entered the main deck but failed to explode. At 9:10, another 16-inch shell was made—again on the quarterdeck—exploding in an after compartment. The *Massachusetts* had fired forty-seven salvos, varying from three to nine guns in each, to achieve these five direct hits on a difficult target, and her achievement is given in some detail as it contrasts so strongly with the hit rate achieved by the *Barham* and *Resolution* on the *Richelieu* at Dakar two years earlier.

Further air attacks failed to score any hits, and by 6:20 that evening, the working turret could traverse once more. The bombardment was resumed on the tenth by the cruiser *Augusta*, which failed to hit, and in the afternoon by the dive-bombers once more from the *Ranger*, which put two more bombs into the *Jean Bart* and one near-miss close alongside. Electrical fires broke out, which were not under control until 9:00 P.M. In all, the *Jean Bart* shipped 4,500 tons of water and settled by the stern, twenty-two of her crew were killed and twenty-two wounded in these attacks, which effectively put her out of action for the rest of the war.[78]

At Algiers and Oran, Force H stood off to the north to maintain a protective patrol between the Italian and French mainland coasts, with the *Duke of York*, *Renown*, two carriers, three cruisers, and sixteen destroyers, but the *Rodney* was detached to give close-in protection against any surface sorties by the local French warships, and to help against the very powerful Vichy-controlled forts controlling the approach to Oran which had so worried Somerville in July 1940.

At Oran, the French resisted as fiercely as they had been expected to. Three Vichy destroyers roared out at dawn to attack the transports but were met by the cruiser *Aurora*. She challenged the first, got no reply and hit her heavily leaving her sinking. A second then appeared, and Captain Agnew, thinking she had come to pick up survivors, held his fire. The French ship replied with a full salvo of torpedoes, whereupon the *Aurora* "rode off" the second ship, which beached itself after being set on fire. A third destroyer then appeared but beat a hasty retreat when a British flotilla came up in support.

A Vichy submarine then tried to torpedo the *Aurora* without success, and she was next straddled at 27,000 yards from a shore battery. The *Aurora* had "polished off her opponents with practiced ease,"[79] as Admiral Cunningham later said, but with six 6-inch guns, she was rather outmatched by the forts, and so the *Rodney* was called in to lend a hand.

The salvos had come from the four 7.6-inch guns of Fort-du-Santon, which was perched up on a hill 1,060 feet. Eyewitnesses aboard the *Rodney* described the fort as one of the most difficult jobs they were ever presented with; low cloud was reducing visibility to between eight and ten miles over the target zone. The *Rodney* fired sixteen 16-inch shells at the fort, and at 1:30 P.M., she reported that although the guns of the fort had been depressed for a while, they had not been hit.

The next day, they had obvious proof that Fort-du-Santon was still alive and kicking, for at 8:30 A.M., the guns there suddenly opened up on the *Rodney* "and came as near to hitting us as anyone has been in this war, the *Bismarck* included."[80] Not for an hour did the *Rodney* get permission to reply in kind, when the fort again fell silent.

On D + 2, the *Rodney* turned her attentions to the three 9.4-inch guns of Canastelle, but before she could do so, she was asked to again engage Santon, which was subjecting the advancing American troops to a heavy bombardment of high-explosive shell. The captain's report of the *Rodney* described the action:

> The decision to open fire at Santon at a range of seventeen miles by chart from a shore fix, in rather bad visibility, with the target and the land near it entirely obscured by cloud, and with the United States troops only 600 yards from it, was only made possible by my complete confidence in the exceptional accuracy of my navigating officer and the exceptional measures which had been taken recently by my gunnery officer to secure reliable and accurate ranging. This confidence was completely justified, and after the first round, which was deliberately fired with a margin of safety for the US troops, the great majority of all subsequent rounds fell within a hundred yards of the target.[81]

After a little of this, they received the signal, "Contact the Navy and tell them to cease fire on shore battery at Oran. Shore battery want to capitulate." And so they did. The *Rodney* later entered Oran and was based there in case her firepower was needed elsewhere along the North African coast. Hers was a more satisfactory role than that played by her companions. Force H cruised in readiness until November 15, but the Italian fleet stayed in harbor. The only move they made was the dispatch of strong submarine forces, which achieved little. On the fifteenth, therefore, Syfret returned to Gibraltar, and the *Duke of York* and *Victorious* were quickly sent back to Scapa Flow to rejoin the Home Fleet.

Adm. François Darlan, who happened to be in North Africa at the time of the landings, was quick to see which way the wind was blowing and ordered the Toulon fleet to sail and join the Allies, but this was ignored by the commanders on the spot, who remained loyal to Vichy, little realizing that as they did so, Hitler was already in the process of snuffing out their illusionary freedom.[82]

On November 27, Operation Lila was put into operation by the 11th SS Armored Corps, and Toulon was occupied. Whereas the Allies in North Africa had been met by shot and shell and the brave and courageous, if futile and wasteful, loss of life,[83] all that met the SS when they entered the port was the sight of the pride of the French Navy sinking at their moorings in a thunder of scuttling charges. Along with four 8-inch cruisers, three light cruisers, a depot ship, and thirty-three destroyers and escorts, plus sixteen submarines, the *Strasbourg, Dunkerque,* and *Provence* committed ritual suicide. Darlan thus claimed that his promise of 1940 was vindicated, but never was there a more wasteful and useless gesture made, for the only person who could possibly benefit from the self-destruction of the French fleet instead of its addition to the Allies as a fighting unit of great power was Adolf Hitler.[84]

Thus passed one of the major navies of World War II. Another was to vanish within six months in the same ocean.

CHAPTER 8

Supporting the Landings

From the poignant and needless passing of a once-great fleet, we must briefly retrace our steps once more and quickly scan events in the other theaters of war up to the spring of 1943.

In the Pacific, the setback at Midway in the summer had not prevented the Japanese from pressing forward with their plans to extend their range of conquests southeast along the chain of the Solomon Islands toward Fiji, with the long-term goal of severing all links between Australia and the United States. We have seen how the commitments elsewhere steadily reduced Admiral Somerville's fleet throughout this period until he was left with no heavy ships or carriers at all and could thus do nothing to take the pressure off the Americans.

By the later months of 1942, however, the U.S. Navy was no longer content to sit passively on the defensive as it had done for the previous year. It was determined to stop the Japanese onslaught, and the island of Guadalcanal was where they drew the line. The Japanese had already constructed an airbase here and developed a forward base at neighboring Tulagi, and were reinforcing both from the main base at Rabaul while their main fleet worked out of the Carolines but was kept very much in the rear.

Despite the generous commitments of battleships and carriers to the Atlantic theater, including the temporary use of even their newest ships—the *Washington, North Carolina, Massachusetts,* and the like, as well as older vessels—by the autumn of 1942, the U.S. Navy was beginning to build up its forces in the southeast Pacific, although they were still vastly inferior to total Japanese strength. In this, as at Midway, Yamamoto played into their hands by conserving his own strength, almost untouched, and feeding in his forces piecemeal. Local equality could often be maintained by the Americans as they drove their way back toward New Britain, and many fierce, close-range actions developed in that murderous stretch of water between the islands, known as the Slot or, later and more accurately, Ironbottom Sound, so great were the numbers of warships that ended their days there.

The fighting was on an intense level not matched elsewhere, and both navies unhesitatingly committed all ships they had on station to the struggle.

From battleship down to the smallest MTB, they exchanged broadsides on an eyeball-to-eyeball basis, and there were no frustrating standoffs as in the European zone, as with the Germans or the Italians. If the Americans wanted a fight, they always knew they would get one without looking far. I will briefly itemize those actions in which battleships were involved, for although this volume is mainly concerned with the British battleship in action, the way other nations utilized their capital ships is illuminating in comparison.[1]

The original landings of the U.S. Marines on Guadalcanal, Operation Watchtower, took place on August 7–9, 1942, guarded by the *North Carolina*, three fleet carriers, five heavy and one light cruiser, and fifteen destroyers. Once the troops were ashore and fierce resistance crushed, the bulk of the fighting consisted of attempts by the Japanese to regain control of the airstrip, which had been renamed Henderson Field by the Americans. This lasted for four months. The day of the landings, Vice Adm. Frank Fletcher withdrew the big ships after fending off air attacks and left the transport anchorage to be protected by the cruiser squadron. A daring and well-executed Japanese riposte by a cruiser force resulted in the battle of Savo Island, during which the Allied force was annihilated, but the Japanese left the transports alone and missed their best chance of a decisive victory.

After both sides had tried piecemeal reinforcing of their troops ashore, the Japanese decided on a major operation, KA, in which 1,500 would be put ashore, covered from American intervention by the main fleet. Yamamoto hoisted his flag aboard the *Yamato* at Truk in the Carolines on August 21 and set the plan in motion. The Japanese main strength was split into two, which were to fall upon and wipe out the American task force east of the Solomons after they had been diverted by a special "shock group" on the twenty-third. The main body was commanded by Adm. Nobutake Kondo, flying his flag aboard the giant *Mutsu*, with five heavy and one light cruiser, a seaplane carrier, and ten destroyers. The carrier strike force, under Vice Adm. Chuichi Nagumo once more, consisted of two fleet carriers, protected by the *Hiei* and *Kirishima*, along with four cruisers and twelve destroyers.

The diversion would be provided by R.Adm. Chuichi Hara, with the small carrier *Ryujo*, one heavy cruiser, and two destroyers. The transport convoy, which was to slip in while the main fleets were engaged, comprised one light cruiser, three, destroyers, and six transport vessels while a further four heavy cruisers and five destroyers were to stand by in close support and to shell Henderson to keep the American aircraft there grounded.

To meet this assembly, Fletcher hurried down from Pearl Harbor with the *North Carolina*, carriers *Saratoga*, *Enterprise*, and *Wasp*, eight cruisers, and eighteen destroyers organized into three task groups.

On the twenty-fourth, the battle got underway when the bait of the *Ryujo* was taken by Fletcher, and this small carrier was quickly dispatched by the *Saratoga*'s aircraft. The Japanese then got in their main blow as planned from the *Shokaku* and *Zuikaku*, hitting the *Enterprise* three times. Admiral Kondo organized the *Hiei* and *Kirishima* with ten cruisers and destroyers to close the American task groups and smash them in a night action with his heavy guns.

It might have worked, but at 11:00 P.M., having sighted nothing, Kondo reversed course at twenty-eight knots to be clear before daylight and instead cruised between Ontong Java and Truk on the twenty-fifth, returning on the twenty-eighth without firm contacts from his scouting aircraft. As at Midway, Fletcher knew the power of the big guns and had prudently retired southward to join up with the *Wasp*, which had been fuelling. The Japanese cruisers bombarded the airstrip, but on the twenty-sixth, dive-bombers from the island were able to operate and caused much damage on the transport group. The first "Tokyo Express" was withdrawn in disorder, and the battle plan had failed.

As some compensation, Japanese submarines scored some notable successes, torpedoing the *Saratoga* on August 31 and sinking the *Wasp* on September 15. The *North Carolina* was also hit by a torpedo at this time and damaged. She returned to Pearl Harbor to repair and was replaced by the *Washington* and *South Dakota*.

Heavy fighting continued almost every night in the Slot, with now one side and then the other inflicting heavy defeats on each other with cruiser and destroyer squadrons. By mid-October, Yamamoto had on hand five battleships, five carriers, fourteen cruisers, and forty-four destroyers to combat American task groups barely half the size of his, but he seemed unable to grasp the nettle. On twenty-sixth, the battle of Santa Cruz Islands developed between Adm. William Halsey with the *South Dakota*, *Washington*, *Enterprise*, *Hornet*, and light forces under R.Adm. Thomas C. Kinkaid.

The Japanese were out with Kondo sailing with the *Haruna* and *Kongo*, four heavy cruisers, and a destroyer flotilla; Kakuta had one small carrier, *Junyo*, and two destroyers; Nagumo had three big carriers, *Shokaku*, *Zuikaku* and *Zuiho*, one heavy cruiser, and destroyers; and the vanguard group had the *Hiei* and *Kirishima* once more, three heavy, and one light cruiser and destroyers. At the same time, Takama was running in another "Tokyo Express" with five light cruisers and fifteen destroyers. On October 24, high-level bombing attacks by the U.S. Army Air Force scored near-misses only on the *Kirishima* and *Zuikaku*, but the Japanese scout planes could locate only the *Washington*; the American carriers remained undetected until the twenty-sixth.

In the exchange of air strikes, the Americans damaged two Japanese carriers while the Japanese damaged the *Enterprise* and sank the *Hornet*. The fierce flak thrown up by the *South Dakota* probably did much to prevent her sharing *Hornet's* fate, and this battleship was taken under attack at 11:27 A.M. by one bomber group, which succeeded in hitting her on her fore turret. The bomb exploded but failed to penetrate the armor of the gunhouse.

The result of the battle was a victory for the Japanese, but again, they failed to follow it up. Once again, a battleship had proven itself an essential working partner to the carrier during heavy air attacks. But now both sides determined to commit their capital ships to the slugging match in the Slot itself.

The Japanese plan was for a battleship bombardment of the airfield by night, which would so immobilize it that their convoys could run in by daylight unmolested. For this, the *Hiei* and *Kirishima* sailed for Guadalcanal on November 12, screened by a light cruiser and fifteen destroyers. The Americans, as usual, got wind of what was in motion, and a cruiser squadron under R.Adm. Daniel Callaghan set course to intercept it, comprising two heavy, three light cruisers, and eight destroyers; the American ships had radar, which in the main the Japanese either lacked or were far behind in. At 1:42 A.M., the two forces collided head on, and a confused and furious close-range action took place:

> The *Hiei* saw a destroyer closing in on her—she was the *Cushing*. The American destroyer's six torpedoes went astray and in a few minutes under a hail of shells she was reduced to a blazing wreck. Another destroyer surged out of the darkness. She was so near the *Hiei* that her torpedoes, unfused through lack of time, rebounded from the hull without bursting. This attacker was also wiped out by two salvos and a torpedo. A third destroyer, the *O'Bannon*, then launched her torpedoes but none of these scored a hit; she was so near that shots from the Japanese battleship passed over her.
>
> In the confusion, [Admiral Abe] could not tell where he was and ordered a slight alteration of course to port. Then the *Hiei* became a target for all the American vessels. In the light of day, his guns would have allowed him to keep any cruiser at bay, their 8-inch guns would have been useless against his heavy armour. But with night's help the American ships could come much closer and at short range their shells caused the enormous vessel much and serious damage. She was at a disadvantage, too, because the shells she fired were intended for land bombardment and were not nearly so effective against the hulls of warships.
>
> The *Kirishima* was farther astern; she was not touched and continued to fire as if on maneuvers.[2]

Such a hot pace could not last; the American cruisers were shot through and through. The *Kirishima*, making undisturbed practice, hit the *San Francisco* with a deluge of shells, turning her upperworks into a colander; Admiral Callaghan died in the shambles of her bridge structure. Only the fact that the heavy shells hit from so close a range saved her and she managed to crawl away to safety. Adm. Norman Scott died aboard the cruiser *Atlanta*, which was hit by shell and torpedo and sank next day; both the *Portland* and *Juneau* were torpedoed and crippled, and four destroyers were sunk. On the Japanese side, two of their destroyers were destroyed, and the *Hiei* was left in a badly damaged state with dawn fast approaching.

> The *Hiei* answered her helm with difficulty. She had been hit more than eighty times, her steering gear was in bad shape, her driving shaft functioned with difficulty and badly-shaken boilers forced her to reduce speed. She dragged herself northwestward to pass to the south of Savo to try to reach a friendly anchorage. Her engineers were worn out. In the suffocating heat deep inside the vessel, that because of her damage now had insufficient ventilation, they opened up the most badly affected boilers, tried to plug leaks, stripped down the steering-gear transmissions and righted twisted machinery. Electricians fixed up emergency lighting. But as soon as one repair was completed another injury was revealed.[3]

Heavy and prolonged air attacks were now launched by the American aircraft carriers to the north. Here Kinkaid lay with the *South Dakota* and *Washington*, the carrier *Enterprise*, and light forces. At 10:20 A.M., torpedo-bombers located the *Hiei*, which was still only ten miles from Savo, and made their attacks against the sluggish moving target. They were rewarded with two hits on her stern which jammed her steering gear. The *Hiei* began to turn in slow circles, a helpless target. At 2:30 P.M., another torpedo-bomber attack put a further pair of torpedoes into her riven hull, flooding her engine rooms. A high-level bombing attack by fourteen B-17s failed to score any hits at all, but at 6:00, there was clearly no chance of saving the old ship, still afloat despite this massive damage and it was decided to scuttle her lest she fall into enemy hands. At 7:00, she finally went down with 450 of her crew, the first Japanese battleship to be lost.[4] It was not long before a sister followed her to the bottom in these waters.

During this period, the Americans decimated the Japanese transport convoy, but the Japanese were still determined to wreck Henderson field. Two heavy cruisers bombarded it on the night of November 13–14, and Admiral Kondo was determined to use the *Kirishima* to finish the job off the following night. With four cruisers and nine destroyers as escorts, the battleship entered the Slot. Unknown to Kondo, fast approaching him on opposite course were the *South Dakota* and *Washington*, with a forward screen of destroyers, under Rear Admiral Lee. At around 10:10 P.M., the outlying destroyers began to clash, and at 11:48, the battleships met at close quarters.

The *South Dakota* led the line, narrowly escaping a whole swarm of torpedoes loosed at her by the Japanese destroyers. Then the *Kirishima* and the two Japanese cruisers opened fire on her at point-blank range, scoring a great number of hits. The radar was out of action and no less than forty-shells of heavy and medium caliber struck her, pulping her superstructure and causing great damage to her upperworks. None, however, penetrated her vitals and she was able to withdraw heavily damaged. But while the *Kirishima* was pouring her fire into her modern opponent, she was being out-flanked by the *Washington*, which remained undetected.

Suddenly, farther west, bright flashes stabbed through the night, and a salvo of 16-inch shells descended on the *Kirishima*. It was the *Washington*, which—her presence unsuspected until that moment—had with the help of her radar been able to calmly prepare her devastating intervention. In seven minutes, the *Kirishima* was put out of action. Her superstructure was hacked away, two of her turrets were disemboweled, her steering was jammed, her electricity supply stopped.[5]

It was enough; the Japanese cruisers withdrew. Although the Americans had one battleship badly damaged and three destroyers sunk out of four, the victory was clearly Lee's. The *Kirishima* was in much the same state as the *Hiei* and was clearly doomed, and at 3:00 A.M. on November 15, she went down to the bottom of Ironbottom Sound northwest of Savo Island.

This final great duel of giants decided Guadalcanal. Although the Tokyo Express continued to run,[6] the issue had been decided, and never again did the Japanese intervene in such strength. A great many other encounters took place as the Japanese retreated up the Solomons chain, but as these did not involve battleships directly, they are not covered here. But without a doubt the daring use of Lee's two ships in these narrow waters proved that for surface actions the battleship was still the decisive weapon. Of all the hundreds of torpedoes fired by the destroyers on both sides, the majority were misses or duds. Heavy shellfire at night had, as with Matapan, finally buried the myth of Jutland.

In trying to judge the value of the battleship at this stage of the war, 1942–43, it is worthwhile remembering that they had already been written off as valueless by many critics before this time. Tedder, for example, claimed that Matapan, as early as March 1941, was the last dying kick of the battleship, which had been replaced by the heavy bomber.[7] Many a post-war historian has come to a similar conclusion, i.e. that by this stage the battleship had finally shot its collective bolt and, if they were still being used, it was either through sentiment or because as they were there something had to be found for them to do. Tedder was clearly wildly wrong in his timing, the heavy bomber up to mid-1943 having failed miserably on almost every occasion it had tried to hit, let alone sink, a battleship, but what of the historians? One wrote:

> It almost seemed that admirals cherished battleships, not for their practical utility in war but because they could display the ultimate pageant of naval seamanship. It was not only British admirals; all navies that had battleships clung to them in face of doubt and criticism. And perhaps it would be foolish now to judge the choice too harshly. Affairs of nations are often guided by sentiment rather than logic, and battleships in every age were wonderful creations. They had a fierce feline beauty like a tiger, a "fearful symmetry"; and even when they proved impracticable, their beauty may have had some material value in itself, to give confidence to a nation that possessed them, and give pause to a nation that did not.[8]

Naturally, battleships were not immediately relegated to the breakers' yard; much capital and ingenuity had gone into their design, while radar and air reconnaissance had increased their effectiveness, and against those European powers that had not developed carrier arms, their usefulness was as great as ever. Even in the Pacific campaign, battleships played a part as the gun component of carrier task forces and by night when air strike forces were blind.[9]

Throughout nearly six years of maritime warfare in European waters and the Atlantic, the small force of British Dreadnoughts was always fully stretched and fully occupied on important duties. They may, indeed, have been made obsolete in tactical terms before the war began; or they may have been almost entirely occupied on functions for which they had never been designed. It could be argued, and was argued, that the wealth and materials expended on the five King George Vs would have been better used on swift armored aircraft carriers with fighters and bombers in their hangars as modern as those possessed by the RAF. But what mattered was that Britain, like all the European great naval powers, had again invested heavily in the Dreadnought, that it again strongly influenced events at sea throughout the war, and that Britain at least, as the perpetrator of the Dreadnought and the builder of more than any other power, employed them busily right up to the end of hostilities.[10]

Certainly, no postwar critic has ever agreed with Lord Chatfield's flat statement that "it is beyond question that if we had failed to rebuild our capital ships we should have lost the war."[11] After what happened to PQ 17 also, one would have thought that the influence of the few enemy battleships would have merited consideration also, but here again the feeling of many historians is that their influence was overrated at the time:

> A person or a group of persons in a section can become interested in a particular place or ship to an extent that distorts their judgment and that of the operational people working with them. For example, the battleship *Tirpitz* was so closely watched day by day, so much reported on, made so much the object of inquiry and discussion that she mesmerized the naval staff by her mere presence, long after the time she was in fact likely—as we now know—to threaten our trade routes either alone or in company with other ships.[12]

Another historian wrote:

> In the same manner the fact that the Italian battleships were used with such caution negates the influence they wielded, on, for example Operation Vigorous, in many people's minds.
>
> Possibly the sinking of HMS *Hood*, the pride of the Royal Navy, in action against the *Bismarck* affected the Sea Lords' outlook, but despite a Churchillian rebuke, the British authorities persisted in erroneously referring to the ship as *Admiral von Tirpitz*, an indication of how great a bogeyman the naval staff had dreamed up. Perhaps a more realistic attitude would have been that of Captain Simpson, commanding the Tenth Submarine Flotilla at Malta, who in 1942 forwarded a patrol report of a missed attack on two Italian battleships with the comment, "but on consideration, these battleships have never done anyone any harm."[13]

Again, maybe so, but had it not been for the vigilance exercised and the fact that the British used their own battleships with much more enthusiasm, the damage these battleships could have done would have been enormous, as Vigorous showed. In the Atlantic, Arctic, and Mediterranean, the enemy heavy ships had caused the complete disruption of the convoys, and the near annihilation of several, whenever they appeared, whereas a prolonged submarine campaign never on a single occasion stopped the convoys from sailing, and nor did bomber attacks.

In September 1942, for example, the passage of Russian Convoy PQ 18 was not disputed by the German heavy ships at all; they stayed in harbor. Plans had been made by the German admirals on the spot to sortie out in a two-pronged attack, Operation *Doppelschlag* (Double-Blow), using the *Admiral Scheer*, *Hipper*, and *Köln*, with the *Tirpitz* as the supporting backup. Preliminary movements of these ships were made because Vice Admiral Kummetz and his staff were eager to carry out the operation. But Hitler proved lukewarm, and his various conditions laid down to Raeder finally made the latter call the surface sortie off, much to the fury of his Norwegian ship commanders.

Instead, PQ 18 faced an all-out assault by the new battle winners, heavy U-boat concentrations and massed torpedo-bomber assaults, the heaviest experienced by any convoy in the entire war. These caused losses but the defence in turn inflicted prohibitive losses on the submarines and aircraft and the convoy reached Russia with far less loss than PQ 17. The conclusions would appear obvious; the influence of the battleship was still decisive and still something that the Admiralty had to guard against, it was not just an illusory paper menace, but a very real threat.

During the passage of PQ 18, Admiral Tovey had remained at Scapa Flow aboard the *King George V* to be in direct touch with London and thus prevent any repetition of the PQ 17 affair, but Vice Admiral Fraser twice put to sea with the *Anson* (flag) and *Duke of York*, one light cruiser, and a destroyer screen to be on hand should they be required for fleet action, operating from Akureyri in Iceland in thick weather.

The position of the two sides over the period 1942–43 again presented a state of flux. The Home Fleet now had three of the King George V class in service, a highly satisfactory state of affairs. The *Anson* had joined in July, while the last, the *Howe*, was due to work up in September 1942. Of his older ships at this time, Tovey was constantly having to detach them for other operations—the *Nelson* for Pedestal, for example, and the *Duke of York* and *Renown* for Torch. For a time, too, the presence of the pocket battleships in Norway gave rise to fears that Atlantic forays were again on the cards and lack of cruisers to reinstate the Northern patrol meant the detaching of the *Anson* to work from Hvalfiord later that autumn.

The German position was less satisfactory because of the combination of the fuel shortage and the German leader's reluctance to unleash his ships lest carrier aircraft cripple them and the Home Fleet battleships wipe them out. The defense of Norway was still his main reason for stationing the ships there at all; the constant pleas of his commanders to go onto the offensive irritated him.

The *Admiral Scheer* was now in need of refitting and returned to Germany early in November. The *Tirpitz* was moved back from Narvik to Trondheim, thus presenting a less immediate threat to the Russia convoys. This was cancelled out, however, by the fact that convoys had to be suspended during the same period to assemble enough close escorts to mount Torch.

The *Tirpitz* was in fact, not operating at full ability and badly needed docking, like the *Scheer,* but Hitler refused to allow her to return to Germany, to have this done, and instead sent the workman to Trondheim from the Kiel dockyards. Some compensation for this dilution of their strength came with the transfer of the *Lützow* from the Baltic to Norway, first to Narvik and then up to Altenfiord, where she joined the *Hipper* and *Köln* and prepared for another attempt at the *Doppelschlag* operation when the Russian convoys were resumed once more. The cruiser *Nürnberg* also arrived at Narvik in December.

Not until December did the German big ships have their chance. When the Russian convoys were resumed, the commander in chief of the British Home Fleet had managed to persuade the higher powers to sail the convoys in smaller, more manageable groups. The first of these, JW 51A, reached Russia safely, mainly because of the appalling weather conditions that shielded them; the second part, JW 51B, left Loch Ewe on December 22 with fourteen freighters and a close escort of seven destroyers and five small craft. Two of the destroyers later lost touch because of bad weather and damage. The cruiser covering force of two 6-inch ships and two destroyers was under Rear Admiral Burnett while the Home Fleet put to sea from Scapa with the *Anson* (flag), one 8-inch cruiser, and three destroyers.

To carry out the interception and destruction of this convoy, which was sighted on the twenty-fourth, Kummetz put to sea with the *Lützow, Admiral Hipper,* and six destroyers in Operation *Regenbogen.* While the cruiser and three destroyers were to approach the convoy and draw off the escorts, the *Lützow* was to fall upon the merchantmen with the other destroyers from a different direction before the Home Fleet could intervene. The plan almost worked, but when the two forces clashed in the Barents Sea on December 31, 1942, skillful and resolute action by the five British destroyers kept the *Hipper* at bay.

This part of the action went according to plan, and the British lost the destroyer *Achates* and had two others badly damaged in the exchange, while the German destroyers sank a minesweeper that had become detached. Then things began to go awry for the Germans.

In the first place, their fear of torpedo attack left the initiative entirely with the British who used it with their normal dash and courage. In the second place the decisive appearance of the *Lützow* was hedged in by the fact that she was under orders to proceed out on an Atlantic raiding mission after dispatching the convoy, this aggravated the already predominant fears of the German captain not to have his ship even slightly damaged lest it hinder his future operations. The result was astounding.

The British destroyers had fought off the *Hipper* group and had lost contact. Nor did the two German squadrons appear to be in touch with each other. While the British knew nothing of the *Lützow* being out, the *Lützow* in turn was unaware of the closeness of Burnett's two light cruisers, which were now fast approaching in support of the hard-pressed destroyers. Nonetheless, from 10:45 to 11:00 A.M., the Germans had the convoy in their grasp. The *Lützow* was sighted by two of the escorts very close to the convoy's southern flank; they made no reports. "Only a providential snow-squall, and the timidity of the German pocket battleship's captain, saved the convoy from a most unpleasant predicament; for the powerful German force had got within a couple of miles of its quarry before being sighted. Fortunately, the *Lützow* stood away, "to wait for the weather to clear."[14]

The *Lützow* was sighted again at 11:00 as the murk lifted, and the *Hipper* also reappeared, pounding the smoke-laying *Achates* into a wreck and then shifting fire to the other undamaged destroyers, who at first thought it was the *Lützow*'s 11-inch—and not the *Hipper*'s 8-inch—guns with which they were dueling with their 4.7- and 4-inch popguns. Things were desperate when at 11:30, the *Sheffield* and *Jamaica* suddenly appeared and opened a heavy fire on the *Hipper*, hitting her three times. Not surprisingly, Kummetz's reaction was to get clear, which he did, but not before losing one of his destroyers.

At 11:40, the *Lützow* opened fire on the convoy from nine miles and hit a merchant ship. The British destroyers laid smoke and moved out to attack. The *Lützow* ceased firing, and then the *Hipper* loomed up once more. All the advantage of firepower still lay with the German squadron, but at 11:49, Kummetz repeated his order to withdraw, and the convoy was saved, with the two British cruisers chasing the heavy ships until they lost contact to the west around 2:00 P.M. The *Lützow* abandoned her Atlantic mission, and all German ships returned to port, maintaining a silence on the operation that drove the Hitler mad with anger. He heard the news of this latest humiliation over the BBC, which did not improve his frame of mind at all.

The Germans gave the usual excuses of the cramping restrictions imposed by the High Command—the fact that at the height of the action, they received a routine signal reminding them that "in spite of operational orders, exercise restraint if you contact enemy of comparable strength, since it is undesirable to run excessive risks to the cruisers"—and by the British use of smoke. Two 6-inch cruisers and five destroyers could hardly be termed a force of "comparable strength"; therefore, that excuse will not hold water. The lack of freedom of action, however, was to be eased during future sorties, although Raeder was not given the chance to benefit. For him, the failure of the *Lützow* and *Hipper*—acknowledged by the Germans as "obviously unsatisfactory to the Germans, but a complete success for the British"—led to his downfall. As supreme champion of the battleship in Germany, he had to pay the price as the wrath of Hitler fell on his head the next day.

The fact that the battleships of the Home Fleet had played no part in this famous victory has further reinforced the claims that they were irrelevant. Tovey had sailed with the *King George V* and *Howe* as soon as news of the fight was received, but the Germans were long gone before he could arrive on the scene. But the fact is, the Germans *had* used their big ships aggressively, and they *had* gotten within two miles of the convoy. Used correctly, the *Lützow* could have annihilated both cruiser and destroyer escorts and the merchantmen with ease. The British could not rely on the enemy staying put in harbor, as this operation showed, and it could not therefore rely absolutely that the next time the Germans appeared, they would act with such lack of spirit.

Adolf Hitler was determined they would not get the chance: Preoccupied with Stalingrad—the first defeat his armies had suffered in this war to date—he had been confident that his surface ships would present him with a naval success with which to greet the new year, and they clearly had not done so. He exploded. Vice Admiral Krancke at his headquarters took the first shock, but Raeder was summoned to hear his leader's viewpoint as well.

> Krancke arranged a delay, which was stretched to five days, but when Raeder arrived on January 6, Hitler's attitude had not changed. Hitler began with a monologue on the German Navy's history, stressing its surface-ship failures and the failure of its leadership. He reiterated his stand on the comparative value of heavy ships, coastal guns, submarines and aircraft. He tried to assure Raeder that scrapping the big ships was no degradation. Then he ordered Raeder to prepare answers on details of decommissioning the ships, utilizing the guns, rebuilding some ships as aircraft-carriers, and speeding the submarine building program. Raeder had little opportunity to speak to Hitler alone, or "under four eyes" as the German expression puts it. He realized that it was his only chance to talk rationally with Hitler, who often behaved quite differently when he had no audience. When the others had left, Raeder tendered his resignation. Hitler tried to dissuade him, but Raeder refused to reconsider.[15]

Before Raeder actually left, he prepared a detailed study refuting most of Hitler's arguments, but the German leader remained disillusioned. [16] He, who had been enormously impressed by the might and power of the battleships he had created, was now firmly convinced that they were merely useless hulks. "Battleships," he had raged, "to which he had always devoted his full attention and which had filled him with so much pride were no longer of the slightest use." He continued, "Large battleships no longer served any purpose and therefore must be taken out of commission, after their guns have been removed. There was an urgent need for their guns on land."[17]

Raeder's successor was the U-boat admiral Karl Dönitz, and most postwar observers have taken his appointment as proof positive that first, Hitler's views on battleships (which coincide almost exactly with numerous postwar historians) were correct and that second, Dönitz, as the best submarine commander of any war on any side, was happy to carry them out.[18] Unfortunately for these observers, Admiral Dönitz himself made quite clear that the reverse happened. He was by no means convinced that Hitler's outlook—that of a landsman backed up by Göring's air-minded incomprehension—was the correct one, and neither did he meekly submit to it.

It is true that when he reported to Hitler on January 30 to take over his new appointment, Hitler took the opportunity to reiterate his "irrevocable decision" to lay up and scrap all the big ships and that just over a week later Dönitz lay before him a detailed plan to do just this, but these moves were only to gain the time to study the matter fully, Raeder having put him in the picture on the handover. He soon came to the conclusion that Raeder had been correct and not merely an elderly admiral clinging to his beloved big ships through a mixture of sentiment and ignorance.[19]

Admiral Dönitz, it is recorded (with some degree of baffled incomprehension), "reacted rather differently than might have been expected."[20] Indeed, he did, and not hastily either. Nor can he be accused of biased sentimentality:

> I very quickly realized, however, that I should have to examine the whole question of this paying off and scrapping of the big ships once again and very thoroughly. As a result of this further scrutiny I came to the conclusion that withdrawing these ships from service would not result in any appreciable increase in either manpower or material, and that the implementation of the project could not but react politically and militarily to our disadvantage. Breaking them up was an even less attractive solution for it made considerable claims on labor and technical resources.
>
> Thus for the same reasons as my predecessor, I came to the conclusion that Hitler's order was wrong. On February 26, I reported to him in this sense. In a brief and reasoned report, I told him that I was unable to give my support to his orders and requested him to cancel them. He was disagreeably surprised, since he had not expected that I, as the former flag officer of submarines and the

man who had always pressed for the expansion of the U-boat war, would adopt this attitude. He was at first extremely immoderate but in the end he very grudgingly agreed, and I was ungraciously dismissed.[21]

The plan as amended by Dönitz was for the cruisers *Hipper*, *Köln* and *Leipzig* to be paid off and later the old pre-Dreadnoughts *Schlesien* and *Schleswig-Holstein* as well. But the major units—the *Tirpitz*, *Scharnhorst*, *Admiral Scheer*, and *Lützow*, along with the cruisers *Prinz Eugen* and *Nürnberg*—were to be retained in full commission, and the two former ships, with all available destroyers, should remain as a powerful group to defend Norway against invasion, and, if a favorable opportunity occurred, to carry on attacking the Russian convoy route. The other units were to be stationed in the Baltic to carry out training duties until an opportunity arose whereupon they could go into action.

Therefore, the German fleet remained a powerfully potent "fleet in being," one still committed to the attack and therefore a real and genuine threat to be guarded against, and not a myth in the minds of the Whitehall planners and the commander in chief of the Home Fleet.

If the resolution to use the big ships had again been restored by the new German commander, then the opportunity to so employ them vanished for the greater part of 1943 because of the opening up of the Mediterranean and the suspension of the Arctic convoy route for the summer and most of the rest of the year. Between January and March, however, before they stopped running, a number of large convoys were sent through in response to the continued demands from Moscow.

The strength of the Home Fleet at this period was reasonable. Admiral Tovey had under his command the *King George V*, *Anson*, and *Howe*, while the *Duke of York* was due to return to him after Torch had been completed. Also on hand was the *Malaya*. She was working up after a refit, but as soon as she was ready, she was detached to provide the heavy escort for an important convoy from England to Freetown between February 25 and March 8, 1943. She did not therefore return to Scapa until the late spring of that year.

To bring about the new desired dispositions, the Germans spent the spring shuffling their heavy ships to and from Norway. The damaged *Hipper* and the light cruiser *Köln* sailed back to Germany in February unscathed leaving only the *Tirpitz*, *Lützow*, and the cruiser *Nürnberg* in Norway at this time. Attempts were made to reinforce them with the *Scharnhorst* and *Prinz Eugen* to bring the combat unit up to full strength in time for the summer. On January 11, both these ships with an escort of three large destroyers were sighted by scouting planes off the Skaw heading northwest. This was no great surprise to

Admiral Tovey, for when he had learned that Dönitz had replaced Raeder, he—contrary to postwar thought—expected this to signal a resumption of surface activity and even a new attempt at Atlantic forays in conjunction with the U-boat campaign.

The Home Fleet therefore prepared to intercept a break-out and six submarines, two cruisers and a destroyer flotilla were deployed off Stadlandet. The Germans ships had turned back on being sighted and eluded the reconnaissance searches of Coastal Command. The two ships tried again two weeks later with exactly the same result, and the dispatch of a strong air striking force came to nothing once again because of bad weather as usual.

The Germans were more successful in March, completely eluding all the air searches flown, despite the fact that considerable thought had been given by Air Marshal Joubert and Admiral Tovey to improve air-shadowing methods. The *Scharnhorst* sailed from Gotenhafen on the eighth and reached Bergen undetected, although the fact that she had left the Baltic had been reported. From Bergen, she moved up the coast to Trondheim to join the *Tirpitz*, and in company, these two powerful ships with an escorting flotilla sailed to the advanced base of Narvik, where they joined the *Lützow* group. Here the whole group was belatedly located in Altenfiord by air searches. Thus, Tovey's fleet was presented with "the most powerful concentration yet assembled in the far north."

The Germans were now in position, but they had missed the chance of striking at Russian convoy JW 53, a twenty-eight ship convoy that had sailed on February 15, and was much beset by storms that damaged many of the merchantmen and their escorts. Likewise, the returning RA 53 of thirty ships only had to face light U-boat and air attacks after leaving Kola on March 1, and then it also was scattered by gales. The *King George V* was out on covering duty, and it was chiefly through the use of her excellent search radars that the bulk of the convoy was finally reassembled in some sort of order and brought home. The *Anson* was up at Hvalfiord at this time.

Nonetheless, although the American Task Force 22, which contained usually one battleship, was placed under Tovey's patrol as further protection for the Atlantic convoys, the combination of this heavy ship force, coupled with demands for Home Fleet destroyers to be sent to the North Atlantic to counter a new U-boat campaign of great intensity, made the suspension of the Russian convoys until November inevitable. Only a maximum effort by the Home Fleet heavy ships in waters dominated by the Luftwaffe could protect them from the Altenfiord squadron, and even had the Admiralty have taken this risk, sacrificing some of their few modern battleships in the hope that the German units would be completely destroyed once and for all, lack of destroyers in those waters made it impossible. As Churchill had by now realized, "The strain upon the British Navy is becoming intolerable." Roosevelt reluctantly accepted this as being the mere, if unpalatable, truth; the Russians refused to accept it at all, and in their pretty chagrin, they obstructed their allies by closing RAF airfields, shutting down radio stations, and similar actions.

Not only were the smaller units of the Home Fleet diluted during the summer of 1943, but the demands of the new operations in the Mediterranean, to which we must again return, caused the transfer thither of both the *King George V* and *Howe*. This was compensated by the return of the *Rodney*, but for only a short period, and the *Malaya* to Scapa Flow. In addition, the modern American battleships *South Dakota* and *Alabama* were transferred to Scapa Flow under Rear Admiral Hustvedt for a time before the former was called away to her duties in the Solomon Islands. Both sides therefore remained in a passive stalemate during the summer of 1943 in the Arctic. In the Mediterranean, things were moving to a grand climax.

At the Casablanca Conference, it had been decided, after much haggling, that once the North African coast had been cleared of Axis forces, the next objective for the Allied armies was to be Sicily, the invasion of which was code-named Operation Husky. As with Torch, Allied troop convoys could be threatened by the Italian Fleet, which, if they had proved a disappointment when North Africa fell, were hardly expected to remain in harbor again while their own homeland was invaded; loss of important ships was not expected to balance the loss of Sicily, but in the event, it did.

Although the bulk of the French Fleet had gone, Churchill still expressed dismay at the reaction of Godfroy's squadron at Alexandria. Despite the scuttling of the Toulon squadron, the occupation of Vichy France by German troops, and considerable pressure from the Allies, he stubbornly refused to bring his ships over to the Allied camp. Churchill wanted to utilize the *Warspite* and *Valiant* from the Eastern Fleet to "persuade" him, but Pound convinced him it was not worth the effort. Not until May 17 did this reluctant sailor notify the authorities that he wished to join the French Navy in North Africa, and docking of his ships after their long immobilization began at once. In the *Lorraine*, ancient as she was, the French had their only active battleship left afloat apart from the two immobilized veterans in British waters. The *Lorraine* ultimately sailed with the cruisers round the Cape of Good Hope to join the French squadron at Dakar.[22]

It was essential that the ships of Force H be fully worked up for the coming showdown (or hoped-for showdown) with Mussolini's navy, and thus, the month of June 1943 saw the confined waters of Scapa Flow as full of ships as they had been at the time of the Grand Fleet. Not only were the four or five heavy ships of the Home Fleet and their American allies there, but also working up at the base were the *Nelson, Rodney, Warspite,* and *Valiant,* as well as two fleet carriers and innumerable cruisers and destroyers. When these units finally sailed south once more, they were followed by the *King George V* and *Howe* since it was essential to have on hand at least two modern ships to help deal with the three available to the Italians at this time. By June, the Home Fleet had been reduced to only three ships: the *Duke of York* (flag), *Anson,* and *Malaya.* Even this strength was further reduced with the decision, because of manpower shortages, to reduce the *Malaya* (the only remaining unmodernized battleship from World War I) to "care and maintenance" in the Clyde. Like the four Royal Sovereigns, it seemed as though her day was finally done, but like them, she had valuable work to do yet in this war.

While the heavy ships were working up to a high state of efficiency, especially in shore bombardment, at Scapa Flow during June, what of their opposite numbers? The sum total of movement by the Italian battleships as North Africa crumbled was the sailing of the *Littorio, Vittorio Veneto,* and *Roma* from La Spezia to Naples; shortage of fuel was blamed for lack of aggressive action. As Husky loomed, the Italian naval command debated about what to do if the Allies landed in Sicily instead of Greece as many expected.

The result was predictable. The Italian capital ships did not intervene to the south of the island. This was because of a decision reached after heated debate in the Italian Navy that a naval battle would be hopeless without trained fighter cover, wrote Admiral Ruge later. [23] He, if anyone, should know, for Dönitz had appointed him director of the German staff attached to Italian naval command.

Captain Roskill has recorded how "the Germans already realized that they could not rely on the Italian navy and air force to carry an appreciable share of the burden of the war—not even if their homeland was threatened with invasion,"[24] and this is confirmed by Dönitz. However, the Allied plan had to provide for the intervention of the six Italian battleships and stated that although on its past record, such intervention seemed unlikely, "if it is ever going to fight, it must fight now in defense of its country . . . and that it is strategically well placed to do so." [25]

The Allied covering force under Rear Admiral Willis (Force H) therefore deployed on July 10 with the *Nelson, Rodney, Warspite,* and *Valiant,* the carriers *Indomitable* and *Formidable,* and light forces, and operated to the east of Sicily. In reserve were the *King George V* and *Howe* and six destroyers, which were kept in the western basin ready to sail to Willis's aid if called upon.[26]

One important diversion was carried out by the Home Fleet at this time to try to divert Axis attention away from the Mediterranean. The new commander in chief, Adm. Bruce Fraser, put to sea with the *Anson, Duke of York, Malaya, Alabama,* and *South Dakota,* the carrier *Furious,* and cruisers and destroyers to make an impressive show of strength off Norway. It was the largest force yet mounted by the Home Fleet, but despite its size, the German air reconnaissance failed to sight it at all.

On the tenth, Husky commenced, with the naval forces under the command of Adm. Andrew Cunningham, and the troops went ashore under cover of massive air and naval bombardments with comparative ease. For the ships waiting at sea, there was little to do but cruise and await events. The *Nelson* and *Rodney* from Oran had earlier rendezvoused with the *Warspite* and *Valiant* from Alexandria, and the main group of Force H cruised in the Ionian Sea, while the *King George V* and *Howe* kept south of Sardinia. No attacks took place on this squadron during the night and at dawn they took up covering positions some forty miles off Cape Passero ready, as American Gen. Dwight Eisenhower signaled them "to take care of anything the enemy is bold enough to send against you." In the event, the enemy sent very little: "We, unfortunately, had only a ringside view. We trailed our coat for days in the lovely Mediterranean waters, longing for the Italian Fleet to appear, or, failing that, for an opportunity to occur for us to test our new and formidable array of close-range weapons, but during the day we were left severely alone."[27]

When the Italian fleet did not appear, the big ships took turns in entering Malta for refueling. When the *Warspite* put into Valletta harbor on the twelfth, it was the first time a British battleship had done so since December 1940. When the *Rodney* was there, she enjoyed a visit from Gen. Bernard Montgomery. While the older battleships briefly enjoyed the fleshpots of Malta, the *King George V* and *Howe* put into Algiers, and then, on the night of July 11-12, they carried out a heavy bombardment of Favignana as a diversion, firmly ramming down Mussolini's throat all his boasts that the Mediterranean was an Italian lake.

The heavy ships were back at sea but again met little opposition; submarine and air attacks were summarily dealt with, and only the carrier *Indomitable* was hit by an aerial torpedo, which caused serious damage, and it was some time before she was back on station again. The success of the warships' heavy guns in support of the troops ashore was again reemphasized, and the big ships of Force H were from time to time now called upon to bring their expertise to bear when bombing attacks proved neither heavy nor precise enough to knock out concealed batteries in concrete bunkers.

On the evening of July 17, for example, the *Warspite* and *Valiant,* lying at the anchorage of Marsaxlokk to the south of Malta, received orders to carry out a bombardment at Catania, where strong German defenses had stopped the British Eighth Army. The bombardment had to start exactly at 6:30 P.M.

and cease precisely half an hour later to coincide with the troop advances; there was no room for error. Unfortunately, the *Valiant* had fouled the anti-submarine defenses earlier and had to be left behind, so the *Warspite* set off alone and, with paravanes streamed, worked up to twenty-three knots.

> Then her steering gear suddenly jammed, she turned a sharp circle and narrowly missed one of her escorts. Precious minutes were lost changing over to emergency steering, but at 6:43, she passed through her initial position for the bombardment and opened fire at a range of about 13,000 yards. Once a minute, she placed a 15-inch salvo on her target. A great mass of smoke and dust rose up out of the town.
>
> Enemy coastal batteries replied, but did not hit her. Submarine contacts were reported on both sides and the escorting destroyers fired great patterns of depth charges to keep them down. Then three Fw 190s skimmed close along the ship's side, but did no damage. At two minutes past seven the last salvo was fired, and the *Warspite* turned south and increased again to full speed. Air alarms continued all night, and the AA [antiaircraft] guns were constantly in action; but by 7 A.M. on the eighteenth, she was safely back in Marsaxlokk harbor, well satisfied with her achievement.[28]

Admiral Cunningham was also delighted to see his old flagship back in the limelight as so often before in these waters, made the famous signal: "Operation well carried out. There is no question when the old lady lifts her skirts, she can run."

By August 17, the last Axis soldier had pulled back across the Straits of Messina, and Sicily was in Allied hands. On August 31, the first Allied troops stormed across in pursuit and landed in Calabria. Their safe passage and arrival was made much easier by the contribution of the *Nelson* and *Rodney*, which, under the command of Admiral Willis, penetrated right into the southern end of the Messina narrows to attack the numerous gun batteries around Reggio. Wrote one observer:

> We proceeded in the most leisurely fashion, in company with the *Nelson* and some cruisers and destroyers, and when we reached the Straits of Messina we were interested to observe that the fields and roads were filled with spectators who had come out to see the fun. We expected heavy air attack and considerable fire from the powerful batteries which bombardment from the air had failed either to damage or to dislodge. Just as the *Nelson* was about to open fire we

received an air-raid warning, and two Junkers 88s appeared on the scene. They did not appear to care very much for the sight that greeted them, however, and they flew off before coming within range of our guns. While the *Nelson* was firing, we could see splashes reasonably near to the screen as other shore batteries opened up. They were, however, quickly silenced by fire from the cruisers and destroyers. When our turn came we did the most perfect shoot. We had a South African pilot in a Spitfire to observe the fall of shot for us, and he completely forgot himself in his excitement and kept sending back such unparliamentary phrases as "Slap in the middle" and "Lovely grub!"

Finally, having fired throughout with exceptional accuracy and precision, we executed our *piece de resistance* and hit an ammunition dump. I have often read in the papers eye-witness accounts from airmen who had hit dumps of various kinds, and I was surprised to see that the result was exactly as they had described it - a huge column of smoke shot vertically into the air to a great height, fanning out when it reached the top into an enormous mushroom. Vivid scarlet flames began to lick the stalk of the mushroom, and, finally, some time afterwards, the shattering sound of the explosion was heard. We came back to port without incident, feeling rather pleased with ourselves, particularly as the *Nelson* had been kind enough to send us a congratulatory signal on our shoot. We were more pleased to read a few days later than when Monty landed the batteries were broken and deserted, and he encountered no opposition from them.[29]

Considering that these operations, described as a striking example of the use of heavy naval guns in restricted waters, were followed on September 2 by bombardments from the *Valiant* and *Warspite* and on the third from the 15-inch guns of the monitors *Abercrombie*, *Erebus*, and *Roberts*, this total lack of resistance is hardly surprising.

Meanwhile, events of great moment had taken place with the fall of Mussolini and his replacement by the government of Pietro Badoglio, which immediately began secret negotiations for surrender, a move that Hitler fully expected. Thus, the final collapse of Italy did not terminate the fight for Italy; the Germans were prepared and took over all the defenses with speed. It did bring about the crowning achievement of the British Mediterranean Fleet, however, with the surrender of the entire Italian Fleet.

This great event took place on the ninth, but even before then, the big ships of Force H were out on other urgent business to cover the invasion of

Salerno. The *Nelson, Rodney, Valiant,* and *Warspite* sailed from Malta on September 7, with the carriers *Illustrious* (replacing the damaged *Indomitable*) and *Formidable* and a strong destroyer screen. They steered south of Malta to give the impression they were merely exercising, and then they passed west about around Sicily and entered the Tyrrhenian Sea. That night, September 8–9, a strong force of more than thirty German torpedo-bombers set out to strike at the invasion convoy but had the misfortune of choosing Force H as their targets instead. The battle was brief but intense, and although aerial torpedoes narrowly missed the *Warspite* and *Formidable,* not a ship was hit, although considerable carnage was inflicted on the attacking aircraft by the massive barrage put up by the fleet.

An observer aboard *Illustrious* later gave this impression:

> It was pitch dark by this time, and when the guns opened up we went out on to the quarter-deck to watch it. The *Nelson* on our beam was firing with everything she had, including her sixteen-inch: as the big guns flashed, the ship's superstructure was briefly and brilliantly lit up, isolated in the surrounding blackness. Then, as one's eyes recovered from the glare, one could see the steams of spark pouring up into the sky; then again the blinding flash and the deafening roar, until one's jaw ached with the noise.[30]

The next day, the fleet cruised north of Sicily, the fighters from the two fleet carriers giving protection to an escort carrier force whose own aircraft were protecting the army ashore, a unique, but highly successful operation.

Meanwhile, the *King George V* and *Howe* had sortied from Augusta to provide their usual backup for both forces. As Operation Avalanche was getting underway, news of the Italian surrender was broadcast. One of the main provisions of the armistice was that "the immediate transfer of the Italian fleet and Italian aircraft to such points as may be designated by the Allied commander in chief . . . be carried out immediately." Thus, the main units of the Italian fleet—the three new battleships *Italia* (as the *Littorio* had recently been renamed), *Roma* (flag), and *Vittorio Veneto,* along with six cruisers and eight destroyers under Admiral Bergamini—left Spezia at 3:00 on the morning of the ninth and steamed down the west coast of Corsica to comply. This force was to surrender itself at Malta, but some confusion arose, and the Italian admiral apparently expected to go to Maddalena in Sardinia instead, for during the afternoon the fleet changed course to the west. He later came back to the prescribed route when he learnt that Sardinia had been taken over by the Germans as had all the other Italian ports, but this diversion had cost him time, which would prove fatal.

The Germans reaction to Italy's "cowardly desertion" of the Axis cause was as ruthless and vigorous as expected. A new bomber unit equipped with a guided bomb was based in southern France, near Marseilles, and it was sent in to extract vengeance from the Italian Fleet. The ships were outside Allied air cover, and worse still, mistook the oncoming bomber formation for friendly escorts. Consequently, no ships opened fire or took any avoiding action whatsoever until it was too late. The bombers approached at a great height and aimed their missiles. One struck the unsuspecting *Roma* fair and square and penetrated to her forward fuel storage before detonating. Uncontrolled fires broke out, sweeping through her decks forward and below her bridge and fore turrets. She listed to port, her magazines ignited and she blew up and sank with heavy loss of life, taking 1,523 of her crew down with her, including Admiral Bergamini.

The *Italia* was also hit by some of these fearsome weapons but stood up well and was not seriously affected. A cruiser and some destroyers stayed behind to pick up the pitifully few survivors of this tragedy while the rest of the fleet steamed on to their rendezvous with the detachment from Force H.

With its radio-controlled bomb, the Luftwaffe had produced the first really effective aerial weapon against the battleship besides the torpedo. It was effective because the aircraft could stay at a height that made them invulnerable to antiaircraft fire and guide the bomb to follow all but the most violent twists and turns that a ship might make (a destroyer at full speed could out-turn the bomb or cause it to stall, a battleship obviously could not); equally important, the missile struck at 400 miles per hour, which gave it the velocity required to penetrate the most modern armored decks (if the angle was right). This weapon tipped the scales against the battleship in its old duel against the bomber.[31] The only drawback of this weapon was that the controlling bomber needed an undisturbed period in which to guide the missile to the target; carrier-borne fighters, if they had sufficient altitude to carry out an interception, could render their accuracy null and void.

It is interesting to note that whereas the Germans used their ingenuity to produce such a potent weapon, which could hit and badly damage the largest of ships at sea, the RAF persisted in their methodical plodding way, to find the answer just by producing bigger and bigger orthodox bombs, until, inevitably they were bound to come up with a bomb large enough to sink a battleship, providing of course it remained absolutely stationary.

The survivors of the Italian fleet were eventually met by the *Warspite* and *Valiant* early the following morning. It was an inspired choice as Captain Roskill pointed out:

In all the annals of military history, there can be few such dramatic events as the submission of an enemy navy. For the victors it is the culmination of the whole process of the application of maritime power; it is the consummation of all their hopes, and the fulfillment of all their purposes. For the vanquished it means, by its very completeness, the abandonment of all ambitions. It is the final and irreversible admission of defeat at sea. To the British race, and especially to the Royal Navy, the significance of the drama of 10th September 1943 was enhanced by the fact that the Italian fleet met our forces in the very waters, which, in so many wars, and not least from 1940 to 1943, we had struggled so arduously to control. There was, moreover, a remarkable coincidence to link the events of that day with the surrender of the German Navy after the 1914-18 war; for the *Warspite* and *Valiant* had both been present when, on November 21, 1918, the Kaiser's fleet had steamed across the North Sea into captivity. Rarely, if ever, in naval history can the same ships have witnessed two such events separated by almost exactly a quarter of a century.[32]

Also appropriate was the fact that Admiral Cunningham, under whose leadership these self-same ships had so often trounced their opponents before them, came out in a destroyer to witness this historic event. He signaled his pleasure at seeing the *Warspite* in her appointed station leading the line of the beaten enemy into Malta, and the next day, he made one of his stirring and always remembered signals to the authorities in London: "Be pleased to inform Their Lordships that the Italian battle fleet now lies at anchor under the guns of the fortress of Malta."

On the ninth, Vice Admiral Power hoisted his flag aboard the *Howe* and in company with the *King George V* and light forces steamed into the former enemy main base at Taranto, thus brilliantly forestalling its occupation by the Germans and ensuring that in the ensuing campaign this vital port was at the Allies' service. On their way, they passed the old *Andrea Doria* and *Caio Duilio* on their way to Malta to surrender. The last active battleship of the Italian Navy, the *Guilio Cesare*—which in a rare flash of spirit had managed to escape from the German-controlled Pola naval base in the northern Adriatic earlier—came into Malta four days later, being met by the *Warspite* at sea. Thus passed a second great navy from the waters of the Mediterranean and the stage of maritime history.[33]

There was severe overcrowding at Valletta with so many large ships, and accordingly, the *Howe* and *King George V* escorted the *Italia* and *Vittorio Veneto*, four cruisers, and four destroyers to Alexandria on September 14–17. On the same day, Admiral Cunningham received a signal from American Vice Admiral Hewitt off the Salerno beachhead, asking desperately for the intervention of heavy ships for bombarding purposes, if there were any to spare. The Germans had counterattacked with great vigor, and for a time, it seemed as if the Allies would be thrown back into the sea. Thus, although the Italian battle fleet had departed from the scene, new and continued demands were made on the British battleships. Cunningham reacted with vigor, sailing the *Warspite* and *Valiant* immediately and informing Hewitt that the *Nelson* and *Rodney* were available from Augusta if required.

At 5:00 P.M. on the fifteenth, the first two battleships arrived off the beachhead and commenced firing from ranges of up to 21,800 yards. The effects of the *Warspite*'s fire were immediate and gratifying, and the American troops were much impressed by her accuracy. She fired sixty-five 15-inch shells, of which thirty-five fell right on the target—eight of them within 100 yards.

By nightfall, what had been a dangerous enemy advance had been stopped dead; the Germans threw in a great weight of aircraft to remove this threat to their success, and heavy air attacks persisted all evening, but without success. The *Warspite* and *Valiant* resumed their operations the next day with similar effect after spending the hours of darkness farther out to sea, and again, their crushing weight of shells had a good effect, although Captain Roskill later stated that the judgment made at the time about their efficiency "now seems to be at fault . . . in attributing too great a share of the success to the heavy ship bombardments of the fifteenth and sixteenth.[34]

After the war, revisionists raised doubts, but at the time, the reaction of the German command gives a different story. Vice Admiral Ruge stated that "fierce German counterattacks collapsed under the concentrated fire of four [*sic*] battleships."[35] To try to remove this threat, the Luftwaffe now threw in their KG 100 units once more, with immediate effect.

The *Warspite* had reopened fire for her third bombardment at 1:00 P.M., firing thirty-two rounds with great accuracy into troop concentrations and ammunition dumps and at the termination of this she started to leave the area at 1400 that afternoon. As she did so, twelve Fw 190 fighter-bombers made a low-level attack out of the sun, which, although scoring no hits, was successful in drawing both the anti-aircraft fire and the attention down to sea-level while Major Jope's Dorniers made an undisturbed approach over the fleet.

At 2:30 came the attack, with three guided bombs being spotted at 3,000 feet. Captain Parker later described these moments:

> The three bombs when directly overhead looked like three very white mushrooms as they turned vertically down and dived for the ship at great speed. From the time of sighting to the time of the

bombs' arrival was only some seven to ten seconds. The ship was making about ten knots through the water at the time, and in the congested area avoiding action was not possible—and would in any case have been ineffective. One bomb came straight for the ship and penetrated to No. 4 boiler room, where it burst. A second bomb was a near-miss amidships abreast the bulge on the starboard side. It burst under water. This bomb had looked like missing by 400 yards, but about two-thirds of its way down it curved in towards the ship. The third bomb was a near-miss on the starboard side aft.[36]

The damage to the old veteran was grave, and for a time it appeared as if it might have been fatal, for it was thought her back had been broken. The direct hit had in fact gone through six decks—a total thickness of several inches—and passed out through the ship's double bottom before detonation. Except for a single diesel generator, all her power failed; she could not steer, and her armament was totally silenced for a period, as was her radar. Through the great gash torn in her starboard bulge, some 5,000 tons of water entered the ship, which settled very low in the water.

Vigorous efforts were made to salvage her, and by 4:15 P.M., a large American tug had her in tow out of Salerno Bay and was joined by two more. Together, they got her moving at a sluggish four knots for the Messina Straits, which she had passed on her way up to the beachhead at twenty three. The antiaircraft cruiser *Delhi* stood by in case the German bombers came back, and she was surrounded by a large destroyer screen. After dark, the Luftwaffe did make another attempt to finish her off, but fortunately, they located the *Valiant* instead. She was well able to take care of herself, passing west of the crippled *Warspite* in the night in "a blaze of tracer" and was undamaged.

Attempts by the cruiser *Euryalus* to take over the tow failed and the tugs took command again, five in all getting lines aboard, but even so the current in the Straits proved too strong, and most of the lines snapped, the *Warspite* going through in spectacular style, broadside on. After a nightmarish journey, she finally reached Malta at 8:00 on the morning of the nineteenth. Admiral Cunningham went aboard her to inspect the damage when she later reached Gibraltar under tow of four more tugs on the November 8. "I walked under her in dry-dock and saw the two enormous cofferdams built on to her bottom. I thought she would require an extensive refit before she fought again," he later recalled.[37]

In fact, she did not get it; two of her 15-inch turrets were completely out of action, and it was beyond the power of Gibraltar to rectify that before she was undocked on December 28. Not until March 1944 did she sail for home waters in company with a large convoy, and after calling at the Clyde, she journeyed around the north of Scotland and anchored at Rosyth on March 16. But even the great dockyard there could restore only one more of her turrets, and for the rest of her life, her main armament was reduced to six guns. During April, she again worked up as a bombardment vessel and rejoined the fleet at Scapa on May 2.

Meanwhile, most of her companions had preceded her home, and for the first time in many years, the Mediterranean was left without a single battleship of the Royal Navy. This movement had commenced once the crisis at Salerno had been resolved. With the Italian Fleet gone, the need now was for the modern ships to return to Scapa to deal with the German Norwegian units and then prepare themselves for the reconquest of the Far East, while the surviving older battleships had to get ready for both the reconquest of northern France—the long-awaited Operation Overlord—and also to once more build up the East Indies Fleet in the Indian Ocean in readiness for the planned retaking of Burma and Malaya. The *King George V* and *Howe* therefore sailed from Alexandria with all available Fleet destroyers on October 1 on the first leg of their homeward journey, and on her return home, the *Howe* commenced a refit in readiness for her eastern move.

The *Nelson* and *Rodney* were at Malta when Admiral Cunningham had rehoisted his flag in the former for the Italian surrender ceremony. This took place aboard the *Nelson* on the forenoon of September 28 and was attended by Gen. Dwight Eisenhower; Gen. Walter Bedell Smith, his chief of staff; and Gen. Harold Alexander, Air Marshal Arthur Tedder, and Admiral Cunningham, the three British commanders in chief of the Mediterranean theater; Lord Gort, the governor of Malta, who had such an honorable place in ensuring the defeat; and Macmillan and Murphy representing the two western governments. Marshal Badoglio and his aides arrived aboard an Italian cruiser and were received aboard the *Nelson* by a full guard of Royal Marines, with the whole of the massive ship's company on parade. The documents were duly signed around a large table in the admiral's quarters. It was a momentous day.[38]

After being based at Augusta for a while, both the Nelsons returned to home waters to recommence battle practice and refit, and here they joined the *Valiant*, which had returned in October and was refitting for the East Indies. Meanwhile, the *Queen Elizabeth* had completed her American refit in July, and after working up, she joined the Home Fleet. The *Renown* meanwhile had been employed in September to bring Winston Churchill home from the Quebec Conference. He boarded her on the twelfth at Halifax, with the already sick and dying Admiral Pound, who had just tendered his resignation. Churchill later recalled, "It was a relief to board the *Renown*. The splendid ship lay alongside the quay. Admiral Pound was already on board, having come through direct from Washington. He bore himself, as erect as ever, and no one looking at him would have dreamed that he was stricken."[39] He died on Trafalgar Day, October 21, 1943.

At once, the *Renown* was prepared to join Admiral Somerville's flag in the Indian Ocean, but her departure via the Mediterranean was delayed in order that she might once again carry Churchill and Admiral Cunningham to the Cairo Conference. The distinguished travelers embarked in the *Renown* at Plymouth on November 12 and sailed via Algiers and Malta. Despite her age, the *Renown* showed on this journey that she was still a flyer; she was the fastest capital ship still in the Royal Navy and remained so for the rest of the war. The captain of one of her escorting destroyers recalled: "It was blowing a full westerly gale as we slipped from our buoys at dusk, and joined the *Renown* just outside the breakwater. Twenty knots was ordered before we reached Eddystone, and then speed was increased to twenty-seven as we turned our noses into the open Atlantic. It was no fun at all for the destroyers; we were taking it green all the time as we slammed our way into the huge rollers."[40] Admiral Cunningham recalled, "I was glad to be on board a ship again, even though a passenger. The weather in the Bay was somewhat boisterous, and our escorting destroyers had difficulty in keeping up. It also reduced the attendance at meals. It was my first trip in the *Renown* and I greatly admired her weatherly qualities at speed."[41]

During the journey, Admiral Cunningham took the opportunity to ask the prime minister about employing the fleet in the Pacific. In view of the widespread understanding that Churchill all along wished to do just that when the opportunity presented itself, it is rather surprising to learn that for a very long time after this skeleton plan had been put to him, Churchill forgot all about it and refused to have anything to do with sending a fleet to the East, except to the East Indies. He required much persuasion.[42]

Somerville's command had by this time fallen to a very low ebb, his only capital ship being the old *Ramillies*, which was scheduled to return home and pay off. The *Renown* was a welcome boost to his strength, and there was the promise of much more to come, including the *Queen Elizabeth*, *Valiant*, and the French *Richelieu* once she had worked up her American equipment at Scapa Flow. The *Renown* arrived at Ceylon flying the flag of Vice Admiral Power on January 27, and no doubt, Somerville was glad to see his old flagship once more.

Meanwhile, the autumn and winter of 1943 had witnessed a startling transformation in the Arctic.

If the suspension of the Arctic convoys had for a time thwarted the German ambitions to use their heavy ships, it was necessary to keep their crews up to scratch while they awaited their opportunity. Casting around for something worthwhile they came up with an operation against the Allied weather reporting station which had been established on the bleak and barren island of Spitzbergen, some 450 miles north of their base at Altenfiord. The information this wireless station transmitted was of great use to the Royal Navy in convoy operations, especially those to Russia, and the Germans had used it for similar functions before being themselves forced out in 1942.

On September 9, 1943, a powerful German squadron comprising the *Tirpitz, Scharnhorst,* and ten destroyers appeared off the island and engaged the main defenses, the two 3-inch guns at Barentsberg. As one observer wryly commented, "It was the last real German squadron ever to go to sea, and to adapt the saying, the Germans were sending twelve men to do a boy's job."[43] This bombardment was carried out with the full power of the *Tirpitz*'s main battery of eight 15-inch guns and the *Scharnhorst*'s nine 11-inch weapons, and it was the only time in her life that the *Tirpitz* fired her main armament at low level against an enemy target. One single salvo from the *Scharnhorst* sufficed to demolish the Norwegian battery, while a pair of Bofors guns ashore—which fired back a gallant 150 rounds at their giant adversaries in futile resistance—were then abandoned.

The German fleet then methodically shelled everything in sight, and landing parties were put ashore to ensure that nothing was left, bringing back a dozen prisoners. The great attack was over by 11:00 A.M., leaving the survivors "to bury their six dead comrades and to get the transmitter in working order." They were confident that the Royal Navy would not desert them, and in the late autumn, ships of the Home Fleet, protected by the *Anson,* brought them supplies that enabled them to carry on their work through the winter.

Back in Altenfiord after this episode, there was some discord between the crews of the two big ships:

> A bitter dispute broke out between the crews of the *Scharnhorst* and *Tirpitz* over the allocation of Second-class Iron Crosses. The men from the *Scharnhorst* who had behind them the tradition of the commerce-raiding expeditions in the Atlantic, the Norwegian campaign, and Operation Cerberus were scornful that there should be a general distribution of Second-class Iron Crosses for such a trifling affair as the Spitzbergen raid, and said so, offensively.[44]

Meanwhile, following the Italian human-torpedo attacks of 1941–42 in the Mediterranean, the British, using a captured Italian model, set about producing their own version, subsequently called Chariots. It was an ordinary 21-torpedo powered by an electric battery to three knots; with an endurance of six hours, it was piloted by a two-man crew and, if successful, could plant a 600-pound warhead where it hurt most—below the waterline.

An early attempt to utilize the early versions of this weapon against the Altenfiord squadron were made in October using an adapted Norwegian fishing boat, the *Arthur*, but despite almost penetrating to the base, the mission failed when the chariots were lost en route. The net defenses in Kaafiord at this time were weak and could be penetrated. On November 1, 1942, the *Arthur* was scuttled, but some of the party were taken prisoner; the wreck was found and examined, and the German defenses were strengthened in the intervening year.

At Scapa, the Home Fleet had been weakened by the departure of the two American battleships to the Pacific in August and by the fact that the *King George V* and *Howe* had been retained in the Mediterranean until October. The Russian convoys were still in suspension however and so the strain was tolerable. A new attempt was launched to disable the German heavy ships at their anchorages, as in the 1942 attempt, but using the more sophisticated "midget submarines" (X craft). Just over fifty foot in length with a crew of four, these vehicles were tiny submarines, but their weapons were detachable two-ton ground mines on each side of the pressure hull, operated with a thirty-six-hour time fuse.[45]

The first of these craft had been launched in March 1942, and after eighteen months of trials and improvements, a force of six of these craft was prepared for the assault. Much of the credit can again be given to Churchill and his prodding memos: "Have you given up all plans for doing anything to *Tirpitz*?" was one such missive that he shot at the Combined Chiefs in February 1943. They had not, but not until September were the X craft fully prepared. On the night of September 11–12, they sailed in tow of six submarines from Loch Cairnbawn and passing between the Faeroes and the Shetland Islands headed north through worsening weather.[46]

The plan called for the parent submarines to unleash the midgets a few miles outside the strong German minefields guarding the approaches to Altenfiord, north and south of Soroy Island. The midgets were then to submerge during the daylight hours of the twenty-first and arrive at dawn on the twenty-second at the entrance to the fiord to commence their attacks. The parent submarines would rendezvous with the survivors later.

The *X-5*, *X-6*, and *X-7* were assigned the *Tirpitz* as their target; the *X-9* and *X-10, the Scharnhorst*; and the *X-8*, the *Lützow*. The first two ships were located at Kaafiord, and the latter at nearby Langefiord. Of the six X craft, two—the *X-9*, which was lost, and the *X-8*, which was scuttled—did not make it to the drop zone. The operational crews now took over the survivors for the actual attacks.[47]

The attacks were made with great bravery but were beset with numerous hazards. The *X-5* may well have placed her charges under her target, but she was lost without a trace (although the search continues to this day), and the Germans claimed to have destroyed one X craft by gunfire outside the nets at 8:43 A.M. The *X-10* lost her periscope, her compass failed, and she was subsequently forced to withdraw without attacking. As the *Scharnhorst* had in the meantime shifted berth, her mission would have been abortive anyway.

The *X-7* led the *X-6* into Kaafiord in the early hours of the twenty-second. The *X-6* inadvertently broke surface at 7:07 and was spotted from the deck of the *Tirpitz* and attacked by small arms and grenades as it surfaced close alongside and laid its charges. The submarine was then scuttled, and the whole four-man crew was taken aboard their intended victim in much the same manner as had the Italians at Alexandria almost two years earlier.

The ships' light gun crews were closed up, and all the battleship's innumerable watertight doors were closed, and at 7:40, the jittery Germans got another fright when the *X-7*, which had become entangled in the netting, bobbed up briefly. The *Tirpitz* was raising steam to put to sea when this happened, but the sight of yet another submarine from a force whose size was unknown caused the cancellation of this idea, and instead, the net gate was closed shut, and the battleship was shifted on her cable as far as she could be from where the *X-6* had settled.

This saved the ship much damage, but not all, for the *X-7* pressed on with her attack undaunted; passing below the *Tirpitz*, this tiny craft systematically placed her charges fore and aft along the giant keel. Her attempts to escape were again frustrated by the nets, and she was still entangled dangerously close to the *Tirpitz* when the charges blew at 8:12. The *X-7* then ran out of control, continually coming to the surface until she was abandoned and sunk; unfortunately, two of the crew went down with her.

The detonation of the two charges beneath the *Tirpitz* was dramatic, as one of the British officers aboard later recorded:

> Then, as I turned to face the guard again, crash! My knees buckled as the explosion hurled the ship out of the water. Complete darkness in the alley as all the lights shattered. Fire sprinklers showered foam on us, I was grabbed by the guard and pushed through the door into bright sunlight. What a change in those few moments!
>
> The ship started to list rapidly to port. Steam gushed from broken pipes. Seamen ran in all directions. Oil flowed from the shattered hull covering the water in the fiord. Injured men were being

brought up on deck. Bursts of machine-gun fire were interspersed with the loud crash of the secondary armament firing wildly. It was impossible to take it all in. All around was confusion.[48]

All four charges laid by the two midgets seem to have gone off, but by shifting her position, the *Tirpitz* avoided the worse effects of three of them. The fourth appears to have detonated directly under her engine rooms, and it was from this explosion that the bulk of the damage was caused. All three of the battleship's main turbines were put out of action by this attack, and thus, the *Tirpitz* was immobilized. The German estimate of the repairs necessary to make her seaworthy again were put at six months. Not until April 1944 would she be considered as a fighting unit again. It was a staggering blow achieved at comparatively slight loss, and both Lieutenant Cameron and Lieutenant Place fully deserved their Victoria Crosses.

Admiral Fraser considered that this damage to the *Tirpitz* at once changed the whole strategic situation in the Arctic and that the Russian convoys could well now be resumed. The fact that both the *Scharnhorst* and *Lützow* were unscathed still meant though that a strong surface fleet had to be retained to deal with them. Even this threat was halved by the end of the month for the *Lützow* to have her ever-troublesome engines overhauled in a German shipyard. Despite the fact that the Admiralty was forewarned of her sailing, she evaded all patrols between leaving Altenfiord on the twenty-third and arriving at Narvik on her first leg.

When she sailed out again on the twenty-seventh, she was again reported, but by an incredible series of muddles on the part of the British—all too strongly like those of February 1942—the only torpedo-bomber striking force available, six Fleet Air Arm Avengers from the *Victorious*'s No. 832 Squadron working from Sumburgh in the Shetlands, were held back until it was too late to intercept her. They arrived late and in bad weather and searched to the north, while astern of them the *Lützow* and her destroyer escorts were speeding south at high speed. By October 1, her high-speed dash had brought her to the safety of the Baltic unharmed. An official inquiry again sat in judgment of this debacle, with the result that, yet again, plans were made to build up Coastal Command's strength, and a more coordinated series of defense measures was thought desirable between the various arms involved, Fighter and Coastal of the RAF and the FAA. Nonetheless, Captain Roskill makes the most pertinent point when he asked just how it could still happen that "after almost exactly four years of war, a German pocket battleship was still able to steam from Vestifiord to the Baltic in complete immunity."[49]

It seems as if the British could never change, and Hitler's verdict of early 1942 appeared just as valid eighteen months after the channel dash had

shaken the nation to the core. This latter episode, however, seems to have
been conveniently ignored by historians, perhaps because it upset too many
convenient theories about the all-powerful torpedo-bomber and the impotent
battleship. Whatever the humiliation of this farce, the fact remained that only
the *Scharnhorst* remained of the German heavy ships in the north. Despite
this, the German resolve to use her against the Russian convoys remained
firm, because of the appalling situation that was now developing on the Eastern Front after the failure of the last German offensive at Kursk with heavy
losses and the crashing forward of the Soviet armies towards the countries of
Eastern Europe. Something had to be done to slow down this onrush, and
the sinking of an Allied convoy laden with tanks and aircraft would be the
equivalent of a major land victory.

The German commanders in the north were firmly resolved to use their
ships aggressively once the chance again presented itself against the Russian
convoys, and this viewpoint was made perfectly clear by Kummetz to Dönitz
and Dönitz to Hitler during 1943. In fact, the German naval staff had, as early
as March 1943, stated quite clearly that the attacking of the convoys of war
material to the Soviet Union was now the *primary* task of their naval units in
the north. "This task is to be given priority" over the "secondary consideration
of the defense of Norway."[50]

Nor did Adolf Hitler, preoccupied by his land reverses in the east and the
defection of his southern ally, do more than wryly note that he would be
proved right should the big ships venture out against the Home Fleet. Apart
from that, he left his new naval commander in chief to get on with his job.
Despite the fact that the chorus of postwar historians in Germany had blamed
Hitler for the many defeats suffered by their armed forces, Admiral Dönitz
refutes this as far as the navy was concerned after 1943: "Hitler never again
attempted to intervene in naval affairs. He had apparently become convinced
that I was doing my utmost and that he could rely on me. When other important people came to him with suggestions or with complaints of some kind
against the Navy, his usual answer was: 'The Grand Admiral will do whatever
is necessary.'"[51]

Thus, when the Russian convoy cycle recommenced homeward with RA
54A on November 1 and outward with JW 54A on the fifteenth, the Germans
examined their plans afresh. In addition to the heavy units sent back for
repair, one of the two destroyer flotillas available had also returned with
them, leaving only the five ships of the 4th Flotilla for operations. Admiral
Kummetz had gone on extended sick leave to Germany, and his place was
temporarily taken by R.Adm. Erich Bey, who was a destroyer officer, and thus,
it was not unexpected that in his mind, any future attack should be a
destroyer-only operation, with, if necessary, the *Scharnhorst* coming out in sup-

port of the light forces. Naval command considered the operation would have more chance of success, however, if overwhelming force could be brought to bear quickly on the close escorts; German destroyer operations up to that point of the war had been, if anything, even more hesitant and unproductive than the activities of the big ships.[52] And so it was decided that the 4th Flotilla should operate as the *Scharnhorst*'s scouting force and screen in the traditional manner, rather than on their own, even though Bey had only a very limited knowledge of big ship operations.

The next obstacle was the cooperation of the Luftwaffe. Just about all the bomber and torpedo-bomber units that had been employed during 1942 had been withdrawn the previous winter, the former to Russia and the latter to the Mediterranean, and in both these new theaters, both forces had been decimated in the subsequent fighting. There was therefore no question of the air fleet being built up again in its 1942 strength to cooperate with the navy. However, as always, the vital aspect of any German sorties was early reconnaissance to give the exact composition and disposition of the usual heavy covering force from the Home Fleet. Göring protested that such a task was now beyond his airmen's strength in the north, but after some argument, the air officer commanding in Norway gave his reluctant consent to provide such air searches to the best of his limited availability. This hurdle over the sortie could go ahead.

Meanwhile, the Russian convoys continued, with, as usual the ultimate protection against such an attack resting, in the winter of 1943, as it had all along, on the covering force of a Home Fleet battleship and escort. It is indeed interesting to note that observers like Tedder had written in June 1942 that Matapan in 1941 had been the battleship's last dying kick and that henceforth the heavy bomber would take over its role by protecting convoys against battleships of the enemy powers. Since that time the call for the battleship had continued and indeed increased, whereas the RAF had still not managed to sink a heavy ship at sea, or indeed, as yet, at anchor. It is also interesting to note that other post-war observers have stated that British battleships were completely helpless without an aircraft-carrier to locate the enemy, provide air cover, damage the enemy and place it on the plate for the battleship to merely administer the *coup de grace*, and yet here again in the winter of 1943–44, the carrier was helpless in the conditions prevailing, as were shore-based aircraft, and only the British battleship remained to give the required protection to the hundreds of tanks and aircraft, the tons of supplies, trucks and ammunition on the way to the vital Eastern Front.

The two convoys that sailed in November had been covered by Vice Admiral Moore in the *Anson*, and both reached their destinations without loss of any kind. The third convoy, JW 55A, left Loch Ewe on December 12, 1943, and again arrived without damage, although it had been sighted by the Luft-waffe en route. Admiral Fraser, however, was informed of the new German resolution to sortie out once more with his big ships and took the new and bold step of going right through to the Kola Inlet himself in the *Duke of York*, the first time a British battleship had sailed into Soviet waters in this war. While there, he conferred with the Soviet admiral, Golovko, who commanded the White Sea Fleet, half a dozen destroyers, and some submarines that helped the convoys over the final few miles into port, and then returned to Iceland aboard his flagship.[53]

On December 20, the fourth convoy of the new cycle put to sea from Loch Ewe, JW 55B, and a homeward-bound group, RA 55A, sailed from Kola on the twenty-third. Both convoys were protected by the usual cruiser squadron under Vice Admiral Burnett, with one heavy cruiser, the *Norfolk*, and two light cruisers, the *Belfast* and *Sheffield*, while from Iceland, Admiral Fraser again sailed with the *Duke of York*; a light cruiser, the *Jamaica*; and four destroyers.

On the twenty-second, the westbound convoy was sighted by the Luft-waffe, which gave its usual interpretation of the event, stating that the convoy consisted of forty troop transports with powerful escort. This led to an alert against the long-expected Allied invasion of Norway before it was realized that this was just the usual air force misinformation and that it was another Russian convoy. All the same, the unreliability of their air searches reports were an ill omen for the operation by the *Scharnhorst*, dependent as she was on their accuracy. Their unreliability was to have a decisive effect.

A U-boat group was put into position west of Bear Island to supplement these reconnaissance reports and to intercept the convoy and Operation *Ost-front* was put into operation. The aircraft which had located the convoys were reinforced by others, but although they actually made a sighting report of the *Duke of York*'s force (closing the convoy at nineteen knots as Fraser knew through Ultra the German big ship would come out this time), this was for-warded by the Luftwaffe officer on the spot merely as five ships, and not a possible heavy ship because it was considered that the aircrew should report only what they had seen and refrain from guessing.

The result was tragedy for the Germans. As Admiral Dönitz recalled: "Our reconnaissance had not discovered the presence of any heavy enemy formation, though that, of course, did not mean that no such force was at sea. But if it were, it must have been a long way from the convoy, and the *Scharn-horst* seemed to have every chance of delivering a rapid and successful attack."[54] At 2:12 P.M. on Christmas Day, therefore, the German naval com-mand signaled the attack order to the *Scharnhorst* and the 4th Flotilla. Dönitz summarized his orders in the following manner: "1. Enemy is trying to hamper the heroic endeavors of our eastern armies by sending valuable convoy of arms and food to the Russians. We must help. 2. The *Scharnhorst* and destroyers will attack the convoy. 3. Engagement will be broken off at your discretion. In principal, you should break off on appearance of strong enemy forces."[55]

So even now, the appearance of "strong enemy forces" gave Bey an out. It was an out he might well need, for Fraser was still closing, the convoy having been ordered to reverse course for a day and Burnett informed so that he could plan to "hold the ring" until the *Duke of York* came up. Bey's doubts about the wisdom of the operation, especially utilizing the *Scharnhorst* and not just the five destroyers, were comprehensive. He doubted whether the *Scharnhorst*'s advantage of heavy gunfire would be of much use in the conditions prevailing at that time of year. "The Fleet Commander warned that only during the brief period of maximum light—at 73 degrees north, lasting from 11:22 to 12:07—could the *Scharnhorst*'s firepower be effectively exploited, and it was more than questionable whether during this short period she could break through the defense screen and get at the convoy itself quite apart from the risk of enemy torpedoes."[56]

But despite these reservations, the battle group put to sea to comply with its orders at 7:00 P.M. on the twenty-fifth, two hours behind schedule. Meanwhile, the appalling weather had grounded all Luftwaffe aircraft, but by 9:00 A.M., the convoy had been located and successfully shadowed by the U-boats, which homed the *Scharnhorst* onto her target. Despite the fact that Admiral Fraser had broken radio silence to inform his commanders of his intentions, the Germans still had no firm information that the *Duke of York* was on the way.

Both big ships were now steaming toward their final rendezvous in terrible weather. The destroyers accompanying the *Scharnhorst* soon began to labor heavily, and doubts were expressed whether they would be able to keep up at all. Thus, already the use of the heavy ship was shown to be practical in these conditions whereas the planned destroyers-only alternative would have proven abortive even before it began. The even smaller destroyers with the *Duke of York* and the convoy were also feeling the effects of the mounting gale, but being British ships and crews, they rode it out and continued operations; they had, after all, been continually at sea in conditions like this for five years now, whereas their German opposite numbers had spent most of the war at anchor in the fiords, year-in, year-out.

The *Duke of York* was also shipping it green over her long, rigid forecastle as she stormed east through the rising gale on the night of December 25–26 at seventeen knots, and at 3:39 A.M., Admiral Fraser received the news from Admiralty intelligence that confirmed his hunch: the *Scharnhorst* was considered likely to be at sea. By 4:00, all the positions of the British forces were plotted as follows.

The convoy—nineteen merchant ships with a close escort of ten destroyers, reinforced by four more from the homeward convoy—was steering northeast at eight knots south of Bear Island. The three cruisers of the covering force were steering southwest toward the North Cape at their best possible speed to interpose themselves between the convoy and any German ships coming up from Altenfiord. They were some 150 miles east of the convoy. The *Duke of York* and light forces were crashing up from the west at twenty-four knots to close the pincers behind Bey's squadron in a gigantic trap. "The wind was blowing strongly from the southwest, and there was a heavy following sea, which made the handling of the destroyers very difficult," wrote Captain Roskill.[57]

The German squadron was finding conditions no less difficult, although they had the advantage in the *Scharnhorst* of the following wind:

Sailing before the wind with the gently swaying motion and rhythmical pitching characteristic of the long ship, the *Scharnhorst* was spared the worst effects of the gale blowing from astern. But snow squalls impeded visibility, the sky was as dark as the sea, and the escorting destroyers were hardly discernible. From time to time, a breaker reared up before the battleship, stood for seconds in a column of pale foam, then collapsed over the bows and ebbed away before the breakwater in gurgling eddies. Smaller breakers, churned up to left and right by the great curving bows, disintegrated in white pennants. The night was icy cold. Cold, too, were the lashes of salty spray, which flung themselves across the armour of the forward triple turrets and whipped up to the bridge.

The dense snow and quickly forming ice obscured the lenses of the range-finders and directors, rendering them practically useless, and the vigilance of the bridge and signal watches, the look-outs on deck, at the searchlight control columns and at the guns was therefore of vital importance. Important too was the Radar apparatus. Although the two radar-sets fitted in the *Scharnhorst* were capable of detecting the approach of enemy units within a limited range, they could not—as the British "Rotterdam apparatus" could—register and make visible the outline and size of any ship so located. However, the captain, squatting on the little emergency seat next to the officer of the watch, his broad frame wrapped in a sheepskin coat and a thick scarf wound several times around his neck, knew that he could depend on his lookouts. They always had been first-class in German warships. Furthermore, the men had recently been issued with the new glasses that gave excellent definition even by night.

From the bridge, nothing could be seen through the driving snow. When the snow flurries abated for a while as though gathering strength for their next onslaught, huge dark waves loomed in sight, rolling alongside, blue-black, white-crested, thundering against the ship's sides. The breakers, coming at long intervals, rushed across the forecastle with deafening roar, shrouded the long bows in a veil of swirling foam, swept across the anchor chains and, as bows rose, drained away through the scuppers.

Little was to be heard above the roar of the sea and the intermittent howling of the gale. Here, a water-tight door would bang; there, the clatter of heavy boots on wooden gratings could be heard as one of the watches on the bridge stamped to keep his feet warm. The soft regular hum of the electrical generating plant spread its soothing sound through the stillness of the control positions and turrets. Otherwise there was silence. Every man was tense with expectancy. Any moment the alarm might sound and the ship that was gliding so smoothly ahead would be suddenly transformed, as if ignited, into a volcano belching fire.[58]

The same air of quiet tension amid the gale could be found aboard the other warships as they pitched and rolled their way across the roof of the world toward their destiny on that Boxing Day of 1943.

At 7:30 A.M., Admiral Bey detached his destroyers to start their reconnaissance sweep along the probable route of the convoy, and the *Scharnhorst* went to action stations in readiness. On their new line of advance, the big German destroyers—never good sea boats because of their heavy main armaments (5.9-inch guns on the latest ships)—found the going ghastly, heading as they now were right into the teeth of the gale. Staggering and clawing their way onward, they quickly lost sight of their big brother and indeed, through signaling confusion, lost touch completely and never regained it. After sweeping west without result, they withdrew and took no part in the battle at all. The *Scharnhorst* was now on her own, but rapidly closing with the convoy. By 8:40, she was within thirty miles of the freighters, but she was destined to get no closer to her prey.

The three cruisers of Admiral Burnett's squadron had closed the gap and in a dead-heat result had arrived on the scene just in time. At 8:40, the *Belfast* obtained a radar contact at 25,000 yards range and closing fast. The three lithe cruisers continued to close the giant adversary, and at 9:21, the range was down to 13,000 yards, and the *Sheffield* reported, "Enemy in sight!"

Aboard the British ships, the four 8-inch turrets of the *Norfolk* and the four 6-inch turrets of the two light cruisers tracked around and locked on, and the eight 8-inch and twenty-four 6-inch guns awaited their moment to loose off at their still unsuspecting opponent. The *Belfast* fired a starshell at 9:24, and five minutes later, the main armament of the British ship opened fire; only the *Norfolk* could engage at that moment because the cruisers were altering course toward the battlecruiser and the arcs of fire of the other two were masked. The battle of North Cape had commenced:

> Short of sinking the *Scharnhorst* with a single broadside—a virtual impossibility—the *Norfolk* could hardly have done better than she did, for her second or third salvo carried away the German's main radar mattress and put her port high-angle fire-control director out of action. With the radar gone the Germans had to fight blind in the darkness of the Arctic winter day. At this stage the destroyers that had left Altenfiord with the *Scharnhorst* would have been invaluable for scouting with their own radar, but they had got lost.[59]

Aboard the German battlecruiser, surprise was complete. No return fire was made from the *Scharnhorst* at this stage; instead, she immediately hauled around to the south, leaving the convoy far astern as she recoiled from the three cruisers at thirty knots. Burnett's ships duly followed her.

At 9:55, Admiral Bey decided to try again and work his way around to the north-east and come in behind the British cruisers. He had at least a five-knot margin of speed over these smaller vessels in the conditions prevailing, but Burnett was still tracking by radar and turned back to cover his convoy. At this point, around 10:00, the British ships lost radar contact, and Admiral Fraser feared she might have retreated for good back to Norway; if so he was still too far distant to intercept her. However he sent four powerful destroyers from the convoy to join Burnett, and this force was now between the *Scharnhorst* and the objective once more. In the meantime, the German destroyers had been searching diligently to the southwest, *away* from the convoy and the scene of action, and despite witnessing the starshell and explosions from a distance, they continued to do so until 10:27, when they broke off and turned back northeast again to try to locate their flagship. They never did.

The *Duke of York* continued to close and was about 160 miles away when the cruisers reported that the *Scharnhorst* was again on their screens resuming her attack, with the *Sheffield* reporting her at 12:21. From 11,000 yards, they reengaged, and after some twenty minutes of inconclusive gunnery, the *Scharnhorst* once more turned away. This time, however, she had retaliated with good effect, hitting the *Norfolk* with two 11-inch shells and knocking out one of her main turrets and most of her radar sets. The British destroyers were unable to get in a torpedo attack, and the *Scharnhorst* drew away for the second time, straddling the *Sheffield* and riddling her hull with shell fragments. Bey now decided to break off the operation and return to Norway, and at 2:18, he signaled his destroyers to do likewise. He headed south at twenty-eight knots, and Burnett ceased fire and followed, knowing the *Scharnhorst* was heading straight for the welcoming arms of Admiral Fraser.

And so it fell out. At 4:17 P.M., the radar of the *Duke of York* picked up the *Scharnhorst* at a range of twenty-two miles to the north-northeast and closing at high speed. The trap was sprung. Admiral Fraser intended to close the range to 12,000 yards and then open fire with his main armament, at the same time he positioned his four destroyers in readiness for a torpedo attack when he judged the time was right. At 4:50, the *Belfast* again illuminated the *Scharnhorst* with star shells, and the *Duke of York*'s opening salvo crashed out.

Once more, the *Scharnhorst* was caught completely unawares. Captain Roskill quotes an eyewitness aboard the destroyer *Scorpion* at this moment: "When the starshell first illuminated the *Scharnhorst*, I could see her so clearly that I noticed her turrets were fore-and-aft; and what a lovely sight she was at full speed. She was almost at once obliterated by a wall of water from the *Duke of York*'s first salvo . . . when she reappeared her turrets wore a different aspect."[60]

Aboard the battlecruiser the effect was immediate, she at once slewed violently around to the north away from this unexpected concentration and increased speed. "Then it came. Blow upon blow. In a matter of seconds ship and crew were swept along in the confused headlong rush of events. Godde [a survivor] observed gigantic splashes 100 to 150 yards on his port side from what must have been shells of the heaviest caliber. Then, while the battleship [*sic*] was still turning round, her own heavy turrets opened fire."[61] But there was no escape for the *Scharnhorst*. The *Duke of York* tracked her remorselessly as she switched and maneuvered to throw off her massive opponent, her 14-inch salvos falling close around the German ship, even though the *Scharnhorst*'s speed enabled her to initially open the range.

At 5:24 P.M., Admiral Bey seemed to realize that he and his ship were doomed. He signaled to Germany: "Am surrounded by heavy units." The battle now settled down to a running duel between the two big ships, a final clash of giants in the Arctic night that was to be a grand finale to all Germany's long efforts to challenge British mastery at sea. At Jutland, at Dogger Bank during World War I, off Norway and in the Atlantic during World War II, the British had taken up the challenge only to have their opponents slip from their grasp. This time Admiral Fraser made no mistake.

The fire from the *Scharnhorst*, in opposition to the usual German practice, was initially wild and inaccurate, but once the long stern chase had been established her accuracy increased for a time and she straddled the British battleship several times at ranges between 17,000 and 20,000 yards. Both the *Duke of York*'s masts were pierced by 11-inch shells during this part of the battle, but these shells failed to explode, and she was virtually unharmed.

By contrast, the steady, accurate salvos crashing out from the *Duke of York*'s ten 14-inch guns were on target and soon began to hit and badly hurt the battlecruiser. An eyewitness aboard one of the cruisers described the scene:

> Then the *Duke of York* fired her fourteen-inch, and even to us, now a thousand yards astern, the noise and concussion was colossal, and the vivid spurt of flame lighted up the whole ship for an instant, leaving a great drift of cordite smoke hanging in the air. Her tracers rose quickly, and, in a bunch, sailed up to the highest point of their trajectory, and then curved down, down towards the target.[62]

The *Scharnhorst* began taking hits:

> At 1655 hours [4:55 P.M.], a 14-inch shell hit the starboard bows abreast of A turret and the blast threw P.O. Godde to the deck. Overcome with shock and greenish-black lyddite fumes he gasped for air and lay for several seconds on the wooden grating of his small platform, incapable of moving. Just at that moment, the captain appeared. The lenses of the optical apparatus had become temporarily unusable from the effects of the hit and the fumes—and had to be cleaned from the outside by ratings sent up from below.[63]

The results of these early hits by the *Duke of York* firmly jammed the *Scharnhorst*'s A turret with its three-gun barrels fully elevated and unattainable. Then within minutes, another hit smashed into the German ship amidships. Despite this the German ship, with half her main armament out of action by this time, continued to draw away from the British battleship, but then followed a further succession of hits, and her speed dropped away.

> On board the German ship, in the second turret, a hit had put the ventilating system out of action and conditions were soon unbearable. Every time the breeches of the guns were opened, thick black smoke belched out, blinding and choking everyone and putting a number of men completely out of action. In spite of powerful lamps, it was impossible to see anything more than a yard away. Guns' crews had to shout their orders at each other, and in doing so filled their lungs with chocking cordite smoke. This, together with

the motion of the ship, combined to make almost every man in the turret violently seasick.

In the 5.9-inch turrets and in the 'tween decks things were horrible, with torn bodies swilling around in a mixture of blood and sea water, while the stretcher parties picked their way through the wreckage with ever increasing numbers of wounded.[64]

At 6:23 P.M., Bey saw the end was inevitable and signaled back to Germany, "We shall fight to the last shell." It was the last message to come from the *Scharnhorst.*

Admiral Fraser now ceased fire for a time and released his four destroyers to make their torpedo attacks. It is interesting to see how the conventional scheme of things was so altered by the conditions. The basis of every fleet action since 1914 was that the destroyers (or aircraft later) would attack with torpedoes and slow down the enemy big ships for the British heavy ships to finish off; so it happened with the *Bismarck*. Fraser's brilliance resulted in the *Duke of York* doing all the initial damage and so knocking the *Scharnhorst* about that she was slowed down sufficiently for the light forces to get back into the fight.[65]

The destroyers attacked in two divisions and scored several hits from point-blank range. Then the *Duke of York* and *Jamaica* came back to resume their pounding, reopening fire from about 14,000 yards with devastating effect:

Hit upon hit crashed on to the *Scharnhorst*. Heavy explosions followed one upon the other, and as each bout of violent rocking subsided it was replaced by a slow vibration as if the very hull were trembling. Steel crashed upon steel; fire broke out and the smoke which billowed from the quickly spreading flames mingled with the acrid cordite fumes of the German salvos and the strangely stinging odor from the British explosives.[66]

"She must have been a hell on earth. The 14-inch [shells] from the flagship were hitting or rocketing off from a ricochet on the sea," wrote one eyewitness at this time, and indeed, the *Scharnhorst* was almost done. By 1930 [7:30 P.M.], her speed was almost zero and all her heavy turrets were out of action. A second destroyer attack went in and more torpedoes slammed into her riven hull. Soon after she went down. "Through the dense smoke nothing could now be seen of the *Scharnhorst* except a dull glow; but she probably sank at about 7:45 P.M. in 72 degrees, 16 minutes north and 28 degrees, 41 minutes east." [67]

Thus passed the *Scharnhorst*, the most successful of the German heavy ships and the most sought-after naval target of the war. As the official historian commented:

Whatever we may think of the faulty planning, weak intelligence and uncertain leadership which led to her doom the *Scharnhorst* had, like the *Bismarck* before her, fought gallantly to the end against overwhelmingly superior forces. And, again like the *Bismarck*, the amount of punishment she withstood without blowing up and before she sank was remarkable. She probably received at least thirteen heavy shell hits from the *Duke of York*, and perhaps a dozen from the smaller weapons of the cruisers; and of the fifty-five torpedoes fired at her it is likely that eleven hit.[68]

All arms concerned, intelligence, the cruiser squadron and the destroyers attacking in terrible weather, duly deserved and received their just credit for the successful outcome of this battle, but it is to the British battleship that the chief honors must go. As Admiral Fraser said at the time, the British battleship was the "principal factor in the battle. She fought the *Scharnhorst* at night, and she won."

Thus, once again was the British battleship vindicated in combat. After the battle, the *Duke of York* again went on to Kola and on her return laid a wreath on the last-known position of her brave adversary. Of the *Scharnhorst*'s crew of almost 2,000 officers and men, including 40 young naval cadets, only 36 survivors were found by the destroyers despite an hour-long search.

With the *Scharnhorst* sunk, the *Lützow* back in Germany, and the *Tirpitz* disabled for six months, nothing remained of the powerful German fleet in northern waters and the supplies to Russia could proceed almost unmolested except for the U-boats, which did little damage. Until the *Tirpitz* was again ready for action, a complete transformation of the entire sea war was achieved by the *Duke of York*'s victory. "Not only was it now acceptable to reduce the Home Fleet's strength to reinforce the Eastern Fleet, but his ships had won for themselves far greater freedom of movement. Continuous offensive operations could henceforth be carried out off the Norwegian coast, and a heavy attack on the *Tirpitz* with naval aircraft was soon being planned."[69]

The Home Fleet still needed to keep some modern ships on hand for a while. "It was still necessary to retain a powerful Home Battle Fleet reinforced by U.S. battleships to contain the Bismarck-class *Tirpitz* and the remaining German pocket battleships and battle cruiser based in Norway,"[70] recalled one historian, but in fact, only the badly damaged *Tirpitz* remained, and all the American battleships had left Scapa many, many months earlier.

It was considered vital that the *Tirpitz* be more completely immobilized than she was if the eastern commitments were to be fulfilled as desired and the Russian convoys were to continue to flow unhindered. The Soviet air force now set out to do what the RAF had so far failed to do. On the night of February 10–11, a force of fifteen bombers was dispatched carrying 2,000-pound bombs to attack the *Tirpitz* while still under repair. Eleven failed to find Kaafiord at all despite the fact that the weather remained clear with bright moonlight over the target zone. Four aircraft made their attacks and scored a single near-miss, which, however, did not cause any serious damage. Later that month, an offensive carrier raid was conducted by the Home Fleet, Operation Bayleaf, against the Norwegian coast with the *Furious*, escorted by the *Anson* and the French battleship *Richelieu*, which was making her operational debut before going to the Indian Ocean.

However, larger carrier forces were now available to the Home fleet with the large number of little escort carriers coming into service and it was decided to carry out a full-scale series of Fleet Air assaults on the *Tirpitz*, which by the end of March was sufficiently repaired to enable her to commence trials again. The *Tirpitz* achieved a speed of twenty-seven knots on these trials and was considered fit enough to take part in a sortie against the next Russian convoy. She was not to get the chance; detailed photo-reconnaissance work had been done by Spitfires from Russian airfields and to coincide with the passage of convoy JW 58 Admiral Fraser sent to sea a considerable force to carry out Operation Tungsten.

The fleet sailed in two groups from Scapa on March 30, ostensibly to provide cover to the convoy, but in reality to attack the *Tirpitz* in her lair. Force I consisted of the *Duke of York* (flag) and *Anson*, the carrier *Victorious*, and light forces while Force II under Rear Admiral Bisset, contained the escort carriers *Emperor*, *Fencer*, *Pursuer*, and *Searcher*, the fleet carrier *Furious*, three more cruisers, and five destroyers. The two forces rendezvoused on April 2, and Admiral Fraser, having decided that a sortie by the *Tirpitz* was unlikely, advanced the attack date to the third.

While the commander in chief continued distant cover in the *Duke of York* with two destroyers, the carrier force, with the *Anson*, turned toward the Norwegian coast and made a brilliantly unobserved approach to their launching-off positions. At dawn on the third from the decks of the six carriers, the largest Fleet Air Arm striking force yet assembled roared off into the lightening sky towards Altenfiord. It consisted of two striking forces of Barracuda torpedo-bombers, a total of forty-two aircraft in all, with the Barracuda bombers being used as dive-bombers for this operation; between them, they carried a total of ten 1,600-pound bombs and sixty-six 500-pound bombs of the armor-piercing type while the remainder carried 500-pound M.C. bombs to decimate the antiaircraft crews. They were given a powerful fighter escort of forty Wildcat, twenty Hellcat, and twenty Corsair fighters.[71]

This great mass of aircraft reached Altenfiord completely undetected, encountering no fighter opposition, and little flak until after they had commenced their attacks. The results were impressive. Although it was fully realized that the bombs they carried were not powerful enough to sink the *Tirpitz* (her position ruled out torpedo-bomber attack), it had been hoped that some of the larger ones would penetrate to her vitals and cause enough damage to put her out of action for another long period.

Because of the nature of the target, the steep sides of the fiord, and the very keenness with which the young aircrew, at last after five years of war equipped with decent aircraft, threw themselves into their task and attacked much lower than the required 3,500 feet, none of the many direct hits did, in fact, penetrate the battleship's armored deck.

The first wave struck at 0530 just as the *Tirpitz* was getting underway to carry out further trials. Her captain had hardly any time to prepare his defenses before the aircraft were upon him, but watertight doors were closed and some light flak defences manned. Strafing by the fighters put most of the fire control out of action and so antiaircraft fire was largely ineffective. Thus, the first wave scored ten direct hits and one very near miss in under a minute.

This attack over, the damaged battleship was nudging back into her berth when the second wave came in at 6:30 A.M., and despite the fact that the barrage was heavier and the smoke screen more effective, they also succeeded in inflicting considerable damage, hitting the *Tirpitz* five more times. Only three Barracudas were lost in this brilliant attack, which left the *Tirpitz* afloat, but a charnel house above her armored decks, of dead and dying. More than 120 of her crew were killed in this attack and more than 300 more wounded. At first, the British thought the great carnage inflicted and the shambles made of the battleship's upperworks had put her out of action for another six month period, but in fact most of it was superficial and the *Tirpitz* was fully operational again after only three months.[72] Nonetheless, it was a wonderful debut by the new Fleet Air Arm.

A second attack had been mooted by the same ships, but Admiral Moore believed the *Tirpitz* had been harder hit than she in fact was and cancelled this; also the weather broke up which would have nullified any subsequent attempt anyway. The fleet returned to Scapa on the sixth to be met with rousing cheers. The First Sea Lord, Admiral Cunningham, was delighted to see this follow-up to Taranto, but in order for it to be effective, he wished to see a repeat attack before the Germans had time to recover, and, after some argument, the Home Fleet did indeed sortie again on April 21, but this attack proved abortive because of the weather and strikes against secondary targets were expensive with little to show.

Nonetheless, the damage inflicted enabled heavy ship cover to be dispensed with for the continuing Russian convoys for some time, and it was especially welcomed that the *Tirpitz* was inoperational because of the Normandy invasion in May when lack of sufficient flotilla craft at Scapa would have hindered Admiral Fraser had she come out.

The Home Fleet returned to Norwegian waters in May with two more attempts to interrupt the repair work the *Tirpitz* was undergoing, with just the *Victorious* and *Furious*, but both attempts were frustrated by weather or by early sighting by the enemy.

Meanwhile, at Scapa, the many great ships of the Overlord bombarding force were being worked up in readiness for June 6. "In April and May four battleships, twenty cruisers, two monitors and many destroyers were given special 'working-up' practices. Even these great bases, which had played such an important part in both world wars, can rarely have been more busy," wrote Captain Roskill.[73]

The battleships thus assigned to the bombardment role for the greatest of the Allied landings were the *Nelson, Rodney, Warspite,* and *Ramillies,* of which the latter two were to be employed initially with Rear-Admiral Patterson's Bombarding Squadron on D-Day itself and the two Nelsons, still earmarked for the East Indies, held in reserve and utilized as required later. The *Malaya* also was held in readiness in case needed. Thus, three old veterans, already "written off" in many people's minds, were again to come into their own for this, the most important event of 1944.

Even so, the Royal Navy had to request that the U.S. Navy send additional ships as reinforcement for the attack. This caused some heart-burn across the Atlantic, for Admiral King considered that the Home Fleet could have contributed more. The Americans did not appreciate the Admiralty's fears (seen to be groundless since then) that the *Admiral Scheer* and *Lützow,* along with two 8-inch and four 6-inch cruisers and destroyer forces might well be sent into the Channel against the invasion convoys, nor the need to maintain a strong force to watch the *Tirpitz,* which *might* have been ready for operations at this time. "To them, the retention of three modern battleships, six cruisers and half a score of destroyers seemed excessive," commented the official historian, who added that "when, however, in April 1944 the needs were fully explained to him, he agreed to send across three of his old battleships . . . which was more than we had originally asked for."[74] These three battleships were the *Arkansas*, *Nevada*, and *Texas*, which joined the Western Task Force in support of the American landings, under Rear Admiral Kirk.[75]

Finally, brief mention should be made of a final, but honorable, role that two even more elderly veterans found at Normandy—the old French *Courbet* being towed across and sunk as a blockship as one of the "Corncobs" for the Mulberry harbor breakwaters along with her equally aged British cousin, the *Centurion*, after her long voyages and many adventures in the Mediterranean earlier.

On the dawn of the great day, the *Warspite* and *Ramillies* moved up with the invasion fleet to take up their bombarding positions with the Eastern Task Force, opposite Sword beaches across from the mouth of the river Seine, having put out from Greenock the night before. The *Warspite*, firing three turret broadsides, was allocated the battery at Villerville which covered the southern flank of the river opposite Le Havre while the *Ramillies* took up position ahead of her and engaged the adjacent battery at Benerville. These batteries were massively protected with concrete and very difficult targets to neutralize for any length of time. Wrote Oscar Parkes:

> While "softening" from the air might knock out or damage some gun positions or batteries, block ammunition supplies and force dazed gunners to take shelter in deep dugouts, they could not destroy the "West Wall" upon which four years of slave labor had been spent. It was during this temporary 'heads down' period that naval units expected to close in and continue the process while the beach assault proceeded. Very thick reinforced concrete meant that nothing short of a direct hit or a shell through a casemate opening could knock a gun out.[76]

The *Warspite* opened fire around 5:30 A.M. against Benerville, "which had injudiciously planted a few shells near her," firing "blind" salvos, without spotters, and continuing to engage this target until 5:58. The *Ramillies* was likewise busily employed to good effect when, around 6:00, the German destroyer force based at Le Havre made a torpedo sortie against them. Both big ships promptly engaged these units who launched their torpedoes at long range and retired without scoring a hit. (The *Warspite* later claimed to have sunk one of these destroyers, her radar observers seeing one 15-inch hit on a destroyer, which disappeared.) This diversion over they resumed their main duties, and the *Warspite* was credited with three direct hits on the Villerville coastal battery soon after.

The *Warspite* continued to divide her attentions between the Villerville and Benerville batteries with the *Ramillies* throughout the day, hitting the former nine times out of seventy-three rounds. She also engaged mobile batteries brought up and knocked out a four gun battery completely. Between them the two battleships and the monitor *Roberts* kept the German heavy batteries mainly silenced throughout the day, while the cruisers and destroyers closed in to saturate the smaller gun positions in a deluge of shell.

Over in the American sector, the *Arkansas* was dealing in a similar manner with the Port-en-Bessin battery, the *Texas* engaged the large Ponte-du-Hoc position, and the *Nevada* dueled with the battery at Azeville. Everywhere save on the Omaha beachhead, the German gunners were silenced and the troops got ashore with astonishingly light casualties. Although as the official historian concedes, these powerful batteries were never completely demolished, the accuracy of the naval gunfire was a decisive element in the success of the operation and German Army reports give glowing testimony to the effect a deluge of heavy naval shells had on concentrations of troops and artillery attempting to re-group many miles behind the beachheads.

The big ships withdrew during the night and next morning they were back on station, the reserve ship *Rodney* joining in the action with considerable effect this day. "Then along came the *Rodney*," recalled the captain of the destroyer *Jervis*:

It was almost incredible to realise that we were off the enemy coast—it was more like Spithead. I had admired the *Rodney* all through the war; she had been one of the ships, which sunk the *Bismarck*, and her shooting on the Pedestal Malta convoy had been memorable. Now here she was, huge and ugly, running close to the shore and training her three triple sixteen-inch turrets ready to bombard. We reckoned some unsuspecting Huns about twenty miles away were going to get a nasty shock.[77]

They did.

We were given three targets altogether and we fired nearly two hundred rounds of 16-inch and a hundred rounds of 6-inch between half-past six and half-past eight in the evening. Each 16-inch shell weighs a ton and a third, and we were using high-explosive shells specially designed to do the maximum amount of damage, so it is not difficult to imagine the demoralizing effect on the enemy of these gigantic explosives fired from a ship nearly twenty miles away. Later in the day, we received the following situation report on our shooting: "Fire, effective, enabling Norfolk's to recapture position."

When this was passed to the ship's company, cheers rang out all round the ship and everyone went about his work with the lightest of hearts. It was one of the unforgettable moments in the *Rodney*'s history.[78]

And so the big ships continued throughout that week to break up enemy troop concentrations and strong-points and again and again returning to the stubborn casemate batteries when called upon by the army. The *Rodney* pulled out for a while, and the *Nelson* took her place thus keeping up the pressure continually.[79]

Throughout the whole of June the bombarding squadrons remained off the Normandy coast, ready to support the Army with their guns whenever the need arose. Ships returned to England to replenish their magazines or to replace worn-out guns; but until the advance inland had reached beyond the range of their guns a large force of battleships, cruisers, monitors and smaller vessels was continuously present and constantly in action. Sometimes ships shifted from one assault area to another, where the need was temporarily greater. Thus, the *Warspite* on her return from Portsmouth on June 10 went to support the Utah force, and engaged four different targets with her 15-inch guns to such good effect that the American army commander signaled his gratitude. Next day, she was in Gold area supporting the 50th Division, and again earned the soldiers' appreciation. The speed with which the great fire power of the heavy ships was repeatedly brought to bear on enemy concentrations certainly emphasized the benefits to be derived from employing warships as mobile heavy artillery.[80]

The great advantage that the *Nelson* and *Rodney* enjoyed was the enormous range at which they could accurately engage their targets. On the seventeenth, the *Rodney* laid down "devastating" fire on armored vehicles some seventeen miles inland south of Gold beach. Dönitz was informed that Rommel had complained to Hitler that the effects of the heavy naval guns made operations within their range "impossible," and the grand admiral was told to do something about it. Hitler saw the only possible relief for the land front in the elimination of enemy naval forces, primarily battleships. This came as a great awakening for him and for many in Britain. In truth, there was absolutely nothing that Dönitz could do about the British battleships; his U-boats were impotent off the beachhead and caused few losses. The biggest hazard the heavy ships had to face was the mine.

On June 13, the *Warspite* had worn out her main armament gun barrels after completing a fifty rounds 15-inch rapid fire' shoot in support of the

army and was sent to Rosyth to replace them, thus becoming the first capital
ship to pass through the Straits of Dover since the *Scharnhorst* and *Gneisenau*
two and a half years before. She evaded the long-range German guns by
blocking their radar but while passing through the swept channel off Harwich
she detonated a large mine, which put all her propeller shafts out of action.
After an hour, she was able to once again proceed but with a six-degree list to
port, and at seven knots under her own power, she managed to reach Rosyth
on the evening of the fourteenth.

"The new battleships *Anson* and *Howe* and other warships lying below the
Forth Bridge all 'cleared lower deck' to cheer the injured *Warspite* as she
slowly passed."[81] Some very temporary repair work was done which left her
with three shafts only, a maximum speed of fifteen knots, and she was pronounced fit for service once again after trials off Scotland, reaching Plymouth
on August 24. The next day, she was in action again off Brest against German
shore batteries holding up the Americans advancing on that port, firing some
147 rounds of her main armament and 66 rounds of armor-piercing shell
from a position north of Ushant, firing across the promontory. She was
engaged in return and near-missed but only suffered light splinter damage.
On September 10, she was back in action off Havre, engaging batteries at
32,000 yards range with the aid of air spotting.

In the interim, the *Ramillies* had fired 1,002 rounds of 15-inch shell at
the enemy fortifications. The *Nelson* had fired 224 16-inch shells and 687 6-
inch during the course of twenty bombardments between June 11 and 18,
and then she too was mined and seriously damaged. She ultimately had to be
sent across the Atlantic to the Philadelphia Navy Yard for repairs, which kept
her out of the war for more than six months and again delayed her journey
eastward, which had been first mooted in 1941.

Meanwhile, the *Malaya* had been commissioned again as a bombarding
ship and, after working up she moved over the Channel to replace these casualties. On September 1, she was in action against the heavy batteries mounted
on the Ile de Cézembre off St. Malo during which she turned in a remarkable
piece of shooting using air spotting. With her fourth salvo she scored a direct
hit on the battery and later shoots landed dead centre on the barracks at
maximum range.

On August 12, the *Rodney* again came into action against the German batteries on Alderney. On this occasion the battleship had fired indirectly over a
hill to reach the enemy guns. Roger Hill in the *Jervis* describes the operation:

> On August 12, we went to Portland and joined two old friends—one
> was the *Rodney* and the other the *Faulknor* with Bill Churchill still in
> command. We screened the *Rodney* to Cherbourg, where she

anchored near the peninsula and bombarded the twelve-inch guns, which were on Alderney. A Spitfire flew over the tops as the shells arrived and a lot of flak went up. The range was eighteen miles, and the *Rodney* signaled: "Spotting aircraft reported shots mostly centered on three Western guns, including direct hits. Fourth gun received near misses. No round more than four hundred yards from centre of target. Seventy-five rounds fired." The enemy guns were in open pits on the high ground in the centre of the island and had a range of twenty-six miles. They were the biggest guns in the heavily fortified Channel Islands and there was a similar battery on Guernsey.[82]

After the completion of this duty, the *Rodney* rejoined the Home Fleet at Scapa Flow. Here the fleet was again at a low ebb. Although the *Tirpitz* was still considered a menace, there was the need to get the modern battleships away to the Pacific to join in the war against Japan, and the *Howe* had already started out, while the *King George V* and *Anson* were refitting in readiness to join her. Only the *Duke of York* remained as flagship of the new commander in chief, Adm. Sir Henry Moore. Great efforts were now made to utilize the fleet carriers, while they were still available (the *Victorious* and *Indomitable* had already gone East and the others were to follow) in further attempts to cripple the *Tirpitz* now that she was again considered operational.

On July 17, the Home Fleet with the *Duke of York* (flag), *Formidable, Indefatigable, Furious,* and light forces launched another air strike, Operation Mascot but the improved German defense measures at Altenfiord gave them at least fifteen minutes' warning of the approach of the forty-four Barracudas and forty-eight fighters. They were met by a massive barrage, including thirty-nine rounds from her main armament directed by an observation post atop a nearby hill. By the time the aircraft arrived, the *Tirpitz* and her anchorage were almost completely hidden by the smoke screens and they had to bomb blind aiming at the flashes of her guns. A single near-miss was scored, doing no damage, and two aircraft were lost.

As if to emphasize that the threat to the Russian convoys was the same as it always had been, the *Tirpitz* herself put to sea for exercises with the five destroyers of the 4th Flotilla between July 31 and August 1. It was to prove her last operational voyage ever. The convoys themselves nonetheless recommenced with JW 59 on August 15, but this time had the added protection of a battleship for most of the journey as the old *Royal Sovereign* was in the vicinity.

The Russians had claimed at least one battleship as their share of the booty from the Italian surrender and this was agreed to unilaterally by Roosevelt, who always went out of his way to appease the Soviet leader in his every request despite Churchill's warnings. It had proven impracticable to implement this demand by sailing the *Guilio Cesare* from the Mediterranean to the Black Sea as the Germans still firmly held the Aegean, and so as a temporary measure, it was agreed to let the Soviets use the *Royal Sovereign* in her place until it could be done.[83] The Soviet crew had been brought back from Russia earlier in the year in a homeward convoy, and they recommissioned the old British veteran and renamed her *Arkhangelsk* on May 30. Along with eight equally aged ex-American four-stackers also to be transferred, she sailed with her 2,300 man crew under Admiral Levchenko and made for Kola, where she finally arrived, but not without incident, on August 24 having left JW 59 earlier on.[84]

The Home Fleet returned to the attack with a series of carrier strikes on August 22, 24, and 29, Operation Goodwood, with the *Duke of York* and the carriers *Indefatigable*, *Formidable*, and *Furious*, the escort carriers *Nabob* and *Trumpeter*, and light forces.

In the first attack by thirty-one Barracudas and fifty-three fighters, the bombers turned back due to bad weather, but the fighters pressed on, bombed through the smoke, but failed to score any hits. A smaller attack launched later the same day with Hellcat fighter-bombers also failed to hit the *Tirpitz*.

On the twenty-fourth, the heaviest strike made so far went in. Again they achieved some surprise but the heavy bombs of the Barracudas had to be released through the smoke. The defences were now much stronger and six aircraft were lost in this attack but they managed to score two hits. A 500-pound bomb struck the roof of B turret, causing slight damage, and a 1,600-pound armor-piercing bomb hit perfectly, just forward of the bridge on the port side.

This bomb penetrated the upper deck and the main armored deck, boring down eight levels through almost six inches of steel armor plate to reach the lower platform deck. Had it gone off here, the damage could have been devastating, and the *Tirpitz* would have been seriously damaged, maybe even sunk. It did not, and when the Germans later examined it they found out why. Instead of 215 pounds of explosive, the bomb contained only 100 pounds. Captain Roskill states that this was "a convincing example of how a failure in manufacture can prejudice an operation of war."[85]

But even though all this gallant effort failed to sink the *Tirpitz*, the combination of the midget submarine attacks and the Fleet Air Arm poundings had in fact, over the year, effectively finished the *Tirpitz* as a fighting unit. She was out of the war for good but the British didn't realise it and kept up the attacks.

The fourth strike was mounted on August 29 by sixty aircraft; again, the Germans were ready for them and covered the area with smoke. Two aircraft were lost and no hits made. The carriers returned to Scapa and their achievements were subsequently classed as "intensely disappointing." They didn't realize that the job was in fact over and had been for some time now.

To protect the next pair of convoys to Russia, the *Rodney* was allocated to escort them right through to Kola Inlet, and here she was inspected by Admiral Golovko. This operation proved to be the last of the war for the *Rodney*. "The ship creaked and groaned her stately way through the waters. She was getting on in years now and was rather proud that she could add North Russia to all her other journeys," wrote her biographer, and indeed, she was but was still in fighting trim, and there was much speculation about whether the *Tirpitz* would come out against her. But the *Tirpitz* could not, even had she so wished. The *Tirpitz* was finished.[86]

CHAPTER 9

The Great Ships Pass

In the Mediterranean, new developments were underway and preparations well advanced for the Allied landings on the southern coast of France, Operation Dragoon. Although the usefulness of this operation was questioned at the time, and seen in perspective it seems a total waste of valuable resources, the Americans were insistent upon it taking place. It was known that the assault area was strongly defended since it stood to the north of the great naval bases of Toulon and Nice, and the attack forces were therefore duly reinforced by the experienced bombardment ships that had been employed off Normandy. Thus, the battleship *Ramillies*, along with the American *Arkansas*, *Nevada*, and *Texas*, and several Allied cruisers and destroyers, were all transferred to the Mediterranean during July in readiness for the assault on this former holiday playground.

In addition to the fixed-gun defenses along the coast, the Germans had been busily reinforcing them with guns of the heaviest caliber—some salvaged from the French battleships scuttled at Toulon in 1942—and they were expected to provide formidable opposition. The *Ramillies* was assigned to Rear Admiral Mansfield's fire-support squadron; the French battleship *Lorraine* also joined the four Allied capital ships for the operation showing that (along with the *Richelieu* at Scapa) the remains of this fleet were once more actively back in the war and pulling their weight.

The landings took place on August 15, 1944, and were completely successful. The strongest coastal defenses were along the sides of the Gulf of St. Tropez, and these were the special targets assigned to the *Ramillies*, *Nevada*, and *Texas*. The *Ramillies* carried out good shoots at Port Cros also, to the south of this area in support of the army, which was soon firmly ashore.

As the main objectives of Toulon and Marseilles were tackled toward the end of the month, the heavy ships were again called upon to tackle the formidable batteries guarding the approaches to Toulon. These emplacements included a pair of twin 13.5-inch mountings on the St. Mandrier peninsula, and to reduce these, Admiral Davidson was allocated the American *Nevada* and the French *Lorraine*, but soon the experienced *Ramillies* was sent to reinforce this squadron and added her 15-inch salvos to the pounding on August 25.

Nonetheless, these defenses proved tough opponents and very hard to silence completely. Once again, the old lessons of ships against shore batteries seemed to swing back against the latter. Some 147 shoots were carried out against the St. Mandrier batteries, but they did not finally surrender until the twenty-eigth, the day after French troops had entered Toulon itself, and one of the four guns was still in use then. With the final clearing of the town, the *Lorraine* led a French squadron into the port of Toulon in a ceremonial return of the French Navy to its principal base on September 13.

Thus, the Mediterranean Sea ceased to be a battleground for the capital ships of the Royal Navy and the entire long struggle from June 1940 had left this great sea clear. Its waters now again functioned as a short-sea route to the Far East for the buildup of Allied fleets there for the final battles.

Only once more did the waters of the Mediterranean ring and vibrate to the sound of a British battleship's main armament fired in anger, and that was when the *King George V*, on her way to the Indian Ocean via the Suez Canal, was diverted to lend the weight of her guns to the reduction of the isolated German garrisons in the Aegean. In November 1944, she engaged the powerful Lakida gun battery on the island of Milos after an Allied landing force had been defeated and forced to withdraw. Despite the pounding she gave them, the German garrisons here, as elsewhere in the Aegean Sea, remained true to their past form, tough and resilient, and they never surrendered. They were sealed up as being too hard a nut to expend lives on and left there.

The decision to rebuild Admiral Somerville's strength in the Indian Ocean during 1944 had dependended upon events in home waters, and until then, his fleet was only slowly reinforced. By the end of January, he had on station the *Renown* (flag), *Queen Elizabeth*, and *Valiant*, along with the new carrier *Illustrious* and light forces. He needed more, much more, and had only two carriers to work with his fleet, having accomplished this by using the *Unicorn* in an operational role for which she had not been truly designed; she nevertheless worked well.

After the great run down of 1943, however, this was more like a fleet, and it was hoped that some form of limited offensive operations could now be carried out against the vulnerable western edge of the Japanese defense perimeter, thus aiding the Americans, who were tackling it head-on from the east. This proved illusory, however. Increased pressure in the Pacific saw the arrival at Singapore of a Japanese fleet of five battleships, three carriers, eighteen cruisers, and light forces. Although a renewed sortie into the Indian Ocean was not the object of this concentration—for they were refitting and preparing themselves for the next decisive battle in the Pacific (which turned out to be the defeat at the Philippine Sea)—they presented a force that Admiral Somerville in 1944, no more than in 1942, felt unable to tackle with his ships as they were.

Instead, a period of intensive training was undertaken while awaiting reinforcements. As soon as he was ready Admiral Mountbatten wished Somerville to start striking with his fleet at the Japanese oil refineries in Sumatra and to assist him, the U.S. Navy again came to the rescue by supplementing his meager air strength with the carrier *Saratoga*. Two escort carriers also arrived on station at this time.

On March 21, Somerville sailed with the *Renown, Queen Elizabeth, Valiant,* and *Illustrious* to both meet the *Saratoga* and try to locate a Japanese cruiser squadron that had been raiding the Middle East-to-Australia convoy route with some success. They also carried out an important refueling at sea exercise, something in which the Royal Navy lagged behind the American and German navies quite considerably, and upon which the future planned operations of the British Pacific Fleet would depend enormously. The whole fleet returned to Trincomalee on April 2 and commenced planning the Sumatra attack.

This operation, timed to coincide with Gen. Douglas MacArthur's assault on Hollandia, was set in motion on April 16. By this time, further reinforcements, in the shape of the French battleship *Richelieu* and the Dutch cruiser *Tromp,* had arrived. Somerville's force had an international air about it as it put to sea flying his flag aboard the *Queen Elizabeth* and accompanied by the *Renown, Valiant,* and *Richelieu* for his battle squadron, the *Illustrious* and *Saratoga* for air, six cruisers, and fourteen destroyers.

This fleet arrived unheralded in its flying-off position some 100 miles southwest of Sabang on the northeast tip of Sumatra on the nineteenth, and at 5:30 A.M., the launching of a strike force of forty-six bombers and thirty-seven fighters began. They achieved complete surprise over the target area and inflicted great damage on oil installations and the enemy's home airfields, although the harbour area was barren of shipping. A counterstrike by a few torpedo-bombers was easily dealt with by the *Saratoga*'s experienced air group, and the whole mission cost only one fighter, whose pilot was rescued by a British submarine.

The *Saratoga* was now recalled to the Pacific, but Somerville was determined to use her once more, and the same ships carried out a similar attack against Soerabaya on May 17 after refueling in Exmouth Gulf. Again, surprise was complete, resistance was minimal, and much damage was done to installations. After parting company with the *Saratoga*, the Eastern Fleet returned to Ceylon in high fettle, having steamed over 7,000 miles in three weeks.

In these operations, as in the air strikes against the *Tirpitz*, it is to be remarked that the battleships played a subordinate role and that the actual fighting was done exclusively by the aircraft from the carriers. That this marked the decline of the battleship from the main protagonist to that of a support vessel would appear an obvious conclusion to draw, and it had its parallels in the Pacific also. Here, as in Europe, the older battleships were mainly used in the bombardment role while the modern battleships accompanied the carrier groups and gave them the colossal support of their myriad anti-aircraft batteries, while awaiting, usually in vain, for their chance to engage the battle line of the enemy.

That the battleship no longer held center stage did not mean, however, that it was thereby rendered completely unnecessary and useless as has been the general verdict of history. The battleship's role might have been merely passive in these instances but it still remained a vital part of a well-balanced fleet. One must ask what would have happened to Admiral Moore's carriers off Norway if, while their aircraft were striking at Altenfiord, one or both of the German pocket battleships, or even heavy cruisers, had appeared on the scene and they had no battleship with them for surface protection. The example of the *Glorious* is the answer that brooks no further arguments. The same can be said of Somerville's carriers off Sumatra if they had run into the five battleships from Singapore, or even the three heavy cruisers that had been active in those waters earlier. It was the interdependence of the battleship and the fleet carrier that should be noted here; each relied on the other for different reasons, and the combination of both in sufficient numbers was unbeatable.

Lest it be argued that the war in the central Pacific showed otherwise or that the carrier could operate without the battleship with complete immunity but that the battleship could not do so without the carrier, as is widely accepted, the battle of Leyte Gulf gave a convincing demonstration that this was not the case, and there were to be other examples.

The strength of the Japanese Navy at this period, after the Philippine Sea battle, was still formidable. Indeed, its battleship strength was hardly impaired at all at this time, while its numbers of carriers were still greater than on the outbreak of the war, although its aircrews were sadly diluted and inferior in expertise.[1]

Large though these forces were, they paled beside the enormous strength of the rebuilt might of the U.S. Navy in the Pacific, which could deploy ten old battleships on bombardment duties, six to eight brand-new ones for fleet duties, and up to sixteen fleet and light fleet carriers organized in four task forces—in addition to scores of escort carriers, modern cruisers of all types, and hundreds of brand-new destroyers. By the summer of 1944, American naval forces in the Pacific exceeded the combined totals of every other navy in the world in size, power, expertise, and organization. There could be little doubt about the ultimate outcome of a major fleet engagement, but the Japanese, unlike the Germans and the Italians, built their warships to be used and had few reservations about using them to the maximum extent. There would be no skulking in harbor for the battleships of Japan.

The great strength of the U.S. Navy led to some disagreement among the Allies as to whether it was either necessary or desirable for the British Pacific Fleet to take its place beside the Americans in the final operations against Japan. It is not the place to go into the many discussions and arguments, involving as they did national prestige, shortage of support shipping, Anglo-American rivalry and other factors, save to record that, ultimately, the participation of the British Pacific Fleet was finally agreed to and that it worked splendidly in the event.[2]

British hopes of mounting large-scale amphibious offensives across the Indian Ocean to recapture Burma—and, ultimately, Malaya—were frustrated by Operation Dragoon, which used up all the vital landing ships, and so the Eastern Fleet continued to build up its experience with a continuation of the carrier raids. These gave the ships of the Pacific Fleet vital training and expertise in readiness for the more protracted operations in their destined area of battle, but although they did considerable damage to the limited Japanese oil reserves in Southeast Asia they failed utterly to draw their strength away from the vital battleground, which now became the Philippines themselves as the Americans prepared for their assault. Some in the fleet at the time, counseled attacking large the few remaining Japanese tankers instead as a more direct means of obliterating Japan's ability to use what oil there was, but this was rejected in favor of the grander gesture.

Thus, on June 20, carrier strikes were made on Port Blair in the Andaman Islands with the *Illustrious*. With the arrival of the *Indomitable* and *Victorious* in July, Somerville could once more plan a more powerful attack, again choosing the island base of Sabang, which he planned to put out of action with a bombardment by the fleet while his carrier aircraft neutralized the surrounding Japanese air bases.

To carry out Operation Crimson, Somerville sailed from Ceylon with his strongest fleet to date. Flying his flag in the *Queen Elizabeth*, Admiral Somerville would have his chance to strike an offensive blow before he hauled down his flag and took up his new appointment in Washington. As well as his flagship, Somerville had, as before, a powerful battle line with the

Renown, Valiant, and *Richelieu,* the *Illustrious* and *Victorious,* one heavy and six light cruisers, and ten destroyers.

The East Indies fleet sailed on July 22, and at dawn on the twenty-fifth, the carriers began flying off their aircraft to attack the airfields and provide spotters for the heavy ships. Eighty Corsairs and nine Barracudas achieved complete surprise, but poor weather conditions hindered their effectiveness and they found few targets. While a standing fighter patrol of twelve aircraft was kept over the fleet, eight more fighters took up their positions to spot targets for the heavy guns of the battle fleet while the destroyers made a "spectacular" gun and torpedo attack on the harbor entrance in grand style.

This was the first real opportunity that the ships of the First Battle Squadron had had to hit back at the Japanese, and they did so with considerable gusto. The fleet's heavy guns opened fire at ranges of 18,000 yards on the harbor and shore installations, doing great damage although, once more, there were few merchant ships to provide targets. However, oil tanks and repair shops were demolished to good effect and the return fire from the shore was ineffective. It was a highly satisfactory close to Admiral Somerville's hitherto frustrating period of command and must have brought back memories of Genoa as the *Renown*'s 15-inch salvos crashed out.

The return of the fleet to Ceylon followed and the heavy ships took the opportunity to refit and refurbish in readiness for the next series of operations. The *Renown* refitted at Durban in December, rejoining the fleet in March. The *Queen Elizabeth* also refitted there during October and November and then returned to become the flagship of the Third Battle Squadron, flying the flag of Vice Admiral Wake-Walker. The *Valiant* was the first to be docked, at Trincomalee, but this resulted in disaster. She was in the floating dock there on August 8 when it suddenly collapsed and sank. The unfortunate *Valiant,* which had been rebuilding at the start of the war, had spent a long period out of action following her mining at Alexandria in December 1941, was now out of action again, for three of her A brackets were broken as the dock buckled.

Repairs to this valuable ship were out of the question there and she accordingly had to sail for home. Her misadventures did not end there however. On her way home she grounded at the entrance to the Suez Canal because of her exceptionally deepened draught from previous rebuilding. She was stuck fast for six-and-a-half hours, "one way of spending Trafalgar Day," and finally had to complete her long voyage home via the Cape. Once back in Britain, she embarked on a prolonged refit which lasted until the end of the war, "a refit which seems to have been somewhat unnecessary," for she took no further part in the fighting.[3]

Meanwhile, further reinforcements for the Pacific Fleet were arriving under Admiral Fraser, and in November, the ships on station were divided into the Pacific Fleet and the East Indies Fleet. The *King George V*, followed by the *Howe*, arrived at Ceylon toward the end of 1944.

Meanwhile, various operations continued to work up the carrier air groups and the heavy ships' gunners. These included air strikes by the *Victorious* and *Indomitable* on Sumatra in August and mid-September. These were followed by more forceful measures in Operation Millet, when, on October 15, the main fleet operated against the Nicobar Islands as a diversion to the American landings on Leyte in the Philippines.

Admiral Power operated between the seventeenth and nineteenth of that month with his flag in the *Renown*, with the carriers *Indomitable* and *Victorious*, heavy cruisers *London*, *Cumberland*, and *Suffolk*, light cruiser *Phoebe*, and eleven destroyers. While the carriers launched air strikes, the heavy cruisers bombarded strong points ashore, and on the eighteenth, the *Renown* joined in these bombardments before proceeding to Durban as recounted.

While the British Pacific Fleet was still in the process of formation, the battleships of America and Japan were clashing again in the greatest naval battle in history, Leyte Gulf. This vast battle extended across hundreds of miles of ocean and involved vast forces on both sides and can only be summarized here briefly.[4]

The Japanese had watched in dismay as first their "outer" and then their "inner" defense bastions in the Pacific had either been overrun or cut off and made useless by the great leapfrogging advances of the Americans. They still had their fleet, but their vital oil supplies, for which they had gone to war in the first place, lay south of the Philippines and a fleet, army, and air force without those supplies would not be able to last but, nor indeed would their homeland. The retention of the Philippines was therefore considered vital to their cause and they decided that they must finally use every ship they had in its defense. They evolved the usual complicated plans for such an eventuality, which called on their fleet to make one final all-out effort to destroy the American invasion convoys as they lay off the beachheads.

They still had a formidable carrier force but hardly any aircraft or fully trained pilots to man it. Carriers without aircraft, as has been pointed out before in this volume, are merely useless targets. The Japanese fully realized this; all their newly trained squadrons had been decimated by the American carrier aircraft in wide-ranging strikes across the South China Sea and on Formosa so they decided to use their useless aircraft carriers merely as bait to lure away the powerful American Fleet to the north.

The battleship—on the Japanese side anyway—had once more resumed its main role as the principal unit of sea power. While Admiral Ozawa, with his four carriers and the battleships *Ise* and *Hyuga*, which had been fitted with flight-decks aft, feinted in from the north and drew upon themselves the full fury of the American airmen their main striking forces would close on the Leyte beach-head from the north, via the Sibuyan Sea and the San Bernardino Strait, and the south, through the Mindanao Sea and the Surigao Strait.

Their command structure was complicated and to force these two entrances and annihilate the assembled troop shipping off the Leyte Gulf beachhead, three separate forces were involved. Under that resolute fighter of old, Admiral Kurita, was the Central Force, which contained the main surface strength of five battleships—the *Yamato, Musashi, Nagato, Kongo,* and *Haruna*—twelve heavy and light cruisers, and fifteen destroyers. From the south came Nishimura with the battleships *Fuso* and *Yamashiro*, one heavy cruiser, and four destroyers, supported by Admiral Shima's squadron of three cruisers and four destroyers.

If Ozawa's decoy operation was successful, all that would stand between the seven battleships and light forces would be the ships of the supporting force, and although these were, on paper, of formidable strength,[5] the ships of the 7th Fleet were equipped mainly for shore support operations and thus supplies of armor- piercing shell for the old American battleships, and AP bombs for the escort carriers present were limited and they would have to combat the Japanese ships with HE instead. The Japanese plan was complicated, but in the event, it almost worked perfectly.

Adm. William Halsey commanded the Third Fleet—Task Force 38— which was organized into four task groups, but one of these was away replenishing when the battle broke and could not immediately rejoin. It was a formidable array of fighting power, one that could crush the Japanese fleet with ease if allowed to. It was organized in three groups during the preliminary operations east of the Philippines about 125 miles, but could be quickly concentrated if the need arose. It totaled six battleships—the *Washington, Massachusetts, Alabama, New Jersey* (flag), *Indiana,* and *Iowa*—eleven fleet and light fleet carriers, two heavy and seven light cruisers, and about fifty destroyers.

Early information of the impending Japanese attack came from submarine patrols west of the Philippines on October 23, which between them sank two heavy cruisers and damaged a third but this failed to deter the Japanese. Air searches were flown on the twenty-fourth to locate these forces, but although they sighted both Japanese battleship groups, Ozawa's decoy force remained unallocated. Meanwhile, shore-based air strikes hit the American Fleet and sank the carrier *Princeton*. Seventy aircraft from Ozawa's carriers— all he could muster—supplemented these attacks, and all but thirty were destroyed; but they drew Halsey's attention northward as it was intended they should. By the time the Americans had located the Japanese carrier force, it was too late to launch air-striking forces against them.

It seemed that the Japanese plan had failed already, for throughout the twenty-fourth, it was the main battleship force of Kurita that was subjected to heavy and prolonged air attack by the American task groups. The Japanese squadron had to fight these out alone, for hardly any shore-based fighters were allocated to their defence. Their antiaircraft armaments had been supplemented accordingly, and they put up a heavy flak barrage. Against the scale of attack to which they were subjected, however, this was not sufficient. A heavy cruiser was damaged and sent back, but the most severe loss to the Japanese was the giant battleship *Musashi.*

Her loss certainly confirmed the trend of the war so far for not even the largest battleship could survive prolonged air attack without adequate fighter protection. The scale of punishment she took before going down was only a small compensation to the enemy against the unpalatable fact that she was destroyed by air attack alone. She certainly stood up far better than the *Prince of Wales* (although the latter was only half her displacement, it must be recalled).

In the first attack, she received slight damage from two near-miss bombs, which merely flooded two small tanks. At the same time, however, she was hit by a torpedo (Japanese sources say three torpedoes) on her starboard side, which resulted in a slight list, which was corrected by counterflooding. These hits did not impair her fighting capacity. The second attack came at 11:40 A.M. Two bombs hit her in this assault, one on the forecastle, which failed to explode, and the second penetrated her upperworks to a port engine compartment, which had to be abandoned. She also took another torpedo hit, this time to port, which flooded a hydraulic machinery space and flooded a port engine room. Again, Japanese reports state that a total of three torpedo hits were made in this attack, all on the port side. The net result of this attack was the loss of her port inboard shaft but the revs on the other three were increased to compensate for this and she stayed in line. A third attack at 12·15 scored only a single near-miss by a heavy bomb, but another torpedo slammed into her. This blow was absorbed with little damage other than that she was down by the bows slightly.

The *Musashi* was still in good fighting condition when the fourth attack developed around 12:50. This attack was much more deadly and no less than four direct hits resulted. The first hit forward, penetrating three decks and exploding in a crew compartment but caused little damage. The second bomb passed through two decks before detonation, but again damage was slight. Number three hit was similar, gouging through two decks and exploding below but failing to penetrate the armored citadel of the ship while the fourth bomb exploded on impact close to the funnel destroying some light antiaircraft positions.

The real damage was done, as always, by the torpedoes. Four certain hits are known to have been scored in this attack, all on her starboard side. The first two opened up her storeroom spaces to flooding but were not serious. The flooding was not increasing, however, and the third torpedo added to it by opening up the starboard hydraulic machinery room. The fourth torpedo caused no damage but the combined effects of the six torpedo hits so far taken had caused her bows to lower until they were almost submerged. She reduced speed to sixteen knots and was left behind by the rest of the force.

The *Musashi* survived a fifth attack at 1:20 although she was now a sitting duck and was almost left to her own devices, with her speed down to twelve knots and the flooding still not rectified. The final blows fell on her in the sixth attack, which developed around 3:20 as she was painfully trying to struggle to safety. One bomb burst atop her fore turret but did no damage— not surprisingly since it had almost eleven inches of armored steel to penetrate. This bomb was followed by nine more direct hits in quick succession. One penetrated the forecastle, another exploded in the ships wardroom, two fell almost together damaging extensively her superstructure while a further pair fell together into the main deck spaces destroying many radio rooms. A bomb exploded against her armored bridge tower while another, hitting the top of this citadel, badly wounded her captain.

A final bomb struck the rear of the tower but did little damage. Although this massive concentration had caused considerable carnage to her upperworks, experience with the *Tirpitz* had shown that this was not sufficient to destroy a modern battleship. Her death blows were once again administered by the Avenger torpedo bombers of the Third Fleet, which, with muchreduced flak now that she was on her own, punished her unmercifully.

During this final attack, it is estimated that the *Musashi* absorbed a further *ten* torpedoes, two of which, it is true, failed to detonate. One hit abreast her fore turret flooding two magazines; another caused further flooding to port. Others opened up her fire room and port outer engine room while another flooded her antiaircraft magazines forward on her starboard side; three others to port and one to starboard cannot be confirmed with accuracy, for by this time, the great vessel was clearly doomed. At the end of this attack, she had a ten-degree list to port with the forecastle underwater, and her speed was down to six knots.

By 7:00 P.M., the water was lapping at the foot of A turret, and her list had increased to fifteen degrees. Attempts to beach her on one of the large islands in the Sibuyan Sea failed, and at 7:35, her list became uncontrollable, and she finally rolled over on her port side going under bows first. Her loss has been given in some detail because it reflects the enormous concentration of effort that had to be devoted to putting down such a ship by air attack. In all, some 259 aircraft had attacked Kurita's force during the twenty-fourth, and besides the sinking of the *Musashi* and the damage to the cruiser *Myoko*, they scored only two bomb hits on the *Yamato* and two on the *Nagato*, while the *Haruna* was near-missed five times. None of these vessels was impaired by these, and Kurita's force was not stopped.

The returning American carrier pilots gave somewhat exaggerated reports of the damage they had inflicted, and when Kurita reversed course for two hours to mark time while Ozawa drew the weight off him, Halsey was convinced that the Japanese had been defeated and were in flight—"no longer," he believed, "a serious menace" to Kinkaid's 7th Fleet off the beaches. The fast carriers and battleships of the 3rd Fleet therefore hauled round and headed north in pursuit of Ozawa as planned, in order to destroy him on the twenty-fifth. Kurita turned back toward the San Bernardino Strait at 5:00 P.M., and that strait was now wide open.

Meanwhile, the smaller force coming up through the Mindanao Sea straight into the Surigao Strait was carefully plotted, and Admiral Kinkaid was left to deal with it. In the immortal words of the American admiral in command of the old battleships of the bombarding force, the U.S. 7th Fleet was not going to "give a sucker an even break." As night fell, Kinkaid made his dispositions. Patrol torpedo boats (PT boats, the equivalent of the British MTB) and destroyers were sent down the sides of the natural trap to deliver massed torpedo attacks from both sides while across the narrow exit steamed the stately forms of his battleships, their great turrets trained into the darkness, ready across the Japanese T to pour in a devastating hail of armor-piercing shells. Into this wall of fire obligingly steamed both Nishimura and Shima.

At 3:00 A.M. on the twenty-fifth, the blackness was opened up as the PT boats launched their first salvos at the oncoming Japanese ships, and one scored a hit on the *Fuso*. She kept coming on. Ten minutes later, another torpedo struck the *Yamashiro*, but she absorbed this without pausing and pressed on into the trap. An hour later, destroyers joined in the carnage and salvo after salvo of torpedoes swished out of their tubes across the narrow straits and into the Japanese formation.

At 3:25, the *Yamashiro* received another hit, but she kept doggedly on. At 3:45, the *Fuso* was struck by one or more torpedoes, which penetrated one of the main magazines. She blew up with an enormous explosion, broke in half, and drifted blazing down the straits sinking later close by Dinagat Island. Further destroyer attacks followed, decimating the ranks of the Japanese squadron until only the *Yamashiro* and the cruiser *Mogami* survived, both damaged, with a solitary and untouched destroyer, the *Shigure*.

At 3:50, the cruisers and battleships of Admiral Elmendorf's waiting battle line opened fire and for twenty minutes poured an overwhelming weight of heavy shell into the two Japanese ships at point-blank range, to which the Japanese could make little reply. The *Yamashiro* was torn apart by heavy shell hits, and the *Mogami* was turned into a flaming inferno. Both ships tried to turn back, but by this time, it was too late, and at 4:19, the battleship capsized, a charnel house of destruction that took to the bottom her obstinate admiral and most of her crew.

The *Mogami* survived a little longer, and creeping away a mass of flame, she almost collided with a cruiser of Shima's force, which now came upon the scene of the earlier carnage. She survived this but finally went down that morning north of Mindanao. Not surprisingly, Shima deemed it prudent not to follow Nishimura's suicidal advance and turned back, but that did not save him from losing another cruiser.

The southern attack then had been decisively beaten, and the old battleships had played their full part in the victory. Their modern sisters were to be denied the chance to share in the honors, for Halsey had taken them with him as he sped off north in pursuit of Ozawa's phantoms. He had earlier signaled that the six modern battleships under Admiral Lee were to be formed into a special task force to take on Kurita's heavy ships at San Bernardino as Oldendorff had at Surigao. The wording is important: "will be formed" did not mean that it had been formed, only that it would be if circumstances called for it. But believing his airmen's reports, Halsey no longer considered this necessary. He therefore wanted the battleships with him to give his carriers their antiaircraft protection in the expected main carrier duel with Ozawa, and away they sailed.

During the chase, Halsey did indeed form the fast battleships into a special task group at 2:45 A.M., but their role was not now to take on Kurita, who was thought now to be in full flight, but to proceed ahead of the carriers and gobble up the cripples from Ozawa's fleet that the American bombers would leave in their wake in the morning. This would have reaped a rich harvest also, for the carrier strikes conducted throughout the early morning of the twenty-fifth sank the carrier *Chitose* but left the other three Japanese aircraft carriers in a damaged state.

The fast battleships were now scenting their prey, and by 11:00, they had pushed on at top speed and were within forty miles of Ozawa's ships, and as their guns ranged twenty miles, they were within hours of reversing the course of Pacific naval fighting and becoming the first battleship force to annihilate a whole enemy carrier group. Ozawa certainly had no aircraft to prevent this happening; his decks were almost empty. While the *Ise* and *Hyuga* might have put up some resistance, they could not have lasted against the mass fire of six of the most powerful battleships in history. Alas, this did not happen, for as the American battleships closed the last few miles, the ether was buzzing with frantic calls for help from farther south. Kurita had broken free from San Bernardino far astern and was closing fast on the beachhead.

Here Oldendorf's battleships after their night victory now began frantically embarking what remained of the limited stocks of armor-piercing shells, but time was not on their side. As Kurita's great ships steamed down the eastern coast of Samar, nothing stood between him and the massed transports and the mountain of war materiel on the beaches other than the little escort carriers of Admiral Sprague's support force. Kurita was therefore faced with an opportunity to do as Halsey—annihilate a carrier force with his battleships and then bring the whole operation to a glorious conclusion by wreaking havoc among the invasion fleet. He failed to do so.

Instead, apparently mistaking the little escort carriers for fleet carriers (part of the 3rd Fleet), he acted with extreme caution, and although his ships were twice as fast as the Americans, he made a slow, deliberate encircling movement to cut them off instead of closing right away and finishing it quickly. As a result, the carriers were able to launch air strikes as fast as the planes could be reloaded, and although they could not sink the battleships, they caused great damage to their exposed gun positions with the bombs and strafing, and even managed to sink three heavy cruisers when torpedoes became available.

By contrast, the huge shells of the Japanese battleships sank only one carrier, the *Gambier Bay*, and damaged others before a gallant destroyer attack caused them to sheer away for a while. Having fended this off, Kurita was even more cautious, and after turning in a huge circle without even penetrating Leyte Gulf, he started his withdrawal at 9:25 A.M. By 9:45, all firing had ceased, and the escort carriers and invasion fleet had been spared.

Kurita's decision was as fatal to his cause as Yamamoto's had been at Midway two and a half years earlier. All the self-sacrifice of Nishimura and Ozawa was thrown away with victory in his grasp. As he called off his battleships and set sail north, far away beyond Luzon, Halsey was doing the same to his battleships. In a futile gesture he now regrouped them and sent them south, but it was far to late to intercept Kurita now, and so the six modern capital ships of the 3rd Fleet spent the entire battle steaming at high speed in pursuit of two enemy fleets without sighting either one of them. It was a terrible waste of striking power and one opportunity that was never to return. Air strikes from the 3rd Fleet carriers were resumed, sinking two more carriers and finishing off one of the cripples. Besides sinking these four carriers, they dispatched a destroyer, and a submarine sank a cruiser, but the *Ise* and *Hyuga*, albeit damaged, made good their escape. And so did Kurita, losing another cruiser on the way.

Despite the misuse of the fast battleships, it had been a striking victory for the Americans—so overwhelming that the Japanese Navy could never again offer a serious threat to the American advance, and it was achieved with remarkably light casualties on the American side.[6]

At Leyte Gulf, the battleship had resumed a greater measure of importance than before, but despite this, most of the sinkings had been achieved by aircraft, which led to some rather questionable conclusions being drawn by postwar historians. For example, one British writer later concluded: "In the vast and complex battle of Leyte Gulf, the principle was the same. Here, in the southern sector of the fight rival surface-ships did come within gun-range, but the carrier-borne plane was by far the main weapon, and the American victory was won when, again, the only four Japanese carriers present were sunk—from the air."[7] I cannot agree with this analysis. The Japanese carriers were there, from the start, as decoys only. The fact that they were sunk was no doubt satisfactory, but even had their diversion succeeded and they made clear their escape without loss, it would have had no effect on the outcome of the battle, for they had no aircraft left. The battle was really decided by Oldendorf's six old battleships at Surigao and Kurita's indecision off Samar.

Another historian greatly critical of the battleship's role tends to agree with this: "It seems, however, that the pendulum had swung too far. Although the war in the Pacific had shown that aircraft over the sea had replaced the battleship as the 'unit of sea power' this did not mean that battleships were impotent. Indeed in this battle they re-established their reputations to quite an extent at the expense of the carrier."[8] As we have seen, they almost achieved two complete victories over carrier forces—one Japanese but impotent, the other American, although not the main force. Be that as it may, he concludes that: "Half the Japanese attacking force had to be left to surface ships to deal with and in the event these proved a more effective stopping agent than aircraft."[9]

Whatever the final verdict on this difference of opinion, it seems clear now that this battle did, in fact, mark the swan song of the classic line-of-battle tactic that had dominated naval thinking for centuries. As Captain Roskill concluded:

Throughout the whole course of the war of 1939–45, only one other battle—that fought by Admiral Cunningham off Cape Matapan on March 28, 1941—bears a resemblance to that which took place in the Surigao Strait three and a half years later; and it seems certain that those two actions will mark the end of the long influence of the "line of battle" on naval warfare, which dates from the seventeenth century.[10]

Nor was this smashing defeat the end of their woes for the Japanese, for their losses continued from other causes, chief of which were the marauding American submarines. On November 21, one of these scored the first success against a Japanese heavy ship by sinking the *Kongo* and a destroyer off northwest Formosa. With the fleet destroyed only the Kamikazes gave them any hope of restoring the balance, but they could not prevent the fall of the Philippines even though they caused serious damage to many of the American warships in the months that followed. For example, on May 7, the battleship *New Mexico*, in which Adm. Sir Bruce Fraser was observing operations, was struck by one of these aircraft in her superstructure, and he was lucky to escape. No doubt it gave him food for thought for his ships were soon to face the same enemy.

With the oil-producing parts of her empire cut off from the home islands, even what heavy ships the Japanese Navy still had left were made largely inoperational through lack of fuel, just as their counterparts in the Italian and German fleets had been earlier, and they were lain up in home waters to await their final missions. The die was now cast, but before concluding the final story of the defeat of Japan and the part played in it by the Allied battleships, we must retrace our steps once more to trace the fate of the heavy ships left in European waters as the war in that theater drew to its conclusion.

At home, the older ships were now going into retirement, having reached the end of their working lives. The *Resolution* had been part of the *Imperieuse* stokers training establishment in Gairloch and then Southampton before settling finally at Devonport. Here in May 1944, she was joined by her sister, the *Revenge*. The *Malaya* and *Ramillies* both completed their final commissions in 1944 as bombardment ships, and on May 15, 1945, they became part of the Torpedo School at HMS *Vernon*, Portsmouth, being collectively known as *Vernon II*, and used as accommodation ships. The *Valiant* continued refitting, but on conclusion, she also joined the *Imperieuse* establishment. Thus, of the old capital ships, only the *Renown* and *Queen Elizabeth* in the East Indies and the patched-up *Warspite* remained in full war service.

The Home Fleet at this time still retained the *Duke of York* as the flagship, her sisters all leaving for the East during the winter of 1944–45—the *King George V* in November, the *Howe* in December, and the *Anson*, after refitting at Devonport, in March 1945. The *Rodney* took over responsibilities as flagship of the Home Fleet for the final time on November 30, 1944, thus releasing the *Duke of York* for refitting and her voyage east in June, but this was only a temporary measure, for the faithful old *Rodney* had now steamed over 156,000 miles since her last refit in 1942 and was in poor shape.

The *Warspite* was, if anything, in worse condition, but her guns—at least those that remained to her—were still useful and needed for one final, vital operation in Europe. When the breakout from the Normandy beachhead had taken place, the British thrust northeast had captured the great port of Antwerp virtually intact and early hopes were expressed by the army commanders that their huge supplies of men, machines, and food would soon be able to pour in through this harbor close to their lines—rather than the channel ports now far behind them. But although Antwerp was in Allied hands in September 1944, the Germans held the estuary of the River Scheldt, and no ships could reach port, the mines could not be swept, and the strain upon the Allies' supplies was so great that it slowed their advance considerably. The Germans were well aware of the effect their garrisons had and were determined to hold those low-lying islets and the heavily fortified linchpin, Walcheren, to the last.

At the end of October, a combined operation was planned to clear the estuary, and a strong force of landing craft was assembled at Ostend under Captain Pugsley to clear the shallow waterways and provide close-in support for the Royal Marine and Army Commando units. Out for the last time to provide really heavy fire support came the *Warspite* with the monitors *Erebus* and *Roberts*.

The heaviest resistance was encountered at Westkapelle, which assaulted by the Royal Marine Commandos. Here along the northwestern and southwestern faces of the island, the Germans had mounted a formidable collection of dug-in coastal batteries, ten in all, mounting forty heavy guns ranging in caliber from 3-inch to 8.7-inch and commanding the whole of the East and West Scheldt estuaries. Moreover, the assault on the breach blown in the dyke wall came some time after the army operations had commenced against Flushing, and so there was no element of surprise.

At 8:15 A.M., the *Warspite* arrived from Deal and took up her bombarding position some dozen miles off the Westkapelle Light and commenced her firing. The Marine Commandos met fierce resistance, as Captain Pugsley later recounted: "It was clear that, for all the thousands of tons of bombs dropped on them, very few of the guns had been silenced. Later, I was to hear it said that the commander in chief of Bomber Command had expressed the opinion that he could capture Walcheren with his batman after all the bombs that had been dropped on it. I could wish that he had been with us that day!"[11]

In truth, RAF Bomber Command continued to live in a different world from the seaman and soldiers, still sticking to its theories of what *should* happen according to their predictions—that Germany would surrender after Bomber Command's great offensives, that air bombardment could neutralize any defense works despite the ample evidence to the contrary at Normandy, and so on. Not that Captain Pugsley had much more faith in the *Warspite*: "As for the bombardment squadron, though it had opened fire at 8:20 and great bursts of smoke and debris were going up as their huge shells landed, without spotting aircraft I knew that I could place little faith in their effectiveness."[12]

This proved to be the *Warspite*'s last shot at an enemy target. Since D-Day, she had fired 1,500 rounds of 15-inch shell, and at the end of the day, she had worn her existing set out and had to return to England and lay at Spithead. As her biographer recalled, "The old ship's life was now plainly drawing to a close. Her armaments and machinery had been driven so hard, and she had so often been damaged by the enemy that to make her fit for further service would necessitate a long and costly refit."[13] In fact, even before Walcheren, it had been decided that she was past repair, for on September 9, it was recorded that she would pay off into the lowest state of reserve, Category C, on completion of her present duties. Of all the British battleships recorded in this volume, it is surely the *Warspite* that holds pride of place both in longevity of service and participation in battle.

And so only the *Rodney* remained in active service in home waters. There was little for her to do, for the *Tirpitz* was finally laid to rest. By the autumn of 1944, the RAF policy of persisting with bigger bombs and bigger bombers had finally resulted in the colossal "earthquake" weapons, the Tallboys and the like—12,000-pound weapons with 5,000 pounds of explosives. Not only did they now have a bomb that could sink any ship afloat, they also had by this date a squadron in service with the skill and expertise to actually hit that type of target, (always with the usual proviso that the ship kept still during the attack). With this combination and the lack of suitable targets in Europe to divert their attention, the fate of the *Tirpitz* was finally settled once and for all.

"It might be said the fate of the battleship was finally sealed in the bath of Air Vice Marshal the Honorable Ralph Cochrane," wrote Paul Brickhill. He does not add whether Cochrane followed Archimedes' example and leapt out crying "Eureka!," but clearly, the reason why Bomber Command had not got round to proving how simple it was, was because they were so busy elsewhere. "In his waking moments, work was rarely absent from his mind; he had been thinking of the *Tirpitz* for a long time, and it was in his bath one morning that he finally made up his mind to get permission for 617 to sink her. He climbed out, dried, dressed, and flew down to see Harris, and Harris said, 'Yes.'"[14] If only this bath had taken place before PQ 17 or all the other futile attempts to sink the *Tirpitz*, so much trouble would have been avoided, but better late than never.

The *Tirpitz* at Altenfiord was unfortunately out of the range of the Lancasters from Britain, but the Soviets cooperated very well in preparing special airstrips for the bombers at Yagodnik, and Operation Source was duly mounted from there on September 17. Twenty-seven Lancasters took off, including twenty-one with 12,000-pound Tallboys and the others with special mines. They were met by the *Tirpitz*'s heavy guns firing shrapnel and other antiaircraft fire and had to bomb through the usual smokescreen. Sixteen of the big bombs were dropped, but the results could not be observed.

Only later was it found that Wing Commander Tait had scored a hit. The huge bomb had hit the *Tirpitz* on her forecastle some fifty feet from her stem and had gone right through her upper deck, coming out through her starboard side below the waterline before exploding. The bows were badly damaged and the concussion of the big bomb jarred much of her delicate machinery so much that the Germans reported that repairs would take nine months to complete, if they could be done at all without further interruption. This was not likely of course and Dönitz wrote her off as an operational unit.

> I thereupon issued orders that in the future the *Tirpitz* would be used merely as a floating battery for the defense of north Norway. It was no longer possible to keep her in a sea-going condition. Only such personnel would remain aboard, I directed, as were required to man the guns. To ensure that the worst did not happen and the *Tirpitz* capsize as the result of one of these air attacks, I ordered that she be berthed in as shallow water as possible.[15]

Unfortunately, Rear Admiral Peters, now in command of the remnants of the German battle group, was unable to find such shallow water any nearer the north than at Tromso. She was therefore brought south under her own power and moored to the south of Haakoy Island where her guns could command the approaches to Tromsoy Island. Her berth was still too deep for the required conditions but he hoped to rectify this by filling in the deep water below her keel with sand. However this move could not have suited No. 617 Squadron better, for now she was within extreme striking range of their bombers, if stripped-down, based in Scotland. It meant taking their guns out and if they were jumped by defending fighters could have resulted in a massacre, but they took that chance.

The final sortie took place on November 12, 1944. Thirty-two Lancasters took off from Lossiemouth for the long flight north. They were aware that if they failed this time there would be no second chance because the light would be insufficient with the coming of winter. For the last time, the *Tirpitz*'s big guns barked in defiance as the Lancasters made their bombing runs but this time the smoke-screen failed to materialize and the fighter squadron at nearby Bardufoss remained on the ground despite calls for help. They missed a sitting target, but the No.617's Lancasters did not.

> One by one the gaggle wheeled as the bombs went. They watched wordless, through the Perspex for thirty seconds till a great yellow flash burst on the battleship's foredeck. From 14,000 feet, they saw her tremble. Another bomb hit the shore, two more in close succession hit the ship, one on the starboard side by the bridge, and another abaft the funnel. Another one split the sea five feet from her bows, and then the smoke pall covered her and only dimly through the smoke they saw the other bursts all inside the crinoline of nets. One constant glare shone through the smoke. She was burning. There came another flash and a plume of steam jetted to 500 feet into the air through the smoke as a magazine went up.[16]

Two direct hits were actually achieved, both on the port side, and these were followed by a number of near misses also on that side of the ship which tore huge holes in the soft sand under her hull into which she listed firstly twenty degrees and then right over to seventy. At about 9:50 A.M., just after the final bomb burst, X magazine detonated, from an interested witness came graphic accounts of the great turret blown whole through the air for forty feet from the ship.

> When the smoke cleared away, the *Tirpitz* was already lying over at an angle, of forty-five degrees, turning slowly. She went on turning until she was nearly upside down, then her upperworks must have hit the bottom, for she stuck as she was, with her red bottom above the surface. Here and there oil fuel on the water was ablaze, and the surface was dotted with the heads of swimmers striking out away from the flames; not all escaped them. The others reached the shore, or the net buoys, or the hull of the ship itself, once it was clear that she would sink no further.[17]

Trapped inside that great hull were more than 1,000 men, and still trapped there, they died by the hundreds as the water rose. Only eighty-seven managed to make their way up to the bottom compartments of the ship, and these were cut out by rescue teams. The remainder stayed with the *Tirpitz*. She had been their bleak home for three years; now she was their tomb.

The RAF was jubilant when it was confirmed the *Tirpitz* was sunk:

Someone [Brickhill never names his source for this rumor] at the Admiralty apparently did not quite agree and said (a little huffily according to the story) that they could not mark her as definitely sunk because her bottom was still showing; but that did not deter a certain dynamic personality at Bomber Command from grunting with deep satisfaction to one of his subordinates when he heard the *Tirpitz* was sunk, "That's one in the eye for the Nautics!"[18]

It was still a game, apparently, of scoring points off the "Nautics," but to the Admiralty, the destruction of the *Tirpitz* came as a considerable relief, although as Admiral Cunningham was to record, "It made little difference to our naval dispositions as she was no longer a fighting unit; but there was always the chance she might have been got back to Germany."[19] With the *Tirpitz* gone, only the abandoned hull of the *Gneisenau* and the two surviving pocket battleships remained of the German surface fleet's heavy ships, and these were all employed in the Baltic.

From the summer of 1944 onward, the Soviet Army mounted attack after attack against which the Germans, now fighting on two fronts, deserted by their allies one by one, outnumbered on the ground and with hardly any air support whatsoever, could only stubbornly give ground and retreat and retreat. It is some measure of their fighting qualities that it still took the Western Allies eleven months to do what the Germans had done in six weeks in 1940, despite the fact the bulk of the Axis troops were engaged in the East. Still, there was no staying the new might of the Russian armies and by October they had broken through to the Baltic coastline at Libau.

From now on, the main task groups of the remainder of the German Navy were engaged in support of the army on this flank and in evacuating over two million soldiers and civilians away from the Soviet advance to the sanctuary of the west. Between October 6 and 13, for example, the task force comprising the pocket battleship *Lützow*, the heavy cruiser *Prinz Eugen*, and six destroyers was employed in firing on Soviet troop concentrations near Memel under heavy air attack. Force 2 was formed under Vice Admiral Thiele, and in addition to the above ships, the *Admiral Scheer*, *Admiral Hipper*, and all available light cruisers and destroyers were in constant action off the Sworbe Peninsula, which, thanks to their firepower, managed to hold out until November 22.

By the beginning of 1945, the Soviet ground forces had reached East Prussia and were still pressing forward. From February 2 to 5, the *Prinz Eugen* was in action against the Fischhausen area, with the *Admiral Scheer* in close support, while a week later, the *Lützow* was bombarding near Frauenburg in support of the 4th Army.

Both pocket battleships continued in action throughout that month in efforts to halt the Russian advance on Königsberg and fired off huge numbers of shells from their 11-inch guns, the effects of which were found to be as devastating by the Soviets as had the Allied naval bombardments by the Germans earlier in the war. Huge efforts by torpedo bombers and MTBs were made by the Russians to eliminate these ships but all survived save a few destroyers.

But all the time, their area of operations was shrinking, and not only from the east. From the west, the continued Allied advance eliminated fighter bases and the heavy bombers of the RAF and USAAF were free to roam at will over the Baltic ports with little or no opposition. Casualties were inevitable and heavy. One by one the big ships were blasted to the bottom as they returned to harbors to renew their guns, which had become worn out by the continual bombardments.

The old *Schleswig Holstein* was sunk in an RAF attack on Gotenhafen on the night of December 18–19, going down in shallow water. The *Admiral Scheer* was in action covering the bridgehead opposite Wollin at the beginning of March, as was the old *Schlesien*, which had to withdraw by the twenty-first because of lack of ammunition. Her place was taken by the *Lützow* and *Leipzig*, and the bombardments went on unabated.

At Gotenhafen, it was clear the port was due to fall soon, and the hulk of the *Gneisenau* found one last employment in the war. She was sunk as a blockship on March 27. The evacuations reached a new peak in the final two months of war, and losses among the merchant vessels were heavy. Off Hela, the *Lützow* was in action again until April 8, when, down to her last drops of precious oil fuel, she had to withdraw to harbor.

On the night of April 9–10, Bomber Command mounted a heavy attack on the harbor at Kiel, dropping 2,600 tons of bombs in a concentrated attack. The pocket battleship *Admiral Scheer* was trapped in this inferno, was hit several times, and capsized with her keel showing above water. No. 617 finished off the *Lützow*, which was lying immobilized in the Kaiserfahrt, to the south of Swinemunde, on April 16. The British used the giant Tallboys that had smashed up the *Tirpitz* against this ship less than one half her size; the results were predictable:

> They picked out the *Lützow* far below, a microbe on the water beside the quay, and as they turned on her the flak burst among them sav-

agely, predicting deadly accurately on the unwavering formation. Clusters of puffs blotched the patch of sky on which they moved, so that nearly every one of the eighteen bombers was hit and holes opened in wings and fuselages as shrapnel ripped through.

It was not for another two days they found out that the *Lützow* had sunk as far as the seabed would let her. The near-miss by the bows had torn out her bottom; the dock was not very deep, but the *Lützow* was finished, lying on the mud. (Someone in the navy claimed she was not really sunk because her decks were still above water).[19]

In fact, some of the turrets were still operational and were kept firing at the advancing Russians until finally, on May 3, she was blown up by her remaining crew when they got too close. The *Schlesien* sortied on May 2 but was heavily damaged by a ground miss near Greifswalder Oie and had to be towed back to Swinemunde and beached not far from the *Lützow*. Both ships were blown up together when the area was evacuated.

With the German surrender, only the *Prinz Eugen*, *Nürnberg*, and a destroyer remained of the German surface fleet. Unlike the Italians, they had fought gamely to the end, and by their rescue operations and bombardments of 1944–45, they had regained much of the honor lost by their ancestors when the High Seas Fleet scuttled itself without a struggle at Scapa Flow in 1919. But the end result was the same, and a third great European navy had gone the way of the bulk of the French and Italian fleets.

The Home Fleet had little to do in these closing months. With all the modern ships on the way east, only the *Rodney* remained in solitary splendor at Scapa. Toward the end, however, there were some fears expressed that the surviving German heavy ships might leave the Baltic and indulge in one last orgy of destruction across the North Sea. "Dönitz's Death Ride" it was called. This was taken quite seriously, and because of it, the *Renown*, having finished her refit at Durban and rejoined the East Indies Fleet at Ceylon, was ordered home "with dispatch" on March 30.

The *Renown* was still the fastest capital ship in the Royal Navy, and for the last time, she was able to prove it. After a high-speed voyage, she arrived at Scapa from Ceylon on April 14, having covered 7,642 miles in 306 steaming hours. It was a fitting ending to such a worthy lifespan. The flag of the commander in chief was duly hauled down from the *Rodney*'s masthead and hoisted at the *Renown*'s, and the *Rodney* steamed away to reserve, her war finally done. The *Renown* did not long outstay her, for with the end of the war in Europe, she had no other duties to fulfill.

One last honor was accorded this grand old ship when in August 1945, at Plymouth, the historic meeting between King George VI and President Harry Truman, on his way home from the Potsdam Conference, took place aboard her in the Sound, under the watchful eye of Drake. By the end of the year, she was at Portsmouth and reduced to two-fifths complement awaiting her fate; later, she finished up as one of the four ships of the *Imperieuse* establishment, at Devonport, along with the other veterans moored there. Her place in the East Indies Fleet was to be taken by the *Nelson*, which had finished her long refit in the United States and was at Malta on her way east when VE Day was celebrated. Meanwhile, the *Queen Elizabeth* was left as the only battleship on that station for several months. She had not been idle.

Although the two fleets, the East Indies and the Pacific, had been formed as separate units in November 1944, both were still based at Ceylon at this period, and the latter's ships were still gaining valuable exercise in strikes at Japanese-held islands. At the end of 1944, Rear Admiral Vian had sailed with the carriers *Indomitable*, *Indefatigable*, and *Victorious*, and light forces and carried out Operation Lentil against the oil refineries at Pankalan Brandan in Sumatra. Meanwhile, the *Howe* had gone on ahead of the rest of the fleet, taking Admiral Fraser and his staff to Australia.

> The battleship *Howe*, having gone on ahead to Australia from Ceylon in December, had already experienced a warm-hearted reception; her crew describing their welcome on the Battle of Sydney, the whole thing had been so boisterous. It had been repeated in New Zealand the following month, when the *Howe* escorted by the light cruiser *Achilles*, and destroyers *Queenborough*, *Quality*, and *Quadrant* took Sir Bruce Fraser to Auckland and there is no doubt that the return of the White Ensign to the Far East was a long and eagerly awaited event.[20]

While the *Howe* was successfully showing the flag, her sister had arrived on station, and on January 16, Vian again sortied out from Ceylon with the *King George V*, four carriers, and light forces to strike at Palembang oil refineries, the largest such in South-East Asia. The attack was duly launched on the 24th with great success and on the 26th he struck at the second group in that area with equal precision after replenishing to the south. Attacks by shore-based aircraft were repulsed with comparative ease and there were no losses to the British force. The fleet then continued on to Freemantle and the British Pacific Fleet had at last reached the Pacific in strength.

The British Fourteenth Army was now on the offensive in Burma and various combined operations were mounted along the coastline to help by cutting off the retreating Japanese forces as they fled south. Complete control of these waters, for so long the exclusive property of the Japanese, was now achieved by the East Indies Fleet. In January, the large island of Ramree was assaulted and taken by the 26th Indian Division in order that air bases could be set up there on the Japanese flanks. The assault went in on the twenty-first and heavy covering fire support was provided by the *Queen Elizabeth*, which opened fire at 7:30 A.M. Her Royal Marine detachment took part in further operations ashore when they landed on the Cheduba Islands on January 26, but the enemy had already fled. The *Queen Elizabeth* herself returned to Trincomalee in readiness for the next assault.

This took place between April 8 and 18 as part of Operation Sunfish. Vice Admiral Wake-Walker flew his flag in the *Queen Elizabeth* and had the *Richelieu* in company for heavy metal, along with two escort carriers and two heavy cruisers with a destroyer flotilla. This force sailed towards Sumatra on April 11 and again subjected Sabang to a heavy bombardment while the carrier planes struck at the Andaman Islands twice.

Rangoon fell to the advancing British army on May 3, while Task Force 67, as it had become known—the *Queen Elizabeth*, *Richelieu*, two escort carriers, two heavy and two light cruisers, and six destroyers—carried out Operation Bishop, shelling and bombing Car Nicobar and Port Blair, destroying a convoy of nine Japanese ships, and generally exercising their mastery of the area between April 30 and May 6, returning to Trincomalee on the ninth.

On May 10, the Japanese had had enough and mounted an evacuation operation to bring her surviving forces out of the Andamans and Nicobars while there was still time. From Singapore, they sailed their last operational ships in those waters, the 8-inch cruiser *Haguro* and the destroyer *Kamikaze*. These were sighted heading north through the Malacca Straits by submarine patrols, and Admiral Wake-Walker sailed with his main strength to intercept them: the *Queen Elizabeth* (flag), *Richelieu*, four escort carriers, one heavy and two light cruisers, and eight destroyers. On the fifteenth, air attacks by the carriers failed to damage the Japanese ships, but the 26th Destroyer Flotilla was sent off to intercept, and in a brilliant night attack—a classic destroyer attack—they dispatched the *Haguro* with torpedoes. The battleships were far behind when this action took place between midnight and 2:00 A.M. and could not help, but it was a satisfactory conclusion to the *Queen Elizabeth*'s fighting life.

The *Nelson* had arrived on station by this time, and on July 12, the flag was transferred to her, and the *Queen Elizabeth* left for home waters, her duty done. The *Nelson* was actively employed during operations to clear the mine-fields off Phuket Island on the west coast of the Kra Isthmus on July 24–26, along with four escort carriers and the cruiser *Sussex*, and on the twenty-sixth, she helped beat off the first *kamikaze* attacks on the fleet. The carrier *Ameer* was hit and damaged and the minesweeper *Vestal* sunk in these attacks, but the operation carried out.

On August 27, Admiral Wake-Walker formed a task group with the *Nelson*, two escort carriers, one heavy and one light cruiser, and light forces and pro-ceeded from Rangoon to Penang to negotiate the surrender of the Japanese forces there. On September 2, Admiral Wake-Walker received Vice Admiral Uzumi aboard the *Nelson*, and the official surrender ceremony of Japanese forces in Southeast Asia was held on board her on the twelfth, the surrender document being signed on the same table in her admiral's cabin as had the surrender of Italy in 1943.

After these great events, the *Nelson* sailed for home for the last time on November 13, and on arrival, she hoisted, as so often before, the flag of the commander in chief of the Home Fleet.

⌁ ⌖ ⌁

While these operations had been taking place in the Indian Ocean the last great act of the drama was being played out in the Pacific Ocean.

We have seen how, after the Battle of Leyte Gulf and subsequent disas-ters, the Japanese battle fleet had been reduced to a mere four ships: the *Yamato, Haruna, Hyuga,* and *Ise*—the latter two damaged and all four handi-capped by lack of oil fuel. All four lay at Kure dockyard, helpless to intervene as the Americans consolidated the Philippines and turned toward their next objective, Okinawa.

The Americans obviously had nothing to fear from these four ships, for they could now muster eight fast modern battleships and ten old ones and two modern battle-cruisers, as well as twenty or so carriers and light carriers. The British planned to add to this mighty concentration two task groups, the first built around the *King George V* and *Howe* and four fleet carriers (initially the *Illustrious, Victorious, Indomitable,* and *Indefatigable,* with the *Formidable* and *Implacable* to replace two of them later); and the second, which would not be ready until July, around the *Duke of York* and *Anson,* with the light fleet carri-ers *Colossus, Glory, Venerable,* and *Vengeance.*

These were the plans, although many Americans still felt that the addi-tion of four battleships and eight to ten carriers to their already sufficient strength was unnecessary and wished to divert it to the reconquest of Malaya, Operation Zipper. But after much discussion, it was decided that Admiral Fraser's fleet would perform a useful function operating with the American fleet, and this was emphasized when the armored carriers showed their resilience to *kamikaze* attack which completely disabled the wooden decked American ships.

The invasion of Okinawa, Operation Iceberg, took place on March 26, and the full strength of the Allied navies was disposed in support. On March 19, Admiral Rawlings, as commander afloat of the British Pacific Fleet, took the bulk of his ships to Ulithi for a final replenishment, and on the twenty-third, he sailed for the battle zone with his flag in the *King George V*, with the *Howe, Indomitable, Victorious, Illustrious,* and *Indefatigable*, five light cruisers, and eleven destroyers. The air striking forces commenced operations against the numerous Japanese airfields on the Sakishima Gunto, which were being used to stage in reinforcements to Okinawa.

Two days of air strikes were followed by two days of refueling, and then Rawlings was in position on April 1, following the usual intensive bombardment from the ten old battleships of Task Force 51.[21] The American landing craft stormed in.

The battle ashore raged with the usual fanatical violence by the Japanese garrison, now fighting on their own land and therefore even more determined. For the Allied warships their main tasks lay in shore bombardment support by the old battleships and aircraft, and in defending themselves against the first great massed Kamikaze attacks, the largest of which developed on the sixth.[22]

On the first, the *West Virginia* and *Indomitable* were both hit by suicide aircraft, although they continued operations. On the third, the escort carrier *Wake Island* was struck, and on the fifth, the battleship *Nevada* took five direct hits by shellfire from Japanese coastal batteries. Up to then, casualties afloat had been light, but the great massed attack launched on the sixth by about 700 aircraft almost swamped the fleet's defenses.

Among the many ships hit by *kamikazes* on this day were the battleship *Maryland* and the carriers *Illustrious* and *San Jacinto*, but the brunt of the assault this day fell on the American picket destroyers, whose losses were heavy. That same day saw the sortie from the Inland Sea of the greatest seagoing *kamikaze* of them all, the battleship *Yamato*, her fuel tanks half full with all the oil that could be scraped together, sailed out with one light cruiser and eight destroyers in a desperate attempt to reach the transport anchorage off Okinawa and there do as much damage as she could before being beached or destroyed. On her way south, however, she was sighted by two American submarines, and after beating off the *kamikaze* attacks, Admirals Spruance and Mitscher prepared to deal with her decisively.

A powerful battle line was formed with the new battleships and stationed to cover the northwestern approaches to Okinawa, and the prospects loomed large for a final battleship action to end the Pacific War. However, when scouting aircraft from his carriers located the Japanese force early on the seventh steaming west into the East China Sea, it was thought they might be turning away before the battleship squadron could come to grips with them.

To prevent such an escape, Spruance changed his plans, to the disgust of the American heavy ships, and organized powerful air striking forces, which he launched from a position east of Amami Gunto at a range of 250 miles. In all, some 380 dive and torpedo-bombers were launched from the decks of the American aircraft carriers to deal with the Japanese squadron, and around noon, they found it, Admiral Ito, the Japanese commander in chief, having by this time turned south to start his final approach for the beachhead.

The *Yamato* was now overwhelmed by this enormous mass of aircraft, but for two and a half hours, she fought back desperately against impossible odds. She was hit by four bombs in the first attack at 12:20 P.M., two detonating on impact and destroying several light antiaircraft gun positions and two more penetrating her armored deck aft close by her after 18.1-inch turret, starting an uncontrolled fire and putting the fire control positions out of action. The fire quickly engulfed the after turret itself, which was gutted completely. In the same attack she took two torpedoes in her port side, which flooded an engine room and gave her a six-degree list, which was rectified by counterflooding.

The second attack hit her around 1:00 P.M., and although no bombs struck her, she took four or five torpedoes, one in her starboard side and the rest along her port side. Widespread flooding took place in her outer engine and hydraulic machinery rooms. She assumed a fifteen-degree list to port, and her speed came down to eighteen knots. Forty-five minutes later, another torpedo hit her to starboard and three more smashed into her mutilated port side, and she was clearly doomed. All power went, and Ito ordered, "Abandon ship."

"The ship's port list was increasing rapidly when the last torpedo hit at 2:17 P.M. Three minutes later, the list had reached twenty degrees, inducing explosions, which sent the ship into a precipitous plunge."[23] This was the death of the *Yamato*, the mightiest battleship to ever sail the high seas. By this time, her escorting cruiser and four of the eight destroyers had also been sunk. The rest managed to pick up a few survivors, but almost all her crew of 2,400 men, including Admiral Ito, perished with their ship. Thus ended the rather one-sided battle of the East China Sea, and with the *Yamato*'s death plunge went the final shreds of the battleship's reputation as mistress of the seas. It cost the Americans merely ten aircraft.

The Allied navies thereafter resumed their poundings of the Japanese defenses, and on April 11 and 12, they had to face redoubled efforts by the *kamikaze* pilots to drive them away. The American fleet suffered heavily, the *Missouri* and the carrier *Enterprise* being among the ships struck and damaged on the eleventh, while the following day suicide aircraft hit both the *Idaho* and *Tennessee.*

On the fourteenth, the attack continued with unmitigated fury, and the battleship *New York* was struck. Three days later, the *Missouri* was hit again, and the carrier *Intrepid* was so badly damaged that she had to pull out, but the bombardments continued.

In support of a new American offensive on April 18–19, the old battleships *Arkansas, Colorado, Idaho, New Mexico, New York,* and *Texas* carried out further heavy shelling of the Japanese defense lines, to which the new *North Carolina* and *South Dakota* later added their quota of heavy shells, but the Japanese continued to hold out. It had been expected that resistance would be fierce, but the Japanese defense was exceptional. The fighting continued through April and May, and even after two months of fighting, the Americans had advanced only four miles.

The British Pacific Fleet had continued striking with its Avenger bombers and cratering the airfields on the islands and on Formosa as well, but it had proved very difficult work to keep so many airstrips out of action for the Japanese merely filled in the craters by night and resumed operations. Admiral Rawlings therefore determined to use his battleships to effect a more complete and widespread devastation. They could after all, deliver a far greater weight of explosive in a far shorter time than the carrier planes, and far more economically too.

Accordingly, on the night of May 4, he took the heavy ships in close to the island of Miyako in the Sakishima group and deployed for a night bombardment:

At 12:05, the ships opened fire. The *Euryalus* and *Black Prince* used their 5.25-inch guns to carry out "air-burst" shots on the antiaircraft positions around Nobara airfield, showering shrapnel down on the exposed guns' crews and decimating them. The *King George V* and *Howe* trained their mighty 14-inch barrels on Hirara airfield and the antiaircraft positions to the north. The *Swiftsure* and *Gambia* bombarded Nobora, and the *Uganda* took on Sukhama. The bombardment was carried out as if on a firing range, with no opposition at all from the enemy. For fifty minutes, the heavy shells smashed their

way up and down the runways, ploughing huge gaps in the installations and parked aircraft; then at 12:50 fire was ceased.[24]

Subsequent aerial photographs revealed that all the rounds fired by the
battleships had fallen in the target area.

Morale among the crews of the heavy guns. was appreciably raised
by this bombardment but the cost to the British force was high for
the carriers were deprived of the battleships' anti-aircraft protection
the following day and the Kamikazes therefore had a field day, both
the *Formidable* and *Indomitable* being hit on the fourth, and the *Victorious* and *Formidable* again on the ninth.

The *Howe* dealt summarily with one *kamikaze* that selected her as
its target this day.

The Rangers set about him and soon it was a blazing mass of fire,
but still it sped towards us only slightly deflected from its course,
and, as more and more 40mm and 20mm shells found their mark, it
passed narrowly over the quarterdeck and fell like a flaming meteor
into the sea some forty or fifty yards from the ship, sending up spray
which the sunshine transformed into a glorious rainbow.[25]

British operations continued until May 25, when the fleet returned to
Manus to refit in readiness for coming operations against Japan proper.
Japanese resistance on Okinawa was not finally crushed until June 21. The
kamikaze attacks and other air attacks cost the Japanese the staggering total of
7,830 aircraft destroyed, for which they could show the destruction of twenty-
four ships—destroyers and smaller—and the damage inflicted on another
200 of all classes.

The British Pacific Fleet now returned to Sydney, and the *Howe* was sent
to Durban in South Africa to refit in June, and she had not completed before
the next operations began. Both the *Duke of York* and *Anson* were on their way
to the Pacific with light fleet carriers, but until they arrived, only the *King
George V* was operational when the fleet sailed from Sydney on June 28, 1945.

By July 10, Admiral Halsey's fleet was back on station after refurbishing
at Leyte, and with his flag in the *Missouri*, he had eight fast battleships and
sixteen carriers with which to soften up the Japanese defenses on the Tokyo
plain in preparation for the intended main invasion. This done, he refueled
and moved north to Hokkaido to strike at that island and Honshu with his
massed air raids, which met surprisingly light opposition as the enemy was
husbanding his strength to oppose the invasion proper.

While these air attacks were sweeping across the home islands of Japan, several battleship striking forces were sent to harry Japanese shipping in their home waters. On the July 16–26, Vice Admiral Oldendorf roamed at will through the East China and Yellow Seas with the battlecruisers *Alaska* and *Guam*, the old battleships *Nevada*, *California*, and *Tennessee*, and light forces. In the enemy backyard, these heavy ships paraded themselves as far as the Yantgtse Estuary off Shanghai in complete immunity. During early August, other battleships, among them the *Pennsylvania*, *Arkansas*, and *Texas*, provided the heavy cover for a strong force of escort carriers operating in the same area, and on August 12, a Japanese torpedo-bomber scored their only success by damaging the *Pennsylvania* off Okinawa.

Nor were the fast battleships left out of these audacious operations. On July 14, Rear Admiral Shafroth took the *Indiana*, *Massachusetts*, and *South Dakota*, with light forces, in close to the Japanese mainland and fired more than eight rounds of 16-inch shell into the Kamaishi iron works. On July 15, Rear Admiral Badger repeated the operation with the *Iowa*, *Missouri*, and *Wisconsin*, which pumped 860 rounds of the heaviest shells into the iron and steel works at Muroran. Aircraft from the American and British carrier fleets were then sent in to finish off the remains of the Japanese Fleet, lying immobilized at their anchorages, and on July 17–18, the *Nagato* was heavily hit but remained operational at Yokohama.

On that same night, the suburbs of Tokyo felt the weight of the Allied battleships when Rear Admiral Badger returned with the *Alabama, Iowa, Missouri, North Carolina, Wisconsin*, and the British *King George V* and carried out an audacious bombardment of Hitachi. The American battleships fired more than 1,200 16-inch shells into the target area, to which the *King George V* added her quota of 267 rounds of 14-inch, her target being an aircraft propeller factory.

On July 24, Halsey returned to the task of wiping out the surviving units of the Imperial Japanese Navy and launched heavy air strikes at Kure Naval Yard, although this time he prevented the British carriers from joining in the destruction. The bombing raids continued for three days and were decisive. All three remaining Japanese heavy ships were hit and hit again and sunk on the bottom of the harbor, the *Hyuga* on July 24 and the *Haruna* and *Ise* on the twenty-eighth. Thus was Pearl Harbor amply avenged, and only the fire-blackened *Nagato* remained afloat to surrender to the Americans when it was all over. In addition, these strikes sank the last carrier, the *Amagi*, five cruisers, and many small craft while the British hit and damaged the light carrier *Kaiyo* in the Inland Sea.

This duty complete, the 3rd Fleet moved on up the coast striking as it went at airfields in central Honshu and at shipping in Nagoya Bay. On the night of July 29–30, the *King George V* joined up with the *Indiana, Massachusetts,* and *South Dakota* and carried out a bombardment of aircraft factories and other industrial targets near Hamamatsu, and this historic bombardment was the last time a British battleship fired its main armament at an enemy target.

Further strikes and bombardments were planned, but all were cancelled, and Japan was subjected to a horror far greater than any bombardment from the air or sea when atomic bombs burned up two of her great cities ushering in a new era. Thereupon, not surprisingly, Japan surrendered.

On August 27, the Allied Fleet arrived in Tokyo Bay, and the formal Japanese surrender was signed aboard the *Missouri.* In that imposing array of fighting power, there assembled the battleships *Alabama, Indiana, Wisconsin, North Carolina, Iowa, Missouri, New Mexico, Mississippi, Idaho, Colorado,* and *West Virginia,* along with the *King George V* and *Duke of York,* just arrived carrying Admiral Fraser to sign for Great Britain and the Commonwealth.

> On the August27, when Admiral Rawlings's flagship anchored at the entrance to Tokyo Bay the snow-capped cone of Fujiyama, the sacred mountain of Japan, stood out exceptionally clearly against the western sky; and as evening drew on, the watchers on the quarterdeck of the *King George V* saw the red orb of the sun go down right into the middle of the volcano's crater. Rarely, if ever, can a heavenly body have appeared to act with such appropriate symbolism.[26]

Thus ended the war at sea. How stood the battleship now at this supreme vindication of the strength of sea power? Without a future at all according to most critics, although in retrospect across the years their strident mockery had been tempered a little with a gentle wistfulness.

> There it was in all its sublime greatness and grandeur, the final manifestation of the work of Cuniberti, Fisher, and Gard, and all the subsequent naval architects of Britain and America, Italy and France and Japan, Russia and Germany. All that mattered was that, where command of the air helped to grant command of the ocean's surface, the battleship performed usefully; scarcely ever in the role for which it was once devised, but very often to good purpose.[27]

Others were more scathing of course: "Their day was done and their expensive lives were ending. In the course of their dominion they fired between them a grand total of 3,557 rounds from their main batteries, or about one round for every £10,000 they cost."[28] This is the summary of the King George V class based on good left-wing principles in which every penny spent on defense is a complete waste (unless, of course, it is spent by a nation like the Soviet Union, North Korea, or Iran). It was a cry that had been heard right up to the outbreak of war in 1939, and after 1945, it was to become ever more dominant until today, when it has become accepted dogma in such media outlets as the BBC and the *Guardian.*

Nonetheless, the battleship, although fighting on to the very end of the war, had become overshadowed by the new weapons developed during that conflict and their final days seemed clearly in sight. To those who expected that the battleship would vanish overnight, however, the postwar years must have come as rather a shock.

True, a great number of the world's battleships did vanish from the oceans in the immediate aftermath of the war, more in fact from the victorious Allied fleets than from their defeated opponents. In the main however these were the older ships, ships already long past their allotted normal life spans before the war had even commenced. There was little surprise in their passing. Britain, as ever, led the way in quickly disposing of her older vessels, most of which had already been laid up for some time anyway.

The first to go was the *Warspite,* which was in very poor condition from her many escapades. Approval to scrap was given in July 1946, and she was taken out from her anchorage into Portsmouth harbour and stripped of all her useful fittings. Metal Industries bought her for scrap, and in April 1947, she left under-tow for the Clyde for breaking up, with an eight-man crew. True to her tradition she put up the toughest fight of her life at the very end, for she slipped her tow in a storm, drifted for three days in the Channel, and finally drove ashore in Prussia Cove, Mounts Bay, Cornwall. It was her final act of defiance, wrote her biographer. She was finally refloated in July 1950 and beached at Marazion and here she was dismantled *in situ,* the work last until 1956. She thus endured longer than her sisters before the end.

Her equally aged companions went more quietly, as if aware of their antiquity and aware that further resistance to their fate, long overdue, was futile. The *Ramillies* was sold in April 1948, the *Resolution* in May of the same year, joined by the *Malaya.* The *Revenge* was not sold until March 1949. None of these old veterans had been modernized, and it was not expected that they would remain in the postwar fleet.

The *Queen Elizabeth* had gone into reserve in March 1946, and the *Nelson* had found useful employment throughout that year as a training battleship at Portland for boy seamen. The *Renown, Rodney,* and *Valiant* had been laid up, however. In February 1948, the Labour government pronounced sentence on all these vessels; the reaction from the country as a whole must have come as a distinct surprise to these unsentimental gentlemen who thought only in figures, loans, and rationings. "Never before had a group of warships been so close to the hearts of the people; each had for long years been a source of pride and confidence, a symbol of naval might. That the time had come when they could no longer be employed was hard to realize, perhaps harder to accept."[29]

Another doughty old veteran rose in their defense. Winston Churchill, now banished by his people to the opposition benches and sharing the memories of these old ships in happier times, pleaded that they be retained—in vain. "But although the First Lord admitted that he had signed the death warrant of five staunch old friends, the Board realized that on the grounds of lack of speed alone they would have to be ruled out of our future fleet organization; besides which there was the disconcerting fact that the battleship could no longer be regarded as the capital ship of today and tomorrow."[30]

And so they were put on the sales list: the *Nelson, Rodney,* and *Renown* being sold in February 1948, the *Queen Elizabeth* in June, and the *Valiant* in August. Before she was finally broken up, the *Rodney* was used as a bombing target, and her old decks were easily penetrated by these huge weapons. (She was, of course, moored to enable the bombers to hit her; things had not moved *that* far since the days of the *Ostfriesland.*)

In 1949, the last of the old veterans returned to home waters. The Allies had finally managed to ensure the delivery of the old Italian *Guilio Cesare* to the Soviet Union as rashly promised in 1943. In return, Stalin was supposed to return the *Royal Sovereign* to Britain, but when it came to it, there was much delay, possibly because the Russians were still unable to handle her properly, or more likely, they yet hoped for a chance to use her against her former owners. Finally, however, on February 4, 1949, she returned to England. Here she received no great welcome and was promptly sold for scrap, being towed to Inverkeithing on May 18 for demolition by T. W. Ward.[31]

Not one of these gallant old ships on which so much had depended over the years was preserved for posterity as a museum to Britain's greatest period of sea power. The Americans were more concerned with their heritage, and both the *Texas* from the old generation and the *Alabama* and *North Carolina* from the new were ultimately so preserved, as were, after further postwar service in Korea, Vietnam, and the Gulf, the *Iowa, Missouri, Wisconsin,* and *New Jersey.*

Nor were the Americans quite so eager to discard their old ships, probably because they had reconstructed them more recently (during 1943-44) and also because they could afford their upkeep as part of their defense budget, which Britain could not, even had she so wished.[32]

All that remained of the once-great British battle fleet were the four King George V–class ships and the brand-new *Vanguard*. Immediately after the war, some limited use was made of the King Georges. The *Anson* had accepted the surrender of Hong Kong in September 1945 and had then sailed to Australia, after a period as guardship at Tokyo. In February 1946, she conveyed the Duke and Duchess of Gloucester to Hobart, Tasmania. The *Anson* then visited Sydney and Japan again and returned home to Portsmouth in July 1946.

The *Anson* underwent a short refit and was then re-commissioned as the Flagship of the Training Squadron, being used as the special training vessel for the new entry of seamen under special service to help man the postwar fleet. The *Howe* completed her refit in September 1945 and replaced the *Nelson* as flagship on the East Indies station, returning to Portsmouth on January 9, 1946.

After recommissioning, the *Howe* became the flagship of Admiral Power with the 2nd Battle Squadron, Home Fleet. The *Duke of York* returned to home waters the same year, arriving at Plymouth in July 1946. In December, Admiral Syfret hoisted his flag aboard her as commander in chief of the Home Fleet.

Finally, the *King George V* herself had returned to Portsmouth on March 2, 1946, and had acted as flagship of the Home Fleet until relieved by the *Duke of York*. She then underwent a long refit following which she also joined the training squadron. Three of these battleships were present at the concentration of the Home Fleet at Portland in the preparation for their cruise to the West Indies in 1948, and the still waters enclosed by the breakwater resembled the great days of 1928 or 1918, for there was only a single flat-top present among this gathering, which included three cruisers and fourteen modern destroyers. It was the last such assembly witnessed in British waters, and one by one, the King Georges began to pay off into reserve.

The *King George V* was the first to be laid up, leaving Portsmouth on June 14, 1950, in tow for lonely Gareloch, where she was sealed up for preservation, or "cocooned" as the press would have it. The *Anson* took then-Princess Elizabeth on a visit to the Channel Islands in June 1949, but in November of that year, she was replaced by the *Vanguard* in the Training Squadron, and in 1950, she joined her sister at Gareloch. The remaining two followed during 1951, "where, to the constant complaint of the advocates of thrift at any price, they still managed to cost the taxpayer three-quarters of a million pounds a year."[33]

Only the *Vanguard* remained in solitary splendor to represent the long line of heavily gunned ships on which Britain's maritime dominance had been built. But that dominance had been signed away in 1922, and lost forever in 1942, and now her appearance on the oceans aroused more controversy than awe. Nobody who had seen her, as this author has, ever doubted she was a great ship and a beautiful ship. The tragedy was that she was built after her time. Although the standard government answer to angry criticisms was that "while other nations have battleships, the British government intends to retain our five," less and less money was made available for defense, and it would not stretch forever for maintaining the big ships.

When the *Vanguard* joined the fleet, it was with a heady confidence that defied the fate of the *Yamato* and the advent of the atomic bomb. She was officially accepted in the Royal Navy on August 9, 1946, and her first duty was to carry the royal family on their tour to South Africa in February and May of 1947. For this, she was extensively fitted out in Portsmouth Dockyard and did not finally undertake her shakedown cruise to Gibraltar until December 1946. All this panoply of empire was received with a somewhat sour response by some critics. "As a ship, the *Vanguard* was judged the most colossal royal yacht ever," wrote one.[34]

As royal yachts rated only second to battleships in the scale of ridicule and anger assigned by those who wished to see the Royal Navy cut down further still, and whose only naval heroes appeared to be the Invergordon mutineers, this type of comment was not unexpected. Nonetheless, the end of this cruise saw her undergoing another refit, this time at Devonport during 1947–48 before she again became operational in the Mediterranean between January and July 1949. In November 1949 she joined the Training Squadron, with reduced complement, but was subsequently commissioned as the flagship of the commander in chief of the Home Fleet for special cruises and exercises.

She was the star attraction at the Coronation Naval Review held at Spithead in 1953, and her sea-keeping performance during the huge NATO Exercise Mariner in 1951 impressed most naval observers. *Flight* magazine was not impressed at all and wondered why the results were always kept secret when the land-based heavy bombers attacked battleships in such exercises. Probably because, as so often before, they failed to hit them, but nonetheless, the *Vanguard* always had a bad press. "Scrap the lot," thundered Cassandra of the *Daily Mirror*, brooding over Spithead in 1953. "The RAF *must* now be the Senior Service," pronounced a *Sunday Express* article around the same time. (Admiral Fraser's quiet letter in reply to this, in which he stated that he served the last three years of war in big ships and had never seen an RAF plane overhead, only the Fleet Air Arm, was printed in rather smaller type.)

The battleship *was* obsolete; there could be no doubt about it in this age of hydrogen bombs and missiles. A few people wondered why, if that was so, the Russians were building the 17,000-ton Sverdolf-class cruisers and just what the Royal Navy was going to pit against them if in the event of a hot war a dozen of these were loosed on British convoy routes with no battleships in reserve. But this did not trouble most, and in 1957, the four King Georges were taken out of their seven-year-old mothballs and towed to the Breakers yards.

Now the *Vanguard* was truly alone. She too was mothballed and placed in reserve at Portsmouth at the disposal of NATO.

The *Vanguard* was permitted the dignity of finishing her fourth refit, at a cost of £720,000, and was eased into the reserve fleet at Portsmouth, across the dockyard from the *Victory*. She was dying but not dead. They made her the administrative headquarters for the reserve fleet and for reserve training in seamanship, at a cost of £230,000 a year. From her moorings she could not have gone to sea to fight even if the legendary drum of Drake had been rolling in the Channel, calling Britain's sea-dogs to arms, without another refit, lasting six weeks. In an age of nuclear missiles, it appeared unlikely there would be time for that.[35]

And so "the battleship, as a class, was dead. The Admiralty scrapped HMS *Vanguard*, the last, the greatest, the most expensive and the least employed in 1961."[36] And so they did, and everyone was happy, except the critics who then turned their attentions to the aircraft carriers with glee and ultimate triumph.

It mattered little by this time, for Britain's days as a great seapower, or even a modest one, were long since done. The French and the Americans still kept their battleships for much longer and usefully employed them. These exceptions apart, it seemed that the days of big ships were gone for ever, almost everyone agreed on that. A big ship was "too many eggs in one basket." "We must stop planning a Jutland-type navy," wrote the *Mirror*. Britain needed only little ships, everyone agreed. So by the 1970s, that is all the British were left with, and not even tiny Icelandic gunboats needed to fear Britain's maritime defenses during the farcical "Cod War." At the Falklands, the whole British Task Force was placed in jeopardy by the presence of just one Argentine warship, the very, very old, ex-American light cruiser *General Belgrano*, for Britain had nothing to oppose with which to oppose her in the way of surface strength, except 4.5-inch guns, had she evaded the British submarine that eventually sank her; our few Sea Harriers could not have sunk her with the weapons they carried. The only group that did not appear to agree with this confident theory of "small is good" for warships were the rulers of the Soviet Union, which was rather a pity for socialist theorists.

In the normal course of logical development, warship types have the habit of starting small and gradually increasing in size. Battleships did not start at any particular tonnage but gradually evolved through 8,000 tonners to 12,000 tonners by the end of the nineteenth century, despite vigorous outcries by the politicians. This growth continued through the First World War despite all attempts to stop it and only at Washington did some check appear, the 35,000-ton limit, to which only Britain rigorously kept.

Thus, in modern times, the Soviet missile cruisers of the Kresta I-class started off at 5,150 tons, developed through the Kresta II type to 6,000 tons, and then to the Kara-class ships of 9,000 tons, all in less than ten years. Likewise, the Moskva-type carriers at 15,000 tons led naturally to the Kiev type at 40,000 tons. These are larger than most World War II battleships.[37] It is not unreasonable to assume therefore that ultimate surface missile ships with the displacement of the old battleships will appear on the scene, again becoming the "battleships" of the twenty-first century (even if they are not so termed), despite the wishful thinking of the many so-called experts.

When these words were originally written in 1977, considerable scorn was thrown by some British self-proclaimed media pundits at this writer's forecasts. However, three decades later, we find the Russian Navy with its four Type 1144.2 Kirov-class ships, like the *Pyotr Velikhiy* (*Peter the Great*). Now even described officially as battlecruisers, they displace 26,190-tons, have an overall length of 255 meters, a breadth of 25.5 meters, and have a speed of thirty-one knots. They are armed with twenty Granite antiship cruiser missiles with a range of 500 kilometers, surface-skimmers with multiple targeting modes. For defense, she has ninety-six vertically mounted Fort antiaircraft missiles on rotating drum launchers, with a 90-kilometer range, and 128 Kinzhal close-range antiaircraft missiles. In addition, she has two Kashtan missile artillery complexes, firing at 5,000 rpm. They were so clearly the battleships of the day that the sneering had to cease.

If that were not sufficient proof that the battleship—in effect, if not title—might be on the way back, in 2005 came the proposal from the Americans for a new surface warship, the arsenal ship—a stealth-designed hull of large displacement, some 825 feet in length, with 4,000 assorted missiles of the strategic and tactical types, including Tomahawk, Standard, and Fast Shot, to attack tanks, ships, and aircraft. This future battleship would have the ability to take out 4,000 enemy targets at a time and could overwhelm the defenses of even the most efficient of the new aggressor nations like Iran if need be. If she is ever built, then truly she will be the battleship of the future.

One thing we can be certain of, however, is that these future "missile battleships" will not fly the White Ensign of the Royal Navy, but the battle ensigns of the United States, Russia, China, and, perhaps, now-resurgent Japan. (The Japanese Navy, totally prostrate in 1945, is in 2007 now larger than the rump Royal Navy.) For even if battleships do reappear in a new guise in the years ahead, only such superpowers will be able to afford them. In Britain's present moral morass and inward-gazing fixation at self-inflicted decline and wounds, it will take enormous effort merely to maintain its present tiny force of nuclear submarines and a score or less destroyers and frigates in full commission.

The days of the British battleships are therefore gone forever, for even though we are told that Britain is still "the world's fourth largest economy" (fifth, if California is included apart from the United States), a British historian has noted from careful study that "Britain's naval growth and decline has always been bound up with her economic growth and decline."[38]

Thus the passed the British battleships. Their final achievements in the service of freedom are here contained. They had seen off three evil would-be enslavers of the British people—Hitler, Mussolini, and Tojo—just as they had seen off the Kaiser, Philip of Spain, and many others throughout the centuries. They had kept Britain free from invasion for more than three centuries and underpinned the abolition of slavery 200 years before. Now they were gone, but the British nation should not be ashamed to look back and be proud of them and of the men who served in them.

Notes

CHAPTER 1: MISTRESS OF THE SEAS?

1. Field Marshal Sir Henry Wilson to Admiral Sir David Beatty, 21 November 1918.

2. What the British blockade meant to the typical German was spelt out by Admiral Meurer to Beatty in October 1918. "It had brought revolution in the north, which had spread to the south, then the east and finally the west; that Anarchy was rampant, the seed was sown . . . men, women and children were dying of starvation and dropping down in the streets and died where they lay; children under six were non-existent; that Germany was destroyed utterly. . . . It had no effect. I [Beatty] only said to myself, 'Thank God for the British Navy. This is your work.' Without it no victory on land would have availed or ever been possible." Rear-Admiral W. S. Chalmers, *Life and Letters of David Beatty* (Hodder & Stoughton, 1951).

3. Commander Randolph Pears, *British Battleships, 1892–1957* (Putnam, 1957). The pathetic state of the German Fleet is described in Schubert and Gibson, *Death of a Fleet* (Hutchinson 1933).

4. Notable among these was Admiral William S. Benson, Chief of Naval Operations. In March 1917, he is alleged to have told Admiral Sims: "Don't let the British pull the wool over your eyes. It is none of our business pulling their chestnuts out of the fire. We would as soon fight the British as the Germans." Elting E. Morison, *Admiral Sims and the Modern American Navy* (Houghton Mifflin Co., 1942).

5. *Congressional Record*, 21 June 1916. Full details of the *Terror* and her design can be found in the article by Ensign A. D. Zimm, U.S.N., *Build the . . . Limit*, contained in *Warship International* XII, No. 1 (1975).

6. Peter Padfield, *The Battleship Era* (Rupert Hart-Davis, 1972).

7. Stephen Roskill, *Naval Policy between the Wars*, Vol. 1, *The Period of Anglo-American Antagonism, 1919–29*, (Collins, 1968).

8. In a lecture delivered in September 1919, Lieutenant Commander H. H. Frost, USN, warned, "The United States is the direct cause of this [British] adverse trade balance. If it develops that we can successfully compete with England on the seas, this adverse balance will be maintained. A nation doomed to commercial defeat will usually demand a military decision before this commercial defeat is complete." Charles M. Melhorn, *Two Block Fox: The Rise of the Aircraft Carrier, 1911–1929* (Naval Institute Press, 1974).

9. H. and M. Sprout, *Towards a New Order of Seapower* (Princeton, 1946).

10. Dr. Oscar Parkes, *British Battleships, 1860–1950* (Seeley Service, 1966).

11. Among those Americans who saw no need for America to fear a dominant British Navy, or any reason why the United States should outbuild her for either

reasons of fear or prestige were ex-President Theodore Roosevelt and Admiral W. S. Sims. In June 1921, the latter addressed the English-Speaking Union and was so pro-British, especially against the activities of the Sinn Fein in Ireland, that it earned him a smart rebuke! See Morison, *Admiral Sims and the Modern American Navy.*

12. Captain Russell Grenfell, RN, *Main Fleet to Singapore* (Faber & Faber, 1951).

13. Sir Oswyn Murray, *The Growth of Admiralty* (Mariners Mirror, Society for Nautical Research, 1937-39).

14. For example, Captain Grenfell estimated that the money spent in maintaining an army of two million men on the Western Front in 1917-18 would have been the equivalent in cost of 7,500 destroyers, when only 400 were actually on hand at that time. And, at the same cost ratio, the shell expenditure *alone* by the British army in this period was the equivalent to their firing off "two battleships every three days"!

     "If we regard the British Armies on the Western Front as being those concerned with the defence of the Channel and North Sea ports, we find that the cost in life amounted to 600,000 dead. By comparison the naval loss of life in all theatres of war incurred in the process of obtaining and exploiting the command of the seas came to 35,000." Captain Russell Grenfell, RN, writing as T124, *Sea Power* (Jonathan Cape, 1940).

15. Of the events leading up to this fateful change of policy in the years before 1914, Captain Grenfell commented, "Thus, we have the strange paradox that while the world's greatest military power was eagerly preparing to seek its further fortune on the water, the world's greatest sea power, alarmed at the menace of its neighbor's growing naval strategy, was working hard, under the guidance of a civilian Foreign Minister, to turn itself into a great land power." Grenfell, *Sea Power.* The BEF of 1940 and the BAOR of 1976 show just how much this astonishing *volte-face*, with its accompanying burden of cost and relative inefficiency *vis-à-vis* a sea-based strategy, which *is* essential, had taken grip on successive British Governments.

16. Statement by Rt. Hon. Leo Amery, Parliamentary secretary to the Admiralty in House of Commons, 3 August 1921. More than eighty-seven years later, it has a depressingly familiar ring to it.

17. The tragic irony of the League of Nations was that the United States, which had done so much to bring it about, turned its back on it and retreated into isolationism, thus depriving it of the stable base it needed to back up its altruistic resolutions. In terms of sea power, Washington gave America the power but no responsibility, while Great Britain was left with the responsibility but inadequate power to enforce it.

18. And not just the Government, the Admiralty itself had already resigned itself to sharing the trident with America. This "One Power Standard" was accepted by the Imperial Conference of 1921 as "The Basis of Imperial Defence" and remained so until the expiration of the Washington and London treaties for the limitation of naval armaments at the end of 1936. Roskill, *Naval Policy between the Wars.*

19. Lloyd George to Woodrow Wilson at Paris Peace Conference, January 1919. Lord Strang, *Britain in World Affairs* (Andre Deutsch, 1961).

20. B. B. Schofield, *British Sea Power* (Batsford, 1967).

21. Ibid.

22. The use of the submarine to make unrestricted attacks on unarmed merchant shipping has become identified as a typical Germanic concept, a product of the "beastly Hun" (and later as a threat poised by the equally despicable Soviets). However, the policy of attacking British merchant shipping, as an alternative to becoming embroiled with her battle fleet to which the French had become traditionally adverse, was of French origin. The classic *guerre de course* that they hoped would one day avenge several centuries of naval defeats was extended to the torpedo boat and then to the submarine. As Admiral Aube wrote of the role of the former, "When night comes on [the torpedo boat] will, unobserved, close with the steamer and send to the bottom cargo, crew and passengers, not only without remorse but proud of the achievement." *Brassey's Naval Annual, 1890.* Certainly between 1921 and 1933, it was the French who opposed abolition.

23. Grenfell, *Main Fleet to Singapore.*

24. Ibid.

25. Padfield, *The Battleship Era.*

26. Ibid. See also Leslie Gardiner, *The British Admiralty* (William Blackmore, 1968). "Beatty's Board, all big-ship advocates, fought hard to keep battleships and build more, against a rising tide of expert opinion which saw no future for the large floating fortress." And again: "The only people, it was alleged, in favour of keeping big ships were those admirals who had a sentimental attachment through having commanded them; a good number of whom served in high places at the Admiralty." However, Lord Chatfield explained just how this "rising tide of *expert* opinion" was demolished when actually faced with the facts, which happened some sixteen years later at the Capital Ship Committee of 1938. In chapter 14 of the second volume of his memoirs, Chatfield describes the case he presented to the numerous critics opposed to the new battleship program. Lord Chatfield, *It Might Happen Again*, Vol. 2, *The Navy and Defence* (William Heinemann, 1947).

On relative costs of bombers and battleships: "Before the conference, the Naval Staff made a calculation, that you could build and maintain over a period of time, including overhead charges, on each side, about forty-five medium bombers for one battleship. We asked the Air Ministry to make their own calculations and they informed us that thirty-seven represented a fair approximation. We fixed on forty-three. These figures were put before the critics when giving their evidence and of course dumbfounded them."

Other criticisms were similarly dealt with, with the result that in 1938 the committee came to the same conclusion, as had the Navy in 1921: "The report of the committee, which was exhaustive, came down heavily and unanimously in support of the capital ship. It was a relief at last to get on to rearming. The whole affair was typical of the difficulty of dealing officially with the *pseudo* expert; he has a clear field for stating a case with a plausible article, or pamphlet, which cannot be technically refuted because the tongue of the Chief of Staff is tied."

Another observer pinpointed the *real* reason for the Government's *volte-face* at this time. Although he also agreed with the popular view that "the supremacy of the British Battlefleet, and even of the battleship itself, was now a thing of the past," which in fact was to be the result of Governmental decision not the *reason* for it. He does specify why this came about when it did. "Britain now no longer ruled the waves unchallenged, not because she had been defeated at sea but because the strain imposed by the war had so weakened her that she was compelled by economic factors to resign herself to position of parity, if not of subordinancy." Christopher Lloyd, *The Nation and the Navy* (The Cresset Press, 1954). The reason for the actual "economic factors" was of course the decision to adopt a continental-style land strategy instead of the traditional sea-based one as related above (see note 15 above). Some ten years after its adoption, therefore, this policy had not only wasted hundreds of thousands of lives in Flanders and bankrupted the country, but also had so impoverished the nation that it could no longer afford to build the fleet necessary to reaffirm its *old* policy, even had it shown the willpower to do so.

A contemporary American attitude is found in the writings of Clark G. Reynolds: "Though the admirals of each country bemoaned these reductions to their operating fleets, they now in fact were unknowingly prevented from expending more funds on the questionably effective battleships while gaining valuable time and freedom to develop the weapons that would eventually dominate future total naval warfare-the airplane and submarine." Clark G. Reynolds, *Command of the Sea: The History and Strategy of Maritime Empires* (Robert Hale, 1974).

But in fact it was Britain who again lost out, for she had the battleship technology available and ready at hand. This was allowed to wither and the RAF, *not* the Royal Navy, funded (or failed to fund) the alternative of an effective naval aircraft program, a crippling handicap which neither America or Japan suffered from.

27. Ibid.
28. Admiralty Policy Statement accompanying Naval Estimates of 1920–21. Schofield, *British Sea Power.*
29. Admiral Sir Frederick C. Dreyer, *The Sea Heritage* (Museum Press, 1955). Admiral Dreyer flew his flag aboard *Hood* from 1928, when she was flagship of the Battlecruiser Squadron, Home Fleet, and had formerly been Director of Admiralty Gunnery Division; his viewpoint therefore seems irrefutable.
30. Admiral S. S. Hall's viewpoint from a letter published in *The Times,* 7 April 1922.
31. The main issues of Trenchard's views were expressed in *The role of the Air Force in the System of Imperial Defence,* a paper circulated to the CID in March 1921. His views remained unaltered to the end.
32. Melhorn, *Two Block Fox.*
33. Ibid.
34. The most comprehensive, clear-sighted, and valuable published documentation available on this episode to date is "More Fiction than Fact: The Sinking of the *Ostfriesland*" by Gene T. Zimmerman in *Warship International* XII, No. 2 (1975). Other books which deal with air attack on battleships, with varying degrees of competence, include the authorative *Air Power and the Royal Navy, 1914–1945: A Historical Survey* by Geoffrey Till (Janes, 1979), which is thoroughly recommended. Less so is the oddly titled *Bombers versus Battleships* by David Hamer (Conway Maritime Press, 1998), which features on the jacket not *Yamato, Musashi, Prince of Wales, Arizona,* or even *Tirpitz* under air attack but an ancient tramp steamer being bombed—as if there were no difference in resistance or capability! Despite the fact that the last British battleship went to the scrap yard a quarter of a century earlier, so that factually there were no battleships at the time, the Falklands War is also featured. Perhaps, like Matthew Hickley, the

Defence Correspondent of the *Daily Mail,* who in an article on January 6, 2007, illustrated the Royal Navy as still possessing three battleships with three more proposed (!) and seemingly somehow managed to equate almost defenseless and totally unarmored helicopter-carrying vessels with battleships. Even "experts" don't know the difference anymore!

35. See also the American *Literary Digest,* 6 August 1921.
36. Roskill, *Naval Policy between the Wars.*
37. Ibid.
38. Wing Commander H. R. Allen, DFC, *The Legacy of Lord Trenchard* (Cassell, 1972).
39. Ibid.
40. Melhorn, *Two Block Fox.*
41. Parkes, *British Battleships.*
42. These facts, and other sobering estimations of the *actual,* rather than the *claimed,* performance of bombers against moving ship targets are contained in *Assessment of Damage due to Aircraft Action in Staff Exercises and War Games 1925–28,* ADM 11G/24G4, Public Record Office, London. In assessing high-altitude bombing as useless against moving warships, this and subsequent reports have been held up to much criticism, but the results gained in war merely proved just how accurate these estimates had been. Dive-bombing and torpedo-bombing were another matter.
43. Allen, *The Legacy of Lord Trenchard.*
44. This is confirmed in letters from the men who actually had to face the dive-bombers of the Luftwaffe in the years 1940–41. Despite the fact that they were serving off Spain in 1939 when the Stukas (Junkers Ju87) were first utilized with enormous success against ships, they echoed the opinions of Captain De Winton: "I don't think I had even heard of a Stuka prewar, and dive-bombing of ships was not ever considered as a likely threat." Letters from Captain F. S. De Winton, Captain Edward Gibbs, the late Admiral Sir Richard Onslow, and others.

    The vulnerability of capital ships (VCS) committee set up under Sir Thomas Inskip, which reported on July 30, 1937, made recommendations that "were singularly anodyne," wrote Roskill, *Naval Policy between the Wars.* What did come out of the trials conducted in the Medway in 1934-36 was that *no* bomb pierced four inches of armor. Another decade was to pass before the RAF developed a bomb that could and the aircraft to carry it as well.
45. In 1925, torpedo-bombers from the *Eagle* took part in a large-scale exercise in the Mediterranean and scored three hits on heavy ships; in September 1930, fifteen torpedo-bombers operating from Lee-on-Solent scored eight hits on the *Nelson* and *Rodney* in fleet exercises off the Isle of Wight; and the following year, torpedo-bombers from *Glorious,* again in the Mediterranean, made *nine* hits on battleship targets. However, this success rate was not repeated in the Home Fleet exercises of 1932.
46. Viscount Cunningham of Hyndhope, Admiral of the Fleet, KT, GCB, OM, DSO, *A Sailor's Odyssey* (Hutchinson, 1951).
47. Roskill, *Naval Policy between the Wars.*
48. Again, this concentration on "re-fighting the Battle of Jutland" instead of concentrating exercises on convoy protection, air-sea warfare and combined operations has recorded almost universal criticism in postwar analysis. But here again the views of officers, at that time in *junior* positions and therefore free from the

blanket accusation of "obsession with the heavy gun," deserve to be heard. Captain Edward Gibbs, for example, wrote that "if a fleet is fully trained to a high pitch for a *fleet* action, then they are as equally ready for any other enemy action." A fleet action, particularly of the "night encounter" type for which the Royal Navy was trained to a high degree, is the most complex and fastest-moving naval action any officer can be expected to participate in. If ships and crews can cope with such high speed and instant reflex training, their years of practice can hardly have been held to have been valueless. Matapan was *not* the sole reward for this effort; its effect was felt in numerous actions in World War II.

Somewhat in contradiction to his earlier statement, Clark Reynolds also maintains that "conservative battleship admirals thus returned to the old prewar anti-intellectualism, their naval war colleges and fleet maneuvred looking to another Jutland and virtually ignoring the promise of the aeroplane and submarine." Reynolds, *Command of the Sea.*

49. Admiral Sir Herbert Richmond, *National Policy and Naval Strategy* (Longmans Green, 1928).

50. Captain S. W. Roskill, DSC, RN. *H.M.S. Warspite: The Story of a Famous Battleship* (Collins, 1957). The *Barham, Malaya, Repulse,* and *Royal Oak* were all scheduled for "partial" modernizations on a lesser scale than these ships, but this never took place. See Roskill, *Naval Policy between the Wars.*

51. Parkes, *British Battleships.*

52. Schofield, *British Sea Power.*

53. The Germans always called them *Panzerschiff* (armored ship), but the term "pocket battleship" much more aptly described their function and power, and since it gained widespread common usage, the term will be used in this book. Likewise, *Scharnhorst* and *Gneisenau,* by their tonnage, armament, and speed, ranked and rated as battlecruisers and are thus so defined in this book.

CHAPTER 2: THE NEW CONFLICT

1. When Inter-Allied Control Commission, set up under the Treaty of Versailles to ensure that Germany *did* disarm, finally disbanded after the Treaty of Locarno in 1925, one British member openly told his German opposite number, "You need not think that we have believed what you have said. You did not speak a single word of truth, but you have given your information so skillfully that we were able to accept it, and for that I am grateful to you." William Shirer, *The Rise and Fall of the Third Reich* (Secker and Warburg, 1962).

2. The great German armaments baron Krupp was to boast in 1942 that "the basic principle of armament and turret design for tanks had already been worked out in 1926. . . . Of the guns being used in 1939–41, the most important ones were already fully complete in 1933." Shirer, *The Rise and Fall of the Third Reich.*

3. Admiral Behncke and Admiral Zenker. Admiral Raeder took over in 1928.

4. Captain Donald Macintyre, DSO, DSC, RN, *The Thunder of the Guns* (Frederick Muller, 1959).

5. This was not apparently appreciated even later. For example, one historian wrote, "In spite of Hitler's alarmingly efficient and coordinated attacks on Poland, the German Navy was not ready to conduct naval warfare on any scale, so the inevitable sole use for her capital ships could only be the *guerre de course,* the attack on enemy trade and shipping routes." Philip Cowburn, *The Warship in History* (Macmillan, 1966). Actually, the whole German battle fleet and the

planned ships of the Z-Plan were built solely with the *guerre de course* in mind. The fact that it might be strong enough to offer battle in direct competition was a sort of bonus brought on more by Britain's weakness at sea rather than German plans to refight Jutland.

6. David Woodward, *The Tirpitz* (William Kimber, 1953).

7. Ibid.

8. "On land I am a hero, at sea I am a coward," Hitler once freely admitted. Hitler never really wanted war against Great Britain anyway, and he always maintained that to challenge her at sea, as the Kaiser had done, was folly. He poured scorn on the efforts of Tirpitz to rival the Royal Navy. "The tendency to build all ships a little smaller than the English ships which were being launched at the same time was hardly farsighted, much less brilliant." The führer was not to repeat *that* particular error! Adolf Hitler, *Mein Kampf* (Hutchinsons, 1974 ed.).

9. H. T. Lenton, *German Surface Vessels—1* (Macdonald, 1966).

10. Shirer, *The Rise and Fall of the Third Reich.*

11. Hoare met Laval on December 7 and asked him straight out whether in the event of an attack Britain could depend on French help. "His answer, though it was in general terms satisfactory, avoided any undertaking to make military preparations, and obviously assumed that French cooperation would depend upon Anglo-French agreement as to our immediate policy." Viscount Templewood, *Nine Troubled Years* (Collins, 1964).

12. At Alexandria were *Queen Elizabeth* (Flag), *Barham, Ramillies,* and *Revenge,* later joined by *Royal Sovereign.* At Gibraltar were *Hood* and *Renown.*

13. Lord Vansittart, *The Mist Procession* (Hutchinson, 1958).

14. Colonel H. R. Pownall, quoted as footnote in Arthur J. Marder, *From the Dardanelles to Oran* (Oxford University Press, 1974).

15. Cunningham, *A Sailor's Odyssey.*

16. The Admiralty had no idea of the numbers of Japanese battleships ready for sea at this period (in fact, half were laid up for refitting); they knew only that they were left with seven British ships in which to counter any sudden move Japan might make during this crisis. Marder, *From the Dardanelles to Oran.*

17. A fact which the Germans had foreseen and were highly pleased with. "The Wilhelmstrasse is delighted. Either Mussolini will stumble and get himself so heavily involved in Africa that he will be greatly weakened in Europe, whereupon Hitler can seize Austria, hitherto protected by the *Duce*; or he will win, defying France and Britain, and therefore be ripe for a tie-up with Hitler against the Western democracies. Either way Hitler wins." Shirer, *Rise and Fall of the Third Reich.*

18. Professor Sir Geoffrey Callender, *The Naval Side of British History* (Christophers, 1924).

19. Roskill, *Naval Policy between the Wars,* Vol. 1. In the spring of 1932 at the disarmament discussions preliminaries in London, Britain unofficially considered the limitations of a top ceiling of 10,000 tons on warships. Later, the American delegate put forward proposals which included a reduction by one-third in total number of arms, including capital ships. Sir John Simon put before the Geneva talks a proposed battleship limitation of 25,000 tons and 12-inch guns, which had been first raised at the Admiralty in 1929.

20. Captain Sir Basil Liddell-Hart, *Memoirs* (Cassell, 1965).

21. John Deane Potter, *Admiral of the Pacific: The Life of Yamamoto* (Heinemann, 1965).

22. Ibid.

23. Ibid.

24. Ibid.

25. Ibid.

26. Ibid.

27. Schofield, *British Sea Power*.

28. Parkes, *British Battleships*.

29. Ibid.

30. Ibid.

31. Charles Owen, *No More Heroes* (George Allen & Unwin, 1975).

32. Roskill, *Naval Policy between the Wars*.

33. Admiral of the Fleet Lord Chatfield, *It Might Happen Again* (Heinemann, 1947).

34. Schofield, *British Sea Power*. In 1935, four designs of battlecruisers—with eight, ten, or twelve 14-inch or nine 16-inch guns—were prepared for study. These were followed by another for twelve 14-inch in quadruple turrets, the genus for the KG5s. In April 1936, Design 14-0 was exhaustively discussed, and ten 14-inch and 291 knots was considered the best one to go for. The tried and tested 15-inch gun (Design 15-C) was rejected since, if improved antiaircraft guns and 29 knots were required, the tonnage would exceed the 35,000 limit. Alternative designs in 1938 for the three later ships (*Duke of York*, *Anson*, and *Howe*) to mount 16-inch guns (Designs 16A-38 and 16G-38) were dropped for similar reasons unfortunately.

    Henderson also later stated that to adopt a modified and updated *Nelson*-type 16-inch gun for these ships the displacement would come out around 45,000 tons instead of 35,000, that magic figure which the Germans, Japanese, Americans, and Soviets had no hesitation in ignoring. See Roskill, *Naval Policy between the Wars*, Vol. 2.

35. Russell Grenfell, *The Bismarck Episode* (Faber & Faber, 1953).

36. Schofield, *British Sea Power*. "With regard to power plants, Admiralty three-drum boilers were also regarded as the standard boilers for capital ships and cruisers although in some cases the working pressure was raised to 400 pounds per square inch, which was about the upper limit for British practice until 1945. Pressures of 650 pounds per square inch were, however, common in the Babcock & Wilcox boilers fitted in many U.S. Navy vessels." K. T. Rowland, *Steam at Sea* (David & Charles, 1970).

37. Macintyre, *The Thunder of the Guns*. Both nations in actual fact did build aircraft carriers. France commissioned the *Béarn* before the war and had another two planned, while Italy converted the liner *Roma* into the aircraft carrier *Aquila*, which was almost ready for trials at the time of the Armistice in June 1943.

38. Parkes, *British Battleships*.

39. Owen, *No More Heroes*.

40. Vice Admiral Sir Peter Gretton, KCB, DSO, OBE, DSC, *Former Naval Person* (Cassell, 1968).

41. Ibid.

42. Grenfell, *Main Fleet to Singapore*.

43. Michael Lewis, *The History of the British Navy* (Allen & Unwin, 1959).

44. Ibid.

45. Gretton, *Former Naval Person*
46. Captain T. D. Manning and Commander C. F. Walker, *British Warship Names* (Putnam, 1959).
47. At the Battle of the Nile in 1798, a former *Bellerophon* tackled the French flagship until she was dismasted. "The *Swiftsure* and *Alexander* were approaching the scene of action when they saw in the darkness a ship's hull drifting by. 'What ship is that?' they hailed. '*Billy Ruff'n* going out of action, disabled,' came the answer." Pears, *British Battleships.*
48. Lieutenant Commander Peter Kemp, *Nine Vanguards* (Hutchinson, 1951).
49. Admiral Beatty put it another way much earlier on; he was determined to station a squadron of battlecruisers at Singapore when the base was finished because without them, "a base without a fleet is a mere hostage to an enemy." Sir Herbert Richmond, *Statesmen and Sea Power* (Oxford University Press, 1928).
50. Cajus Bekker, *Hitler's Naval War* (Macdonald, 1974).
51. Ibid.
52. Woodward, *The Tirpitz.*
53. Lenton, *German Surface Vessels—1.*
54. Woodward, *The Tirpitz.*
55. Bekker, *Hitler's Naval War.*
56. See, for example, R. Erikson, "Soviet Battleships" in *Warship International* 2 (1974); and the letter from B. Lemachko in *Warship International* 2 (1975).
57. Owen, *No More Heroes.*
58. Marder, *From the Dardanelles to Oran.*
59. Captain S. W. Roskill, DSC, FR Hist.S, RN, Rtd., *The Strategy of Seapower: Its Development and Application* (Collins, 1962).
60. Vice Admiral Friedrich Ruge, *Sea Warfare, 1939–45* (Cassell, 1957).
61. Ernle Bradford, *The Mighty Hood* (Hodder & Stoughton, 1959).
62. Count Ciano, Italian Foreign Minister, had been having a hard time convincing Mussolini to stay out of the conflict due to Italy's precarious financial and industrial position. Throughout August and September, he strove to convince him of the nation's military weaknesses as well. In October, he wrote of the *Duce* that he had never seen him so depressed now he realized that the war was "inevitable," and he knew he had to stay out of it. Count Galeazzo Ciano, *Diaries, 1939–43* (Heinemann, 1947).

CHAPTER 3: OLD TRUTHS, NEW LESSONS

1. Only the battleships *Cavour* and *Cesare* were ready at this time. Dating from 1914–15, they were sister ships and both had been extensively modernized during 1933–37. Their details were:

   Battleships (2): *Conte di Cavour, Giulio Cesare*

   23,622 tons, 10 12.6-inch, 12 4.7-inch, 8 3.9-inch guns, 27 knots.

   Two other battleships, near sisters of these vessels, were due to complete similar modernizations in mid-1940. Built in 1915–16, their details were:

   Battleships (2): *Andrea Doria, Caio Duilio.*

   23,622 tons, 10 12.6-inch, 12 5.3-inch, 10 3.5-inch guns, 27 knots.

   All four of these old Italian ships were therefore faster than the modernized British ships of similar vintage, and, although the caliber of their main armaments was inferior they had been given greater elevation, and therefore range, and thus outclassed the unmodernised British battleships. In addition to these four of course the Italian replacement programs had started earlier and the first brace of the new battleships were also due for completion in mid-1940, over a year before the first "King George V" could arrive on the scene.

2. The Italians could both intercept and read British coded cables at this time. Count Ciano recorded in his diary on June 8, 1940, two days before Italy entered the war that he received from Hong Kong a document of the highest interest; it was a study made by Admiral Noble (then Commander in Chief, China) of British possibilities against the Axis forces. It "was couched in pessimistic terms," especially with regard to the Mediterranean, which he saw dominated by the forces of Fascist Italy. Ciano duly handed a copy of this document to the Japanese ambassador on the eve of that gentleman's departure for Berlin. Ciano found the gloomy contents of the message, understandably enough, "very impressive."

3. In January 1940, reconnaissance photos of *Bismarck* and the carrier *Graf Zeppelin* seemed to indicate that both ships might be ready for action as early as June. Despite an all-out effort presided over by Churchill himself, neither *King George V* nor *Prince of Wales* could be ready until well after that date. Air strikes were considered against both ships in order to damage and delay them but later observations showed that they were not so far advanced as first thought. Also the German practice of long and elaborate work-ups and trials before sending their ships to sea meant that both British ships beat her into operational service, although in *Prince of Wales*'s case this typical British policy of initial delay followed by panic and rush may not have necessarily have been a good thing, as we will see.

4. Philip Cosgrave, *Churchill at War*, Vol. 1, *Alone, 1939–40* (Collins, 1974). Another factor in the abandonment of these ships (and the delay to *Vanguard*) may have been the factor noted by Roskill. The acute shortage of manufacturing capacity for armour plate had led, in 1937, to the ordering of much of it for our capital ship program from the Skoda works in Czechoslovakia. This source naturally dried up when the British Government handed that nation over to our likeliest enemy Roskill, *Naval Policy between the Wars*, Vol. 2. Captain Roskill actually states that the German invasion of Poland cut off this source to us, but of course Czechoslovakia and the Skoda works became Hitler's property some months earlier, in March.

5. Gretton, *Former Naval Person*.

6. Cosgrave, *Churchill at War*, Vol. 1

7. Marder, *From the Dardanelles to Oran*.

8. Ibid.

9. Ibid.

10. Ibid.

11. Ibid.

12. A former official naval historian, Lieutenant Commander P. K. Kemp, has stated that the name *Vanguard* was originally allocated to a projected fifth *Lion*-class ship. See Kemp, *Nine Vanguards*. While one must respect such a source, with unreleased documentation to draw on, there is no confirmation of this by either Oscar Parkes in his definitive volume *British Battleships* nor by Manning and Walker in their equally exhaustive study *British Warship Names*.

With regard to the slow time of construction of this vessel, Kemp stated in his highly detailed work that "her construction went ahead comparatively fast, considering the two factors which operated most in holding her back. The first of these was the natural difficulty in wartime of the allocation of materials and the competing pressure of other work, both in new building and in repair work in British yards." In other words then she was reduced to a low priority project very early on despite the original desire to finish her before the projected *Lions*. The second factor Kemp describes as "the result of experience gained in action." He stated that "during her actual construction there were four major alterations in structural design, an indication of the thoroughness with which currently learned lessons were being applied in the new ship." These alterations he cites as the adding of the high sheer to her bows, by the fitting of an entirely new bow, increased protection against air attack, improved subdivision and damage control facilities, while, for good measure, "wireless-controlled glider-bombs, magnetic and acoustic mines and torpedoes, and the like have all been taken into account in her building."

Even so, it is surely rather overstating the case to claim that "the actual time between her laying down and her launching compares favorably with normal peacetime experience in the construction of battleships." If this is so, it invalidates the Churchillian arguments for building her in the first place, and the *Lion* could have been completed anyway in the same timeframe to give a more powerful end result. Here are some comparison dates for other battleships

	Laid Down	Launched	Months
Queen Elizabeth	Oct 1912	Oct 1913	12
Nelson	Dec 1922	Sept 1925	33
King George V	Jan 1937	Feb 1939	25
Vanguard	Oct 1941	Nov 1944	37

In fairness Lenton and Colledge state that "the construction of the *Vanguard*, although not pushed, could have been expedited if required." H. T. Lenton and J. J. Colledge, *Warships of World War II* (Ian Allan, 1965).

13. Marder, *From Dardanelles to Oran.*
14. Winston S. Churchill, *The Second World War*, Vol. 1 (Cassell, 1949).
15. Denis Richards, *Royal Air Force, 1939–45*, Vol. 1, *The Fight at Odds* (Her Majesty's Stationery Office, 1953).
16. Cajus Bekker, *The Luftwaffe War Diaries* (Macdonald, 1967).
17. Captain S. W Roskill, *The War at Sea*, Vol. 1, *The Defensive* (Her Majesty's Stationery Office, 1954).
18. Air Ministry, *The Rise and Fall of the German Air Force, 1933–45* (Air Ministry, 1948).
19. Roskill, *The War at Sea*, Vol. 1.
20. Bradford, *The Mighty Hood.*
21. Roskill, *The War at Sea*, Vol. 1.
22. Richards, *Royal Air Force, 1939–45*, Vol. 1.
23. Bekker, *The Luftwaffe War Diaries.*
24. Richards, *Royal Air Force, 1939–5*, Vol. 1.
25. Vice-Admiral Sir Arthur Hezlet, KBE, CB, DSO, DSC, *Aircraft and Seapower* (Peter Davies, 1970).
26. A full examination of these failures, their causes and also their ultimate remedy is contained in Bekker, *Hitler's Naval War.*

27. Macintyre, *The Thunder of the Guns.*
28. The slowest battleships in service with the Royal Navy were the *Royal Sovereign* class with a *maximum* speed of 21 knots. The *Nelson* had 23 knots, the *Queen Elizabeth* 25 knots. One could usually take off a couple of knots after hard war service without proper refits. In contrast the main types of German submarine in service during 1939-44 had the following speeds credited to them:

Type	Maximum Submerged Speed	Maximum Surfaced Speed
VIIC	7.6 knots	17.1 knots
IXC	7.3 knots	18.3 knots
XXI	17 knots	15 knots
XXIII	12.5 knots	9.7 knots

29. Schofield, *British Sea Power.*
30. Ibid.
31. See, for example, Alexandre Korganoff, *The Phantom of Scapa Flow* (Ian Allan, 1974).
32. The sinking of the *Royal Oak,* is examined in great depth, which gives a good insight to the whole affair, in Gerald S. Snyder, *The Royal Oak Disaster* (William Kimber 1976), and Alexander McKee, *Black Saturday* (Souvenir Press, 1959). The only significant new details confirmed in the former volume are the extracts from the Board of Enquiry report (Appendix A) and the report of divers on the wreck (Appendix B), both of which confirm the *Royal Oak* was sunk by submarine torpedoes and not sabotage, as is sometimes alleged.
33. Roskill, *The War at Sea,* Vol. 1.
34. Another German myth, which seems to be self-perpetuating despite the true facts long being made known, is the claim that when the *Nelson* was attacked on this occasion, she had aboard Winston Churchill, Admiral Pound, and Air Vice-Marshal Peirse. This is simply not true. The U-boat attack took place on the morning of October 30, at sea, whereas the First Lord, First Sea Lord, and the Deputy Chief of the Air Staff did not step aboard the *Nelson,* at anchor in the Clyde, until the next day, October 31, to discuss the problems of defense of the fleet base.
35. The effects of a battleship hitting a destroyer thus, even at a slow speed, were quite devastating. The *Barham* was moving slowly up the Clyde, escorted by the destroyers *Dainty, Diana,* and *Duchess* at 3:00 A.M. during a jet-black winter's night.
"There was a sudden great jarring crash, then a violent shuddering as *Barham* went full astern. Diving out of their hammocks they saw, in the light of searchlights, what looked like a submarine with a few men clinging on to her. Then they realized that it was the upturned hull of the *Duchess. Barham* had rammed and overturned her. One or two of her scuttles were still above the water-line and Ted could see men trying to climb out of the small openings." Kenneth Poolman, *Ark Royal* (William Kimber, 1956). Only 23 from a crew of 140 were rescued from the icy water.
36. The original vessels were
Old Battleships (8): *Zähringen*
11,800 tons, 4 9.4-inch, 18 5.9-inch guns, 18 knots (1902).
Braunschweig, Elsass, Hessen, Lothringen, Preussen.
13,200 tons, 4 11-inch, 14 6.7-inch guns, 18 knots. (1904–6)

Schleswig-Holstein, Schlesien.
13,200 tons, 4 11-inch, 14 6.7-inch, 20 3-inch guns, 18 knots. (1908)
   Of these eight, four—*Braunschweig, Elsass, Lothringen,* and *Preussen*—had been scrapped in 1931. *Zähringen* and *Hessen* had been converted into radio-controlled target ships and served through the war, the former being sunk in a bombing raid on Gotenhafen in December 1944 and the latter surviving to be handed over to the Russians in 1946.

37. Ruge, *Sea Warfare.*
38. Under this name the ex-*Deutschland* should not be confused with the 14,800-ton heavy cruiser *Lützow,* a half-sister of the *Admiral Hipper.* This latter vessel was sold, still unfinished but afloat, to the Russians in March, 1940 as part of a deal between these two allied nations involving food, oil, and war material. Eager as he was to placate Hitler, even Stalin jibbed at the asking price for this vessel, 150 million Reichsmarks. "One should not take advantage of the Soviet Union's good nature!" Shirer, *The Rise and Fall of the Third Reich.* The Soviet Navy never had time to complete her.
39. Probably due to the fact that this episode took place at a time when little else was happening, the River Plate battle has been given saturation coverage by naval historians, and the reader is offered enormous scope for further research. Among the mountain of volumes are *Battle of the River Plate* by Commander A. B. Campbell, *Battle of the River Plate* by Dudley Pope, *Battle of the River Plate* by Lord Strabolgi, *The Drama of the Graf Spee and the Battle of the Plate,* perhaps the best of them all, by Sir Eugen Millington-Drake. For the prisoners' viewpoint, see *I was Graf Spee's Prisoner* by Captain Patrick Dove and *The Navy's Here* by W. Frischauer and R. Jackson. Despite such a wealth of material, fresh books still appear, including among a veritable host of others *Battle of the River Plate* by Geoffrey Bennett (Ian Allan, 1972).
40. Willi Frischauer and Robert Jackson, *The Navy's Here* (Victor Gollancz, 1955).
41. For an excellent study of German afloat support methods and practice during the war, see Geoffrey P. Jones, *Under Three Flags* (William Kimber, 1972).
42. Although the development of radar had proceeded almost step-by-step simultaneously in Great Britain and in Germany, the two navies adopted it for different prime functions initially. The Germans regarded it as an aid for surface gunnery ranging, the British for the detection of aircraft as its prime function, with its surface warning spin-off, as a sort of bonus. The first British ship-borne radar set went to sea in the cruiser *Sheffield* in August 1938; it was known as RDF (Radio Detection and Ranging) set, Type 79. The first British battleship to be equipped was the *Rodney,* later the same year.
   A good description of the comparative merits of British and German rangefinders is to be found in Peter Padfield, *Guns at Sea* (Hugh Evelyn, 1973).
43. Bekker, *Hitler's Naval War.*
44. Roskill, *The War at Sea,* Vol. 1.
45. The fact that the German capital ships of the *Deutschland, Gneisenau,* and *Bismarck* classes, and also the heavy cruisers like *Prinz Eugen,* were endlessly confused with one another, despite the great differences in size and armament, may cause the reader to assume that British recognition efficiency throughout the war was rather poor. While this may in fact be so, it is also true that the German ships' silhouettes were remarkably similar. All were single-funneled, with the distinctive German raking funnel cap, and their hull lines were also similar, with

clipper stems. They were, indeed, outstandingly graceful, as well as powerful, warships for their day. Such similarity of design was an accident; they were *not* quite deliberately designed this way in order to cause confusion. See Donald MacLachlan, *Room 39: Naval Intelligence in Action* (Weidenfeld & Nicolson, 1968).

46. Corvette-Captain Fritz-Otto Busch, *The Drama of the Scharnhorst* (Robert Hale, 1956). "We are coming like rats out of their holes," a sub-lieutenant remarked happily. "And we'll show them we can bite."

47. Roskill, *The War at Sea*, Vol. 1.

48. Apart from the contributions of the battlecruisers to the Atlantic Hunting Groups, about the only French movement of heavy ships was the cross-Atlantic trip by the old *Bretagne* carrying 1,200 bars of gold from Toulon to Halifax, to pay for vital war supplies, which took place between March 11 and April 10. Otherwise, not much stirred in French ports, although, because of the expected lateness of the *King George V*s, much pressure was put on the French to complete the *Jean Bart* and *Richelieu* earlier than planned. The French response to this British request was good, and they *were* hastened. Unfortunately, Hitler was moving at a much faster pace than either ally, and their completion was overtaken by events.

49. The reconstruction plans put forward for the *Hood* were first made in 1939, and she would have followed *Queen Elizabeth* into the yards. According to Dr. Parkes, the reconstruction would have involved

1. Provision of new machinery
2. Modifications to underwater protection
3. Removal of the conning tower.
4. Removal of the above-water torpedo tubes.
5. Replacing the obsolete 5.5-inch and 4-inch guns with a modern dual- purpose battery of sixteen 5.25-inch, like *King George V* and *Lion*.
6. Fitting hangars, etc.
7. Increase of horizontal and vertical protection.

The first five would certainly have much improved the twenty-year-old battle-cruiser; (6) would have been a heedless expense and waste of space. Whether (7) would have prevented her subsequent demise is open to question; it would have certainly helped. What in fact she *did* get in this refit was something not mentioned above, the addition of five UPs. These latter were an antiaircraft device developed by Professor Lindemann's department as a "more efficient" weapon for use against low-flying enemy aircraft. It was a multiple rocket launcher, each outfit carrying fourteen 3-inch rockets (UP = unrotating projectile). Each rocket projected a 7-inch container carrying 2,000 feet of wire to which was attached a small parachute and a 2-pound bomb. The theory was that an aircraft would become entangled in the wire and pulled the explosive down into itself whereupon it would detonate. Both the DNO and the majority of experts shared Admiral Nicholl's view, expressed in Arthur J. Marder's book *From the Dardanelles to Oran*, that this device was "considered by everyone, except Winston as 'plumb crazy.'" Nonetheless, Churchill had his way and by the autumn of 1940 twenty-nine such sets had been installed in British capital ships. There is no record of them ever having brought down an enemy aircraft, other than a "probable" at Dover on November 14, 1940. This UP equipment certainly increased *Hood*'s capacity for modern warfare by not one jot; quite the reverse, for there is much speculation that they in fact contributed directly to her loss. This will be discussed in the appropriate section.

50. As with most campaigns, the literature available is of gigantic proportions. Apart from the official British history, *The Campaign in Norway* by T. K. Derry (HMSO, 1952), which is the best overall volume on the campaign, both on land and at sea, the better books on the various aspects of the fighting are Bernard Ash, *Norway 1940* (Cassell, 1964); Captain D. F. W. Macintyre, *Narvik* (Evans, 1959), which gives a general view of the sea operations similar to that contained in Captain Stephen Roskill's first volume; and Captain Peter Dickens, *Narvik* (Ian Allan, 1974), a first-rate description and analysis of the two naval battles of that name.

51. Bekker, *Hitler's Naval War.*

52. Richards, *Royal Air Force, 1939-45*

53. Macintyre, *Narvik.*

54. Busch, *The Drama of the Scharnhorst.*

55. Roskill, *The War at Sea, Vol. 1.*

56. Ruge, *Sea Warfare.*

57. Strangely enough, even the outstanding Dr. Parkes describes the German ships in this action as being "the *Scharnhorst* and *Admiral Hipper* off Narvik" and the date as April 8. See Parkes, *British Battleships* (this being the new and revised edition of 1966).

58. Richards, *Royal Air Force, 1939-45.*

59. Admiral of the Fleet Sir Philip Vian, *Action this Day* (Frederick Muller, 1960).

60. Ash, *Norway 1940.*

61. The first attack had sunk the destroyers *Heidkamp* and *Schmitt* and damaged the destroyers *Roeder, Thiele,* and *Arnim* severely and the *Ludemann* and *Künne* lightly. Of the three undamaged vessels of the German destroyer flotilla, the *Zenker, Kollner,* and *Giese,* the first pair were damaged by running aground because of bad navigation on the eleventh after a half-hearted attempt at escape. Thus, all eight remained trapped in the fjord on the thirteenth. They had been joined by the two U-boats; all had their torpedo outfits in good order and ample ammunition, although magazines in some ships were reported as half-empty.

62. Dickens, *Narvik.*

63. Roskill, *HMS Warspite.*

64. Macintyre, *Narvik.*

65. Ibid.

66. The extent in which Churchill intervened in the day-to-day operations of the Fleet while First Lord is the subject of some differences of opinion. See Captain S.W. Roskill's article "Marder, Churchill and the Admiralty, 1939–42," *Royal United Services Institute Journal* CXVII (December 1972) in reply to Arthur J. Marder's study "Winston is Back" in his *Dardanelles to Oran.* Marder's counterblast, *Musings on a Bolt from Olympus,* are contained in this book, the original article appearing as Supplement Five of the *English Historical Review* (Longman, 1972). Not wishing to take sides against such combatants, it is fair to comment that the actual commanders, Forbes, Cunningham, Somerville, and others, *did* frequently feel that the more prodding and intolerant of such signals originated from Churchill. Whether they actually did so I leave others to judge; however,

Winston's "prayers" were well-known, as were his more emphatic "Action This Day" memos.

67. The heavy cruiser *Suffolk* (10,000 tons; eight 8-inch, eight 4-inch, eight 2-pound guns; 31 knots) was one of the "County"-class Washington Treaty ships built in 1927. She was sent from Scapa, alone and unescorted, to bombard the airfield at Stavanger on the night of April 16-17, which she did, firing 250 rounds of 8-inch shell in three unspotted runs at 20,000 yards range. Damage was moderate; the airfield was certainly not put out of action. During the daylight hours of the seventeenth, her fighter cover having failed to materialize as usual, she was subjected to over six hours' continuous aerial attack. Thirty-three attacks were made during this period, twenty-one by altitude bombers which were not effective and twelve by Stukas, which *were*. She fired off all her ammunition, including practice shells, repeated calls for fighter defense were ignored, and after eighty-eight near-misses, the Stukas planted a 1,100-pound bomb, which went right through the lightly armored deck aft. It penetrated the upper deck at the base of X turret, went through the wardroom and warrant officers' mess, and burst in a storeroom, close to the after engine room. The resulting explosion caused severe damage, casualties and flooding here, while the blast ignited the cordite in the handling room which, in turn, triggered off a massive explosion in the after turret which blew off the roof. Thirty-three men were killed and thirty-eight wounded. The magazines were flooded, 1,500 tons of water entering in twenty minutes. Further near-misses increased this to 2,500 tons, and she was unable to steer save by her engines. The first fighters arrived at 2:15 P.M., almost six hours after the first attacks, and she finally crawled into Scapa Flow, with her quarterdeck awash, on the seventeenth, after covering the last 164 miles by her screws only. She was not sunk, but was put out of the war for almost a year.

68. Donald Forbes, *Two Small Ships* (Hutchinsons, 1957).

69. Ash, *Norway 1940*. Presumably, the author had in mind the plans for Operation Catherine already discussed above. A similar project later resulted when the old demilitarized radio-controlled target ship, *Centurion* (built 1913 as one of the four *King George V* battleships of the 1910 Program and used as a target ship, 1927-39) was converted in a special operation, to resemble the new battleship *Anson*. She had an armament which consisted solely of 2-pounders and 20-millimeter Oerlikons. She saw service with the Home Fleet in 1939–41 and went to Bombay in 1941–42. She took part in Convoy Vigorous from Alexandria to Malta in June 1942, but fooled nobody, least of all the enemy, as we describe later.

70. Bekker, *Hitler's Naval War*.

71. Ibid.

72. Ibid.

73. As Bernard Ash reveals, the German squadron *had* been reported at sea despite official accounts to the contrary. The Norwegian coast watch had reported them to Wing Commander Atcherley's operations room, the telephone girls describing them as "two German battleships." As Ash remarks, "the report caused two reactions. In the first place, it was thought very funny, and in the second place, it was assumed (pardonably but, one sees now, unjustifiably) that the Navy, who knew everything, knew all about these ships. Atcherley distinctly remembers that the last words said to him before he himself embarked after the fighters had been finally flown away were 'Look out for the bloody battleships!' and this,

in fact, became a catch-phrase that was current for quite a time afterwards." As Ash also states, his joke was, in the event, "tragically unfunny." It is also equally tragic and ironic that the OIC reading of the German W/T traffic, which led one member to believe that the German heavy ships *were* out, were treated with extreme—one is tempted to say *ultra*—caution. Patrick Beesley states that as these readings and conclusions could not be checked or confirmed by other sources, they were not acted upon. "To alert the Home Fleet on this insubstantial and untested basis," he recalls, "seemed to be running too great a risk." Patrick Beesley, *Very Special Intelligence* (Hamish Hamilton, 1977). And so *Glorious, Ardent*, and *Acasta* died.

74. Busch, *The Drama of the Scharnhorst.*
75. A vexing puzzle this. Both Dr. Derry, the official historian of the Norwegian campaign, and Captain Roskill, the official naval historian, assume that the reason no antisubmarine patrol was aloft at this time, which would have almost certainly given *Glorious* enough time to evade interception, maybe even mount a torpedo strike from out of the blue, was because of the congestion aboard the carrier due to the RAF fighters. Ash remarks that this made no difference to normal flying operations on the outward voyage with an equal number of "visiting" RAF aircraft aboard (eight Gladiators and ten Hurricanes). Macintyre also assumes that hangars were cluttered with the Hurricanes and Gladiators, whose wings, unlike those of the Fleet Air aircraft, did not fold. However, he adds the valid point that her commander had reported that she was too short of fuel for the high-speed steaming required for flying aircraft, on and off. Because of this she was routed home independently, although it would have surely have been better, for this very reason, to attach her to one of the convoys for her own protection. Ash adds the cryptic note that *Glorious*'s captain "was well known in the service for swarming off on his own whenever he got the chance; so much so in fact that his ship had earned the nickname of Carter Paterson." Her captain also appears to have been obsessed with the court-martialing of his Air Commander, whom he had left ashore after the last sortie. Whether this had any bearing on the actual granting of permission which resulted in her being alone seems doubtful; that order came from above. But for further speculation along those lines, see John Winton (pseudonym of John Pratt), *Carrier Glorious* (London, 1982).
76. Busch, *The Drama of the Scharnhorst.*
77. Ash, *Norway 1940.*
78. Bekker, *Hitler's Naval War.*
79. Statement of Leading Seaman Carter, the sole survivor of *Acasta*. His story was recently amplified in the book *The Man Who Hit the Scharnhorst* (Leo Cooper, 1974).
80. Bekker, *Hitler's Naval War.*
81. Busch, *The Drama of the Scharnhorst.*

CHAPTER 4: MEDITERRANEAN BATTLEGROUND

1. The confidence that the Royal Navy would be able to contain without difficulty and defeat with ease, the Italian Navy was widespread among all British ranks. During the Ethiopian crisis, as we have already noted, British morale was at a high peak. As Chatfield remarked on September 13, 1935, at a Combined Chiefs of Staff meeting, he "thought it improbable that the Italian Navy would

ever prove really efficient at sea." In this opinion, he was backed up by Italy's Axis partner. Admiral Ruge wrote: "There had been much talk of *Mare Nostrum,* yet although Mussolini had created a modern fleet, it was apparent that he did not know how to use it. The ships were good, though they possessed more speed than staying power. The Italian Navy had wanted aircraft carriers, but Mussolini had thought them unnecessary because of the numerous aerodromes on land. The gun and torpedo armaments of the ships were sound, but the anti-aircraft armament was too weak, as indeed it was with most navies at the outset of the war Italian industry was too small to produce any rapid changes in armaments or in radar. The naval officers were mostly of a good type, but their education, with its emphasis on mathematics, had perhaps crammed them with theory at the expense of practical experience. They handled their ships well and could shoot straight, though they lacked training in night fighting. They were also somewhat subject to the vagaries of the southern temperament. The submarine arm, though numerically powerful, was not very efficient technically or operationally, but the small battle units—midget submarines and motor torpedo boats - were surprisingly good. Their personnel suffered from an inferiority complex in relation to the British navy; it might have disappeared if the Italians had achieved some initial success." Vice Adm. Friedrich Ruge, *Sea Power, 1939–45*. This initial success they were never to get, and the Royal Navy was determined to ensure that they *never* got it at all. As Lord Chatfield again commented, "The bumptiousness of Italy is so great that it may be worth fighting her now to re-assert our dominance over an inferior race."

Chatfield's wartime successor put it more subtly than that but was equally determined to force the loud Italian boasts of invulnerability right down their throats at the earliest, and at every subsequent, opportunity. As he signaled on June 6, "You may be sure that all in the fleet are imbued with a burning desire to get at the Italian fleet." This superiority was to become more and more marked as the war progressed.

2. Count Ciano, *Ciano's Diary.*
3. Captain Sir Lewis Anselmo Ritchie, *East of Malta, West of Suez* (HMSO, 1942).
4. Cunningham, *A Sailor's Odyssey.*
5. Winston Churchill wrote later that "at the end of June that Admiralty's first thoughts contemplated the abandonment of the Eastern Mediterranean and concentration at Gibraltar." Churchill, *The Second World War*, Vol. 2. Churchill's resolution soon resulted in his veto on this plan. As Admiral Cunningham had pointed out to Admiral Pound, "I hope it will not be necessary to abandon the Eastern Mediterranean: the landslide would be frightful." Cunningham to First Sea Lord, June 27, 1940. Despite the perils facing the Home islands Churchill stood firm and this decision impressed the Germans a great deal. "That Great Britain was ready, despite her difficult position, to station half her capital ships and thirty-three of her irreplaceable destroyers in the Mediterranean was proof of the importance she attached to that part of the world, and also showed that she was confident of the failure of any German attempt to invade England." Ruge, *Sea Warfare.*
6. The affair of Mers-el-Kebir—or as it is more commonly, but incorrectly, cited, Oran—was charged with so much emotion and aroused such fierce controversy that books on it are legion. Here we can list a few that reflect all the varying shades of opinion, and leave the reader to draw their own conclusions. At the

time, in Britain, the decision seemed clear-cut and justified. Churchill was the prime mover in this, and his memoirs should be consulted as a primary source. Churchill, *Their Finest Hour.* So too should the Official British Histories, of which Captain Roskill's is, as always, the most clear and concise. *War at Sea*, Vol. 1.

Turning to more emotional accounts, perhaps a typical British wartime reflection on the matter is that contained in A. D. Divine, *Destroyers' War* (John Murray, 1942): "The French Navy as a fighting ally was gone from us in the very instant of our direst need. It was not defeated, for it never fought. It did not go in the shock of battle, for it saw no battle. It went because its High Command chose to use it as a bargaining counter to save the French *rentier*—a navy balanced in the scales against the money-bags of the middle class and the power of the Two Hundred." And again, "Admiral Darlan sold honour and dignity, and, worst of all, the brotherhood of the sea."

Postwar analysis has swung right round the opposite way and the majority of volumes that have subsequently appeared on the subject hold out the view that the action was both unnecessary and indeed harmful to the British cause. For instance see John Vader, *The Fleet Without a Friend* (New English Library, 1971): "It is now possible to surmise that had Britain not antagonized France by first of all distrusting her admirals and then bombarding her battleships at Mers-el-Kebir, the war may have ended earlier than it did: the French could have resisted the German invasion of Tunisia and when the Unoccupied Zone was invaded the Toulon fleet may have joined the Allied Navy, as the armistice terms would have been broken."

Other viewpoints are contained in A. Heckstall-Smith, *The Fleet That Faced Both Ways* (Blonde, 1963), and Warren Tute, *The Deadly Stroke* (Collins, 1973). A similar viewpoint is naturally contained in the French versions. See, for example, R.Adm. Paul Auphan and Capt. Herve Cras, *The French Navy in World War II* (United States Naval Institute Press, 1959).

Neutral opinions also vary considerably. Ruge, *Sea Warfare*, is typically Germanic and uses the opportunity to reinforce another German "fact" of the war up to that date. Thus: "This aggression against a former ally, no less than the earlier treatment of Norway showed clearly how Great Britain adapted the laws of nations to benefit her sea power and to serve her naval interests." In strict contrast, no doubt, to the way in which Germany treated Norway in 1940!

Ciano's wartime viewpoint showed the action impressed the Axis however. "It is too early to judge the consequences of the British action. For the moment it proves that the fighting spirit of His Britannic Majesty's fleet is quite alive, and still has the aggressive ruthlessness of the captains and pirates of the seventeenth century." *Ciano Diaries.*

De Gaulle was, of course, prone to extremes: "In spite of the pain and anger into which I and my companions were plunged by the tragedy of Mers-el-Kebir, by the behavior of the British and by the way they gloried in it, I considered that the saving of France ranked above everything, even above the fate of her ships, and that our duty was still to go on with the fight." Charles de Gaulle, *Call to Honour* (Collins, 1955). That the British "gloried" in the destruction of the French ships is quite untrue. As Marder wrote in his work on the subject, which is by far and away the best to date: "I can find no such note in the principal London dailies and weeklies, but rather warm approval of the action and praise of Churchill and the Navy, mixed with profound regret." Marder, *From the Dard-anelles to Oran.*

Captain Roskill wrote: "The necessity for this violent action by the Royal Navy against its former Ally has been hotly debated ever since that fateful day. What can be said with confidence is that three British Flag officers involved in it— Admiral Sir Dudley North on shore at Gibraltar, Admiral Cunningham at Alexandria and Admiral Somerville himself—all viewed the government's orders with something approaching horror." S. W. Roskill, *The Navy at War, 1939–45* (Collins, 1965). And not only the men on the spot either: "I think it probable that when other factors operate in France—great distress and probably famine, also the feeling of the French (played on of course by the Germans)—may result in their giving facilities to those we are fighting, if not actually taking up arms against us. The war will take on a far more bitter aspect." R.Adm. W. S. Chalmers, *Max Horton and the Western Approaches* (Hodder & Stoughton, 1954). Prophetic words indeed from Admiral Horton.

In the author's own strictly personal viewpoint, whatever the rights or wrongs of this incident, all the frothy French appeals about their "honor" being at stake if they took their ships away from German and Italian supervision were nonsense. If honor, as the French interpreted it in this incident, is taken as a major factor, then the French forfeited all claims to that quality when they unilaterally signed an armistice with Germany and Italy, having categorically undertaken just three months beforehand, on March 28, that they would "neither negotiate nor conclude an armistice or treaty of peace except by mutual agreement." Honor would therefore seem to be a one-sided commodity. If, as Marder concludes, the action taken by Great Britain at Mers-el-Kebir was, in the context of the situation on July 3, 1940, "both intelligible and defensible," in that it ensured that Britain (and therefore ultimately a Free France rather than a Vichy puppet-France) would emerge as a victor from the war, then at least the job should have been done more completely and finally than it was.

7. Admiralty to Somerville, 1:03 A.M., July 2, 1940 (CAB65/8).
8. "It is difficult to adjudicate between Churchill and Pound on their respective parts in these attacks on officers in high commands at sea, but it was certainly Churchill who demanded the immediate relief of Admiral Sir Dudley North from the Gibraltar Command because of his criticism of the attack on the French Fleet in Oran harbour on 3rd July 1940—for which Churchill, advised by Beaverbrook, was chiefly responsible." Roskill, *Marder, Churchill, and the Admiralty, 1939-42.*
9. Capt. Donald Macintyre, *Fighting Admiral* (Evans, 1961).
10. Ibid.
11. Imposing as this force appeared, it did *not* impress naval commentators. Adm. Sir Ralph Edwards described them in his diary as "an ill-assorted party. None of 'em can concentrate with the other."
12. Macintyre, *Fighting Admiral.*
13. Churchill, *Their Finest Hour.*
14. Bradford, *The Mighty Hood.*
15. Times vary according to sources: 1804 in Somerville's report, 1810 in the Official History of the Mediterranean War, 1812 according to *Hood*'s log.

16. Macintyre, *Fighting Admiral.* He in fact survived this *faux pas* but went on to make several other operational decisions that led Churchill, and others, to have doubts as to his required aggressiveness, as we shall see.

17. This effectively put her out of the running for the rest of the war as Somerville had thought. It is relevant if we here trace the movements of Vichy France's heavy ships for the rest of their brief, and ineffective, lives. Darlan, ablaze with rage, had ordered the *Strasbourg* and the Algiers cruiser squadron to put to sea on the fourth to give battle to Force H, but wiser counsels prevailed, and she stayed in Toulon in safety. She later made her way to become the flagship of Admiral Laborde's fleet, but rarely, if ever, ventured out on the high seas. She was joined by the *Provence* in November 1940, after she had been made seaworthy. She joined the units there commanded by Marquis, Maritime Prefect of Toulon. The repairs to *Dunkerque* took much longer, and it was not until February 1942 that she too sailed for Toulon, still damaged. All three ships were still there in November 1942, when the Germans arrived to take over the yards and the fleet. These great ships met them, not with shells, but with suicide; all three were scuttled and settled on the bottom of Toulon Harbor. *Dunkerque* and *Strasbourg* had their guns blown up, but *Provence*'s commander acted rather too late to effect such complete destruction to his command. The Germans later utilized two of her 13.4-inch guns as coastal defense weapons at St. Mandrier, where they fired on Allied ships in July 1944. See Jacques Robichon, *The Second D-Day* (Arthur Barker, 1969).

   On the results of the action itself, Churchill wrote, "The elimination of the French Navy as an important factor almost at a single stroke by violent action produced a profound impression in every country. Here was this Britain, which so many had counted down and out, which strangers had supposed to be quivering on the brink of surrender to the mighty power arrayed against her, striking ruthlessly at her dearest friends of yesterday and securing for a while in herself the undisputed command of the sea." Churchill, *Their Finest Hour.*

   Whether the French fleet had been so eliminated has been disputed. Certainly Auphan and Mordal do not agree. Furthermore, they state that "if it had not been for the aggression of the British, the principal French squadrons would have remained in North Africa, out of reach of the Germans." But after Mers-el-Kebir and Dakar, "the remaining capital ships of the French Navy—including the *Dunkerque* when she was temporarily repaired—took cover under the protection of the powerful coastal batteries of Toulon. They thus came nearer to the German forces in the Occupied Zone." *The French Navy in World War II.*

   This point is valid: the blow had to be complete to be of any use, and it was not. As Sir Samuel Hoare wrote to Lord Halifax, "My conclusion would be that so far as Spain is concerned, we may get away with it, provided our action is really justified by success. By this I mean that we have really captured, immobilized or destroyed the effective part of the French fleet. If we cannot point to successful results, Spain will regard it as a mad dog act against one of the Latin countries." Viscount Templewood, *Ambassador on Special Mission* (Collins, 1946).

18. Of all the Italian front-line bomber strength—which in July and August 1940 was at a peak of efficiency and numerically very strong—it was the SM 79-II which constituted the greater part.

"Eleven *Stormi* [groups], each comprising four *Squadriglie* [squadrons], were equipped with a total of 385 SM 79-Is based in Italy, Albania, and the Aegean Isles, and by June 16, 1940, when Italy entered World War II on Germany's side, the number of SM 79-I and Sm 79-II aircraft possessed by the *Regia Aeronautica* had increased to 594 machines, of which 403 were ready for immediate offensive operations. The *Regia Aeronautica* possessed a first-line strength of 975 bombers, and thus, the Sparviero equipped nearly two-thirds of Italy's bomber forces." William Green, *Famous Bombers of the Second World War* (Macdonald, 1959).

The other principal altitude bombers employed against ships in attacks on the British fleet were the Savoia Marchetti SM 81 and the Cant CZ 506. The following units were involved during operations on July 8-10, 1940:

Attacks on Cunningham's fleet, July 8: sixty-one SM 79s of 10, 11, 12, 14, and 15 *Stormo.*

Attacks on Cunningham's fleet, July 9: eighty-two SM 79s of the above units; thirty-five SM 81s of 37, 39, and 40 *Stormo*; nine CZ 506s.

Attacks on Somerville's fleet, July 9: forty-one SM 79s of 32 *Stormo* and local defense units from Decimomannu and Villacidro.

Attacks on Cunningham's fleet, July 11: eighty-one SM 79s of 30, 34, 36, and 41 *Stormo*; twenty-four SM 79s of 15 and 33 *Stormo* from Libya.

Attacks on Cunningham's fleet, July 12: 112 SM 79s of 10, 11, 12, 14, 15, and 33 *Stormo.*

A total of 404 bombers directed at Cunningham in a four-day period and 41 against Somerville in one day. Dimensione Cielo, *Bombardieri Ricognitori, Aerei Italiani nella 2a Guerra Mondiale* (Rome, 1972).

19. Roskill, *HMS Warspite.*
20. Vice Adm. Sir Arthur Hezlet. *Aircraft and Sea Power* (Peter Davies, 1970).
21. Ibid.
22. "It was most frightening. At times a ship would completely disappear behind the great splashes, to emerge as though from a dark, thick wood of enormous fir trees. I was seriously alarmed for the old ships *Royal Sovereign* and *Eagle*, which were not well protected. A clutch of those eggs hitting either must have sent her to the bottom." Cunningham, *A Sailor's Odyssey.*
23. "'People at home will be thinking I hadn't the guts to go on. Seemed to me it required far more not to,' he wrote bitterly. If such a sentiment seems to show a lack of confidence out of keeping with the character of a great leader, the pressure from the Admiralty at this time to undertake foolhardy operations must be remembered and the chair-borne taste for fire-eating, which Somerville already sensed and of which he was later to have proof." Macintyre, *Fighting Admiral.*

Admiral Cunningham wrote that "it is not too much to say of those early months that the Italian high-level bombing was the best I have ever seen, far better than the German. Later, when our anti-aircraft fire improved and the trained squadrons of the *Regia Aeronautica* came to be knocked about by our fleet fighters, their air work over the sea deteriorated. But I shall always remember it with respect. There was some consolation in realizing that there was always more water than ship." Cunningham, *A Sailor's Odyssey.*
24. Bradford, *The Mighty Hood.*
25. Report of Adm. A. B. Cunningham, commander in chief Mediterranean, submitted to Lords Commissioners of the Admiralty as a "Despatch" on January 29,

1941, and published as a supplement in the *London Gazette* on April 28, 1948. See also *La Marina Guerra Mondiale* (*Ufficio Storico Della Marina Militare*, 1960).

26. Cunningham, *A Sailor's Odyssey.*
27. Ibid.
28. Roskill, *HMS Warspite.*
29. Report of Adm. A. B. Cunningham.
30. Cunningham, *A Sailor's Odyssey.*
31. Report of Adm. A. B. Cunningham. It is interesting to note that, despite these sentiments on airpower, which seem clear enough, Admiral Somerville was to write a week later, "I am amused to find that Andrew B. had quite changed his tune as a result of his recent experiences." This does not seem apparent. Nor did Admiral Somerville "change his tune," it should be said.
32. Cunningham of Hyndhope, A Sailor's Odyssey, op cit.
33. Ciano, *Diaries.*
34. Ibid.
35. Ibid. The actual translation states "naval armament," but this is merely poor translation, and "naval engagement" or "battle" is what Ciano is actually referring to here.
36. For example, see David Howarth, *Sovereign of the Seas: The Story of British Sea Power* (Collins, 1974). "But in the whole age of steam, the British Battlefleet never fought as a tactical unit except at Jutland, when it was engaged in the work it was built to do for a total of forty minutes. Indeed, the battle fleet was a splendid monster that had outgrown its use. It was such an immense industrial investment and such a precious source of pride that no nation that owned one could afford to run a serious risk of losing it."

   The statement that follows is, in my opinion, equally unsound: "Other weapons in modern times, gas, disease and atomic bombs, have been unused for fear of reprisal, but the battle fleet under steam was the only weapon that could not fulfill its primary function because it was too grand and too expensive."

   Apart from the fact that the British battle fleets in both world wars spent the greater part of their time *deliberately seeking* the enemy to bring it to battle, thus making a nonsense of the claim that it was not used in battle because of the risk of loss, the point surely is that it was because the British battle fleet was so "grand" that the enemy did not dare face it and that therefore it did, in fact, perform its real function, control of the sea. If it were any less grand and expensive, the enemy could have come out and sunk it, and anything else it cared to tackle as well. As for being expensive, this is relative, as we have discussed in the respective costs for the Grand Fleet and the army on the Western Front. Wing Commander Allen's cost analysis of the strategic bombing offensive of the Second World War shows just how "value-for-money-spent" the battle fleet was in comparison.
37. Cunningham, *A Sailor's Odyssey.*
38. Ibid.
39. The Italians made a brief foray from Taranto during this operation and were now able to field their full strength as both the *Littorio* and *Veneto* took part with three of the old battleships, thirteen cruisers, and forty destroyers. The five battleships were in fact sighted by the *Eagle's* aircraft some ninety miles north of

Cunningham, but the Italians had already turned back, and it was too late to mount an air strike against them.

40. See "The Strange Silence" in part 2 of Peter C. Smith, *Action Imminent: Three Studies of the Naval War in the Mediterranean Theatre during 1940* (William Kimber, 1980) for the fullest account of the so-called Dudley North Affair. Another good, but less detailed, account is Arthur J. Marder, *Operation Menace: The Dakar Expedition and the Dudley North Affair* (Oxford University Press, 1976), which tells the story, told and researched with Marder's usual expertise. Admiral North's case was given an earlier, though far less professional and far more biased, airing in Noel Monks, *That Day at Gibraltar* (Frederick Muller, 1957).

41. Smith, *Action Imminent.*

42. Another viewpoint on this affair was given in Leslie Gardiner, *The British Admiralty* (William Blackwood, 1968): "Admiral North was not the first flag officer in British history to have been ordered to haul down his flag and no reason given. The Admiralty would preserve its venerable privilege of doing what it thought fit with officers of the Royal Navy. What the Admiral's parliamentary champions called 'injustice' had little to do with it; nor did the matter concern Parliament."

43. Hezlet, *Aircraft and Sea Power.*

44. J. Rohwer and G. Hummelchen, *Chronology of the War at Sea, 1939–45* (Ian Allan, 1972). This is normal German interpretation of events, common in such books. British hits are usually "lucky"; Axis successes are not so termed of course.

45. Cunningham, *A Sailor's Odyssey.*

46. Ibid.

47. Roskill, *HMS Warspite.*

48. Roskill, *The War at Sea*, vol. 1.

49. Ciano, *Diaries.*

50. Admiral Cunningham later described this situation, which, according to General Wavell, was due mainly to the complete shortage of all equipment in the Middle East, the army suffering as much as the navy and air force, if not more so. The matter was never completely resolved. "While the fleet was in harbour, the volume of gunfire was imposing enough," Cunningham recalled. "In its absence at sea the gun defence was quite another matter."

51. Known to the Axis as the battle of Tenleda. Likewise, the battle of Calabria is termed by Axis sources as the battle of Punta Stilio.

52. For which decision he received no acclaim from the Axis side whatsoever and considerable contempt from contemporary British observers. Admiral Ruge, for example, made the following cryptic comments: "Admiral Campioni, commanding the Italian force, felt himself severely handicapped for lack of an aircraft-carrier. But land-based aircraft were available in Sardinia—less than sixty miles away—and should have been able to provide him with full fighter protection as well as air reconnaissance." However, he places the chief blame, not on Campioni, but "chiefly due to lack of cooperation between the air force and navy; but a contributory factor was that the Italian Admiralty attempted to direct the operation from Rome without possessing the requisite information."

   The British Admirals were to be frequently subjected to the same type of treatment, with equally dire results, in the years that followed. Whatever the cause it cost Campioni his job; Iachino replaced him. However, Ruge reminds us that "the fact remains that in his new command he achieved even less than his predecessor." Ruge, *Sea Warfare.*

53. Divine, *Destroyer's War.*
54. Ibid.
55. Report of Vice Adm. Sir James F. Somerville, flag officer of Force H, published as a supplement to the *London Gazette* on May 5, 1948.
56. Admiral Somerville had an idea that his breaking off the pursuit might not go down well at home: "I shouldn't be surprised if some of them at the Admiralty don't argue that I should have continued the chase," he wrote. He was right, for while still at sea on the way back to Gibraltar, he learned that the Admiralty had set up a board of inquiry under Admiral of the Fleet, the Earl of Cork and Orrery, which was even now flying out to Gibraltar to investigate his conduct. As his biographer was to comment, this was a procedure without precedent in naval history, "which gave Somerville the impression that the Admiralty or the Government behind the Board had seized what appeared a welcome opportunity to get rid of a tiresome critic of their policy." Donald Macintyre, *Fighting Admiral.*

Such high-handedness did not go down well with the fleet; Cunningham was very critical of it in a letter to the First Sea Lord at the time, and he later recalled that he thought it "intolerable that a flag officer, doing his utmost in difficult circumstances, should be continuously under the threat of finding a Board of Enquiry waiting for him on his return to harbour if his actions failed to commend themselves to those at home who knew little or nothing of the real facts of the case. Such prejudgment is not the best way to get loyal service." Cunningham of Hyndhope, *A Sailor's Odyssey.*

The fact that the commander of Force H had not enamored himself to the government was no secret. The escape of the *Strasbourg,* the Dudley North affair, and the abandoning of the first sortie into the Mediterranean under threat of air attacks—all these isolated incidents had made their mark, and the decision to break off the Spartivento sortie was taken as another example of lack of resolution in London before all the full facts of the matter had been examined. Somerville's criticism of the government's handling of the Vichy threat had been far from muted, and a good example of how they currently viewed his performance was given to Admiral North in a brief interview with the First Lord, A. N. Alexander, in January 1941. Alexander is said to have told North quite firmly that "it is not your business to decide who are the King's enemies." Presumably, this applied equally to Somerville, and Alexander added the further point: "By the way, Somerville messed the job [Mers-el-Kebir]. He should have sunk all the French ships. He had a powerful force." Noel Monks, *That Day at Gibraltar.*

Captain Roskill has it exactly right in the official history: "Admiral Somerville was criticized in London for abandoning the pursuit. This criticism, by itself, may not have been unreasonable." However, it was, again, the *manner* in which it was done, as with North, that was lacking in tact. Again, "though the right of the Admiralty to criticize and, if need be, to chastise its flag officers is indisputable, the handling of the whole matter was certainly unfortunate." Roskill, *The War at Sea,* Vol. 1.

In the event, the board's findings upheld Somerville's action, although the Admiralty did not entirely endorse their findings wholeheartedly, adding that Somerville was "over-influenced by his anxiety for the security of his convoy." In their final judgement, the board's findings notwithstanding, "he could have continued the pursuit until it was clear beyond doubt that no possibility of the destruction of any of the enemy units remained."

57. Ruge, *Sea Warfare.*
58. Roskill, *HMS Warspite.*
59. Cunningham, *A Sailor's Odyssey.*
60. Should the reader wish to study further the development of this particular aircraft, its design, and use, especially at sea, my book *Luftwaffe Colors: Ju 87 Dive Bomber Units* (Classic/Ian Allen, 2006) gives a working outline, with many illustrations.

     The despatch of these units to the Mediterranean and their primary functions were laid down on Hitler's orders. Directive No. 22, issued on January 11, 1941, the day after the attack on the *Illustrious*, reemphasized its role thus: "2. X Air Corps will continue to operate from Sicily. Its chief task will be to attack British naval forces and British sea communications between the Western and Eastern Mediterranean." See Trevor-Roper, *Hitler's War Directives, 1939–1945* (Sidgwick & Jackson, 1964). It may be added that the Italians, at first, were none to keen on the idea.

61. Ian Cameron, *Red Duster, White Ensign: The Story of the Malta Convoys* (Frederick Muller, 1959).
62. Howarth, *Sovereign of the Seas.*
63. Roskill, *HMS Warspite.*
64. Macintyre, *Fighting Admiral.* See also Duff Hart-Davis, "Navy's 'filthy job' at last cleared up," *Sunday Telegraph*, December 9, 1973, for some relevant background on Churchill's and Alexander's feelings after Mers-el-Kebir.
65. Macintyre, *Fighting Admiral.*
66. Among the many works dealing with this battle other than the official histories of both Britain and Italy and the Cunningham autobiography, the most concise is S. W. C. Pack, *Night Action off Cape Matapan* (Ian Allan, 1972), which has some useful data and tries to be objective. Recommended also is Ronald Seth, Ronald, *Two Fleets Surprised* (Geoffrey Bles, 1960), which is a very well-written and researched book, although it tends to give the Italians the benefit of every possible doubt. Iachino's own version of events is contained in *Gaudo e Matapan* (Arnoldo Mondadori Editore, Rome, 1956). The most useful still remains the report of Adm. A. B. Cunningham, commander in chief of the Mediterranean, submitted as a dispatch and published as a supplement in the *London Gazette* on July 29, 1947.
67. There is no dispute that the British fleet was well served by the few Fleet Air Arm aircraft carried by the *Formidable*, whose torpedo-bomber attacks had at last had the desired affect on a flying enemy fleet. The battle would not have been possible without them. That the Italians were badly let down by the numerically overwhelmingly superior land-based air formations available to them was equally undisputed. Nor is it denied that the fact the British fleet was well-equipped with radar while the Italians had none (and thought that the British had none either) was equally decisive. All these points have received their justified allotment of praise. Without detracting from this, however, the main point is that the final destruction of the enemy squadron was brought about by the accurate salvos of the British battleships, without which all else would have been wasted and unfulfilled effort.

The British had learned the lessons of night-fighting from Jutland, as Admiral Dreyer fully admits: "We learned that the German method of night action apparently was to train a searchlight on to any ship at which they wanted to fire. It appeared that the light was burning, but obscured perhaps by a large iris diaphragm. When the guns were on the target the order 'Fire' was given. Only then was the iris diaphragm opened, when the searchlight illuminated our ship, and practically simultaneously a devastating fire from turret and other guns was opened. In addition, the Germans used star shell, which, bursting by time fuse, released parachutes carrying the illumination, which lit, up a large area. We were ready to learn anything useful, and largely adopted the German night-fighting procedure, and in 1917 achieved star shell which do not disclose the firing-ship and her course." Sir Frederick C. Dryer, *The Sea Heritage* (Museum Press, 1955). Between the wars, these techniques were brought to a fine art, in endless night-encounter exercises with the main fleets. As Marder records:

> Apart from the establishment of the Staff College, there were various ways in which the lessons of the First War had obviously been learned and were well applied. Thus, enemy reporting was much improved and the Navy had good success in solving the problem of a massed torpedo attack by destroyers on a battle fleet, which had hobbled Grand Fleet tactics. The Grand Fleet doctrine of not committing a fleet to night action was rejected, and improvements were introduced in night fighting (as through the introduction of star shell and improved searchlight control), with the reward of Matapan. Ernle Chatfield, and W. W. Fisher in the Mediterranean in the early thirties placed great emphasis on night-action training. (Marder, *From the Dardanelles to Oran.*

See also Roskill, *British Naval Policy Between the Wars.* Thus, at Matapan, the British had Type 279 RDF, with a sweeping aerial fitted aboard the *Valiant, Formidable,* and *Ajax* (a light cruiser). But *all* the battleships were equipped fully with both the well-established Evershed searchlight control system and searchlights fitted with the Iris shutter. Conversely, the Italian prewar experiments had led them to abandon searchlights for main armament night work completely.

68. Cunningham, *A Sailor's Odyssey.*
69. Ibid.

CHAPTER 5: THE BROAD ATLANTIC

1. Heckstall-Smith, *The Fleet That Faced Both Ways.* As stated, this is a detailed study, very sympathetic to the French case, but valuable still if read with this in mind. Darlan's change of heart came very quickly after these gallant exploits but were deep-rooted in the past. As David Woodward wrote, "It has always been suspected that somewhere at the heart of Darlan's ambition was the vision of himself as commander in chief of a European fleet. Thus he could avenge himself on Britain for a series of events beginning with the killing of an ancestor at Trafalgar, passing through a supposed lack of politeness shown him in London during the coronation of King George VI, and ending with the crippling of the French fleet at Oran by the British in July 1940." Woodward, *The Tirpitz.*

2. From the strictly immediate British viewpoint the operations against the French fleet just completed, when computed on the strict basis of numbers and poten-

tial, and actual, Axis battleships on a debit and credit sheet, came out entirely satisfactory. As Marder summed up, "At any rate, the Admiralty and Churchill viewed the situation differently. For them all that mattered was the capital-ship position and they had no doubt about the crucial gains made." Marder, *From the Dardanelles to Oran.*

3. Roskill, *The War at Sea,* Vol. 1.
4. Hezlet, *Aircraft and Sea Power.*
5. Cajus Bekker's book, *Hitler's Naval War,* contains a highly interesting appendix that shows very clearly and precisely the state of the German Navy on August 31, 1940. From it, it is clear that Raeder had a hopeless task on his hands and that the German troops would have had to rely almost entirely on the Luftwaffe for their protection. As Bekker recounts, the German soldiers seemed resigned to their probable final mode of transportation to the British beaches: "'If you want to swim, cross the water with Raeder!' became one of the whispered jokes of the time."
6. Churchill, *The Second World War,* Vol. 2, *Their Finest Hour.*
7. Grenfell, *Sea Power.*
8. Churchill, *The Second World War,* Vol. 2, *Their Finest Hour.*
9. One of Churchill's biographers describes the situation in this fashion: "By early July the Admiralty and Admiral Forbes had completed their plans, which Pound read to the War Cabinet on July 9. There was some concern about which bases were most suitable for the dual task now facing the Royal Navy—guarding the coast against invasion while protecting the trade routes. The *Nelson* and *Barham,* for example, *two of the great ships in the new construction* [emphasis added], were to go to Scapa, while Churchill thought they might be more suitably based at Rosyth. His view was accepted, although it was nonetheless agreed that the running-in period for both vessels should be spent at the navy's traditional base, which was now after so many months work, the most secure available in Britain." Cosgrave, *Churchill at War,* Vol. 1., *Alone.*

While both the fourteen-year-old *Nelson* and the twenty-five-year-old *Barham* might have been highly flattered at being described as "new construction," Churchill' further ideas were soon to render at least part of this design null and void.
10. R.Adm. A. F. Pugsley, *Destroyer Man* (Weidenfeld & Nicolson, 1957).
11. Admiral Forbes's views were not shared by his brother naval officers in the south and the continued retention of so many of his light craft long after he felt it was necessary to do so, continued to cause friction. Ultimately, it was realized that he had been right. But as Captain Roskill sagely summed up, "If Admiral Forbes's belief that the invasion attempt had been defeated by the end of September was ahead of the intelligence available in London, a similar realization did gradually spread over the country as the autumn nights began to lengthen into winter with all its accompaniment of gales, cold and fog in the North Sea and English Channel. Thus, gradually, the disturbance to our maritime strategy was relaxed and the Home Fleet and all the varied instruments of our maritime power reverted to their normal functions of 'acting offensively against the enemy and in defence of our trade.'" Roskill, *The War at Sea,* Vol. 1.
12. Arthur J. Marder, *Operation Menace: The Dakar Expedition and the Dudley North Affair* (Oxford University Press, 1976).

13. On August 8, Churchill was writing enthusiastically to General Ismay, ordering the Dakar operation into being, and he included, "We should of course in any case take over *Richelieu* under the French flag and have her repaired."

14. The British ships mounted four (the *Faulknor* five) 4.7-inch guns and one quadruple torpedo tube. The other had been replaced by a single 3-inch HA gun against Stuka attack, but there were no Stukas closer than Northern France at that moment however. The French destroyers carried five 5.5-inch guns. It is an interesting footnote to notice that Marder calls both French and British destroyers TBDs (torpedo boat destroyers), the old classification for the type that had been discontinued in the Royal Navy in 1925—a hangover, no doubt, from his *Dreadnought to Scapa Flow* series of volumes covering 1904 to 1919.

15. Donald Forbes, *Two Small Ships*.

16. It is ironic to note that the captain of the Vichy submarine was later to be awarded a British decoration when the French again changed sides—from Admiral Cunningham himself. When told that it was this officer who had hit the *Resolution*, Cunningham's reply was to congratulate him for a "good shot."

17. Churchill, *The Second World War*, Vol. 2, *Their Finest Hour*.

18. This was not the *Resolution*'s first voyage to a North American port, for on October 7, 1939, she and the *Revenge* had successfully carried gold bullion from England's reserves to safety in Canada, sailing from Portland and disembarking their cargo at Halifax, Nova Scotia.

19. Divine, *Destroyers' War*.

20. Churchill, *The Second World War*, Vol. 2, *Their Finest Hour*.

21. Bekker, *Hitler's Naval War*.

22. Roskill, *The War at Sea*, Vol. 1.

23. The old myth about battleships always being in harbor aground on their own beer cans still persisted among small-ship men, false though this picture was known to be even then. Since the war, this impression has been reinforced and embellished by many writers of popular fiction of the Royal Navy.

24. Kenneth Thompson, *HMS Rodney at War* (Hollis and Carter, 1946).

25. For one example of this: "Even then it was only in combination with aircraft-carriers that they were able to achieve any success. Prior to the entry of Japan into the war Britain's sea power was threatened at two principal points. In the wide spaces of the Atlantic a long-drawn out running fight was waged against her merchant convoys by German U-boats. *In this battle the battleship had no part.* [emphasis added]." Macintyre, *The Thunder of the Guns*.

    The occasions when the battleships encountered the raiders and thus saved a North Atlantic convoy are recorded in this chapter, so they certainly played a part, a significant one, in the battle of the Atlantic. On none of these occasions, except the *Bismarck* operation, did the battleships thus employed ever see a carrier let alone were they rendered impotent by their absence.

    Another historian wrote that "it was easy to see that the Germans, as aggressors at sea, would have done better to use their money and time and shipyard space in building a hundred more submarines than in building a few big ships; and also easy to see that if they had, the British big ships *would not have had anything to do* [emphasis added]. It was a most unwelcome thought: the British had trusted big ships so long for their security, and few people had the agility of mind, like Fisher in 1920, suddenly to discard such a long-standing national sentiment." David Howarth, *Sovereign of the Seas: The Story of British Sea Power* (Collins, 1974).

Again, I beg to differ. Even at the *worst* of the U-boat campaign, no Atlantic convoys were halted or stopped, as when the *Scheer* or another big ship broke loose. Men employed in manning battleships (or cruisers, destroyers or minesweepers for that matter) were not necessarily suitable submarine sailors, nor did the shipyards that built one type have the expertise to build the other in every case. As for saying that had there been no German big ships there need not have been any British big ships the argument is both obviously inaccurate and meaningless. If there had been no Luftwaffe, there would have been no need of RAF Fighter Command; if no Panzers, no need for anti-tank guns; no U-boats, no need for many thousands of escort vessels. The fact is, there *were* German big ships, with more planned. And even had there *not* been German battleships, there were Italian and Japanese battleships, and also a large number of heavy cruisers belonging to those nations, against which nothing less than a battleship could have stood up.

Another historian got it right inadvertently: "When war came again, the main roles of the one-time battle-winner, the capital ship, were commerce raiding and protection and the task of covering invasion by fire power." Douglas G. Browne, *The Floating Bulwark* (Cassell, 1963). To which I say bravo and yes indeed. It was for the purpose of commerce protection and the (secondary) task of covering invasion by fire-power that the Royal Navy had existed at all and every one of its major fights, from time immemorial, was to achieve these ends. In other words,

Then, the "one-time battle-winner," by carrying out these duties, continued to play its vital role.

26. Jones, *Under Three Flags*, contains a complete account of the war service of this vessel in particular and of the German Navy's floating support system at this time, which was unequalled.

27. Grand Admiral Raeder was so elated at this successful pulling of the lion's tail that he personally met both ships and congratulated them according to Bekker.

28. As usual, the official historian was not allowed to reveal any more than this on just what the sources were. Fortunately, books like F. W. Winterbotham's *The Ultra Secret* (Weidenfeld & Nicolson, 1974) have lifted some of this unnecessary veil a little, although Winterbotham's chapter ten, "Naval Affairs and Briefing the Americans," is frustratingly brief. However, the publication in 1977 of Patrick Beesley's *Very Special Intelligence* (Hamish Hamilton) redresses the balance telling the story of Naval intelligence throughout the war, and the large part played in it by the decoding of the German Enigma cipher machine.

29. Bekker possibly welcomed this interpretation of it, for it certainly reinforces one recurring theme in his book—that all battleship operations were futile and a waste of time and effort. His arguments are almost identical to the many British conclusions reached after the war, some of which we have already quoted. Bekker writes: "Yet, considering the potential of the German heavy ships, such achievements were not an adequate contribution to the success of the German Navy as a whole: Man for man, and ton for ton, the contribution of the U-boats was both absolutely and relatively far greater. . . . Without the menace presented by the German ships, the much greater potential of the British battle fleet would have been largely wasted—if one discounts operations in the Mediter-

ranean. . . . Though battleships were designed to fight battles at sea, such battles had become outmoded as a means of winning a war." Bekker, *Hitler's Naval War.*

30. Ibid.
31. Peter C. Smith, *Destroyer Leader* (William Kimber, 1968).
32. Busch, *The Drama of the Scharnhorst.*
33. Thompson, *HMS Rodney at War.*
34. Rohwer and Hummelchen, *Chronology of the War at Sea.*
35. Roskill, *The War at Sea,* Vol. 1.
36. Ibid.
37. The voyage and destruction of the *Bismarck*, with all its many facets of high drama, has of course resulted in a large number of books on the subject, of varying degrees of accuracy and usefulness. A film was made of the subject also, which reached far greater audiences than any book—a fact that made it all the more regrettable that parts of it were pure fantasy. (The "sinking" by gunfire of the purely imaginary destroyer, the *Solent*, was the most blatant example of rewriting of history in the film, which was presented as "a factual account.)

    Among those accounts that I have studied are the following: Francis McMurtrie, *The Cruise of the Bismarck* (Hutchinsons, 1942), a wartime account written soon after the event; Russell Grenfell, *The Bismarck Episode* (Faber & Faber, 1948), the first postwar analysis, which, although some material is missing, still remains one of the most accurate and worthwhile versions of the action in print; Will Bethold, *Sink the Bismarck* (Longmans, 1958); William L. Shirer, *All about the Sinking of the Bismarck* (W. H. Allen, 1963, which is unfortunately mistitled; Vice Adm. B. B. Schofield, *The Loss of the Bismarck* (Ian Allen, 1972), one of the useful minihistories with a great deal of interesting facts and figures; and Ludovic Kennedy, *Pursuit: The Sinking of the Bismarck* (Collins, 1974), a very well presented account that unearthed most of the salient facts known at the time. More recently, there is an excellent portrait of the battle in part 2, chapter 7, of Geoffrey Bennett, *Naval Battles of World War II* (B. T. Batsford, 1975). There are many lesser accounts, but the only other one of value is the German viewpoint contained in Jochen Brennecke, *Schlachtschiff Bismarck* (U.S. Naval Institute Press, 1960).
38. Grand-Admiral Erich Raeder, *Struggle for the Sea* (William Kimber, 1959).
39. The *Prinz Eugen* was damaged by a mine in the Baltic, which put off the operation until the end of May when the conditions of the new moon would again be right for the break out. The Germans were still not aware of how much the advanced British radar had changed sea warfare. Waiting for the *Tirpitz* to complete was brought up by Lütjens, who felt the effect of both ships on the initial assault would be greater and be more certain of success, whereas single operations by both in turn would give the British time to prepare against them. The Germans, quite rightly, stuck to their policy of not sending a warship into battle until she was fully worked up and efficient. The *Tirpitz* might be completed but she was not operational. According to C. D. Bekker in *Swastika at Sea* (William Kimber, 1953):

    At the time, the crew of the *Tirpitz* had not been able to understand why, in May 1941, "big brother" *Bismarck* had been allowed to break out into the Atlantic all alone. When, chased by the whole British fleet [*sic*], the *Bismarck* finally succumbed; the news was an especially heavy blow to the men of the *Tirpitz*.

The two ships had trained together in the Baltic; they had often taken each other in tow. However, the naval command had decided that the *Tirpitz*, which first became operational at the end of February 1941, was not ready two months later to be sent into action along with the *Bismarck*.

This was in strict contrast to the Royal Navy, which was forced to send ships straight out from the builders into combat due to the severe shortages of all types. Thus, for example, the destroyer *Havant* was sent straight to the bedlam of Dunkirk in June 1940 and sunk after an operational life of less than a week, and we have seen how the *Barham* at Dakar and the *Queen Elizabeth* and *Hood* more recently in the Atlantic were used in the same manner. Both the *Prince of Wales* and the new carrier *Victorious* were to be thrown in at the deep end in exactly the same way.

40. On September 7, 1940, Churchill had again reaised this pet scheme with the First Lord, but this time with their employment in the Mediterranean in mind. "I should be glad if you would let me have a short resume of the different occasions when I pressed, as First Lord, for the preparation of the Ramillies-class ships [*sic*] to withstand air bombardment by thick deck armour and larger bulges. If those ships had been put in hand when I repeatedly pressed for them to be, we should now have the means of attacking the Italian shores."

The Admiralty had other priorities, and the prime minister continued to growl at intervals at the stonewalling of Pound on this project. Thus, on September 9, Churchill said, "I am not content at all with the refusal to reconstruct the Royal Sovereign class." And again on fifteenth: "I should be content if two R-class vessels were taken in hand as soon as the invasion situation has cleared and we get *King George V* in commission. Meanwhile material can be collected and preparations made. This should enable them to be ready in eighteen months from now—i.e., the summer of 1942." Churchill, *The Second World War*, Vol. 2.

41. It seems an appropriate place to briefly at this point go into the differences between the battleship proper and the battlecruiser. As originally conceived, the battlecruiser was an enlarged armored cruiser with the speed (and therefore lack of protection) of the latter, but with the guns of the same caliber (although usually fewer in number) as the battleships of the same period. As such they could act as the fast scouting force for the main fleets, using their heavy guns to brush aside an enemy cruiser screen and their high speed to evade the enemy battle squadrons salvos and report back his strength to the main British fleet. They could also use this combination of speed and hitting power to annihilate any enemy raiding squadron composed of armored or light cruisers with absolute immunity to themselves, being able to choose their own range and course.

They were correctly used in the latter way at the Battle of the Falkland Islands in 1914 and Beatty used them in the same way at Dogger Bank and Heligoland Bight. However, in a navy dominated by the gun and its power, and steeped in the tradition of engaging the enemy, rather than retreating no matter what the odds, it was perhaps inevitable that they became utilized more and more as fast battleships. Fast they were, battleships they were *not*, their great guns notwithstanding. They could not, indeed they were not expected to, stand up to heavy bombardment by the conventional battleship. But under the guidance of leaders like the gallant Hood they scorned to stand off when the opportunity arose. The results were well-known, at Jutland three of the British battle-cruisers went up like Roman Candles after heavy shells had penetrated their flimsy armour and detonated their magazines. Being in too advanced state to cancel, the *Renown* and *Repulse* were completed after Jutland, as were the *Courageous* and *Glorious*, although their half-sister *Furious* became an early aircraft carrier with the Grand Fleet.* Even in 1917, their weakness was the cause of much adverse comment in the fleet. The *Hood* was the sole survivor of four such ships of a greatly enlarged design built to combat German battlecruisers, which, in the event, were never completed. Because of her enormous size and tonnage, and the fact that she carried eight 15-inch guns, the same number as the latest battleships, the *Hood*, when she was completed in 1920, had gained an aura of invulnerability and might. She was still not a battleship, however. Most of that extra size had been to give her the thirty knots plus bonus of a battlecruiser over the twenty-one or twenty-five knot speeds of the best battleships. We have seen how her protection was suspect as early as the 1920s and how the attitude of the Treasury and the policy of the government had ensured that no funds were available to remedy that defect until it was too late. Now they were never to be remedied. The *Renown* and *Repulse* were even weaker, and only their speed kept them in the postwar fleet when the Emperor of India-class battleships with 13 5-inch guns were scrapped. The six 15-inch guns of these two ships (known as the *Refit* and *Repair* to the canny seaman of the Grand Fleet) after all matched that of the newer battleships. During the Washington Conference, the Americans insisted on classing them with the battleship on account of their guns and not their all-round ability to stand in line of battle.

Between the wars, subsequent development made the type largely irrelevant because all the new battleships laid down in the 1930s matched their speed while at the same time incorporating even more massive armour protection than before. The fast battleship replaced the battleship *and* the battlecruiser in fact, although France and Japan, and later America, brought back the type for slightly different reasons.

42. Just how the two types differed in protection can best be judged by a comparison between the ships engaged in the *Bismarck* Operation:

Ship	Type	Nationality	Max. Side Armor	Max. Armor
King George V	BB	British	15 inches	6 inches
Prince of Wales	BB	British	15 inches	6 inches
Bismarck	BB	German	12½ inches	7½ inches
Hood	BC	British	12 inches	3½ inches

In side armor, the new British pair demonstrated that they were designed to take punishment in the traditional British battleship manner. With her 12-inch belt, it was little wonder that the *Hood* was thought to have incorporated "the lessons of Jutland" when she joined the fleet in 1920. When the relative deck armor is examined, however, it can be seen that the German designers had the better conception of things. From the enormous ranges surface actions were likely to be fought, plunging fire was the crucial consideration. Here the *Bismarck* showed a marked superiority over even the new British ships, while the *Hood*'s 3½-inch decks were pathetic, even against the shells carried by the Grand Fleet in 1918. She was still *not* a battleship.

It must be remembered too that the design and forging of the armor carried by these giants was subject to exactly the same technological advances between

1920 and 1940 as were the engines, guns, and everything else. Nothing stood still. For a very interesting study on this subject and the relative merits of the various types used, see Nathun Okun, *Armor and Its Application to Warships* (Warship International, 1976).

43. It is interesting to note that Vice Admiral Holland's squadron was entitled the Battlecruiser Squadron.

44. Winston S. Churchill, *The Second World War*, Vol. 3, *The Grand Alliance* (Cassell 1950).

45. Bekker, *Hitler's Naval War*.

46. Grenfell, *The Bismarck Episode*.

47. T. J. Cain and A. V. Sellwood, *HMS Electra* (Muller, 1959). It should, in fairness, be pointed out that although much indignation has been voiced over this German "cheating" on tonnages, the ships of the King George V class were also "over the limit" of the sacrosanct 35,000 tons. As Churchill was informed by the First Sea Lord, Admiral Pound, in a memo dated October 2, 1941: "In *King George V*, we set out to build a ship of 35,000 tons standard displacement, but additions were made during construction and some of the estimated weights (principally armament) were not realized. Hence the ship came out 1,750 tons heavy." Since Great Britain, alone of all the great powers to make any attempt to keep to these internationally agreed limits, failed to do so by the margin of a large destroyer in tonnage, it was hardly to be wondered at that the German ships, which had been lied about since the 1920s, and the Pocket Battleships would be anywhere near to this mystic figure. If the Royal Navy was as surprised by this as the historians were alleged to have been—which is doubtful—then it was the surprise of supreme naivety, but see *Room 39*.

48. Grenfell, *The Bismarck Episode*. Grenfell completed this before he found out that the *Hood* was, in fact, firing at the *Prinz Eugen*, not the *Bismarck*; he noted this in a footnote added at the last minute.

49. Ibid. This fire on the upper deck raises the possibility of the fire in the UP ammunition that resulted in the loss of the ship (see note 49, chapter 3).

The two Boards of Inquiry on the loss of the *Hood*, which reported on June 2 and September 12, both reached the same conclusions on this point. The second stated that the UP or the 4-inch ammunition was ignited by this hit but that the resulting cordite fire did not lead to her loss. They came to the conclusion that a 15-inch shell had later penetrated the *Hood*'s armor and had exploded in or near her after magazines, with the "possibility" that the after 4-inch magazine had exploded first.

Captain Philips of the *Norfolk* thought the *Prinz Eugen*'s hit might have landed on the above deck torpedo tubes there, but this is discounted by Bradford because of the type of fire described by most onlookers, which identified it as a cordite blaze. It would seem as good an explanation as any that the nine-and-a-half tons of UP ammunition stored in light steel lockers in exposed positions would be the most likely source of a fire of this nature, being susceptible to even splinter damage or a grazing blow. Admiral Schofield states that, although this fire spread forward rapidly, whether or not it contributed to the loss of the ship will never be known for certain, but he considered it "unlikely."

Captain Roskill's official history follows the line of the Admiralty inquiry all the way, but Professor Marder goes deeper into the matter than this. In particular, he quotes the reported verbal convictions of Captain Leach and Commander Lawson of the *Prince of Wales*, the two senior naval officers of either side, that both survived this action and were closest to the *Hood* when she received her mortal blow. They gave their views to Captain Oswald immediately after the battle, at Scapa Flow, and they both considered that the "rocket weapons and the unsafely stowed ammunition were the direct cause of the loss of the ship, probably through the explosion of the ready-use cordite penetrating the flash-proofing of X turret." Marder, *From the Dardanelles to Oran.* Captain Roskill later disputed this possibility, again quoting from Admiral Blake's two inquiries, in the article, "Marder, Churchill and the Admiralty," to furnish proof. Whatever the truth, the fact is that soon after the *Hood*'s loss, these useless weapons were promptly removed from Britain's ships.

All the authorities consulted seem in general agreement on one point, however: no matter how many inquiries or post mortems were held and debated over the years, the final story would probably never be known for sure. Despite this, the issue has again been raised repeatedly (see *Warship International,* January 1975 and subsequent editions) by an American naval officer who prefers to discount the British versions and cites Cmdr. Gerhard F. Bidlingmaier's German version as the most reliable evidence (see "Exploits and End of the Bismarck," *USNI Proceedings,* July 1958), even though the conclusions are not much different from the Admiralty Reports: i.e, that the *Hood*'s loss resulted from a 15-inch shell that penetrated a main magazine. For readers wishing to study the matter in more detail, the most recommended publication on the *Hood* is Maurice Northcott, *Hood: Design and Construction* (Ensign Special; Bivouac Books, 1975).

Perhaps the rest of us should be content with the expert summary of Admiral of the Fleet Lord Chatfield, who, in a letter to *The Times* (May 26, 1941), laid out in detail the five main points of the *Hood*'s loss and concluded his findings with the flat statement—an indictment of the whole futile fumbling policy of British governments toward defense from 1919 to the present day—that "the *Hood* was destroyed because she had to fight a ship twenty-two years more modern than herself."

50. Quoted in *World War II*, Vol. 2. (Orbis, 1972).
51. Bradford, *The Mighty Hood.*
52. Cmdr. Thomas Dailey, who has made a detailed study of this action, discounts the oft-quoted figure of seven hits on the *Prince of Wales* in this action and concludes, after much research, that only six shells struck her *for certain.* Roskill, Schofield, and most other British sources state that seven is the correct figure, but more recently, the subject has been made more confusing by Geoffrey Bennett, who comes up with a total of eight: "This blow [the hit on the *Prince of Wales* bridge] was followed by four more 15-inch shells and three 8-inch shells." He does not give the source of this new information. See *Naval Battles of World War II.*
53. Alan Franklin and Gordon Franklin, *One Year of Life: The Story of HMS Prince of Wales,* (William Blackwood & Sons Ltd, 1944).
54. Bennett states that Churchill was so angry about the *Hood*'s loss and *Bismarck*'s near-escape that he persuaded Pound to require Tovey to charge both Wake-Walker and Leach before courts martial for failure to reengage the enemy. Tovey refused to be a party to this and threatened to haul down his flag if the matter was pressed. It was not. It was almost the North-Somerville affair all over again.
55. Thompson, *HMS Rodney at War.* The *Rodney* finally got her refit after this operation, which led to the typical German postwar claim that because of this, the *Bis-*

marck may well have caused heavy damage in the last fight: "American reports told of severe damage to the *Rodney,*which subsequently had to go to the shipyard in Boston." Cmdr. Paul K. M. Schmalenbach, *Bismarck* (Profile Publications, 1972). That such an unfounded implication should be blithely published by a British publisher in 1972 shows just how the wish to believe anything asserted by our former enemies as true and discard the British version as a "cover up" has spread. As with the *Royal Oak* affair, the mining of the *Nelson,* the sinking of the *Helle,* and many other instances, the rewriting of history goes on at an alarming pace until shortly we shall all be told how terrible it was that the Axis lost the war.

56. "Early on May 25, Admiral Lutjens, thinking that he was still being shadowed by a British warship, sent a long signal to his Naval Headquarters in Germany. It listed all his difficulties but mainly the loss of fuel from his earlier battle and he asked what he was to do now. It was this signal, picked up by us, which gave away once more his position." Winterbotham, *The Ultra Secret.* This has now been refuted by Patrick Beesley in *Very Special Intelligence.* Although "accurate and rapid intelligence had enabled the Admiralty and commander in chief to concentrate overwhelming force at the decisive point," Ultra or special intelligence "played only a minor part" since it was not available until the point where it provided confirmation of what. was already known or deduced. Special intelligence's "enormous contribution to the war at sea was still to be made."

57. "The old *Renown* was, of course, no match for the splendid German battleship. Though Somerville had planned how he would engage her if it became necessary, he did not demur when the Admiralty gave him orders that his flagship was not to do so unless the *Bismarck* was already being engaged by the *King George V* and *Rodney.* The crew of the *Renown* could not understand this and were firmly convinced that their admiral had held the battle-tried *Renown* back to allow the *King George V* and *Rodney,* which had never experienced action, to be 'blooded.'" Macintyre, *Fighting Admiral.*

58. Hart-Davis, "Navy's Filthy Job."

59. McMurtrie, *The Cruise of the Bismarck.*

60. Thompson, *HMS Rodney at War.*

61. Lieutenant Commander Wellings of the U.S. Navy, taking passage aboard the *Rodney,* reported that because of the firing over the forecastle, the deck as far back as B turret had to be removed to repair leakages and that some bulkheads and stanchions were strained for the same reason.

It is interesting to recall Lord Chatfield's experiences of the blast-fire from these weapons before the war: "The gun-trials were carried out off Portland, and as controller, I attended them. One trial was for blast effect. It will be remembered that these three turrets, each of three guns, were all placed immediately before the bridge superstructure, and the problem was: what would be the effect on the persons on the bridge, if the turrets were fired on an extreme afterbearing. So we trained the after turret right aft, and elevated *one gun* [emphasis added] to its extreme elevation so that its muzzle was not more than a few feet from the bridge. With three others, I went to the bridge and awaited the firing of the gun! The shock of the full charge was very severe and gave a feeling of one's chest being crushed, but actually the result on those present was very slight. The bridge structure however, in which we were enclosed, was con-

siderably damaged in places and in consequence modifications were made."
Chatfield, *It Might Happen Again.*
62. According to Grenfell, *The Bismarck Episode:*

> The truth was that there were faulty details in the design of their new-
> pattern 14-in turrets. It is said that so many defects came to light during
> the *Bismarck* actions which would otherwise have remained longer con-
> cealed that more progress was made in perfecting. the 14-inch turrets
> in the two months after the operation than would have ordinarily have
> taken a year or more. In other words had the actions taken place in
> 1942 instead of 1941, the 14-in turrets would probably have shown up
> nearly as poorly as they did on. the earlier date.
>
> These turrets were therefore manifesting the same characteristics
> that had marred most of their predecessors in the inter-war period.

63. Gerhard Junack, *The Last Hours of the Bismarck* (Purnell, 1967).
64. Thompson, *HMS Rodney at War.*
65. McMurtrie, *The Cruise of the Bismarck.*
66. Bennett, *Naval Battles of World War II.*
67. In all, the *Rodney* fired off six of these torpedoes during the action. There is no
    proof that any hit, but if one did, it was a unique event in naval history. The
    crew were convinced that they had scored at least one hit on the *Bismarck:* "The
    last torpedo was traversed in the same way, and a huge cheer went up from the
    crew when Commander (T) Lewis DSO, reported that the last torpedo had hit
    the *Bismarck* right amidships." Thompson, *HMS Rodney at War.* This is dis-
    counted by most British and German sources
68. It will come as no surprise to learn that postwar German historians have
    claimed that the *Bismarck* was sunk by her own crew with scuttling charges and
    not destroyed by British torpedoes at all.
69. Adm. Sir John Tovey, *Despatch on the Sinking of the Bismarck,* published as a sup-
    plement to the *London Gazette.*
70. Admiralty 1610/27: "For political reasons it is essential that nothing of the
    nature of the sentiments expressed in your 1119 should be given publicity, how-
    ever much we admire a gallant fight."

CHAPTER 6: THE FLEET IN BEING
"The point seems to have been reached where fleets cannot be kept clear of
shore-based aircraft, and will have to put up with air attack in their bases if they
are to continue to exercise their proper functions." Cmdr. Russell Grenfell, *Sea
Power in the Next War* (Faber, 1938).
2. All these air forces had, of course, continued experiments with torpedo dropping from aircraft and development of the most suitable types during the
   period 1919-1939, but in all three countries the torpedo took very much of a
   back-seat to the heavy bomber. There were, in all these countries, a nucleus of
   experts and enthusiasts in the art of torpedo-bombing, but they were starved of
   funds and viewed as "cranks." The Luftwaffe was developing its army-support
   role that resulted in the blitzkrieg success; the Italians were firmly sold on the
   fast bomber, which, on the principle expounded by Douhet, would "always get
   through." The RAF similarly pinned its hopes on the altitude bomber, which
   many of their leaders honestly believed could win wars on its own, making all

other arms unnecessary. In this conviction, they were as set in their ways as the admirals they despised, and it took several years of high casualties to expose the fallibility of their arguments.

3. Thus, the RAF adapted the Hampden, the Beaufort, and finally—and more successfully—the Beaufighter. The Italians utilized the SM 79 in the main, with some success, while in 1942 the Luftwaffe converted the He 111 and the Ju 88 into torpedo-bombers. By contrast, the Japanese carrier-borne Kate and the long-range Nell, Betty, and others were custom-built to naval requirements and specifications. For a brief pictorial outline of the development of these aircraft, see, Peter C. Smith, *The Story of the Torpedo Bomber* (Pen & Sword, 2007).

4. One historian has alleged that the torpedo-bombers' effectiveness was not so much underrated as deliberately suppressed: "The activities of the torpedo planes on fleet manoeuvred, and the calculated disparagement of its record on exercises—when battleships were often "torpedoed" with astonishing ease—closely followed those of its predecessor, the submarine, in the period before the First World War, and the torpedo boat earlier still; just as naval air officers lacked certain customary privileges and were regarded as socially inferior." Richard Hough, *The Hunting of Force Z* (Collins, 1963).

5. As an interesting side-light to these events, this campaign witnessed the first sinking of battleships by dive-bombing attack. These unfortunate vessels were, however, the two ancient Greek vessels *Kilkis* and *Lemnos*, two pre-Dreadnought ships originally built for the U.S. Navy in 1908 and handed over to Greece in July 1913. They were smaller than most of their contemporaries, even when first built, and the U.S. Navy never found much use for them. Their details were 13,000 tons; four 12-inch, eight 8-inch, and eight 7-inch guns; and seventeen knots. Both these old veterans were sunk in harbor, and although hardly viable fighting units, even in the First World War, they gave the Luftwaffe the *kudos* of claiming the dispatch of two "battleships." The photo, in full colour, of the *Kilkis* resting on the bottom of Salamis harbor was certainly an impressive propaganda point for the Germans.

6. Of the large number of books on the battle for Crete, those which deal with the purely naval side of the battle are few. Recommended are S. W. C. Pack, *The Battle for Crete* (Ian Allan, 1973), which is marred only by being rather one-sided in sources and conclusions; Anthony Heckstall-Smith and Vice Adm. H. T. Baillie-Grohman, *Greek Tragedy* (Antony Blond, 1961); and David A. Thomas, *Crete 1941: The Battle at Sea* (Andre Deutsch, 1972), which is the best book on this subject for both research and narrative clarity. In addition, the official histories include Roskill, *The War at Sea*, Vol. 1, and Christopher Buckley, *Greece and Crete 1941* (HMSO, 1952).

7. Richards, *Royal Air Force, 1939–45*, Vol. 1, *The Fight at Odds*.

8. Thomas, *Crete 1941.*

9. It is a remarkable comment on Italian efficiency that the passage of the *Queen Elizabeth* right through the whole length of the Mediterranean, from Gibraltar to Alexandria, which took place between May 4 and 9 in conjunction with convoy Operation Tiger, remained unknown to them. Thus, "the information received in those days from air reconnaissance service was so confused that *Supermarina* [Italian naval command] did not have the least idea that a British battleship, the *Queen Elizabeth*, had made the passage eastward with the convoy." See Cmdr. Marc Bragadin, *The Italian Navy in World War II* (U.S. Naval Institute Press, 1957).

The Tiger convoy was escorted by the *Renown* and *Ark Royal*, with other ships of Force H, prior to their *Bismarck* triumph, and Bragadin states that the *Renown* was damaged by air attacks. In fact, an attack by eight torpedo-bombers on the *Renown* on the eighth resulted in three aircraft being brought down and no hits on the *Renown* at all, although one torpedo came to the end of its run scant yards short of the battlecruiser. A subsequent attack by a further three aircraft, although well pushed home, also failed to score a hit. In fact, the only damage that the *Renown* suffered on this operation was from her own guns. A fail-safe mechanism on one of the twin 4.5-inch guns failed, and the guns continued firing when trained beyond a safety stop. As a result, one turret put two 4.5-inch shells into the back of the turret in front, killing six men and wounding twenty-six others.

South of Malta on the ninth, the *Queen Elizabeth* and the convoy had been met by the Mediterranean Fleet, which had filled in their waiting time by covering another convoy to Malta from Alexandria and shooting up Benghazi—all without loss.

10. Pack, *The Battle for Crete*.
11. Roskill, *H.M.S. Warspite*.
12. Admiral King had taken over command when the *Warspite* was damaged. Because of an error of signaling, Admiral King had no idea that the antiaircraft outfits of the two cruisers were almost exhausted. Had he known, it is doubtful whether he would have sent them out in support. It was another hard lesson in the operating of a fleet under air attack. As Admiral Cunningham summed up, "One of the reasons for all these losses was the disregard of the golden rule which we had long since found essential in all our previous encounters with aircraft, and that was never to detach ships for any particular tasks. The fleet should remain concentrated and move in formation to wherever any rescue or other work had to be done. The detachment of the *Greyhound* was a mistake, as was that of the *Gloucester, Fiji*, and other ships. Together, the fleet's volume of antiaircraft fire might have prevented some of our casualties." Cunningham, *A Sailor's Odyssey*. Despite this, the detaching of light vessels away from the covering fire of the battleships continued during these and many subsequent operations.
13. The two damaged battleships were out of action for a considerable period. Both were patched up temporarily at Alexandria, the *Warspite* narrowly escaping further damage when she was near-missed by a heavy bomb on the night of June 23-24. On the twenty-sixth, she passed south through the canal and voyaged, via Colombo, Singapore, Manila, and Honolulu, to Esquimault on Canada's west coast, where she arrived on August 10. The next day, she arrived at the Bremerton Navy Yard in Seattle. Here she underwent an extensive refit, during which time five of her 15-inch guns were replaced and her bomb damage made good. She did not recommission again until December 28. The *Barham* was similarly patched up at Alexandria and sailed through the Suez Canal to Durban, South Africa. Her damage was less extensive and she was ready for service again by July, when she again rejoined Cunningham's flag.
14. Albert Kesselring, *Memoirs* (William Kimber, 1953).
15. Ruge, *Sea Warfare, 1939–45*.
16. Hezlet, *Aircraft and Seapower*.
17. Thomas, *Crete 1941*.
18. Cunningham, *A Sailor's Odyssey*.

19. In February 2007, the Royal Navy's promised two new aircraft carriers where again under threat of cancellation by myopic civil servants at the Ministry of Defence, and the head of the navy was being forced to plead in an uncomprehending and unsympathetic media for their retention.

20. The cabinet had this particular brain wave in April. The idea was that the blocking of Tripoli harbor, the Axis land forces main supply line, would be a vital blow in slowing up their advance on Egypt. Cunningham had asked for the dispatch of heavy bombers to do the job, but these were all busily employed making large holes in the German countryside and could not be spared, or transported in time, apparently, although the Luftwaffe could switch whole air fleets around Europe in a matter of days. Bombardment by the Mediterranean Fleet was considered too risky, and the lasting results too uncertain.

    Churchill recorded how Pound signaled the alternative policy to Cunningham on April 15. After careful consideration, Their Lordships decided that an attempt should be made to block the harbour instead, on the lines of Zeebrugge in the Great War (which was not completely successful incidentally). To do this, they considered that Cunningham should use the *Barham* and an old C-class light cruiser which had not been modernized (like the *Caradoc*). Although it was stated that to use the *Barham* thus would probably cause "the deepest regret," they considered that the price was worthwhile if something of lasting effect was achieved. Not surprisingly, Cunningham was aghast at such panic-stricken reasoning. Even supposing the blocking attempt *was* successful, which was by no means certain, there was the probable loss of 1,000 highly skilled men to the fleet and other considerations. "We shall have lost a first-class fighting unit whose passing is liable to give an inestimable fillip to Italian naval morale." In addition, there was nothing to stop them using alternative ports for disembarkation. To replace the *Barham*, a ship would have to be withdrawn from the vital Atlantic battle. Rather than carry out such a policy, Cunningham said, he would withdraw his reservations about a bombardment by the fleet. This may have been what the cabinet was really after in using the Admiralty as their mouthpiece, without consulting the man on the spot, again. Through Pound, Churchill cordially agreed to let Cunningham run the risks against his better judgment.

    When Cunningham stated that he could not see how either the *Nelson* or *Rodney* could be spared from the Atlantic to replace the *Barham*, Churchill replied, thus showing himself to be the real moving force of the whole scheme. The *Nelson* and *Rodney* were much better suited to the Mediterranean for their armored decks could better withstand dive-bombing. This was certainly true. They would be sent from the Atlantic because, with the establishment of the American neutrality patrols west of 26 degrees west, British forces could be reduced. Within a few weeks, the *Bismarck* was on the loose, and the *Rodney* was found not to be so surplus to requirements in that ocean as had been thought (and anyway she was due to refit).

    In the event, Cunningham sailed with the *Warspite, Valiant, Barham, Formidable* to provide spotters, two small cruisers, and a destroyer screen, on the eighteenth, apparently to cover a Malta convoy. This force arrived unheralded off Tripoli at daybreak on April 21. Opening fire at 5:00 A.M., the three battleships, joined by the cruiser *Gloucester*, for forty-five minutes steamed up and down, pumping 15-inch and 6-inch shells into the port. Although the target was obscured by the dust raised by inaccurate bombing earlier, great damage was inflicted on the port installations, oil installations engaged by the *Valiant* were set alight and six freighters and a destroyer were hit and damaged. The Italian coastal batteries did not make reply for twenty minutes and then the firing was wild and inaccurate. There was no aerial opposition and not a ship was hit or a man hurt in the fleet.

Cunningham considered they had only gotten away with it because the Luftwaffe was busy elsewhere, leaving the defenses to the Italians. Churchill considered the results satisfactory and added a fascinating snippet, which put the bomber firmly in its place in the scale of things. "The Chief of the Air Staff tells me that the same weight of bombs as you fired of shells into Tripoli in 42 minutes, viz 530 tons, might have been dropped: (a) by one Wellington squadron from Malta in 10 weeks, or (b) by one Stirling squadron from Egypt in about thirty weeks.

Still not satisfied, the Admiralty began pressing Cunningham to station one of his battleships (presumably, they still had the *Barham* in mind) at Malta and operate her against the Axis supply convoys. This took no consideration of the heavy drain on Malta's already marginal oil stocks, and such continued unrealism made Cunningham "seriously annoyed. This constant advice, not to say interference, in how to run our own business from those who seemed to be unaware of the real facts of our situation did not help us at all. They were merely a source of worry." Cunningham, *A Sailor's Odyssey*. As we have seen, Cunningham was not the first, nor by any means the last, naval commander to be so cursed.

21. "The two-months cruise had revealed serious defects in the *Scharnhorst's* boilers. The tubes of the super-heaters, especially, had given constant trouble threatening a major breakdown. German dockyard engineers who examined her estimated ten weeks would be needed for repairs. When her Kapitän, Kurt Hoffmann, reported this news to Grand Admiral Erich Raeder, head of the German Navy in Berlin, the German Admiralty staff were shocked at the extent of the repairs necessary." Potter, *Fiasco*.

We have seen how similar problems affected the pocket battleships and German destroyers were also badly affected. It was not altogether a German problem, however. "There is evidence to show that the use of superheated steam at very high pressures and temperatures during the inter-war years gave rise to many difficulties, mainly due to the fact that the materials of the day were unsuitable for prolonged service at elevated temperatures." K. T. Rowland, *Steam at Sea* (David & Charles, 1973).

22. Churchill, *The Second World War*, Vol. 2.

23. Ibid.

(24) For example, the commander in chief of RAF Coastal Command, Air Chief Marshal Joubert, made this interesting observation on the torpedo-bomber, which one would have thought represented his commands' main unit of offensive power: "I could not see the sense in carrying a weapon at, say, 150 mph to the vicinity of the target and then dropping it into the water where its motors could only drive it at 50 mph and where it might or might not adopt a stable path to its hoped-for destination." Philip Joubert, *Birds and Fishes* (Hutchinson, 1960).

25. Richards, *Royal Air Force*, Vol. 1.

26. Ibid.

27. Roskill, *The War at Sea*, Vol. 1.

28. Ibid.
29. Ibid.
30. Richards, *Royal Air Force, 1939–45*, Vol. 1.
31. See chapters 1 and 2.
32. In July 1941, the American general staff had confidentially informed American editors and Washington correspondents that the collapse of the Soviet Union was only a matter of a few weeks. William L. Shirer, *Rise and Fall of the Third Reich.*
33. These two old ships were the *Marat* (formerly the *Petropavlovsk*) first commissioned January 1915, and the *Oktyabrskaya Revolutsiya* (the former *Gamgut*) first commissioned in the same month. They had a face-lift in the late thirties but were not counted as front-line vessels by modern standards, and the *Royal Sovereign*'s far outclassed them. Their basic details when first completed were 23,400 tons; twelve 12-inch and sixteen 4.7-inch guns; and twenty-three knots. These two old veterans were formed into Kronstadt-Oranienbaum, part of the Baltic Fleet's artillery support force, on August 30.
34. Paul Carell, *Hitler's War on Russia* (Harrap, 1964).
35. Hans-Ulrich Rudel, *Stuka Pilot* (Euphonon Books, 1952).
36. Ibid.
37. Postwar claims that the *Marat* was not sunk and that the *Oktyabrskaya Revolutsiya* was not damaged in these air attacks appear to be ill-founded because there is ample photographic evidence, taken at the time, to show conclusively that they were. The hulk of the *Marat* was finally renamed *Volkhov* and used as an artillery ship, while her sister ship graced the reference books of the world's navies as a "fighting unit" until 1956 at Kronstadt; then she too went to the breakers' yard at Leningrad in 1958.
38. Details of the old battleship *Parizhskaya Kommuna* (formerly the *Sebastopol*) were 23,400 tons; twelve 12-inch and sixteen 4.7-inch guns; and twenty-three knots. First commissioned in 1914, it served in the Great War and was later renamed *Poltava* and then *Parizhskaya Kommuna.* She was scrapped in 1956–57.
39. A detailed account of this attack and a good account of the buildup and subsequent work of the RAF torpedo-bomber units is contained in Ralph Barker, *The Ship Busters* (Chatto & Windus, 1957).
40. Admitted in German records.
41. Details of these ships were the *Arkansas* (1912)—26,100 tons; twelve 12-inch and sixteen 5-inch guns; and twenty-one knots; the *New York* and *Texas* (1913)— 27,000 tons; ten 14-inch and sixteen 5-inch guns; and twenty-one knots; and the *New Mexico* (1918)—33,400 tons; twelve 14-inch and twelve 5-inch guns; and twenty-one knots. All had been modernized in the period 1925-34.
42. Thus, "plans for an Atlantic operation by *Tirpitz* and *Hipper* in conjunction with the Brest Squadron remained in the paper stage." Ruge, *Sea Warfare, 1939–45.*
43. On November 13, Raeder told Hitler that the Brest Squadron would be ready for action by February 1942. Atlantic operations could then resume when the crews were worked up. In addition, the *Admiral Scheer* was ready for a long-range penetration into the Indian Ocean once more. Hitler refused to sanction this at all; the loss of the *Scheer* would mean a heavy loss of prestige. Instead, said Hitler, the Brest Squadron could be brought home through the English Channel. The *Scheer* was to go to Norway.

His fears about the vulnerability of Norway were further expressed in a meeting on December 29: "If the British go about things properly, they will attack

northern Norway at several points using an all-out attack with their fleet and
landing troops, taking Narvik. Such an event [would] be of decisive importance
for the outcome of the war." See *Führer Conferences on Naval Affairs* (Brassey's
Naval Annual, 1948).

44. After completing her battle damage, the *Prince of Wales* had taken Winston
Churchill and Harry Hopkins to the famous Atlantic Charter meeting at Pla-
centia Bay, Newfoundland, on August 4, returning on the eighteenth. That the
prime minister was proud of his new ships is very evident. As one historian
wrote:

> It would clearly have been unseemly for Winston Churchill to have
> arrived in Newfoundland in an aeroplane or passenger liner to meet
> the President. It was, however, eminently appropriate to steam into Pla-
> centia Bay in a 35,900 ton battleship, scarred by the rigors of war but
> disdainful of German bombers and U-boats alike (for much of her jour-
> ney she had lacked even a destroyer escort), to parley with the leader of
> the world's second maritime power, who was using only a ten-year-old
> 9,000 ton cruiser for the occasion. The situation was in accord with the
> Prime Minister's sense of propriety for these circumstances, and there
> can be no doubt that he was largely instrumental in bringing it about.
> [Richard Hough, *The Hunting of Force Z* (Collins, 1963)]

Churchill's pride is reflected in a message he sent to Roosevelt in January
when Halifax went in her sister ship, the *King George V*: "I don't know whether
you would be interested to see her. We should be proud to show her to you, or
to any of your high naval authorities, if you could arrange that." Churchill, *Second World War*, Vol. 2. He made sure Roosevelt saw the *Prince of Wales*. On Sunday, August 10, the president, with his staff and several hundred men of the U.S.
Navy, joined the ship's company in Divine Service on the battleship's quarterdeck. "It was a great hour to live. Nearly half those who sang were soon to die."
During the voyage home, Churchill also indulged in a little showmanship. On
meeting a homeward-bound convoy of seventy-three merchant ships, he got the
Prince of Wales to steam through their ranks. And at Iceland on the sixteenth, he
took time out to pay a visit to the *Ramillies* based there on Atlantic escort duties.

45. The *Resolution, Rodney,* and *Warspite* were refitting in America; the *Repulse,
Malaya,* and *Royal Sovereign* in England; the *Queen Elizabeth, Valiant,* and *Barham*
in the Mediterranean Fleet; the *Nelson* and *Renown* with Force H; the *Ramillies*
and *Revenge* in the North Atlantic Escort Force.

46. Macintyre, *Fighting Admiral.*

47. Divine, *Destroyers' War.*

48. Both these ships, so invaluable in the western Mediterranean at this time, were
earmarked for the Far East. Neither eventually got there, as we shall see.

49. Macintyre, *Fighting Admiral.*

50. This vessel was one of a class of four Dreadnought-type battleships built by Aus-
tro-Hungary. Her details were 20,000 tons; twelve 12-inch and twelve 5.9-inch
guns; and twenty-one knots. She was completed 1912–14. Her sister ship was
equally unfortunate, being sunk by the Italian E-boat *MAS15* in June 1918. The
two sister ships were disposed of by the Allies during 1922–24.

51. Macintyre, *Fighting Admiral.*

52. Thomas Woodrooffe, *In Good Company* (Faber & Faber, 1952).
53. Macintyre, *Fighting Admiral.*
54. Thompson, *H.M.S. Rodney at War.*
55. This was a very unpopular move with the *Rodney*'s company since, after fifteen months of operations without home leave, they had expected to go home. "This period spent in Iceland was about the worst of the war, for the ship's company generally. Men who had cheerfully endured Atlantic and Malta convoys and the action with the *Bismarck* now seemed to be remote from the war, and they could not understand why, if they were to be inactive, they should not be sent home for the much-needed refit." Thompson, *H.M.S. Rodney at War.*
56. For example see, Hough, *The Hunting of Force Z*; Grenfell, *Main Fleet to Singapore*; Roskill, *British Naval Policy between the Wars*, Vol. 2; and Maj. Gen. Woodburn Kirby, *The War against Japan*, (HMSO, 1960), for details of the movement of the "main fleet" to the Far East.
57. See Chapter 2.
58. Churchill, *The Second World War*, Vol. 2.
59. Ibid.
60. In view of the fact that the tag "floating coffins" stuck to the Royal Sovereign class, it is worthwhile comparing them with their Japanese opponents. The British quartet had been completed in the years 1916–17 and had been modernized in the 1920s but none had been given a rebuild in the 1930s. Their best speed was probably around 18-20 knots; they mounted eight 15-inch guns but poor antiaircraft weaponry. Thus, they were old and slow, but they were tough— far tougher than the *Repulse*, or even the rebuilt *Renown*, whose saving grace was speed (her antiaircraft firepower was also up to date).

At the time of these discussions, neither of the two new Japanese battleships was completed; the battle line of the Imperial Japanese Navy therefore comprised the following ten vessels, none of which were in their first flush of youth either. The majority had been rebuilt to a far greater extent than the Royal Sovereigns between the wars, and thus, both completion dates and modernization dates are given.

The *Haruna*, *Kirishima*, and *Kongo* (completed 1914-16, modernized 1930–36): 31,720 tons; eight 14-inch, fourteen 6-inch, and eight 5-inch guns; and 30.5 knots. These were completed as battlecruisers but during their modifications they had their hulls lengthened, extra armour worked in, changed from coal to oil fuel and their speed increased from 26 to 30.5 knots. These were the vessels that Churchill probably had in mind as fast raiders, although they were in fact several years older than the *Royal Sovereign* and battlecruisers in origin rather than battleships.

The *Hiei* (completed 1914, modernized 1936–40): 31,980 tons; eight 14-inch, fourteen 6-inch, and eight 5-inch guns; and 30.5 knots. She had been demilitarized under the First London Treaty in the same manner as the *Iron Duke* and *Centurion*, but whereas these two old veterans remained noncombatants in all but the most limited sense, the *Hiei* was quickly rebuilt using modern techniques in time for the war.

The *Fuso* and *Yamashiro* (completed 1914-15, modernized 1932–35): 34,700 tons; twelve 14-inch, fourteen 6-inch, and eight 5-inch guns; and twenty-five knots.

The *Hyuga* and *Ise* (completed 1917–18, modernized 1936): 36,000 tons; twelve 14-inch, sixteen 5.5-inch, and eight 5-inch guns; and twenty-six knots. This pair were converted during the war (1943–4) to the first hybrid battle-ship/carriers, losing their after turrets and having a flight deck and hangar for twenty-two seaplanes built on. They still carried eighty heavy guns and a host of antiaircraft weapons after this conversion. (They were no more a success than the *Furious* had been in 1917, but these failures did not prevent the Admiralty from repeating the mistake in the 1960s with the Tiger-class cruiser abortions.)

The *Mutsu* and *Nagato* (completed 1920–21): 39,130 tons; eight 16-inch, eighteen 5.5-inch, and eight 5-inch guns; and twenty-five knots. They were not modernized. The *Nagato* was the first battleship of the post-Great War period to mount the 16-inch gun.

61. Even so ardent a defender of Churchill's degree of intervention in Admiralty decisions as Arthur Marder states in a footnote that "Pound regretted his having yielded over the *Prince of Wales* and *Repulse* against his better judgment. He never got over it." Marder, *From the Dardanelles to Oran*. At the same time, he quotes Lord Mountbatten's viewpoint, expressed to historian Richard Hough, that "the only time he [Pound] was finally defeated was on the *Repulse* and *Prince of Wales*." Captain Roskill revealed how, after the disaster, Pound wrote a letter to Churchill insisting that the despatch of the *Prince of Wales* to the east was "in accordance with my advice." "Loyalty to one's superior could scarcely go further than this," comments Hough, *The Hunting of Force Z*.

62. This refit was scheduled to take place in an American yard, and she was to have shipped fourteen of the latest Mk.16 4-inch antiaircraft guns in place of the far from successful triple mountings as well as three sets of 282 and three sets of 285 radar. "There is no record that she ever received the other sets, and this is significant as 282 and 285 sets much improved anitiaircraft gunfire." Parkes, *British Battleships*.

63. The choice of Admiral Phillips has been almost universally criticized after the war on the grounds that he overrated the defensive power of the battleship and grossly under-estimated the effect of bombing at sea. This author does not share these views to any great extent, as might be expected. In fact, far from underes-timating the extent of bombing, Phillips was one of few naval officers who made a special study of it before the war and worked out a series of evolutions espe-cially to combat this. Nor had the achievements of the airmen at sea up to this date given him much reason to upgrade their ability. It was his misfortune that one of his ships lacked modern antiaircraft equipment and the other had not had the chance to develop it correctly, but this was not his doing. It must be remembered also that Force Z was to have included the modern carrier *Indomitable*, which would have made all the difference. The fact that she ran her-self aground in the West Indies cannot be laid at Phillips's door. He was blamed for being too aggressive and not cautious enough in his handling of his reduced command, but timidity and hesitancy are not qualities that win wars, even if they preserved ships. It is notable that Philip had as his most sour and scathing critic Admiral Somerville, but the latter came within an ace of losing a far greater size fleet by taking enormous risks just a few months later.

64. Cunningham, *A Sailor's Odyssey*.

65. Hugh Hodgkinson, *Before the Tide Turned* (George Harrap, 1945).

66. Cunningham, *A Sailor's Odyssey*.

67. As the dispatch of the two British heavy ships was done as a decisive deterrent, it was essential that the Japanese be made aware of it, and this was done on a grand scale. Unfortunately, the manner in which it was done was far from tactful, at least as far as the crew of the *Repulse* were concerned. The official communique set the tone: "HMS *Prince of Wales* and other heavy units," it began and was repeated in a broadcast by Churchill in the same words. But there was only *one* other "heavy unit," the *Repulse*, and this led to considerable ill-feeling between the two ships' companies, so much so that their commanding officers had to clear the lower decks and explain that this was official governmental policy and not a deliberate slight upon the battlecruiser men. They were far from convinced. They wryly dubbed themselves "HMS Anonymous," and it is fair to say that as a crew the *Repulse* was worked up to a much higher degree of efficiency than her modern, larger, and more "glamorous" sister. But this was not the serious part of it. The Japanese knew very well that there were only two big ships from the moment they entered the Johore Straits. As Captain Grenfell put it: "The deception was therefore a dangerous one to attempt, since a Japanese discovery that the strength of the British force was being exaggerated was one from which they would draw obvious conclusions. A bluff that can readily be seen through is worse than no bluff at all. Those who would be deceived without possibility of enlightenment were, of course, the British public." Grenfell, *Main Fleet to Singapore.* Just so, and a cursory examination of much of the wartime pap fed the British public leads one to conclude that they were indeed just about the only ones so continually taken in.

68. The original timetable as discussed in August had the following dispositions planned for the Rs: *Revenge*, mid-September; *Royal Sovereign*, mid-November; *Ramillies*, mid-December; and *Resolution*, early January.

69. The *Prince of Wales* had picked up some extra Bofors guns at Colombo, and these had to be bolted into place. Of the destroyers from the Mediterranean, the following is a description of their state: "The *Jupiter* and *Encounter*, which he transferred, were not in fact in good structural order. One of them had something wrong with her fuel tanks, so that when completed to full capacity she took on a list of about ten degrees, which gradually lost as she got through her oil. The other had a corrugated bottom due to too close an acquaintance with the bottom of the sea on some previous occasion." Grenfell, *Main Fleet to Singapore.*

 Their places were taken for the time being by two very ancient veterans relegated to the Far Eastern waters earlier for their own safety as much as anything else, the Australian destroyer *Vampire* and the little *Tenedos*, one of the smallest and oldest ships in the navy. One of Philips's first duties on reaching Singapore had been to fly to confer with the commander of the U.S. Asian Fleet to beg the loan of some destroyers while his few were repaired, in order to have sufficient screening ships to operate. The American was willing, but the two heavy ships were lost before these reinforcements could reach him.

70. Of the many excellent accounts of the Pearl Harbor attack available, I have consulted: Samuel Eliot Morison, *History of United States Naval Operations in World War II*, Vol. 3 (Oxford University Press, 1948), for the American viewpoint, and Masatake Okumiya and Jiro Horokoshi, *Zero! The Story of the Japanese Navy Air Force, 1937–1945* (Cassell, 1957), as my main sources. There are many more books of course on this subject.

Brief details of the American battleships at Pearl Harbor at the time of the attack include the *Utah* (1910)—19,800 tons; no armament; and twenty-one knots. This old vessel was the equivalent to the *Iron Duke* or *Centurion*. It is ironic that her Japanese counterpart should have taken part in this strike as a fully operational fleet unit. The *Wyoming* was used as a gunnery ship. Also included were the *Nevada* and *Oklahoma* (completed 1915, modernized 1927–29)—29,000 tons; ten 14-inch and twelve 5-inch guns; and twenty knots; the *Arizona* and *Pennsylvania* (completed 1916, modernized 1928–31)—33,100 tons; twelve 14-inch guns, twelve 5-inch guns, and twelve 5-inch antiaircraft guns; and twenty knots; the *California* and *Tennessee* (1920–21)—32,600 tons; twelve 14-inch guns, twelve 5-inch guns, and twelve 5-inch antiaircraft guns; and twenty-one knots; and the *Maryland* and *West Virginia* (1921–22)—31,500 tons; eight 16-inch guns, ten 5-inch guns, and eight 5-inch antiaircraft guns; and twenty-one knots.

Of these, the *Utah* and *Arizona* were write-offs, as was the *Oklahoma*, which, although raised, was never repaired. All the rest were extensively refitted or rebuilt and subsequently served in later campaigns with great distinction.

71. Okumiya and Horikoshi, *Zero!*
72. Ibid.
73. Apart from Marder, some sources for the details of this battle include Grenfell, *Main Fleet to Singapore*; Hough, *The Hunting of Force Z*; and Geoffrey Bennett, *The Loss of the Prince of Wales and Repulse* (Ian Allan, 1973).

   The composition of the Japanese squadrons engaged in the attack was as follows: Eleventh Air Fleet (under R.Adm. Sadaichi Matsunga)—21st and 22nd Air Flotillas based at Thudaumot and Soctrang; Mihoro Air Corps with forty-eight Mitsubishi G3M2 Navy Type 96 twin-engine bombers (Nells); Genzan Air Corps with forty-eight Nells; Kanoya Air Corps with seventy-two Mitsubishi G4M2 Navy Type I twin-engine bombers (Bettys).

   The *Repulse* was the target of thirty-six torpedoes and was hit by five of them. Sixteen heavy bombs were dropped; one hit. The *Prince of Wales* was the target of fifteen torpedoes and was hit by five of them. Thirty-two heavy bombs were dropped; one hit. Japanese casualties were only three bombers, although several more were damaged but reached their bases.

74. Franklin, *One Year of Life*.
75. Sellwood and Cain, *H.M.S. Electra*.
76. Okumiya and Horikoshi, *Zero!*
77. Franklin, *One Year of Life*.
78. Grenfell, *Main Fleet to Singapore*.
79. Sellwood and Cain, *H.M.S. Electra*.
80. Roskill, *The War at Sea*, Vol. 1.
81. Grenfell, *Main Fleet to Singapore*.
82. The loss of these two ships was not the decisive element that it was claimed to be, according to Admiral Hezlet:

> In many people's minds the subsequent loss of Singapore was mainly attributable to this disaster, but it is very doubtful whether it made much difference except to morale. It was a great shock to those who still believed that sea power depended on the battleship but it was not the cause of the loss of Malaya. What had been suspected for many years was now proved beyond doubt. Even modern battleships fitted

with the latest anti-aircraft gunnery systems could be sunk by aircraft at sea. On the Japanese side there is little doubt that it was the 22nd Air Flotilla, which covered the landings at Singapore rather than Admiral Kondo's battleship force. It was now clear to the most reactionary of the nautical faction that the battleship was no longer the only counter to the battleship and a battle-fleet by itself could no longer claim to be the arbiter of sea power. (Hezlet, *Aircraft and Sea Power*)

Such a popular conclusion was not shared by other observers who probed a little more deeply. Long before, Captain Grenfell had anticipated the conclusion and given the riposte:

There at once arose a clamor of propaganda among the professionally air-minded that the loss of the ships by air attack conclusively proved the superiority of shore-based aircraft over the heaviest surface ship. It proved, of course, nothing of the kind; but only that battleships with no anti-aircraft defence could be sunk by air attack- quite a different thing. On subsequent occasions, when battleships had suitable anti-aircraft protection, they retained their operational value. (Grenfell, *Main Fleet to Singapore*)

The two viewpoints are further shown to be irreconcilable by the verdicts of the two nations' historians. Thus Okumiya and Horikoshi in *Zero!* : "The battle of Malaya illustrated in the most forcible manner that a surface fleet without fighter protection was helpless under enemy air attack. The battleship, long ruler of the seas, had been toppled from its dominant position and was now just another warship to be destroyed by aerial assault."

Whether the decision to send the two ships to Singapore was right has also been the subject of much digression, but once there Admiral Phillips' acceptance of battle, despite the long odds involved are less justifiably attacked. Captain Roskill's viewpoint in *The War at Sea*, Vol. 1, is perhaps the fairest of many: "As to the conduct of his operations after Admiral Phillips had arrived on his station and Japan had launched his attack, the attempt to destroy the enemy landing forces is surely not open to criticism; for the Admiral could not possibly ignore such a threat to the base on which our whole position in his theatre depended."'

The French historian Andrieu D'Albas in *Death of a Navy* (Robert Hale, 1957) states that the conduct of the admiral "had done honor to the traditions of the Royal Navy." A similar verdict is given by the Swiss historian Bauer: "As for the initiative taken by the ill-fated Sir Tom Phillips, it was that to be expected of a British sailor, bred in the tradition of taking the offensive and promoted to his high command by virtue of this very fighting spirit which was admired by all." Bauer, *World War II*.

A different viewpoint was expressed by a fellow admiral: "Somerville was shocked and dismayed but hardly surprised at the news. He had privately expressed his misgivings at the appointment as commander in chief of our Eastern Fleet of Sir Tom Phillips, who in his view, was inexperienced in the practicalities of modern war at sea. He knew him for an advocate of 'pushing on regardless of cost' and ignorant of the effect of well-handled air power on naval operations." Macintyre, *Fighting Admiral.* Admiral Somerville was soon to be given the opportunity of demonstrating the effectiveness of his alternative measures.

83. Churchill, *The Second World War,* Vol. 2.
84. Cunningham, *A Sailor's Odyssey.*
85. Donald Macintyre, *The Battle of the Mediterranean* (Batsford, 1964).

CHAPTER 7: BROADER HORIZONS

1. Lloyd, *The Nation and the Navy.*
2. "When the *Prince of Wales* was sunk off the coast of Malaya after having been hit by six Japanese torpedoes, the fact was so recorded in WIR (Weekly Intelligence Report) and somehow found its way into the notice board version of the Report which could be read by ships' companies. As the ship had been constructed to withstand a dozen torpedoes, it was read firstly as an affront to the Controller and Naval Constructors and secondly as a threat to the morale of her sister ship the *King George V.* A personal and incredulous call from Admiral Tovey, commander in chief of the Home Fleet, who had seen the offending version ashore at Scapa, was the first that Godfrey knew of the matter. The point was conceded and the notice went no further." McLachlan, *Room 39.*
3. Ciano, *Diaries, 1939–45.*
4. S. W. Roskill, *The War at Sea,* Vol. 2, *The Period of Balance* (H.M.S.O., 1956).
5. Sir Philip Vian, *Action This Day* (Frederick Muller, 1960).
6. Peter C. Smith, *Fighting Flotilla* (William Kimber, 1976).
7. Cameron, *Red Ensign; White Duster.*
8. Roskill, *The War at Sea,* Vol. 2.
9. Ibid. It was only on June 27 that the *Queen Elizabeth* was finally undocked and sailed through the Suez Canal for Port Sudan after completing temporary repairs and during July she sailed for the United States. The *Valiant,* her repairs completed locally, was allocated for the Eastern Fleet and joined that station in August. The only capital ship the British had in the whole Mediterranean at this time was the *Malaya,* just returned to Gibraltar. Her other vital duties had been listed earlier as escorting important troop convoys, giving cover to convoys east of 26 degrees west in emergency, and backing up Force H for operations in the western Mediterranean when necessary. This she had just done.
10. The escape of the *Scharnhorst* and *Gneisenau* through the English Channel is the subject of the following books: Terence Robertson, *Channel Dash* (Evans, 1958); John Deane Potter, *Fiasco* (Heinemann, 1970); and Peter Kemp, *Escape of the Scharnhorst and Gneisenau* (Ian Allan, 1975).
11. Churchill, *The Second World War,* Vol. 4.
12. "You can count on this," Hitler told Raeder, "from my previous experience, I do not believe the British capable of the conception and execution of lightning decisions such as will be required for the transfer of their air and sea forces to meet the boldness of our operation."
13. Quoted in Robertson, *Channel Dash.*
14. Roskill, *The War at Sea,* Vol. 2.
15. In fairness, it should be added that the estimate of the RAF on February 2 contained the telling line: "Our bombers have shown that we cannot place much reliance on them to damage the enemy. . . . This was far from the opinion of most senior RAF commanders even at this date. For example, after the farcical

failure of the Liberators in June against the Italian Fleet had long been history Lord Tedder was to write how: 'A number of hits were scored and there was no doubt that both the bomb and torpedo attacks were well executed," and that "the Italian Fleet soon made off to the north after our attacks.' He further claimed from these attacks that the main lessons were that 'given the right aircraft carrying the right bombs we can restore the situation in the Mediterranean, deny the sea to enemy capital ships and so free our own sea communications.'" Tedder, *With Prejudice.*

16. Robertson, *Channel Dash.*
17. Bekker, *Swastika at Sea.*
18. Ibid.
19. Robertson, *Channel Dash.*
20. Churchill, *The Second World War,* Vol. 3.
21. Potter, *Fiasco.*
22. Hezlet, *Aircraft and Sea Power.*
23. Chatfield, *It Might Happen Again,* Vol. 2, *The Navy and Defence.*
24. The same problems beset the *Scharnhorst,* and she was not finally ready for operations again until October 1942, also at Gotenhafen, but she never received her 15-inch guns either.
25. Had the *Tirpitz* ever got to St. Nazaire and entered the dock incidentally, she would have been unable to get out again for a year. This useful tip was given to the German admiral Schultze by Admiral Darlan at a dinner party in Paris for which the German was duly thankful.
26. Churchill, *The Second World War,* Vol. 4. The prime minister's anxiety was well founded; a year before, he had been confidently predicting that the *Nelson* and *Rodney* would be able to join the American 16-inch-gun battleships in the Pacific to present an all-powerful homogeneous squadron, which it was hoped, would confront and defeat the Japanese battle line in the expected decisive set-piece battle. Now the whole British position in the Indian Ocean was at some risk, although the Premier confidently stated that he did not expect the Japanese fleet to venture into that area in any strength, an opinion that was rather ill-founded. The *Anson* was not expected to complete until August.
27. After the vital operations with Force H at the western end of the Mediterranean, the *Malaya* went on to carry out vital convoy escort work escorting WS convoys down from Freetown to the Cape during July and August 1942. Admiral Somerville had earlier criticized her allocation as his flagship, apparently because of her fighting ability, although her lack of comfort is the main point featured by his biographer. "This ship does not please me a bit. She's never been a flagship and has none of the proper arrangements or fittings. My bridge forward has no protection from the weather and must be absolutely bloody at sea. As for my sea cabin, words fail me." Macintyre, *Fighting Admiral.*
28. Woodward, *The Tirpitz.*
29. The only air operations against the Home Fleet had been a feeble attack by three Ju 88s at 3:45 A.M. on the ninth while the fleet was off Vestifiord. No damage was done.
30. Two carriers were planned before the war, of which the *Graf Zeppelin* had been launched before the outbreak of hostilities. An experimental air group was actually already formed for her at this time. She would have carried eight fighters and twenty-two adapted Ju 87 dive-bombers. The dive-bombers, converted

Stukas with hooks, were utilized in the Polish campaign sinking several Polish warships but no torpedo bombers were envisaged for her. The development of specialized, rather than converted types, naval aircraft for her would, Goering stated, postpone her completion until 1946.

31. The first experimental squadrons of these were working up at Grossetto on the west coast of Italy because the Luftwaffe was learning much of its technique of this new arm from the Italians, past masters at it. The first experienced squadrons started to come to Norway in May and were at once used with success against Russian convoys. See: Peter C. Smith, *Arctic Victory* (Crécy, 2001), for a full description of the history, training, and use of the torpedo-bomber in the Luftwaffe at this period.

32. Despite this, Churchill was writing to Roosevelt in April requesting that her brand-new sister, the *North Carolina*, be sent to join her so that both the *Duke of York* and *Renown* could go east.

33. This damage and the loss of the *Prince of Wales* is ironic in view of the prewar emphasis placed on underwater protection at the expense of offensive power. Lord Chatfield described how he spent "many hours from 1936 to 1938 in considering the design of our new ships. I brought all the six Sea Lords into the discussions." He goes on to stress how the importance of underwater protection was reflected in the design of the King George V class, these vessels which "originally were designed to carry twelve, but we removed two guns in order that the large saving of weight could be put into underwater protection." Chatfield, *It Might Happen Again*, Vol. 2.

   Churchill, typically, came up with a unique idea of his own to make the best of a bad situation, combining the damage to the *King George V* and the late delivery of the *Anson*. His proposal was that the whole crew of the damaged flagship be sent on leave simultaneously "for a fortnight, or whatever is the proper period." While they were away, the crew allocated to stand by the *Anson* could instead be assigned to the *King George*, while the latter's crew on return would go as "a complete, integral, highly trained unit to the *Anson*, which is an identical ship in almost every respect." This, he estimated, would save a month or six weeks in the *Anson*'s working up time. Quite how the very patient Pound reacted to that brainchild is not revealed. What *did* happen is that King George VI paid a surprise visit to Scapa Flow, staying aboard the *King George V* and visiting the *Washington*.

34. A detailed account of the attacks on the *Prinz Eugen*, their failure, and the gallantry of the crews is given in chapter 7 of Barker, *The Ship Busters*.

35. Of all the reams of paper and gallons of ink expended in analyzing this particular disaster, I have examined the majority published in English. Of these, David Irving, *The Destruction of Convoy P.Q.17* (Cassell, 1968), gives the most precise details available of the German big ship movements and the plan of the "Knights Move" operation. As it is with the work of battleships with which this book is concerned rather than the close escort, other sources are less relevant, but for the reader who wishes to go deeper into this affair, the following works by those who were present are the best available, although there is much more—of uneven accuracy—available: Jack Broomem, *Convoy is to Scatter* (William Kimber, 1972); Roger Hill, *Destroyer Captain* (William Kimber, 1975); Graeme Ogden, *My Sea Lady* (Hutchinson, 1963); and Godfrey Winn, *PQ 17: The Story of a Ship* (Hutchinson, 1947). The most valuable account of the trau-

matic hours in the Citadel which led to the withdrawal of the cruiser squadron is Patrick Beasley, *Very Special Intelligence*.

36. Irving, *The Destruction of Convoy P.Q.17*.

37. In big ships, that is. Three of the escorting destroyers hit a submerged rock in Gimsoy narrows badly damaging their propeller-shafts and screws and were forced to drop out of the operation.

38. This grounding effectively put paid to the *Lützow*'s part in operations against the Russian convoys for four months. She sailed for Kiel on August 9, arriving intact on the twenty-first. Repairs to her hull were not finally complete until November 5, 1942.

39. Stumpff, the commander of the 5th Air Fleet, was one of the few who thought otherwise. He claimed the honor of the annihilation of PQ 17 to his air force alone. "I beg to report," he wrote to Goering on July 12, "the destruction of Convoy PQ 17. I report the sinking of the Fifth Air Force of one cruiser, one destroyer, two small escorts totaling 4,000 tons. 22 merchant ships totaling 142,216 tons." In fact, the convoy had lost only twenty-three ships in all, and of these, at least ten of them had been sunk by submarines. No warships at all had been lost. After the war, Hezlet, *Aircraft and Sea Power*, also gives the credit to the Luftwaffe: "It was primarily the strengthening of the Luftwaffe in Northern waters rather than the arrival of the German heavy ships which was responsible for the disaster to PQ 17, and which for three months afterwards, stopped the North Russian convoys."

   However, any close study of this Russian convoy at this period seems to indicate exactly the opposite conclusion to this one. The air attacks had caused some losses to previous convoys, but had never stopped one or caused it to break up in confusion, nor had these losses been unbearable in any degree. Subsequently the next convoy PQ 18 was subjected to air attack on a far greater scale and intensity and came through with much smaller casualties while inflicting prohibitive losses on the elite group of German torpedo-bomber crews.

   Moreover, study of all the available records of the time shows how it was the German battleships that weighed the most heavily on those given the unenviable task of fighting these convoys through. Only the heavy ships had the power to cause a convoy to be scattered in this way, the Luftwaffe had nothing to do with it apart from mopping up later.

40. Churchill, *The Second World War*, Vol. 4.

41. Ibid.

42. Ibid.

43. Roskill, *The War at Sea*, Vol. 2.

44. Woodward, *The Tirpitz*.

45. For a very different viewpoint of the situation in the Indian Ocean at this time, see Michael Tomlinson, *The Most Dangerous Moment* (William Kimber, 1976). Writing from an air force background, he does not seems to understand the naval problems and situation.

46. As this did not feature battleships, this battle is not described here. For a clear description, see David A. Thomas, *Battle of the Java Sea* (Andre Deutsch, 1968). In the operations that finally wrapped up their conquest of Java, the Japanese sailed their Southern Striking Force under Admiral Kondo, and comprising the battleships *Hiei* and *Kirishima*, two heavy cruisers, and a flotilla, they intercepted the U.S. destroyer *Edsall*; on March 1, they sank her south of Christmas Island.

Five merchant ships were also destroyed. On March 3, they sank the American gunboat *Asheville* in the same area. The *Hiei* and *Kirishima*, with four destroyers, rounded off their foray with a bombardment of Christmas Island on March 7, during which another freighter was sunk.

47. "[T]he message, as we got it, was somewhat as follows: 'With your heads held high, and your hearts beating proudly, I leave the defence of Singapore in your strong and capable hands. I am off to Colombo to collect a new fleet.' Well doubtless the admiral had only meant to be encouraging; but the retort of the messdeck was inevitable . . . 'Up ladder Jack—I'm inboard!'" Cain and Sellwood, *HMS Electra*.

48. For example, he wrote to the Chiefs of Staff Committee on March 27 that the fleets base at Colombo was the highest priority for defence so that the fleet could operate from there into the Bay of Bengal, e.g., offensively. "One had hoped that *Warspite* and two armored carriers would be able to play an important part in the Bay of Bengal. It seems a great loss to have to send one of these fast carriers to Port T [Addu Atoll] to guard the fairly useless R class. If they are no use and only an encumbrance, why don't they get out of the way, say to Aden or cruising, and give the aircraft carriers a chance?" Churchill, *The Second World War*, Vol. 4. In actual fact, the Rs and the *Indomitable* were detached to Addu for badly needed training programs, which could be carried out, by both types of ship in safety there and not at Colombo.

49. Macintyre, *Fighting Admiral*. All the R-class ships had been operating independently as convoy escorts for most of the war and therefore, as Somerville recorded for all the ships, "Everyone is naturally very rusty about doing their Fleet stuff most ships have hardly been in company with another ship during the war."

50. Because the *King George V* was damaged (and the *Washington*, far from being reinforced by her sister, the *North Carolina*, understandably being withdrawn for the Pacific), the *Duke of York* had to stay at home. Both the *Illustrious* and *Valiant* finally got to Somerville, but too late to affect the issue, which was decided almost at once. Likewise, the *Nelson* and *Rodney* had other commitments which prevented them sailing eastward until July, and by then, the crisis was over, and by the time they got to Freetown, they were needed in the Mediterranean again.

51. Grenfell, *Main Fleet to Singapore*.

52. Ibid.

53. Ibid.

54. Macintyre, *Fighting Admiral*.

55. Nor was there. The Japanese remained in complete ignorance of Port T throughout the entire operation.

56. The official historian concludes that Somerville's actions were "premature." At the time, Somerville was confident, writing, "I fear they have taken fright, which is a pity because if I could have given them a good crack now it would have been very timely." As his biographer noted, "He must have looked back with embarrassment on this judgment in time to come when the full strength of the Japanese raiding squadron came to be known." Macintyre, *Fighting Admiral*. Churchill later publicly stated that Somerville still enjoyed the cabinet's confidence.

57. Macintyre, *Fighting Admiral*.

58. Grenfell, *Main Fleet to Singapore*.

59. Macintyre, *Fighting Admiral.*
60. Ibid.
61. "The numerous enemy reports and the fate of the two cruisers were bringing it home to Sir James that his own force was in some danger, divided as it was. He therefore decided to rejoin his Force B (the R-class battleships) and turned back accordingly. In fact, his previous decision to push on ahead with one battleship and two carriers only, though gallant and forceful was distinctly rash." Grenfell, *Main Fleet to Singapore.* This is strange in view of his expressed feelings over Tom Phillips's earlier strategy. As the official historian put it, Somerville's search, had it have been successful, would have probably ended in tragedy on an even greater scale than the Malayan episode. "We may be thankful that they never found him [Nagumo]." Even the aggressive Churchill seems to have realized this point, commenting later: "We had narrowly escaped a disastrous fleet action." Churchill, *The Second World War*, Vol. 4.
62. Churchill wrote to Roosevelt, "The four 'R' class battleships were good enough, in combination with the others, to meet the three Kongos [in actual fact, there were four, the *Haruna* having been falsely reported sunk by the USAAF earlier off the Philippines] which were all we believed were over our side. They cannot of course cope with modernized Japanese ships." Churchill, *The Second World War*, Vol. 4.

He expressed the views of himself and the Admiralty somewhat more forcefully: "On one point we were all agreed. The 'Rs' should get out of danger at the earliest moment. When I put this to the First Sea Lord, there was no need for argument. Orders were sent accordingly, and the Admiralty authorised Admiral Somerville to withdraw his fleet 2,000 miles westward to East Africa." Ibid.
63. On March 10, Churchill had written to the First Lord and First Sea Lord, "Is it credible that the Japanese have at present time nine capital ships and two large aircraft-carriers all building simultaneously?" When he was assured that it was, he replied on the seventeenth: "The assumption is that all these ships are completed punctually. *Kuro*, laid down in 1937, should have been finished in 1941. She is only now thought to have joined the fleet, a year later. Five years are assigned for *Sasebo*, but *Maizuru* is given only four years. How does this compare with the five ships of the King George V class or the contemporary American vessels?" Churchill, *The Second World War*, Vol. 4.

In case the reader is puzzled by these names, it should be pointed out that, not knowing anything much about the Japanese warships being built, except that they were battleships with 16-inch guns (in fact, they were 18.1-inch weapons), or their names, the Admiralty assigned codenames to them pertaining to their port of construction. This *Kuro* is probably the *Yamato*, built at Kure, and which joined the fleet early in 1942. The *Maizuru* is possibly her sister, the *Musashi*, building at Mitsubishi yard in Nagasaki, while the *Sasebo* could be the third of these giants, the *Shinano*, subsequently completed as an aircraft carrier at Yokosuka Navy Yard.

For a complete list of the fighting ships actually completed for the Imperial Navy at this time and during the war, see the definitive volume, Anthony J. Watts and Brian G. Gordon, *The Imperial Japanese Navy* (Macdonald, 1971). For the most complete description of the Yamato-class ships, the reader should consult W. David Dickson, *I.J.N. Yamato* (International Naval Research Organization, 1975).

64. A very detailed account of this battle and its importance world-wide is contained in: Peter C. Smith, *Midway: Dauntless Victory* (Pen & Sword Publishing, 2007).

65. Browne, *The Floating Bulwark.*

66. Laval had just come to power in Vichy-France and was working even more closely with his Axis opposite numbers. A Japanese pilot recalled how, when they landed at their Indochina base in December, French pilots ran up to them cheering the news of Pearl Harbor and other Allied defeats. See *Zero!*

67. In April, Churchill had signaled Pound that he could not understand why this ship would not be operational until June as Admiral Cunningham had informed him that her crew, who had rejoined her in bulk, were in "perfect order."

68. They had got as far as Freetown when recalled to Scapa Flow. Admiral Syfret flew home and hoisted his flag in the *Nelson* and began the detailed planning of the operation using a direct telephone link to Norfolk House in London.

69. When it was proposed to bring the *Valiant* home for a time in December, since many of her crew had not had leave for more than two years, the prime minister objected, "I do not know why special favour should be shown the Navy." When the *Warspite* returned home later, it was the first time her crew had seen England in thirty-seven months.

70. Churchill, *The Second World War*, Vol. 4.

71. Bernard Fergusson, *The Watery Maze* (Collins, 1961).

72. Roskill, *The War at Sea*, Vol. 2.

73. Roskill, *HMS Warspite.*

74. The most complete account of this battle is contained in Peter C. Smith, *Pedestal: The Convoy That Saved Malta* (Goodall, 2002).

75. Thompson, *HMS Rodney at War.*

76. Churchill, *The Second World War*, Vol. 4.

77. Ibid.

78. The *Jean Bart* remained out of action for the duration of the war. Not until November 1945 was she sailed to Cherbourg to dock and repair, and then she went to Brest in 1946 to complete. She carried out her acceptance trials in July 1949 and achieved almost thirty-two knots, the last battleship in the world to enter service. She finally paid off at Toulon in 1961 and was hulked as an accommodation ship, almost the last of her line to serve in an active capacity.

80. Thompson, *HMS Rodney at War.*

81. Ibid.

82. Most Frenchmen remained convinced that Vichy France was a nation free to do as it wished and follow the path it chose. Its high priest of illusion was Laval. By 11:30 A.M., they had already agreed to let the Axis powers move their bombers into Tunisia, and that same evening, November 9, Hitler summoned Laval to Berchtesgaden: He arrived on the tenth, and Hitler then proceeded to show the Vichy leader just how much of a puppet he really was. "The poor man," wrote Ciano, who was present, "could not even imagine the fait accompli that the Germans were to place before him. Not a word was said to Laval about the impending action—that the orders to occupy France were being given while he was smoking his cigarette and conversing with various people in the next room." Ciano, *Diaries, 1939–43.*

     Darlan's appeal, as respected chief of the French Navy, for the Toulon Fleet to make a dash to join the Allies in North Africa received from Admiral de

Laborde just one word in reply: "an answer in one expressive—if indelicate—word: '*Merde*'." Shirer, *The Rise and Fall of the Third Reich.*

83. Nobody questioned the bravery of the French sailors who died in this way, only the pointlessness of it all. Had they have fought the Axis with such fanaticism as they did the British and Americans, World War II may indeed have ended some months earlier than it did.

84. If, as the French historians have always maintained, the Germans would never have taken over their fleet in 1940 because they could not operate French ships, then the scuttling at Toulon becomes even more unnecessary. They cannot have it both ways.

CHAPTER 8: SUPPORTING THE LANDINGS

1. For the fullest descriptions of the events described here and those omitted, the reader should consult the complete set of volumes by Samuel E. Morison, *History of United States Naval Operations in World War II* (Oxford University Press).

2. D'Albas, *Death of a Navy.*

3. Ibid.

4. Roskill remarked, "It is interesting to recall that the *Hiei* and her three sister ships (laid down 1911-12 in Japanese yards) were designed by Sir George Thurston, one of the most distinguished British naval architects of the time. The large amount of punishment she withstood more than thirty years later, without sinking or blowing up, appears to be a remarkable tribute to the man who designed her." Roskill, *The War at Sea*, Vol. 2.

5. D'Albas, *Death of a Navy.*

6. For a detailed and highly personal account from the Japanese side of the campaign at sea in the Solomons, the reader is recommended to read Tameichi Hara, *Japanese Destroyer Captain* (Ballantine Books, New York, 1963).

7. Tedder, *With Prejudice.*

8. Howarth, *Sovereign of the Seas.*

9. Padfield, *The Battleship Era.*

10. Hough, *Dreadnought.*

11. Chatfield, *It Might Happen Again*, Vol. 2, *The Navy and Defence.*

12. McLachlan, *Room 39.*

13. Gervis Frere-Cook, *The Attacks on the Tirpitz* (Ian Allan, 1973).

14. Roskill, *The War at Sea*, Vol. 2.

15. Edward Von der Porten, *The German Navy in World War II* (Arthur Baker, 1969).

16. Raeder actually resigned on January 30, 1943, having been supreme commander since October 1928. He was given the honorary post of Inspector General of the Navy, but the job was meaningless and only utilized to lessen the effect of his departure on the nation's morale.

17. For a fuller account of these monologues, see *Führer Conferences on Naval Affairs* contained in *Brassey's Naval Annual, 1948* (William Clowes, 1948), and Admiral Raeder's autobiography, *Struggle for the Sea* (William Kimber, 1959). A complete account of the New Year's Eve battle is contained in Pope, *73 North.*

18. See, for example, Shirer, *Rise and Fall of the Third Reich.* "Dönitz, the new commander in chief, had been commander of U-boats, knew very little of the problems of surface vessels, and henceforth concentrated on submarine warfare."

19. "For one who held the supreme command of the Navy for over fourteen years, battleships remained a basic instrument of world-wide naval strategy. Though he

accepted the aeroplane as a new and important factor, he regarded a naval air force mainly as an auxiliary to the Fleet. That air power had brought to war a new dimension, rendering former naval concepts outmoded and virtually consigning battle fleets to the scrapheap, was beyond him. On giving up his post he was, after all, in his sixty-seventh year." Bekker, *Hitler's Naval War.*

20. Ibid.
21. Karl Dönitz, *Ten Years and Twenty Days* (Weidenfeld & Nicolson, 1958).
22. Admiral Cunningham wrote on December 1 that "they have now no excuse for remaining inert, except perhaps that so many Frenchmen at the present time appear to have lost all their spirit. Doubtless it will revive; but at the moment the will to fight for their country is completely absent." When Godfroy finally changed his mind, Cunningham in conversation with Churchill drew his attention to the penultimate chapter of Ecclesiastes: "Cast thy bread upon the waters: for thou shall find it after many days." "My innocent remark," he recalled later, "was rather ill received." Cunningham, *A Sailor's Odyssey.*
23. Ruge, *Sea Warfare, 1939–45.*
24. Roskill, *The War at Sea,* Vol. 3.
25. Before moving to Naples, the three new battleships had been caught in an American air attack on La Spezia on June 5, suffering slight superficial damage only. The three old battleships *Cesare, Doria,* and *Duilio* had been laid up inactive because of shortage of fuel, the former at Pola and the other two at Taranto, but all efforts were made in July to commission them again, and the *Caio Duilio* and *Andrea Doria* were ready for service again at the time of Husky, with the *Giulio Cesare* being prepared.
26. Of passing interest is the old *Centurion.* After the *Vigorous* episode and the damage she underwent, the earlier plans to change her from a replica of the *Anson* into one of the *Malaya* in the Indian Ocean were abandoned and she was not used in her dummy role again. The unfortunate fact that Axis scout planes over Alexandria had spotted one of her dummy wooden 14-inch guns floating in the water alongside her had always invalidated this role anyway. She was therefore sent back through the Suez Canal and used as a floating anitaircraft battery at Port Said with her thirteen Oerlikons. Here she remained until March 1944, when she was brought home again.
27. Thompson, *HMS Rodney at War.* Availability of short-range antiaircraft weapons had now permitted the close-range armaments of most of the old battleships to be built up into a daunting array by this stage of the war. The two Nelsons ultimately shipped an extra thirty-two 2-pounder pom-poms, sixteen 40mm Bofors, and sixty or more 20mm Oerlikons while the Queen Elizabeths were similarly equipped on a lighter scale. This made the capital ships bristly targets for dive-bomber and torpedo-bomber alike.
28. Roskill, *HMS Warspite.*
29. Thompson, *HMS Rodney at War.*
30. Hugh Popham, *Sea Flight* (William Kimber, 1954).
31. The Luftwaffe unit involved was KG 100, a special unit that had pioneered many of the revolutionary German airborne inventions over the years. See Peter C. Smith, *Ship Strike* (Airlife, 1998).
At this time, Major Bernhard Jope commanded it and they were equipped with the Dornier Do 217K-2 aircraft, which was a specially modified version of this twin-engined aircraft, with a longer wingspan, which enabled it to climb above

20,000 feet and still carry two of the guided bombs under its wings. Eleven of these aircraft belonging to III/KG 100 were used in this attack; the pilot of the aircraft that scored the hit on the *Roma* was Oberleutnant Schmetz.

The weapon itself was the FX 1400, known as the Fritz X, which was a 3,000-pound weapon which had no propulsion unit of its own but free-fell from heights of 19,000 to 12,000 feet striking their target with a terminal velocity of around 800 feet per second. The aircraft were based at Istres airfield.

32. Roskill, *The War at Sea*, Vol. 3.
33. On September 27, an agreement was signed by Admiral Cunningham whereby some of these surrendered units would be able to join the Allies in the fight against Germany. The disposal of the still large fleet caused some problems for the Allies also. Russia claimed a share of the spoils, which was agreed to but could not be carried out immediately.
34. Roskill, *The War at Sea*, Vol. 3.
35. Ruge, *Sea Warfare, 1939–45*.
36. Roskill, *H.M.S. Warspite*.
37. Cunningham, *A Sailor's Odyssey*.
38. Although Admiral Cunningham was not satisfied because the problem of the Italian Fleet was not faced. Its disposal was omitted "greatly to my disgust," and had later to be settled by an additional clause, added to "The Cunningham-de Courton Agreement," signed later on by Rear Admiral McGrigor. Admiral Cunningham had meanwhile flown home to take up the appointment of First Sea Lord owing to the death of Admiral Pound.
39. Churchill, *The Second World War*, Vol. 5, *Triumph and Tragedy* (Cassell, 1949).
40. William Donald, *Stand by for Action* (William Kimber, 1956).
41. Cunningham, *A Sailor's Odyssey*.
42. Ibid.
43. Woodward, *The Tirpitz*.
44. Ibid.
45. For a more detailed account on the many attempts to put the *Tirpitz* out of action, the following books should be consulted in conjunction with David Woodward's study: David Brown, *Tirpitz: A Pictorial History* (Gentry Books, 1975); Frere-Cook, *The Attacks on the Tirpitz*; L. Peillard, *Sink the Tirpitz* (Jonathan Cape, 1965); David Howard, *The Shetland Bus* (Nelson, 1951); H. J. Brennecke, *The Tirpitz: The Drama of the Lone Queen of the North* (Robert Hale, 1963); and C. E. T. Warren and James Benson, *Above us the Waves* (Harrap, 1953).
46. The X craft and their towing submarines were the *X-6* (Lieutenant Alexander), *Truculent*; *X-9* (Lieutenant Jupp), *Syrtis*; *X-8* (Lieutenant Oackley), *Seanymphe*; *X-7* (Lieutenant Duff), *Stubborn*; *X-5* (Lieutenant Hezlet), *Thrasher*; and *X-10* (Lieutenant McIntosh), *Sceptre*.
47. The operational commanders were the *X-5*, Lieutenant Henty-Creer; *X-6*, Lieutenant Cameron; *X-7*, Lieutenant Place; and *X-10*, Lieutenant Hudspeth.
48. As quoted in Peillard, *Sink the Tirpitz*.
49. Roskill, *The War at Sea*, Vol. 3.
50. By far the most comprehensive account of the loss of the *Scharnhorst*, giving a detailed analysis of the gunnery duel and other data, is Anthony P. Watts, *The Loss of the Scharnhorst* (Ian Allan, 1971). Other books include Busch, *The Drama of the Scharnhorst*, a really excellent study from the German viewpoint with much additional information not contained in British accounts; and Fraser, *Despatch*

on the sinking of the Scharnhorst (*London Gazette,* Supplement 38038). The volume that gives an absolutely fascinating insight into the vital role Ultra played in this operation and the way in which several warnings were ignored on the German side that the *Duke of York* was out is Patrick Beesley, *Very Special Intelligence.* At one stage, he recalls, Admiral Burnett with the British cruiser force, was receiving decoded signals from the German High Command as soon as the naval staff in Berlin.

51. Dönitz, *Ten Years and Twenty Days.*

52. For example, at Narvik, the New Year's Eve battle, and, even more so, in an action between two British light cruisers and eleven German destroyers in the Bay of Biscay in December 1943 when the *Glasgow* and *Enterprise* had sunk three of them, plus a blockade runner, and forced the others to withdraw, all without loss of a man.

53. For the Soviet reaction to this visit and the subsequent battle, see Arseni Golovko, *With the Red Fleet* (Putnam, 1965), a remarkable insight on Russian naval thinking and the rewriting of history.

54. Dönitz, *Ten Years and Twenty Days.*

55. Ibid.

56. Bekker, *Hitler's Naval War.*

57. Roskill, *The War at Sea,* Vol. 3.

58. Busch, *The Drama of the Scharnhorst.*

59. Woodward, *The Tirpitz.*

60. Roskill, *The War at Sea,* Vol. 3.

61. Busch, *The Drama of the Scharnhorst.*

62. B. B. Ramsden, *Sea Tales from Blackwoods* (Blackwoods, 1960).

63. Busch, *The Drama of the Scharnhorst.*

64. Woodward, *The Tirpitz.*

65. The *Duke of York* had up to that time fired some fifty-two broadsides, thirty-one of which straddled the target, sixteen falling within 200 yards of the *Scharnhorst.* See Anthony Watts's book for more detailed analysis. Roskill commented: "This was remarkable shooting, even when allowing for the efficiency of her radar control and spotting. But at such comparatively short ranges her 14-inch shell were unlikely, due to the flatness of the trajectory, to penetrate the enemy's main armored deck and so do her lethal injury." Nonetheless, the culmination of so many hits did the job.

The *Scharnhorst's* tactics had been to make a turn to southward and fire a broadside, then turn end-on away to the east until ready to fire the next one, which made the *Duke of York's* gunnery more difficult, and her accuracy thus even more credible. Oscar Parkes commented that "the engagement was marked by speedy radio communication and exceptional performance by radar personnel, which largely contributed to the success of a night action fought in heavy weather." Parkes, *British Battleships.*

The clarity of the British radar was remarkable, it being possible for them to watch on the screen the *Scharnhorst's* return salvos emerging from out of the target echo. "The visible approach of the enemy salvos had no effect other than stimulating interest in the operations, and I learned about each salvo from a cheerful voice of warning saying to me, 'One's coming,'" wrote the *Duke of York's* gunnery officer in his report.

66. Busch, *The Drama of the Scharnhorst.*

67. Roskill, *The War at Sea*, Vol. 3.
68. Ibid.
69. Ibid.
70. Padfield, *The Battleship Era.*
71. These aircraft—Corsair, Hellcat, and Wildcat—were all standard U.S. Navy or U.S. Marine Corps fighters of high quality, faster, more powerfully armed and much more rugged than their British equivalents and made available under Lease-Lend. With them a British fleet could approach the strongest Axis coastline with complete confidence against air attack. The Barracuda was a British aircraft which tried to combine several duties and was not really good at any of them as a result. They were phased out and replaced by the much more reliable American Avenger torpedo-bomber soon after this operation, although the British used them more as glide-bombers than in their correct role, The true dive-bombers, of the Dauntless and Helldiver types, were not available from the U.S. at this time, in the latter case because of the antipathy of Adm. Ernest King. See Peter C. Smith, *Curtiss SB2C Helldiver* (Crowood, 2004).
72. Although the upper decks were a shambles, the Germans were quick to realize that this was only superficial damage, and even the shipping of 875 tons of water in the bilges was something that could be quickly rectified. Had they but known it, the Fleet Air Arm pilots had delivered a more telling blow than they realized. Operation Tungsten marked the end of the *Tirpitz*'s operational life, as Admiral Dönitz has since confirmed.
73. Roskill, *The War at Sea*, Vol. 3. Patrick Beesley has now revealed how the accuracy of the intelligence reports was now such that the precise time when the *Tirpitz* would be leaving port but not yet at speed at sea, could be transmitted to the Naval commanders on the spot which enabled the attack to go in at precisely the most vulnerable moment. Beesley, *Very Special Intelligence.*
74. Beesley, *Very Special Intelligence.*
75. It is a measure of the American navy's newfound power that at the same time as these three battleships were firing at Normandy their own huge invasion fleet was carrying out the colossal Saipan landings. The heavy bombardment force for this operation included the battleships *California, Colorado, Idaho, Maryland, New Mexico, Pennsylvania,* and *Tennessee.* Covering the operation and engaged in the battle of the Philippine Sea later in the month was Task Force 58 under Admiral Spruance, which included in its massive array of fifteen aircraft carriers, twenty cruisers, and sixty-seven destroyers a backbone of seven modern battleships: *North Carolina, South Dakota, Indiana, Alabama, Iowa, New Jersey,* and *Washington.* Also, although famous as a carrier battle, perhaps the largest such fought, it is interesting that Spruance was as overcautious as Yamamoto at Midway and refused to allow Mitscher to despatch his fast battleships to finish off the enemy after his aircraft had been decimated, and therefore the bulk of Ozawa's fleet got away to fight again at Leyte and elsewhere.

   With the older British battleships laid up in home waters, there should have been absolutely no need whatsoever to make this request of the Americans at all. This point was not overlooked by the prime minister, who had a late change of heart about his coffin ships, realizing that they were at least four years younger and much more powerful than the *Arkansas,* which the Americans were using most effectively. He accordingly raised the point with the First Lord and First Sea Lord on June 22: "It is much better to rely on the 15-inch than the 16-inch, because of the larger stocks of ammunition and replacement mountings and tubes," he noted. He then observed that the *Revenge* and *Resolution* were being used merely as stoker training ships. "These vessels should be put to a higher use," he correctly observed. "It would surely be wrong to use important fighting vessels as stoker training-schools in the height of a great battle, when either they or their armament or equipment are urgently needed." What Churchill had in mind was the reduction of Cherbourg. He emphasized that the *Warspite* should be used as much as possible while she could still "swim and her guns can fire" and hoped that the *Malaya* would then take over, which in fact she did, but he got no response from the Navy on the other veterans and the American ships had to stay and be used for the South of France landings despite the need for them in the Pacific. Britain now had severe manpower shortages.

76. Parkes, *British Battleships*.
77. Hill, *Destroyer Captain* (William Kimber, 1975).
78. Thompson, *HMS Rodney at War*.
79. The *Nelson* and *Ramillies*, with the monitors *Robert* and *Erebus*, fired a total of 218 rounds of 16- and 15-inch at the Houlgate battery. The *Rodney*, *Warspite*, *Ramillies*, and *Roberts* fired 284 rounds of 16- and 15-inch into Benerville during the bombardments that followed. An investigation made in 1945 by the joint Technical Warfare Committee carefully analyzed the effects of the various methods of bombardment, sea and air, during the Normandy operation and their findings seem conclusive enough. "[T]he only weapon which was capable of penetrating the strong concrete protection of casemated guns was the armor-piercing shell from the main armament of battleships or monitors. None of the bombs used was adequate, nor were they expected to be." See also Belfied and Essame, *The Battle for Normandy* (Batsford, 1965).
80. Roskill, *The War at Sea*, Vol. 3.
81. Roskill, *HMS Warspite*.
82. Hill, *Destroyer Captain*.
83. It is convenient here to relate the subsequent fate of the six surrendered Italian battleships which for some period lay in the Bitter Lakes south of the Suez Canal awaiting their ultimate fates. Churchill was in no doubt that the new Littorios, being splendid ships in excellent condition, would have a vital role to play in the war against Japan. He suggested that they be refitted in an American navy yard to bring them up to standard and then sail to the Pacific.

This excellent idea was rejected, and both these modern ships, the *Italia* and *Vittorio Veneto*, lay in useless idleness until the end of the war while the great powers vacillated over what to do with them, their reduced crews kept in a state of practical internment. Not surprisingly, they deteriorated in such conditions. The *Vittorio Veneto* was stricken from the navy list on February 1, 1948, and the *Italia* followed on June 1, 1948, and both were laid up at La Spezia. The Russians were now in their full cold-war blast, and everything that could be done to weaken the defenses of Western Europe was done. Britain and America could not agree even at this date and meekly submitted when Stalin insisted that the ships be made completely inoperational. The gun barrels of their 15-inch main armaments were burnt off in 1948, their machinery gearwheels were broken with sledgehammer blows and their hulls began to be dismantled, despite reports that they were to be publicly auctioned to pay off debts of the Ministry of Marine. By 1951, these two vessels were almost totally demolished, their hulls lingering on at La Spezia for several years after this, finally being scrapped in 1960.

Of the older ships surrendered, the *Giulio Cesare* was allocated to the Soviet Union. All three, the *Doria*, *Duilio*, and *Cesare*, were allowed to return to Augusta before the war's end, where they were used by the Italians for training purposes. The former two were reassigned to the Italian Navy as "cobelligerents" but were never actively employed again. Both remained on the Italian Navy active list after the war for many years, but the *Duilio* was finally stricken on September 15, 1956, and scrapped at La Spezia the next year, while the *Doria* was stricken on November 1, 1956, being towed from Taranto to La Spezia in 1961, where she was also scrapped.

The unfinished *Imperio*, sister of the ill-fated *Roma*, was found half submerged at Trieste when the Allies finally occupied that port, and had probably been damaged in a heavy air attack on February 12. The same air attacks accounted for the *Cavour*, which had finally been refloated at Taranto and transferred to Trieste for reconstruction. She capsized in the port and settled on the bottom. The hulk of the *Imperio* was scrapped at Venice in 1947-48, and the wreck of the *Cavour* was raised and scrapped after the war as well.

Thus passed the Italian battle fleet. See also Loewenheim et al., *Roosevelt and Churchill: Their Secret Wartime Correspondence* (Barrie & Jenkins, 1975).

84. Quite what the Soviets intended to do with their new addition is not quite clear, they could certainly not have fought the old veteran with much efficiency despite having almost double her normal complement aboard. In fact it has since transpired that their chiefly used her as a Training Ship. The first voyage as the *Arkhangelsk* was almost her last, for on twenty-third she was sighted and stalked by the *U-711*, which fired two acoustic torpedoes at her, one of which detonated prematurely. The next month, at Kola Inlet, she was lying at anchor when a second German attack was made on her, by the *U-315*. The attack, on September 14, was also unsuccessful. The Germans tried again on January 5, 1945, using the midget submarines of the Biber type. The *Arkhangelsk* was lying behind her own torpedo net defences at Murmansk but the operation was called off due to weather damage to the midgets en route. Her war career as a Soviet ship was limited to say the least. Between her arrival in August 1944 and the end of hostilities she did not venture out of the Kola Inlet once. Not until June 1945 did she go out for two trial runs in the Barents Sea, and the next month she sailed on a two-month cadet-training voyage into the White Sea. Great difficulties were apparently encountered in handling such a large vessel and after a further few trips she ran aground in the autumn of 1947 and was later re-floated. Nor were the remaining Soviet veterans much more active. The surviving vessel at Leningrad continued to carry out shore bombardments while the German siege lasted but, in between 4th and 30th April 1942 further heavy German air attacks were mounted against them, Operation *Eisstoss*, some sixty-two Stukas and sixty medium bombers being utilized. Many of the smaller ships of the Baltic Fleet were hit and seriously damaged, and the *Oktyabrskaya Revolut-siya* was damaged by four bombs.

Despite this, both she and the workable turrets of the sunken *Petropavlovsk* (formerly the *Marat*) gave valuable support to the Soviet Army when they finally launched their break-out attacks against the German encirclement in January 1944, which finally lifted the siege. In June 1944, the *Oktyabrskaya Revolutsiya* also gave fire support to the Soviet operations against the Finnish Army on the offshore islands of the Karelian Isthmus.

85. Roskill, *The War at Sea*, Vol. 3.
86. Thompson, *HMS Rodney at War.*

CHAPTER 9: THE GREAT SHIPS PASS

1. At this time, Japan had nine battleships in commission. The new *Yamato* and *Musashi* replaced the old *Hiei* and *Kirishima*, which had been lost at Guadalcanal. The only other heavy ship loss up to this stage of the war had been the *Mutsu*. She was not lost through enemy action however but had blown up with appalling loss of life while at anchor in Hiroshima Bay on June 8, 1943. In a tragedy strongly reminiscent of the loss of the *Vanguard* at Scapa Flow in 1917, the great ship was torn apart by a magazine explosion, the exact cause of which is still not certain.

2. For a full account of the operations and planning of the British Pacific Fleet, see the definitive account contained in Peter C. Smith, *Task Force 57* (Crécy, 2005). Note also that Barrett Tillman's forthcoming detailed study, *Whirlwind: Bombing Japan, 1944–45*, is currently in preparation.

3. Randolph Pears, *British Battleships, 1892–1957.*

4. A very graphic account of this battle, with some important conclusions often overlooked or ignored, can be found in: C. Vann Woodward, *The Battle of Leyte Gulf* (Macmillan, 1947).

5. The six battleships of Oldendorf's force were the *Pennsylvania, Tennessee, California, West Virginia, Maryland,* and *Mississippi.*

6. Japanese losses were three battleships (the *Musashi, Yamashiro,* and *Fuso*), four carriers, six heavy and six light cruisers, and nine destroyers. The Americans lost one light carrier; two escort carriers (the *St. Lo* was sunk by *kamikazes*), three destroyers, two submarines, and a PT boat.

7. Lewis, *The History of the British Navy.*

8. Hezlet, *Aircraft and Sea Power.*

9. Ibid.

10. Roskill, *The War at Sea*, Vol. 3.

11. Pugsley, *Destroyer Man.*

12. Ibid.

13. Roskill, *HMS Warspite.*

14. Paul Brickhill, *The Dam Busters* (Evans, 1951).

15. Dönitz, *Ten Years and Twenty Days.*

16. Brickhill, *The Dam Busters.*

17. Woodward, *The Tirpitz.*

18. Cunningham, *A Sailor's Odyssey.*

19. Brickhill, *The Dam Busters.*

20. Smith, *Task Force 57.*

21. Okinawa had already been heavily shelled by the new battleships *New Jersey, Wisconsin,* and *Missouri* and the *Massachusetts* and *Indiana* on the twenty-fourth. The battleships of Rear Admiral Deyo's fire-support group were Group 1, *Maryland* and *Texas;* Group 2, *Arkansas* and *Colorado;* Group 3, *Nevada* and *Tennessee;* Group 4, *Idaho* and *West Virginia;* and Group 5, *New Mexico* and *New York.* Operating with Task Force 58 were Task Group 58.1, *Indiana* and *Massachusetts;* Task

Group 58.2, *North Carolina* and *Washington*; Task Group 58.3, *New Jersey* and *South Dakota*; and Task Group 58.4, *Alaska, Guam, Missouri*, and *Wisconsin*.

22. The training and use of the *kamikaze* aircraft are fully tabulated in the book Nakajima Inoguchi, *The Divine Wind* (Hutchinson, 1959), while the list of Allied casualties is fully documented in Morison's volumes. See also Peter C. Smith, *Aichi D3A1/2 Val* (Crowood Press,1999).

23. Tameichi Hara, *Japanese Destroyer Captain* (Ballantine Books, 1961).

24. Smith, *Task Force 57*.

25. *HMS Howe, 1944–45* (John Singleton, 1945).

26. Roskill, *The War at Sea*, Vol. 3.

27. Hough, *Dreadnought*.

28. Stanley Bonnett, *The Price of Admiralty* (Robert Hale, 1968).

20. Parkes, *British Battleships*.

30. Ibid.

31. The addition of the old *Cesare* proved no more help to them than had the *Royal Sovereign*, and after serving for many years in the Black Sea Fleet, her end was tragic. On November 4, 1955, the fleet was assembling in the Sevastopol roadstead to celebrate the thirty-eighth anniversary of the Bolshevik revolution when the *Novorossiisk* (as they had renamed the *Cesare*) suddenly was torn apart by a violent explosion, the cause of which was concealed for many years by the Soviet Union. Apparently the ship's anchor touched undiscovered mines which had been laid in Sebastopol harbor by the Germans during their occupation of the Crimea. For a hundred minutes the crew and rescue teams tried to save the vessel but she suddenly turned-turtle trapping more than six-hundred-and-three men. All but six were drowned. She sank quickly, going down in almost the identical spot to where the old tsarist battleship *Imperatritsa Maria* had sunk thirty-nine years earlier. A total blackout of the loss was imposed and still remains, the names of the dead never being divulged by the authorities. A list was found by a former warrant officer, which had been callously thrown into the rubbish bin by the authorities, and it was finally published by *Slava Sevastopolya*.

　Some indication of how the Soviet Navy coped with the *Royal Sovereign* can be gauged from the following: "She was returned after the war in a dreadful state, covered in rust, all her guns loaded with live ammunition and much of it rusted in place." David and Hugh Lyon, *World War II Warships* (Orbis Publishing, 1976).

32. The fates of the American battleships were as follows. The *Mississippi* was used as an experimental gunnery ship to evaluate new types of weaponry and as such she lasted in the fleet for many years. She was finally scrapped at Baltimore in December 1956. The *New Mexico* and *Idaho* were scrapped at Newark in November and December 1947. The *Arkansas, New York, Nevada*, and *Pennsylvania*, along with the *Nagato* and *Prinz Eugen* (the Americans' share of the major war prizes), were utilized in the atomic bomb tests at Bikini atoll in July 1946. The *Arkansas* was one of the centre target ships the others were spaced at varying distances out from ground zero. The effects were stunning, the *Arkansas* herself achieving a sort of immortality as she was captured in the last split-second of her life as a tiny dot ascending into the base of the gigantic mushroom cloud, totally vanishing at about 4,000 feet. The others survived the detonation in floating condition, which gave rise to some limited hopes that properly protected warships, sealed against radio-active fallout, could still operate in the aftermath of

an atomic explosion. The *New York*, *Nevada*, and *Pennsylvania*, after they had "cooled down," were sunk during 1948.

The following old battleships, somewhat surprisingly, survived for another ten years or more in reserve. The *California* and *Tennessee* were finally scrapped at Baltimore in 1959. The *Colorado* and *Maryland* were scrapped at Seattle and Oakland respectively in July and August 1959. The *West Virginia* was scrapped at Seattle in January 1961. The *Texas* was saved and preserved, however.

Of the new ships, all survived until the 1960s. Then the *Washington* was scrapped at Newark in October 1961. The *South Dakota* was broken up in late 1962. The *Indiana* was scrapped at Richmond in December 1963. The *Iowa*, *New Jersey*, *Missouri*, and *Wisconsin* survived to serve at Korea and Vietnam, were modernized in 1982-84, and saw combat in the Middle East including the First Gulf War and Bosnia. This author was a guest aboard the *Iowa* when she visited Portsmouth harbor, presenting a copy of this book to her ships' library during a conducted tour of the ship, which I found to be still a very impressive and battleworthy vessel. All her class have been since preserved to the great delight of ship lovers, plus three of the older battleships. The American public has shown far more interest in their maritime history than the British, and the eight battleships preserved as museums and open to the public are the *Alabama* at Battleship Parkway, Mobile Bay, Alabama; the *Iowa* at Stockton, California; the *Massachusetts*, at Battleship Cove, Fall River, Massachusetts; the *Missouri* at the old Battleship Row, Ford Island, Pearl Harbor; the *New Jersey* at Camden, New Jersey; the *North Carolina* at Eagles Island, Wilmington, North Carolina; the *Texas* at San Jacinto State Historical Park, Houston, Texas; and the *Wisconsin* at Elizabeth River Waterfront, Norfolk, Virginia.

33. Gardiner, Leslie, *The British Admiralty*.
34. Bonnett, *The Price of Admiralty*.
35. Ibid.
36. Gardiner, *The British Admiralty*.
37. For those interested in the history of how Russia under the Soviets built up its strength with the amazing growth of the Russian maritime forces—remembering that that nation depends not a wit on the sea for defense, but knows from the past how valuable it is for offense—it is recommended they turn to *The Soviet War Machine: An Encyclopedia of Russian Military Equipment and Strategy* (Salamander Books, Hamlyn, 1976). Since the downfall of the Stalinist empire, much of that massive force has sunk into disrepair and many ships have been laid up or scrapped. However, there is now a new resurgence under President Putin's more aggressively nationalistic leadership.
38. Paul M. Kennedy, *The Rise and Fall of British Naval Mastery* (Allen Lane, 1976). Much the same line of argument has been followed, conclusively in my opinion, by Correlli Barnett in his definitive book *The Collapse of British Power* (Eyre & Spottiswood, 1974). The conclusion he reaches, that this collapse started long before 1945, is to a certain extent confirmed by the findings of David Divine in his book *The Blunted Sword* (Hutchinson, 1964). While agreeing with both Barnett and Divine to a great extent, I hold firmly to the viewpoint that it is more the puerile defense policies of successive weak governments since 1919 that carry the greatest blame for Britain's present headlong decline. A further viewpoint that carries weight is that of Adm. Sir Herbert Richmond, *Statesmen and Sea Power* (Oxford University Press, 1948).

Acknowledgments

I have drawn on many published sources, for *The Great Ships* is a treatise of how the British battleship is recorded in history as much as an account of the war records of the ships themselves. I am therefore deeply indebted to the authors, publishers, and agents who kindly made it possible for me to quote at such length from the books consulted. These were chosen carefully in order to present *both* sides of the story, for and against the battleship, so that the reader may draw his own conclusions of the battleship's role in the greatest sea conflict in history.

Special thanks and acknowledgements are given to Evans Brothers Limited for permission to quote from *The Dam Busters* by Paul Brickhill, *Narvik* by Donald Macintyre, *Channel Dash* by Terence Robertson, and *Fighting Admiral* by Donald Macintyre; A. N. Sellwood for quotations from his *HMS Electra*, coauthored with T. J. Cain; William S. Donald for quotations from his *Stand by for Action*; Lt. Col. Eddy Bauer and Orbis Publishing Limited for quotations from *World War II*; Edita S. A. Lausanne and Donald Macintyre for quotations from their *The Thunder of the Guns*, to be reissued in a revised edition as *The Twentieth Century Battleship* by Donald Macintyre and Charles Owen; Cassell & Collier Macmillan Publishers Limited and John Farquharson Limited for quotations from *Floating Bulwark* by Douglas Browne; Hugh Popham for quotations from his *Sea Flight*; Blond & Briggs Publishers for quotations from *The Fleet That Faced Both Ways* by Anthony Heckstall-Smith; David & Charles (Holdings) Limited and K. T. Rowland for quotations from *Steam at Sea* by K. T. Rowland; Hans-Ulrich Rudel for quotations from his *Stuka Pilot*; Collins Publishers for quotations from *Ambassador on Special Missions* by Viscount Templewood, *Call to Honour: The Memoirs of General De Gaulle* by Aidan Crawley, *Churchill at War* by Patrick Cosgrave, *Sovereign of the Seas* by David Howarth, *The Strategy of Sea Power* by Capt. S. W. Roskill, and *HMS Warspite* by Capt. S. W. Roskill; Patrick Stephens Limited and Richard Hough for quotations from *Dreadnought* by Richard Hough; Weidenfeld & Nicolson Limited for quotations from *Destroyer Man* by Rear Adm. A. F. Pugsley, *The Ultra Secret* by F. W. Winterbotham, *Room 39* by Donald McLachlan, and *The German Navy in World War II* by Edward Von der Porten; Peter Davies Limited and

Vice Adm. Sir Arthur Hezlet for quotations from *Aircraft and Sea Power* by Vice Adm. Sir Arthur Hezlet; Jonathan Cape Limited and Leone Peillard for quotations from *Sink the Tirpitz* by Leone Peillard; Curtis Brown Limited and Hodder & Stoughton for quotations from *Max Horton and the Western Approaches* by Rear Adm. W. S. Chalmers; Macdonald & Janes Publishers Limited and William Green for quotations from *Famous Bombers of World War II* by William Green; Arthur J. Marder and Oxford University Press for quotations from *From the Dardanelles to Oran* and *Operation Menace* by Arthur J. Marder; A. P. Watt & Son and the estate of the late Admiral Cunningham for quotations from *A Sailor's Odyssey* by Admiral of the Fleet Viscount Cunningham of Hyndhope; David Higham Associates Limited for quotations from *Main Fleet to Singapore* and *The Bismarck Episode* by Russell Grenfell; The Controller of Her Majesty's Stationery Office for quotations from *The War at Sea* by Capt. S. W. Roskill and *The Royal Air Force, 1939–45* by Denis Richards; A. M. Heath & Company Limited and Ernle Bradford for quotations from *The Mighty Hood* by Ernle Bradford; William Heinemann Limited for quotations from *Fiasco* by John Deane Potter; Weidenfeld & Nicolson and the author for quotations from *Memoirs: Ten Years and Twenty Days* by Adm. Karl Donitz; A.P. Watt & Son and the estate of the late Thomas Woodroofe for quotations from *In Good Company* by Thomas Woodrooffe; George G. Harrap & Company Limited and Paul Carell for quotations from *Hitler's War on Russia* by Paul Carell; Andre Deutsch and David Thomas for quotations from *Crete 1941: The Battle at Sea* by David A. Thomas; The Bodley Head for quotations from *HMS Rodney at War* by Kenneth Thompson and *British Warship Names* by Capt. T. D. Manning and Cmdr. C. F. Walker; David Higham Associates Limited for quotations from *The Navy and Defence*, Vol. 2: *It Might Happen Again* by Lord Chatfield; John Murray and A. D. Divine for quotations from *Destroyers' War* by A. D. Divine; George Allen & Unwin Limited and Charles Owen for quotations from *No More Heroes* by Charles Owen; George G. Harrap & Company Limited and Hugh Hodgkinson for quotations from *Before the Tide Turned* by Hugh Hodgkinson; David Higham Associates Limited and Donald Gordon Payne for quotations from *Red Duster, White Ensign* by Ian Cameron; Ian Allan Limited for quotations from *Chronology of the War at Sea* by J. Rohwer and G. Hummelchen, *The Battle of Matapan* by S. W. C. Pack, and *The Attacks on the Tirpitz* by Gervis Frere-Cook; Laurence Pollinger Limited and the authors for quotations from *Zero: The Story of the Japanese Navy Air Force, 1937-45* by Masatake Okumiya and Jiro Horikoshi with Martin Caidin, *Command of the Sea* by Clark G. Reynolds, *Death of a Navy* by Andrieu D'Albas, and *Norway 1940* by Bernard Ash; Cassell & Collier Macmillan Publishers Limited for quotations from *The Second World War* by Winston S. Churchill, *With Prejudice* by Lord Tedder, *Former Naval Person* by Vice Adm. Sir Peter Gretton, *Sea Warfare* by

Vice Adm. F. Ruge; George Allen & Unwin and Professor Michael Lewis for quotations from *The History of the British Navy*; Robert Hale Limited and the author for quotations from *The Drama of the Scharnhorst* by Fritz Otto-Busch and *The Price of Admiralty* by Stanley Bonnet; Victor Gollancz Limited and the author for quotations from *The Navy's Here* by Willi Frischauer and Robert Jackson; Granada Publishing Limited and the author for quotations from *The Battleship Era* by Peter Padfield; Martin Secker & Warburg Limited and William L. Shirer for quotations from *The Rise and Fall of the Third Reich*; Hutchinson Publishing Group and authors for quotations from *Birds and Fishes* by Sir Philip Joubert de la Ferte and *Two Small Ships* by Donald Forbes; William Blackwood & Sons Limited for quotations from *One Year of Life: The Story of HMS Prince of Wales* by Alan Franklin and Gordon Franklin, *Sea Tales from Blackwoods* (which includes the account of the *Barham*'s sinking by Lt. B. B. Ramsden), and *The British Admiralty* by Leslie Gardiner; Pitman Publishing Limited for quotations from *The Sea Heritage* by Adm. Sir Frederick C. Dreyer; William Heinemann Limited and the author for quotations from *Admiral of the Pacific* by John Deane Potter; Jonathan Cape Limited and the author's estate for quotations from *Sea Power* by T124; B. T. Batsford Limited for quotations from *British Sea Power* by B. B. Schofield; Seeley, Service & Cooper Limited for quotations from *British Battleships* by Oscar Parkes; Macdonald and Janes Publishers Limited for quotations from *The Luftwaffe War Diaries* and *Hitler's Naval War* by Cajjus Bekker and *German Surface Vessels*, Vol. 1, by H. T. Lenton; Wing Cmdr. H. R. Allen for quotations from his *The Legacy of Lord Trenchard*; William Kimber Limited for quotations from *The Tirpitz* by David Woodward, *Swastika at Sea* by C. D. Bekker, *Memoirs* by Admiral Raeder, and *Destroyer Captain* by Roger Hill.

The full details of the above books plus the other volumes consulted but not directly quoted from are contained in the source notes.

Index

Stackpole Military History Series

Real battles. Real soldiers. Real stories.

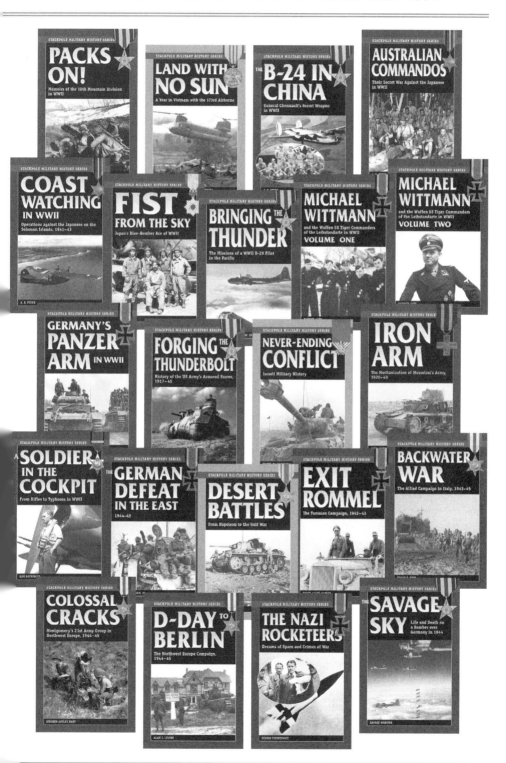

Stackpole Military History Series

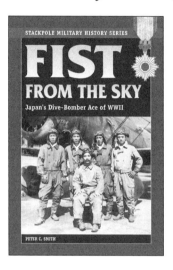

Stackpole Military History Series

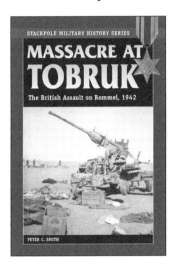

MASSACRE AT TOBRUK
THE BRITISH ASSAULT ON ROMMEL, 1942
Peter C. Smith

By September 1942, Erwin Rommel's Afrika Korps stood
perilously close to breaking through to Cairo and the Nile.
The Desert Fox had captured Tobruk three months earlier
and turned the city into a vital Axis supply port. In a
desperate attempt to halt the Germans and buy time for the
Allies, the British launched a daring amphibious raid on
Tobruk, combining forces from the Royal Marines, Royal
Navy, SAS, Long Range Desert Group, and other secret
units. Boldly conceived and bravely conducted, the assault
nevertheless failed with terrible losses.

$16.95 • Paperback • 6 x 9 • 272 pages • 38 photos, 2 maps

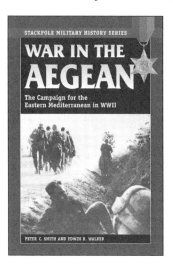

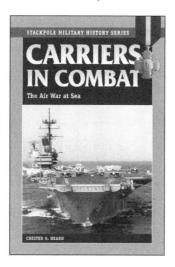

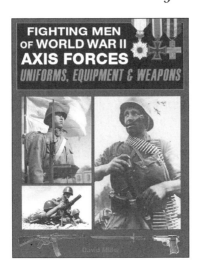
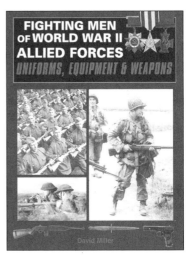